STRATEGIC MANAGEMENT FOR NON-PROFIT ORGANIZATION

STRATEGIC MANAGEMENT FOR NON-PROFIT ORGANIZATION

Dr. G. Rama Krishna

MANGLAM PUBLICATIONS
DELHI-110053 (INDIA)

Published by :

MANGLAM PUBLICATIONS

L-21/1, Street No. 5, Shivaji Marg, Near Kali Mandir,
J.P. Nagar, Kartar Nagar, West Ghonda, Delhi-110053
Phone : 011-22945677, (M.) 9968367559, 9868572512
E-mail: manglam.books2007@rediffmail.com
manglam.publications2007@rediffmail.com

Strategic Management For Non-Profit Organization

First Edition 2010

ISBN 978-93-80013-40-4

PRINTED IN INDIA

Published by Ravindra Kumar Yadav for Manglam Publications, Delhi-110053 Laser Typeset by Amandeep Singh Bansal, (Graphic Era), Delhi- 92, Printed at Sachin Printers, Moujpur Delhi- 53

PREFACE

This book is intended to increase the efficiency by which the financial and the strategic management of nonprofit organizations are conducted. For top management, the two perspectives must be seen as a cohesive whole. Finance is simply a necessary tool to meet the organization's strategic goals. The challenge before all top managers, therefore, is how to develop and use financial and other tools successfully in a coordinated strategy to meet the responsibilities of the organization as these responsibilities fall on the managers themselves and on the trustees.

This book has a distinct managerial orientation. The core questions at every turn are the following: What should all managers and trustees of all nonprofit organizations and associations know in order to be very successful in moving their organizations forward? What are their legal responsibilities and barriers? What are the penalties on these managers and trustees and on their organizations when they fail?

This book presumes that active managers, as well as persons aspiring to be managers, are closer to Rodin's Thinker than to short-order cooks. Therefore, it first undertakes to explore fully the factual bases that undergird key topics, and only after that is satisfactorily done, does it proceed to recommend specific steps that managers should consider in altering their operations for the better. As a result, the readers of this book will get not only the technical, often legal facts, but will learn how to think about them and how they may continuously support his or her own managerial imagination and ambition.

To enhance its completeness as a reference and guide, the book provides a comprehensive reference to all types of nonprofits, from charities to associations. Chapters are self-contained, but readers are pointed to related topics covered in the book. Therefore, readers get a gestalt—a rounded, interconnected picture of subjects as they impact readers' own and other organizations. Occurrences tend to have ramifications throughout and across organizations. A successful manager never misses the bigger picture, even as he or she masters the details.

The book continues what the author introduced in the second edition as the 4Ms of nonprofit management. These are mission, money, management, and marketing. It begins by firmly establishing in the very first chapter that mission, money, marketing, and management are the fundamental pillars of every nonprofit operation. It is the role of management and the trustees to create the environment and to instill the practices that make these 4Ms fully realized ethically, legally, and efficiently. This book builds on this core competency.

—*Author*

CONTENTS

Preface

1. Introduction 1

2. Nonprofit Organization 37

3. The Challenge of Corporate Responsibility 47

4. Governance for Nonprofit Organizations 77

5. Financial Management of Nonprofit Organizations 103

6. The Non-profit Paradox 108

7. Tax Exemptions for Nonprofit Organisations 130

8. Non-profit Organizations: Legal Risks and Protections 145

9. Enhancing Organisational Performance Through Strategic Management 179

10. The Nonprofit Strategic Management 209

11. The New Institutionalism in Strategic Management 226

12. The Process of Strategic Management 258

Bibliography 279

Index 280

1

INTRODUCTION

Strategic or institutional management is the conduct of drafting, implementing and evaluating cross-functional decisions that will enable an organization to achieve its long-term objectives. It is the process of specifying the organization's mission, vision and objectives, developing policies and plans, often in terms of projects and programs, which are designed to achieve these objectives, and then allocating resources to implement the policies and plans, projects and programs. A balanced scorecard is often used to evaluate the overall performance of the business and its progress towards objectives.

Strategic management is a level of managerial activity under setting goals and over Tactics. Strategic management provides overall direction to the enterprise and is closely related to the field of Organization Studies. In the field of business administration it is useful to talk about "strategic alignment" between the organization and its environment or "strategic consistency". According to Arieu (2007), "there is strategic consistency when the actions of an organization are consistent with the expectations of management, and these in turn are with the market and the context."

"Strategic management is an ongoing process that evaluates and controls the business and the industries in which the company is involved; assesses its competitors and sets goals and strategies to meet all existing and potential competitors; and then reassesses each strategy annually or quarterly [i.e. regularly] to determine how it has been implemented and whether it has succeeded or needs replacement by a new strategy to meet changed circumstances, new technology, new competitors, a new economic environment., or a new social, financial, or political environment." Strategic management is a combination of three main processes which are as follows:

Strategy Formulation

- Performing a situation analysis, self-evaluation and competitor analysis: both internal and external; both micro-environmental and macro-environmental.
- Concurrent with this assessment, objectives are set. These objectives should be parallel to a timeline; some are in the short-term and others on the long-term. This involves crafting vision statements (long term view of a possible future), mission statements (the role that the organization gives itself in society), overall corporate objectives (both financial and strategic), strategic business unit objectives (both financial and strategic), and tactical objectives.
- These objectives should, in the light of the situation analysis, suggest a strategic plan. The plan provides the details of how to achieve these objectives.

This three-step strategy formulation process is sometimes referred to as determining where you are now, determining where you want to go, and then determining how to get there. These three questions are the essence of strategic planning. I/O Economics for the external factors and RBV for the internal factors.

Strategy implementation

- Allocation and management of sufficient resources (financial, personnel, operational support, time, technology support)
- Establishing a chain of command or some alternative structure (such as cross functional teams)
- Assigning responsibility of specific tasks or processes to specific individuals or groups
- It also involves managing the process. This includes monitoring results, comparing to benchmarks and best practices, evaluating the efficacy and efficiency of the process, controlling for variances, and making adjustments to the process as necessary.

- When implementing specific programs, this involves acquiring the requisite resources, developing the process, training, process testing, documentation, and integration with (and/or conversion from) legacy processes.

Thus, when the strategy implementation processes, there have been many problems arising such as human relations and/or the employee-communication. At this stage, the greatest implementation problem usually involves marketing strategy, with emphasis on the appropriate timing of new products. An organization, with a effective management, should try to implement its plans without signaling the fact to its competitors.

In order for a policy to work, there must be a level of consistency from every person in an organization, including from the management. This is what needs to occur on the tactical level of management as well as strategic.

Strategy evaluation

- Measuring the effectiveness of the organizational strategy, it's extremely important to conduct a SWOT analysis to figure out the strengths, weaknesses, opportunities and threats (both internal and external) of the entity in question. This may require to take certain precautionary measures or even to change the entire strategy.

In corporate strategy, Johnson and Scholes present a model in which strategic options are evaluated against three key success criteria:

- Suitability (would it work?)
- Feasibility (can it be made to work?)
- Acceptability (will they work it?)

SUITABILITY

Suitability deals with the overall rationale of the strategy. The key point to consider is whether the strategy would address the key strategic issues underlined by the organisation's strategic position.

- Does it make economic sense?
- Would the organisation obtain economies of scale, economies of scope or experience economy?

- Would it be suitable in terms of environment and capabilities?

Tools that can be used to evaluate suitability include:

- Ranking strategic options
- Decision trees
- What-if analysis

Feasibility

Feasibility is concerned with the resources required to implement the strategy are available, can be developed or obtained. Resources include funding, people, time and information.

Tools that can be used to evaluate feasibility include:

- cash flow analysis and forecasting
- break-even analysis
- resource deployment analysis

Acceptability

Acceptability is concerned with the expectations of the identified stakeholders (mainly shareholders, employees and customers) with the expected performance outcomes, which can be return, risk and stakeholder reactions.

- Return deals with the benefits expected by the stakeholders (financial and non-financial). For example, shareholders would expect the increase of their wealth, employees would expect improvement in their careers and customers would expect better value for money.
- Risk deals with the probability and consequences of failure of a strategy (financial and non-financial).
- Stakeholder reactions deals with anticipating the likely reaction of stakeholders. Shareholders could oppose the issuing of new shares, employees and unions could oppose outsourcing for fear of losing their jobs, customers could have concerns over a merger with regards to quality and support.

Tools that can be used to evaluate acceptability include:

- what-if analysis
- stakeholder mapping

General Approaches

In general terms, there are two main approaches, which are opposite but complement each other in some ways, to strategic management:

- The Industrial Organizational Approach
  * based on economic theory — deals with issues like competitive rivalry, resource allocation, economies of scale
  * assumptions — rationality, self discipline behaviour, profit maximization
- The Sociological Approach
  * deals primarily with human interactions
  * assumptions — bounded rationality, satisfying behaviour, profit sub-optimality. An example of a company that currently operates this way is Google

Strategic management techniques can be viewed as bottom-up, top-down, or collaborative processes. In the bottom-up approach, employees submit proposals to their managers who, in turn, funnel the best ideas further up the organization. This is often accomplished by a capital budgeting process. Proposals are assessed using financial criteria such as return on investment or cost-benefit analysis. Cost underestimation and benefit overestimation are major sources of error. The proposals that are approved form the substance of a new strategy, all of which is done without a grand strategic design or a strategic architect. The top-down approach is the most common by far. In it, the CEO, possibly with the assistance of a strategic planning team, decides on the overall direction the company should take. Some organizations are starting to experiment with collaborative strategic planning techniques that recognize the emergent nature of strategic decisions.

THE STRATEGY HIERARCHY

In most (large) corporations there are several levels of management. Strategic management is the highest of these levels in the sense that it is the broadest - applying to all parts of the firm - while also incorporating the longest time horizon. It gives direction to corporate values, corporate culture, corporate goals, and corporate missions. Under this broad corporate strategy there are typically business-level competitive strategies and functional unit strategies.

Corporate strategy refers to the overarching strategy of the diversified firm. Such a corporate strategy answers the questions of "in which businesses should we be in?" and "how does being in these business create synergy and/or add to the competitive advantage of the corporation as a whole?"

Business strategy refers to the aggregated strategies of single business firm or a strategic business unit (SBU) in a diversified corporation. According to Michael Porter, a firm must formulate a business strategy that incorporates either cost leadership, differentiation or focus in order to achieve a sustainable competitive advantage and long-term success in its chosen arenas or industries.

Functional strategies include marketing strategies, new product development strategies, human resource strategies, financial strategies, legal strategies, supply-chain strategies, and information technology management strategies. The emphasis is on short and medium term plans and is limited to the domain of each department's functional responsibility. Each functional department attempts to do its part in meeting overall corporate objectives, and hence to some extent their strategies are derived from broader corporate strategies.

Many companies feel that a functional organizational structure is not an efficient way to organize activities so they have reengineered according to processes or SBUs. A strategic business unit is a semi-autonomous unit that is usually responsible for its own budgeting, new product decisions, hiring decisions, and price setting. An SBU is treated as an internal profit centre by corporate headquarters.

An additional level of strategy called operational strategy was encouraged by Peter Drucker in his theory of management by objectives (MBO). It is very narrow in focus and deals with day-to-day operational activities such as scheduling criteria. It must operate within a budget but is not at liberty to adjust or create that budget. Operational level strategies are informed by business level strategies which, in turn, are informed by corporate level strategies. Since the turn of the millennium, some firms have reverted to a simpler strategic structure driven by advances in information technology. It is felt that knowledge management systems should be used to share information and create common goals. Strategic divisions are thought to hamper this process. This notion of strategy has been captured under the rubric of dynamic strategy, popularized by Carpenter and Sanders's textbook . This work builds on that of Brown and Eisenhart as well as Christensen and portrays firm strategy, both business and corporate, as necessarily embracing ongoing strategic change, and the seamless integration of strategy formulation and implementation. Such change and implementation are usually built into the strategy through the staging and pacing facets.

HISTORICAL DEVELOPMENT OF STRATEGIC MANAGEMENT

Birth of Strategic Management

Strategic management as a discipline originated in the 1950s and 60s. Although there were numerous early contributors to the literature, the most influential pioneers were Alfred D. Chandler, Philip Selznick, Igor Ansoff, and Peter Drucker.

Alfred Chandler recognized the importance of coordinating the various aspects of management under one all-encompassing strategy. Prior to this time the various functions of management were separate with little overall coordination or strategy. Interactions between functions or between departments were typically handled by a boundary position, that is, there were one or two managers that relayed information back and forth between two departments. Chandler also stressed the importance of taking a long term perspective when looking to the future. In his 1962 groundbreaking work *Strategy and Structure,* Chandler showed that a long-term coordinated strategy was necessary to give a company structure, direction, and focus. He says it concisely, "structure follows strategy."

In 1957, Philip Selznick introduced the idea of matching the organization's internal factors with external environmental circumstances. This core idea was developed into what we now call SWOT analysis by Learned, Andrews, and others at the Harvard Business School General Management Group. Strengths and weaknesses of the firm are assessed in light of the opportunities and threats from the business environment.

Igor Ansoff built on Chandler's work by adding a range of strategic concepts and inventing a whole new vocabulary. He developed a strategy grid that compared market penetration strategies, product development strategies, market development strategies and horizontal and vertical integration and diversification strategies. He felt that management could use these strategies to systematically prepare for future opportunities and challenges. In his 1965 classic *Corporate Strategy*, he developed the gap analysis still used today in which we must understand the gap between where we are currently and where we would like to be, then develop what he called "gap reducing actions".

Peter Drucker was a prolific strategy theorist, author of dozens of management books, with a career spanning five decades. His contributions to strategic management were many but two are most important. Firstly, he stressed the importance of objectives. An organization without clear objectives is like a ship without a rudder. As early as 1954 he was developing a theory of management based on objectives. This evolved into his theory of management by objectives (MBO). According to Drucker, the procedure of setting objectives and monitoring your progress towards them should permeate the entire organization, top to bottom. His other seminal contribution was in predicting the importance of what today we would call intellectual capital. He predicted the rise of what he called the "knowledge worker" and explained the consequences of this for management. He said that knowledge work is non-hierarchical. Work would be carried out in teams with the person most knowledgeable in the task at hand being the temporary leader.

In 1985, Ellen-Earle Chaffee summarized what she thought were the main elements of strategic management theory by the 1970s:

- Strategic management involves adapting the organization to its business environment.

- Strategic management is fluid and complex. Change creates novel combinations of circumstances requiring unstructured non-repetitive responses.
- Strategic management affects the entire organization by providing direction.
- Strategic management involves both strategy formation (she called it content) and also strategy implementation (she called it process).
- Strategic management is partially planned and partially unplanned.
- Strategic management is done at several levels: overall corporate strategy, and individual business strategies.
- Strategic management involves both conceptual and analytical thought processes.

GROWTH AND PORTFOLIO THEORY

In the 1970s much of strategic management dealt with size, growth, and portfolio theory. The PIMS study was a long term study, started in the 1960s and lasted for 19 years, that attempted to understand the Profit Impact of Marketing Strategies (PIMS), particularly the effect of market share. Started at General Electric, moved to Harvard in the early 1970s, and then moved to the Strategic Planning Institute in the late 1970s, it now contains decades of information on the relationship between profitability and strategy. Their initial conclusion was unambiguous: The greater a company's market share, the greater will be their rate of profit. The high market share provides volume and economies of scale. It also provides experience and learning curve advantages. The combined effect is increased profits. The studies conclusions continue to be drawn on by academics and companies today: "PIMS provides compelling quantitative evidence as to which business strategies work and don't work" - Tom Peters.

The benefits of high market share naturally lead to an interest in growth strategies. The relative advantages of horizontal integration, vertical integration, diversification, franchises, mergers and acquisitions, joint ventures, and organic growth were discussed. The most appropriate market dominance strategies were assessed given the competitive and regulatory environment. There was also research that indicated that a low market share strategy could also be very profitable. Schumacher (1973), Woo and Cooper (1982), Levenson (1984), and later Traverso (2002) showed how smaller niche players obtained very high returns.

By the early 1980s the paradoxical conclusion was that high market share and low market share companies were often very profitable but most of the companies in between were not. This was sometimes called the "hole in the middle" problem. This anomaly would be explained by Michael Porter in the 1980s.

The management of diversified organizations required new techniques and new ways of thinking. The first CEO to address the problem of a multi-divisional company was Alfred Sloan at General Motors. GM was decentralized into semi-autonomous "strategic business units" (SBU's), but with centralized support functions.

One of the most valuable concepts in the strategic management of multi-divisional companies was portfolio theory. In the previous decade Harry Markowitz and other financial theorists developed the theory of portfolio analysis. It was concluded that a broad portfolio of financial assets could reduce specific risk. In the 1970s marketers extended the theory to product portfolio decisions and managerial strategists extended it to operating division portfolios. Each of a company's operating divisions were seen as an element in the corporate portfolio.

Each operating division (also called strategic business units) was treated as a semi-independent profit center with its own revenues, costs, objectives, and strategies. Several techniques were developed to analyze the relationships between elements in a portfolio. B.C.G. Analysis, for example, was developed by the Boston Consulting Group in the early 1970s. This was the theory that gave us the wonderful image of a CEO sitting on a stool milking a cash cow. Shortly after that the G.E. multi factoral model was developed by General Electric. Companies continued to diversify until the 1980s when it was realized that in many cases a portfolio of operating divisions was worth more as separate completely independent companies.

THE MARKETING REVOLUTION

The 1970s also saw the rise of the marketing oriented firm. From the beginnings of capitalism it was assumed that the key requirement of business success was a product of high technical quality. If you produced a product that worked well and was durable, it was assumed you would have no difficulty selling them at a profit. This was called the production orientation and it was generally true that good products could be sold without effort, encapsulated in the saying "Build a better mousetrap and the world will beat a path to your door." This was largely due to the growing numbers of affluent and middle class people that capitalism had created. But after the untapped demand caused by the second world war was saturated in the 1950s it became obvious that products were not selling as easily as they had been. The answer was to concentrate on selling. The 1950s and 1960s is known as the sales era and the guiding philosophy of business of the time is today called the sales orientation. In the early 1970s Theodore Levitt and others at Harvard argued that the sales orientation had things backward. They claimed that instead of producing products then trying to sell them to the customer, businesses should start with the customer, find out what they wanted, and then produce it for them. The customer became the driving force behind all strategic business decisions. This marketing orientation, in the decades since its introduction, has been reformulated and repackaged under numerous names including customer orientation, marketing philosophy, customer intimacy, customer focus, customer driven, and market focused.

THE JAPANESE CHALLENGE

By the late 70s people had started to notice how successful Japanese industry had become. In industry after industry, including steel, watches, ship building, cameras, autos, and electronics, the Japanese were surpassing American and European companies. Westerners wanted to know why. Numerous theories purported to explain the Japanese success including:

- Higher employee morale, dedication, and loyalty;
- Lower cost structure, including wages;

- Effective government industrial policy;
- Modernization after WWII leading to high capital intensity and productivity;
- Economies of scale associated with increased exporting;
- Relatively low value of the Yen leading to low interest rates and capital costs, low dividend expectations, and inexpensive exports;
- Superior quality control techniques such as Total Quality Management and other systems introduced by W. Edwards Deming in the 1950s and 60s.

Although there was some truth to all these potential explanations, there was clearly something missing. In fact by 1980 the Japanese cost structure was higher than the American. And post WWII reconstruction was nearly 40 years in the past. The first management theorist to suggest an explanation was Richard Pascale.

In 1981 Richard Pascale and Anthony Athos in *The Art of Japanese Management* claimed that the main reason for Japanese success was their superior management techniques. They divided management into 7 aspects (which are also known as McKinsey 7S Framework): Strategy, Structure, Systems, Skills, Staff, Style, and Supraordinate goals (which we would now call shared values). The first three of the 7 S's were called hard factors and this is where American companies excelled. The remaining four factors (skills, staff, style, and shared values) were called soft factors and were not well understood by American businesses of the time (for details on the role of soft and hard factors see Wickens P.D. 1995.) Americans did not yet place great value on corporate culture, shared values and beliefs, and social cohesion in the workplace. In Japan the task of management was seen as managing the whole complex of human needs, economic, social, psychological, and spiritual. In America work was seen as something that was separate from the rest of one's life. It was quite common for Americans to exhibit a very different personality at work compared to the rest of their lives. Pascale also highlighted the difference between decision making styles; hierarchical in America, and consensus in Japan. He also claimed that American business lacked long term vision, preferring instead to apply management fads and theories in a piecemeal fashion.

One year later *The Mind of the Strategist* was released in America by Kenichi Ohmae, the head of McKinsey & Co.'s Tokyo office. (It was originally published in Japan in 1975.) He claimed that strategy in America was too analytical. Strategy should be a creative art: It is a frame of mind that requires intuition and intellectual flexibility. He claimed that Americans constrained their strategic options by thinking in terms of analytical techniques, rote formula, and step-by-step processes. He compared the culture of Japan in which vagueness, ambiguity, and tentative decisions were acceptable, to American culture that valued fast decisions.

Also in 1982 Tom Peters and Robert Waterman released a study that would respond to the Japanese challenge head on. Peters and Waterman, who had several years earlier collaborated with Pascale and Athos at McKinsey & Co. asked "What makes an excellent company?".

They looked at 62 companies that they thought were fairly successful. Each was subject to six performance criteria. To be classified as an excellent company, it had to be above the 50th percentile in 4 of the 6 performance metrics for 20 consecutive years. Forty-three companies passed the test. They then studied these successful companies and interviewed key executives. They concluded in *In Search of Excellence* that there were 8 keys to excellence that were shared by all 43 firms. They are:

- A bias for action — Do it. Try it. Don't waste time studying it with multiple reports and committees.
- Customer focus — Get close to the customer. Know your customer.
- Entrepreneurship — Even big companies act and think small by giving people the authority to take initiatives.
- Productivity through people — Treat your people with respect and they will reward you with productivity.
- Value-oriented CEOs — The CEO should actively propagate corporate values throughout the organization.
- Stick to the knitting — Do what you know well.

- Keep things simple and lean — Complexity encourages waste and confusion.
- Simultaneously centralized and decentralized — Have tight centralized control while also allowing maximum individual autonomy.

The basic blueprint on how to compete against the Japanese had been drawn. But as J.E. Rehfeld (1994) explains it is not a straight forward task due to differences in culture. A certain type of alchemy was required to transform knowledge from various cultures into a management style that allows a specific company to compete in a globally diverse world. He says, for example, that Japanese style kaizen (continuous improvement) techniques, although suitable for people socialized in Japanese culture, have not been successful when implemented in the U.S. unless they are modified significantly.

In 2009, industry consultants Mark Blaxill and Ralph Eckardt suggested that much of the Japanese business dominance that began in the mid 1970s was the direct result of competition enforcement efforts by the Federal Trade Commission (FTC) and U.S. Department of Justice (DOJ). In 1975 the FTC reached a settlement with Xerox Corporation in its anti-trust lawsuit. (At the time, the FTC was under the direction of Frederic M. Scherer). The 1975 Xerox consent decree forced the licensing of the company's entire patent portfolio, mainly to Japanese competitors. (See "compulsory license".) This action marked the start of an activist approach to managing competition by the FTC and DOJ, which resulted in the compulsory licensing of tens of thousands of patent from some of America's leading companies, including IBM, AT&T, DuPont, Bausch & Lomb, and Eastman Kodak.[*original research?*]

Within four years of the consent decree, Xerox's share of the U.S. copier market dropped from nearly 100% to less than 14%. Between 1950 and 1980 Japanese companies consummated more than 35,000 foreign licensing agreements, mostly with U.S. companies, for free or low-cost licenses made possible by the FTC and DOJ. The post-1975 era of anti-trust initiatives by Washington D.C. economists at the FTC corresponded directly with the rapid, unprecedented rise in Japanese competitiveness and a simultaneous stalling of the U.S. manufacturing economy.

GAINING COMPETITIVE ADVANTAGE

The Japanese challenge shook the confidence of the western business elite, but detailed comparisons of the two management styles and examinations of successful businesses convinced westerners that they could overcome the challenge. The 1980s and early 1990s saw a plethora of theories explaining exactly how this could be done. They cannot all be detailed here, but some of the more important strategic advances of the decade are explained below.

Gary Hamel and C. K. Prahalad declared that strategy needs to be more active and interactive; less "arm-chair planning" was needed. They introduced terms like strategic intent and strategic architecture. Their most well known advance was the idea of core competency. They showed how important it was to know the one or two key things that your company does better than the competition.

Active strategic management required active information gathering and active problem solving. In the early days of Hewlett-Packard (H-P), Dave Packard and Bill Hewlett devised an active management style that they called Management By Walking Around (MBWA). Senior H-P managers were seldom at their desks. They spent most of their days visiting employees, customers, and suppliers. This direct contact with key people provided them with a solid grounding from which viable strategies could be crafted. The MBWA concept was popularized in 1985 by a book by Tom Peters and Nancy Austin. Japanese managers employ a similar system, which originated at Honda, and is sometimes called the 3 G's (Genba, Genbutsu, and Genjitsu, which translate into "actual place", "actual thing", and "actual situation").

Probably the most influential strategist of the decade was Michael Porter. He introduced many new concepts including; 5 forces analysis, generic strategies, the value chain, strategic groups, and clusters. In 5 forces analysis he identifies the forces that shape a firm's strategic environment. It is like a SWOT analysis with structure and purpose. It shows how a firm can use these forces to obtain a sustainable competitive advantage. Porter modifies Chandler's dictum about structure following strategy by introducing a second level of structure: Organizational structure follows strategy, which in turn follows industry structure. Porter's generic strategies detail the interaction between cost minimization strategies, product differentiation strategies, and market focus strategies. Although he did not introduce these terms, he showed the importance of choosing one of them rather than trying to position your company between them. He also challenged managers to see their industry in terms of a value chain. A firm will be successful only to the extent that it contributes to the industry's value chain. This forced management to look at its operations from the customer's point of view. Every operation should be examined in terms of what value it adds in the eyes of the final customer.

In 1993, John Kay took the idea of the value chain to a financial level claiming " Adding value is the central purpose of business activity", where adding value is defined as the difference between the market value of outputs and the cost of inputs including capital, all divided by the firm's net output. Borrowing from Gary Hamel and Michael Porter, Kay claims that the role of strategic management is to identify your core competencies, and then assemble a collection of assets that will increase value added and provide a competitive advantage. He claims that there are 3 types of capabilities that can do this; innovation, reputation, and organizational structure.

The 1980s also saw the widespread acceptance of positioning theory. Although the theory originated with Jack Trout in 1969, it didn't gain wide acceptance until Al Ries and Jack Trout wrote their classic book "Positioning: The Battle For Your Mind" (1979). The basic premise is that a strategy should not be judged by internal company factors but by the way customers see it relative to the competition. Crafting and implementing a strategy involves creating a position in the mind of the collective consumer. Several techniques were applied to positioning theory, some newly invented but most borrowed from other disciplines. Perceptual mapping for example, creates visual displays of the relationships between positions. Multidimensional scaling, discriminant analysis, factor analysis, and conjoint analysis are mathematical techniques used to determine the most relevant characteristics (called dimensions or factors) upon which positions should be based.

Preference regression can be used to determine vectors of ideal positions and cluster analysis can identify clusters of positions.

Others felt that internal company resources were the key. In 1992, Jay Barney, for example, saw strategy as assembling the optimum mix of resources, including human, technology, and suppliers, and then configure them in unique and sustainable ways.

Michael Hammer and James Champy felt that these resources needed to be restructured. This process, that they labeled reengineering, involved organizing a firm's assets around whole processes rather than tasks. In this way a team of people saw a project through, from inception to completion. This avoided functional silos where isolated departments seldom talked to each other. It also eliminated waste due to functional overlap and interdepartmental communications.

In 1989 Richard Lester and the researchers at the MIT Industrial Performance Center identified seven best practices and concluded that firms must accelerate the shift away from the mass production of low cost standardized products. The seven areas of best practice were:

- Simultaneous continuous improvement in cost, quality, service, and product innovation
- Breaking down organizational barriers between departments
- Eliminating layers of management creating flatter organizational hierarchies.
- Closer relationships with customers and suppliers
- Intelligent use of new technology
- Global focus
- Improving human resource skills

The search for "best practices" is also called benchmarking. This involves determining where you need to improve, finding an organization that is exceptional in this area, then studying the company and applying its best practices in your firm.

A large group of theorists felt the area where western business was most lacking was product quality. People like W. Edwards

Deming, Joseph M. Juran, A. Kearney, Philip Crosby, and Armand Feignbaum suggested quality improvement techniques like Total Quality Management (TQM), continuous improvement, lean manufacturing, Six Sigma, and Return on Quality (ROQ).

An equally large group of theorists felt that poor customer service was the problem. People like James Heskett (1988), Earl Sasser (1995), William Davidow, Len Schlesinger, A. Paraurgman (1988), Len Berry, Jane Kingman-Brundage, Christopher Hart, and Christopher Lovelock (1994), gave us fishbone diagramming, service charting, Total Customer Service (TCS), the service profit chain, service gaps analysis, the service encounter, strategic service vision, service mapping, and service teams. Their underlying assumption was that there is no better source of competitive advantage than a continuous stream of delighted customers.

Process management uses some of the techniques from product quality management and some of the techniques from customer service management. It looks at an activity as a sequential process. The objective is to find inefficiencies and make the process more effective. Although the procedures have a long history, dating back to Taylorism, the scope of their applicability has been greatly widened, leaving no aspect of the firm free from potential process improvements. Because of the broad applicability of process management techniques, they can be used as a basis for competitive advantage.

Some realized that businesses were spending much more on acquiring new customers than on retaining current ones. Carl Sewell, Frederick F. Reichheld, C. Gronroos, and Earl Sasser showed us how a competitive advantage could be found in ensuring that customers returned again and again. This has come to be known as the loyalty effect after Reicheld's book of the same name in which he broadens the concept to include employee loyalty, supplier loyalty, distributor loyalty, and shareholder loyalty. They also developed techniques for estimating the lifetime value of a loyal customer, called customer lifetime value (CLV). A significant movement started that attempted to recast selling and marketing techniques into a long term endeavor that created a sustained relationship with customers (called relationship selling, relationship marketing, and customer relationship management).

Customer relationship management (CRM) software (and its many variants) became an integral tool that sustained this trend.

James Gilmore and Joseph Pine found competitive advantage in mass customization. Flexible manufacturing techniques allowed businesses to individualize products for each customer without losing economies of scale. This effectively turned the product into a service. They also realized that if a service is mass customized by creating a "performance" for each individual client, that service would be transformed into an "experience". Their book, *The Experience Economy*, along with the work of Bernd Schmitt convinced many to see service provision as a form of theatre. This school of thought is sometimes referred to as customer experience management (CEM). Like Peters and Waterman a decade earlier, James Collins and Jerry Porras spent years conducting empirical research on what makes great companies. Six years of research uncovered a key underlying principle behind the 19 successful companies that they studied: They all encourage and preserve a core ideology that nurtures the company. Even though strategy and tactics change daily, the companies, nevertheless, were able to maintain a core set of values. These core values encourage employees to build an organization that lasts. In *Built To Last* (1994) they claim that short term profit goals, cost cutting, and restructuring will not stimulate dedicated employees to build a great company that will endure. In 2000 Collins coined the term "built to flip" to describe the prevailing business attitudes in Silicon Valley. It describes a business culture where technological change inhibits a long term focus. He also popularized the concept of the BHAG (Big Hairy Audacious Goal).

Arie de Geus (1997) undertook a similar study and obtained similar results. He identified four key traits of companies that had prospered for 50 years or more. They are:

- Sensitivity to the business environment — the ability to learn and adjust
- Cohesion and identity — the ability to build a community with personality, vision, and purpose
- Tolerance and decentralization — the ability to build relationships
- Conservative financing

A company with these key characteristics he called a living company because it is able to perpetuate itself. If a company emphasizes knowledge rather than finance, and sees itself as an ongoing community of human beings, it has the potential to become great and endure for decades. Such an organization is an organic entity capable of learning (he called it a "learning organization") and capable of creating its own processes, goals, and persona.

THE MILITARY THEORISTS

In the 1980s some business strategists realized that there was a vast knowledge base stretching back thousands of years that they had barely examined. They turned to military strategy for guidance. Military strategy books such as *The Art of War* by Sun Tzu, *On War* by von Clausewitz, and *The Red Book* by Mao Zedong became instant business classics. From Sun Tzu they learned the tactical side of military strategy and specific tactical prescriptions. From Von Clausewitz they learned the dynamic and unpredictable nature of military strategy. From Mao Zedong they learned the principles of guerrilla warfare. The main marketing warfare books were:

- *Business War Games* by Barrie James, 1984
- *Marketing Warfare* by Al Ries and Jack Trout, 1986
- Leadership Secrets of Attila the Hun by Wess Roberts, 1987

Philip Kotler was a well-known proponent of marketing warfare strategy.

There were generally thought to be four types of business warfare theories. They are:

- Offensive marketing warfare strategies
- Defensive marketing warfare strategies
- Flanking marketing warfare strategies
- Guerrilla marketing warfare strategies

The marketing warfare literature also examined leadership and motivation, intelligence gathering, types of marketing weapons, logistics, and communications.

By the turn of the century marketing warfare strategies had gone out of favour. It was felt that they were limiting. There were many situations in which non-confrontational approaches were more appropriate. The "Strategy of the Dolphin" was developed in the mid 1990s to give guidance as to when to use aggressive strategies and when to use passive strategies. A variety of aggressiveness strategies were developed.

In 1993, J. Moore used a similar metaphor. Instead of using military terms, he created an ecological theory of predators and prey, a sort of Darwinian management strategy in which market interactions mimic long term ecological stability.

Strategic Change

In 1970, Alvin Toffler in *Future Shock* described a trend towards accelerating rates of change. He illustrated how social and technological norms had shorter lifespans with each generation, and he questioned society's ability to cope with the resulting turmoil and anxiety. In past generations periods of change were always punctuated with times of stability. This allowed society to assimilate the change and deal with it before the next change arrived. But these periods of stability are getting shorter and by the late 20th century had all but disappeared. In 1980 in *The Third Wave*, Toffler characterized this shift to relentless change as the defining feature of the third phase of civilization (the first two phases being the agricultural and industrial waves). He claimed that the dawn of this new phase will cause great anxiety for those that grew up in the previous phases, and will cause much conflict and opportunity in the business world. Hundreds of authors, particularly since the early 1990s, have attempted to explain what this means for business strategy.

In 1997, Watts Waker and Jim Taylor called this upheaval a "500 year delta." They claimed these major upheavals occur every 5 centuries. They said we are currently making the transition from the "Age of Reason" to a new chaotic Age of Access. Jeremy Rifkin (2000) popularized and expanded this term, "age of access" three years later in his book of the same name.

In 1968, Peter Drucker (1969) coined the phrase Age of Discontinuity to describe the way change forces disruptions into the continuity of our lives. In an age of continuity attempts to predict the future by extrapolating from the past can be somewhat accurate. But according to Drucker, we are now in an age of discontinuity and extrapolating from the past is hopelessly ineffective. We cannot assume that trends that exist today will continue into the future. He identifies four sources of discontinuity: new technologies, globalization, cultural pluralism, and knowledge capital.

In 2000, Gary Hamel discussed strategic decay, the notion that the value of all strategies, no matter how brilliant, decays over time.

In 1978, Dereck Abell (Abell, D. 1978) described strategic windows and stressed the importance of the timing (both entrance and exit) of any given strategy. This has led some strategic planners to build planned obsolescence into their strategies.

In 1989, Charles Handy identified two types of change. Strategic drift is a gradual change that occurs so subtly that it is not noticed until it is too late. By contrast, transformational change is sudden and radical. It is typically caused by discontinuities (or exogenous shocks) in the business environment. The point where a new trend is initiated is called a strategic inflection point by Andy Grove. Inflection points can be subtle or radical.

In 2000, Malcolm Gladwell discussed the importance of the tipping point, that point where a trend or fad acquires critical mass and takes off.

In 1983, Noel Tichy recognized that because we are all beings of habit we tend to repeat what we are comfortable with. He wrote that this is a trap that constrains our creativity, prevents us from exploring new ideas, and hampers our dealing with the full complexity of new issues. He developed a systematic method of dealing with change that involved looking at any new issue from three angles: technical and production, political and resource allocation, and corporate culture.

In 1990, Richard Pascale (Pascale, R. 1990) wrote that relentless change requires that businesses continuously reinvent themselves. His famous maxim is "Nothing fails like success" by which he means that what was a strength yesterday becomes the root of weakness today, We tend to depend on what worked yesterday and refuse to let go of what worked so well for us in the past.

Prevailing strategies become self-confirming. In order to avoid this trap, businesses must stimulate a spirit of inquiry and healthy debate. They must encourage a creative process of self renewal based on constructive conflict.

In 1996, Art Kleiner (1996) claimed that to foster a corporate culture that embraces change, you have to hire the right people; heretics, heroes, outlaws, and visionaries. The conservative bureaucrat that made such a good middle manager in yesterday's hierarchical organizations is of little use today. A decade earlier Peters and Austin (1985) had stressed the importance of nurturing champions and heroes. They said we have a tendency to dismiss new ideas, so to overcome this, we should support those few people in the organization that have the courage to put their career and reputation on the line for an unproven idea.

In 1996, Adrian Slywotzky showed how changes in the business environment are reflected in value migrations between industries, between companies, and within companies. He claimed that recognizing the patterns behind these value migrations is necessary if we wish to understand the world of chaotic change. In "Profit Patterns" (1999) he described businesses as being in a state of strategic anticipation as they try to spot emerging patterns. Slywotsky and his team identified 30 patterns that have transformed industry after industry.

In 1997, Clayton Christensen (1997) took the position that great companies can fail precisely because they do everything right since the capabilities of the organization also defines its disabilities. Christensen's thesis is that outstanding companies lose their market leadership when confronted with disruptive technology. He called the approach to discovering the emerging markets for disruptive technologies agnostic marketing, i.e., marketing under the implicit assumption that no one - not the company, not the customers - can know how or in what quantities a disruptive product can or will be used before they have experience using it.

A number of strategists use scenario planning techniques to deal with change. Kees van der Heijden (1996), for example, says that change and uncertainty make "optimum strategy" determination impossible. We have neither the time nor the information required for such a calculation. The best we can hope for is what he calls "the most skillful process". The way Peter Schwartz put it in 1991 is that strategic outcomes cannot be known in advance so the sources of competitive advantage cannot be predetermined. The fast changing business environment is too uncertain for us to find sustainable value in formulas of excellence or competitive advantage. Instead, scenario planning is a technique in which multiple outcomes can be developed, their implications assessed, and their likeliness of occurrence evaluated. According to Pierre Wack, scenario planning is about insight, complexity, and subtlety, not about formal analysis and numbers.

In 1988, Henry Mintzberg looked at the changing world around him and decided it was time to reexamine how strategic management was done. He examined the strategic process and concluded it was much more fluid and unpredictable than people had thought. Because of this, he could not point to one process that could be called strategic planning. Instead he concludes that there are five types of strategies. They are:

- Strategy as plan - a direction, guide, course of action - intention rather than actual
- Strategy as ploy - a maneuver intended to outwit a competitor
- Strategy as pattern - a consistent pattern of past behaviour - realized rather than intended
- Strategy as position - locating of brands, products, or companies within the conceptual framework of consumers or other stakeholders - strategy determined primarily by factors outside the firm
- Strategy as perspective - strategy determined primarily by a master strategist

In 1998, Mintzberg developed these five types of management strategy into 10 "schools of thought". These 10 schools are grouped into three categories. The first group is prescriptive or normative. It consists of the informal design and conception school, the formal planning school, and the analytical positioning school.

The second group, consisting of six schools, is more concerned with how strategic management is actually done, rather than prescribing optimal plans or positions. The six schools are the entrepreneurial, visionary, or great leader school, the cognitive or mental process school, the learning, adaptive, or emergent process school, the power or negotiation school, the corporate culture or collective process school, and the business environment or reactive school. The third and final group consists of one school, the configuration or transformation school, an hybrid of the other schools organized into stages, organizational life cycles, or "episodes".

In 1999, Constantinos Markides also wanted to reexamine the nature of strategic planning itself. He describes strategy formation and implementation as an on-going, never-ending, integrated process requiring continuous reassessment and reformation. Strategic management is planned and emergent, dynamic, and interactive. J. Moncrieff (1999) also stresses strategy dynamics. He recognized that strategy is partially deliberate and partially unplanned. The unplanned element comes from two sources: emergent strategies (result from the emergence of opportunities and threats in the environment) and Strategies in action (ad hoc actions by many people from all parts of the organization).

Some business planners are starting to use a complexity theory approach to strategy. Complexity can be thought of as chaos with a dash of order. Chaos theory deals with turbulent systems that rapidly become disordered. Complexity is not quite so unpredictable.

It involves multiple agents interacting in such a way that a glimpse of structure may appear. Axelrod, R., Holland, J., and Kelly, S. and Allison, M.A., call these systems of multiple actions and reactions complex adaptive systems.

Axelrod asserts that rather than fear complexity, business should harness it. He says this can best be done when "there are many participants, numerous interactions, much trial and error learning, and abundant attempts to imitate each others' successes". In 2000, E. Dudik wrote that an organization must develop a mechanism for understanding the source and level of complexity it will face in the future and then transform itself into a complex adaptive system in order to deal with it.

INFORMATION AND TECHNOLOGY DRIVEN STRATEGY

Peter Drucker had theorized the rise of the "knowledge worker" back in the 1950s. He described how fewer workers would be doing physical labor, and more would be applying their minds. In 1984, John Nesbitt theorized that the future would be driven largely by information: companies that managed information well could obtain an advantage, however the profitability of what he calls the "information float" (information that the company had and others desired) would all but disappear as inexpensive computers made information more accessible.

Daniel Bell (1985) examined the sociological consequences of information technology, while Gloria Schuck and Shoshana Zuboff looked at psychological factors. Zuboff, in her five year study of eight pioneering corporations made the important distinction between "automating technologies" and "infomating technologies". She studied the effect that both had on individual workers, managers, and organizational structures. She largely confirmed Peter Drucker's predictions three decades earlier, about the importance of flexible decentralized structure, work teams, knowledge sharing, and the central role of the knowledge worker. Zuboff also detected a new basis for managerial authority, based not on position or hierarchy, but on knowledge (also predicted by Drucker) which she called "participative management".

In 1990, Peter Senge, who had collaborated with Arie de Geus at Dutch Shell, borrowed de Geus' notion of the learning organization, expanded it, and popularized it. The underlying theory is that a company's ability to gather, analyze, and use information is a necessary requirement for business success in the information age. In order to do this, Senge claimed that an organization would need to be structured such that:

- People can continuously expand their capacity to learn and be productive,
- New patterns of thinking are nurtured,
- Collective aspirations are encouraged, and
- People are encouraged to see the "whole picture" together.

Senge identified five disciplines of a learning organization. They are:

- Personal responsibility, self reliance, and mastery — We accept that we are the masters of our own destiny. We make decisions and live with the consequences of them. When a problem needs to be fixed, or an opportunity exploited, we take the initiative to learn the required skills to get it done.
- Mental models — We need to explore our personal mental models to understand the subtle effect they have on our behaviour.
- Shared vision — The vision of where we want to be in the future is discussed and communicated to all. It provides guidance and energy for the journey ahead.
- Team learning — We learn together in teams. This involves a shift from "a spirit of advocacy to a spirit of enquiry".
- Systems thinking — We look at the whole rather than the parts. This is what Senge calls the "Fifth discipline". It is the glue that integrates the other four into a coherent strategy. For an alternative approach to the "learning organization", see Garratt, B. (1987).

Since 1990 many theorists have written on the strategic importance of information, including J.B. Quinn, J. Carlos Jarillo,D.L. Barton, Manuel Castells, J.P. Lieleskin, Thomas Stewart, K.E. Sveiby, Gilbert J. Probst, and Shapiro and Varian to name just a few.

Thomas A. Stewart, for example, uses the term intellectual capital to describe the investment an organization makes in knowledge. It is composed of human capital (the knowledge inside the heads of employees), customer capital (the knowledge inside the heads of customers that decide to buy from you), and structural capital (the knowledge that resides in the company itself).

Manuel Castells, describes a network society characterized by: globalization, organizations structured as a network, instability of employment, and a social divide between those with access to information technology and those without.

Stan Davis and Christopher Meyer (1998) have combined three variables to define what they call the BLUR equation. The speed of change, Internet connectivity, and intangible knowledge value, when multiplied together yields a society's rate of BLUR. The three variables interact and reinforce each other making this relationship highly non-linear.

Regis McKenna posits that life in the high tech information age is what he called a "real time experience". Events occur in real time. To ever more demanding customers "now" is what matters. Pricing will more and more become variable pricing changing with each transaction, often exhibiting first degree price discrimination. Customers expect immediate service, customized to their needs, and will be prepared to pay a premium price for it. He claimed that the new basis for competition will be time based competition.

Geoffrey Moore (1991) and R. Frank and P. Cook also detected a shift in the nature of competition. In industries with high technology content, technical standards become established and this gives the dominant firm a near monopoly. The same is true of networked industries in which interoperability requires compatibility between users. An example is word processor documents. Once a product has gained market dominance, other products, even far superior products, cannot compete. Moore showed how firms could attain this enviable position by using E.M. Rogers five stage adoption process and focusing on one group of customers at a time, using each group as a base for marketing to the next group. The most difficult step is making the transition between visionaries and pragmatists. If successful a firm can create a bandwagon effect in which the momentum builds and your product becomes a de facto standard.

Evans and Wurster describe how industries with a high information component are being transformed. They cite Encarta's demolition of the Encyclopedia Britannica (whose sales have plummeted 80% since their peak of $650 million in 1990). Many speculate that Encarta's reign will be short-lived, eclipsed by collaborative encyclopedias like Wikipedia that can operate at very low marginal costs. Evans also mentions the music industry which is desperately looking for a new business model. The upstart information savvy firms, unburdened by cumbersome physical assets, are changing the competitive landscape, redefining market segments, and disintermediating some channels. One manifestation of this is personalized marketing. Information technology allows marketers to treat each individual as its own market, a market of one. Traditional ideas of market segments will no longer be relevant if personalized marketing is successful.

The technology sector has provided some strategies directly. For example, from the software development industry agile software development provides a model for shared development processes. Access to information systems have allowed senior managers to take a much more comprehensive view of strategic management than ever before. The most notable of the comprehensive systems is the balanced scorecard approach developed in the early 1990s by Drs. Robert S. Kaplan (Harvard Business School) and David Norton (Kaplan, R. and Norton, D. 1992). It measures several factors financial, marketing, production, organizational development, and new product development in order to achieve a 'balanced' perspective.

KNOWLEDGE DRIVEN STRATEGY

In 2009, Mark Blaxill and Ralph Eckardt suggested that in a knowledge economy all business strategy boils down to intellectual property (IP) strategy.

By contrast, most current approaches to business "strategy" focus on the mechanics of management — e.g., Drucker's operational "strategies" — and as such are not true business strategy. In a post-industrial world these operationally focused business strategies hinge on conventional sources of advantage have essentially been eliminated:

- Scale used to be very important. But now, with access to capital and a global marketplace, scale is achievable by multiple organizations simultaneously. In many cases, it can literally be rented.
- Process improvement or "best practices" were once a favored source of advantage, but they were at best temporary, as they could be copied and adapted by competitors.
- Owning the customer had always been thought of as an important form of competitive advantage. Now, however,

customer loyalty is far less important and difficult to maintain as new brands and products emerge all the time.

In such a world, differentiation, as elicudated by Michael Porter, is the only way to maintain economic or market superiority (i.e., comparative advantage) over competitors. A company must OWN the thing that differentitates it from competitors. Without IP ownership and protection, any product, process or scale advantage can be compromised or entirely lost. Competitors can copy them without fear of economic or legal consequences, thereby eliminating the advantage.

THE PSYCHOLOGY OF STRATEGIC MANAGEMENT

Several psychologists have conducted studies to determine the psychological patterns involved in strategic management. Typically senior managers have been asked how they go about making strategic decisions. A 1938 treatise by Chester Barnard, that was based on his own experience as a business executive, sees the process as informal, intuitive, non-routinized, and involving primarily oral, 2-way communications. Bernard says "The process is the sensing of the organization as a whole and the total situation relevant to it. It transcends the capacity of merely intellectual methods, and the techniques of discriminating the factors of the situation. The terms pertinent to it are "feeling", "judgement", "sense", "proportion", "balance", "appropriateness". It is a matter of art rather than science."

In 1973, Henry Mintzberg found that senior managers typically deal with unpredictable situations so they strategize in *ad hoc*, flexible, dynamic, and implicit ways. He says, "The job breeds adaptive information-manipulators who prefer the live concrete situation. The manager works in an environment of stimulous-response, and he develops in his work a clear preference for live action."

In 1982, John Kotter studied the daily activities of 15 executives and concluded that they spent most of their time developing and working a network of relationships from which they gained general insights and specific details to be used in making strategic decisions. They tended to use "mental road maps" rather than systematic planning techniques.

Daniel Isēnberg's 1984 study of senior managers found that their decisions were highly intuitive. Executives often sensed what they were going to do before they could explain why. He claimed in 1986 that one of the reasons for this is the complexity of strategic decisions and the resultant information uncertainty.

Shoshana Zuboff (1988) claims that information technology is widening the divide between senior managers (who typically make strategic decisions) and operational level managers (who typically make routine decisions). She claims that prior to the widespread use of computer systems, managers, even at the most senior level, engaged in both strategic decisions and routine administration, but as computers facilitated (She called it "deskilled") routine processes, these activities were moved further down the hierarchy, leaving senior management free for strategic decions making.

In 1977, Abraham Zaleznik identified a difference between leaders and managers. He describes leadershipleaders as visionaries who inspire. They care about substance. Whereas managers are claimed to care about process, plans, and form. He also claimed in 1989 that the rise of the manager was the main factor that caused the decline of American business in the 1970s and 80s. Lack of leadership is most damaging at the level of strategic management where it can paralyze an entire organization.

According to Corner, Kinichi, and Keats, strategic decision making in organizations occurs at two levels: individual and aggregate. They have developed a model of parallel strategic decision making. The model identifies two parallel processes both of which involve getting attention, encoding information, storage and retrieval of information, strategic choice, strategic outcome, and feedback. The individual and organizational processes are not independent however. They interact at each stage of the process.

REASONS WHY STRATEGIC PLANS FAIL

- There are many reasons why strategic plans fail, especially:
  - Failure to understand the customer
    - * Why do they buy
    - * Is there a real need for the product
    - * inadequate or incorrect marketing research

- Inability to predict environmental reaction
  * What will competitors do
    - Fighting brands
    - Price wars
  * Will government intervene
- Over-estimation of resource competence
  * Can the staff, equipment, and processes handle the new strategy
  * Failure to develop new employee and management skills
- Failure to coordinate
  * Reporting and control relationships not adequate
  * Organizational structure not flexible enough
- Failure to obtain senior management commitment
  * Failure to get management involved right from the start
  * Failure to obtain sufficient company resources to accomplish task
- Failure to obtain employee commitment
  * New strategy not well explained to employees
  * No incentives given to workers to embrace the new strategy
- Under-estimation of time requirements
  * No critical path analysis done
- Failure to follow the plan
  * No follow through after initial planning
  * No tracking of progress against plan
  * No consequences for above
- Failure to manage change
  * Inadequate understanding of the internal resistance to change
  * Lack of vision on the relationships between processes, technology and organization
- Poor communications

* Insufficient information sharing among stakeholders
* Exclusion of stakeholders and delegates

LIMITATIONS OF STRATEGIC MANAGEMENT

Although a sense of direction is important, it can also stifle creativity, especially if it is rigidly enforced. In an uncertain and ambiguous world, fluidity can be more important than a finely tuned strategic compass. When a strategy becomes internalized into a corporate culture, it can lead to group think. It can also cause an organization to define itself too narrowly. An example of this is marketing myopia.

Many theories of strategic management tend to undergo only brief periods of popularity. A summary of these theories thus inevitably exhibits survivorship bias (itself an area of research in strategic management).

Many theories tend either to be too narrow in focus to build a complete corporate strategy on, or too general and abstract to be applicable to specific situations. Populism or faddishness can have an impact on a particular theory's life cycle and may see application in inappropriate circumstances. See business philosophies and popular management theories for a more critical view of management theories.

In 2000, Gary Hamel coined the term strategic convergence to explain the limited scope of the strategies being used by rivals in greatly differing circumstances. He lamented that strategies converge more than they should, because the more successful ones are imitated by firms that do not understand that the strategic process involves designing a custom strategy for the specifics of each situation.

Ram Charan, aligning with a popular marketing tagline, believes that strategic planning must not dominate action. "Just do it!", while not quite what he meant, is a phrase that nevertheless comes to mind when combatting analysis paralysis.

The Linearity Trap

It is tempting to think that the elements of strategic management – (i) reaching consensus on corporate objectives;

(ii) developing a plan for achieving the objectives; and (iii) marshalling and allocating the resources required to implement the plan – can be approached sequentially. It would be convenient, in other words, if one could deal first with the noble question of ends, and then address the mundane question of means.

But in the world in which strategies have to be implemented, the three elements are interdependent. Means are as likely to determine ends as ends are to determine means. The objectives that an organization might wish to pursue are limited by the range of feasible approaches to implementation. (There will usually be only a small number of approaches that will not only be technically and administratively possible, but also satisfactory to the full range of organizational stakeholders.) In turn, the range of feasible implementation approaches is determined by the availability of resources.

And so, although participants in a typical "strategy session" may be asked to do "blue sky" thinking where they pretend that the usual constraints – resources, acceptability to stakeholders , administrative feasibility – have been lifted, the fact is that it rarely makes sense to divorce oneself from the environment in which a strategy will have to be implemented. It's probably impossible to think in any meaningful way about strategy in an unconstrained environment.

Our brains can't process "boundless possibilities", and the very idea of strategy only has meaning in the context of challenges or obstacles to be overcome. It's at least as plausible to argue that acute awareness of constraints is the very thing that stimulates creativity by forcing us to constantly reassess both means and ends in light of circumstances.

The key question, then, is, "How can individuals, organizations and societies cope as well as possible with ... issues too complex to be fully understood, given the fact that actions initiated on the basis of inadequate understanding may lead to significant regret?"

The answer is that the process of developing organizational strategy must be iterative. It involves toggling back and forth between questions about objectives, implementation planning and resources. An initial idea about corporate objectives may have to be altered if there is no feasible implementation plan that will meet with a sufficient level of acceptance among the full range of stakeholders, or because the necessary resources are not available, or both.

Even the most talented manager would no doubt agree that "comprehensive analysis is impossible" for complex problems. Formulation and implementation of strategy must thus occur side-by-side rather than sequentially, because strategies are built on assumptions which, in the absence of perfect knowledge, will never be perfectly correct.

Strategic management is necessarily a "repetitive learning cycle [rather than] a linear progression towards a clearly defined final destination." While assumptions can and should be tested in advance, the ultimate test is implementation. You will inevitably need to adjust corporate objectives and/or your approach to pursuing outcomes and/or assumptions about required resources. Thus a strategy will get remade during implementation because "humans rarely can proceed satisfactorily except by learning from experience; and modest probes, serially modified on the basis of feedback, usually are the best method for such learning."

It serves little purpose (other than to provide a false aura of certainty sometimes demanded by corporate strategists and planners) to pretend to anticipate every possible consequence of a corporate decision, every possible constraining or enabling factor, and every possible point of view.

At the end of the day, what matters for the purposes of strategic management is having a clear view – based on the best available evidence and on defensible assumptions – of what it seems possible to accomplish within the constraints of a given set of circumstances. As the situation changes, some opportunities for pursuing objectives will disappear and others arise. Some implementation approaches will become impossible, while others, previously impossible or unimagined, will become viable.

The essence of being "strategic" thus lies in a capacity for "intelligent trial-and error" rather than linear adherence to finally honed and detailed strategic plans. Strategic management will add little value — indeed, it may well do harm — if organizational strategies are designed to be used as a detailed blueprints for managers. Strategy should be seen, rather, as laying out the general path - but not the precise steps - by which an organization intends to create value.

Strategic management is a question of interpreting, and continuously reinterpreting, the possibilities presented by shifting circumstances for advancing an organization's objectives. Doing so requires strategists to think *simultaneously* about desired objectives, the best approach for achieving them, and the resources implied by the chosen approach. It requires a frame of mind that admits of no boundary between means and ends.

2

NONPROFIT ORGANIZATION

Surprisingly, there is no legal definition of a nonprofit organization. In general, a nonprofit organization is one that is organized to achieve a purpose other than generating profit. Despite this, a nonprofit organization is not precluded from making a profit or engaging in profit-making activities. It *is* prohibited from passing along any profits to those individuals who control it, like founders, directors, officers, employees, and members. Nothing, however, prevents a nonprofit from paying reasonable salaries to officers, employees, and others who perform a service for it.

This section is aimed at those seeking to start and operate a nonprofit corporation that is a public charity under section 501(c)(3) of the U.S. Internal Revenue Code (the "tax code"). A corporation is the most common and generally most appropriate structure used to create a nonprofit organization. You should seek the advice of an experienced nonprofit lawyer if you wish to establish a nonprofit organization using some other business structure.

Section 501(c)(3) of the tax code exempts certain nonprofit organizations from federal corporate income taxes. Gaining tax-exempt status gives a nonprofit corporation credibility with potential donors because it shows that the organization has a legitimate charitable purpose, a formal structure for accomplishing its goals, and is publicly accountable. Section 501(c)(3) tax exemptions are denied to any nonprofit organization engaging in certain political or legislative activities, which will be discussed below.

Section 501(c)(3) classifies nonprofit organizations into private foundations and public charities. In all likelihood, you want your nonprofit organization to avoid being classified as a private foundation because a number of complex additional regulations and restrictions apply to them. When you fill out your application for 501(c)(3) tax-exempt status, you should request to be classified as a public charity in Part X of Form 1023, usually by checking the box in Line 5g, 5h, or 5i (depending on the nature of your funding). In order to qualify as a public charity, a nonprofit corporation must be formed and operated for a charitable purpose. "Charitable" is a narrow descriptor given the many types of organizations covered under section 501(c)(3). The section also applies to organizations with religious, educational, scientific, or literary purposes, among others. These purposes must be for the benefit of some significant section of society, whether it be the general public or a specific community.

Additionally, a public charity must be publicly supported. This means that the nonprofit corporation must normally receive funds from governmental entities or multiple private donors. Contrast this with a private foundation, which typically gets its funds from a single source. The calculations behind what "public support" means are complicated, see the Nonprofit Law Blog's Public Support Tests for details.

Keep in mind the following factors as you consider whether to operate as a nonprofit public charity corporation:

Liability

Like other corporate entities, nonprofit organizations can be sued for any number of reasons, including:

- publishing defamatory statements
- neglecting to pay taxes (tax exemptions under 501(c)(3) only cover federal corporate income tax; the nonprofit is still responsible for other taxes)
- violating state charitable solicitation laws, antitrust laws, or the tax code by engaging in prohibited political activity or substantial lobbying
- lawsuits common to any business: wrongful termination, employment discrimination, personal injury, and breach of contract

Like shareholders in a for-profit corporation, directors of a nonprofit corporation, and other individuals who participate in the founding and/or operating of the nonprofit organization, enjoy limited liability for the debts and obligations of the organization, including for the unlawful acts of other directors, officers, and employees.

- For example, assume you are a director of a nonprofit corporation for which you and others operate a blog about the environmental impacts of deep-sea fishing. If a fellow director or employee publishes a defamatory blog post or posts copyright infringing material on the nonprofit organization's website, you are not personally liable by virtue of your status as a director of the organization, and your liability ordinarily is limited to the amount you contributed to the nonprofit organization (if any).

However, directors, officers, and employees may be personally liable for their own wrongful conduct, regardless of whether they are paid for their work or are volunteers.

- For example, assume that you make defamatory statements about one of the larger fishing companies. The fishing company can sue you personally and satisfy the judgment out of your personal assets.

Note that if you apply for a small business loan to help fund your nonprofit corporation, the lender probably will require you to give a personal guarantee. In that case, you are personally responsible for the paying back the debt, even if your business is a nonprofit corporation and even if there is no basis for piercing the corporate veil.

Formation

Nonprofit organizations usually incorporate in the state where they expect to do business. Forming a nonprofit 501(c)(3) corporation is burdensome. The section on Forming a Nonprofit Corporation provides the steps necessary to get established in general; the section on State Law: Forming a Nonprofit Corporation outlines what is required by the fifteen most populous U.S. states and the District of Columbia.

There are two main steps involved in forming a nonprofit corporation:

1. Incorporating as a nonprofit corporation at the state level

If you want to incorporate, you must file articles of incorporation with a state office, usually the Secretary of State. Creating articles of incorporation for a nonprofit corporation can be more involved than creating one for a for-profit corporation because you will need to include language about the purpose of your nonprofit corporation in order to be eligible for 501(c)(3) tax exemptions. Drafting the articles of incorporation generally does not require the assistance of a lawyer, and usually the filing fees are significantly less than the filing fees for incorporating as a for-profit corporation.

You will also need to create corporate bylaws which are the internal rules and procedures of the nonprofit corporation. Drafting bylaws that are highly customized to your business may involve some complexity. Additionally, you must keep a records book at the nonprofit's place of business.

The incorporators and/or directors of a newly formed nonprofit corporation should hold an initial organizational meeting to adopt bylaws and elect initial directors (if not named in the articles of incorporation), among other things. Minutes of this meeting must be recorded.

2. Applying for 501(c)(3) corporate income tax exemptions at the federal level

You need to file Form 1023 in order to apply for tax-exempt status under 501(c)(3). The application process is complicated, but can be done without the assistance of a lawyer if you are willing to devote the requisite time and energy in to the process. IRS resources (both the website and the call centers) are of immense help as is Anthony Mancuso's book on "How to form a Nonprofit Corporation" which provides line-by-line guidance on how to complete the application form. The filing fee for the application is high: \$300 if your gross receipts have not exceeded or will not exceed \$10,000 annually over a 4-year period, and \$750 otherwise. You do not have to apply for tax-exempt status if you anticipate bringing in gross receipts of less than $5,000 per year. If you actually bring in more than $5,000 in any particular year, however, you will need to file Form 1023 within 90 days of the end of the year. See Application for 501(c)(3) Tax Exemption for details.

Note that if the IRS classifies you as a private foundation and not a public charity, you should contact an experienced nonprofit lawyer immediately to understand the implications of such a classification.

MANAGEMENT STRUCTURE

Like other corporations, a nonprofit corporation consists of the following classes of people:

- Incorporators:Incorporators form the nonprofit corporation.
- Board of Directors:The board of directors makes major strategic and financial decisions for the organization and ensures compliance with relevant legal and accounting requirements.
- Officers: Officers oversee day-to-day affairs; usually officers consist of the president, vice-president, secretary, and treasurer.
- Employees: Employees execute the decisions made by the directors and officers.

Note that any or all of these people may be volunteers and that the categories bleed into each other. Especially in nonprofit settings, force of personality becomes the key to the identity of the decision makers.

Another category unique to nonprofits is members. Members are a special class of individuals and/or organizations that have rights to participate in the current and future affairs of the nonprofit organization. Nonprofit organizations are not required to have members. You should consult with an experienced nonprofit lawyer if you wish to become a membership organization.

State corporate laws and the nonprofit organization's corporate bylaws govern such things as:

- the required number of directors, or minimum and maximum sizes of the board

- voting requirements for valid board action, such as how many directors are needed to constitute a quorum
- whether action in writing without a formal meeting is permitted

The full array of issues surrounding nonprofit governance is beyond the scope of this Guide. For example, there are reasons to both limit a board's numbers (concentrate control) and broaden a board's numbers (live up to the ideals of representation). A good legal professional or legal resource should be able to help you find the best structure for your nonprofit. For the board example above, in "Starting and Managing a Nonprofit Organization," Bruce R. Hopkins suggests creating an additional advisory committee, thus satisfying concerns of representation and control. You should seek out resources such as Hopkins' book, or consult with a lawyer experienced in nonprofit matters.

Operation

Operating a nonprofit organization is often burdensome and costly. There are reporting requirements and operating restrictions that you need to keep in mind in order to to comply with the law and maintain 501(c)(3) exempt status. Expect increased paperwork and red tape in order to comply with:

- state corporate laws' formalities for corporate governance
- state laws on charitable organizations' record-keeping requirements
- IRS regulations on tax exemptions (do not underestimate the time and energy that you will need to spend organizing the fundraising arm of your nonprofit corporation in order to solicit and accept donations and remain a publicly supported public charity)
- the public's right to inspect your nonprofit organization's corporate records book

Note that the operating restrictions and requirements are even more stringent if your organization qualifies as a private foundation and not as a public charity.

Additionally, you will also be responsible for the tax and other regulatory obligations imposed on all small businesses. For more on the tax obligations of small businesses, see the Tax Obligations of Small Businesses section and the IRS's informational guide, Publication 583 (1/2007), Starting a Business and Keeping Records.

OWNERSHIP OF ASSETS/DISTRIBUTION OF PROFITS

Once incorporated, the newly created nonprofit organization is a separate legal entity from its incorporators, directors, and employees. In fact, a nonprofit has no owners, at least not in any ordinary sense.

The nonprofit corporation owns all assets of the business and is entitled to receive all profits from its operation. Among the most important assets of any nonprofit corporation that operates a website or blog are its articles, posts, videos, and other content. For details on who owns what from a copyright perspective, see the Copyright Ownership of Articles and Posts section.

Despite its name, a nonprofit organization is not precluded from making a profit or engaging in profit-making activities. However, a nonprofit is prohibited from passing along any profits to those individuals who control them, like founders, directors, officers, key employees, and members. (A handful of states allow a nonprofit corporation to issue stock as a mechanism of control, but no dividend rights accompany the issued stock.)

Instead, a nonprofit organization must use any profits to further its program activities or "exempt functions." It may also invest profits in another tax-exempt organization.

Although a nonprofit organization may not distribute profits to its directors, officers, key employees, or members, a nonprofit organization may pay its employees a salary and give them benefits. A nonprofit organization may also pay directors for their expenses and time spent attending director meetings. The key is that the salaries and payments must be reasonable. Excessive payments or exorbitant amounts posturing as salaries or compensation violate the tax code and may lead to penalties and a loss of tax-exempt status.

Note: If you dissolve your nonprofit organization, you must invest all profits into another nonprofit organization.

Tax Treatment

If you obtain 501(c)(3) tax-exempt status, your nonprofit corporation will be exempt from paying federal corporate income tax. However, the 501(c)(3) tax exemption does not apply to unrelated business taxable income or "UBTI," which refers to income generated from regular trade or business activity that is not substantially related to the nonprofit organization's exempt purpose. Consult the IRS publication, Tax on Unrelated Business Income of Exempt Organizations, for examples of what constitutes "unrelated business income."

Note that your nonprofit corporation may engage in unrelated trade or business activity, but will be liable for the taxes on the gross income exceeding $1,000 generated by it. In this situation, you will need to file Form 990T, the UBTI return, with the IRS.

If you achieve 501(c)(3) tax-exempt status, you will still need to file an annual tax return with the IRS, unless your organization's gross receipts are normally $25,000 or less. Organizations beyond the $25,000 threshold with gross receipts below $100,000 and total assets at the end of the year less than $250,000 can file the return on Form 990EZ. Organizations with gross receipts above $100,000 and assets above $250,000 must file the return on Form 990. For details, including how to calculate gross receipts, see the Instructions for Form 990 and Form 990-EZ.

Beyond exemption for federal income tax, qualifying under 501(c)(3) provides another important benefit: donations to the organization will be tax deductible by donor, making fundraising easier. Moreover, some donors, like foundations and the federal government, are barred from funding projects that don't have 501(c)(3) status).

You may also be eligible for other special benefits, such as:

- discounted postal rates
- state tax exemptions (such as sales tax), and limited tort liability
- local tax exemptions, including property tax

Taxation is a very technical subject and you should consider having the nonprofit corporation's tax returns and reports handled by an experienced tax accountant.

PROHIBITION ON POLITICAL AND LEGISLATIVE ACTIVITIES

An important issue is the federal tax code's rule against 501(c)(3) organizations engaging in political and legislative activities. Because the proscribed activities violate the tax code (and may result in the revocation of the organization's tax-exempt status, the imposition of an excise tax, and liability for back taxes), you must understand how 501(c)(3) defines each type of activity. See the section on Prohibitions on Political and Legislative Activities in this guide for more information.

Other Considerations

As discussed above, forming and maintaining a 501(c)(3) nonprofit corporation can take a lot of time, energy, and money, especially if you are beyond the gross receipts threshold requiring you to formally apply for 501(c)(3) exempt status. You may worry that the work needed to incorporate will distract you from your online publishing activities, but also believe that the benefits of tax-exempt status are too important to pass up.

One option to explore is whether a relationship with a "fiscal sponsor" is right for you. Fiscal sponsorship is the mechanism by which a nonprofit organization with 501(c)(3) status lends its legal and nonprofit status to persons, groups, or businesses that engage in activities related to the sponsor's mission. Through fiscal sponsorship, you may be able to function as a nonprofit organization (including receiving tax-deductible donations) without going through the hassle of forming your own independent organization. Fiscal sponsorship also offers the possibility of benefiting from the sponsor's established administrative infrastructure, financial liquidity, and expertise. In exchange for these services, the fiscal sponsor generally keeps a percentage of each financial transaction or charges a monthly or yearly membership fee. Note that fiscal sponsors that work on a percentage basis or provide services beyond simply acting as an umbrella organization often have a minimum fundraising requirement for eligibility.

Seeking a fiscal sponsor may be best if you are:

- working on a short-term project

- initiating a project that has yet to show long-term viability (in some cases fiscal sponsors may help a new project spin off as an independent nonprofit organization)
- waiting for IRS approval on your application for the 501(c)(3) tax exemption
- performing work effectively, but without access to support staff

You will need to weigh the benefits of gaining immediate tax-exempt status and administrative support (if selected) against taking the time and effort to apply for fiscal sponsorship, relinquishing some control, and paying the fees charged by a sponsor.

Some examples of fiscal sponsors include:

- Fractured Atlas is an organization that offers fiscal sponsorship as well as other services (such as event liability insurance and even health insurance) to individuals or groups involved in the arts (including publishing). In order to apply, you must become a member. While rates for membership start at $7.50/month, there is no fee to apply for fiscal sponsorship. Once you are sponsored, Fractured Atlas will accept donations for you and act as a bank from which you can withdraw funds at any time. When you withdraw from your account, you are charged an administrative fee of the greater of $10 or 6% of the funds withdrawn. Fractured Atlas has a requirement that $1,000 be raised prior to sponsorship.
- The Tides Center is a large fiscal sponsor supporting programs that seek to accelerate social change. In addition to sponsorship, the Tides Center offers other office-related services such as human resources management and payroll management. Tides offers more comprehensive services and greater availability of experts than most fiscal sponsors and charges a fee equal to 9% of gross annual revenue. The Tides Center does not offer sponsorship to projects with less than $30,000 in annual funding and does not offer sponsorship to individuals.

3

THE CHALLENGE OF CORPORATE RESPONSIBILITY

To augment the Essential Knowledge Project, this essay discusses the perplexities and challenges of corporate social responsibility (CSR). The essay features the "what," "why," and "how" of CSR. As they help formulate CSR standards and give voice to organizations, public relations practitioners can use experts' carefully considered thoughts as well as research findings to determine the best plan of action. Internally and externally, practitioners can help build a foundation for image/reputation management, brand equity, relationship management, issues management, and crisis management.

"Are you a good corporate citizen?" That rhetorical question was asked by Ben W. Heineman Jr., senior vice president for law and public affairs at General Electric Corporation, writing in the Wall Street Journal (6/28/2005). His question helps set the tone for the topic of corporate social responsibility as a vital part of the Essential Knowledge Project. The column explained how GE"sets a challenging goal—high performance with high integrity—for successful companies and, indeed, for 21st-century capitalism" (p. B2). High performance and high integrity are good for the bottom line. Citizenship requires a "rigorous, unwavering compliance with the law." It blends strict adherence to capital performance with integrity to never allow that commitment to corrode those principles. Quality judgments support, rather than defeat, a commitment to financial standards and to the globe where the organization works, including commitment to "reduce greenhouse gases and increase energy conservation" (p. B2).

What is CSR?

When discussing CSR, some prefer corporate responsibility (CR) to avoid the assumption that it is limited to "social" concerns (strategic philanthropy and community relations). Others use "social" responsibility to avoid the stigma that this topic only relates to businesses driven to place profit over social principle. Those who prefer "social" without the modifier "corporate" recognize that non-profits and governmental organizations are and should be held to responsibility standards. By whatever name, interests of organizations cannot long be at odds with mutual interest and common good.

Consideration of corporate social responsibility is as old as organizations themselves. The central question always has been this: Does each organization, as it strives to achieve its mission and vision, add value to the society which franchises its existence? Long before consideration focused on business, especially large corporations, questions about CSR addressed the rationale and acceptability of government and church.

HISTORY: A LONG-TERM PERSPECTIVE

Despite this timeless concern, the topic came to receive serious discussion and management policy development during the 1950's in nations with large corporations—or those working to overthrow governmental and capitalist colonialism. In developed nations, social movement activism and principles of social democracy offered not only a rationale but also a voice for the concern that mass production/mass consumption societies had spawned large corporations that were slowly dominating the standards of business performance in ways that distorted not only their rationale in society but also the wholesomeness of the private sector. Efficient and rational business practices could in fact harm the society that franchised the organizations to operate.

In the 1960s, interest in CSR became feverish as activists at all points of the ideological and geographical compass called for higher standards of business and government performance. Non-profits asked to share business profits. Academics argued over the differences between the modern and post-modern organization.

As Basu and Palazzo (2008) observed: "The last three decades have witnessed a lively debate over the role of corporations in society" (p. 122). This scrutiny revealed how CSR standards are defined by the ideology of each society. Public relations practitioners contribute to this ideology as they discuss business performance internally and externally. Critics have reasoned that CSR can become insulated, self-serving, and self-affirming—often to the detriment of the society where it was supposed to be a social, political, technical, and financial benefit. Public relations can help organizations craft their standards and implement them through actions and statements.

One of the primary discussants in that 30 year-long dialogue, Freeman Freeman & Liedtka, 1991) observed 17 years ago: "The idea of corporate social responsibility has failed to help create the good society. Long seen by academics and managers alike as the missing link in capitalism, the concept of corporate social responsibility has not delivered on its promise" (p. 92). Convinced of its failure, they reasoned that it is a "dangerous idea" (p. 92), which led them to agree in principle but not detail with Freidman (1970).

DEBATE AROUND FRIEDMAN'S ARGUMENTS

In one way or another, all discussions of CSR recall the famous, or infamous, claim of economist Milton Friedman (1970) that CSR is bunk. He sparked decades of controversy by arguing that the only responsibility of publicly held companies is to increase profits—the efficiency paradigm of organizational excellence. Companies should pay only as much wage/salary as necessary to operate efficiently and pay taxes reluctantly. Some today laud his sentiments, and indeed many empirical tests have not found a positive relationship between CSR activities and major corporate financial performance indicators such as profit (e.g., Agle, Mitchell, & Sonnenfeld, 1999; Auppede, Carroll, & Hatfield, 1985). Agle et al. (1999) stressed the methodological challenge: "Corporate social performance is notoriously difficult to quantify" (p. 515).

Others argue that Friedman's view of the role of companies too narrowly addresses the key issue. Stovali, Neill, and Perkins (2004) fought the traditional interpretation of the Invisible Hand of Adam Smith, which serves to legitimize the maximization of shareholder wealth, and as a result, shareholder-dominant corporate governance. A broader view of the Invisible Hand considers a "sympathy principle," or the ability and propensity of human beings to consider the interests of others. This view may be more aligned with the dominant concept of CSR and promote a broader, multiple stakeholder approach to corporate governance. If sympathy suggests only philanthropy, we add that CSR demands empathy, an outside-in way of thinking and planning to help management reflect on its role in and impact on the society where it operates. Critics believe that Friedman failed to understand the positive advantages to be gained from CSR: Reduce business costs and bolster profits (See the section on Profits and CSR).

Public Relations Practitioners' Views

Public relations practitioners added their voices to this controversy. Senior public relations practitioner, John L. Paluszek (1995) reasoned that advocates of CSR can be committed to profits and the community where they are generated,

> Business is increasingly in society not only in its traditional role of improving the standard of living—by generating jobs, offering products and services and paying taxes—but also via an overlay of sensitivity that supports employees, empowers customers and investors, and relates to the needs of local, national and international communities. (p. 49)

The daunting question raised by this debate is this: Does the price of enjoying the franchise to operate in a society where profits are generated include increasing operating standards so that the organization adds value to that society beyond merely making a profit? Clark (2000) quoted public relations giant Arthur Page: "All business in a democratic country begins with the public's permission and exists by public approval" (p. 364). In fact, he might say the same of business in "undemocratic countries." If it lacks public support, it operates on a questionable franchise.

The legendary John W. Hill (1958) (co-founder of Hill & Knowlton) advised us to understand sound management as the initial step toward appreciating the roles and challenges facing public relations professionals.

It is not the work of public relations—let it always be emphasized—to outsmart the American public in helping management build profits. It is the job of public relations to help management find ways of identifying its own interests with the public interest—ways so clear that the profit earned by the company may be viewed as contributing to the progress of everybody in the American economy. (p. 21)

Another senior practitioner, Raymond Ewing (Allstate Insurance) (1987) reasoned, "A corporation exists for the optimization of the satisfactions of its stakeholders" (p. 32).

This history of CSR discussions leads to many conclusions, including the following ones:

- Knowing and achieving legal and ethical standards are not inherently opposed to one another, but they are not one and the same (Bowen & Heath, 2005);
- Knowing and achieving engineering and operating standards that advance quality of work life, product quality and the community well-being where organizations operate is fundamental to CSR;
- Understanding and appreciating that the franchise to operate is granted by and required to serve the positive interests of society;
- Adopting standards that blend the public and private interest is basic to achieving aligned and mutual interest.

Thus, higher standards of employee or consumer safety help manage risks and reduce the likelihood of crisis related to employment and consumption.

Source of the Controversies

The Role of Business in Society: (Is CSR a Responsibility, an Advantage, or a Just a Liability?)

During the 1980s, discussion of CSR progressed logically from responsiveness to responsibility and rectitude: The ability "to act with rectitude, to refer their policies and plans to a culture of ethics that embraces the most fundamental moral principles of humankind" (Frederick, 1986, p. 136). The heart of CSR is a firm interdependence between business and society.

Although his statement is fraught with the irony surrounding the tobacco industry, George Weissman (1984), former Chairman and Chief Executive Officer of Philip Morris, Inc., set corporate responsibility into its sociopolitical context: "Like property, the corporation is a creation of the state. It gets its charter from the government. To survive, the corporation subjects itself to regulation by government, and to serving the needs of government and the commonwealth." This point "is fundamental to understanding the concept of corporate responsibility in its current context; to understanding that we are not dealing with a fad; and to understanding that we are dealing with the fundamental existence and survival of the corporation" (p. 67). Businesses are expected to be involved in community affairs, formerly the exclusive responsibility of government, reasoned Chrisman and Carroll (1984) in their efforts to reconcile profits, business goals, and society.

CSR is basic to each organization's character, good, bad, or in between. Its character depends on how well it can align its interests with those of consumers, audiences, and publics. For this reason, CSR is not merely a communication challenge; it is a management planning and performance challenge.

Public relations can help an organization know the standards needed to achieve CSR through issue monitoring. Such issue monitoring facilitates an outside-in approach to considering what makes an organization good—the standards and expectations by which it is judged. An outside-in approach makes pragmatic and ethical sense because activists and other critics play a significant role in the raising of CSR standards and in evaluating private sector performance.

Platitudes are likely to foster as well as frustrate efforts to discover which standards of corporate responsibility truly make a difference in the quality of relationships with key stakeholders. The challenge is to know how the organization's interests align with those of its stakeholders. One goal of such discussions is to achieve the common good (Mahon & McGowan, 1991) and to enhance community (Heerema & Giannini, 1991).

Meeting stakeholder expectations is a vital part of achieving the legitimacy needed to operate. Sethi (1977) coined the legitimacy gap between organizational performance and the expectations of myriad stakeholders. At least in part, questions about legitimacy express "concern for a corporation's image" (Clark, 2000, p. 364). Is it a crisis (therefore the rationale for crisis management and communication) when an organization's image is damaged because its legitimacy is questioned because it fails to meet established CSR principles?

Heath (1997) featured the legitimacy gap as the rationale for his discussion of the four pillars of strategic issues management (SIM):

- Strategic business planning which includes foresight judgment, budgeting, and choices among options that lead to organizational success within a sociopolitical environment.
- Issue monitoring which can help organizations understand the alignment of interests, points of misalignment, as well as power resources and challenges by various stakeholders.
- Corporate responsibility, the standards by which an organization is judged.
- Issues communication, the dialogue to better understand facts, develop appropriate evaluations, create vital identifications, advance reputations, and foster public policy positions that achieve mutually beneficial interests. Such discourse defines terms, establishes principles and standards, and thereby creates the socially constructed meaning that guides CSR.

SIM sees CSR/CR as the socially approved expenditure of material and human resources to advance the strategic business plans in ways that meet stakeholder expectations. When firms' operations offend stakeholder expectations, legitimacy gaps motivate stakeholders to correct those operations. Such logic applies not only to the private sector, but also to non-profit organizations and government agencies.

Without oversimplifying the topic, four general themes seem to dominate the discussion of business CSR/CR:

- Profits efficiently earned may not constitute a sufficient CSR standard.

- Companies should engage in strategic philanthropy whereby good acts improve operating conditions and quality of life—and serve society.
- Companies should partner with non-profits and government agencies to solve social, economic, and psychological problems in society.
- Companies should meet or exceed stakeholder expectations of performance standards needed to satisfy the moral rectitude that business contributes to the long-term business climate by collaborative decision making and operating in the public interest.

In such matters, CSR might be defined as corporate strategic philanthropy, even narrowed to "effective public relations" where images are massaged by wordsmiths who tout the excellence of the organization and build accommodating relationships with stakeholders. It can be viewed as cause-related marketing. At best, it can be conceived of as knowing, achieving, and communicating about higher standards of performance in the public or community interest. Profits and CSR: Partners or Opponents? (Are We More Able to Generate and Use Revenue Wisely by Meeting Stakeholder CSR Expectations?)

Does the cost of achieving CSR decrease, increase, or have no effect on "profit" –the cost-benefit residual? What communication activities add impact to CSR performance? In addition to making general claims that corporate responsibility is good for business (Makower, 1994) and observing the trend that companies are integrating environmental values and competitive strategizing (Elkington, 1994), many empirical studies offer data that demonstrate the relationship between profits and CSR.

Most studies have identified a positive relationship (although not always linear) between CSR activities and organization performance as measured by various indicators such as shareholder returns, profit, or marketing impact. For example, the data from Ogden and Watson (1999) suggested that despite the cost of improving the quality of customer service performance, "shareholder returns respond in a significantly positive manner to such improvements" (p. 526).

Beliveau, Cottrill, and O'Neill (1994) found that the CSR-profit relationship is not linear and varies by industry as well as by different company performance indicators. For instance, some industries are rewarded for being innovative more than others. In addition, stock market measures lead in CSR performance, while accounting measures lag CSR. Including sociological factors (such as social impact of an industry) can help explain CSR impact on performance measures. Finally, perceptions of management reputation can have a social and economic advantage.

Sen and Bhattacharya (2001) discovered that CSR performance can increase marketing clout if it relates to product quality and/or consumers' personal preference views on key social issues. This study suggests that aligned interest is crucial to and accountable for positive impact of CSR, but also cautions that such facts don't count if key stakeholders don't know about the organization's accomplishments.

Awareness counts. Sen, Bhattacharya, and Korschun (2006) used survey data to conclude that knowledge of companies' CSR (primarily defined as strategic philanthropy) is fairly low. When consumers are more aware of what companies are doing philanthropically, that knowledge increases desire to purchase from the company, and makes it more attractive as a place to work and in which to invest. The motives (positive or negative) attributed to companies for this action affect the perception of and motivation to respond favorably to the company.

Rochlin, Witter, Monagahn, and Murray (2005) discovered that "by building a business strategy that aligns social, environmental, and economic performance with long-term business value, corporate responsibility becomes part of core business and is tied to long-term value creation for both business and society" (p. 8).

Other studies have shown how CSR decisions relate to people's attitudes and behaviors toward organizations. CR can sell products (Gildea, 1994-1995) but is best when CR decisions lead to increased sales and reputation management, rather than when sales drive CR. Based on ranking data, the following list was compiled, ranging from most important to least important factors in making decisions relevant to a specific company: business practices, community support, employee treatment, quality, environment, service, price, convenience, and stability. Analysis revealed that:

- 34% of the respondents would avoid buying a product or service from a company they perceived as unethical.
- 16% seek information to consider a company's business practices and ethics as part of their decision making.
- 50% intended not to purchase a product or service from a company they considered not to be socially responsible.

Ellen, Webb, and Mohr (2006) found consumer opinions on CSR performance are complex rather than simple—either serving economic or social ends. Customers are more positive when they see CSR as being values driven and strategic. They think badly of companies whose efforts are attributed to egotism or as merely accommodating.

Using social identity theory, Cornwell and Coote (2005) found that if supporters of a non-profit organization know of a mutually beneficial relationship between it and a company that knowledge and the identification with the non-profit positively predict consumer purchase intentions. Barone, Miyazaki, and Taylor (2000) found a positive connection between cause-oriented marketing and consumer relations.

CR also has shown value by reducing costs and gaining support. Carroll (1991) argued that CR pays for itself. Other assumptions relevant to the bottom line are these:

- CR reduces the propensity and rationale activists have to call for excessive and punitive legislation/regulation and the cost of such mistakes.
- CR protects organizations, at least for a while, during a crisis and can reduce various costs, such as litigation and related punitive damages.
- CR increases the likelihood, on the part of non-profits and governmental agencies, that they will get funding they need because they are accomplishing a mission which stakeholders support.

These factors translate into axioms that Carroll (1991) argued serve the good of the company and community: Do good for the community, be ethical, obey the law in spirit as well as principle, and make a profit (or generate revenue regardless of the type of organization) that is put to proper purpose.

Carroll (1991) used these principles to formulate the pyramid of corporate social responsibility:

- The foundation is economic responsibility (to produce an acceptable return on investment)
- Legal responsibilities (to act within the legal framework),
- Ethical responsibility (to do no harm to its stakeholders and operating environment),
- Philanthropic responsibility (or more proactive, strategic behaviors that can benefit the firm and society, or both):

"Be a good corporate citizen; contribute resources to the community; improve quality of life" (p. 42). To accomplish CSR, effective management requires the appropriate balance between an orientation toward owner/shareholders, and employee stakeholders, customer stakeholders, and community stakeholders. To make society "good" becomes a reality only when this high expectation "becomes the aspiration and preoccupation of management" (p. 48).

DEFINING CSR: AN EVOLVING CONCEPT AND STANDARDS

A Variety of Definitions

As is often the case on thought provoking topics, the CSR literature has produced a variety of definitions, each of which features the advantages to be accrued from CSR.

- Kotler and Lee (2005) defined it as "a commitment to improve community well-being through discretionary business practices and contribution of corporate resources" (p. 3). These authors found an increased commitment to give more, to report on the giving, to set high social goals for organizational success, and to use such details to build corporate reputation and brand equity.
- Basu and Palazzo (2008) reasoned that CSR is "the process by which managers within an organization think about

and discuss relationships with stakeholders as well as their roles in relation to the common good, along with their behavioral disposition with respect to the fulfillment and achievement of these roles and relationships" (p. 124; italics in the original). CSR is "the continuing commitment by business to behaving ethically and contributing to economic development while improving the quality of life of the work force and their family as well as the community and society at large" (Watts & Holmes, 1999 cited in Sims, 2003, p. 43).

- Mahon and McGowan (1991) adopted common-good principles of CSR: "it is clear that most authors mean corporate social responsibility to include behavior and actions beyond merely profit making that serve to improve the conditions of society and individuals within that society" (p. 80).
- Ihlen (2005) suggested that Bourdieu's (1986) concept of social capital offers a constructive approach to the power elements within a relationship between an organization and those on whom its success or failure depends. Whether instrumental, symbolic, or purely relational, the quality of each relationship rests on whether one entity wants another to continue operation in the current fashion.
- In his entry on Corporate Social Responsibility in the Encyclopedia of Public Relations, Rawlins (2005) proposed that CSR means "doing well by doing good." That means, for instance, that organizations with high CSR become the employers of choice (an excellent place to work), a neighbor of choice (community where it operates is pleased to have it operating there), and vendor of choice (avoiding bad product design and safety issues—giving full value). The real challenge is for organizations to be accountable beyond financial obligations.

Main Themes

However platitudinous various CSR definitions are, at least four realities are ever present in management discussions and strategic planning regarding CSR:

- Every organization operates in a multiple stakeholder arena where each stakeholder is likely to hold different expectations of how it should operate.
- No absolute standards of corporate responsibility exist; they are defined (socially constructed) by each generation.
- Executives are outraged by accusations that they prefer unethical business practices. For this reason, how discussion transpires within an organization accounts substantially for its positive or negative impact on helping management to be reflective: take an outside-in approach to their planning, operations, and evaluations.
- Calls for operating in the public interest, or community interest, often requires profoundly complicated analysis that defines this interest as an interlocking set of multidimensional determinants of mutual interest. The details move discussions beyond platitude. The devil is in the detail.

Such considerations demand that CSR is more than strategic philanthropy or community relations, such as efforts to sponsor little league teams and engage in goodwill fundraising. It is more than the sort of odious public relations where accommodation and being nice is seen to be more effective than engaging in policy development and implementation that achieves a true community of interest, now ever more global and focused on sustainability.

Expectations of how organizations should perform change over time. "Reshaping the corporate citizenship debate poses challenges to both the advocates and critics of corporate social responsibility. But it is where the debate should occur" (Heineman, 2005, p. B2). Advocacy over standards is likely to occur within as well as outside of each organization (Berger & Reber, 2006; Heath, 2007). The broadest set of ethical concerns arises from the organization's economic, social, and political interests (Wartick & Cochran, 1985).

Why is CSR Important?

Answers to this question, partially addressed in the previous section, depend on how CSR is defined and what obligations that definition hold for an organization's mission and vision, its standards of corporate performance, as fundamental to its planning and operations—and the conceptualization of the societal obligation of the organization to satisfy its franchise. As Basu and Palazzo (2008) concluded, "Such a process view of CSR locates the phenomenon as an intrinsic part of an organization's character (i.e., the way it goes about making sense of its world), with the potential to discriminate it from other organizations that might adopt different types of sense making processes" (p. 124).

One of the strongest CSR roles of public relations is to participate in the social construction of the meaning that defines and evaluates CSR standards by type of organization and during a given era. In contrast to Milton Friedman's narrow and conservative concern, a more reflective answer to the question of CSR's importance can be seen in the metaphor that once offered the challenge: What is good for General Motors is good for America. The contrasting point, and the theme of post-modern discussions of corporate responsibility, is this: What is good for society is good for General Motors.

Framed this way, CSR is important for an organization's success for two primary reasons: (1) To enhance its reputation as being morally bound to rectitude, a rational discretionary choice bringing in economic benefits (Werther & Chandler, 2006), a means for boosting brand equity and sales, and (2) to advance the organization's credibility and character in public policy battles and during the early stages of a crisis.

Mutual, Aligned Interests and Moral Argument

CSR is the foundation for achieving mutually aligned interests and winning the moral argument about the social relevance of the organization. The modern approach to organizational management was to communicate in ways that shaped markets to the advantage of businesses—an inside-out approach to relationships. A post modern approach suggests that an outside-in approach is more capable of creating and sustaining relationships by achieving truly mutual and aligned interests.

This attention to mutual and aligned interests forms a moral argument for CSR. This argument, similar to the business citizenship perspective, also known as normative stakeholder management (Donaldson & Preston, 1995; Jones & Wicks, 1999), states that organizations consider themselves to be duty bound and deeply embedded in the strength and wholesomeness of community.

A large part of corporations' success comes from the values, expectations, and principles of the wider society within which they operate and which franchises them to operate. In a sense, a social contract exists and conforms corporations to society's objectives (Wartick & Cochran, 1985). Within the corporate social performance (CSP) framework, Carroll (1979) stated that corporate social responsiveness is measured by the degree to which management responds to the social sphere by enacting each of the firm's social responsibilities.

Systematic consideration of CSR can be used to reduce friction and increase harmony with stakeholders and increase the organization's strategic business advantage. To do so requires issue monitoring and critical thinking which are second nature to effective strategic issues management as public relations:

- Ascertain the standards of corporate responsibility held by key stakeholders.
- Compare those standards to those preferred and used by the organization.
- Determine whether differences exist and, if so, whether they strain the relationship.
- Ascertain whether differences in facts account for the disparity in expectations.
- Decide whether value differences constitute the disparity between the organization and its key stakeholders.
- Budget for change options, whether communication strategies, public policy efforts, or redefined strategic business strategies to respond to stakeholder expectations.
- Alter performance or operating standards to lessen the legitimacy gap.
- Take a communication or public policy stance based on correct facts or preferred values when the community interest would be better served.

- Eliminate misunderstanding and disagreement by supplying facts or redefining standards vital to the community interest.
- Incorporate preferred standards of corporate responsibility in strategic business planning, and communicate with key external stakeholders.
- Integrate standards into individual, unit, and corporate performance review, including efforts to achieve total quality management.
- Use improved standards of corporate responsibility to achieve competitive advantage.
- Integrate these standards into product, service, and organizational reputation messages.
- Achieving mutually beneficial interests is not easy in a multiple-stakeholder- environment.

Not all stakeholders see the world in the same way. Interests often conflict. Priorities differ. High standards of corporate responsibility foster aligned relationships and can avoid costly conflict. Good performance is a bottom-line issue.

Cost Reduction and Marketing Advantage (Rational and Economic Arguments)

CSR is important because it is the foundation for reducing cost and gaining marketing advantage.

- Cost reduction (outcome): CSR can reduce cost. Conflict can raise costs, through litigation, legislation, and regulation. These can be dysfunctional means for making decisions of public policy when outrage drives the discussion of stakeholder expectation.
- Marketing advantage (outcome): By achieving appropriate standards of CSR, an organization has a more favorable image and is preferred by customers and other commercial stakeholders. Thus, CSR can increase revenue. CSR is more important when customers can vote their performance expectation with purchase dollars. It has advantage when market conditions prevail so some can achieve market advantage through higher standards. David, Kline, and

> Dai (2005) offered this challenge: "consumers' knowledge of CSR practices of an organization is a function of corporate communication activities" (p. 298). This knowledge can lead to positive perceptions of the company, as well as purchase intention and behavior. Perception of an organization's willingness to engage in discretionary CSR practices and moral/ethics predict belief that the organization has strong corporate social values. Using the theory of reasoned action, Werder (2008) reasoned that knowledge of CSR initiatives can foster salient beliefs about the company, but do not predict attitudes toward it or behavior intention. Luo and Bhattacharya (2006) reasoned that CSR initiatives with stated financial, marketing, and communication objectives can enhance company visibility, enhance customer satisfaction, and generate financial gain. Impact is greater when CSR standards are perceived to be more altruistic than self-interested. As Porter and Kramer (2002) claimed, "The acid test of good corporate philanthropy is whether the desired social change is so beneficial to the company that the organization would pursue the change even if no one ever knew about it" (p. 67).

These two outcomes build a rational or economic argument for CSR. CSR offers a rational argument for managers who seek to maximize their performance by minimizing operational and financial constraints, especially in today's globalizing world, where activist organizations feel empowered to enact change. This view of CSR builds on what is best about the efficiency and rational market argument supporting the private sector. In addition, CSR is an argument of economic self-interest for business because it allows companies to reflect the needs and concerns of their various stakeholder groups and thus gain its societal legitimacy and maximize its financial viability.

Indeed, Clarkson's (1995) ten years of research project on corporate social performance found a clear distinction between stakeholder issues and social issues. Similarly, Freeman (1984) suggested the stakeholder framework argues the firm is not responsible to society at large, but to specific stakeholders. Different from the moral argument, this view is similar to strategic philanthropy, or instrumental stakeholder management (Donaldson & Preston, 1995). CSR should focus on specific activities and target publics that are most desirable in terms of loyalty, trust, and goodwill (Fombrun, 1996), consumer purchase decisions, and the goals of the corporation so that ultimately the shareholder value is increased in ways that affirm the franchise to operate.

Globalization/Free Flow of Information and Changing Trends (Reflectiveness and Stakeholder Expectations)

CSR is the foundation for understanding and meeting the challenges of global stakeholders. In the last half of the 20th Century, activist publics formed to change every aspect of business and government. What tended to start as local concern and networking increased to global proportion. With the Internet, virtually every aspect of business and government around the globe can receive instant and detailed attention 24/7.

For this reason, the stakeholders of any organization play an increasingly important role in its standards of CSR. This stakeholder reciprocity/common good rationale for CSR was introduced by Freeman (1984) for strategic management and effective public affairs. This approach reasoned that key stakeholder expectations were crucial to building harmony with targeted organizations.

Basu and Palazzo (2008) highlighted the stakeholder driven approach to CSR is fundamental to a content approach whereby stakeholder standards are important for an organization to know and implement. Planning and performance combine to achieve those standards. The motivation for achievement rests on the principle that reputation counts; it can bring revenue and reduce costs.

This stakeholder rationale motivates authors such as Fombrun (1996) to merge public policy battles and crisis response. Stakeholder adjustments are important. The foundation of successful CSR rests on outside to in thinking: effective CSR goes beyond the question "what's in it for us" to focus on the higher moral position, "what's in it for them" or even for "us"?

Related to the stakeholder argument, social capital is thought to be a "stockpile of goodwill" that can aid an organization in addressing and recovering from crisis. It can also increase the likelihood that it will be a desirable relational partner in many ways such as a preferred provider of products or services.

Discussing social capital and its specific role in collective action regarding climate change, Adger (2003) reasoned that such topics "inform the nature of adaptive capacity and normative prescriptions of policies of adaptation. Specifically, social capital is increasingly understood within economics to have public and private elements, both of which are based on trust, reputation, and reciprocal action" (p. 387). Such dialogue can be framed as matters of the public good and ability of organizations to make appropriate adaptations to change. As a resource challenge is framed in terms of economics, CSR (as related to social capital) must come to grips with this reality: "...adaptation processes involve the interdependence of agents through their relationships with each other, with the institutions in which they reside, and with the resource based on which they depend" (p. 388). By this analysis, "social capital is an important determinant of human well-being, along with the traditional factors of production and natural capital" (p. 391). As a force in organizational and societal decision making, social capital can be seen as both bonding through shared meaning and governmental intervention and networking through shared interests and expectations. Such reasoning agrees with Bowie's (1991) challenge that a stakeholder CSR features "reciprocal duties" (p. 62).

In similar fashion, Clark (2000) concluded that CSR and public relations "have much in common" (p. 369). Her communication-management approach (CMA) works "to join the most compelling arguments made by CSR and public relations, that is, to use the knowledge of identifying stakeholder groups and a corporation's responsibility to them with the ability to strengthen these relationships through effective communication" (p. 373).

To achieve the fully functioning quality of each relationship, the client organization must have the management procedures and cultural commitment that lead to admiration rather than condemnation. No efforts to foster effective relationships can preclude the need for the organization to be good, as a first step to being a good communicator (Heath, 2001).

How to Implement CSR

How organizations implement CSR depends on how they define it, whether as a moral obligation and a rational approach to stakeholder satisfaction. It serves best when it is part of organizations' culture, planning, and management. It has implications for budgeting, return on investment, and measures of effectiveness. As mentioned above, public relations practitioners not only participate in the dialogue to define CSR standards but they also play a crucial role in helping markets, audiences, and publics to be aware of the standards client organizations are willing and able to implement.

Plan of Action: Three-factor Model of CSR Implementation and Application to Public Relations

CSR requires a comprehensive approach that, according to Basu and Palazzo (2008, see especially page 208), features the classic troika of human nature:

- Cognitive: Matters of identity and legitimacy that define what and how firms think
- Linguistic: Matters of justification, positioning, and transparency that define what firms say
- Conative: Matters of posture, consistency, and commitment that define how firms behave.

Practitioners can participate in the cognitive, linguistic, and conative aspects of their organizations to foster the alignment of mutually beneficial interests in society.

Cognitive: Public relations, through issues monitoring, can play a vital role in helping the organization to know and think about changing CSR standards and the means for achieving them. The reality, however, is that beyond scanning for changing stakeholder expectations and helping to create a matrix of multidisciplinary players to learn about and analyze such changes, public relations is not expert on many of the matters that are at the core of CSR standards and performance management. Others in management must commit to a strong CSR program. Accountants must recognize, appreciate, and implement higher financial management standards, as must general counsel, engineers, process experts, human resources specialists, nutritionists, environmental impact specialists, to mention only a few of the key disciplines.

Effective public relations and CSR requires every discipline in an organization to understand how an organization can improve, how that improvement enhances stakeholder relationships, and how it can be communicated. Such planning often requires practitioners to convince management that stakeholders are calling for higher engineering standards and processes to achieve employee or product safety, or even more daunting—sustainability. Practitioners may not know what is required in terms of engineering standards or accounting practices. But, practitioners can ascertain that strains occur when key stakeholders expectations are not being met—or when they are being met but the stakeholders do not know that fact.

Linguistic: Exploring the interconnection of communication and management (public relations and CSR), Clark (2000) observed that these two disciplines "have similar objectives: both disciplines are seeking to enhance the quality of the relationship of an organization among key stakeholder groups. Both disciplines recognize that to do so makes good business sense" (p. 376). Making this conclusion, she also noted that "questions as to the chosen message and how it affects the reputation or perception of an organization as responsible remain" (p. 376). Relevant to reputation and issue position are the terms that define a good organization and the socially responsible position on key issues. In such matters, meaning matters.

From this linguistic perspective, public relations can play a leadership role in understanding the terminology or linguistic changes in the communities where each organization operates—outside-in thinking. As the famous language theorist Kenneth Burke (1973) observed, we are interested in co-created meaning. Human experience can never free itself from the terminology operating at a given moment that filters views of physical and social realities (including standards of corporate responsibility). As Burke reasoned, "We must use terministic screens, since we can't say anything without the use of terms; whatever terms we use, they necessarily constitute a corresponding kind of screen; and any such screen necessarily directs the attention to one field rather than another" (p. 50). Looking as he did so well for the chinks in the armor of communication, he warned: "If language is the fundamental instrument of human cooperation, and if there is an 'organic flaw' in the nature of language, we may well expect to find this organic flaw revealing itself through the texture of society" (Burke, 1934, p. 330).

No useful discussion of CSR can ignore the terminological challenges, and the role of public relations in such efforts. "In any process of institutionalization, meaningfulness is never 'given' but has to be struggled for, has to be secured, even against the resistance of others" (Clegg, Courpasson, & Phillips, 2006, p. 8). Public relations helps to define key terms that become part of the general dialogue which influences how the ideology of and evaluation of CSR performance is conceived in each society in any era. Therefore, practitioners should be especially trained and positioned to understand, appreciate, and respect the development of idioms that are current in private and public sector thinking and decision making.

Conative: Discussing the conative dimension of CSR, Basu and Palazzo (2008) reasoned that it focuses on matters of posture, consistency, and commitment that define how firms tend and prefer to behave. Organizations enact the standards of CSR in all that they say and do. The operational enactment of each organization's standards of CSR occurs by "putting their money where their mind and mouth are." This enactment opens the door for another key role of public relations: To help the organization communicate internally and externally its commitment to various standards and goals and the actions that demonstrate that commitment. Best practices companies believe transparency includes stating their CSR goals and then reporting how well they meet those goals. Such statements can help reduce any legitimacy gap by demonstrating how organizations meet or exceed the expectations of others. In this way, effective public relations can foster mutually beneficial relationships, which Heath and Coombs (2006) reasoned exhibit the following characteristics:

- Openness and transparency: Letting others see whether the organization has sound CSR principles and whether it meets them

- Trustworthiness: Demonstrating that the organization uses CSR principles to be seen as reliable, non-exploitative, and dependable.
- Cooperation: Enacting collaborative decision making regarding what standards should be met and the measures needed to achieve them
- Alignment: Showing that the organization is responsible, responsive, and able to achieve rectitude through shared interests, rewards, and goals with its stakeholders
- Compatibility of views/opinions: Co-creating (socially constructing) through dialogue the standards and implementation of CSR
- Commitment: Planning and operating in ways that achieve a balance between the interests of the organization and those of the persons whom the organization affects and whose support the organization needs for its success

Although CSR and public relations are not identical they must be interdependent to be effective: Being the good organization as prerequisite for being a good communicator.

In truth, few articles on CSR focus on how it can be communicated. Clark (2000) sought to correct this flaw by showing the parallels between CSR and communication management approaches to public relations which features problem identification, conflict resolution, and relationship quality.

We may add scope to Clark's argument and show public relations to have a dynamic role in the processes by which organizations advance their CSR performance, in pursuit of strengthening the relationships between them and their stakeholders. In this way, public relations can help organizations to make society more fully functioning (Heath 2006) by solving collective problems rather than merely managing relationships in ways that can accommodate various entities to one another. Having a good relationship does not mean that organizational standards of CSR will be raised. In fact, an antagonistic relationship is more predictive of the kind of change that has led to higher standards of CSR. They have been forged through heated debates (issue communication focusing on fact, value, and policy) by various groups engaged in power resource management, at various times with the good of society genuinely not under consideration but merely the good of a sector of the society, perhaps to the disadvantage of some other sector.

As cases, Enron and other businesses in crisis demonstrate that often the organization with what seems to enjoy the best relationships with stakeholders may not actually—and substantively—be the ones adhering to high CSR standards. The paradox is image driving substance rather than substance driving image. The quality of such relationships needs to be based on solid principles and the willingness and ability of each organization to meet or exceed stakeholder expectations over the long term. Sometimes, and cases are ample to demonstrate this point, organizations foster positive relationships to seem to be good when those relationships actually mask a crisis in the making. Once the crisis manifests itself, the relationships are not only demonstrated to be based on false assumptions and performance standards, but the damage of falsely built relationships makes crisis response and recovery difficult, and even impossible. A sound foundation of CSR commitment can help an organization recover from crisis. In sharp contrast, if the crisis results from inadequate or fraudulent CSR commitment, it is very likely to be even more damaging.

Black and Hartel (2004) conceptualized a model which they tested empirically to better understand the connections between their concepts and the way that public affairs and CSR can make organizations more effective.

- Public relations can support value attuned behavior and dialogue.
- CSR can define and support ethical business behavior and accountability.
- More socially aware organizations exhibit a higher commitment to and ability to achieve genuine dialogue and engagement with stakeholders,
- Organizations with higher CSR exhibit a caring atmosphere (commitment) in the workplace and higher standards of business ethics and

- "foster employee beliefs about the value of accountability" (p. 140).

In such matters, organizations under attack may smooth relationships instead of making true change in ways to reduce the honest hostility of critics. Advocacy as a cognitive variable can, and probably should, be seen as a positive communication option since it addresses from many perspectives the key issues upon which standards of corporate responsibility are forged and framed.

IMPLEMENTABLE STRATEGIES AND TACTICS

However hard an organization strives to meet high CSR standards, that effort can be squandered if targeted publics do not know of this accomplishment as evidence of the organization's commitment to CSR. Reputation, crisis response, relationship development and other benefits of public relations depend on how well it can communicate about an organizations' CSR performance.

Fundamentally, public relations practitioners can and must bring discussions of CSR into management decision making to refine and implement mission/vision statements, budgeting, performance standards, and a philosophy or culture of working for a fully functioning society that defines and supports the organization. It must engage in outside-in thinking, issues monitoring, by which it aids other disciplines as well as brings its own expertise to play on knowing the standards expected by various stakeholders. It must engage with other voices to discover, consider, evaluate, and implement facts and opinions that individually and collectively advance the common good. Finally, it must not only help to create and define the culture of CSR excellence internally, but also report the organization's achievement and commitments externally. Finally,

Specific action steps identified by Werther and Chandler (2006) and discussed by other authors offer short-term strategies including top down commitment, the creation of a CSR framework, CSR position statement, CSR ombudsman, CSR audit and report, and awareness creation. After these basic conditions are created, organizations may engage in more long-term strategies such as stakeholder involvement, corporate governance, and managing key messages. Not all of these strategies should or can be managed by public relations practitioners—but they can add value to internal discussions and planning and are essential to external communication.

Short-term Strategies:

Top down commitment: The integration of CSR into an organization's operational culture should start with top management, preferably the CEO (or the other top organizational leader such as a vice president of corporate responsibility), who should collaboratively establish the necessary components of an effective CSR policy and institutionalize it within the firm—and use the standards for the assessment of individual, unit, and organizational effectiveness. To this end, the leadership must take a stakeholder perspective rather than input/output approach to strategic management (Donaldson & Preston, 1995).

CSR framework: Structural support for CSR is needed. CSR should be at the same executive level as other key corporate governance issues. To gain visibility and sponsorship, ideally a CSR officer position should be taken by a company executive and must be backed by the CEO.

CSR position statement: This statement, with the CEO's active support, should involve the organization's key stakeholders and their perspectives and contain a conflict resolution process that seeks mutually beneficial solutions. It also provides practical guidance by reinforcing the importance of CSR through rewards and sanctions and by specifying how CSR is to be implemented on a day-to-day basis. From a business perspective, Hess, Rogovsky and Dunfee (2004) suggested that the CSR process needs to connect to the company's core values and core competencies, the response to moral pressures, and set clear objectives and means of measurement.

CSR audit: CSR audit with published results will further awareness among internal and external stakeholders. Using survey methodologies in consultation with stakeholders has been considered an effective method (Jackson & Bundgard, 2002) in this procedure. One of the earlier efforts in public relations to facilitate the CSR auditing process was reported by J. Grunig (1979) who used situational theory to explain communication behavior and attitudes of publics arising around issues of CSR. Essentially that study helped managers to select certain social issues for attention and auditing as well as to devise a communication program to inform publics about responsible corporate acts.

CSR annual report: This report should incorporate triple bottom line thinking: financial, environmental, and social performance. For an "ideal" CSR report, Middlemiss (2004) suggested the following:

- Takes account of the demand (stakeholders) and not of the supply (company).
- Focuses on management systems and doesn't list too many detailed indicators.
- Doesn't consist of more than 50 pages and is complemented by the internet and special publications.
- Reveals its key messages within, at most, 30-minutes reading time.
- Is written in a business like fashion and sparsely illustrated.

Financial report (report to shareholders or donors/followers): Financial stakeholders appreciate firms' ability to generate profits in ways that demonstrate preferred standards of responsibility. Some mutual funds are designed and managed to feature CSR standards to justify why organizations deserve investment dollars. Such claims are strengthened when they demonstrate how improved ethical standards increase profits, especially by avoiding increased amounts of regulatory constraint, limiting legal liability, increasing market share, or operating efficiently.

Sometimes, companies realize that by improving their engineering standards, for instance, they can use more of the feedstock materials they purchase while reducing environmentally damaging wastes and emissions, thereby avoiding unnecessary regulatory constraints. Companies can tout the reduction in raw materials used, improved processes to lessen environmental impact, lowered accident rates, and other practices that mark financial and ethical improvements. They can avoid crises associated with discoveries such as child labor practices, sweatshop conditions, and economic colonialism.

Online Reports: Printed reports have traditionally been circulated to tout an organization's CSR standards and accomplishments. Many printed documents never get circulated or only reach those who are not particularly interested in such reading.

Today, many organizations place such reports, or at least summaries of such reports with the full report available by link, on their home pages. In this venue, organizations tout their standards of CSR with text and even pictures (including video). Rather than languishing on shelves of public relations practitioners, online versions are available 24/7. The interested reader can even follow links to find additional comments by organizations that positively comment on the focal organization's standards and achievements. Links can be used to bridge between a business and its non-profit partners in CSR. It is wise as well to continually report on progress and be willing to combat against unsupported or biased claims to the opposite. This online venue can allow for CSR accomplishments to be attached to related messages such as marketing and organizational history.

Employee communication: Another means for communicating corporate responsibility lies in the array of vehicles, including executive statements and the intranet, used to reach employees. Organizational culture is vital to the way employees conduct themselves and perform their work. This culture is crucial to the ability of an organization to achieve CSR (Hosmer, 1991).

Advertising and other promotional options: These tools can integrate CSR claims into product and service advertising, as well as arguments by government agencies for funding and by nonprofits for fund-raising. Such claims demonstrate how an organization's actions truly benefit its stakeholders.

CSR ombudsman: This position serves as a key component of the continuous internal reinforcement necessary for an effective CSR policy.

Awareness creation: Rewards and measures are key in creating an organizational culture that is sensitive to CSR. Many articles report that key stakeholders are less aware of CSR performance than the sponsoring organization should prefer.

Medium to Long-term Strategies:

Stakeholder involvement: Here public relations practitioners can, for instance, change the focus from financial reporting and investor relations to include social issues and relationship building with all key publics. Smith (2003) indicated that such stakeholder engagement should be at the core of designing any CSR strategy. Lack of awareness about a firm's obligations to its stakeholders can produce a legitimacy gap. Therefore, stakeholders' engagement is more likely to lead to informed management thinking and decision making. Given the foreseeable difficulties in this process (such as a lack of skill set and openness of the management), diverse perspectives of stakeholders and management, and the unwillingness of certain stakeholder groups to engage in such a dialogue, some firms hire talent from the non-profit sector.

- Corporate governance: Transparency and accountability are the key words. Shareholder activism is increasing and drives reform in the area of corporate law.
- Manage the message: Strategic CSR requires that stakeholder expectations are met in reality and that excessive self-promotion should be avoided otherwise CSR efforts fail to demonstrate the other interest or mutual interest orientation needed.
- Measure social performance: Smith (2003) suggested developing appropriate metrics, essentially benchmarks for measuring social and environmental performance and goal setting.
- Communication strategy guidelines: Framing strategies for communicating about corporate responsibility, Sims (1992) offered the following sage bits of advice:
  (a) Be realistic and do not promise what the organization or industry cannot deliver,
  (b) encourage organization or industry-wide input into the standards and the best means for accomplishing them (as well as the stumbling blocks),
  (c) allow diversity,
  (d) allow whistle-blowing,
  (e) provide ethics training,

(f) recognize the ambiguity that is inherent in ethical standards and their implementation, and

(g) integrate ethical decision making into employee and operating unit appraisal.

SUMMARY

Public relations is ideally positioned to help organizations make communities more fully functioning because of its close interdependency with CSR. CSR is the means by which an organization is good first as a foundation for being an effective communicator. Organizational culture and character count. Both as a "listener" and communicator, public relations can aid organizations' ability to foster mutually beneficial interests proactively as a problem solver rather than reactively as lessons learned.

The constructive role of public relations in CSR planning, implementation, and communication simply must be reflective (van Ruler & Vercic, 2005; see also, Black & Hartel, 2004 and Holmstrom, 2004). One size of CSR does not fit all. In such matters, "it depends" is not a stumbling block but a foundational principle.

4

GOVERNANCE FOR NONPROFIT ORGANIZATIONS

BOARD OF DIRECTORS/TRUSTEES: LEGAL OBLIGATIONS

In conducting the business of an organization, directors have certain legal obligations. Failure to observe these obligations may subject nonprofit directors to liability. It's a mistake to believe you can't be sued just because you are a volunteer director serving an organization with a great cause.

a. Duty of Care and Duty of Loyalty

Directors of for-profit and nonprofit institutions have the same two basic legal obligations:

Duty of Care. The duty of care requires directors to exercise the care, diligence and skill that an ordinary, prudent person would exhibit under similar circumstances. For directors, this means, at the least, understanding and paying attention to the substantive matters brought before the board, attending meetings, asking questions, challenging assumptions, following up on issues that may not have been resolved, consulting with experts if needed, reading and understanding materials and reports given to the board.

Duty of Loyalty. The duty of loyalty requires pursuit of the organization's best interest, avoidance of self dealing and conflicts of interests, as well as disclosure of potential conflicts and obtaining prior board approval of any transactions or situations that might be considered self-dealing or a conflict. For example, it would be a breach of the duty of loyalty for a director, or another organization with which the director is affiliated, to profit financially from a transaction with your nonprofit organization, unless all the facts surrounding the transaction had been disclosed to the board and the board approves the transaction as in the interest of the organization in advance. Many boards have formal conflict of interest policies and codes of conduct to help directors understand when a situation might be considered a conflict. The duty of loyalty includes a duty of confidentiality, a duty not to speak about board matters to non-board members unless authorized. For nonprofits, the duty of loyalty also includes the duty of obedience which requires directors to act in accordance with the organization's charter and bylaws and in furtherance of its mission.

As noted above, breaches of the duty of care or duty of loyalty can result in personal liability for directors, although some states have legislatively limited the liability of volunteer directors in some circumstances, and some organizations have Directors and Officers' Liability Insurance that may protect directors from personal financial liability in certain situations. However, aside from helping to avoid liability, paying attention to the duty of care and duty of loyalty helps prevent organizational crises as well negative publicity which might raise the question, "Where was the board?" in large, banner headlines.

b. Federal and State Laws

Specific federal and state laws also may place responsibilities on directors of nonprofits. In addition, good corporate governance practices in the for-profit world are migrating to the nonprofit arena. For example, the Sarbanes-Oxley Act of 2002 set new standards of governance for publicly traded companies in the wake of Enron and other notorious scandals. While most provisions of "SOX" do not directly apply to nonprofits or their directors, trustees or officers, SOX is still important to nonprofits, even with limited legal connection. Many commentators now recommend that nonprofits adopt the generally applicable governance principles embodied in SOX. The concepts embodied in SOX are fast becoming the standard by which the governance of all organizations will be judged.

Furthermore, two provisions of SOX, those protecting "whistleblowers" and penalizing the destruction of documents, are applicable to nonprofits. These provisions require organizations to have a process to protect whistleblowers and to establish policies for the retention of documents and to prevent their destruction in certain circumstances.

In considering how the governance of the nonprofit you serve measures up to SOX standards, ask yourself the following questions:

- Are the directors independent of the management?
- Do the directors-or their family members-have a financial interest in the organization (such as vendors or professional consultants to the organization would have) that creates a conflict of interest? If there are any potentially conflicted directors, is a majority of the board free of conflicts and fully independent?
- Does the board meet regularly, including in executive session without the presence of management?
- Does the board have a finance committee and an audit committee or a full board process for reviewing the financial statements, evaluating internal controls, and interacting with the independent auditors?
- Does the board have a compensation committee or a full board process for regularly evaluating the performance of senior staff and setting their compensation?
- Does the board have a nominating/governance committee or a full board process for identifying new directors?
- Is there an ethics code or code of conduct for the directors and the employees? Do the directors have a way to evaluate compliance with that code? Is there an annual certificate of compliance required?
- Is there an organizational policy to protect whistleblowers?
- Is there a written document retention/destruction policy for the organization and how often is it reviewed?

If you can answer positively to these questions, your organization has gone a long way toward protecting directors against personal liability.

Some nonprofit organizations have for-profit subsidiaries. Federal and state laws place a number of restrictions on such organizations and may limit the interaction between the nonprofit and the for-profit subsidiary, creating additional governance and compliance complexities for boards of both the for-profit and nonprofit organizations charged with ensuring such restrictions are followed. Some states have laws that place particular and quite specific governance requirements on nonprofit organizations once they reach a certain size.

c. Tax Regulations

Tax exemption is not automatic for nonprofit organizations. Organizations that wish to obtain federal tax-exempt status must file for approval with the IRS. There are various types of exempt organizations recognized in the Internal Revenue Code. Charitable organizations typically apply to the IRS to qualify as 501(c)(3) organizations, and, upon approval, receive a letter from the IRS confirming this status. Assurance that the organization has this letter is important to donors because it is the basis on which they can claim a tax deduction on their income tax for a donation.

Although 501(c)(3) organizations are exempt from paying income tax, they must nonetheless file an annual return with the IRS-a Form 990. While the IRS does not directly regulate corporate governance, the information on the Form 990 enables the IRS to watch for evidence of excessive compensation of the staff or transactions which create a conflict of interest, either of which can be the basis for the IRS to withdraw the exempt status or impose other penalties. New applicants for 501(c)(3) letters should consider developing a conflict of interest policy consistent with the IRS' model that can be included with the application.

The IRS has also published a staff discussion draft of good governance practices for charitable organizations. While not technically part of the IRS rules for nonprofits, it indicates those governance practices which are important to the IRS when it has an organization under review. This IRS draft discusses a nonprofit's mission statement, code of ethics, due diligence, duty of loyalty, transparency, fundraising policy, financial audits, compensation practices and document retention policy.

Exemptions from state taxes, such as sales taxes, are available in many states, but the rules and procedures necessary to obtain these exemptions vary from state to state. Nonprofit organizations typically work with professionals for help in establishing and maintaining their federal and state tax-exempt status.

BOARD OF DIRECTORS/TRUSTEES: PERSONAL QUALITIES OF EFFECTIVE BOARD MEMBERS

a. Fundamental Characteristics

Great boards don't just happen. It takes a lot of work to make a board effective. That work begins with selection of individual board members who, regardless of the type of organization, have certain fundamental characteristics:

- Vision and Leadership: the ability to see the big picture, and to help create and, if necessary, re-set strategy and policy to help the organization achieve its mission.
- Advocacy, Stewardship and Integrity: the ability to serve and promote the interests and goals of the organization without forgetting the interests of the public and the organization's intended beneficiaries.
- Knowledge: the willingness to become thoroughly familiar with the mission and how the organization actually carries out the mission day-to-day through its organizational structure and operations.
- Personal Commitment and Diligence: the willingness to take the necessary time and make the necessary effort to fulfill director responsibilities, including understanding strategic, financial and operational issues facing the organization, asking questions and following up as needed, engaging personally with the organization, whether through financial support, advocacy, networking, personal service, or other personal support activities, and staying current on sound governance principles and working to apply them to the organization.
- Collegiality: the ability to work well with others and to show respect for the ideas and views of fellow board members and staff; the understanding that boards operate as a body.

Beyond these fundamental characteristics, nonprofit boards typically seek directors with particular backgrounds or types of expertise, financial capacity, positions in the community, or access to key constituents or professionals that can be helpful to the organization.

In recent years there is a trend for boards to seek individuals representing specific ethnic or minority groups, or women, so that the board has an ethnically or gender diverse membership.

One effective way to help make sure that boards are sourcing directors who meet the needs of the organization is for the board, or nominating committee, to create and maintain written criteria for board membership focusing on key characteristics being sought and, in addition, to conduct an annual review of the strengths and weaknesses of the existing board so that future recruiting can focus on the organization's needs. (The Society website has samples of written criteria that have been developed by some nonprofit boards.)

Having a good understanding of a board's criteria for membership, and the specific reasons why the organization has selected you as a director, can go a long way in helping you determine whether service on a particular board is right for you. Don't be afraid to ask!

This is particularly true with respect to financial commitment expectations, or for operating boards, anticipated time commitments. Understanding these matters at the outset can help keep embarrassing situations from arising as a result of mutual expectations not being met.

Similarly, understanding the board dynamic, how board members work together and with staff, is an important topic to explore in advance of joining a board. In the nonprofit world, founders of an organization may still be involved and cast a long shadow over board deliberations.

Sometimes organizations may be in a period where there is a disconnect or distrust between the board and current management. Sometimes the sheer size and diversity of members on a board may make communication and consensus difficult. Sometimes the number of "old guard" board members may inhibit participation by new members. Occasionally, lack of staff may limit time and attention that are given to directors or to board matters by management. While none of these issues may be enough to discourage you from joining the board of an organization you care about, understanding how things are can make it easier for you to understand the nature of the task facing the board in achieving good governance.

b. Personal Commitment

Your own ability to be effective as a director is another factor to take into account in considering board service. Expertise, reputation, financial donations and support may have played a role in your being asked to join a board. They alone do not make you a good director. Although there is no magic formula for being a good director, there are a number of actions and practices which are generally considered to represent excellence in board service, including the following:

- Understanding the mission of your organization and helping to keep it current and relevant.
- Becoming familiar with the organization's basic governance documents.
- Staying current on governance trends.
- Staying current on business and societal issues that may affect the operation or mission of the organization.
- Attending board and committee meetings regularly.
- Actively contributing to the work of the board and the organization.
- Reading board and committee materials in advance.
- Asking questions at meetings on issues you don't understand.
- Offering suggestions and comments in a positive manner.
- Avoiding micromanaging or nit-picking.
- Being respectful of the management team and other directors.
- Being collegial; refraining from dominating meetings or personalizing debate.

- Supporting the chair in efforts to keep meetings moving.
- Keeping questions and comments relevant.
- Knowing key staff and their roles, but refraining from contacting lower level staff without advising the executive director.
- Meeting periodically with the executive director.
- Getting to know the other board members.
- Supporting the organization financially.
- Attending functions of the organization in the community.
- Helping raise funds from others for the organization.
- Being an advocate for the organization in your community.
- Engaging others in the work of the organization.
- Keeping alert for warning signs of potential trouble-disaffected directors, arrogant or ineffectual executive director, sloppy reports, lack of forward momentum, poor accounting, shortage of funds, etc.
- When you have concerns about the organization or board or staff, raising them with sensitivity to the appropriate person (board or committee chair or executive director) and working to correct the problems.
- Knowing when it's time for you to rotate off the board in order to help keep the board fresh and viable.

Comparing your performance against these actions and practices will give you a good idea of whether the organization you serve will consider you a valued and effective director.

BOARD OF DIRECTORS/TRUSTEES: BOARD STRUCTURE AND OPERATIONS

The size and sophistication of the organization and the size and function of the board (i.e. governing/oversight board or operating/hands-on board) tend to determine how often a board meets and whether a majority of the work is done at board meetings or through committees of the board.

In the corporate for-profit arena, the trend has been to reduce the size of boards to allow for greater discussion and interchange and to increase efficiency and accountability. However, in the nonprofit world, particularly with respect to educational and arts organizations where directors play a major role in fundraising and the desire to engage a wide variety of constituencies is common, it is not unusual to have boards with 30 or more members, and sometimes as many as 75-100 members.

Boards of this size clearly must rely on committees to do much of the work on behalf of the board, either with delegated authority to act on behalf of the board, or with a mandate to present well-vetted recommendations to the board to facilitate full board action.

Committees vary with the needs of each organization. Smaller boards may not need committees and may perform many of the functions mentioned below at the board level itself. However, fairly typical standing committees (i.e., committees which stay in existence year after year) would include:

- The Executive Committee - empowered to act between board meetings if necessary, and sometimes with specifically delegated authority to act in particular areas on behalf of the full board. The make-up of executive committees will vary with the organization, but many such committees are made up of the board officers and committee chairs.
- The Finance Committee - typically assigned to provide detailed review of financial statements and issues, including budget, accounting, tax and investment issues, and, if there is no separate audit committee, audit issues.
- The Nominating/Governance Committee - typically charged with finding and recommending new directors for board approval, but sometimes also charged with recommending officer and committee appointments, establishing criteria for board service, reviewing performance of existing directors, and providing orientation for new directors. Some nonprofit nominating committees have taken on the additional role of reviewing and making recommendations on governance issues and otherwise playing a leadership role in shaping the nonprofit's corporate governance.

- The Development Committee - typically oversees the fund raising process of the organization.

Larger boards and organizations may also have additional committees, such as:

- The Audit Committee - responsible for oversight of the independent audit process and for overseeing the financial integrity and finance/accounting controls of the organization. The trend is for members of audit committees to be "independent" board members (i.e., with no significant financial or other relationship to the organization), and to have substantial financial expertise (i.e., experience in reading financial statements and at least one member with an understanding of accounting principles and practices). Audit committees and their membership may be legislatively mandated in certain states for organizations of a certain size.
- Personnel Committee - typically charged with overseeing the development of compensation and benefit programs and guidelines for any paid staff. In some cases, this committee actually approves salaries of the top executives, reviews their expenses, and oversees their formal evaluation. Committee or board approval of the executive/managing director's (i.e. CEO-equivalent) salary and expenses may be legislatively mandated in certain states for organizations of a certain size.
- Investment Committee - responsible for oversight of the investment of funds, typically endowment funds, of the organization and for creating or recommending investment policies.

In addition to standing committees, many boards create ad hoc committees for particular, short term projects. Typical examples would include a strategic planning committee when the organization's strategic plan needs updating, or a facilities committee when new premises are needed, or a search committee when a new executive director is sought.

Regardless of the role of standing or ad hoc committees, their effectiveness can be improved by making sure that each one understands its mandate. An excellent way to achieve this is to create written charters for each committee. Some organizations include these charters in their bylaws. (The Society has sample charters.) Effective staffing of committees by management can also help committees function more efficiently.

Committees also need to report all their activities to the full board, so that body is aware of their work. Depending on the size of the board, or the tradition of the organization, reports can be oral or written.

Nonprofit boards frequently add non-board members to committees, either to broaden the expertise of the committee or to provide an opportunity for getting to know potential board candidates before nominating them for a director role. State law varies on whether such non-director members can actually participate as voting members.

Effective meetings can mean the difference between an engaged, effective board and one that doesn't accomplish much. Running effective meetings is the role of the chair, whether of the board or of a committee.

This is an art, in many ways dependent on the interpersonal skills of the chair. However, there are certain basics which can help:

- Written agendas focus everyone on the matters to be covered and aid the chair in keeping the meeting on schedule. Agendas are typically developed jointly by the chair and the executive director (or in the case of committees, the staff person assigned to support the committee chair).
- Limiting agenda items helps allow for adequate discussion.
- Focusing principally on strategic and forward-looking issues, rather than reviewing past history, helps keep meetings interesting for board and committee members, and makes the discussion more useful to the organization.
- Providing regular opportunities for discussion of the work of the organization and offering directors key insights into substantive issues allows directors to learn more and to feel more connected to the organization.

- Using executive summaries and cover memos to help guide board and committee members through financial statements or other reports can help focus attention on important issues and eliminate confusion and the need for time consuming questions.
- Using written reports rather than oral reports from committees can be an effective way to deliver a great deal of information without taking much time at board meetings.
- Gathering routine, general business items all together at either the end or beginning of the meeting (sometimes referred to as the 'consent agenda') allows the board or committee to act quickly and all at once on matters that don't require much discussion.
- Having draft resolutions prepared in advance and distributed to directors prior to a vote helps insure that everyone clearly understands what action is being requested.
- Maintaining order, not allowing small side discussions, or dominance of discussion by a small group, helps keep everyone focused and the meeting moving.
- Establishing a culture of open discussion, respect for all views, and free exchange of information, helps ensure that all views are heard and no one is intimidated.
- Holding regularly scheduled executive sessions (where some or all members of staff are excused from the meeting) provides an opportunity for directors to ask questions or raise issues they might not feel as free to do in the presence of management and can help ensure that such concerns are surfaced and addressed in a timely manner.
- Documenting actions of the board in concise, written minutes not only facilitates tracking of board actions, but also provides a useful mechanism for keeping directors who could not attend a prior meeting informed and up-to-date on board deliberations, particularly if draft minutes are sent out promptly following a meeting.
- Meetings between the chair and the executive director promptly after a board meeting to discuss what went well,

what needs to be improved, and what follow up is needed, helps create both improvement and continuity from meeting to meeting.

Effective boards come in many forms, but they generally have several things in common: They understand the business or mission of the organization; they help move the organization's business or mission forward; and they understand and operate in accordance with legal and fiduciary responsibilities. Increasingly, nonprofit boards are adapting governance practices from the for-profit arena to help them maintain or improve their effectiveness. While good governance practices cannot absolutely assure board or organizational effectiveness, they certainly can help make it more likely than not that the affairs of an organization are well-managed.

Dysfunctional or ineffective boards are usually easy to spot. Typically they are characterized by one or more of the following:

- The board does not have, or does not abide by, a regular meeting schedule.
- At board meetings nothing much happens, and many board members don't attend or are disaffected.
- Directors don't understand the mission or business of the organization and aren't passionate about either.
- Directors don't understand the financial underpinnings of the organization.
- Directors attempt to micromanage the staff.
- There's a lack of trust and confidence between the board and management.
- Directors or management speak disrespectfully of others on the board and/or of management.
- Directors or management speak publicly, without permission, about confidential board matters.
- A few directors dominate meetings.
- Directors don't understand basic governance principles.
- The organization is floundering.

To help gauge the effectiveness of a board on which you serve or are thinking of joining, try asking the following governance-related questions:

YES	NO	
☐	☐	Does the board get enough information of the right kinds, at the right time, from the right members of management?
☐	☐	Does the board have an effective director-orientation program?
☐	☐	Does the board have active committees composed of a small, effective number of members to tackle audit, development/fund-raising, finance, governance, nomination, personnel, program and other key matters?
☐	☐	Does the board rotate committee members and chairs at appropriate intervals?
☐	☐	Are meetings conducted effectively, with appropriate frequency, on time and according to well-thought-out agendas circulated in advance?
☐	☐	Are meetings characterized by open communication and diligent questions discussed in a collegial manner?
☐	☐	Does the board meet regularly in private apart from the executive director and other managers?
☐	☐	Are the board's actions motivated by and designed in furtherance of the organization's mission?
☐	☐	Does the board periodically review the organization's mission statement and implementation strategy?
☐	☐	Does the board act as if it is accountable to contributors and beneficiaries?
☐	☐	Does the board communicate effectively on a regular basis with its stakeholders, contributors and beneficiaries?
☐	☐	Does the board establish goals for the chief executive and review his or her effectiveness and performance on at least an annual basis?
☐	☐	Does the board have effective processes and structures to evaluate, communicate with and counsel the chief executive?
☐	☐	Does the board have guidelines for managers clearly specifying their authority?
☐	☐	Does the board micromanage the organization's operations or, at the other extreme, does it ignore them and let management handle everything with little board oversight?
☐	☐	Has the board reviewed the operation's significant legal exposures and assessed the organization's legal compliance processes and record?
☐	☐	Does the board have effective audit and financial oversight processes?
☐	☐	Does the board review and adopt the organization's capital and operating budgets?
☐	☐	Does the board have clear and effective procedures on handling funds, contributions and assets?
☐	☐	Does the board have effective standards and procedures to minimize and disclose potential conflicts of interest?
☐	☐	Does the board governance and nominating committee regularly assess board practices and structures for effectiveness; evaluate current directors and counsel those whose performance is less than ideal; and continually look for talented potential new directors?
☐	☐	Does the board have an appropriate level of turnover in its membership -- new members and ideas balanced with experience and continuity?

If you end up with a number of "no" answers, it may be time to suggest a board-effectiveness study. Conducting regular board-effectiveness studies can keep boards from drifting into dysfunctional behavior, help cure them if they are already there, and also help increase the effectiveness of already effective boards. Furthermore, the effectiveness of boards and the implementation of good governance practices are now both of great interest to funders of nonprofit organizations, making it ever more essential for nonprofits to focus on strengthening their governance and their board effectiveness. A board-effectiveness survey:

- Polls the board on a number of issues related to the effective operation of the board, focusing on both substance and process.
- Provides a base line for looking at how the board itself believes it is doing, and for comparing board practices to those of other boards and to governance trends.
- Becomes a starting point for making adjustments and improvements.

The process is relatively simple: A series of questions is developed by the director appointed to lead the project, with input from management and other directors, and if desired with assistance from an outside consultant. Questions typically range from the level of "housekeeping" (e.g., time, place and length of meetings) to the more substantive (e.g., what do you think are the critical issues facing the organization in the next two years?). These questions are used as the basis for eliciting information from directors, although it is common for the answers to bring up issues beyond the questions asked. More detailed and representative results will be obtained by using face-to-face interviews rather than written responses to questions and by interviewing as many of the full board as possible, although that process can be quite time consuming. In addition, responses must be summarized in a format that will be useful to the board and also protect the confidentiality of those who participated.

Once results are summarized, they are shared with the board and a process created for follow-up and adjustments to board procedures and organization. Most effectiveness surveys will not be self-executing, but require changes in how committees or the board operate, who is on the board, what is expected of board members, etc. Issues raised in the survey may need to be worked on by a variety of board committees. But the effort can be well worth it if it improves the effectiveness of the board.

Even without a board-effectiveness study, there are a number of steps which can help improve board effectiveness, including one or more of the following:

- Make a board committee responsible for governance issues:
  * Possibilities include the executive committee, nominating committee, or a separate governance committee.
- At least once a year, have the committee responsible for governance:
  * Look at external trends in governance.
  * Compare trends to board practices.
  * Recommend adjustments as needed.
  * Inform the board about its legal/governance responsibilities.
- Review articles of incorporation, bylaws, committee charters, the board's own governance guidelines and key policies to make sure:
  * They meet changing governance and legal requirements/standards.
  * - The organization actually conducts its affairs in accordance with those documents.
- Create a written document outlining expectations or responsibilities of directors:
  * Be specific, especially about time and money expectations.
  * Have the full board approve it so all directors know exactly what is expected.
  * Use this in recruiting new directors.
- Define other roles:
  * Define the role of the board-is it an operating board, a governing board, does it set strategy, hire/fire the CEO, review finances, approve budgets, etc. Write it down!

  * Create written job descriptions for executive management.
  * Create written job description for the board chair/president.
  * Create written charters for board committees.
- Define what you are looking for in board members:
  * Be rigorous in seeking board members who meet these criteria.
  * Determine an optimum size for the board and do not allow it to become too large or too small.
  * But save a little room to be opportunistic.
- Review who is on the board in comparison to what you need/are looking for:
  * What background and skills do they have?
  * How engaged are they-time, money, attendance, etc.?
  * How do they compare to what you need?
- Establish a process for meeting with directors to re-engage those not meeting expectations or to prepare them to leave the board.
- Consider establishing term limits to ensure that there is always "new blood" on the board.
- Create active dialog with management so the board stays informed:
  * About the accomplishment of the organization's mission and day-to-day operations-what's happening: good and bad.
  * About the organization's financial situation-compare budget to actual performance, conduct tutorials on how to read/understand financial statements (don't take financial expertise for granted).
  * About the organization's competition.
  * About the organization's strategy.
  * About executive management's "dreams."
- Keep board members engaged-make sure meetings give them something they can't get except for being on your board and participating in board meetings.

- Keep committees meaningful and helpful:
  * Review the need for each standing and ad hoc committee annually. Is the charter still viable, is the committee actually doing what it is supposed to, is it helpful to the board or to management, or a drain on resources?
  * Establish committee goals annually and have committees report on what was accomplished by year-end.
  * Rotate committee members to avoid entrenched thinking and to spread expertise.
- Establish a board orientation process for new directors and a "board book" to help them get up to speed quickly. Such an orientation might include:
  * Meetings with key staff to understand the role of their departments and strategic issues facing the organization.
  * Meetings with the chair of the board and committee chairs.
  * Delivery of a book containing key organizational documents, such as the organization's charter, bylaws, mission statement, annual tax report, code of conduct or conflict of interest policy, other critical board policies, any written expectations of directors, contact information for other directors and key staff, and perhaps a "glossary" of terms and acronyms used in the organization that outsiders might not know.

Do all these ideas sound too daunting? Well, building and maintaining an effective board is not a process that happens overnight. It requires leadership from both the executive director and the chair, or another member of the board. The good news is that building an effective board can be done in stages. If your organization is not ready for some of the effectiveness practices described above, start with one or two-perhaps strengthening agendas so they focus on strategic, important issues based on both director and staff input, or strengthening the board based on clear criteria developed jointly with the board. With leadership from the chair or another senior director and executive director it's relatively easy to bring the board into the process of improving governance over time. Without such leadership, nothing much is likely to improve.

MAKING BOARD SERVICE FULFILLING

As suggested at the beginning of this document, board service on nonprofits can be fulfilling and engaging, or the opposite.

Following is a checklist which summarizes a number of the issues that you may want to consider in reviewing directorship opportunities or in examining your role as a director of a nonprofit. This checklist is not necessarily all inclusive, but reflecting on the issues raised in this checklist can help you determine whether you want to join a particular board or, if you are already on the board, whether there are important issues that may need to be addressed either personally or organizationally.

1. Do you know why you were asked, or are being recruited, to serve on the board and what the board's expectations of you are, including any financial support or time commitment obligations?
2. Are you committed to being a good director and helping advance not only the mission of the organization, but the governance of the organization?
3. Do you have a copy of the organization's charter, bylaws and mission statement, and have you read them? Does the board periodically review these documents to make sure they are current with changes in law or practice, or strategy?
4. Is there a code of conduct for directors and do you have a copy? Do you understand your responsibility under the code and know who is responsible for enforcement of the code?
5. Is there a conflicts of interest policy (either in a code of conduct or a separate document)? Do you understand your responsibilities under the policy and know who is responsible for enforcement of the policy?
6. Does the organization provide Directors and Officers' Insurance?

7. Do you and other directors have copies of other critical board policies and are you aware of other policies that may be legally required for your organization (such as a document retention policy, or whistleblower policy)?
8. Who in the organization is responsible for filing tax forms related to the organization's nonprofit status and who reviews those forms?
9. Are financial performance and budget documents understandable and regularly monitored by the board or a committee of the board?
10. Are financial statements audited?
11. Are there policies in place to monitor donor designations on donations to the organization and who monitors compliance with them?
12. Do you know who else is on the board and how to contact other members?
13. Are you and other directors engaged in the work of the board and the organization?
14. How well do you and other directors understand the mission of the organization?
15. Do you and other directors preserve the confidentiality of material and information given or presented to the board?
16. Is the board functioning effectively, with regular well-attended and well-run meetings addressing important issues?
17. Does the board periodically review its own effectiveness?
18. Is the board up-to-date in its governance practices and, specifically, has the board considered the applicability to the organization of principles contained in Sarbanes Oxley and other governance legislation?
19. Do you and other directors understand your legal obligations as directors, including the duty of care and duty of loyalty, and the fact that board must act as a body, not through individual directors?
20. Do committees function well and serve the current needs of the organization?

21. Is there a well-understood process for recruiting new directors, with established criteria for seeking particular directors?
22. Is there a well-understood process for development and succession of officers of the board?
23. Is there a board orientation program or manual?
24. Is there a well-understood process for management development and succession planning?
25. Are key staff members formally evaluated by the chief executive and those evaluations shared with the board?
26. Are key staff salaries and expenditures approved by the chief executive and reviewed by the board or a committee of the board?

Aside from making sure there is a good fit between your expectations and those of the organization, considering the governance practices of the organization may also help you understand how well the organization functions and accomplishes its mission and how effective your service as a director may be.

Given the great differences in size, strength, and missions of nonprofits, not all governance principles common in the for-profit arena will make sense for nonprofits. However, we hope that the principles and ideas identified in this document provide you and the organization you serve with food for thought and a roadmap for improving governance to the benefit of both.

GUIDES AND TIPS: SAMPLE MEETING RULES

Following is a much abridged version of Robert's Rules as they might be adapted for nonprofit meetings. Their goal is to promote a balance of fairness and efficiency. Tailor them to fit your own culture. Meetings should be fair so that people who have a point to make are given an opportunity. Meetings should be efficient so that time is spent on discussion relevant to the matter at hand.

Discussion

Only members and guests recognized by the chair may speak.

Motions & Voting

Only members of the board who are present at the meeting may vote. Before an item can be voted, there must be a quorum as well as a motion and a second from two different members of the board. Discussion may precede or follow these motions, or both, depending on how closely the organization follows Robert's Rules. After discussion and motions, one of four things can happen:

- There can be a vote on the motion.
- The motion may be amended (second required), discussion on the amendment may follow and a vote taken on the amendment. If the amendment passes, the motion automatically passes. If the amendment fails, the motion still stands and can be discussed until voted.
- The motion can be tabled (second required). There can be no discussion on a motion to table — a vote must be taken immediately. If the vote is to table, no further discussion can take place on the motion.
- There may be no action on the motion —therefore it becomes old business at a future meeting.

Motions must be clear and concise. A motion to "improve fund-raising" would be vague and discussions could meander. However, a motion to "sponsor a benefit golf tournament" is specific and could be effectively discussed and acted on.

To help clarify exactly what is being voted upon, it is useful to distribute written draft resolutions spelling out the desired action. There is no prescribed form for a resolution. Traditionally, many start out with a series of "whereas" clauses indicating the background or reasons for the proposed action, but such clauses are not required. The most important thing to keep in mind in drafting resolutions is clarity.

Committees

Make general board meetings more productive by use of committees and rely on committee reports as a basis for action. The idea is for committees to sort through minutiae and come forward with a well-developed proposal for the whole board to consider. Committee reports can be oral or written. Written reports, distributed in advance of the meeting, tend to save time at the meeting. Bylaws of some organizations may require that the board vote to accept committee reports of certain committees.

Disagreements

The chair of the meeting is responsible for maintaining order. On procedural questions, the chair's ruling is determinative and final.

Executive Sessions

Executive sessions are generally for the purpose of discussing sensitive issues, such as personnel matters, outside the presence of non-board members. They also provide a forum to help ensure board members feel free to raise any issues they are concerned about but which they might feel awkward raising in the presence of staff. If the executive director is a member of the board, he or she must consent to being asked to leave the meeting. While minutes are not generally kept of executive sessions, it can be helpful for the chair to report the discussion in general terms to the executive director, particularly if the discussion raised major concerns or issues of continuing interest to the board. Such communication can also reduce stress and the sense of being excluded that may arise for an executive director who is excused from a portion of the meeting. Holding executive sessions regularly also minimizes the stress or alarm to the organization that can be occur if such sessions are called only sporadically or only when a real crisis arises.

Possible Order of Business —Per Agenda Circulated in Advance

Common Order of Business

1. Opening of meeting and introductions (Chair)
2. Approval of minutes of previous meeting (Secretary)
3. Reports and discussion, i.e. chair calls for reports from the treasurer, executive director, development committee, or program committee
4. Old business to be brought up (Chair)

5. Unfinished business from previous meetings
6. Motions that were tabled from previous meetings
7. New business - motions to be made for voting by the board (Chair)
8. Executive Session (Chair)
9. Adjournment (Chair)

Alternative Order of Business

1. Opening of meeting and introductions (Chair)
2. Comments from chair or executive director
3. Discussion of strategic issues (Executive Director)
4. Review of financial performance (Treasurer or CFO)
5. General business/Consent Items (i.e., no significant discussion needed)
6. Minutes of previous meeting
7. Written committee reports
8. General business resolutions
9. Executive Session (Chair)
10. Adjournment (Chair)

   - Minutes: The purpose of minutes and reports is to document what was done (i.e., what action was taken), not what was said.
     a. Minutes are not intended to be a verbatim report.
     b. It's okay to re-organize comments-e.g., if a relevant comment comes at the end of meeting related to an item in the beginning of the meeting, you can report it with the discussion at the beginning.
     c. Describe what topics were covered rather than trying to summarize what was actually said. For example: "The committee discussed the size of the staff in relation to available space, future staff needs and the possibility of reconfiguring space, the feasibility of renting additional space or of implementing telecommuting." Avoid characterizations and adjectives, either favorable or unfavorable. Stick to facts and stay away from opinions.

d. Remember, boards and committees take action as a group. It is usually not important to "name names" in summarizing discussions. However, minutes typically start off with a list of directors who were present and those who were absent.

e. When action is taken it is typical to indicate what was basis for the action-e.g., after discussion, after review of material, after the presentation, etc.

f. When reporting action taken, be as specific as possible. If a resolution is needed, try to have it drafted before the meeting, though sometimes it may be necessary to draft the specific wording after the fact.

g. It's okay to be repetitious in style. Minutes are meant to be a record, not literature.

h. In general, shorter or medium length minutes are likely to generate less legal risk than very detailed long-form minutes, especially if counsel is not involved in reviewing them.

i. Consider using headings for each section to help you decide if something is really worth mentioning. E.g., if you have a heading followed by an offhand remark or very short discussion, it may not be worth even including as a separate topic.

j. You can also append committee reports or presentation documents as attachments to minutes if it helps the reader of the minutes. This isn't generally done for regular reports such as finance or committee reports-though you certainly could re-circulate such reports if it helps. There is a big legal difference between appending a report to the minutes, which makes it part of the minutes, and just re-circulating a report to help people remember something or learn what was said if they weren't there.

k. Executive Sessions are not generally minuted, although sometimes it can be helpful to list the general topic discussed.

l. Try to write minutes as soon as practicable after a meeting-at least an initial draft. Adopting this practice makes it much easier to remember key points.

- Reports: In drafting reports of meetings, try not to reinvent the wheel. If possible, just shorten the minutes and take out what isn't relevant for a report.e.g., no need to list attendance, no need to list specific comings and goings, no need to include a call to order or adjournment, etc.
- Record Keeping: Minutes, including those of committees, are typically kept in a notebook or a folder titled Minutes, organized by date of meeting. It can also be helpful to keep a separate list or index of resolutions adopted and, particularly, of policies adopted, so they are easier to find in the future when someone may ask for them. Once minutes are approved, most secretaries dispose of any handwritten notes or tapes that were used to create them. The approved minutes are the official record and it can be confusing, and inadvisable from a legal standpoint, to keep prior drafts or handwritten notes.

5

FINANCIAL MANAGEMENT OF NONPROFIT ORGANIZATIONS

RATIONALE

Finance is the art of managing an organization's resources to bring about operational outcomes. For a manager of a nonprofit organization, managing the organization's finances is especially challenging. A nonprofit organization's revenue sources are frequently subject to changes in both economic forces and political climate. Yet, it has to compete for labor and other inputs just like any other organization. Accurate recording and reliable reporting of financial information are the preconditions for financial management. Public accountability also requires a high degree of accuracy and reliability of financial data. The financial statements of a nonprofit organization provide a useful overview of the organization's fiscal health.

Financial management involves both planning and implementation. A nonprofit manager needs to be able to analyze and interpret historical and current financial information and to prepare financial plans to ensure the effective operations of an organization. Financial management may entail both short-term day-to-day operation and long term capital investment that require advance planning. Central to the analysis is an understanding of the cost structure of the organization. Increasingly, creative revenue strategies are called upon to offset diminished public funding sources in cyclical economic downturns. A financial plan is seldom implemented as is. Changes in circumstances or lack of perfect foresight require frequent financial adjustments that may have significant operational implications. This competency requires students to be able to understand the basic accounting tasks of recording transactions and producing financial statements, to demonstrate skills in utilizing financial information to conduct analyses and address common financial management issues of a non-profit organization.

PREREQUISITES: Quantitative Reasoning.

COMPETENCY: Can explain the compilation of financial statements, prepare budgets, analyze costs and revenue structure, and conduct necessary financial analysis to address issues arises in the implementation of financial plans of nonprofit organizations.

CRITERIA:

1. Explain the purpose of each financial statement of a nonprofit organization and define the terms used within the statements. Take a set of sample transactions through the accounting cycle from books of original entry to basic financial statements. Explain the difference between cash and accrual accounting.
2. Explain the resource allocation and financing decision functions of a nonprofit organization. Describe the basic elements of financial management, including developing and maintaining financial goals. Describe the IRS requirements for obtaining and retaining tax-exempt status and the reporting requirements imposed by the various state and federal tax authorities. Explain the importance of tax-exempt status to the organizations.
3. Explain the basic methods and tools (e.g. financial ratios) used in analyzing financial information to determine trends, measure progress towards stated goals, and help in assessing future prospects.
4. Define and explain the techniques for developing operating budgets, including: line item budgeting, performance budgeting, and program budgeting. Develop a budget for an organization based on its financial information.
5. Define direct and indirect costs, fixed costs, cost allocation, and unit costs, and explain how these concepts are used in making decisions on resource allocation.

6. Explain the differences between operating budgets and capital budgets, and describe the steps in planning for capital expenditures, including estimating cost with discounting, bidding, financing options, depreciation, and budgeting for the future surplus needs of an organization.
7. Conduct a cash flow analysis using financial data, and describe the methods of cash flow planning and control, including sources and uses of cash, cash flow budgeting, and cash flow management techniques.
8. Explain the importance of internal controls and the role of outside auditors. Explain the responsibility of the manager in establishing and maintaining adequate controls.

STANDARDS:

1. For Criterion 1, record a minimum of 10 financial transactions in the general journal, the general ledger of t-accounts. Then, utilize the information to prepare a trial balance and the financial statements. Explain the purpose of each statement, define the terms used, and explain the source of the information. Discuss the advantages and disadvantages of cash and accrual accounting, and the implications for decision-making.
2. Explanations and definitions must follow standard accounting practice and must be referenced. Describe the process of applying for tax-exempt status with the IRS, and the requirements for retaining that status. Explain the reporting requirements imposed by the IRS and the state payroll taxing authorities.
3. Explanation of the financial methods and tools must include what they are, the circumstances under which they are useful, as well as their limitations. The financial analysis may include the use of vertical and horizontal analysis, comparative analysis, and completion of financial ratios. Numerical calculations need to be supplemented by narrative discussion. Financial data used for Criteria 4 - 8 may be provided by the faculty evaluator, or (with prior approval from the evaluator) from the student's own experience.

4. The budget developed for Criterion 5 must include narrative description of the method used, all relevant assumptions, and objectives to be achieved during the budget period.
5. Demonstration of understanding various cost concepts must include a numerical example showing the calculations leading to the cost amount, as well as a discussion of how changes in them affect resource allocation within the organization.
6. Demonstration of understanding a capital budget must include a numerical example showing the calculations for various relevant budget items, as well as a discussion of the risks a capital budget necessarily entails.
7. Cash flow analysis for Criterion 8 is to be completed monthly for a 12-month period. All relevant assumptions need to be outlined. Steps of calculation must be clear. Numerical results must be accompanied by a narrative summary.
8. Give examples of controls for various assets of the organization. Describe and explain the purpose of various internal control mechanisms: bank statement reconciliation; periodic inventories; petty cash systems; separation of function; purchase order systems. Discuss the criteria and process used in selecting external auditors.

EXAMPLES OF DEMONSTRATION:

1. Prior Learning: You have worked for a community organization as a staff person responsible for managing its finances. You may provide written documents of actual financial tasks you have performed for the organization, like the historical analysis, the preparation, and the implementation of its budgets. These tasks must address the criteria in the competency. Based on the documentation you submit, the evaluator may discuss with you further details not apparent in the written documents.
2. Independent Learning: You make arrangements with an independent evaluator to write critical summaries of selected relevant readings, and to complete various

hypothetical financial management exercises and/or real-life case studies.

3. Course: You complete all the requirements of CPCS course addressing this competency.
4. Field Project: Under the close supervision of a faculty-evaluator and cooperation of a nonprofit agency, you participated in a field project to examine the financial statements and relevant budget documents of the agency. Based on this information, you analyzed the various financial management aspects of the agency, covering all the criteria of the competency.

6

THE NON-PROFIT PARADOX

In a competitive business environment, with shrinking support from both government contracts and private donors, and with society's increasing need for its services, the nonprofit must embrace the best practices of the commercial, for-profit world in order to survive. Yet for-profit strategies can become the nonprofit's downfall by undermining its culture, mission, and public image. In an effort to save its bottom line, the modern nonprofit risks losing its soul. This article discusses the paradox—its causes, symptoms, and possible remedies.

INTRODUCTION

It has become a generally accepted truth in the nonprofit world that third-sector organizations must embrace the best practices of the for-profit, business world in order to survive. The mantra "no money, no mission," is heard throughout the third sector. The loftiest mission will fail if its delivering organization lacks the financial stability to stay afloat. An increasingly competitive business environment, with shrinking support from government and private donors, dictates that nonprofits acquire the efficiency, flexibility, innovativeness, and discipline traditionally represented in the competitive for-profit sector.

But does this solution carry the seeds of destruction? Others have argued that for-profit commercialization and resulting revenue streams threaten the nonprofit sector (Weisbord, 1998). Here the focus is on not the dollars but the for-profit model itself. The position proposed in this article is that the modern nonprofit faces a paradox. The business practices the nonprofit embraces to assure its survival threaten to undermine its culture, mission, and public image. In an effort to save its bottom line, the modern nonprofit risks losing its soul.

The first section of this article discusses some of the characteristics of the for-profit business model and demonstrates how, like a virus in a new organism, they can become fundamentally unhealthy to the nonprofit. The second section suggests several underlying reasons for the paradox. The third section presents the case of a large community mental health center; its success in incorporating the efficiency, flexibility, innovativeness, and discipline of the for-profit business world; and the resulting dangers to its culture, public image, and mission. The fourth section reviews the tradition of the nonprofit sector in American culture and various theories for its success. Finally, this article concludes with suggestions for solving the nonprofit paradox. Strategies call for reexamining board governance and staff management, constantly reevaluating mission relevance, and even asking whether to retain nonprofit status.

THE DYNAMICS OF THE NONPROFIT PARADOX

There can be no doubt about the general trend of nonprofits embracing the concepts and techniques of for-profit business and industry. For years, the task of operating a nonprofit was considered *administration*, from the Latin *administrare*, "to serve." The term was used as a substitute for *management*, which was associated in the public mind with business and profit making (Mulhare, 1999). In 1973, the Commission on Private Philanthropy and Public Needs, known as the Filer Commission, was formed to conduct a comprehensive, multidisciplinary survey of the nation's nonprofit sector (Hall, 1987: 20; Commission on Private Philanthropy and Public Needs, 1975a, 1975b, 1977). The commission concluded that the nonprofit sector faced serious problems, including a shortage of pertinent research and no academic programs to prepare nonprofit leaders. Yale University created the Program on Nonprofit Organizations in 1976, the first research center of its kind (Powell, 1987: xi). In 1980, the Independent Sector was formed as a permanent consortium dedicated to strengthening nonprofit organizations through research, education, and advocacy (Independent Sector, 1989).

Research centers, academic programs awarding degrees or certificates in nonprofit management, and continuing education programs developed during the 1980s (Hodgkinson, 1988: 3-5, 13). New trade periodicals and scholarly journals gained in popularity, including *Nonprofit and Voluntary Sector Quarterly, Nonprofit Management and Leadership, Nonprofit World Report, Chronicle of Philanthropy,* and *Nonprofit Times.* For-profit organizations underwrote research projects on nonprofit management issues (e.g., Independent Sector 1986). Today more than 60 U.S. colleges and universities offer coursework or research opportunities in nonprofit management (Whittaker, 1995: 59-62). From coast to coast, highly rated programs flourish: Harvard University, University of Indiana at Bloomington, University of Minnesota, Yale University, Northwestern University, University of Michigan at Ann Arbor, and Stanford University.

Professionalized nonprofit management incorporates concepts and techniques almost exclusively from for-profit business and industry (Bailey, Grochau, and Speltz, 1990). Perhaps this reliance on for-profit models stems from the financial uncertainty in which nonprofit organizations have found themselves during the past several decades. Government budgets have been cut even while needs have continued to grow. Organizations under stress look to outside models they perceive as successful and promising (DiMaggio and Powell, 1983). A related explanation is offered by Ryan (1999), who notes that the social services industry in the United States is in a period of transition marked by the entry of for-profit organizations that compete directly with nonprofits for government contracts. According to Ryan, for-profits entering the social services industry enjoy four distinct advantages: size, capital means capability, mobility, and responsiveness. In an attempt to compete head to head with for-profits, nonprofits in the industry are adopting for-profit management models in hopes of sharing these advantages.

What is this for-profit business model to which the nonprofit sector has looked for salvation? Generally, it has been a developing series of management models emphasizing quality (of products or services), efficiency (cost management), flexibility (assuring adaptation to change), innovation (striving for improvements in products and services), and above all a disciplined focus on the financial bottom line, the for-profit's raison d'etre.

But adoption of this model has not occurred without consequences. Consider the following:

1. More business people are recruited for nonprofit boards of trustees because of their influence, money, and business expertise.
2. Nonprofits are understandably encouraged to hire staff, especially senior executive staff, with business expertise and skill as opposed to mission-related acumen. In addition, non-mission-related outside consultants, such as accountants and attorneys, are brought in to address issues such issues as financial accountability and risk management.
3. New for-profit management systems, which emphasize productivity, quality assurance, budget discipline, or strategic planning, are forced on a mission-oriented staff.
4. Even the lexicon of business has effloresced in the nonprofit world.

Much of the above is undeniably good for public charities, especially those plagued by financial ills or lackluster delivery of services. However, the following side-effects are often troubling:

1. Boards of directors tend to be underused for their proper role of assuring mission integrity, strategic planning, and high-level policy-making. Business-oriented board members are inclined to emphasize financial issues over mission issues. When they micromanage, their focus on financial issues exacerbates the problem by diverting even more staff time and resources away from mission activities.
2. Psychological distancing develops between management and program staff. People of different orientations are drawn to these different roles. Management's focus on financial health and program staff's concerns with mission delivery create two camps in the organization, each failing to understand and communicate with the other.
3. As management's decisions are increasingly driven by managers' natural interests and familiarity with financial

issues, mission concerns are deemphasized. This can diminish morale among program staff members who are uncomfortable with the new procedures and unfamiliar with their advantages.

4. Public image suffers. To paraphrase an old saying, "If you walk like a duck and quack like a duck, eventually people will think that you are a duck." As nonprofit organizations increasingly resemble for-profit organizations, they look less and less like the public charities they are meant to be. Donors are less inclined to support organizations outside their traditional notions of public charities. When donors cease to recognize these organizations as public charities, they stop supporting them. This in turn causes management to rely on commercialism to sustain financial viability. The problem compounds itself. With the best of intentions, an organization seeking to assure its financial health ends up trading one set of problems for another.

Reasons for the Paradox

The management strategies borrowed from the for-profit world threaten to undermine the culture, mission, and public image of the nonprofit. Why? Four answers are suggested. They have to do with complexity, transferability, motivation, and values.

Nonprofits are surprisingly complex by comparison to for-profits. The "law of nonprofit complexity" argues that they "tend to be more complex than business firms of comparable size" (Anheier, 2000: 7). Anheier (2000) proposes that the nonprofit environment requires managing diverse constituencies and stakeholders, including a professional core of managers, a governing board of experts and community representatives, a client or user base and their representatives, a volunteer and membership component, and actual service providers. He adds that the nonprofit also must manage a set of contractual relations with both government and business, as well as multiple revenue sources, including donations, fees, charges, subsidies, grants, and contracts.

As a result of this diverse list of constituents, stakeholders, obligations, and revenue sources, nonprofits have, in effect, multiple bottom lines. A recognition of nonprofits as uniquely complex suggests one problem with incorporating ready-made management models from the business world, where prices, wages, profits, and taxes drop down into a single bottom line (Anheier, 2000). In sum, the for-profit model may be too unsophisticated to meet the needs of the non-profit organization.

Some for-profit management models need serious modification for the nonprofit environment. Take, for example, financial management. Bryce (1999) argues that the financial functions in nonprofits and for-profit organizations differ in fundamental ways:

1. For-profit organizations fund growth and finance new initiatives through retained earnings, stock sales, and borrowing. There are no stockholders in a nonprofit. Nonprofit leaders therefore need to be more innovative in exploiting other revenue sources, such as contributions and assessments of membership.
2. For-profit organizations commonly have large investors who own the organizations and may even exercise total control. In nonprofit organizations, large contributors are prohibited from exercising unbridled control.
3. Non-profit public charities must demonstrate that a large portion of their revenues comes from public support or that they are owned by a publicly supported organization. For-profits face no such requirement.
4. The nonprofit sector often has prohibitions against certain types of investments or investment strategies, such as commodity and options trading. Again, for-profits face no such rule.

No judgment of motivation or values is intended here. The motivations of for-profit organizations and those of nonprofit organizations are both perfectly appropriate. Likewise, the values of each sector may be exemplary. The problem is that they differ. It is also important to note that the problem is not that business people are stingy. Quite the contrary, it is impressive how much time and energy business leaders invest in nonprofit work (McFarlan, 1999). The goal of a commercial business enterprise is profitability, not the specific product or service it provides. This differs fundamentally from a nonprofit organization that exists solely to accomplish its mission. For the nonprofit, financial health is a means to the end; for the for-profit, financial health is the end. When people from these two sectors come together in an organization, whether as staff or board members, ambiguity develops around mission, especially when business-oriented people predominate. After all, as Young states, "Calvin Coolidge would not have said, 'The business of nonprofits is not business'" (Young, 2001: 8).

Regarding values, one view holds that a fundamental conflict exists between the moral foundations of the public sectors (government and nonprofits) and those of commerce. Jane Jacobs (1992) describes the "guardian moral syndrome" and the "commercial moral syndrome," both valid and necessary moral systems in their respective contexts. However, when one sort of organization adopts the other's moral system, it will sink into "functional and moral quagmire." Kolthoff and Huberts (2002) hypothesize similarities as well as differences and contradictions between public- and private-sector ethics. They also hypothesize that by adopting a business-style approach to management, nonprofits adopt some values of the business sector.

On a less complimentary note, deLeon and Denhart (2000) discuss the values associated with "entrepreneurial management." They maintain that entrepreneurs are creative and innovative, but also characterized by a narrow focus, an unwillingness to follow rules and stay within boundaries, and so strong a preference for action as to threaten accountability. These are values opposed to those found traditionally in the nonprofit sector. Going further, and assuming that one can closely relate the values of the public sector with those of the nonprofit sector, Bellone and Goerl (1992) argue that entrepreneurship values autonomy, personal vision, secrecy, and risk taking, which may be opposed to administrating values such as democratic accountability, participation, openness, and stewardship.

Less judgmentally, I prefer the example of a city that hires a stonemason and a sculptor to create a memorial for the city square. Both bring valuable talents to the project. However, the stonemason may be primarily motivated to create a structurally sound, lasting memorial, while the sculptor's primary motivation is to create a work of art. Their values of practicality and beauty may also conflict. Each possesses appropriate motivation and values, but they differ, and that creates a problem.

Young (2001) discusses ways that entanglement with business can endanger nonprofits. He notes that nonprofit leaders have few strong counterbalancing influences when faced with financial temptations. They must rely on internalized values and an understanding of the mission if they are to stay on course. Mulgan (2000) acknowledges evidence of a growing convergence between public and private sectors. The continued use of private-sector management practices as the model for public-sector management is bringing pressure to bear on public accountability, as is the growing tendency to appoint private-sector managers to public-sector positions. Mulgan maintains that private, business-oriented managers, when suddenly operating in the non-private sector, resist the comparatively higher degree of scrutiny.

Case in Point

I studied the case of a large community mental health center through interviews and questionnaires of management and program staff, interviews of board members, and observations of the organization over a four-year period. Pikes Peak Mental Health is the name used to refer to a group of associated companies that provide comprehensive mental health and chemical-dependency treatment services to residents of the greater metropolitan area of Colorado Springs, Colorado, and seven surrounding counties in the southern part of the state. Pikes Peak Mental Health employs more than 400 people. It serves more than 13,000 consumers annually. The combined budgets of the four companies exceed $35 million. Comprehensive behavioral health-care services are provided through 21 company-owned facilities and 26 additional off-site programs that supplement public and private endeavors, including services to schools, jails, and nursing homes. The organization is a 501 (c)(3) private nonprofit corporation with funding from Medicaid, public support, local government contracts, state contracts, and client and third-party insurance. The organization's greatest challenge is securing the funding to continue to treat the indigent mentally ill population. The original Pikes Peak Mental Health Center first became a comprehensive community mental health provider in 1970. Legislation of the 1960s, enacted under President John F. Kennedy, resulted in mentally ill patients being moved out of institutions and into community mental health centers that were multipurpose and comprehensive. The chief executive officer at the outset had originally trained as a mental health therapist, and he continued to run the organization for 30 years. In 2000, he retired and was replaced by a new CEO, who also had been trained as a mental health therapist and who had been with the organization for 25 years. Obviously, leadership had been stable and closely tied to mission.

Under state fee-for-service contracts, the Mental Health Center grew slowly but consistently. With the fee-for-service model, relatively little concern was given to business efficiencies, because the way to earn more revenue to cover expenses was simply to provide more services. In addition, the organization, through its original CEO, developed a reputation for entrepreneurship by creating new revenue sources to supplement fee-for-service. It purchased real estate, some quite profitable. Property that had been a motel was leveled and leased to a Wendy's fast-food franchise, which paid a percentage of its earnings to the Mental Health Center. Following the savings and loan crisis of the 1980s, the Mental Health Center purchased a large apartment complex from the Resolution Trust Corporation at a depressed price. Sound management and a rising real estate market have turned that property into a substantial revenue source. These types of real-estate activities have given Pikes Peak Mental Health something of a national reputation as an innovative entrepreneurial nonprofit. Another prominent source of revenue developed under a state Medicaid contract for providing behavior health-care services to Medicaid patients in the area.

From time to time, it was suggested that a more efficient business model be implemented. However, the organization had little financial motivation to change, and it grew without any fundamental alteration in the way it managed business. That all changed in 1996, when Medicaid went from a fee-for-service model to a capitation model. With profits now based on the difference between costs and the captivated fee provided under the contract, the organization immediately had an incentive to become more efficient. In addition, the margin earned under the Medicaid contract had provided much of the funding for treating the indigent mentally ill. With this new incentive, the organization began to emphasize efficient business practices. While management personnel made this transition, clinical personnel providing health services lagged behind, as might be expected. Clinical personnel, many of whom had not appreciated the earlier entrepreneurial investments, likewise did not appreciate the need for a new, more efficient way of doing business. With every change toward more professional, business-oriented management, clinical staff morale suffered.

For a period in the late 1990s, Medicaid grew but general funds from the State of Colorado for treating the indigent stayed level and then began to decline. The situation reached crisis proportions in 2002, when both Medicaid and general fund monies were cut.

The new Chief Executive Officer undertook a number of changes in an effort to gain even more efficiency and professionalism in management. The organization restructured itself as a family of four separate companies, each providing different services for the mentally ill. The Pikes Peak Mental Health Center continued to provide therapy for the mentally ill; Aspen Diversified Industries provided job training and employment for the mentally disabled; Connect Care provided managed-care contract administration in the behavior health field; and the Pikes Peak Foundation for Mental Health provided fundraising and asset management for all of the companies. More business-trained senior staff came in to run these companies.

The organization adopted updated financial management techniques and tried to acquire the latest in information-technology infrastructure. Eventually, in 2003, a corporate restructuring resulted in the elimination or reduction of the operating companies' boards of directors and the creation of the overarching holding company board of directors to oversee and coordinate the activities of all the companies. The theory was that this new emphasis on sound business management would minimize cost and maximize profits in an environment of decreasing government support, and also would encourage growth and revenue among three of the companies even while the original Mental Health Center suffered under state budget cuts. Working together, the family of companies would support one another through bad times. The organization had been proactive, even bold, in anticipating the challenges facing it.

Today the organization continues in transition, and the news is mixed. The senior executive staff is highly trained and experienced in professional business management. Best business practices are incorporated in all areas of administration. Accountability and profitability are emphasized. The organization has been updated in its technology, management efficiencies, and clinical models. Despite a crisis in funding, it has found innovative financing solutions and continues to provide behavioral health-care services in a difficult financial environment, though some services for the indigent are still seriously limited. Several of the companies are actually growing. However, not all news is good.

Board of Directors

The members of the new holding company board of directors are unsure of their new role. What were once four separate boards have now been consolidated into one overarching, managing board of directors. While their opportunity for micro-management has been decreased, they are uncertain about their new role in leading the combined organizations. Remaining foundation board members, traditionally asset managers, are now being asked to move into the area of fundraising, and they are finding this transition difficult. Other board members, who have concerned themselves with the issues of individual companies, hesitate to take on broad leadership and strategic issues for the family of companies. How well these board members will rise to the new challenge of strategic leadership for the families of companies is yet unknown.

Staff

Morale among clinical staff suffers. Clinical staff is uncomfortable with the changes made toward more business-like management. Staff members are not convinced of the necessity for these changes. There is concern that the organizations are not living up to their mission of providing sufficient mental health services to the indigent community. Staff members question the priorities of senior management, financial versus mission. They feel that they are not sufficiently consulted and that management does not always value their opinions. Clinical staff members do not feel connected to the members of the board of directors, with whom they say they have little to no contact.

Public Image

The public image of the companies is not clear. Many people in the region mistakenly view the organizations as a quasi-government mental health center, totally supported by government funds in providing mental health treatment. The organization is not widely understood as a public charity in need of public support. Even among those who do understand the organization as a nonprofit mental health-care provider, there has been some resentment over its entrepreneurial endeavors and its failure to act like a more traditional nonprofit organization. All this has inhibited fundraising efforts.

Mission

The integrity of the mission of the affiliated companies of Pikes Peak Mental Health remains a concern. As earlier stated, clinicians continue to worry that financial issues are placed ahead of mission issues. The chief executive officer, while having achieved significant success in maintaining the financial health of the organizations, is also concerned with this mission dilemma. He speaks of the importance of remaining "relevant" to the community. He asks senior staff rhetorically, "If tomorrow Pikes Peak Mental Health ceased to exist, would our community notice?" He is asking the right questions. Is the organization's mission important to the needs of its community? Is this nonprofit meeting those needs? If the future of Pikes Peak Mental Health is bright, it is so precisely because the CEO is confronting this issue of mission. Having spent his professional career in community mental health, he is not about to let the organization drift away from its purpose.

The Nonprofit Tradition in America: Does It Matter?

So what if nonprofits evolve into for-profits providing the same services? Does it matter?

Indeed, it matters a great deal. In the United States, the concept of voluntary association and its evolution into the nonprofit sector are unique in the world. It has provided our society with services considered vital yet unprofitable.

Alexis de Tocqueville traveled the United States in 1831 as an early observer of American traditions. He described voluntary association as uniquely American and influential in promoting America's democratic character (de Tocqueville, 1848). He noted examples of voluntary association, including planting and harvesting, militias, self-protection from hostiles, and barn raisings. He found that four characteristics contributed to this phenomenon of voluntary association:

1. A lack of class structure.
2. Frontier dangers and difficulties.
3. Open spaces.
4. A lack of governing presence to do the job.

These associations were motivated to provide services seen as vital to American life yet unavailable from third-party businesses or government because they were not seen as profitable or practical. From this beginning the nonprofit sector evolved.

Americans have never been comfortable with the idea of private institutions controlling large amounts of wealth, but at the same time, they place great value on such concepts as individualism, self-expression, personal initiative, and private-over-public action to pursue even public ends. The resulting compromise supported private nonprofit institutions but required that they remain largely volunteer-based, separate from government, and dedicated to those most in need (Salamon, 1997).

Other paradigms may also help us understand the nonprofit sector's value in American society. Hansmann (1980) and others have argued for a view they call "contract failure." Hansmann (1980: page 835) argues that "nonprofits typically arise and are preferred in situations in which, either owing to the circumstances under which a service is purchased or consumed or to the nature of the service itself, customers feel unable to evaluate accurately the quantity or quality of the service a firm produces for them." Customers therefore distrust for-profit organizations and look to the nonprofit whose bottom line is supposedly providing the service and not making a profit. Imagine yourself visiting nursing homes in an attempt to find a comfortable home and a competent and caring staff for your elderly and failing parents. Which are you going to trust most: the for-profit organization with its eye on the bottom line or the nonprofit organization focused on its charitable mission?

Douglas (1987) added to this model the concept of "government failure." In order for government to provide expensive public goods, the goods are subject to what he calls "categorical restraints." The service they offer must be equitable, equal, uniform, and universal. Douglas finds government failure when the categorical restraints, together with the need for popular political support, prevent the government from offering diverse, experimental, or flexible non-bureaucratic services. When these services are needed, the nonprofit organization again fills the void.

Another compelling theory for the purpose and function of a nonprofit organization is proposed by Berger and Neuhaus (1977). They argue that there are two contradicting realities in American life. The first, despite much rhetoric to the contrary, is the continuing desire on the part of Americans for most of the services provided by the modern welfare state. The second is Americans' strong animus against the government, big bureaucracy, and indeed any large institutions of public life, including large economic conglomerates of capitalistic enterprise and big labor. These "mega structures" are a fact of life, yet people look to their private lives for meaning, fulfillment, and personal identity. Nonprofits organizations act as "mediating structures," institutions that mediate and prevent the political order from becoming detached from the values and realities of individual life. Mediating structures are as fundamental as neighborhood organizations.

Families, churches, voluntary associations, and others are the value-generating and value-maintaining agencies in society. In a society as conflicting as ours, they are vital. Democracy is more vulnerable to the erosion of meaning in its institutions compared to totalitarianism, which, although a terrible system, tends to be very stable and long-lasting.

Berger and Neuhaus conclude that mediating structures are essential to any vital democracy, and public policy should protect and foster them. Further, public policy should use these mediating structures, these nonprofit organizations, for the realization of social purposes.

Galambros (1993) proposes that nonprofits act as "institutional facilitators." Historically, American society has come to embrace certain dominant values: equity, security, efficiency, and innovation. As these values came to the fore, nonprofit organizations acting as institutional facilitators were largely responsible for transforming these concepts into reality. Examples include the labor movement; trade associations; and science, engineering, and education associations.

Ryan (1999) notes unique advantages non-profits have traditionally brought to the third sector: better services, due to longer experience and special commitment; unsubsidized services, due to the reinvestment of surplus revenue into more services that government contracts may leave unfulfilled; promotion of civic virtues, by offering opportunities for citizens to become involved in community affairs as volunteers and trustees; and advocacy, by acting as educators, advocates, and vigorous agents of social change. Ryan argues that for-profits are simply unmotivated or ill-equipped to provide these added values.

We make a grave mistake if we forget the nonprofit models and their advantages described by such scholars as Solomon, Hansmann, Douglas, Berger and Neuhaus, Galambros, and Ryan. It is within these models that nonprofit organizations find their intellectual, moral, and practical effectiveness. Here nonprofits, better than any other sector, provide services recognized by our society as vital. The American public will continue to value and support the nonprofit sector as long as it satisfies these needs.

Solutions

Solutions to the nonprofit dilemma involve addressing issues of governance, management, mission, and nonprofit status.

Governance

Strong nonprofit organizations have strong boards of directors. Organizations that make the mistake of developing over-controlled, rubber-stamp boards will be handicapped by their shortsightedness. Visionary, passionate boards of directors lead nonprofit organizations to excellence and relevancy for their communities.

They focus on strategic goals, mission integrity, and high-level policy decisions (Stone, 1991). Boards of directors need to recruit members who are driven by passion for the mission of the organization and who possess particular skills. Staff and board members should join in a partnership dedicated to providing boards with the information and education that will enable them to focus on high-level mission-related issues. Board members should insist on board agendas that promote this focus and discourage preoccupation with operational matters.

Choosing the right CEO may be the most important duty of any nonprofit board. The right CEO for a nonprofit is mission-driven and understands the unique complexities of governance under a nonprofit board of directors (McFarland, 1999). A CEO not motivated by the organization's mission will be seduced by profitability, the marker of for-profit success. A successful nonprofit CEO needs to understand how very different a for-profit board of directors is from a nonprofit board (McFarland, 1999). Unlike the for-profit CEO, who is often the chairman of the board and his own boss, the nonprofit CEO almost always reports to a separate board chairperson. A good working relationship is absolutely essential. McFarland adds that, unlike most for-profit boards, nonprofit boards tend to be large, with active and powerful standing committees. A new CEO who does not know how to work within this framework is destined for trouble.

Boards of directors are a nonprofit's most important link to the community it serves. They, more than anyone else, can create and promote the appropriate image in the community. Public image-building, community connections, and fundraising should be accepted unconditionally as primary board responsibilities and integral to board members' leadership.

Management

In nonprofit organizations, flat, horizontal organizational and management structures promote closer connections between management and program staff, who are the organizations' best connection to mission. Program staff professionals and, if possible, program clientele should be involved in high-level decision-making whenever appropriate. This includes both management decisions and board activities. Some program professionals should attend senior management meetings and board meetings. Their connection to programs and the clientele served will be a constant reminder to staff and board of mission priority (Young, 2001).

As CEOs lead organizations in change, especially management change, justification to staff and board should always be made in terms of the advantage to mission, not financial health, efficiency, or productivity. This message should also be central to an on-going educational effort directed toward management and program staff. There must be no question of senior management's priorities.

On a related issue, nonprofit leadership should ask whether business management tools are actually promoting mission. The answer may be surprising.

Okrepkie and Goodman (2003) investigated whether churches that operate like businesses are significantly more successful than those that do not. Analysis of their survey data showed a statistically significant growth in receipts for churches employing a high level of professional management. However, the statistics did not necessarily support the same conclusions regarding church attendance, which, after all, seems more relevant to a religious mission. Mulharv (1999) suggests that the widespread use of strategic planning by nonprofit organizations today may have more to do with the growing influence of professional management than with strategic planning's efficacies as a management technique. He recommends that applied anthropologists and other management advisers consider whether the nonprofit's customary style of decision-making (an aspect of its organization culture) can be adapted to making wiser decisions about the future. The result may suggest that strategic planning is unnecessary and even counterproductive.

Compared to for-profit businesses, nonprofit organizations are more complex, with more stakeholders, more components, more cultures, more goals, and more operating procedures. This multiplicity requires that management develop multiple models of management to fit the "multiple bottom lines" (Anheier 2000). Professional budget management, for example, doesn't address important areas such as volunteer management, fundraising, and program management.

Mission Relevancy

The American public will continue to value and support the nonprofit sector as long as it satisfies recognized needs not addressed by government or the for-profit sector. The nonprofit sector provides historically valued services that, because they bring no profit, no one else provides. Do the services protect and preserve personal values of private life? Do the services require the hallmark of trustworthiness? Does the organization promote new ideas and theories and policies that have not yet developed a foothold in society? Nonprofits stray from these questions at their own risk.

Changing Nonprofit Status to For-Profit

Perhaps some nonprofits should become for-profit organizations. The nonprofit organization is uniquely complex and multi-functional. If, over time, a single component becomes more market-driven and begins to dominate the organization, consideration should be given to turning this simpler component into a for-profit (Anheier, 2000). Anheier notes that this decision has been made in the U.S. health-care field, where for-profit hospitals and clinics are on the increase. A nonprofit organization that has lost its distinctive multiplicity may function much more smoothly in the for-profit arena. For example, a hospital may partner with for-profit pharmaceutical companies and engage in lucrative research. If the research component of the hospital activities becomes predominant, overshadowing indigent health-care, should that organization consider giving up its tax-exempt status and operating in a sector where it is more recognizable? To carry the conceit to its conclusion, shouldn't a duck admit it's a duck?

SUMMARY AND CONCLUSION

The nonprofit sector has looked to the for-profit professional management model for solutions to the challenges it faces, including the loss of government support, increased competition from the for-profit sector, and society's growing need for services. Greater professionalism in management is needed to ensure financial health, which supports the missions of nonprofit organizations.

"Whether an organization's goals be lofty or modest, public serving or private, they can be achieved only with appropriate financial support. This is no less true of nonprofit universities, hospitals, museums, homeless shelters, and disease research organizations, than it is true for Marshall Fields or General Motors" (Weisbrod, 1998: page 167).

For-profit business models have emphasized efficiency, flexibility, innovation, quality, and a disciplined focus on the bottom line. However, adoption of for-profit management models has not been without consequences for nonprofits. They include the following:

1. More business people recruited for boards of directors, resulting in a greater emphasis on financial concerns over mission-related issues.
2. Senior management staff with greater business experience and skill, but less emotional connection to the mission of the organization.
3. An increased use of outside professional consultants to address such issues as risk management and accountability.
4. A variety of management systems focusing on quality, productivity, accountability, and financial health over mission.
5. Adoption of much of the culture and lexicon of business in the nonprofit organization.

The results may be troubling and problematic:

1. Boards tend to be underused for their proper role of mission integrity, strategic planning, and high-level policy-making.
2. A psychological distancing develops between management staff and program staff. Management's focus on financial

health and program staff's concern about mission serve to create two camps in the organization, each failing to understand and communicate with the other.

3. As management decisions are more and more driven by financial issues, mission concerns are deemphasized, and morale suffers among program staff.
4. Public image suffers as the public begins to see the organization as a for-profit organization rather than as a public charity.
5. Donors are less inclined to support charitable organizations they no longer recognize as such.
6. This lack of public charitable support encourages nonprofit managers to rely more on commercialism for funding. The problem compounds itself.

Four reasons are suggested for the development of this scenario:

1. Nonprofit complexity and multiplicity make the typical nonprofit organization too complex for the comparably simple design of for-profit management models.
2. Transferability of for-profit management models is not always effective. Because of the differing functions and limitations of nonprofits, for-profit management models can be ineffective without serious modifications.
3. Differing motivations underlie the for-profit and not-for-profit organizations: for-profit—bottom line; nonprofit—mission.
4. Conflicts exist between the values expressed in the for-profit sector and those of the nonprofit sector.

These issues were illustrated by the case of a large community mental health center; its success incorporating the entrepreneurial spirit, efficiency, flexibility, innovativeness, and discipline of the for-profit business world, and the consequential dangers to its culture, staff morale, public image, and mission.

It matters a great deal that the nonprofit sector not evolve into another version of the for-profit sector with an emphasis on profitability. At stake is the cultural relevance of the nonprofit sector and the needs that it has served so well, vital services that nobody else can or wants to provide. Public policy writers have offered examples of effective nonprofit models that include the following:

1. Organizations that provide vital services that no other sector provides because there is no profit or no governmental consensus.
2. Services that protect and preserve personal values of private life.
3. Organizations whose services require the hallmark of trustworthiness.
4. Organizations that promote new ideas, theories, and policies that have not yet developed a foothold in society.

Solutions to this paradox are offered:

1. Governance: Boards of directors need to focus on mission integrity, strategic goals, and high-level policy decisions, which are the hallmark of board leadership. Board members need to be recruited for their mission passion as well as their skills. Boards of directors need to connect with the community by promoting the organization's image and fundraising. Boards of directors need to choose the right CEO, one motivated by mission and skilled in the unique characteristics of nonprofit governance.
2. Management: Flat organizational and management structures promote closer connections between management staff and program staff, with their passion for mission. Program professionals should be included at high-level staff and board discussions whenever appropriate. Nonprofit organizations should incorporate multiple management models to address the multiple bottom lines characteristic of nonprofits. Some models, such as financial management, need significant modification to meet nonprofit needs. Management must continually educate program staff on the importance of management tools to accomplish mission. CEOs must lead by a commitment to the mission, with financial health, accountability, and productivity as means to that end.

3. Mission Relevancy: An organization must constantly reevaluate the relevance of its mission against the changing environment. Is its mission needed in the community? If so, is the organization meeting those needs?
4. Nonprofit Status: Some nonprofits should consider changing to for-profit status. As a nonprofit loses its character and acquires a more market-driven character, consideration should be given to the appropriateness of becoming a for-profit organization.

7

TAX EXEMPTIONS FOR NONPROFIT ORGANISATIONS

In recent years, a number of tax-exempt organizations have pursued related activities that normally qualify for tax exemption as for-profit, taxable enterprises. Examples include a university opting to create a for-profit distance learning program, a hospital packaging software for commercial sale, an art museum selling special reproductions, or a housing group participating in a consortium to build low-income housing.

When a nonprofit engages in business activities unrelated to its nonprofit purposes, taxability is usually not a question of choice; various laws and regulations require that the organization pay taxes on this income and, typically, on sales and property. For related activities, however, a nonprofit that can claim tax exemption sometimes chooses to carry out these activities in the form of a taxable enterprise. But why would an organization decide to pay more tax—or at least appear to pay more tax—than the law requires?

This puzzling question was the subject of the fourth seminar on emerging issues in philanthropy sponsored by the Urban Institute's Center on Nonprofits and Philanthropy and the Hauser Center at Harvard University. The seminar, held on November 30, 2000, brought together a wide range of private practitioners representing nonprofit organizations, clients, legal counsel to nonprofit organizations, academics, and researchers.

Information on nonprofits that structure certain activities as for-profit enterprises is scarce because most data on for-profit enterprises of exempt organizations are not public. But the anecdotal evidence suggests that this type of activity, while still only a small part of the nonprofit sector's overall activity, reflects an increasing desire among nonprofits to take advantage of perceived market opportunities—in particular, through the co-investment of taxable parties.

According to the participants' discussion, the taxable form appears desirable when a nonprofit would like to attract out-side capital; more efficiently apportion control among private and nonprofit participants and among various parts of the non-profit itself; provide certain forms of incentive compensation to nonprofit executives or other key employees; or show good citizenship by paying property taxes in the local community.

TAX-EXEMPT ACTIVITY IN NONPROFITS

Has reliance on revenues ancillary to non-profit organizations' exempt purposes—from fees, sales, or royalties—increased in recent years? Ancillary revenue can come from both related activities and unrelated activities. Although no overall measure of such income is available, tax return records filed by nonprofit organizations provide .some insight into their taxable activities. In a panel of 6,000 nonprofit organizations that filed IRS Form 990 returns in 1993 and 1998,[1] the number of taxable subsidiaries grew by more than 50 percent—from 1,449 in 1993 to 2,244 in 1998. Nonprofit organizations with one or more taxable subsidiaries also increased 35 percent, from 980 in 1993 to 1,324 in 1998.

Over the same period, median ownership in a taxable subsidiary among the 6,000 nonprofits dropped from about 90 percent in 1993 to about 50 percent in 1998. This drop, given the rise in taxable subsidiaries, suggests that the number of partners to such activities has increased. In dollar terms, the most material shift has been in income from the "related income" to "unrelated, excluded" category—probably as a result of increased royalties. By contrast, the level of unrelated, taxable income has not changed very much; indeed, about a third of organizations reported net taxable losses, implying that nonprofit organizations classify income and expenses in a way that keeps the amount of tax on unrelated income quite small.

Still, commercial income for nonprofits as a whole has increased in terms of absolute dollars. In a panel of 130,000 organizations that filed IRS Form 990 returns in both 1993 and 1998, 2 66 percent reported an increase in the amount of commercial income. The increase was most prevalent among higher education organizations and hospitals; commercial income rose in three out of four of these types of organizations. Much of that increase may reflect greater sales of related services within the exempt part of the organization, but we have no way of knowing for sure. The growth in commercial revenue may simply reflect the rapidly expanding health sector, which generates a sizable share of its revenues from hospital fees for service. It would not be surprising, however, if growth in program revenue and growth in nonexempt revenue were strongly correlated over time, since both types of revenue generally come from the sale of goods and services.

Taxable Activity: Well Considered and Diverse

Panelists concluded that most activities undertaken as taxable by non-profits appear to be well planned and designed to meet a definite purpose. Beyond this common feature, the taxable activity of nonprofits varies considerably and can take many forms, including limited liability companies, partnerships, trusts, or corporations. Participants named several types of activities that have been pursued under a for-profit structure:

- *Low-income housing* (e.g., a community development corporation engaging in a consortium to build the housing).
- *Other rental housing* (e.g., a non-profit with large property ownership in a community).
- *Distance learning and executive education* (e.g., a university capitalizing on what it already does).
- *Biotechnology* (e.g., a nonprofit research organization engaging in a venture with a profit-making research organization).
- *Business incubators* (e.g., a start-up software company flowing out of a health or educational organization).
- *Information systems* (e.g., disease-management software developed by a large health system to be spun off).

- *Dot-coms* (e.g., a sales operation conducted by commercial businesses for dot-orgs, museum stores, and other nonprofits, often with a percentage of the sales going to the nonprofit).

The Search for For-Profit Partners

Participants identified several reasons for adopting a taxable entity. Often, such initiatives are designed to acquire the expertise of, and coordinate activities with, a particular for-profit partner. The presence of a business partner does not require that a nonprofit give up exemption for the activity in question; the organization usually makes that choice.

Often, the decision to acquire a nonexempt partner is a matter of convenience and will have little effect on the overall activity of both parties. As one panelist observed, "Nonprofits often resist furthering their core mission?through a taxable entity, and the for-profit participant probably doesn't want to learn too much about the nonprofit world."

Panelists described several reasons why nonprofits sometimes forgo tax-exempt status:

To raise financial capital or gain access to human capital. For enterprises that require a great deal of start-up risk capital, a nonprofit may want to lay off the cost of developing programs to a for-profit partner in exchange for giving up a share of the resulting revenues. By creating or partnering with a for-profit entity, a nonprofit can allocate shares of ownership relatively easily. The pure for-profit form also helps minimize the risk that profits will be siphoned off or used to subsidize another2group (e.g., a nonprofit-related organization). To the for-profit partners, taxable status increases the likelihood that management of the activity will be directed toward maximizing profit.

Participants pointed out that in some cases, such as electronic commerce, a business initiative might be taken more seriously if organized as a for-profit activity. Such partnering seems especially fruitful when the nonprofit does not have the necessary internal business expertise to ensure the initiative's success. One panelist noted that a for-profit partner can add a dose of pragmatism to a business plan: "A nonprofit's projections of profitability—like

Ambrose Bierce's definition of remarriage *The Devil's Dictionary*—represent the triumph of hope over experience. By contrast, venture capitalists are particularly realistic."

To cash in and sell a new venture. A clearly separate for-profit venture (especially one that begins as a partnership with one or more for-profit organizations) may be easier to sell successfully in the open market. For example, some ventures may create attractive short-term opportunities. Running an enterprise for decades, however, is not always in the long-term interest of the nonprofit organization as a whole. Thus, a nonprofit might raise capital, act as a partner or shareholder for a short time, and then sell the venture. Even when a new venture is pursued as a for-profit activity, the tax consequences of investing in it are often minimal for two reasons:

- When an organization expects most income to come in the form of future capital gains, the venture's early net operating income often will be negative or very small and require minimal to no income tax payments. In general, a tax-exempt organization's sales of capital shares are not subject to tax. Another possibility is to structure any income generated during the start-up phase as royalty payments, which are deductible by the enterprise and nontaxable to the exempt recipient. In effect, then, operation as a for-profit subsidiary would leave most of the nonprofit's returns tax-exempt.
- A nonprofit might develop a product for internal purposes that has large initial costs but potential external application (e.g., a large health care organization develops fee-tracking software). If development costs can be pushed into a for-profit subsidiary, these costs can then be written off against taxable income rather than simply reported as an expense incurred by the nonprofit.

To address tax aspects of the activity itself. In joint ventures between exempt and taxable participants, an important IRS concern is that impermissible private benefit might result. Accordingly, the IRS carefully screens such joint ventures and looks for evidence that the exempt participant controls the enterprise in a way that protects its primary exempt purpose. In some transactions, before giving clearance the IRS calls upon the exempt organization to make a guarantee, such as meeting an environmental condition or dedicating a percentage of revenues to services to low-income individuals.

Using a taxable vehicle for the nonprofit's investment can eliminate the need for such close scrutiny, although it raises other problematic issues. In particular, for-profit initiatives often raise questions about how expenses are allocated between partners and about compensation paid to staff with dual employment.

In addition, recent changes to the tax laws limit a nonprofit's ability to exclude certain income. Under the revised law, a tax-exempt organization must report as income all interest, rents, and royalties paid by taxable subsidiaries in which it directly or indirectly owns more than a 50 percent stake. Thus, economically equivalent transactions can produce different tax results. For example, to exclude royalties from licensing arrangements, the nonprofit must take a passive role and let the for-profit partner regulate the activity. By contrast, to exclude income from a joint venture with a taxable partner, the nonprofit must retain control over the activity.

To simplify tax filing for certain activities. For initiatives that are financed by commercial or similar revenue, a nonprofit may be subject to unrelated business income tax (UBIT). For example, some organizations finance Web sites or television activities with advertising revenues. By setting up taxable affiliates or subsidiaries, a nonprofit can simplify accounting procedures and steer clear of UBIT requirements. Moreover, the tax consequences are sometimes favorable when expenses can be allocated to an affiliate.

To make payments in lieu of taxes. Nonprofit organizations that own large amounts of commercial or residential real estate typically try to maintain good relations with the local governments supplying important services, such as roads, water, police, and fire protection. Some nonprofit organizations achieve this goal by making payments in lieu of taxes (PILOTs).

Nonprofits with large amounts of rental real estate, however, may forgo exemption on some portion of their real estate and pay the appropriate property tax. By moving this real estate into the profit sector, an organization will pay some property tax; because of depreciation and interest expenses, however, it often will incur little or no income tax.

ESTABLISHING SEPARATE FOR-PROFIT ENTITIES

In addition to engaging in taxable activities with for-profit partners, nonprofit organizations can establish separate entities to pursue related or unrelated activities. An organization can structure these separate entities as for-profit to meet certain objectives.

To ensure accountability to the IRS. A nonprofit that operates a for-profit activity directly may face increased scrutiny from the IRS. The IRS generally wants to ensure that the nonprofit governing board protects the charitable purposes of the exempt organization. The nonprofit needs to appropriately reflect any sharing of personnel, facilities, or resources between its for-profit and nonprofit arms. The IRS considers some types of activity, such as management services, to be inherently taxable. To minimize any threat to the exempt status of the nonprofit—especially when net income is not likely to be significant—the nonprofit might prefer to relegate the activity to a for-profit subsidiary.

To maintain accountability to the nonprofit's board and members. In addition to the IRS, a non-profit's board and members monitor an organization's adherence to its mission. Several participants gave examples of nonprofits that did not want to give even the appearance of tainted activities or a weakening commitment to their organizations' primary purposes. As one panelist put it, "Losing your soul is even worse than losing your tax-exempt status—and you might even be able to keep your tax-exempt status." The nonprofit board may lead the charge toward separating nonprofit and for-profit functions, or the officers of the nonprofit may make the separation to ensure that contributors are not misinformed about the exempt organization's main pursuits.

To limit nonprofit's liability. By separating activities into different corporations, a nonprofit can sometimes take advantage of the limited liability laws that apply to individual corporations. Bankruptcy laws can make it easier to abandon a failed venture; the ability to contain lawsuits helps protect other parts of the nonprofit.

To gain some flexibility in compensation. A taxable entity has more flexibility in the area of compensation. Particular nonprofits may have explicit or implicit caps on employees' salaries to reflect the culture of the organization or to keep salaries from discouraging outside contributions. Within a for-profit entity, such limits often do not apply. When compensation can help attract or retain the talent needed to run a separate activity, an organization might set up a for-profit subsidiary.

A for-profit can also offer additional types of compensation, such as deferred compensation and equity-based compensation (e.g., participating stock, deeply discounted stock, stock appreciation rights, and options of all kinds) to potential leaders of the enterprise. In other cases, the exempt organization might try to increase the compensation of some its own employees by putting them on the for-profit board or by making them officers with a significant stake in the venture. Enhanced compensation, however, can be a mixed blessing. First, in some circumstances, the goal of the for-profit entity may be to reduce transparency of the organization's activities. Unlike compensation paid to top officers and board members of the nonprofit, compensation paid by the for-profit subsidiary is not disclosed to the public. With less disclosure, a nonprofit risks becoming less accountable to the public whose support it seeks. Moreover, recent legislation imposes penalties on nonprofit insiders who receive "excess benefits" from the nonprofit and its affiliate combined.

Second, compensation packages offered in the for-profit subsidiary can cause dissension in the ranks. Employees of the exempt entity might want to shift to the for-profit venture if compensation gains are potentially higher. In addition, within a complex organization, these structures can create winners and losers. For example, within a university conducting for-profit scientific research, the biology staff stands to gain more than, say, the humanities staff.

CONCERNS RAISED BY THE TAXABLE ACTIVITIES OF NONPROFITS

Most participants at the meeting agreed that the level of taxable activity among nonprofits is small relative to the level of assets.

Moreover, this activity is generally confined to well-defined marketplaces and, in many cases, comprises one-time or limited profitability opportunities. Nonetheless, even a small increase in taxable activities has important implications for the nonprofit sector. All charities have some obligation to ensure that assets and human capital within the organization are not diverted toward noncharitable purposes. In addition to legal and tax consequences, nonprofits are governed by other fiduciary obligations to the public and to past donors.

Given the unique legal and social position of nonprofits, the structuring of normally exempt activities as for-profit business raises important regulatory, competitive, and structural questions. As one panelist stated, "We're used to thinking about abuses from for-profits using the exempt form to conduct business activities, but this is the other way around. Instead of tax avoidance, the issues are strategic and philosophical: Is this a prudent or program-related investment? Is there a diversion of charitable assets or nonprofit managers' attention? Do private parties inappropriately benefit?"

States attorneys general and the IRS often find it difficult to measure and monitor a nonprofit's unrelated business activities. Regulating nonprofits has become even more difficult as a result of the inexpensive, universal marketing opportunities made possible by the Internet. At the same time, nonprofits would like to avoid calls for disclosure of all activities by exempt organizations—not just of unrelated business income earned directly, but of income earned by a taxable affiliate or subsidiary. Any stringent reporting requirement would make nonprofits a less appealing source of capital to commercial partners making taxable investments. It could also provide an unfair advantage to taxable competitors that do not have exempt investors.

The current tax-exemption structure is based on organizational form rather than on specific activities. Nonprofit outputs, however, are difficult to observe and quantify. Consequently, we must rely on proxies to try to ensure that truly charitable activity is undertaken with the charitable contributions of donors. For example, the law, as well as nonprofit boards themselves, prohibits payment of excess compensation or profits to executives.

Profit-seeking activities put pressure on these form-based rules. Moreover, if a nonprofit charges full market prices for otherwise program-related activities—as is clearly the case with taxable subsidiaries—it can ultimately price some of the very people that it wants to help out of the market. In the long term, the visible commercial activity of a few nonprofits could invite closer scrutiny of the unrelated business income tax. If this kind of activity increases significantly, it could call into question the tax exemption of certain nonprofit industries, or even the exemption of the entire sector.

This line of discussion left participants with a broad, thought-provoking question by the meeting's end: Will we see a transformation of entity-based exemption that requires activities with different levels of social value to adhere to different tax regimes?

The NGO Entrepreneur: Nonprofit in Purpose, For-Profit in Approach

The question of how to financially sustain and support the activities of nongovernmental organizations (NGOs) has been one of the most recurrent challenges for nonprofit leaders around the world. There is an increasingly urgent need to address this fundamental question for NGOs in the Newly Independent States (NIS) as NGOs expand and diversify, struggling to fill the gap left as the role of the public sector recedes.

Diversifying NGO Resources

As the diagram (next page) illustrates, there are three sectors from which NGOs can derive their resources: the private sector, the general public and the government/public sector. Resources from each of these sectors can originate from both "external" sources (i.e. international) and "local" (i.e., domestic or municipal public and private donors). One area which is often overlooked are those resources generated from "internal" sources (i.e., self-generated income from fees, sales or investments).

The most "sustainable" financing strategy consists of diversifying sources of income and thus minimizing dependency on any single source-reducing vulnerability to shifts in fund availability or donor preferences. A sustainable approach to NGO financing is an approach that avoids dependency on any one source of revenue, whether external or internal. It is impossible to prescribe any formula for the percentages that need to be derived from various sources to constitute a "financially sustainable NGO." However, a balance between externally and internally generated resources is necessary in order for an organization to meet its operating and administrative expenses while maintaining the freedom to determine its programmatic priorities and projects, irrespective of donor preferences. A rule of thumb is that an NGO try to raise sufficient funds from internal sources to cover its basic operating costs but approach external donors for its program costs.

Most NGOs in the NIS (as in many regions of the world) remain heavily dependent on the external financial assistance of foreign, primarily Western, donors. The support provided by international donors accounts for the single largest source of NGO funding in the region. This has presented a two-part problem for local NGOs. First, the level of international funding is unstable. Resources for NGOs have not been as forthcoming as had been anticipated in NIS countries, and many donors have shifted their attention to other priorities-more needy, politically expedient or publicly popular regions of the world.

Second, existing international donor funds in the region are often earmarked for particular projects or for limited project cycles. Donors often attach very specific limitations on how money can be spent, designating particular issues or themes or supporting only programmatic expenses. This has made it tremendously difficulty for NGOs to raise adequate support for their ongoing, operational expenses. The current donor enthusiasm for project-based funding puts the focus on the activities of NGOs rather than on sustaining the organizations themselves. In practice, institutional or organizational development remains a lower priority. NGOs are forced to "go where the money is" regardless of whether the project priorities identified by a perspective funder suit the long-term strategic plans of the NGO. This approach has led NGOs into an endless cycle of resource dependency.

Meanwhile, the local sources of NGO funding in the NIS-from local or national agencies, private sources or public donations-have not yet developed to a level sufficient to meet demand. The poverty, corruption and social unrest in many NIS countries present major obstacles to local philanthropy. The discretionary income of the general population is generally not high enough to support philanthropy, especially given the lack of a recent local tradition of private charity. Therefore, while the development of a local philanthropic base for NGO initiatives may represent the most preferable solution to NGO financing problems in the NIS in the long-term, this is a process which will take years of cultural, social and economic change.

The New NGO Entrepreneur

Mounting frustration with the current funding status quo and the desire to avoid donor control has led many NGOs to examine the entrepreneurial principles of the private sector. NGO leaders are defining a completely new breed of "entrepreneur" to stimulate the creation of a larger, sustainable pool of resources for NGO initiatives. Going beyond traditional donor-grantee relationships, they have created a new organizational "hybrid"-nonprofit in purpose and for-profit in approach. These new NGO entrepreneurs have developed unique strategies for creating sustainable funds for their activities by employing creative and sometimes lucrative "self-financing" enterprises. Self-financing activities include both mission-related and non-related ventures-direct for-profit, resource-generating activity conducted to create new resources for the NGO. Some forms of self-financing are identified in the box at the left.

NGOs around the world have already begun to employ creative and sometimes lucrative self-financing strategies-albeit with mixed success. The Organizacao de Ajuda Fraterna, a center for street children in Brazil, covers all of its annual expenses from the sale of furniture and hospital equipment, while simultaneously providing job training and income for its constituents. Ekocenter, a coordinating body for environmental NGOs in Yugoslavia, is using publishing and an organic wine project to generate income. Child Relief and You (CRY), in India, generates nearly 50 percent of its annual income through the sale of greeting cards, office paper products and children's toys in India and the US. FUNREDES, in the Dominican Republic, covers over 70 percent of its operational expenses by offering internet and website design services to for-profit companies. The Lotus Foundation, a Czech environmental NGO, has succeeded in generating about a third of its annual operating budget through its desktop publishing services for NGO and for-profit clients. Also in the Czech Republic, the environmental NGO Adonis has started a for-profit tourist office to attract eco-tourists to the region. These are but a few success stories of NGO entrepreneurs who are attempting to shift from purely resource consumers to resource creators.

Obstacles to NGO Self-Financing

It would be unrealistic to assume that NGOs in the NIS region could solve all of their financial problems overnight by utilizing self-financing strategies. Self-financing is not a panacea. If typical success rates of small businesses are any indication, then the majority of NGO enterprise efforts are destined to fail. Meanwhile, critics point to philosophical and practical problems with NGO self-financing. Some fear the "commercialization" of NGOs, believing that self-financing approaches will "contaminate" NGO initiatives with market philosophies and distort NGO mission-related activities in favor of profit-making priorities.

NGOs and community groups face a nember of important problems in developing the human, financial and institutional capacity necessary to effectively implement self-financing approaches. Several philosophical and practical obstacles may exist within organizations. First, some may find accepting private-sector, market-oriented approaches to generating NGO resources unethical or even antithetical to NGO values. Second, most people working in NGOs lack the necessary business and financial management skills necessary to effectively run a for-profit enterprise. Third, NGOs face difficulty in allocating their internal resource capacities-both financial and human-to undertake the business activity and continue their nonprofit work. Fourth, determining the most effective structure for management and accountability is critical. NGOs must choose carefully between managing the activity within the existing organizational structure, through a separate department or team, or establishing a completely separate subsidiary or other legal entity to manage the venture. Other obstacles to NGO self-financing are external. Access to the necessary financial capital to launch or expand self-financing activities is a significant problem for NGOs, which are often denied access to traditional small business loan funds from private banks or other lending agencies. Using internally generated funds, donor funds, in-kind donations and contributions from staff, members, boards, or friends is often the only alternative. Second, NGOs need to be concerned about public perceptions of NGO enterprise. Poorly marketed or misunderstood intentions can bring unwanted negative public opinion that the NGOs are evading taxes or "cashing in" on the poor or the environment.

Particularly in countries of the NIS where corruption scandals are common, NGOs need to be transparent in their financial transactions and instill confidence in the public by establishing clear and rigorous self-regulatory and ethical standards. Third, there is wide variation from country to country regarding the legal and tax treatment of economic and commercial activities of NGOs, as well as to the levels of monitoring and enforcement of these regulations. One for-profit enterprise of an Azerbaijani NGO found the lack of clarity in nonprofit law and commercial regulation so frustrating that it was forced to register as a nonprofit organization in the United States. Fourth, in some countries, private small-businesses have raised objection to the entrance of NGOs into local markets, saying they enjoy "unfair" competitive advantages in the form of tax exemptions, etc. As self-financing activities among NGOs increase around the world, the potential competition and/or conflict between NGO and for-profit entrepreneurs has the potential to increase as well.

CONCLUSIONS

While not new, NGO self-financing is relatively unknown to many in the NGO community. A great deal more attention needs to be paid to how best to facilitate this alternative revenue generating strategy among NGOs in the NIS and other regions of the world, as well as to its overall effectiveness as a self-sustainability strategy. There is a significant need to document, analyze and assess self-financing initiatives. Little is known about the prevalence of self-financing among NGOs, the types of self-financing strategies used, and the impact of self-financing on the missions, internal management and values of NGOs. An assessment of the wide range of fiscal, legal and tax policies affecting self-financing is needed to encourage NGO entrepreneurs and to educate donors, policymakers and the public about its benefits and costs. Successful NGO self-financing cases need to be documented and promoted to illustrate the benefits of shifting from short-term, project-based funding to long-term "investments" in organizational development. This is especially necessary in regions like the NIS where international donors are beginning to exit or reduce their commitments and are searching for ways to lay the foundation for long-term NGO sustainability.

NGOs themselves must begin by questioning their growing dependence on international donors for both its practical limitations and philosophical consequences. Donors and international intermediaries must work to help stimulate viable local funding alternatives by providing flexible resources, information and capacity-building to foster NGO self-financing initiatives. NGOs require assistance to develop appropriate management strategies, staff capacity and skills, organizational and legal structures, start-up funding, financial and accountability mechanisms, business planning and marketing strategies.

Collectively, such efforts can help NGOs move beyond well-intentioned discussions of "sustainability" toward the development of concrete alternative strategies-like self-financing-and from resource dependency to greater autonomy and self-reliance.

8

NON-PROFIT ORGANIZATIONS: LEGAL RISKS AND PROTECTIONS

INTRODUCTION

Non-profits face exposure to a wide array of legal risks. Some risks are unique to non-profits – they may arise, for example, from an organization's tax-exempt status or from the inherent nature of association activity. As non-profits increasingly feel pressure to do more with fewer resources, however, many non-profits have turned to business models traditionally maintained by for-profit enterprises to increase efficiency and impact by developing new ways of creating revenue, increasing employee utilization and enhancing marketing techniques. "Capacity building," as this process has been called, is a growing trend in the operation of non-profits. Not surprisingly, as non-profits become more like their for-profit counterparts, the laws and duties that apply to – and the claims that are asserted against – non-profits likewise evolve. The result is that non-profits face more exposure to legal risks. Moreover, even the successful resolution of a matter may leave a non-profit facing significant legal defense costs.

When faced with such potential liabilities, non-profits and their management should weigh carefully how best to protect their organizations as well as their own personal assets. Given the limitations of indemnification and statutory immunity, one of the most effective protections available is insurance coverage. Among the primary types of insurance that a non-profit may wish to consider are directors and officers liability policies and employment practices liability policies.

This article provides an overview of the potential legal risks that today's non-profit organizations and their directors and officers may encounter. It also discusses certain statutory and other protections that may be afforded to non-profits which are at risk of legal liability. Finally, the article discusses the availability of insurance coverage to better protect non-profits and those who oversee and operate them.

LEGAL RISKS OF NON-PROFITS AND THEIR DIRECTORS AND OFFICERS

Non-profits and their directors and officers are susceptible to numerous types of claims. Such claims may include allegations concerning employment , civil rights, defamationor other assertions by employees, clients, members or other individuals who seek to hold the organization or its directors and officers liable for an injury suffered as a result of actions taken by the non-profit. Directors and officers may be sued for breaches of fiduciary duties that they owe to the organization.

Non-profits may be subject to government enforcement actions by state or federal officials to enforce the organization's compliance with applicable statutes and regulations. In addition, some non-profits may face liability for antitrust claims or other claims asserted by creative litigants.

In fact, in some respects directors and officers may be at a greater risk of liability in a non-profit than they would be in a for-profit corporation given that many non-profits have smaller budgets, fewer personnel performing more functions, and less defined policies and procedures (particularly with respect to employment practices). Moreover, for financial reasons non-profits may be unable to retain or consult professionals such as accountants and lawyers on as frequent a basis as for-profit companies. All of these factors and others may increase the likelihood of supervisory lapses or other errors.

The potential for liability may be of particular concern for directors, who very often serve on the boards of non-profits without compensation. The most common types of liability confronting non-profits and their directors and officers are discussed below.

A. Employment Claims

Employment-related disputes comprise the largest source of claims asserted against non-profits and their directors and officers. These claims involve a wide array of workplace issues that may be brought under general legal principles (common law causes of action) and a broad network of federal, state and local laws designed to protect employees (statutory causes of action). As a predicate to certain employment litigation, a claimant also may be required first to pursue his or her claims in administrative proceedings.

While potential defenses to the employment claims exist, the potential damages are great. Although some claims are dismissed quickly, others may result in protracted and expensive litigation even if the non-profit ultimately prevails. Most claimants are entitled to a jury trial. The relief that may be awarded to a successful claimant ranges from reinstatement of employment to monetary damages, including, in some instances, reimbursement of attorney's fees.

1. *Types of Claims*

Although most individuals in the workplace are "at-will" employees (without contracts for a definite term) – and thus their employment may be terminated with or without cause – employers must assure that employment is not terminated for legally prohibited reasons. An employee may sue on behalf of himself or herself, but also may bring suit on behalf of a similarly situated class of individuals (often referred to as a "class action"). Depending upon the employment claim asserted, an employee may sue the non-profit itself. Under most federal statutes the organization, rather than an individual, is considered to be the "employer."

In other instances, however, an employee may name directors and officers as defendants, particularly if those individuals were involved in decisions relating to that employee's hiring, evaluations, training and termination. Employment claims may pose a special risk for non-profit directors and officers because employment claims brought under federal statutes are beyond the protection of state liability-limiting statutes that grant immunity to non-profits' directors and officers in certain circumstances.

(a) Statutory Causes of Action: Federal, state and local governments over the last several decades have enacted a variety of legislation to protect employees from discrimination in the workplace. The most commonly cited federal statute is Title VII of the Civil Rights Act of 1964, which prohibits employment discrimination against individuals on the basis of race, color, religion, sex or national origin. Notably, Title VII also prohibits sexual harassment in the workplace. States and local jurisdictions may have analogous statutes or regulations that may expand the protected classes to include, for example, sexual orientation. Some of these statutes, though, may apply only to employers with a specified number of employees.

Other federal statutes prohibit discrimination based on an individual's mental or physical disability (the Americans with Disabilities Act (" ADA")), age (the Age Discrimination in Employment Act ("ADEA")), or sex-based wage differentials where the work involves the same skill, effort and responsibility performed under the same working conditions (the Equal Pay Act). Other frequently litigated employment statutes include the Family and Medical Leave Act ("FMLA"), which entitles employees in certain circumstances to take leave without losing their position, seniority or health insurance benefits and the Fair Labor Standards Act ("FLSA"), which regulates minimum wages, overtime compensation and child labor. Many of these statutes also prohibit retaliation by an employer against an employee who pursues his or her statutory rights and protections or who discloses wrongful or illegal activities. "Whistle-blower" provisions in the Sarbanes-Oxley Act also may be triggered.

Many other state and local statutes and regulations also may govern an employment relationship.

(b) Administrative Proceedings: Some statutes – federal, state and local – require that an individual complaining about employment discrimination first seek resolution of the claim through a designated government agency. For example, to advance a claim of race discrimination under

Title VII, an employee first must file a complaint or "charge" with the United States Equal Employment Opportunity Commission ("EEOC"). (The employee also may be required to file with an analogous state or local agency.) The EEOC (or other agency) considers the charge and may take a variety of actions – it may investigate and ask the employer to respond and/or to provide documents, suggest alternative dispute resolution, effectuate a resolution, or pursue the action on behalf of the employee. Often, the EEOC concludes its review by issuing the employee a "right to sue letter," a prerequisite for filing suit in court. At each step of the process, the non-profit may be asked to defend its employment decision.

(c) Common Law Causes of Action: A non-profit also may be the target of an employment claim based upon "common law" (non-statutory) causes of action. Such actions include wrongful termination, termination in violation of public policy, breach of contract (*e.g.*, an express employment contract or an implied contract such as an employee handbook), constructive discharge (where an employer allegedly makes working conditions so intolerable that an employee is forced to resign), defamation, invasion of privacy, intentional infliction of emotional distress, torts based on negligence (*e.g.*, negligent hiring, negligent training, negligent supervision, or negligent evaluation), and intentional/fraudulent misrepresentation (*e.g.*, in providing substantive recommendations for former employees).

In sum, employment claims run the gamut and often are restricted only by the creativity of legal counsel for the claimant. This is true whether the employer is a non-profit or a for-profit enterprise.

2. *Potential Defenses*

For as many types of wrongful employment claims as exist, a myriad of defenses also may be available. These include "technical" defenses such as a statute of limitations, or a failure to exhaust administrative remedies, that may be fatal to the claim.

Other defenses may be more substantive in nature, including that the non-profit's employment decision was not prohibited by law and, moreover, was supported by a bona fide business reason. Each employment claim is likely to be factually unique.

3. Potential Damages

The relief that may be awarded in employment claims varies depending upon the type of action asserted. It may include injunctive relief, which is non-monetary in nature. Such relief may require an employer, for example, to reinstate an employee to his or her job or prohibit certain employment practices or, in the case of a disability, to provide an employee with an accommodation, which enables the employee to enjoy equal employment opportunities. An employee also may recover monetary damages in the form of back pay, front pay (future damages), compensation for non-economic damages such as emotional distress, punitive damages or, in some cases, liquidated damages. Title VII, however, imposes caps on compensatory damages (not including back pay or front pay) depending upon the number of employees in an organization. Of particular note is that some statutes, including Title VII, provide that a successful employee also may recover his or her attorney's fees. Employment cases often are expensive to litigate for both sides, which makes the recovery of attorney's fees a factor in assessing a case against a non-profit (or any organization). Similarly, it is not uncommon for a non-profit's legal defense costs to exceed a settlement amount or a judicial/jury award.

B. Civil Rights Claims

Federal and state civil rights law are not limited to the employment context; they also prohibit discrimination in, among other things, education, housing, public accommodations, public facilities, and certain federally funded programs. Various statutes, including 42 U.S.C. § 1981 and Title VII, prohibit discrimination on the basis of race, sex, disability, religion and national origin.

C. Defamation, Libel and Slander Claims

"Defamation" is commonly defined as an "intentional false communication, either published or publicly spoken, that injures another's reputation or good name." Libel is written defamation, while slander is oral defamation. Defamation claims are governed by state law and defined either by state statutes or state court decisions.

Defamation claims against non-profits may arise from numerous circumstances. For example, an employee filing a wrongful discharge action may include a defamation claim, alleging that the employer slandered her when providing a reference. Improper handling of confidential or sensitive client information may lead to a defamation claim. Statements on a non-profit's website may be the subject of a defamation claim.

The primary defenses to a defamation claim are truth and privilege. There may be an "absolute privilege" defense when public policy or the administration of justice requires complete immunity, such as statements made by a witness in an EEOC proceeding. A "qualified privilege" prohibits recovery when the communication at issue was made in good faith to someone who had a legitimate interest in hearing it. Thus, for example, employee references may be protected by a qualified privilege – so long as a court does not conclude that the employer abused the privilege or acted with malice.

Some, but not all states, have recognized that defamation claims can be thinly-disguised attacks on exercising First Amendment/free speech rights, and have enacted statutes aimed at discouraging strategic litigation against public participation ("SLAPP"). Anti-SLAPP statutes generally are limited to statements that concern an issue of widespread public interest, and not all states offer this form of statutory protection.

D. Breaches of Fiduciary Duty

Directors and officers of non-profits owe "fiduciary duties" to the organization, *i.e.*, specific legal duties which may be generally characterized as ensuring that the interests of the organization are paramount. Specifically, directors and officers owe a non-profit three fiduciary duties:

(1) the duty of care, which requires that the directors and officers act reasonably with respect to the management of the organization's affairs;

(2) the duty of loyalty, which prohibits directors and officers from using their positions in the organization to further their own personal interests; and

(3) the duty of obedience, which requires directors and officers to ensure that the organization is run in accordance with its charter and bylaws, and that the organization complies with applicable laws.

Fiduciary duties generally are governed by state law. Representative provisions defining fiduciary duties may be found in the Revised Model Non-profit Corporation Act (1987) (the "Model Non-Profit Act"), a draft statute that serves as guideline legislation for states to enact in whole or in part.

A number of states have adopted some version of the Model Non-Profit Act, including Alabama, Nebraska, North Carolina, North Dakota, Oregon, Tennessee, Texas, Virginia, and Wisconsin, as well as the District of Columbia. While California and New York have separate not-for-profit statutes that differ significantly from the Model Non-Profit Act, some of their provisions - such as the standard for the duty of care – are nonetheless substantially similar to the Model Non-Profit Act. Delaware's corporations law governs both non-profit and for-profit corporations.

1. Standing: Who May Sue for Breach of Fiduciary Duties

Because fiduciary duties are owed to the organization, there are restrictions on who may bring suit against directors and officers who allegedly have breached their fiduciary duties. In a for-profit corporation, for example, the company's shareholders may bring suit against the directors and officers for mismanagement of the corporation.

Such an action is referred to as a " derivative action," and the shareholders, as owners of the company, sue on behalf of the company on the theory that the company's directors and officers have failed to take actions to rectify abuses or errors by management. While non-profits do not have shareholders, their directors and officers may still be sued to enforce compliance with their fiduciary duties by certain classes of individuals or entities possessing legal eligibility, or "standing," to bring a lawsuit.

The first group of individuals that may sue directors and officers for possible breaches of their fiduciary duties are fellow directors and officers of the organization.

Second, where the non-profit has members, such as trade associations composed of businesses in the same industry, the members usually have standing to bring an action against the organization's directors and officers. Because the members are analogous to shareholders in a for-profit corporation, these suits are also often referred to as derivative actions. For example, the Model Non-Profit Act permits an action to be brought in the name of the non-profit corporation by "any member or members having five percent or more of the voting power or by fifty members, whichever is less." Similarly, New York permits an action to be brought by "five percent or more of any class of members." Even where a state statute does not explicitly grant standing, state court decisions may. Thus, Florida, Indiana, and Massachusetts also permit members to sue directors and officers of non-profits to which they belong.

A third group of potential adversaries are state attorneys general, who are often authorized by statute to enforce the directors' and officers' fiduciary responsibilities to the organization.

Another group of persons or entities that may possess standing to sue directors and officers includes the ill-defined class of those who are in a "special relationship" with the non-profit. The existence of a special relationship is largely the product of judicial decisions finding such a relationship under very specific facts. Although courts generally disfavor the creation of new classes of individuals with standing to sue non-profits, it is nevertheless uncertain in any given case whether a court will find such a relationship and permit a suit to go forward. Even if the court eventually concludes that the plaintiff lacks standing, the directors and officers may incur significant legal expenses and fees in the meantime.

Finally, as a result of the tax-exempt status of many non-profits, the fiduciary duties of non-profits' directors and officers also may be enforced by the Internal Revenue Service ("IRS"). The Internal Revenue Code provides that no part of the net earnings of a tax exempt organization is to inure to the benefit of any private shareholder or individual. Courts have interpreted the non-inurement requirement as a restriction on self-dealing by directors of tax-exempt organizations. As a penalty for directors' breach of their fiduciary duties, the IRS may revoke the organization's tax-exempt status, and, in the case of private foundations, may include an excise tax on the self-dealing party. State tax law may impose similar constraints on directors.

2. Duty of Care

The responsibilities of non-profits' boards of directors have been defined as including the following activities:

- Establishing and overseeing the organization's policies;
- Monitoring the conduct of the staff to ensure the organization is being properly managed;
- Reviewing the organization's finances, including approving the annual budget, to ensure resources are expended only to further organizational activities;
- Defining, modifying and communicating the organization's mission;
- Hiring and firing the chief executives and establishing compensation for the executive leadership;
- Securing the resources necessary to enable the organization to fulfill its mission;
- Serving as an advocate for the organization;
- Ensuring compliance with rules or standards established by law, mandated by accreditation agencies, or required by the organization's articles of incorporation and bylaws;
- Recruiting new board members and evaluating the performance of fellow board members; and
- Establishing procedures to ensure that each board member understands and complies with his or her duties as a board member.

In order to ensure that the foregoing responsibilities are fulfilled, directors and officers have a fiduciary duty of care to the non-profit.

There has been recent debate over whether non-profits' directors and officers should be held to the standard of care applied to directors and officers of for-profit corporations, or whether the more stringent standard applied to "trustees" is appropriate. The trend in the law, however, has been to apply the corporate standard to non-profits' directors and officers, which requires that a director or officer act with the care that a reasonably prudent person in a similar position would exercise under the same circumstances. Specifically, the Model Non-Profit Act defines the director's duty of care as follows:

A director shall discharge his or her duties as a director, including his or her duties as a member of a committee:

(1) in good faith;

(2) with the care an ordinarily prudent person in a like position would exercise under similar circumstances; and

(3) in a manner the director reasonably believes to be in the best interests of the corporation.

Although California and New York have not enacted the Model Non-Profit Act, their provisions governing the standard of care are substantially similar.

In order to fulfill the duty of care, directors must regularly attend meetings of the board, as well as meetings of any committees of which they are members. In most states, a director may not vote by proxy at meetings. Directors and officers must exercise their independent judgment, which means the judgment must be an informed one and should not be dominated by the opinion of other directors or officers. Directors and officers, however, are permitted to rely upon information and reports provided by:

(1) officers or employees of the non-profit "whom the director reasonably believes to be reliable and competent in the matters presented";

(2) professionals and other persons retained by the organization "as to matters the director reasonably believes are within the person's professional or expert competence"; and

(3) a committee of the board "as to matters within its jurisdiction, if the director reasonably believes the committee merits confidence."

A director, however, is not acting "in good faith" if he or she relies upon information where the director's own personal knowledge renders such reliance unwarranted. Further, in delegating the responsibilities of the organization's management to others, the directors must implement appropriate policies and procedures that provide for the oversight of personnel. Directors and officers must not willfully avoid learning information that, if known, would reveal problems in the organization. If, however, directors and officers act in good faith, and in a prudent, diligent and informed manner, they will be protected from liability under a legal defense known as the "business judgment rule" for any corporate actions that later events show to have been unwise or mistaken.

3. *Duty of Loyalty*

Under the duty of loyalty, directors and officers owe their non-profit an undivided allegiance to the organization's interests, which means that directors and officers may not use their positions to further their own interests or those of another person or entity unconnected with the organization. The duty of loyalty also requires that directors and officers always act to further the best interests of the organization as a whole, and not merely for the benefit of a particular constituency. The duty of loyalty is generally regarded as encompassing three related areas:

(1) conflicts of interest between directors and officers and the interests of the organization;
(2) corporate opportunities that become available to the organization; and
(3) confidentiality of non-public information regarding the organization.

(a) Conflicts of Interest

A conflict of interest arises when a director or officer has a direct or indirect personal interest in a transaction involving the organization. For example, a director or officer may be personally involved in the transaction, or have a financial or investment interest that would be furthered as a result of the transaction. A conflict may also exist if the interest of a family member of the director or officer would be furthered by the transaction. The concern is that in such instances, the director or officer may approve of the transaction for reasons other than the benefits that would accrue to the organization.

Conflicts of interest are not, however, *per se* prohibited. Indeed, many individuals are recruited to serve on the boards of non-profits because of their professional or business affiliations and activities. There may be situations in which, as a result of a director's or officer's connection or affiliation with other persons or entities, the non-profit is able to engage in a transaction on terms more favorable than it could have obtained on its own. Liability, therefore, is not imposed on a director or officer for the mere approval of a transaction in which he or she may have a conflict of interest. Instead, the focus is on the process by which the transaction was reviewed and approved by the board.

Under the Model Non-Profit Act, and the laws of many states, the existence of a conflict of interest will not be deemed a breach of fiduciary duty if the transaction was approved under certain conditions. First, the director with the conflict should disclose the material facts regarding the conflict to the other board members and refrain from participating in the deliberations and vote on the matter. Second, it must be shown that the disinterested directors approved the transaction in good faith and reasonably believed it was fair to the organization. In some cases, the directors may insulate themselves from liability by obtaining the approval of the state attorney general or a court either before or after consummation of the transaction. Some transactions, however, may be prohibited entirely by state non-profit laws. For example, the Model Non-Profit Act bars a non-profit corporation from lending money to or guaranteeing the obligation of a director or officer of the corporation.

(b) Corporate Opportunities

Directors and officers also generally are prohibited from "usurping" corporate opportunities and competing with their non-profit organization. The corporate opportunity doctrine involves any situation where a director or officer is presented with a business opportunity, whether or not she learned of it through her position with the organization, which she reasonably should know may be of interest to the non-profit's present or future activities. In such circumstances, most states require that the director or officer disclose the transaction to the board so that its disinterested members may determine whether the organization should act or decline to act with respect to the opportunity. Only after the board has declined the opportunity on the record should the director or officer take advantage of the opportunity.

(c) Confidentiality

Directors and officers are under a duty to treat as confidential the organization's internal activities, unless there has been general public disclosure or the information is a matter of public record or public knowledge. There appears to be little or no litigation relating to this duty.

4. Duty of Obedience

The duties of care and loyalty are common to both for-profit and non-profit corporations. The duty of obedience, however, is unique to non-profits. The duty of obedience encompasses two related obligations:

(1) adherence to the non-profit's mission, and
(2) compliance with applicable laws. Organizations failing to comply with federal, state and local law run the risk of government enforcement actions.

(a) Adherence to the Non-Profit's Mission

Non-profits' directors are required to adhere to the purposes, or "mission," for which the organization was established. It is crucial that non-profits follow their enunciated purposes, in part, because the public's trust that the organization will apply funds in conformity with its mission is the motive for donations and grants made to the organization. A non-profit's mission often is found in its articles of incorporation (also referred to as its charter), its by-laws, and/or a "mission statement" that has been adopted by the board of directors. Where the organization is viewed as veering from its core purposes, fellow directors, members of the organization and/or the general public may bring this fact to the attention of the state attorney general, who is empowered in many states to enforce compliance with the mission. In fact, the attorney general or a court may be empowered to unwind any transaction that contravenes the organization's mission or changes the organization's character. If such an improper transaction is found to have occurred, the directors may be liable under state statutes for damages that the organization incurred as a result of the prohibited transaction.

(b) Compliance with Applicable Laws/Government Enforcement Actions

Directors also must ensure that the organization is acting in compliance with the laws and regulations that apply to it. This is especially important because if, for example, the organization fails to comply with the restrictions imposed by the tax laws, it may lose its tax-exempt status and possibly incur other penalties. Additional laws that may apply to non-profits include:

- Income withholding and employment tax requirements;
- Discrimination, equal protection and civil rights laws, including Title VII and the Americans with Disabilities Act;
- State solicitation laws;
- The Employee Retirement Income Security Act of 1974 ("ERISA");
- The Labor-Management Reporting and Disclosure Act;
- The Health Insurance and Portability and Accountability Act of 1996 ("HIPAA"); and
- Restrictions under tax laws on the political activity of tax-exempt organizations.

Failure to adhere to the organization's mission may result in civil litigation by private individuals or entities. Statutory violations, however, may lead to government enforcement actions by either state or federal officials to ensure that non-profits comply with applicable statutes and regulations.

Because non-profit corporations are governed by state corporations law, state officials may bring actions for dissolution of the corporation or revocation of its charter if the non-profit engages in fraudulent or illegal conduct. Federal enforcement actions against non-profits are most likely to be brought under the tax laws, which may impose penalties on non-profits' directors and officers for noncompliance with various statutory duties. Penalties may be imposed, for exampie, for failure to timely file tax returns or to withhold income tax and social security taxes from employees' income. Additionally, the IRS may impose an excise tax on "disqualified persons" who participate in "excess benefit transactions" with tax exempt non-profits. A disqualified person is a person who was in a position to exercise substantial influence over the organization within five years of the transaction, such as officers, directors, high-level employees and major donors to the organization.

An excess benefit transaction is a financial transaction in which a disqualified person receives in excess of fair market value from the organization or pays less than fair market value to the organization. In the case of an excess benefit transaction, the IRS can impose a tax of twenty-five percent of the excess benefit amount on the disqualified person, and, if the transaction is not "corrected," an additional two hundred percent of the excess benefit amount may be imposed. Further, "organization managers" (which include officers, directors, trustees, or other persons holding similar powers) who knowingly approve an excess benefit transaction may be liable for a ten percent excise tax on the excess benefit, up to a maximum of $10,000, for each transaction. With respect to non-profits that qualify as "private foundations," similar excise taxes may be imposed against "foundation mangers" for self-dealing transactions.

E. Miscellaneous Actions

1. *Antitrust Claims*

Federal and state antitrust laws are another source of potential liability for various non-profits. Since non-profit trade associations are, by definition, groups of competitors gathered to share common interests and seek solutions to common problems, antitrust laws have special relevance to trade associations and may be implicated in a variety of association activities. But it is well-settled that membership in an association or attendance at association meetings may not be considered evidence of a conspiracy to restrain trade or competition. Because associations often provide benefits that allow members to more effectively compete in the industry, however, membership criteria that create a barrier to membership may give rise to antitrust liability.

Sports-related organizations also may find themselves the subject of antitrust claims because of their authority to establish rules, regulations and standards which may have financial consequences on businesses whose activity is tied to that particular sport or sports organization.

Similar to sports organizations, other non-profits that have the authority to establish trade standards that influence an industry, or control membership admittance into the industry, may be subject to antitrust claims by individuals or entities who allege that the non-profit's actions have anticompetitive effects with respect to them. The risk of antitrust claims is greater where the non-profit exercises powers of accreditation or certification over individuals or institutions.

Hospitals increasingly have become the target of antitrust claims brought by physicians who have been denied staff privileges, or by clinic and physician practice groups in competition with local area hospitals who may be injured by favorable contractual relations between a hospital and healthcare insurance companies.

2. *Other Claims*

While the most frequent types of claims brought against non-profits are described above, the reality is that non-profits and their officers and directors may be the targets of claims arising from a wide variety of acts and concerning any area of law. For example, commentators have noted that some non-profits may be exposed to liability under securities laws where they issue notes, bonds or other debt instruments in connection with fundraising activities. Another source of potential liability facing non-profits is claims related to internet activities, such as defamation, engaging in fundraising activities through websites without registering them under state solicitation laws, improperly permitting the advertisement of for-profit entities on the non-profit's website, and infringing on the intellectual property of others.

In summary, the universe of claims that may be asserted against a non-profit and its directors and officers is limited only by the imagination of litigants and their lawyers. At any moment, a non-profit may find itself the subject of an unforeseen – and unpredictable – claim. And, even the successful defense of a claim may nonetheless leave a non-profit facing significant legal defense fees and costs.

GOVERNANCE REFORMS

A. The Sarbanes-Oxley Act and Its Impact on Non-Profits

A new potential source of liability is the Sarbanes-Oxley Act (the "SOX Act") and similar state legislation. The SOX Act generally does not apply to non-profits – with two exceptions (whistleblower protection and document preservation), the SOX Act applies only to publicly traded companies – and, to date, there does not appear to have been any litigation involving non-profits and the SOX Act. Nevertheless, the SOX Act should be of concern to non-profits. Several states have enacted, or have proposed enacting, governance reforms modeled on the SOX Act for charities. Inspired in part by the SOX Act's provisions, the IRS has increased its oversight of tax-exempt entities, revising Form 1023 by which organizations seek new tax-exempt status, developing a new Form 990 tax return for tax-exempt organizations, and proposing to conduct more audits. Some non-profits themselves have proposed governance reforms based upon selected provisions of the SOX Act. The SOX Act likely has increased the expectations of regulators, donors, and others with respect to non-profits' financial reporting and accountability. Future plaintiffs may argue, therefore, that non-profits' directors and officers breach their fiduciary duties if they fail to act in accordance with the SOX Act's reforms which they may claim now may represent "best practices." Thus, non-profits should be aware of the SOX Act and its key provisions.

1. Sarbanes-Oxley Act Provisions Applicable to Non-Profits and For-Profits

Whistleblower Protection: The SOX Act extends protection for whistleblowers who report what they reasonably believe to be illegal activities. Employers – whether for-profit or non-profit corporations – may not "discharge, demote, suspend, threaten, harass, or in any other manner discriminate" against such whistleblowers. The SOX Act grants whistleblowers the right to file a civil suit against their employers for retaliatory actions, and successful whistleblower plaintiffs may obtain compensatory damages and reimbursement of their attorneys' fees.

Document Preservation: The SOX Act makes it a federal crime to destroy, alter, or falsify any document, including audit records, to prevent its use in an official proceeding such as a federal investigation or bankruptcy proceeding. The document preservation requirements apply to both for-profits and non-profits.

2. *Sarbanes-Oxley Act Provisions Currently Applicable Only to For-Profits*

- Audit Committee: Generally, an audit committee hires, sets compensation for, and oversees the auditor's activities, and establishes rules and processes for accounting and internal control practices. The SOX Act requires each member of a company's audit committee to be a member of the board of directors and "independent," *i.e.*, not part of the management team and not receiving any consulting fee or other compensation from the company, either directly or indirectly, except for compensation for board services. The company must disclose whether or not they have at least one financial expert on the committee and, if not, why.
- Auditors' Responsibilities: The SOX Act prohibits a company's auditor from providing the company with any non-audit services (*e.g.*, bookkeeping, appraisals or valuations, actuarial services, investment banking services, etc.) concurrent with its auditing services, although the board may pre-approve certain services such as tax preparation. The auditor must report to the audit committee about the organization's "critical accounting policies and practices," alternative treatments of financial information within generally accepted accounting principles ("GAAP") that were discussed with the company's management, and other significant written

communications with management. The SOX Act requires that the auditing firm's lead partner and reviewing partner rotate off the audit every five years.

- Certification of Financial Statements : Under the SOX Act, the CEO and the CFO must certify, among other things, that the financial statements and disclosures in the company's quarterly and annual reports "fairly present in all material respects the operations and financial condition" of the company; that they have disclosed to the audit committee and the auditors "all significant deficiencies in the design or operation of internal controls which could adversely impact" the company's ability to report financial data, and that they have disclosed any fraud that involves management or other employees who have a significant role in the company's internal controls.
- Conflicts of Interest: The SOX Act generally prohibits a company from providing loans to any of its directors or executives. The SOX Act also prohibits the CEO, CFO, controller, and chief accounting officer from working for the company's auditing firm for one year before the audit.
- Disclosure Requirements: The SOX Act prescribes several disclosure requirements, including disclosure of significant corrections to financial statements, material off-balance sheet transactions, the structure and an assessment of internal controls, transactions involving management and principal stockholders, and whether or not the company has adopted a code of ethics for senior financial officers. The SOX Act also requires companies to disclose "on a rapid and current basis" any material changes in the company's operations or financial situation.

B. State Governance Reforms for Non-Profits

Several states have enacted reforms apparently inspired by the Sarbanes-Oxley Act. California, Connecticut, Kansas, Massachusetts and New Hampshire now mandate that certain charities (the revenue threshold varies by state) file audited financial statements with a state agency or attorney general. The Attorney General of Hawaii now is authorized to require a charitable organization to submit audited financial statements. California charities with gross revenues of $2 million or greater now must have an audit committee with independent members. Connecticut recently enacted conflict-of-interest standards for charities. Iowa enacted new standards for board conduct for non-profits, related party transactions and loans. Maine also expanded its attorney general's oversight of non-profits and enacted new conflict of interest provisions for non-profits. Many other states have considered – or currently are considering – similar reforms.

PROTECTION FOR NON-PROFITS' DIRECTORS AND OFFICERS

As described above, non-profits' directors and officers may face substantial liability for a variety of claims, ranging from employment claims to derivative actions for breaches of fiduciary duties. Even when the directors and officers ultimately prevail, they may incur significant legal defense costs in the interim. To encourage individuals to serve non-profits, despite the potential liability, several forms of protection have been developed. First, a non-profit itself may provide "indemnification" to its directors and officers. Second, liability-limiting statutes may protect the directors and officers of non-profits. The protection afforded by such statutes varies from state to state, but there is more uniform protection for volunteers since the enactment of the federal Volunteer Protection Act. Finally, a non-profit may obtain insurance, particularly directors and officers liability coverage and employment practices liability coverage, tailored to fill the significant gaps left by other forms of protection.

A. Indemnification

Generally speaking, "indemnification," in the context of corporate governance, means the financial protection that a corporation provides to its directors and officers for expenses incurred by them in lawsuits alleging that they breached a duty in their service to or on behalf of the organization. State law generally governs indemnification, establishing the scope and terms of permissive (or "discretionary") indemnification (*i.e.*, when the corporation *may* indemnify its directors and officers) and mandatory indemnification (*i.e.*, when the corporation *must* indemnify its directors and officers). State law also describes when corporations are prohibited from indemnifying their directors and officers. Most states have modeled their indemnification provisions either on the Model Business Corporation Act or the Revised Model Non-Profit Act but state laws may vary considerably. Non-statutory indemnification also may be available for certain claims. Finally, the limitations to indemnification may be significant, depending upon the circumstances.

1. *Permissive Indemnification*

State law generally permits a non-profit corporation to indemnify its directors and officers where (1) the director or officer is a party in the action because of his or her status as such, (2) the individual "conducted himself or herself in good faith," (3) the individual "reasonably believed" that either "in the case of conduct in his or her official capacity with the corporation, that his or her conduct was in its best interest," or "in all other cases, that his or her conduct was at least not opposed to its best interests." A corporation also generally may indemnify its directors and officers in a criminal proceeding if the individual "had no reasonable cause to believe his or her conduct was unlawful."

A director or officer may satisfy the prescribed standard of conduct for discretionary indemnification whether the proceeding is terminated "by judgment, order, settlement, conviction, or upon a plea of nolo contendere or its equivalent." Indemnification generally is prohibited if a court finds the director improperly received a "personal benefit" or if the director is found liable to the corporation in a derivative action. A non-profit generally may indemnify "reasonable expenses incurred in connection with the proceeding."

For lawsuits other than derivative actions, "expenses" may include attorneys' fees and costs, judgments, fines, penalties, and settlement amounts. For derivative actions, state law usually limits indemnification to legal defense costs. Directors and officers typically must pay the judgment or settlement for a derivative action with personal assets, unless they have insurance providing directors and officers liability coverage.

Permissive indemnification generally must be authorized on a case-by-case basis and may be subject to statutory requirements. Typically, the decision to indemnify must be reflected in the non-profit corporation's charter or by-laws or by formal board action. Discretionary indemnification, however, may be made mandatory by the organization's own articles of incorporation or bylaws.

2. *Mandatory Indemnification*

Unless otherwise limited by the organization's articles of incorporation, indemnification generally is mandatory under state law if the director or officer was "wholly successful, on the merits or otherwise" in a lawsuit in which she was a party because of her position with the corporation. A director likely would be deemed to be "wholly successful" if there is a verdict or final ruling in the director's favor. Whether a director would be entitled to mandatory indemnification for a settlement likely would depend upon the circumstances and applicable state law.

"On the merits or otherwise" means that the director or officer may be entitled to mandatory indemnification if he has a valid defense, whether it is substantive (*e.g.*, he did not breach his fiduciary duties) or procedural (*e.g.*, lack of jurisdiction, standing, or the statute of limitations). Mandatory indemnification is limited to "reasonable expenses actually incurred by the director in connection with the proceeding." Unlike permissive indemnification, however, the director or officer need not establish that she acted in good faith and in a manner she reasonably believed to be in the best interests of the corporation. As noted above, permissive indemnification may be made mandatory by the organization's own articles of incorporation or bylaws. Finally, a court may order indemnification.

3. *Non-Statutory Indemnification*

Many states' indemnification statutes contain "nonexclusivity provisions" which allow organizations to provide indemnification beyond that described in the statute's permissive indemnification and mandatory indemnification provisions, such as for litigation where the directors or officers are not sued in their official capacities. Even such indemnification, however, may be limited by public policy. In addition to statutory or corporate indemnification, contractual or "third-party" indemnification may be available. For example, as part of a contract of sale, the sellers may agree to indemnify the organization and/or its directors and officers from any claims that arise from that sale. Whether third-party indemnification is available will depend upon the nature of the claim and the nature of the agreement.

4. Limitations to Indemnification

Indemnification may provide some protection to non-profits' directors and officers – but its protection may be limited. First, the value of indemnification may be limited by the organization's resources. As a practical matter, many non-profits may be unable to pay significant sums to defend directors and officers involved in a lawsuit. If the non-profit is insolvent – or if indemnification would cause insolvency – indemnification likely will be unavailable. Second, unless state law or the organization's by-laws provide otherwise, indemnification may be limited to *reimbursement* of expenses at the conclusion of the lawsuit, rather than *advancement* of legal expenses as the lawsuit is ongoing.

Third, indemnification may be limited or prohibited by law or public policy. For example, public policy may preclude the indemnification of directors or officers who engaged in intentional or illegal misconduct. Fourth, if the board's composition changes, the new board may not be sympathetic to the previous directors or officers and decline to make the necessary authorization for permissive indemnification. Finally, the non-profit's own internal policies may limit indemnification. For example, a non-profit may consider it inappropriate to use donations or other contributions for defending lawsuits against its directors and officers. Consequently, the protection of indemnification is far from absolute.

B. Liability-Limiting Statutes/ Volunteer Protection Statutes

Beginning in the 1980s, a combination of factors – including the rising number of lawsuits and large jury awards – raised concerns that fear of liability might discourage individuals from serving non-profits. All fifty states and the District of Columbia subsequently enacted some form of limited statutory immunity for non-profits' directors and officers and/or volunteer protection statutes. There are significant differences among the states' liability-limiting laws, although the federal Volunteer Protection Act sets the floor for volunteer protection.

Notably, these statutes generally provide immunity to individuals and *not* to the non-profit itself. Charitable immunity – full protection for the non-profit itself – has been largely abolished in most states, although some states continue to offer limited immunity. The immunity afforded by liability-limiting statutes, however, applies only to damages: the statutes will not necessarily prevent lawsuits from being filed in the first instance, nor protect a non-profit and its directors and officers from incurring legal defense costs while arguing that the statutes apply.

1. *Statutory Immunity for Non-Profits' Directors and Officers*

Many states have statutorily limited the liability of non-profits' directors and officers under certain circumstances. Such protection may be conditioned, for example, on the officer's compliance with a specified standard of conduct. Thus, the Model Non-Profit Act provides that if an officer acts in good faith, "with the care an ordinarily prudent person in like position would exercise under similar circumstances," and "in a manner the officer reasonably believes to be in the best interests of the corporation and its members, if any," then that "officer is not liable to the corporation, any member, or other person for any action taken or not taken as an officer . . . ." A state may dictate, however, that limited liability applies only to non-profits' directors who serve with no or limited compensation.

Statutory protection may extend only to certain types of cases: for example, only to lawsuits alleging negligence, and not alleging willful, wanton, or intentional misconduct. Under the Supremacy Clause of the United States Constitution, state statutes cannot eliminate directors' and officers' liability for violations of federal law. This exception to state statutory immunity represents a significant "loophole" given that a frequent source of non-profits' liability exposure is employment claims under Title VII, the Americans with Disabilities Act, and other federal statutes.

2. State Volunteer Protection Statutes

Most states have enacted some form of statutory protection for individuals acting in their capacity as volunteers, although the scope varies widely since states reached different solutions when attempting to balance the protection of volunteers against assuring compensation for innocent victims of a volunteer's negligence. First, although states commonly define a volunteer as one who does not receive compensation for his or her services, there may be questions about what constitutes "compensation" if it is not clearly defined by statute. In some jurisdictions, volunteers specifically may include directors and officers; in others, the immunity of directors and officers is governed by separate statutes, as discussed above.

Second, the extent of immunity may vary depending on the type of organization or volunteer activity. Some states provide expanded protection for firefighters, sports program volunteers, or volunteers in small non-profits with assets less than $50,000. Those providing medical services may enjoy enhanced protection under a volunteer protection statute or a good Samaritan law. Third, although most states include some exclusions to statutory volunteer protection, the precise exclusions vary. Typically, volunteer protection statutes include exceptions for actions (1) based on willful, wanton, or grossly negligent misconduct, (2) involving operation of a motor vehicle, or (3) brought by government official to enforce federal, state or local law. As discussed above, state statutes cannot provide immunity for federal law violations. Finally, some states either condition immunity on whether the organization has general liability insurance, or provide that volunteers will be subject to liability only to the extent of the available insurance.

3. Federal Volunteer Protection Act

Enacted in 1997, the federal Volunteer Protection Act (the "VPA") was designed to establish certain minimum, uniform protections for volunteers from liability for alleged negligence. The VPA provides that "no volunteer of a non-profit organization . . . shall be liable for harm caused by an act or omission of the volunteer on behalf of the organization or entity" if the volunteer satisfies certain prerequisites. The VPA defines "volunteers" to include directors and officers, so long as they do not receive compensation "other than reasonable reimbursement or allowance for expenses actually incurred" *or* anything in lieu of compensation valued at more than $500. Organizations covered by the VPA include tax-exempt organizations and any "not-for-profit organization which is conducted for public benefit and operated primarily for charitable, civil, educational, religious, welfare or health purposes" who do not practice hate crimes.

To qualify for immunity under the VPA, the volunteer must satisfy the following prerequisites:

(1) the volunteer was acting within the scope of the volunteer's responsibilities in the non-profit organization at the time of the act or omission at issue;

(2) "if appropriate or required," the volunteer was properly licensed or certified in the State in which the harm occurred for the activities undertaken as a volunteer;

(3) the harm was not caused by "willful or criminal misconduct, gross negligence, reckless misconduct or a conscious, flagrant indifference to the rights or safety" of the person harmed; and

(4) the harm was not caused by the volunteer's operation of a vehicle for which the state requires the owner or operator to possess an operator's license or maintain insurance.

The VPA also generally prohibits the recovery of punitive damages against volunteers, and mandates that a volunteer shall be liable for non-economic loss only "in direct proportion to the percentage of responsibility of" the volunteer to the claimant. The VPA does not protect a volunteer from liability arising from violent crimes, terrorism, hate crimes, sexual offenses, civil rights violations under either federal or state law (including employment discrimination claims), or when the volunteer was under the influence of drugs or alcohol. The VPA does not prohibit a governmental entity or the non-profit from bringing an action against a volunteer. Finally, the VPA does not protect the non-profit itself. The VPA preempts state laws "to the extent that such laws are inconsistent" with the Act, although a State may provide *additional* protection or, alternatively, "opt-out" of the VPA's coverage. The VPA does not preempt state statutory provisions:

(1) requiring a non-profit to adhere to risk management procedures, including mandatory volunteer training;

(2) making a non-profit liable for the acts or omissions of its volunteers to the same extent that an employer is liable for the acts or omissions of its employees;

(3) rendering the immunity inapplicable if the action is brought by an officer of a state or local government pursuant to state or local law, or

(4) limiting the applicability of immunity to non-profits that provide a "financially secure source of recovery," such as insurance.

4. *Charitable Immunity*

Even if state or federal law provides immunity for individuals serving a non-profit, the non-profit itself still may be held liable for the actions of its directors and officers. The historic immunity charities formerly enjoyed no longer exists in most states, although some limited immunity may still be available in certain states, either by statute or by common law. The scope of charitable immunity varies from state to state. For example, New Jersey non-profits are not liable for negligently causing injury to their beneficiaries, but only where the non-profit is a corporation, society or association organized exclusively for charitable, religious, education or hospital purposes. Georgia law provides charitable immunity to hospitals in certain circumstances. Some states have provided a form of charitable immunity by imposing a cap on monetary damages. In Massachusetts, for example, damages are limited to $20,000 for torts occurring in the course of activity related directly to the organization's charitable purpose, while in Colorado, judgments against non-profits are limited to the extent of existing insurance coverage. State liability caps, however, may not apply to claims under federal law.

C. Insurance Coverage

A third source of protection for non-profits and their directors and officers is insurance, particularly directors and officers liability insurance coverage and/or employment practices liability insurance coverage. Although traditionally non-profits have limited insurance coverage to commercial general liability policies, such coverage may be insufficient to protect against the wide array of risk for their organizations and their directors and officers. Similarly, homeowners' insurance and professional liability (*e.g.*, attorney malpractice) policies generally are not tailored for non-profits' directors and officers. Directors and officers' insurance can specifically fill many of the gaps in the protection afforded by indemnification and liability-limiting statutes, particularly with respect to coverage for legal defense costs.

1. Commercial General Liability Insurance

Despite the expansion of potential liability, many non-profits and their directors and officers continue to maintain only basic commercial general liability ("CGL") coverage. CGL coverage applies to claims for bodily injury, personal injury, advertising liability and damage to, or destruction of, tangible property. Such basic coverage, however, often will not respond to breach of fiduciary duty claims, antitrust claims, government enforcement actions or any other type claim not involving bodily injury, personal injury, advertising liability or property damage. In particular, it is important to note that CGL policies generally do not cover employment claims for a number of reasons. First, most employment claims allege solely emotional distress and/or mental anguish which many jurisdictions do not consider "bodily injury" under CGL policies unless it is accompanied by physical symptoms or manifestations. Second, CGL policies are intended to cover occurrences or events which are not "expected or intended" by the insured. The acts giving rise to many employment claims are not unexpected or unintended and therefore may not be covered under CGL policies. Finally, many CGL policies contain a specific exclusion for employment-related claims.

2. Directors and Officers Liability Insurance

Given the limitations of other types of protection, directors and officers ("D&O") liability insurance may be an important component of risk management strategies for many non-profits. Such coverage also may be referred to as "Organization and

Management Liability" coverage, thus underscoring that coverage may be available to all participating in the non-profits' management, and that the organization itself may be covered by the policy. Notably, under several states' law, insurance may protect directors and officers in situations where the non-profit itself otherwise would be prohibited by applicable law from providing indemnification, such as for settlement of a derivative action. Unlike various liability-limiting statutes, a D&O insurance policy applies to both damages *and* defense costs.

Specific terms vary from insurance policy to insurance policy. The policy "form" often may be modified by "endorsements" negotiated with insurers. The following outlines some typical elements in a D&O liability insurance policy.

A D&O policy usually has separate insuring agreements for:

(a) "management liability" coverage which directly pays directors and officers for losses which are not indemnified by the organization,

(b) reimbursement to the organization for indemnification of its directors and officers and, in some policies,

(c) "entity coverage" that reimburses an organization for loss from its own direct liability. Entity coverage may be particularly beneficial to non-profits since such organizations themselves frequently are the target of lawsuits and usually are not protected by liability-limiting statutes.

Broadly speaking, D&O insurance generally provides coverage for "loss" from "claims" against "insured persons" for "wrongful acts." Policies usually define "loss" as judgments, settlements, and reasonable and necessary legal defense fees and costs. "Loss" typically does not include fines, penalties, taxes, restitution, or matters which may be deemed uninsurable under applicable law. Policies vary on whether "loss" includes punitive or multiplied damages. A "claim" generally includes a lawsuit and, depending upon the policy's definition, may include a regulatory proceeding or a government investigation. "Insured persons" include directors and officers, and may also include employees, trustees, or volunteers. As noted above, some D&O policies may provide coverage for the wrongful acts of the organization itself. A "wrongful act" typically is defined as any actual or alleged breach of duty, neglect, error, misstatement, misleading statement, act or omission by an insured person in his or her capacity as a director or officer (or employee, trustee, etc.) of the insured organization. Such policy definitions are critically important because they define the scope of coverage under the policy.

Most D&O policies currently are "claims-made" policies, *i.e.*, they provide coverage for claims first asserted during the policy period, regardless of when the wrongful act occurred. If the insured provides a detailed notice of circumstances that may give rise to a claim, and a claim subsequently develops, that claim may be deemed "first made" when notice is given even if the claim itself is not actually made until after the policy's expiration. The policy may have "extended reporting" or "discovery" provisions that allow an insured to pay an additional sum to obtain more time in which to report a claim. Most policies require prompt notice of a claim, and non-compliance with a policy's notice provisions may eliminate coverage.

D&O policies usually exclude coverage for claims arising out of or based upon:

(1) litigation or another proceeding that began before the policy period,

(2) intentional conduct, including dishonest, fraudulent or criminal conduct,

(3) an insured person's obtaining a personal profit or advantage to which he was not entitled,

(4) pollution, and

(5) bodily injury and property damage (which usually are covered by CGL insurance).

If other insurance is available, a D&O policy typically does not provide coverage. Some D&O policies exclude coverage for claims by one insured person against another insured person. Many D&O policies also exclude coverage for libel or slander. D&O policies also may specifically exclude employment claims (unless employment practices liability coverage is part of the policy). Similarly, ERISA claims usually are excluded from coverage unless the policy specifically provides fiduciary liability coverage.

If a claim is within a D&O policy's scope of coverage, and is not otherwise excluded, the organization generally must first pay a deductible (or retention) specified in the policy. If, however, the organization may not indemnify the director or officer, usually the individual need not pay a deductible. The maximum amount of coverage is the "limit of liability."

In most D&O policies, legal defense costs are "within limits," *i.e.*, payment of defense costs will reduce the remaining available limit of liability. Depending on the policy, the insurer may have a duty to defend the insured (*i.e.*, hire a lawyer to represent the insured) or it may simply pay legal defense costs incurred by the lawyer representing the insured. The policy usually will specify whether the insurer will "advance" legal defense costs or "reimburse" defense costs which have been paid by the insured. The former generally presents less of a strain on a non-profit's resources. Generally, the insured must have the insurer's prior written consent to incur legal defense costs or to enter into a settlement. Failure to obtain consent may result in elimination of coverage.

Often, the D&O policy will incorporate the insurance application into the policy. A misstatement in the application may void coverage.

3. Employment Practices Liability Insurance

In the last decade, the right to a jury trial to recover damages in a discrimination case combined with the heightened social attention on workplace conduct, including sexual harassment, have resulted in a significant increase in employment claims. From 2000 through 2004, approximately 80,000 charges of discrimination were filed each year with the United States Equal Employment Opportunity Commission ("EEOC"). Nearly 90% of all claims against non-profits were employment-related. To better protect themselves, employers, including non-profits, have turned to employment practices liability ("EPL") insurance policies. EPL coverage may be provided as part of a standard D&O policy, by endorsement or as a stand-alone policy.

EPL policies typically provide coverage for an insured entity, its directors and officers and its employees. In the non-profit context, coverage also may extend to volunteers. EPL policies generally are claims-made policies (*i.e.*, triggered when the claim is first made versus when the alleged incident occurred), contain specific requirements for reporting of a claim, and provide coverage for indemnity (*e.g.*, a judgment or settlement) and legal defense costs (*i.e.*, attorneys' fees and costs of litigation). Typically, the legal defense costs are considered to be a part of, or within, the limits of liability under the policy and subject to the policy's retention or deductible.

Most EPL policies specifically address issues of control – which defense counsel will represent the employer, who will control litigation decisions and who will decide whether and when to settle litigation – the insured or the insurer. However, policy provisions vary. EPL policies typically define an "employment claim," but the scope and breadth of potential coverage will depend on the definition. Most EPL policies currently cover claims for wrongful termination, discrimination and sexual harassment. Beyond these basic, traditional employment claims, EPL policies may cover a wide variety of workplace torts, *e.g.*, wrongful failure to employ or promote, negligent supervision, negligent hiring, wrongful reference, employment-related infliction of emotional distress, wrongful deprivation of a career opportunity, wrongful demotion and negligent job performance evaluation. Again, EPL policy provisions and definitions vary depending upon the policy and its language.

While EPL policies typically provide coverage for emotional distress, they usually do not provide coverage for bodily injury, sickness, disease or death, or property damage. Such claims are more likely to be covered by CGL policies because they involve actions that are not "expected" or "intended" by the insured. Conversely, however, CGL policies generally will not provide, and often expressly exclude, coverage for employment-related claims, which frequently involve intentional employment actions. EPL policies also often exclude coverage for certain statutory claims related to workers compensation, pensions, ERISA, and HIPAA. And, as with more traditional D&O policies, EPL policies often do not provide coverage for punitive damages, fines, contractual agreements or non-monetary relief.

CONCLUSION

Non-profit organizations and their directors and officers face a wide variety of legal risks including but not limited to lawsuits by employees, government authorities, members of the non-profit and individuals that the non-profit serves. Awareness of potential legal exposures is critical for prudent management. Although directors, officers and volunteers of non-profits may be entitled, under some circumstances, to statutory and other limitations on their liability and legal expenses, those protections vary greatly and are neither complete nor universal. And the non-profit itself typically does not receive comparable protections from liability or legal expenses. Insurance coverage, including D&O and EPL policies, affords non-profit directors and officers and their organizations broader and more effective protections in a world awash in litigation risks. Once aware of the risks that face them and their organizations, non-profit managers should be prepared and assured that they and their organization are protected adequately.

9

ENHANCING ORGANISATIONAL PERFORMANCE THROUGH STRATEGIC MANAGEMENT

INTRODUCTION

Strategic management is a disciplined approach utilizing the principles and process of management to identify the corporate objective or mission of any business. It determines an appropriate target to satisfy the objective, recognize existing opportunities and constraints in the environment, and device a rational practical way by which objective can be achieved.

Strategic management is both the process and philosophy for determining and controlling the organizational relationship in its dynamic environment. As a process, it attempts to define approaches and techniques to assist management adapt to the dynamic of today, through the use of objectives and strategies. Strategic management endeavours to achieve effective and efficient programs to accomplish the organization's mission. As a philosophy, it changes how manager looks at competitors, customers, markets and even the organization itself. Its objective is to stimulate management's awareness of the strategic implication of environmental events and internal decision.

Lawrence and William (1988) defined strategic management as a stream of decisions and actions, which leads to the development of an effective strategy or strategies to help achieve corporate objectives. The strategic management process is the way in which strategists determine objectives and make strategic decisions.

Strategic management's main focus is the achievement of organizational goals taking into consideration the internal and external environmental factors.

Porter (1985) argues that the essence of formulating comprehensive strategy is relating a company to its environment. Strategic management permits the systematic management of change. It enables organization to purposefully mobilize resources towards a desired future.

Chandler (1962) also posited that any effective successful strategy is dependent on structure, thus to achieve any effective economic performance the organization needs to alter its structure.

The objective of this paper is to examine the conceptual and theoretical approach of strategic management on the performance of business organization.

The objectives of the paper are:

i. To examine the importance and relevance of strategic management in an organization.
ii. To examine the effectiveness of strategic management.
iii. To see how strategic management influence performance of the business organization.

LITERATURE REVIEW/ THEORETICAL FRAMEWORK

Strategy is the determination of the basic term goals and objectives of an enterprise, and the adoption of course of action and the allocation of resources necessary for carrying out those goals Chandler (1962).

In Chandler definition of strategy he attempts to view that strategy is as much as about defining goals and objectives as it is about providing the means for achieving them. Ansoff and McDonnell (1990) also separate goal setting (concerned with ends) from strategy (concerned with means). On the subject of strategic management they provide the following definition:

Strategic management is a systematic approach for managing strategic change, which consists of the following:

a. Positioning of the firm through strategy and capability planning.

b. Real-time strategic response through issue management.
c. Systematic management of resistance during strategic implementation.

Strategy and market positions are necessary to set directions for a firm and to outsmart competitors or at least enable it to overcome threatening environment. A good strategy when adequately implemented can ensure a topmost position for the weakest firm among other superior competitors, but without good strategies.

Strategic planning if well conceptualized and implemented with an organization should result in strategic management. Strategic management treats strategic thinking as a pervasive concept for running a business organization and regards strategic planning as an instrument around which all other control system budgeting, information, reward and organization can be integrated. Strategic planning specifically entails the allocation of resources to programmed activities in such a way as to achieve a set of business goals in a dynamic competitive environment. Glueck and Jauch (1984) posited that strategic management as a steam of decisions and actions that lead to the development od effective strategies to help achieve corporate objectives.

Mintzberg (1991) sees strategy as 5 P's – plans, ploys, patterns, position and perspective. He describes a plan as 'some sort of consciously intended course of action'. In this situation organizations are expected to decide what they want to do and how they intend to achieve it. Failure of many organizations in recent time has been attributed to poor plan.

A ploy is a sub-set of a plan, and is a strategy in the sense of a strategies (i.e. a ruse or trick designed to put a rival company off the sent by disguising the real intention of the company).

Mintzberg (1991) describes pattern as the consistent behaviour and processes that emerge from strategic thinking, due to intended or unintended actions. He sees plans and ploys as deliberate strategy use by an organization, but considers pattern as emergent strategies.

According to Mintzberg position is acceptable location for the organization in an environment. In business organization position boils down to its product market position in its chosen market. This is what Nigeria Bottling Company (NBC) has been using over other any soft drink industry. Perspective is looking inside the organization. Any of business organization with high degree of perspective approach will have management that have shared view and vision and make a positive impact on the environment where it operates.

Strategy is needed to focus effort and promote coordination of activities. Without strategy an organization becomes bunch of individuals, hence strategy is required to ensure collective actions and concentration of efforts towards achieving organizational plans and objective.

Johnson and Scholes (1993) view corporate strategy from cultural perspective, they described it as a strategy based on the experiences, assumptions and beliefs of management overtime and which may eventually permeate the whole organization.

Henceforth, strategy can help in defining an organization to both insiders and outsiders. Strategy as plan, ploy pattern, position and perspectives defines the organization by providing proper understanding of the organization to the people and a way of differentiating it from others. One needs to understand that a clearly defined strategy that will lead to enthusiasm among various stakeholders – shareholders, suppliers, creditors, customers, promoter and employees as a result promote commitment that will enhance better performance of business organization.

Strategy provides consistency and stability. It deals with irregularity in behaviour and reduces uncertainty about the operation of an organization. It resist changes thereby ensuring consistency which gives a sense of being in control to the management and relief from the anxiety created by complexity.

This does not mean a static or stationary situation but rather it implies an efficient response to the environment to ensure stability and continual domination or retention of market leadership by the business organization involved. This assists the organization to focus its resources and exploit its opportunities, skill and knowledge to the fullest.

Strategy is a broad based formular for how business is going to compete (Porter 1980), that is, what its goal should be, and what policies will be needed to carryout these goals.

An organization strategic management has its ultimate objective in the development of its corporate values, managerial capabilities, organizational responsibilities and operational decision making at all hierarchical levels and across all business and functional lines of authority.

According to Child (1972) strategic decision making is seen as a crucial part of the process by which organization adapt to their environments. It is argued that those decision that actually succeed in creating or changing organizations do so via complex iterative process, which strategy theorists subsume under the concept of strategy implementation.

IMPORTANCE OF STRATEGIC PLANNING

The importance of strategic planning in any business organization can not be overemphasized. Most of the organizations recently recognized the role of strategic planning to the long range growth and survival of their business organization. Most of the managers have observed that by specifically defining the mission of their organization they are better able to give it direction and focus its activities.

Some Nigerian Business Organizations are without formal plans or where there are formal plans they do operate without adhering to them. Some argued that the market place changes so fast for a plan to be useful. All business organizations are heading somewhere but unfortunately some do not know where they are going, then any road will lead them there. This therefore emphasizes the need for organizations to utilize strategic planning concepts.

Planning remains the key to organization success because absence of proper planning could lead to confusion and unethical practices. However, despite the importance of strategic planning many organizations still fail to plan, hence planning to fail.

In recent times, the study of strategic management is being given much attention Lambo (1986) studies bank portfolio management examining profit maximization and accommodation principle models in Nigeria commercial banks. Adeyemi (1992) who established that there is a positive correlation between strategic management and organizational performance in some Nigeria banks also carried out another study.

It is worthy of note that whatever conclusions are made, it has been empirically stated that the success or failure of strategic planning is determined by a number of components which include the environment, organization structure and strategic decision making. According to Ansoff (1979), when these three components are properly matched, the performance of any organization is optimized.

Lorange (1979) posited that the importance of strategic planning is to accomplish a sufficient process of innovation to support and enhance the planning process. He further argues that effective strategic planning does not have to be elaborate or complicated but must be logical and focused on strategic decisions to be undertaken.

EFFECTIVENESS OF STRATEGIC MANAGEMENT

Alli (1992) gives the characteristics of an effective strategic management as follows:

a. Clear direction and purpose
b. Objectives, goals, and strategic consistency
c. Continuous monitoring of internal and external (environment)
d. Integration of operating budget and profit plans with strategic plan
e. Continuous monitoring of progress with revision of plan and programs as appropriate
f. Creation of strategic atmosphere that foresters a team spirit
g. Commitment of necessary resources and the development of system to provide necessary management information.

Basically, there are three major perspectives of studying strategic management effectiveness in literature.

Firstly, uses of goal centered approach to assess organizational effectiveness. In this situation, individual organization seeks to analyze the extent of fulfillment of important planning objectives. Cameron and Whitton (1983), King (1987) and Steiner (1979) also support this.

Secondly, specific capabilities to develop a 'generic view' if system capabilities as stated by Lorange (1979) a generic capability required of every formal strategic planning system is the ability to encourage both creativity and control (Camillus 1975). In this perspective, creativity and control are used here not as opposite objective but as requisite properties of an effective planning system.

The third perspective traditionally examines the role and impact of corporate planning on organizational effectiveness. Although, the link may be a little bit difficult however, there are strong arguments that the ultimate test of the system's effectiveness and justification for its existence is the impact on organizational performance (Henry 1979).

Methodology

For this study the researcher designed questionnaire and was administered to the First Bank of Nigeria, Plc. Ilorin Branch. The researcher administered thirty-five (35) questionnaires, which was divided into two parts. This first part contained demographic characteristics of the respondents while the second part was used to tap information on how strategic management enhances organization performance.

The researcher was able to retrieved twenty-nine (29) questionnaires from the respondents. This represents eighty-three per cent (83%) rate. The respondents for the study were randomly selected and stratified into male and female. The collected data were analysed descriptively.

Analysis and Discussion

The first part of the questionnaire which is on demographic characteristic of the respondents revealed that 72.4% of the sample were male while 27.6% of the respondents were female. This shows that majority of the respondents interviewed are male.

The ages of the respondents were between 21 to 50, although about 62.1% of the respondents fall within 31-40 age bracket. While only 13.8% were between 41-50 age group.

The study also revealed that 75.9% of the respondents were married while 24.1% were still single.

About 44.8% of the respondents have spent above 11 years with the organisation.

This shows that information was collected from the well-experienced personnel from the organisation, and this is an indication of the reliability of the information obtained.

Table 1: Demographic characteristics of the respondents

SEX	*frequency*	*percentage*
Male	21	72.4
Female	8	27.6
Total	29	100
Age	*frequency*	*percentage*
Under 21	-	-
21-30	7	24.1
31-40	18	62.1
41-50	4	13.8
Total	29	100
length of service	*frequency*	*percentage*
1-5 yrs	6	20.7
6-10yrs	13	44.8
11-15yrs	5	17.2
16-above	5	17.2
Total	29	100
Education qualification	*frequency*	*percentage*
WASC / GCE	2	6.9
NCE/OND	1	3.4
HND/B.Sc./B.A.	16	55.2
M.Sc./MBA/MPA	10	34.5
Total	29	100

Table 2: Staff responses on the adoption of strategic management by their organisation

Variables	*Frequency*	*Percentage*
Strongly agree	9	31.0
Agree	15	51.7
Disagree	3	10.3
Strongly disagree	-	-
Undecided	2	6.9
Total	29	100

Source: researcher findings.

Table 3: Adoption of strategic management has enhanced the organisation performance.

Variables	*Frequency*	*Percentage*
Strongly agree	15	51.7
Agree	11	37.9
Disagree	2	6.9
Strongly disagree	1	3.4
Undecided	-	-
Total	29	100

Source: researcher findings.

The table 2 above shows that the responses of the respondents as regards to the adoption of strategic management in their organisation. 31.0% of the people interviewed strongly agreed while 51.7% also agreed that their organisation is fully adopted strategic management in its operation.

Although, about 10.3% of the respondents disagreed that their operation has not fully adopted strategic management in their operation.

The study also revealed that 51.7% and 37.9% of the respondents strongly agreed and agreed respectively that adoption of strategic management has enhanced the organisation performance. This shows that management recognition of strategic management has enabled it to make a sound decision, which has enhanced its successful operation in its environment.

However, 10.3% of the respondents disagreed with that position, according to them their organisation performance was due to other factors, which is outside the scope of this paper. It was also revealed from the study that strategic planning in the organiation is occassionally handled by the consultant, and also done at the top management level.

CONCLUSION AND SUMMARY

This paper examines the enhancement of Organisational performance through strategic management: conceptual theoretical and approach. In recent times world economy has witnessed a lot of dynamism and challenges. Therefore, there is need to take longer perspectives of operations so as to ensure that available resources are purposely harnessed for the optimal direction of the affairs of the business organizations.

An enhancement of business organization performance through strategic management will depend on management's recognition of the following functions: setting objectives, establishing policies with which to work towards objectives, assign responsibilities and provide for coordinated action, selecting and developing key personnel, helping them adjust to change, motivating and stimulating them to think creatively and measuring progress and evaluating results.

Strategic management allows an organization to make its decisions based on long-range forecast and not on the spur of the moment reaction. It also allows the establishment to make action at an early stage of new trend and consider the lead-time for effective management.

Ansoff et al (1979) studies ninety-three large firms, all of which have made acquisition between 1946 and 1965 and their financial and sales measure. They found that managers were able to predict outcomes better than non-planners.

The business organizations should adopt a competitive position, which will allow them to defend themselves against any forces in the industry environment. Harmnermesh (1993) proposed three broad generic strategies which if adopted by business organization will enable it to compete in a given business and position itself among it's competitors. These strategies are: overall cost leadership (achieve lower cost than competitors; differentiation (creating something unique and superior) and focus that is, selecting a particular buyer group or segment of the market as the basis for competition.

In order to achieve better performance, business organizations need to take bold step of adopting strategic management in their various organizations. Knowing fully well that the level and intensity of the competition between the organizations is fast increasing as the level of business organizations and individual.

In meeting the current challenges by the business organizations call for application of better and more meaningful strategic management which would transcend all categories of worker within the business organization.

STRATEGIC POSITIONING AND STRATEGIC MANAGEMENT

Strategic positioning is the positioning of an organization (unit) in the future, while taking into account the changing environment, plus the systematic realization of that positioning.

The strategic positioning of an organization includes the devising of the desired future position of the organization on the basis of present and foreseeable developments, and the making of plans to realize that positioning.

The strategic positioning method is derived from the business world. The method is aimed at ensuring the continuity of the organization. The strategy determines the contents and the character of the organization's activities.

Terms, such as survival, legitimacy, market positioning, relationship with environment and choice for a certain work area, come up in this context.

Subjects which have been developed reasonably well in literature on strategic management include: information collection techniques, analysis techniques and planning schemes. Not or hardly developed are methods for exploring the future.

Various questions must be asked with strategic positioning:

- How does the future look like?

- How could the organization be roughly positioned in the future?
- How are things in the organization at present?
- How can opportunities be seized and how can threats be met?
- How can this be put into practice in a systematic way?

We will deal with the following aspects:

1. the future;
2. information collection;
3. analysis;
4. choice of strategy;
5. implementation.

The Future

Each futurology is based on the past and present. Whether the future is predicted from the flight of a flock of ducks, or from the way in which coffee grounds spread under a turned cup, or from thoughts of wise men: the waves of the future are always interpreted on the basis of the wavelets which are already visible in the present.

Trend research according to Naisbitt (shifts in the basically closed news circuit) is based on small shifts which announce future developments. If we can get hold of today's trends, we may perhaps extrapolate them into the future.

It is important for everybody to map the non-volatile developments which are relevant to the own organization. A first exploration of the strategic positioning can be constituted by extrapolating the trends and by gearing them to the field in which the own organization operates.

Information Collection

The steps to be taken are internal research and external research.

Internal Research

Where does our organization stand? What internal factors are decisive for survival and for failure or success, both in a positive and in a negative sense? It is advisable to draw up a list of own relevant criteria, which are applicable to the branch you are working in.

This will help determine the strong and weak points of the own organization.

External Research

What influences from outside can be of decisive importance to the realization of the organization's objectives? Or: what external critical factors are there?

Model lists of such factors are available but the organization should come up with its own relevant criteria, which do not only belong to the sector but also, for instance, to region-specific developments. This will help describe the opportunities and threats of the organization.

Future opportunities and threats are also mapped occasionally by making use of extrapolation (trend curves or mathematical models) or by consulting experts in a systemized way. Or by making one or more empirically founded, plausible constructions of the anticipated developments (scenarios).

Analysis

One can make an analysis of the strategic position by confronting the data of the internal and external researches with each other. An often used method is the SWOT analysis. Four lists of factors are drawn up: Strong Weak Opportunity and Threat. This is usually done in a group meeting of members of the organisation.

Another method is the Product/Market Matrix. Questions raised with this method are: Can you, departing from the existing product range, think of new applications (markets)? And can you supply markets where you are already on firm ground with a variation on your product? (Example: New Zealand sheep farms inventing a new application of wool at times of stiff competition on the wool market: absorption of oil spills at sea, being an existing product on a new market.)

A third method is the Portfolio analysis, which is derived from stock exchange operators wondering: "Which securities must we keep and which must we sell?". A specific portfolio is that of the Boston Consultants Group, which holds the investment or the growth of the branch of industry (Y-axis) against the profit or the market share (X-axis). Four fields then come into being: the stars, the milk cows, the wild cats and the dogs.

Note: for NGO's, the term profit has to be translated in the immaterial yield that should be derived: some distress that is eased; some social interest that is served. The instruments of strategic positioning are derived from business but are fit to serve NGO's as well.

Choice of Strategy

On the basis of the analysis of internal and external critical factors - so, on basis of the estimated chances of seizing opportunities and meeting threats - the positioning will be determined. It would be quite nice to make a very specific positioning choice: we aim at becoming an organization which ..... (a description follows, by what the position choice is characterized, in terms of products, customers and image).

Once such a choice has been made, it should be studied what strategy is appropriate to realize that choice of position. In literature rough strategies are indicated, such as stabilization, growth, shrinking and turnaround. The organization can probably indicate much more specifically and accurately what strategy must be opted for. Growth in a certain direction, orientation towards a certain market, etc.

Implementation

The main thing of implementation is that, departing from the future positioning choice, theory is translated into what is to be done in order to realize that positioning.

Example of Elements of a Strategic Plan

Business plan, for instance aimed at:

- internal growth: strengthening of the own position on the existing market;
- market penetration: introduction of products on new market;

- market development: new product on existing market;
- product development or diversification: new product on new market.

Product plan, selection of products or services, determination of their quality, effect of a product (result for customer).

Marketing plan, aimed at marketing mix: product policy, promotion policy, distribution policy and price policy (cost price/ market price/ competition price?).

Production plan, choice of location, choice of equipment and of the production process, production standards, layout. Production planning, production management, stock control, quality control, cost control, maintenance.

Research plan, technological innovation or product modification.

Personnel & Organization plan, positions, recruitment and selection, career development, organizational structure, training and education, organization culture, performance assessment, terms of employment, relationship with the representative advisory committee, organized consultations, trade unions, promotion policy.

Purchase plan, evaluation of suppliers, account management, make-or-buy.

Logistical plan, transport management, stock and handling, run-through times, term of delivery.

Financial plan, registration and evaluation of financial data, responsibility for availability of financing.

Information plan, gathering and processing of data.

Quality plan, consistency, competence, responsibility, accessibility, respect, communication, credibility, understanding, safety, appearance.

Public Relations plan, both internal (mission, propagation of business objectives, motivation of staff) and external.

STRATEGIZING CHANGE AND IMPLEMENTATION OF CHANGES

The process of consulting is approaching its finish. Ideas are being transformed to operational plans.

Most of the time the process of change is described as if we are dealing with a fixed procedure and as if consultants are following the path of the theory: intake, dynamic analysis, recommendations, implementation. But life itself is more complex and chaotic.

Implementation of changes in an organisation can be compared with action research in investigation. The moment the consultant makes his or her appearance in the organisation, its reality starts to be influenced.

The mere announcement of change causes already changes.

The art of consulting is to push those changes in the desired direction.

Consulting is not dealing with a scientific determination of the effect of recommendations. The heart of the matter is bringing about feasible and effective changes.

So defined, implementation covers far more than carrying out recommendations in the last phase of a consultancy process. Other topics are also part of the process, like sensitizing the organisation for the problem at hand, strengthening the support for the recommendations and making the organisation susceptible for change. Implementation is an ongoing process, right from the start.

The core question of implementation is: how to use the energy, available in the organisation, in behalf of the realisation of the intended change.

E=KxA, effectivity and acceptation.

The famous formula: E=KxA is applicable: the effectiveness of the recommendation equals the quality of that recommendation multiplied by its acceptation.

The consultant/change agent considers the development of the acceptance as part of the job. Consultant who are blaming the organisation not being fit for their recommendations, those consultants will find the cynics on their hands, but will not manage to put the organisation in motion.

It can happen that an organisation turns out not being able to realize the consultants recommendations. Thinking in terms of action research: in such a case something in the recommendations will be deficient too. Probably the consultant has taken the role of the expert who has not taken into account the possibilities or capacities of the organisation.

Working on acceptation is the part of the process of implementation that always need attention. Because if the right breeding ground is available, the organisation probably had thought itself of a solution. The presence of a consultant indicates the need for help of an organisation in adjusting itself to a changing reality.

Some recommendations can be introduced top down, neglecting the level of acceptance. But such recommendations are rare. When the turning point of the change has to do with (the knowledge, attitude or skills of) people, an active support will be needed for a successful implementation.

Support and Energy

To change an organisation, passive support is not sufficient. What we need is active and dynamic support. Like said before: when the turning point of the change has to do with (the knowledge, attitude or skills of) people, it is not enough that people acquiesce in a new policy, structure or culture. People have to consider the change necessary, and they have to feel the need to support it.

Only then the change has a chance to be integrated in the realm of action. Such a support requires energy.

The Energy-scan

Studying the ways an organisation tries to tackle problems (or how it was done in the past) can reveal the employment of energy of an organisation. Sometimes the organisation stresses the possibilities and chances and everyone is mobilised to think about solutions. Such an organisation has forward directed energy. Other organisations are primarily preoccupied with the threats and run the risk to get stuck in that phase. The energy is frozen. Some organisations put their energy in looking for the guilty ones or a scapegoat and keep themselves busy with the question: how could it happen? The energy has a backwards direction. Some organisations only want to be put in the right (I warned several times....)

The ways to cope with problems are not accidental nor incidental. The way an organisation directs its energy is comparable with the current of a river. It is not a choice, it is the resultant of the past. The direction of the stream creates the bed of the river which makes the same direction for the next time more probable.

A consultant cannot just order another flow. The art of consulting is to use the common direction of the energy on behalf of the solution of the problem. Not only by placing the problem in the middle of the stream, but by joining the motion of the stream and using its force.

The change itself generates the motion.

Sometimes the intended change itself generates the energy for its realisation. The ideas ignite the enthusiasm of people and all that should be done is to use and direct the ebullition of energy.

In some organisation such positive use of energy lies ready to be used. The work of the consultant is to think about ways to employ the energy. Sometimes an extra ignition is needed for a take-off speed to break away. Take-off ignition can be found for example in an opening conference or start-meeting that stimulates the existing energy and offers an approach to the problem, directed to solutions.

Sometimes it is necessary to temporarily evade structural obstacles in order to provide the process of a successful start. For that reason some organisations make use of a temporary infra-structure (a task force with a specific assignment and own channels of communications) by which blockages in the line -or in the communication- no longer are obstacles for the process of change.

How to join the motion.

The intended change not always finds a favourable breeding ground. Maybe the organisation has some energy, but that is being used for other purposes. The consultant could try to apply judo techniques: take advantage of the forces on behalf of the change. The most important activity for implementation in such a case is joining the motion.

The consultant should investigate by what kind of topics people tend to be mobilised. The next step is to join the change-topic to the existing stream of energy: i.e. to the mobilising-topic. This activity can be compared with the smart habits of the small white heron that pokes about in the presence of a cow, making profit of its abundance of food. Use the richness of energy of something else for your own purpose.

A smart energy-seeker always finds streams of energy that can be used.

A disadvantage of this strategy is its inevitable invisibility. If we should make the strategy visible, the change topic becomes visible. But that change topic is not able to generate enough energy under its own steam, otherwise it should be placed in the category above (the change generates the motion).

Joining the motion as a strategy can be used on content and process. For instance: the heron of the gender-approach can make use of for instance the energy of the cow: personnel policy or the quality policy (using another content). Or: the heron gender-approach makes use of the energy of the cow: lunch meetings (using another process).

Using the culture.

The consultant who is invited as a change agent often feels the existing culture as a major obstacle. An example: the organisational culture is procedure driven, while the core of the intended change is to turn the organisation towards an external orientation. Being driven by procedures is a sign of an internal orientation, so at first sight the assignment of the consultant seems to be to fight the existing culture. But organisational culture is never trivial and organisational culture is never composed of only useless elements. It is the task of the consultant to recognise those elements in the existing culture that can be used as materials for improvement.

For instance: we begin to look closer to what we called procedure driven. It turns out to be a summary of a variety of actions (habits): people are used to describe in detail whàt should be done before doing it, hòw it should be done, whò is doing what, in which order and whò will be responsible. What could the consultant use this culture on behalf of the development of an external orientation?? For instance by organising a series of individual agreements (!) with members of the organisation in order to map out in detail (!) in which networks they participate. Those individual networks will be joined to one external map (!) of the organisation. In a general meeting it will be determined (!) which connections are missing and which should be used better. This common analysis (!) is followed by the precise distribution of tasks (!) and the planning (!) of agreements. To round it off the evaluation (!) is planned.

The consultant uses the existing stream of the culture and makes his or her own preference (for instance to celebrate the start of becoming external orientation with a tremendous party) of minor importance.

Ostentatious challenging the existing culture sometimes brings about admiration, but seldom success.

The impossible culture.

Using the culture (as the heron uses the cow) is not always possible. There are some organisational cultures which make a favourable turn impossible

An example is the organisational culture which is called: popular cynicism. In an organisation suffering from cynicism the people have given up the hope of improvement. In fact they are in a state of collective depression, which is not expressed in the blues. On the contrary, people seem to rejoice that things are rotten. There is a collective ambition to amuse each other with bitter jokes at the expense of the organisation.

An organisation in deep sombreness is a difficult but not impossible challenge for a consultant. Helping an organisation that amuses itself with its misery is well-nigh impossible. The reason for that is because the cynics have committed themselves to a certain attitude and each opening to improvement would strike at the roots of their certainties. People have to reject ideas for improvement because the risk of loosing one's footing is too big.

There are more examples of impossible cultures, but the consultant is not always empty-handed. It is important to explore quietly the spreading of the popular cynicism over the organisation. Is it really uniformly spread, or are there differences in the organisation? The outcome of such an exploration often is that it is only a minority that defines the expressions and the manners and that the majority would like to be hopeful, if they only dared.

The consultant should work with those people in small groups, avoiding for the time being plenary sessions in which the cynics set the tone.

How to make use of people: supporters, opponents and bystanders.

In a lot of change processes the consultant will detect three types of people in the organisation: supporters, opponents and bystanders. It is necessary to begin with the process of change with supporters. Even if the organisation proposes to compose a task force "in which also some critical people who are not in favour of changes" (in a sincere attempt to provide the consultant of a representative group) the consultant should choose for a group that feels like help thinking.

After a while the Help Thinking-group should deal with the question: how to reach the probably biggest group in the organisation, the bystanders, those people who sit on the fence. What could we do to make them enthusiastic?

By displacement of the enthusiasm to the middle group one could try to reach the opponents. In a successful process the opponents have sometimes simply disappeared. Sometimes they wait in the wings in case the project yet happens to fail. Sometimes they develop themselves into people with a positive critical function.

It is important for the consultant to realise that the question of failure or success is not decided by the supporters or the opponents, but that the critical mass is decisive. In a succeeding project the number of people who are joining in swells and at a certain moment it will pass a limit that makes the change inevitable.

Consultants should bear this in mind and should try to recognise this phenomenon, because opponents can have a massive negative effect on their energy and attention. One gruff man who is shaking his head in an audience that is generally enthusiastic, one such a person is able to absorb the energy of the speaker. We call this phenomenon the power of distraction. The consultant in the role as speaker should be aware of this phenomenon. A firm intention to direct the own energy towards the supporters and bystanders may help prevent this unbelievably annoying experience.

The use of necessity.

Generally spoken: the forces in an organisation always tend to continue the once taken direction. Even if the consultant is recruited on behalf of a desired change, even then the energy of an organisation will be directed primarily on continuation of what people were doing. Probably we are dealing here with a pattern of a social psychological nature. Though some experts' starting point is people liking change (as for instance Moss Kanter), the most common point of view is that an organisation is likely to show resistance to change.

The practise of change shows that the most successful changes are realised if a clear necessity for change is apparent. The more tight the link of the necessity is to the survival of the organisation, the more complete and quick will be the change of the organisation.

If the board of an health institution wants to integrate a gender approach in its treatment this will be easier accomplished when the institution has a fast growing number of female patients.

A new policy alone causes no organisational necessity. The change in the group of clients does. That is why consultants speak of a *workable necessity.*

CHANGE AND THE SENSE OF URGENCY

Realising changes in organisations requires investment in terms of time and money, but most important in terms of people's attention, reflection and energy to do things differently. Not everybody will accept the intended changes with the same level of willing. People are busy, are more or less content with the way things go or have other priorities. In other words: change is not happening only because someone says it should happen. People change (their habits or working methods) because they believe in the necessity. Because they feel the sense of urgency.

That sense of urgency is not equally clear for everyone in the organisation.

The crucial activity in change is to induce people to do things differently. In most cases this means also a change in organisational culture: in values and norms and in habits and working methods they once developed and agreed to. Culture is a powerful force in the organisation. If the intended change follows naturally the way people are used to do their job, then the characteristics of the organisational culture can be used completely. But if the intended change requires new cultural aspects, then the change will be more difficult to realise. Not because the workers are on beforehand unwilling, but because a change of the organisational culture will fail if it is only based on a declaration of intent. If compelling reasons to change are lacking, then a relapse in old habits is most likely.

Organisational culture can be considered as the personality of the organisation. Like in the case of someone's personality, one can change some aspects of behaviour, but structural changes are far more difficult to obtain and require deep investments. Far reaching changes are only feasible if people feel the urgency to change. (Comparable with psychotherapy: clients can only bear the burden of a therapy if they consider the burden of their suffering heavier.)

An example of a change like that is the change over to market oriented working methods, a process of conversion for a lot of institutions in the non-profit sector in Western countries. Being market oriented requires another attitude. Concepts like price quality ratio, measuring output or getting the targets are abominations to those workers in the non-profit sector who work with their clients (or on a topic) from a feeling of solidarity. Such workers can only be motivated to change their working methods if they have a sense of urgency, for instance because the survival of the organisation is at stake.

External necessity.

Far reaching changes need a clear external necessity. The management (or the change agent) has to make visible and perceptible that change is needed in order to survive. Sometimes such an external necessity is clearly present. For instance because the subsidy is reallocated or finished, because the clientele is changing or because of an increase in complaints.

The making of necessity.

The existence of a necessity to change may be clear for the change agent, but sometimes it has to be made visible and perceptible for other people as well. Sometimes it is needed to look for changes in the outside world that can act as motivators for changes inside the organisation.

One way of doing it is *benchmarking*. Benchmarking is a method of investigation in which products or services are compared with those of another (peer or competitive) organisation. Benchmarking can reveal the (lack of) quality of the own organisation, in comparison to similar organisations. Such results can mean a threat for the future, certainly if competition will play an important role in the future. So benchmarking can help prove that performance should improve (in order to keep joining) and that it can improve (others can do it, so why don't we?)

Sometimes the external necessity is caused by *changes in the outside world*, may it be a threat or an opportunity.

Some institutions are able to change by seizing opportunities. An organisation for instance seizes the opportunities to change its profile thereby promoting the stream of a new segment of the market. Or an organisation develops in a relatively simple way a new supply and puts it on the market that seems ready for it (a training preventing work-stress for example).

Other organisations are more likely to be motivated by rising threats: aggressive competition, decreasing profits, threatening reduction. External threats, like increasing competition or decreasing subsidy are not always experienced as the most powerful motivating stimuli. The first reaction to such threats is rather anger, defence or paralysis. The skill of the change agent is to bend such (understandable) reactions to external threats towards a certain level of enthusiasm. For instance by showing that such a threat can offer new perspectives. For example: a situation of intensified competition offers the opportunity to concentrate more than before on the own core competence.

Finally: the urge for change can be underlined by pointing to relevant *trends and developments.* We mention some examples of trends that can stress the external necessity for the introduction of gender specific health care:

- individualisation: clients increasingly expect care that corresponds to their specific interests and needs.
- emancipation nowadays belongs to the mainstream: the last few years, problems of women and the way to understand those problems are convincingly related by the women movement to gender socialisation. As a result a lot of women came to see their own complaints and problems in a different light. (A Dutch example: before 1980 hardly any woman was seeking help because of sexual abuse. The percentage of women seeking help for that reason increased significantly after 1980, when the women movement brought to light that sexual abuse was a common problem.) Women are liberated and they expect from health care institutions that they have emancipated in a same degree.
- women in societal functions and positions: slowly but surely women get higher positions. This brings new problems, for instance problems of burning out, double burden because of the combination of work and domestic care. Not only men but also women of forty year old land in a midlife crisis. This social upgrading causes gender specific complaints.
- increased freedom of choice: people seem to have more and more choices. The path of life is no longer outlined at the moment of birth. The idea of freedom of choice (apart from the question if such freedom really exists) may intensify feelings of guilt. "It is my own fault, I went with him completely voluntarily.") Most people have indeed more choices, but the wealth of choices held out to them isn't within easy reach. The fact that one cannot realise one's wishes is more and more felt as a personal failure, while the real cause may lie in societal exclusion.

Resistance to Change

Resistance has many faces: open resistance, passive resistance, resistance in disguise. Resistance will bother the change agent, especially as the type of change (change of values or norms which need to be rooted in the behaviour of people) requires participation, active cooperation or even enthusiasm.

Resistance may show up in all phases of the change process. Resistance can be present at the start, when the necessity to change is investigated, if people do not enough accept or experience the necessity. Resistance will be painfully perceptible in the phase of implementation, when the objectives of change have to be translated to actual actions.

And again: the more active participation plays a role, the more it will be difficult to deal with resistance. Changes, in which training and coaching of workers are crucial elements, can be fairly well obstructed by resistance. In other words: resistance can lead to a lack of support of those people who are at stake.

Expressions of such a lack of support go from passively waiting and negating the changes, via delay and misunderstandings, via impalpable sabotage to finally open opposition.

An obvious way to break resistance is to launch the intended changes more forcefully. But such a counter pressure leads often to intensified resistance. Something different has to be done.

The change agent has to begin to understand, decode and re-code the resistance.

A positive scheme of thinking about people implies that people want to change. If people in an organisation do not join the changes, then their natural willingness is blocked by something. Such a blockage can be a consequence of a lack of a feeling of urgence, a lack of wanting the change or a lack of capacity to change.

- The feeling of urgence. Someone will be willing to change if he or she really experiences the urge to change and if the people in the workplace have a positive attitude towards the change. Thus if the boss and the colleagues agree with the change or when they show some enthusiasm because of the change. The sense of urgency can be influenced by information on the actual performance of the organisation and the (future) demands.

- The will to change. Someone will be willing to change if (s)he is convinced of the positive results of the change and believes in the positive effects on the work and on the organisation. The will to change can be influenced by motivating.
- The capacity to change. Someone will be willing to change if (s)he is running the process of change her/him-self, as much as possible. Thus if someone can agree with the way the process is directed, if money and time are supplied, if the involvement is as big as possible and if the complexity of the change can be overlooked. Good experiences with previous changes can be helpful.

The capacity to change can be influenced by a high degree of participation.

The change agent will be able, with he help of this decoding key, to investigate the willingness to change and to predict the presence of resistance.

Questions:

- which consequences for the work do the workers expect of the intended change?
- what kind of emotions are evoked by the intended change?
- are the workers convinced of the positive effects of the change?
- are they involved in the process of change?
- what is the attitude of others (management, colleagues) towards the change?
- what is the experience of the workers with previous changes?
- have the workers enough time and other means to their disposal, in order to realise the change successfully?
- is the process of change well-directed guided?
- do the workers consider the change complex?
- is the process of change at the right moment?

Wanting to (motivation), having to (urge) and being able to (capacity) are three necessary ingredients for a successful implementation.

A combination of presence and absence of those three ingredients can lead to specific problems:

- motivation OK, but no capacity: frustration. Solution: training.
- motivation OK, but no urge: delay. Solution: anticipatory experiments.
- urge OK, but no motivation: reactive attitude of personnel. Solution: motivation.
- urge OK, but no capacity: paralysis. Solution: capacity building
- capacity OK, but no motivation: nothing happens. Solution: create take-off energy
- capacity OK, but no urge: everything waits till the market forces a change. Solution: look for other urge.

The urge (to have to change) is the crucial element at the start and the decision making of the change process. Action: mobilise.

The motivation (wanting to change) is important in the phase of acceptation. Action: negotiate, coach and convince.

The capacity (being able to change) is crucial in the phase of implementation. Action: support, plan and simplify.

Resuming:

- do ask yourself if the resistance can be understood as deficits in the willingness to change
- check in which phase the process of change is
- think if actions are possible that will cover fully the (decoded) diagnosis of the resistance.

Trends

The American author John Naisbitt has developed a method for gaining an impression of future developments. This is based on a content analysis of a large amount of print media. The news segment of the newspaper is a closed system. For economic reasons the relative amount of space for news (relationship between advertising and news) changes little in the course of time. If a topic is added, something else has to be left out.

By keeping careful track of the new and the omitted topics, we can in a certain sense get a picture of the changing market share of competing social aspects.

Naisbitt's content analysis makes use of a monthly evaluation of 6,000 local newspapers. The shifts he reveals in this manner, he refers to as *trends* or *megatrends.*

Trends appear gradually, fads are faster and less long-lasting, they have more to do with fashion. Trends are massive shifts in what is regarded as important by public opinion, regardless of their "objective" importance.

In his book Naisbitt gives impressive examples of the operation of trends. He points out, for instance, that interest in drugs in the news has dropped dramatically in the past ten years, although the problem itself has become progressively greater. In other words, there is no relationship between the attention the topic receives and its objective or "real" importance.

Another example from Naisbitt: in the sixties the "space" for discrimination was filled with worries about racism; in 1969 sexism began to appear in the columns. By 1975 half the space was devoted to racism and half to sexism. From 1977 onwards these topics lost out to increasing concern about discrimination against older people. In the end, two-thirds of the space for discrimination was filled with reports about the problems of "ageism" and the remaining third was shared by racism and sexism. However, as soon as the US Congress raised the age of compulsory retirement in industry from 65 to 70 and abolished the limit for the public sector, stories about age discrimination began to decrease.

Naisbitt wrote *Megatrends* in 1982 and *Megatrends 2000* in 1990. His first book was concerned with the following trends, which, in his view, "shaped the eighties":

1. From an industrial society to an information society
2. From imposed technology to technology processing
3. From a national economy to a world economy
4. From short term to long term

5. From centralisation to decentralisation of power
6. From welfare to self-help
7. From representational democracy to direct democracy
8. From hierarchies to networks
9. From north to south
10. From limited choice to multiple choice

Megatrends 2000 is about the last ten years prior to the 21st century. In that decade, the "most important trends that affect our lives" are, according to Naisbitt:

1. The explosive development of the world economy
2. A renaissance in art
3. The rise of free market socialism
4. Global lifestyles and cultural nationalism
5. The privatisation of the welfare state
6. The rise of the Pacific Rim countries
7. The decade of women at the top
8. The age of biology
9. The religious revival in the third millennium
10. The triumph of the individual

The most all-encompassing trend playing a role in social developments in a large part of the world is Naisbitt's number ten, individualisation. Many "sub-trends" derive from this: quality, success, emancipation of the citizen, etc.

It can be useful for an organisation to research which trends are important to its own field of operation. What are the non-trivial developments which can be derived from trends. And to what extent does a development bring opportunity or danger.

10

THE NONPROFIT STRATEGIC MANAGEMENT

USES OF STRATEGIC MANAGEMENT:

Strategic management can be used to determine mission, vision, values, goals, objectives, roles and responsibilities, timelines, etc.

Definition: Strategic management is that set of managerial decisions and actions aimed at the generation of sustainable competitive advantage that determines the long-run performance of a corporation. It includes environmental scanning, strategy formulation, strategy implementation and evaluation and control.

Overview

An organization's strategy must be appropriate for its resources, environmental circumstances, and core objectives. The process involves matching the company's internal resources (*e.g. IT*)and capabilities e.g. (*quality management)* to the *external business environment* the organization faces. Strategy formulation involves:

- Doing a situation analysis: both internal and external; both micro-environmental and macro-environmental.
- Concurrent with this assessment, objectives are set. This involves crafting vision statements (long term view of a possible future), mission statements (the role that the organization gives itself in society), overall corporate objectives (both financial and strategic), strategic business unit objectives (both financial and strategic), and tactical objectives.

- These objectives should, in the light of the situation analysis, suggest a strategic plan. The plan provides the details of how to achieve these objectives.

This three-step strategy formulation process is sometimes referred to as determining where you are now, determining where you want to go, and then determining how to get there. These three questions are the essence of *strategic planning. SWOT Analysis: I/O Economics for the external factors and RBV* for the internal factors.

Strategy implementation involves:

- Allocation of sufficient resources (financial, personnel, time, technology support)
- Establishing a chain of command or some alternative structure (such as cross functional teams)
- Assigning responsibility of specific tasks or processes to specific individuals or groups
- It also involves managing the process. This includes monitoring results, comparing to benchmarks and best practices, evaluating the efficacy and efficiency of the process, controlling for variances, and making adjustments to the process as necessary.
- When implementing specific programs, this involves acquiring the requisite resources, developing the process, training, process testing, documentation, and integration with (and/or conversion from) legacy processes.

Strategy formulation and implementation is an on-going, never-ending, integrated process requiring continuous reassessment and reformation. Strategic management is dynamic. It involves a complex pattern of actions and reactions. It is partially planned and partially unplanned. Strategy is planned and emergent, dynamic, and interactive. Some people (such as *Andy Grove* at Intel) feel that there are critical points at which a strategy must take a new direction in order to be in step with a changing business environment. These critical points of change are called strategic inflection points.

Time Scales

Strategic management operates on several time scales. Short term strategies involve planning and managing for the present.

Long term strategies involve preparing for and pre-empting the future. Marketing strategist Derek Abell (1993), has suggested that understanding this dual nature of strategic management is the least understood part of the process. He claims that balancing the temporal aspects of strategic planning requires the use of dual strategies simultaneously.

Strategic Management is actually a solid foundation or a framework within which all the functioning managerial operations are bundled together. This is the highest level corporate activity that sets the terms and goals for a company that it should follow for prosperity.

General Approaches

In general terms, there are two main approaches to strategic management which are opposite but complement each other in some ways:

'The Industrial Organization Approach'

* based on *economic theory* — deals with issues like competitive rivalry, *resource allocation, economies of scale*
* assumptions — rationality, self discipline behaviour, profit maximization

The Sociological Approach

* deals primarily with human interactions
* Assumptions — bounded rationality, satisfying behaviour, profit sub-optimality. An example of a company that currently operates this way is *Google*

Strategic management techniques can be viewed as bottom-up, top-down, or collaborative processes. In the bottom-up approach, employees submit proposals to their managers who, in turn, funnel the best ideas further up the organization. This is often accomplished by a capital budgeting process. Proposals are assessed using financial criteria such as *return on investment or cost-benefit analysis.* The proposals that are approved form the substance of a new strategy, all of which is done without a grand strategic design or a strategic architect. The top-down approach is the most common by far. In it, the CEO, possibly with the assistance of a strategic planning team, decides on the overall direction the company should take. Some organizations are starting to experiment with collaborative strategic planning techniques that recognize the emergent nature of strategic decisions.

THE STRATEGY HIERARCHY

In most (large) corporations there are several levels of strategy. Strategic management is the highest in the sense that it is the broadest, applying to all parts of the firm. It gives direction to corporate values, corporate culture, corporate goals, and corporate missions. Under this broad corporate strategy there are often functional or business unit strategies.

Functional strategies include marketing strategies, new product development strategies, human resource strategies, financial strategies, legal strategies, and information technology management strategies. The emphasis is on short and medium term plans and is limited to the domain of each department's functional responsibility. Each functional department attempts to do its part in meeting overall corporate objectives, and hence to some extent their strategies are derived from broader corporate strategies.

Many companies feel that a functional organizational structure is not an efficient way to organize activities so they have *reengineered* according to processes or strategic business units (called SBUs). A strategic business unit is a semi-autonomous unit within an organization. It is usually responsible for its own budgeting, new product decisions, hiring decisions, and price setting. An SBU is treated as an internal profit centre by corporate headquarters. Each SBU is responsible for developing its business strategies, strategies that must be in tune with broader corporate strategies.

The "lowest" level of strategy is operational strategy. It is very narrow in focus and deals with day-to-day operational activities such as scheduling criteria. It must operate within a budget but is not at liberty to adjust or create that budget. Operational level strategy was encouraged by *Peter Drucker* in his theory of *management by objectives* (MBO).

Operational level strategies are informed by business level strategies which, in turn, are informed by corporate level strategies.

Business strategy, which refers to the aggregated operational strategies of single business firm or that of an SBU in a diversified corporation refers to the way in which a firm competes in its chosen arenas.

Corporate strategy, then, refers to the overarching strategy of the diversified firm. Such corporate strategy answers the questions of "in which businesses should we compete?" and "how does being in one business add to the competitive advantage of another portfolio firm, as well as the competitive advantage of the corporation as a whole?"

Since the turn of the millennium, there has been a tendency in some firms to revert to a simpler strategic structure. This is being driven by information technology. It is felt that *knowledge management* systems should be used to share information and create common goals. Strategic divisions are thought to hamper this process. Most recently, this notion of strategy has been captured under the rubric of dynamic strategy, popularized by the strategic management textbook authored by Carpenter and Sanders

This work builds on that of Brown and Eisenhart as well as Christensen and portrays firm strategy, both business and corporate, as necessarily embracing ongoing strategic change, and the seamless integration of strategy formulation and implementation. Such change and implementation are usually built into the strategy through the staging and pacing facets.

Reasons Why Strategic Plans Fail

There are many reasons why strategic plans fail, especially:

Failure to understand the customer

* Why do they buy
* Is there a real need for the product
* inadequate or incorrect *marketing research*

Inability to predict *environmental reaction*

* What will competitors do
    - Fighting *brands*
    - *Price wars*
* Will government intervene

Over-estimation of resource competence

* Can the staff, equipment, and processes handle the new strategy
* Failure to develop new employee and management skills

Failure to coordinate

* Reporting and control relationships not adequate
* Organizational structure not flexible enough

Failure to obtain senior management commitment

* Failure to get management involved right from the start
* Failure to obtain sufficient company resources to accomplish task

Failure to obtain employee commitment

* New strategy not well explained to employees
* No incentives given to workers to embrace the new strategy

Under-estimation of time requirements

* No *critical path* analysis done

Failure to follow the plan

* No follow through after initial planning
* No tracking of progress against plan
* No consequences for above

Failure to manage change

* Inadequate understanding of the internal resistance to change
* Lack of vision on the relationships between processes, technology and organization

Poor communications

* Insufficient information sharing among stakeholders
* Exclusion of stakeholders and delegates

Failure to focus

* Inability or unwillingness to make choices which are true to the strategic mission (i.e. to do fewer things, better), leads to mediocrity, inability to compete

CRITICISMS OF STRATEGIC MANAGEMENT

Although a sense of direction is important, it can also stifle creativity, especially if it is rigidly enforced. In an uncertain and ambiguous world, fluidity can be more important than a finely tuned strategic compass. When a strategy becomes internalized into a corporate culture, it can lead to *group think*. It can also cause an organization to define itself too narrowly. An example of this is *marketing myopia*.

Most theories of strategic management seem to have a lifespan less than that of the popularity of the latest teen music idol. Many critics claim that this is because most of them generally do not work. Keep in mind that this article describes only the 50 or so most successful theories, thus exhibiting survivorship bias (ironically, itself an area of research in strategic management).

For every theory that gets incorporated into strategic management textbooks there are many that are quickly forgotten. Many theories tend either to be too narrow in focus to build a complete corporate strategy on, or too general and abstract to be applicable to specific situations.

The low success rate is further fuelled by the management lecture circuit in which hundreds of self-appointed gurus, many without serious academic credentials or substantial expertise, attempt to sell books and explain their "revolutionary" and "groundbreaking" theories to audiences of business executives for a sizable fee.

While there are undoubtedly inspirational ideas contained in these seminars, the theories expounded therein have not, for the most part, been subjected to serious study. Some critics take thc opposite approach claiming effectively that there are not enough theories, and when they arrive they are too late to help managers make any important decisions.

These commentators remind us that the basic, everyday purpose of strategic management is to match a company's strategy with the business environment that the organization is in. Because the environment is constantly changing, effective strategic management requires a continuous flow of new theories suitable for the new circumstances.

The problem with most theories is that they solve yesterday's problems, similar to a business *Maginot Line.* Various approaches to solve this problem have emerged, however, including Mintzberg's ideas of 'emergent strategies' and use of ideas from *complexity theory* in what is often called *complexity strategy.*

Gary Hamel (2000) coined the term strategic convergence to explain the limited scope of the strategies being used by rivals in greatly differing circumstances. He lamented that strategies converge more than they should, because the more successful ones get imitated by firms that do not understand that the strategic process involves designing a custom strategy for the specifics of each situation.

International Strategic Management

International Strategic Management is an ongoing management planning process aimed at developing strategies to enable an organization to compete internationally. The process of developing a particular international strategy is referred to as 'strategic planning'. International strategies for multiple countries are similar to the strategies used in a single country. An organization must be able to answer the following questions:

- What products or services does the organization intend to sell?
- Where and how will the organization make those products or services?
- Where and how will the organization sell those products or services?
- Where and how will the organization acquire the resources?
- How does the organization expect to outperform its *competitors?*

Complexity in Developing an International Strategy

Developing an international strategy for an organization in a foreign country is more complex than developing a strategy for an organization in a domestic country.

In a domestic country, you only have to consider one *national government,* one *currency, one accounting system, one political and legal system* and usually a similar culture. In foreign countries, you are talking about multiple governments, multiple currencies, multiple accounting systems, multiple political and legal systems and a large variety of languages and cultures.

In foreign countries, there is the possibility of:

- local languages required in many situations
- very diverse cultures, both between countries and sometimes even within countries
- often volatile politics
- varied *economic systems*
- scarcity of skilled labor, in which case you would be talking about training or redesigning methods
- poorly-developed *financial markets* and government-controlled capital flows, in some of the countries
- problems and exorbitant costs in obtaining *market research* data
- limited *advertising*, subjected to lots of restrictions
- possible low *literacy rates*, not to mention the possibility of making mistakes in the language when advertising
- currency exchange fluctuations
- inadequate or limited communication
- mandatory worker participation in management in some countries
- Legal restrictions on lying off of workers.

International strategic management is therefore a whole lot more difficult than strategic management in one nation.

SCHOOLS IN STRATEGIC MANAGEMENT

Strategic management is not a task, but a rather a set of managerial skills that should be used throughout the organization, in a wide variety of functions.

Strategic cross-functional management is central to capitalizing on functional excellence, and in order for functional specialists to make the greatest possible contribution, managers must take *a broader view of their functions* and understand how they fit into the web of the organizational processes and, ultimately, into the overall *strategy.*

New Systemic Approach to Strategic Management

All the above schools, often fighting between themselves, favour different single-sided approaches to strategy formulation. They represent both different approaches to strategy formulation and different parts of the same process. Today's managers have to deal with the entire business systems – as opposed to dealing with its different parts independently - not only to keep strategy formulation as a vital force but also to impart real energy to the strategic process. They must practice balanced results-based leadership strategies and apply a balanced approach to business systems.

Certain positive moves in this direction have been seen recently. Some of the more recent approaches to strategy formulation take a wider perspective and cut across the above ten schools in eclectic and interesting ways, for example learning and Design in the "Dynamic Capabilities" approach, or the "Dynamic Strategy" one based on knowledge working.

The currently dominant view of business strategy – resource-based theory – is based on the concept of economic rent and the view of the company as a collection of capabilities. This view of strategy has a coherence and integrative role that places it well ahead of other mechanisms of strategic decision making.

What is Strategic Planning?

Strategic planning is a management tool, period. As with any management tool, it is used for one purpose only: to help an organization do a better job - to focus its energy, to ensure that members of the organization are working toward the same goals, to assess and adjust the organization's direction in response to a changing environment. In short, strategic planning is a disciplined effort to produce fundamental decisions and actions that shape and guide what an organization is, what it does, and why it does it, with a focus on the future.

A word by word dissection of this definition provides the key elements that underlie the meaning and success of a strategic planning process: The process is strategic because it involves preparing the best way to respond to the circumstances of the organization's environment, whether or not its circumstances are known in advance; nonprofits often must respond to dynamic and even hostile environments.

Being strategic means being clear about the organization's objectives, being aware of the organization's resources, and incorporating both into being consciously responsive to a dynamic environment.

The process is about planning because it involves intentionally setting goals (i.e., choosing a desired future) and developing an approach to achieving those goals. The process is disciplined in that it calls for a certain order and pattern to keep it focused and productive.

The process raises a sequence of questions that helps planners examine experience, test assumptions, gather and incorporate information about the present, and anticipate the environment in which the organization will be working in the future.

Finally, the process is about fundamental decisions and actions because choices must be made in order to answer the sequence of questions mentioned above. The plan is ultimately no more, and no less, than a set of decisions about what to do, why to do it, and how to do it.

Because it is impossible to do everything that needs to be done in this world, strategic planning implies that some organizational decisions and actions are more important than others - and that much of the strategy lies in making the tough decisions about what is most important to achieving organizational success.

The strategic planning can be complex, challenging, and even messy, but it is always defined by the basic ideas outlined above - and you can always return to these basics for insight into your own strategic planning process.

What is the difference between strategic planning and long-range planning?

Although many use these terms interchangeably, strategic planning and long-range planning differ in their emphasis on the "assumed" environment.

Long-range planning is generally considered to mean the development of a plan for accomplishing a goal or set of goals over a period of several years, with the assumption that current knowledge about future conditions is sufficiently reliable to ensure the plan's reliability over the duration of its implementation.

In the late fifties and early sixties, for example, the US economy was relatively stable and somewhat predictable, and, therefore, long-range planning was both fashionable and useful. On the other hand, strategic planning assumes that an organization must be responsive to a dynamic, changing environment (not the more stable environment assumed for long-range planning).

Certainly a common assumption has emerged in the non-profit sector that the environment is indeed changeable, often in unpredictable ways. Strategic planning, then, stresses the importance of making decisions that will ensure the organization's ability to successfully respond to changes in the environment.

What is strategic thinking and strategic management?

Strategic planning is only useful if it supports strategic thinking and leads to strategic management - the basis for an effective organization.

Strategic thinking means asking, "Are we doing the right thing?" Perhaps, more precisely, it means making that assessment using three key requirements about strategic thinking: a definite purpose be in mind; an understanding of the environment, particularly of the forces that affect or impede the fulfilment of that purpose; and creativity in developing effective responses to those forces.

It follows, then, that strategic management is the application of strategic thinking to the job of leading an organization.

Dr. Jagdish Sheth, a respected authority on marketing and strategic planning, provides the following framework for understanding strategic management: continually asking the question, "Are we doing the right thing?"

It entails attention to the "big picture" and the willingness to adapt to changing circumstances, and consists of the following three elements: formulation of the organization's future mission in light of changing external factors such as regulation, competition, technology, and customers development of a competitive strategy to achieve the mission creation of an organizational structure which will deploy resources to successfully carry out its competitive strategy.

Strategic management is adaptive and keeps an organization relevant. In these dynamic times it is more likely to succeed than the traditional approach of "if it ain't broke, don't fix it."

What Strategic Planning Is Not!

Everything said above to describe what strategic planning is can also provide an understanding of what it is not. For example, it is about fundamental decisions and actions, but it does not attempt to make future decisions (Steiner, 1979).

Strategic planning involves anticipating the future environment, but the decisions are made in the present. This means that over time, the organization must stay abreast of changes in order to make the best decisions it can at any given point - it must manage, as well as plan, strategically.

Strategic planning has also been described as a tool - but it is not a substitute for the exercise of judgment by leadership.

Ultimately, the leaders of any enterprise need to sit back and ask, and answer, "What are the most important issues to respond to?" and "How shall we respond?" Just as the hammer does not create the bookshelf, so the data analysis and decision-making tools of strategic planning do not make the organization work - they can only support the intuition, reasoning skills, and judgment that people bring to their organization.

Finally, strategic planning, though described as disciplined, does not typically flow smoothly from one step to the next. It is a creative process, and the fresh insight arrived at today might very well alter the decision made yesterday. Inevitably the process moves forward and back several times before arriving at the final set of decisions. Therefore, no one should be surprised if the process feels less like a comfortable trip on a commuter train, but rather like a ride on a roller coaster. But even roller coaster cars arrive at their destination, as long as they stay on track!

What is a strategic plan?

In strategic planning it is critical to formally consider how your organization will accomplish its goals. The answer to this question is a strategy.

There are a variety of formal definitions for strategies, but everyone fundamentally agrees that a strategy is the answer to the question, "How?"

"Strategies are simply a set of actions that enable an organization to achieve results." MAP for Nonprofits, St. Paul, MN. "Strategy is a way of comparing your organization's strengths with the changing environment in order to get an idea of how best to complete or serve client needs."(Jim Fisk & Robert Barron, The Official MBA Handbook.)

Essentially, there are three different categories of strategies: organizational, programmatic, and functional. The difference among the categories is the focus of the strategy:

Organizational strategy outlines the planned avenue for organizational development (e.g., collaborations, earned income, selection of businesses, mergers, etc.). Programmatic strategy addresses how to develop, manage and deliver programs (e.g., market a prenatal care service to disadvantaged expectant mothers by providing information and intake services in welfare offices).

Functional strategies articulate how to manage administration and support needs that impact the organization's efficiency and effectiveness (e.g., develop a financial system that provides accurate information using a cash accrual method).

When should a strategic plan be developed?

Strategy development follows the creation and affirmation of the organization's purpose statement, environmental and program data collection and analysis, and identification of critical issues.

It is critical that strategy development follow these steps because the information gathered and decisions made in these phases are the foundation for strategy creation and selection. Each of these steps provides the following: The purpose statement, the statement of the organization's ultimate goal, provides the direction to which the strategies should ultimately lead.

External market data and program evaluation results provide critical data to support strategy development. Without this information and insight, the organization's strategies will not be in alignment with or effective in the marketplace.

The critical issues list serves as the specific focus and framework for the activities of the organization and the pattern of these activities (developing and selecting the strategies).

How are strategies developed?

Strategy formulation is a combination of rational, scientific examinations and educated, intuitive best guesses. Many individuals are overwhelmed by the idea of developing strategies, but it can be a fun and invigorating process.

The process entails: examining the organization's critical issues determining how the organization's strengths and skills can be employed to address the critical issues analyzing opportunities and strengths and looking for ways to synthesize the two exploring and choosing the best approaches for the organization. During this evaluation ask these key questions: Does the strategy meet/ address critical issues? Is this aligned with our mission? Is this approach financially viable?

One effective method of strategy generation is to list critical issues and organizational strengths onto flipcharts and then have staff or board members brainstorm possible uses of those strengths or other skills to address the critical issues.

Once the brainstorm session is completed, use a roundtable discussion to investigate and evaluate the possible strategies. Remember to develop a list of alternative strategies to investigate and keep in the contingency planning file. It is important not to discount the ideas that come to people during non-working hours.

The Polaroid camera is the result of a three year olds question to her father: "Dad, why can't I see the picture now?"

What are some tools for analysis and planning?

A number of analytical tools have been developed to assist organizations with the planning process. Many non-profit organizations have adapted these tools, modifying the questions and criteria to align with their own specific services and markets.

Listed below are analytical tools frequently used by non-profit and for-profit organizations?

What is SWOT Analysis?

SWOT analysis is a methodology of examining potential strategies derived from the synthesis of organizational strengths, weaknesses, opportunities and threats (SWOT). The partnering of the different elements and the extensive data collected as a result of the analysis can serve as a spark for roundtable discussions and refinement of current strategies or generation of new strategies.

What is the Macmillan Matrix?

This strategy grid, developed by Dr. Ian Macmillan, is specifically designed to assist non-profit organizations to formulate organizational strategies. There are three assumptions underlying this approach: the need for resources is essentially competitive and all agencies wanting to survive must acknowledge this dynamic given that resources are scarce, there is no room for direct duplication of services to a single constituency — this is wasteful and inefficient mediocre or low quality service to a large client population is less preferable to delivering higher quality services to a more focused population. These assumptions have implications that are difficult and painful for many organizations and individuals. It might mean terminating some programs to improve core services and competencies, giving programs and clients to more efficient, effective agencies, or competing aggressively with those programs that are less effective or efficient. Mac Milan's matrix examines four program dimensions that guide placement on the strategy grid and indicate implied strategies.

- Alignment with Mission Statement: Services or programs that are not in alignment with the organizational mission, unable to draw on existing organizational skills or knowledge, unable to share resources, and/or unable to coordinate activities across programs should be divested.
- Competitive Position: Competitive position addresses the degree to which the organization has a stronger capability and potential to fund the program and serve the client base than the competitive agencies.

- Program Attractiveness: Program attractiveness is the complexity associated with managing a program. Programs that have low client resistance, a growing client base, easy exit barriers, and stable financial resources are considered simple or "easy to administer." The level of program attractiveness also includes an economic perspective or a review of current and future resource investments.
- Alternative Coverage: Alternative coverage is the number of other organizations attempting to deliver or succeeding in delivering a similar program in the same region to similar constituents.

The Macmillan Matrix provides ten cells in which to place programs that have been reviewed in terms of these four dimensions. Each cell is assigned a strategy that directs the future of the program (s) listed in the cell (e.g., aggressive competition, joint venture, orderly divestment, etc.). One cell of the matrix, "Soul of the Agency," requires additional explanation. These are the difficult programs for which the organization is often the clients' "last, best hope." Management must find ways to use the programs in other cells to develop, piggyback, subsidize, leverage, promote, or otherwise support the programs in this category.

11

THE NEW INSTITUTIONALISM IN STRATEGIC MANAGEMENT

The recent collapse of the huge energy-trading company Enron has prompted a cry rarely heard in the American economy: to increase regulation. All the more rare, this call is coming from both consumers and employees, who fear the power of large corporations, as well as from the corporations themselves, who fear that an erosion in the trust and confidence of employees, investors, customers and suppliers will cripple their capacity to do business. The effect of the Enron shock is to remind us of something that strategists, managers, and designers of organizations frequently ignore—that the economy rests on an institutional bedrock. Particularly in the United States, where fundamental institutions have been so effective and so stable for so long, it is easy to forget that the state, along with the various organizations and social norms that promote trust and confidence in economic transactions, have a critical influence on which organizations and strategies will succeed.

This volume examines new-institutional theory, which takes as its explicit focus the influences that were hidden, or taken for granted, in the Enron debacle. The core claim of this theory is that actors pursue their interests within institutional constraints, such as the regulations that constrained (or were presumed to constrain) Enron. This idea is the basis of a growing, pan-disciplinary literature that seeks to explain the conduct and performance of individuals, organizations, and states. As the foundational theory about the nature and operation of institutions has been established, and as evidence on the operation and inter-relationship of alternative institutional forms has grown, the tools available for constructing new institutional explanations have been established. The accumulated research has reached a critical mass that creates numerous theoretical and empirical opportunities.

We begin this introductory chapter by addressing the question "why now?" for the new institutionalism in strategy. We identify a number of economic developments and scholarly advances that have helped to make clear the significance of institutions for strategic management. We then explain just what we mean by institutions, with a quick survey of the most relevant literature. In this survey we give explicit attention to the fact that there are a number of variants of new-institutional theory, which tend to emphasize different types of institutions.

Our response to this variety is to present a classification of institutional forms, and identify the literatures that have focused on each. Our own view is that a complete theory of institutions must be comprehensive in its definition of institutions, but also explicit about differences among institutional forms and interdependencies between them. In the third section of this introduction we identify a number of pressing questions for new-institutional theory. By applying the chapters of this volume to those questions, we show that research in strategic management can play an important role in the development of new-institutional theory, particularly by helping to explain how organizations affect institutions of other types. In the fourth and final section, we make the literature on strategic management the focus, and describe how new-institutional theory can help solve pressing questions in that literature.

Why the Growing Interest in the New Institutionalism in Strategy?

Until recently, the idea of explicitly considering institutions to explain the content and effectiveness of organizational strategies would have seemed a little like building theories of strategy based on the fact that the human subjects of the organizations we study breathe air. Institutions, like air, probably make a difference, but why, given their constancy and pervasiveness, should we invest in understanding that difference? The naiveté of this position has been made clear by a number of recent developments in the international economy, and in the scholarly field of strategy.

Transition from state socialism. The most significant of these developments is the transition from state socialism among countries of the former Soviet-bloc and China. The theme of the somewhat crude analysis of the early days of this transition was that capitalist economies were more productive than state-socialist ones; the prescription was for the latter economies to adopt features of the former. The result of these early changes was a range of unintended consequences (Murphy, Shleifer & Vishny, 1992; Nee, 1992; Stark, 1996). These surprise outcomes of piecemeal changes indicated something under-appreciated about the economies in question—laws, organizations, and norms operated together in a complex fashion. Economies that were made to be similar on a subset of these might yet exhibit very different performance outcomes.

As Spicer and Pyle (this volume) show, attempts to create western-style markets in formerly state-socialist economies have been crippled by malfeasance on the part of some organizations, and the corresponding distrust that developed among the public. Simply, these problems arose because the designers of new institutions and organizations paid insufficient attention to the complex interdependence of the institutions that facilitate exchange in "free" markets. For example, Spicer and Pyle document the failure of the market for household savings in Russia.

On the surface, that market looks something like markets in the United States—indeed some of the most prominent American financial organizations tried to extend their operations to Russia. However, important institutional constraints that in the U.S. are provided by the state (regulation), organizations (auditing and rating of investments) and civil society (public awareness of the operation and risks of financial markets) were missing in Russia. The patchwork institutional framework that resulted enabled some organizational strategies and frustrated others.

Internationalization of business. Another development that points to the strategic significance of institutions is the recent increase in international trade, as well as the multinational operations of specific organizations. To be fair, international business is the one area where there is a long intellectual history of considering the impact of institutions on strategy. For example, concerns surrounding differences in national cultures (Hofstede 1980), and the risk of expropriation of capital by a host nation (Teece 1981), enter into prescriptions for operating a business internationally. Even in this area, however, there is rapid growth in attention to institutions. The significance of the international context for highlighting the role of institutions is that cross-national comparisons highlight institutional differences that may be taken for granted within a country.

Henisz and Delios (this volume) consider how multinational organizations can learn, and exploit their knowledge of institutions in the countries in which they operate. This is an integration of institutional forms that have been considered separately. There is a substantial literature that measures the legal and social environment for doing business in a given country (e.g. Henisz, 2000). And multinational organization has been characterized as an institutional mechanism for overcoming business risks, or other institutional shortcomings that exist in some countries. The learning theory that Henisz and Delios present forges a strategic link between those two literatures. Their arguments suggest patterns of design and expansion that can help multinationals succeed across a range of institutional environments.

Technological development. The interdependence between institutions and technology has been prominent in the new institutionalism. For example, North (1993) claims that technological advance by organizations forms the impetus for changing institutions—as new technologies develop, new institutions are required to effectively exploit them. Sometimes, changing technology highlights the significance of institutions because it exposes gaps in the institutional structure. For example, advances in medical transplant technology have created a market for the exchange of human organs, and exposed the unpreparedness of the law, the medical profession, and even the value-system of our culture, to govern that market (Healy, 2002).

In other instances, technological development makes institutions salient by setting off an episode of institutional creation or change. This is illustrated by Dowell, Swaminathan and Wade (this volume). They examine the role of social movements to create institutions around the technology of high definition television (HDTV). The development of HDTV created an interest in changing institutions—for example the rights over the spectrum related to television broadcasts, and the standard that HDTV would follow in the U.S. Further, organizations that had previously been unsuccessful in their campaign to influence spectrum allocation were able to harness the interest associated with HDTV to affect institutional change in their favor. Dowell, Swaminathan and Wade's account of this campaign highlights the strategic use of cultural concepts (framing) by the champions of various HDTV schemes.

Compromise and manipulation of existing institutions. The attention generated by the Enron collapse is not the result of new technology, internationalization, or the shift of political regimes. Instead, it emerges because institutions which were assumed to be stable and reliable were undermined, or otherwise shown to be lacking. For example, the failure of Enron's auditors, Arthur Andersen, to identify questionable financial reporting practices is a violation of the role that auditors are expected to play in the institutional framework of western capitalism. Audit firms are in the business of selling surety.

They vouch for the compliance by the auditee to familiar and accepted accounting principles, and thus allow investors to more reliably value the company (Strange, 1996). The objectivity of the auditor is key to providing this surety, and many of the professional policies of accountants—which include rules against accepting gifts from clients, and rules prohibiting over-reliance by the auditor on the fees of any single client—are designed to maintain objectivity. The very necessity of these rules points to a weak spot in the institutional framework. If an auditor could be influenced by the auditee, and convinced or deceived into inappropriately validating improper accounting practices, then stakeholders of many types—banks, shareholders, employees, customers—might be convinced to over-invest in the auditee.

The point of this is not to criticize a particular corporation, or auditor, but to illustrate that sometimes institutions, even those that are as venerable as auditing, are malleable and at risk of influence by their subject organizations. This malleability creates strategic opportunities for organizations. And although collusion with or deception of an auditor is illegitimate (although potentially profitable), other forms of institutional influence are more acceptable. Specifically, there is a growing attention to the possibility that organizations may influence for good or ill the institutions provided by the state, such as laws and regulations (Baron, 2001; Murphy, Shleifer & Vishny, 1993). In this volume, Holburn and Vanden Bergh, as well as De Figueiredo and de Figueiredo, build on this idea, using strikingly different methodologies. Holburn and Vanden Bergh present a formal model that helps to identify where organizations should aim their lobbying efforts. De Figueiredo and de Figueiredo use an experimental methodology to examine the question "how good are strategists at recognizing the opportunity to influence the state?" The clear significance of these questions, and the diversity of the research methods employed, point to the great opportunities for the organizations that make institutions the focus of their strategies, and the scholars that study them.

Collapse of the tyranny of the here and now. The new institutionalism has always emphasized historical research. Classics in the field examine economic and organizational outcomes from the deep past (North & Weingast, 1989; Greif, 1994). The willingness to embrace history derives from two core precepts of new-institutional theory. The first is that core elements of the theory are timeless. The behavioral assumptions of the new institutionalism amount to bounded rationality. Institutions, as we will describe, are simply the rules that constrain the interest-seeking behavior of actors.

The manner in which institutions operate is basically the same, whether the institutions are the self-policing policies of 11th century traders on the Mediterranean, or 21st century tax laws in Munich. Therefore, old institutions are understood to be as valuable as new ones for understanding economic performance—perhaps even more valuable, because historical institutions can sometimes be studied with fuller information and more objectivity. The second element of new-institutional theory that leads to historical research is the path dependence of institutions. We don't have complete theories of institutional change, but one thing that seems certain is that the options for new institutions derive in a large way from pre-existing institutions (North, 1990). So, even forward-looking analysts must understand old institutions, as they are the roots of future institutions.

The treatment of history in the new institutionalism stands in sharp contrast to the normal practice in research on business strategy. Strategy often suffers from a tyranny of the here and now, a desire to celebrate contemporary phenomena and slight historical ones. This ahistoricism is one reason why research in strategy struggles for social-scientific legitimacy. By reveling in current affairs, and de-emphasizing their underpinnings in the past, strategy scholarship often undermines its own claims to develop explanations that transcend their contemporary context. In other words, the field of strategy struggles to develop good theory, because it downplays temporal transitivity and generalizability.

Clay and Strauss (this volume) illustrate these arguments. They provide a new institutional analysis of the phenomenon of Internet commerce. The treatment of this phenomenon in strategic management is a classic example of the cost of ahistoricism. The fashion (fortunately, not universal) in strategy has been to approach Internet commerce as "new"—it was a new economy, operated by new organizational forms, requiring new strategies. This approach has yielded a set of thoroughly forgettable scholarship, which has not endured even the recent downturn in the technology sector, let alone provided a theoretical basis to guide organizations that attempt to transact in evolving internet-related markets.

In contrast, Clay and Strauss begin by identifying the historical precedents for the contemporary struggles of those who transact over the Internet. They identify an analog to the challenges of Internet commerce in Richard Sears' attempts to conduct business by mail in the late nineteenth century. Sears and his customers had the problem of building trust with strangers—for their transaction to be successful the customers needed to be confident that Sears would deliver high-quality goods, and Sears had to be confident that the customers would pay what they owed. Similar challenges arose for credit card providers and users in the mid-twentieth century. These problems are strikingly similar to those faced by sellers and buyers over the internet.

As Clay and Strauss argue, potential solutions for contemporary internet businesses are similar to those employed by nineteenth century mail-order businesses and 1950s credit card issuers—institutions can modify the transaction so that both parties can approach it with confidence.

AN INTRODUCTION TO THE NEW INSTITUTIONALISM

There are a number of variants of "new-institutional theory" (Fligstein, 1997), so it is important to be clear just what we mean by institutions, and how we understand them to operate. We'll begin with this statement, which for us explains action in the new institutionalism: Actors pursue their interests by making choices within institutional constraints. This simple statement contains three elements that must be explained: who are the actors, how do they make choices, and what are the institutional constraints?

The Actors

The actors in the new institutionalism are individuals, organizations, or states. Each of these classes contains components that pursue interests, are subject to institutional constraints, and which supply institutional constraints that affect other actors. For researchers of strategic management, the idea that an organization can be, like an individual, an actor that pursues an interest, is uncontroversial. Without trivializing the fact that organizations have numerous and diverse stakeholders, the field of strategic management has shown repeatedly that there is utility in the simplification of organizations as actors.

For example, in game theoretic treatments of entry deterrence, or models of competitive dynamics, an organization is an actor that can make "moves." Likewise, it is central to the field that organizations have interests (otherwise, to what end would they have strategies?). New institutional arguments tend to be agnostic as to what the interests of individuals or organizations are, so the familiar candidates from strategic management—profit, market share, growth of employment, survival—are all feasible.

It may be more of a stretch to think of states as actors. This position reflects a recent trend in political science to characterize states as sets of organizations (ministries and agencies), which are like other organizations in that they are populated with individuals (bureaucrats and politicians) who use the state to achieve their goals (a paycheck, re-election; control over many subordinates, furtherance of an ideological value). This is not to say that the state is just another organization—it has capabilities that other organizations can't match, such as the legitimate right to employ violence. The key, however, is that states represent interests, and take action to achieve those interests. We'll employ the typical definition of the state in the new institutionalism, as an organizational actor which, at a minimum, attempts to maintain its authority by exchanging justice and order for revenue and power (North, 1981; Skocpol, 1985).

Each class of actors produces its own form of institutional constraint: individuals produce norms (private-decentralized institutions in the classification we present below), organizations produce their rules (private-centralized institutions), and states produce laws and regulations (public-centralized institutions). In this sense, it can be said that actors lead a double life in the new institutionalism, pursuing their own interests within constraints, while producing constraints for other actors. The interplay between the actors can best be understood as a three-layered hierarchy, with states superordinate to organizations, which are superordinate to individuals (Williamson, 1994; Nee & Ingram 1998). States constrain organizations and individuals that are their subjects, and organizations constrain the individuals that are their participants. There is also upward influence in the hierarchy, as actors try to affect the institutions that constrain them.

Finally, we introduce a fourth relevant class, which we'll call civil society. It would be incorrect to call civil society an actor—it doesn't have identifiable interests, and it is incapable of forming or pursuing a strategy. Yet, in the catholic version of new institutionalism that we are developing, civil society has a role as the source of a fourth type of institution—culture (public-decentralized). As we describe below, culture constrains action in a manner that is comparable to other institutional forms. Culture also influences those forms, as when it is used to create favor for one legal option or governance form over another.

Choice: Bounded Rationality

The new institutionalism treats actors as rational in the basic sense of making choices that further their interests, but distinguishes itself from neo-classical assumptions of rationality by attending to "cognitive costs" of decision making. The pursuit of benefits is limited by individuals' capacity to retain and process information; in other words, individuals are boundedly rational (Coase 1937, Simon 1957). Further, information is often costly (Barzel 1989). These two factors create transactions costs – the costs of writing and enforcing contracts – because individuals cannot foresee at the time of writing all contingencies that might be relevant nor can they observe all of the actions of their partners. And transaction costs give rise to the possibility of opportunism (Williamson 1975, 1985).

In the new institutionalism, a key implication of opportunism is the problem of credible commitment. It is illustrated by the dilemma faced by a kidnap victim whose kidnapper has a change of heart and decides to set her free (Schelling, 1960). The victim gladly promises not to reveal the kidnapper to the authorities in exchange for her freedom. However, the kidnapper realizes that once the victim is free she will have no incentive to keep her promise, and reluctantly decides the victim must be killed. More generally, the problem of credible commitment is faced by any party to an exchange that wants to promise in the present to do something in the future that may not be in their interests to do when the future actually arrives. The problem is endemic because in almost every exchange there is at least a moment where one of the parties has control over all or most of the goods, and must decide whether to follow through on the agreed upon bargain, or make a grab for more. It is clearly present, for example, in Richard Sears' attempt to get farmers to send him money for goods that he promised to subsequently send to them (Clay and Strauss, this volume).

The problem of credible commitment illustrates the positive role that institutions can play to smooth exchange (and by extension, to resolve all sorts of collective-action problems). Ideally, an institution can re-arrange the incentives of the parties of an exchange to allow them to make credible commitments. For example, what if it was possible for the kidnapper's victim to somehow post a bond that she would forfeit if she revealed the kidnapper's identity? And what if the farmer's friends maintained a norm to punish any vendor that mistreated any one of them, such that it was in Sears' interest to follow through on the bargain once he had the farmer's money? As we'll see, these examples do not describe all of the ways that institutions can affect economic performance of individuals, organizations and states. However, solving problems of credible commitment is one of the most positive functions of institutions, and one of the most significant for business strategy.

Institutional Forms

We employ an extension of the classification system for institutions that was first introduced in Ingram and Clay (2000). That system classifies institutions based on their scope (public or private), and how are they made and enforced (in centralized or decentralized fashion). The scope dimension defines which actors are subject to the institution. Public institutions apply without discrimination to all actors of a type. It is impossible to opt in or out of a public institution. Private institutions apply only to actors that are part of some group or organization, so actors have some influence over the institutions that affect them as long as they can choose which associations they are part of.

The centralized-decentralized dimension refers to whether or not there are designated functionaries charged with creating and enforcing the institution. Centralized institutions rely on such functionaries, for example, laws may be made by legislatures and enforced by the police. The legislature and police are "third parties" in that they make and enforce the laws, even if they are not directly affected by their violation. Decentralized institutions, on the other hand, emerge from unorganized social interaction, and really on diffuse individuals (often those directly affected) to punish institutional violations. These two dimensions create four institutional forms. We describe each form, as well as research on the form that is relevant for strategic management. Figure 1 portrays these basic institutional forms, and summarizes key information about each.

Figure 1. A Typology of Institutional Forms

	Decentralized	Centralized
Private	Archetypal form: norms Chief actor: social groups Representative theorists: Homans, 1950; Granovetter, 1985 Levers for strategy: human resource policy; corporate-culture building; inter-organizational networks	Archetypal form: rules Chief actor: organizations Representative theorists: Williamson, 1975; Greif, 1994 Levers for strategy: conventional strategy and structure tools; business groups
Public	Archetypal form: culture Chief actor: civil society Representative theorists: Meyer & Rowan, 1977, DiMaggio & Powell, 1983 Levers for strategy: partnerships with mobilized social groups outside the firm; framing	Archetypal form: laws Chief actor: states Representative theorists: North, 1990; North & Weingast, 1989 Levers for strategy: non-market strategy; business political activity

Public-Centralized Institutions

There are at least five ways that the public institutions provided by the state can be understood to affect its choices, and those of organizations and individuals. The first is particularly relevant to strategic management. The state may smooth exchange between its subjects by providing institutions that allow them to make credible commitments. This can be achieved if the state provides a legal system to protect property rights, decrease transaction costs, and enforce contracts (North, 1990). This function is particularly vital in modern economies, in which specialization and the division of labor give rise to the need for sustaining complex exchanges over time, across space, and between strangers, creating the need for trust between disconnected actors. An effective institutional framework facilitates this trust by penalizing actors who break the rules of exchange, for example, by applying legal sanctions to actors who violate contracts.

There is quantitative evidence of the role of public-centralized institutions for enabling credible commitments. Some studies exploit changes in laws governing specific industries to show that increased legal constraint on organizations causes them to flourish. Studies of populations as diverse as U.S. health maintenance organizations and telephone companies, Toronto day-care centers, Niagara Falls hotels, and Singapore banks have demonstrated that their failure is reduced by increasing government involvement in monitoring, certifying, authorizing and endorsing their activities (Wholey et al 1992, Barnett & Carroll 1993, Baum & Oliver 1992, Ingram & Inman 1996, Carroll & Teo 1998).

Such government involvement can also affect the pattern of competition between incumbent firms and potential entrants, as demonstrated in Calabrese et al's (2000) study of the Canadian biotechnology industry. In the human therapeutics/diagnostics sectors, where FDA regulation is most strict, new products take a decade to come to market and short technological leads can become entrenched as regulators demand evidence of superior efficacy for later-to-market drugs. Incumbent firms' innovative activity suppresses new entry significantly more in human subsectors than in subsectors characterized by less onerous regulatory scrutiny.

The effects of broader changes in public institutions are seen in Ingram & Simons' (2000) analysis of the effect of the formation of the Israeli State on the failure rates of workers' cooperatives in many industries. The transition from the weak British Mandate for Palestine to the strong Israeli State caused a radical improvement in the institutional support for credible commitment, and a corresponding sixty-percent decrease in organizational failure rates. The second key feature of public-centralized institutions is whether or not the state can credibly commit to not subsidize subject organizations when they struggle. The recent transitions from state socialism have demonstrated that absent such a commitment, entrepreneurs will direct their energies towards "holding up" the state treasury rather than to producing economic value. As Stark & Bruszt (1998:119) put it, when the state hears organizations' "siren cry, 'Give me a hand, give me your hand,' it must be bound to respond not simply that it should not, or that it will not, but that it cannot."

The third key feature of public institutions is an outgrowth of the first two. A state strong enough to guarantee the property rights of its subjects, and to resist their calls for subsidies, is also strong enough to appropriate their wealth. Unless the state can credibly commit against such appropriations, its subjects' incentives for productive economic activity will be greatly curtailed. Evans (1995) uses the term "predatory" to describe states that exploit their subjects for short-term gain. He cites Zaire of the Mobutu regime (1965 to the present) as an archetype. Mobutu and his state cronies "systematically looted Zaire's vast deposits of copper, cobalt, and diamonds, extracting vast personal fortunes...In return for their taxes, Zairians could not even count on their government to provide minimal infrastructure." The gains from this strategy to the state, and those who dominate it, are, however, short lived. Predation on the part of the state has the effect of discouraging productive activities by organizations of all types—why invest capital or labor if the state is likely to appropriate the rewards of this activity? This effect is apparent in the deceleration of the Zairian economy—GNP per capita declined 2 percent per year over the first twenty-five years of Mobutu's rule. Eventually, there will be little left to plunder.

A classic illustration of the cost of a predatory state, and the institutional solution that eliminated that cost, is North & Weingast's (1989) account of the Stuarts' impact on the economy of 17th century England. After coming to the Crown in 1612, the Stuarts exploited their subjects in numerous ways: they sold monopolies (at the expense of industry incumbents and potential entrants), they sold special dispensations from laws, and even committed outright theft, as in 1640 when they seized £130,000 that private merchants had placed in the Tower of London for safekeeping. These abuses led eventually to the Glorious Revolution of 1688, which resulted in numerous institutional changes to reduce the Crown's capacity to act independently of Parliament and the courts. This loss of Crown autonomy had, however, positive implications in that it enabled the Crown to make a credible commitment not to appropriate subjects' wealth. The value of this commitment can be seen, for example, in the dramatic increase in the Stuarts' capacity to borrow funds. More generally, a national constitution, with its delineation of enduring limits to government power, may be interpreted as an attempt by a state to commit not to become predatory over time (Weingast 1993).

Public-centralized institutions provided by the state are not always part of a grand effort to facilitate the credible commitments of actors. Sometimes they influence distributional battles over zero-sum interests, which is their fourth role (Knight 1992). These may be the battles between suppliers and consumers, as shown in analyses of the effects of regulatory policy on railroad foundings in early Massachussetts (Dobbin & Dowd 1997) or interstate trucking firm failures in the 1980s (Silverman, Nickerson & Freeman 1997).

Or they may be the battles between rival organizational forms without apparent efficiency differences, as in the case of thrift-savings organizations that fought as much in the legislative arena as in the market (Haveman & Rao 1997), or national coffee roasters in the U.S., that derived a competitive advantage over regional roasters through an international treaty (Bates 1997). Evans (1995) detailed numerous ways that states act to create economic transformations, for example, by lending money or taking responsibility for high-risk activities such as research and development. Such efforts are overwhelmingly selective, aimed at promoting particular sectors over others.

Fifth and finally, public-centralized institutions may affect the legitimacy of particular organizational forms by influencing the definition of organizational propriety. This influence may be concrete, as when a law requires a certain organizational practice or office, or intangible, as when myths of efficiency develop to justify a practice that the state endorses but does not enforce (Dobbin & Sutton, 1998). Legitimacy, in turn, affects organizations' capacity to obtain the resources they need to survive (Meyer & Rowan, 1977). This feature of public-centralized institutions represents a link between this institutional form and the public-decentralized institutional form. Essentially, the state is in a particular position to influence culture—this is one of the characteristics that differentiates the state from other types of organizations.

Private-Centralized Institutions

The most ubiquitous role of private-centralized institutions is to internalize transactions in an organization. In his seminal paper, Coase (1937) addressed the question of why organizations exist. His central insight was that the governance of exchange within organizations as opposed to markets depended on the cost of transacting in each type of institution. In more recent work, Williamson (1985) and others have systematically investigated the effect of information, opportunism, and asset specificity on the governance of exchange, concluding that in some transaction environments, exchange is more efficient within an organization than the market. Further, the prevailing public-centralized institutions influence the attractiveness of various governance arrangements (Nee 1992).

Ficker (1999) illustrates the relationship between the environment of public-centralized institutions and other factors, and the market/organization trade-off in the evolution of the Mexican Central Railroad (MCR). The MCR was founded in 1880 into "a country characterized by economic backwardness and an incipient and precarious institutional framework." The company initially pursued a strategy of building main lines and depending on market transactions with railroads and other types of transportation organizations to supply freight. These market transactions did not materialize, however, due to the weak Mexican infrastructure, and the difficulties of organizational and technological coordination. In response to this failing of the market, the MCR switched to a strategy of internalization, extending its trunk lines and building branch lines to supply itself with freight. Private-centralized institutions can also facilitate exchange between organizations. This can occur when organizations are part of a "super-organization" with its own rules and policies. An example is the diamond industry. Bernstein (1992) examines the rules that govern transactions in that industry, which rely on private-centralized institutions, and not the law.

Members of a diamond bourse are governed by formal written rules that represent the codification of and are supported by industry norms. Bernstein finds that use of arbitration panels and mandatory pre-arbitration conciliation is a response to members' need for speed, secrecy, and specialized knowledge of the industry. The industry enforces arbitration decisions with the threat of suspension of membership in the diamond bourse. In the case of noncompliance, a bourse faxes the individual's picture to all other diamond bourses worldwide. Informed of noncompliance, members then refuse to trade with the individual in question because of the risk that they will be cheated. Through this reputation mechanism, the institution creates incentives for members to adhere to industry rules and norms in their transactions with other members.

Ingram & Simons (2000) describe a private-centralized institution that is even more comprehensive than the diamond bourse. They explain that in Palestine under the British Mandate (1922-1948), the state failed to provide public-centralized institutions to support economic exchange. A large group of cooperative organizations created a private-centralized substitute for these missing institutions, in the form of a comprehensive federation, called the Histadrut. The Histadrut has had as members, at various times, agricultural cooperatives (the kibbutzim and moshavim), workers' cooperatives (in services, manufacturing and transportation), Israel's largest conglomerate, a bank, credit cooperatives, housing cooperatives and consumer cooperatives. The Histadrut did a number of things to smooth transactions between these members.

For example, the Histadrut directed its affiliated bank and its major marketing cooperative to give preferential service to other Histadrut members. It also arbitrated disputes for members, provided auditing services, gave seminars in accounting and management, arranged bulk purchases of raw materials, and maintained a pension fund. The institutional framework provided by the Histadrut was a major benefit to its members—they had a failure rate one-fifth that of non-members during the period of the British Mandate.

Private-Decentralized Institutions

The archetype of the private-decentralized institution is the norm. Although norms are often unwritten and unspoken, the real contrast to centralized institutions is in enforcement. Norms rely on social relationships for their enforcement—the ultimate penalty for violating a norm is the cessation of a relationship, or in the extreme, ostracism from a group. Penalizing violations of norms typically falls to the affected parties rather than third parties, and it is the value of the relationship itself that provides the motivation to maintain the norms that surround it. As Homans ([1961] 1974: 76) puts it, "the great bulk of controls over social behavior are not external but built into the relationship themselves, in the sense that either party is worse off if he changes his behavior toward the other."

The operation of norms among individuals within organizations is familiar. An illustrative case is Homans (1950) re-analysis of the bank-wiring room from the Hawthorne studies. That study documents the norms of the workers, governing how much to produce on a shift. Normative enforcement through relationships is clear—workers who did not work hard enough were insulted, and excluded from games, gambling, and the sharing of candy. Although such group processes may at first seem tangential to the organization's strategy and performance, the truth is that norms interact with the rules of the organization, and that interaction has a fundamental influence on organizational success (Nee & Ingram, 1998; Zenger, Lazzarini & Poppo, this volume). It was General Electric's group piece-rate incentive system that set the background for the development of the norms in the bank-wiring room, which generally acted to encourage productivity. In other instances, sub-organizational norms undermine the control system of the organization, and inhibit its pursuit of its goals (Shibutani, 1978). Norms, or their analogs, also operate in the inter-organizational context. There is important historical research that illustrates the function of private-decentralized institutions in long-distance trade. With this type of trade, merchants can often profit from using other merchants as agents to sell goods, collect debts, and so forth. This agency relationship, however, raises the possibility that the agent will act opportunistically, keeping some or all of the monies owed.

The Maghribi traders in the 11th century Western Mediterranean (Greif 1994), and American merchants on the 19th century California coast (Clay 1997) overcame this problem by forming coalitions, which allowed exchange to flourish. In both cases, merchants in the coalition conditioned future use of other merchants as agents on those merchants' having acted in accordance with group norms in the past. For instance, when a Maghribi merchant was accused of cheating in 1041-42, he found that "people became agitated and hostile and whoever owed [me money] conspired to keep it from me (Greif 1994: 925)." By tying future economic gains to past behavior as an agent, merchants were able to ensure that the future gains to membership in the coalition were greater than the gains to cheating and being punished.

Additionally, there is a rapidly expanding body of empirical research on the relational governance of inter-organizational exchange. Uzzi (1996) describes the embeddedness of exchange in the Manhattan garment industry. As in the examples above, participants in that industry followed norms that encouraged them to deal fairly and flexibly with each other. Zaheer, McEvily & Perrone (1998) apply related arguments to explain the purchasing practices of large organizations. They find that even among large corporations, trust between buyers and sellers is an important input to reducing transaction costs. There is also a developing literature in strategic management that focuses on the role of relationships for the interorganizational transfer of knowledge (e.g., Darr, Argote & Epple, 1995).

Public-Decentralized Institutions

We have left public-decentralized institutions for last because they are different from the previous three institutional forms. The difference is in terms of intentionality. Laws, organizational rules, and norms are provided consciously and even strategically by states, organizations and individuals. These institutions don't always have the effects that their designers and enforcers intend, but none the less, they emerge from some intent. In contrast, public-decentralized institutions might be called "pre-conscious". As we have described, they are provided by amorphous civil society, and not by a specific actor. Public-decentralized institutions amount to culture—they are ideas about what practices and social designs are acceptable and desirable.

So why include public-decentralized institutions in the same theory as other institutional forms? The best reason is that despite their origins, public-decentralized institutions are comparable to other institutional forms in their operation (Scott, 1995). Cultural values structure the choices of actors, partly determining the alternatives that are considered and the attractiveness of each alternative. For example, a manager's evaluation of an alternative for an organization's strategy might be influenced by the alternative's propriety and legitimacy in much the same way that it might be affected by its legality (DiMaggio & Powell, 1983; Carroll & Hannan, 2000). Indeed, work on the cognitive processes by which public-decentralized institutions operate indicate that they influence the value of alternatives—for example, the stock of a company may be discounted because the company's activities do not fit legitimate categories (Zuckerman, 1999).

Additionally, although public-decentralized institutions are not controlled by any specific actor, actors may still be strategic in the face of them (DiMaggio, 1988; Roberts & Greenwood, 1997). All of this is not to oversimplify this institutional form. It is particular among the institutional classes in the pre-conscious manner in which it may emerge, and operate to affect action. Still, public-decentralized institutions fit the description of new-institutional action that we began with. The influence of propriety and legitimacy on the effectiveness of organizational designs and strategies is undeniable. Likewise, as we describe below, public-decentralized institutions have a critical affect on the development of other institutional forms, and thereby present important strategic opportunities for organizations.

What can strategy do for the new institutionalism?

So far, we've explained what the new institutionalism is, and why scholars in strategic management are paying more attention to it. But what is to be gained by the whole enterprise? Of course, the subsequent chapters will provide the answer to that question. But before we turn you loose on them, we'll give you our own interpretation. From the inception of this volume, we were convinced that there was a real promise of "gains from trade" by bringing together new institutional and strategy research. We see the benefits flowing both ways—strategy research can help solve some of the core problems of the new institutionalism, and vice versa.

The potential contribution of strategy to the new institutionalism comes from its sophisticated conceptualization of the action of organizations. Organizations are obviously key to new-institutional theory, not only as a source of private-centralized institutions, but even more importantly as the vehicles for the pursuit of the most important human interests, both economic and social (Hannan & Freeman, 1977). Yet, the treatment of organizations in the various institutional theories has been soundly criticized. DiMaggio (1988) charged theories of public-decentralized institutions with suffering from a "metaphysical pathos", denying the capacity of organizations and individuals for self-interested, and strategic, action.

Similarly, Granovetter (1985) claimed the same theories presented an "oversocialized" view of organizations and other actors, underestimating their autonomy from cultural influence. Institutional economists on the other hand, have erred in the opposite direction in their treatment of organizations. North (1993), for example, identifies organizations as the chief vehicles of institutional change. Yet, his characterization of organizations as malleable, rational and decisive entities is in contrast to what we know about organizational change and strategy making.

Without a doubt one of the prime contributions of the chapters in this book is to develop more informed theories of the role of organizations in institutional change. Indeed, many of the chapters represent great leaps forward for this critical but understudied topic. Jaffee and Freeman, for example, offer a thrilling account of institutional change in real time.

They courageously make predictions about the evolution of German taxation of stock options as the institutions are unfolding. Their analysis highlights the role of interest-seeking organizations in institutional change. German tax law forms the background for competition among established organizational forms and their challengers. The authors challenge and refine existing ideas (e.g., North, 1993) by identifying organizational inertia as a key determinant of the strategies that organizations pursue to maintain or change specific institutions.

The idea that legal institutions can be the object of organizational strategies is also prominent in other chapters. Holburn & Vanden Bergh present a formal model of lobbying. Their model explicitly reflects a key challenge to any organizational attempt to influence the law—that there are multiple options as to where lobbying efforts should be targeted. Should an organization lobby a state's executive, or its legislators? Or perhaps the organization should bypass the law makers and go directly to the agencies that enforce laws and regulations? The model presented in this paper yields prescriptions that organizations can apply to their lobbying strategies.

De Figueiredo and De Figueiredo address a different stage of the same problem, using a radically different methodology. They follow on the under-developed literature on strategic decision making (e.g., Schwenk, 1984; Zajac & Bazerman, 1991). Implicit in their approach is a sophisticated idea that has been slighted in the new institutionalism, that the influence of institutions depends on the perception of those institutions by the relevant actors. Their experiments yield insights into the very practical problem of how to help strategists to correctly analyze the institutional environment, and recognize the opportunities and challenges that it presents. Their results are cause for optimism, evidencing the utility of business-school courses on the strategy of dealing with institutions.

Two other papers in the volume examine organizations' role in institutional change, but focus on culture, rather than the law, as the context for organizations' strategies. In other words, they venture bravely into the void between established institutional theories. Dowell, Swaminathan and Wade examine a fascinating instance of institutional entrepreneurship, the effort to establish standards for HDTV in the U.S. This chapter provides a uniquely lucid explanation of the sociology and psychology of "framing." Framing is a conscious attempt to use cultural values to support a given action, or in this case, a direction for institutional change. Framing therefore represents a vast set of strategic opportunities for institutional entrepreneurs. The clear and compelling treatment of the topic in this chapter will encourage its application to other strategies and studies.

Rao's chapter is similar in that it considers organizations' influence on public-decentralized institutions, but it considers taken-for-grantedness, rather than a technological standard. Taken-for-grantedness presents a dilemma for strategy—it has been convincingly shown to influence organizational performance, but what can be done with that knowledge? How can organizations affect what others take for granted? Rao's answer is that they can do so through demonstration. Specifically, he examines the demonstrations of reliability and quality that seeded the taken-for-grantedness of the automobile. In doing so, he gives fair treatment to the many other influences on the perception of the automobile. The result is a necessarily complex, but original and very promising set of ideas about the interdependence of organizations and public-decentralized institutions.

The interdependence between institutional forms demonstrated in Rao's paper (and in most of the papers in this volume) is itself a substantial contribution to the new institutionalism. Research has so far been mainly within the quadrants of figure 1, with interdependencies between the quadrants going unexamined to the detriment of the theory. While the multi-form emphasis of so many of this volume's papers redresses that theoretical neglect, it also has implications for the field of strategy. Unpacking the simultaneous influence of different types of institutions is necessary for effective strategizing. In many ways the theoretical and applied contributions of these papers are intertwined, as the next section demonstrates.

What can the new institutionalism do for strategy?

The previous section described the benefits that new institutional scholars can gain from taking strategy research seriously. But this is by no means a one-way street. Our rationale for including a volume on new institutionalism in the *Advances in Strategic Management* series is predicated on the idea that the new institutionalism can help surmount some of the core challenges in strategy research.

The potential contribution of new institutional research to strategy comes from its highlighting of the interactive role that institutions play in both constraining and enabling organizational action. Institutions are frequently seen as background conditions or "shift parameters" that contour the expected payoffs associated with particular strategic actions (Williamson 1991). But more than that, institutions directly determine what arrows a firm has in its quiver as it struggles to formulate and implement strategy, and to create competitive advantage. Given the importance of institutions for determining the success or failure of specific strategies or actors, consideration of ways to influence the creation and maintenance of favorable institutions is fundamental to any organization's strategy. Hence, an understanding of institutional change, and the ways that firms can influence such change, becomes central to the study and practice of strategy.

Consider the taxonomy of institutions in Figure 1. The vast majority of strategy research focuses on private-centralized institutions such as firms and the formal actions that they undertake. Strategy research has generated a post-adolescent, if not quite mature, body of literature that offers strong predictions and prescriptions for firms' boundaries and competitive activity. Yet direct application of traditional strategy prescriptions to managing other types of institutions offers far less utility. How can a firm deal with private-decentralized institutions such as norms? Use of traditional strategic levers without consideration of variance in underlying norms of organization members can be ineffective, or can even backfire, as in Simon's (1957) "unintended consequences." As for altering norms themselves, this is frequently perceived as an organizational behavior or human resource management issue, and consequently outside the purview of strategy. Similarly, how can a firm deal with public-centralized institutions?

With the exception of what is sometimes called the "non-market strategy" literature (Baron 2001), these are largely seen as exogenous institutions that influence strategic and organizational choices in much the same way as production technology. Finally, the link between strategy research and public-decentralized institutions has generally been limited to the use of cultural distance measures (Hofstede 1980) to predict the rate and mode of entry of multinational firms into specific host markets (Kogut & Singh 1988; Hennart & Park 1993).

The chapters in this book contribute to the development of deep insights into the influence of all four types of institutions on firm strategy, and vice versa. Even more exciting, many of the chapters set forth into new terrain regarding the *interactions* across types of institutions as well as their relationship to strategy. For example, Zenger, Lazzarini and Poppo propose a novel and compelling extension to the theory of the firm by considering interactions between private-centralized and private-decentralized (or "formal" and "informal") institutions.

Starting from a few basic assumptions about differences in the characteristics of each of these types of institutions, they develop a series of bold propositions that potentially resolve several puzzles in the strategy and organization literature. The authors argue that although an organization cannot quickly alter private-decentralized institutions through the usual methods of changing formal organization structures, such formal changes can spark gradual changes in such norms. Coupling this argument with the common assumption that formal organizational structures are discrete (and hence can not be incrementally tweaked to achieve an optimal form), they provide a rationale for the seemingly constant oscillation of structures that many organizations demonstrate (Nickerson & Zenger 2002).

SPECIFIC RESEARCH QUESTIONS, AND THE LAYOUT OF THIS VOLUME

The above discussion noted general insights that can be fruitfully drawn from the new institutionalism into strategy research. We have organized the volume so as to highlight insights related to specific research questions in strategy. In their manifesto for the strategy field, Rumelt, Schendel & Teece (1994) suggest four fundamental questions in strategy research: 1) How do firms behave? 2) Why are firms different? 3) What limits the scope of the firm? 4) What determines success or failure in international competition? New institutional research, and in particular the research in this volume, speaks to each of these questions.

How do firms behave? Or, do firms really behave like rational actors, and, if not, what models of their behavior should be used by researchers and policy makers?

In "Policy and process: A game-theoretic framework for the design of non-market strategy," Guy Holburn and Richard Vanden Bergh adopt a far-sighted rational action lens to explore interactions among agents of the state and their effect on how firms should try to influence legal/institutional framework. Expanding on positive political theory models of lobbying in the U.S., they demonstrate that different agents – regulatory agency officials, legislators, other elected officials – become the pivotal actors depending on the distribution of preferences across these actors. Thus, a firm that wishes to influence a specific regulation should not necessarily lobby the regulator directly, but in many cases will need to direct its lobbying efforts towards other political actors.

In "Managerial decision-making in non-market environments: A survey experiment," John de Figueiredo and Rui de Figueiredo test the assumption that managers are able to pursue far-sighted rational action. Noting that a large body of experimental literature raises questions about the rationality of managers, they conduct a series of experiments designed to test the ability of managers to make "optimal" decisions about activities designed to influence legal institutions, such as investing in lobbying activity. Their results indicate that although managers are competent at making optimal decisions when confronted with simple, single-stage problems, managerial decisions deviate significantly from optimal choices as problems become more complex.

In "Pretty pictures and ugly scenes: Political and technological maneuvers in high definition television," Glen Dowell, Anand

Swaminathan, and Jim Wade study institutional change regarding the allocation of broadcasting spectrum in the U.S. They provide a case study of the various attempts by television broadcasters to fight FCC regulations in the mid-1980s that would take away unused spectrum from broadcasters and allocate it to other uses such as cellular communication. Initial attempts to get Congress to overturn this regulation foundered, due both to the difficulty of overcoming a "collective action" problem among the diverse broadcasters and to the lack of a resonant "frame" to motivate Congress. Yet subsequent attempts succeeded, once the broadcasters found a way to frame their need for spectrum in terms of U.S. manufacturing competitiveness vis-à-vis Japan, a particularly resonant frame in the late 1980s. Dowell et al. explain these outcomes through the lens of social movement theory, and particularly the role of framing problems in ways that motivate desired action. Rather than far-sighted rational actors, the managers and policymakers in this lens are characterized by subjective perception, and the institutional outcome is determined during the battle to socially construct the frame of the institutional change.

In "The evolution of university patenting and licensing procedures: An empirical study of institutional change," Bhaven Sampat and Richard Nelson take a still different view of actors' behavior and motivation. Drawing on a routine-based view of organizational action, they argue that actors develop "social technologies" to manage their various activities. As these social technologies diffuse and harden into standardized patterns of behavior, they become institutions. Hence, institutions arise through the boundedly rational attempts of actors to solve problems, notably problems associated with production and exchange. Sampat and Nelson study the diffusion of different social technologies used by universities to manage their patenting and licensing activities, culminating in the technology transfer office commonly found at research universities today. Interestingly, they note that the diffusion of this institution was facilitated by the passage of the Bayh-Dole Act of 1980, for which universities actively lobbied – and the motivation for which seems to have been based on erroneous and inaccurate evidence of a university-industry technology transfer "market failure."

Thus the four chapters in this section all focus on firms' efforts to influence public and/or private institutions, and each takes a slightly different perspective on the fundamental strategic question: How do firms behave? It is interesting to note that this difference mirrors the differences in strategy literature writ large. But the consecutive presentation of these perspectives in this volume is informative in a way that heterogeneity in the broader literature is not. The papers here point to the fact that styles of choice depend on their context. The types of institutions that most constrain an actor greatly affect the appearance of the actor's decisions. Actors attempting to influence the complex, but well-defined institutional structure represented by the U.S. government may seem intentional and calculative, but occasionally confused. When culture is the object or key constraint, decisions follow different styles because the rules of decision-making are different. For example, the symbolic value of behavior may become more important.

Why are firms different? Or, what sustains the heterogeneity in resources and performance among close competitors despite competition and imitative attempts?

In "Competition, contingency, and the external structure of markets," Ron Burt, Miguel Guilarte, Holly Raider, and Yuki Yasuda explore the implicit institutional foundation of market structure among industry competitors. They propose and demonstrate a network-based measurement of "effective competition" among rivals. They find that an apparent puzzle in prior literature can be explained by incorporating effective competition. Specifically, prior research has found that strong corporate culture is only erratically associated with firm performance. Burt et al. demonstrate that the relationship between corporate culture and firm performance is contingent on the level of effective competition faced by the firm – in highly competitive markets, strong culture enhances performance, while in low-competition markets culture has no impact on performance.

In "Institutional change in 'real-time': The development of employee stock options in German venture capital contracts, 1997 to 2000," Jonathan Jaffee and John Freeman analyze the attempt by several young German law firms to gain legal clearance to implement "American-style" employee stock ownership plans for their clients who were start-up and venture capital firms, and the opposition to this from several large, well-established law firms who did less work with start-ups. Conceptually, their study shows how firms can influence the institutional framework – in this case, concerning the legality of certain stock compensation policies – to further entrench their relative advantages over competitors. Institutions (and the ability to enact institutional change) thus become central features explaining sustainable performance differences among firms.

In "Institutional barriers to electronic commerce: An historical perspective," Karen Clay and Robert Strauss study several historical precedents to Internet commerce. They note that Richard Sears, and later various credit card companies, faced challenges of opportunism associated with remote commerce that sound very familiar today, and they analyze the emergence of several institutions that ameliorated such opportunism in the past. In addition to pointing us toward institution-based solutions to the challenges facing current Internet businesses, Clay and Strauss underscore the competitive advantage that can accrue to a firm, or a group of firms, that successfully undertakes institutional innovation. By "solving" the remote commerce problem, Sears was able to grow quickly to dominate the mail order business in the late nineteenth century; thus, Sears's institutional innovation provided the firm with a first-mover advantage that endured for nearly a century. Those businesses that establish private institutions to solve current challenges to Internet commerce may similarly enjoy enduring performance benefits. And, as in the preceding chapter, Clay and Strauss argue that performance differences between Internet- and brick-and-mortar businesses will turn largely on the outcome of battles over broad institutional issues such as taxation of Internet commerce.

These papers illustrate that sound new-institutional arguments are in the spirit of Henderson & Mitchell's (1997) call for research that explores interactions between market effects and internal capabilities, Burt et al.'s study demonstrates how the competitive environment influences the value of a organization-specific institution (culture). Similarly, Jaffee & Freeman emphasize the significance of compliance between organizational form and the institutional environment. This valuable compliance creates strategic opportunities for organizations to manipulate the institutions that surround them. Finally, Clay and Strauss remind us that, given the appropriate market structure, a firm's institutional innovations can potentially provide a source of sustained competitive advantage.

What limits the scope of the firm? Or, what is the function of or value added by the headquarters unit in a diversified firm?

In "Informal and formal organization in new institutional economics," Todd Zenger, Sergio Lazzarini, and Laura Poppo note that prior scholarship on the theory of the firm has largely focused on either formal institutions such as contracts, or on informal institutions such as norms, and rarely on the interactions between the two. Beginning with a few basic assumptions about the characteristics of each type of institution, they explicitly analyze interactions between formal and informal institutions. Zenger et al. derive a series of startling propositions that potentially resolve a number of puzzles that have challenged the theory of the firm over the last thirty years. Chief among these are 1) when will formal and informal institutions act as substitutes, and when as complements; 2) what explains some organizations' apparent predilection for cycling (and recycling) through organization structures frequently; and 3) what precisely limits the size of the firm? The chapter suggests a number of fruitful directions for empirical testing as well.

In "'Tests tell:' Constitutive legitimacy and consumer acceptance of the automobile, 1895-1912," Hayagreeva Rao explores the growth in consumer acceptance of the automobile in the years following its initial commercialization. In particular, he examines the role of several activities – both those managed by the firm, such as advertising, and those propelled by actors outside the firm, such as auto demonstration races sponsored by social movement-like organizations of car enthusiasts – on auto sales. This study contributes a novel look at the way that social movement theory may explain the effectiveness of particular public-decentralized institutions, such as auto clubs. It also demonstrates how advertising and social movement things are differentially effective at different times, and also work as substitutes. As such, the chapter provokes consideration of the conditions under which a firm should strategically consider mobilizing forces outside its formal boundaries to enhance its competitive strategy.

These papers suggest a reframing of the definition, often used in strategy, of the firm as a nexus of contracts. It may be more useful to consider the firm as a nexus of institutions. This broader characterization takes explicit account of the multiple institutional forms that affect behavior or and within organizations. A more strategically tractable understanding emerges by recognizing the multiple institutional forms that constitute organizations—law, culture, norms, and rules. As Zenger et al. show, an organization is not merely the agency-theory driven rules of employment, but also the norms that are associated, but not completely coupled to them. As Rao shows, organizations have cultural identities that are separate from their product profiles, but fundamental to their effectiveness.

What determines success and failure in international competition? Or, what are the origins of success and what are their particular manifestations in international settings of global competition?

In "Learning about the institutional environment," Witold Henisz and Andrew Delios note that prior literature on FDI typically treats firms as homogeneous while examining the relationship between FDI and national variation, or treats national institutions as homogeneous while examining the firm variation-FDI relationship. They explore the joint roles of heterogeneous firm experience and heterogeneous institutional environments in explaining the direction and mode of foreign direct investment. In their framework, a firm's experience provides firm-specific knowledge that moderates the influence of variation in institutional environment, thus leading multinational corporations with different patterns of experience to pursue different entry strategies and expect different performance outcomes in international competition. By recognizing variation in both firm experience and institutional environments, they are able to propose a wide range of empirically refutable implications that significantly extend current strategy research on international business.

In "Institutions and the vicious circle of distrust in the Russian market for household deposits, 1992-1999," Andrew Spicer and William Pyle explore the apparent failure of public and private institutions in Russia to support the development of a private market for household savings deposits. They analyze the events associated with these development attempts, and argue that the initial "institutional backdrop" at the birth of this sector contributed to a self-reinforcing cycle in which private commercial banks were unable, either individually or collectively, to win the trust of potential depositors. Of particular interest to strategy researchers, their research demonstrates how several traditional strategic prescriptions are implicitly predicated on deep assumptions about the institutional backdrop. For example, although advertising is often seen as an investment to demonstrate high quality, Spicer and Pyle suggest that in Russia, where consumers had a low level of market savvy and where regulatory institutions were not set up to enforce certain behaviors among banks, advertising apparently had either no relationship, or even an inverse relationship, with bank quality. Their analysis reinforces our understanding of the difficulty of simply "porting" from one nation to another successful businesses, or even successful institutions, without the appropriate supporting institutional backdrop.

These papers point the way towards a theoretically-informed refinement of the international business environment. They illustrate that every country represents a complex web of characteristics. Traditional ideas of "foreign and local" or one dimensional characterizations of a country (e.g., collectivist of individualist; common-law or Napoleonic Code) are insufficient. But beyond that point, which should be uncontroversial, new-institutional theory can pave the way for a rigorous analysis of the multi-faceted institutional environment that each country represents. Indexes of institutional stability or the environment for investing (e.g., Henisz, 2000) present a real opportunity for both researchers and strategists to incorporate institutional sophistication into their country-characterizations.

12

THE PROCESS OF STRATEGIC MANAGEMENT

The primary purpose of the strategic management process is to enable companies to achieve strategic competitiveness and earn above-average returns. Research indicates that companies that engage in strategic management generally outperform those that do not. The attainment of an appropriate match or fit between a company's environment and its strategy, structure, and processes has positive effects on the company's performance. Bruce Henderson, founder of the Boston Consulting Group, pointed out that a company cannot afford to follow intuitive strategies once it becomes large, has layers of management, or its environment changes substantially. As the world's environment becomes increasingly complex and changing, today's companies as one way to make the environment more manageable use strategic management.

Strategic competitiveness is achieved when a company successfully formulates and implements a value-creating strategy. By implementing a value-creating strategy that current and potential competitors are not simultaneously implementing and that competitors are unable to duplicate, a company achieves a sustained or sustainable competitive advantage.

So long as a company can sustain (or maintain) a competitive advantage, investors will earn above-average returns. Above-average returns represent returns that exceed returns that investors expect to earn from other investments with similar levels of risk (investor uncertainty about the economic gains or losses that will result from a particular investment). In other words, above average-returns exceed investors' expected levels of return for given levels of risk.

In the long run, companies must earn at least average returns and provide investors with average returns if they are to survive. If a company earns below-average returns and provides investors with below-average returns, investors will withdraw their funds and place them in investments that earn at least average returns. Internationally these types of companies are prime take-over targets, a concept that is picking up in India.

COLOURS OF CHANGE

At one extreme you had the internet start-ups with almost-teenagers strategising for the company. At the other, you have companies like the Godrej group — over a hundred years old, with legacy systems of managing and strategising. Now the group's infusing a little colour into those processes. Godrej's new colour-coded approach to rejuvenating the group is a careful balance between both — involve youngsters in decision-making, access all those bright young ideas, and also bring a touch of sobriety (plum, a mix of red and blue) to weigh the final approach.

A young executives board, comprising a group of youngsters with functions similar to that of the company's board of directors, gives its recommendations to the board.

Meet Adi Godrej, the new Chief Personnel Officer of Group Godrej, and the man behind the red and blue teams. "Post the dissolution of our JV with P&G in 1996, we did a lot of introspection, which led us to the realisation that we needed to change dramatically if we wanted to progress," he explains. Godrej isn't preaching what he doesn't practice. When you're a managing director trying to ensure people-focus and youthfulness in your group, you set an example. When he decided that all managers have to go through extensive feedback sessions — not just from peers and subordinates, but also from vendors and suppliers — he underwent one himself. Says a deadpan Godrej: "My evaluation said that I'm too autocratic and not a good listener. People also felt that I do not encourage teamwork."

Adi Godrej was inspired to start the red and blue teams after a CEO's forum held by US-based management guru CK Prahalad. Godrej modified the plan, and got the guru himself to speak to his teams about the concept's methodology and relevance to the group's needs. Now red and blue are the colours of change at the lush green premises of the Godrej group in suburban Mumbai. In an interesting experiment to evolve out-of-the-box thinking, various group businesses have formed two eight-member teams called the red team and the blue team, made up of young employees whose mandate is to come up with recommendations on future growth prospects for their divisions, strategies and business directions.

Working independently of each other, the red and blue teams meet with opinion makers from all walks of life for a period of 3-4 months in order to chalk out a strategic plan for the next three years. These teams then present their plan to the 'plum team', a team of senior managers from the respective businesses, sometimes including chairman Adi Godrej. The senior team's job is to review the two plans, distil the best suggestions, and come up with a final plan to be implemented. It was tried at Godrej Agrovet last year, and has been rolled out to the rest of the group now.

So far, the teams have come up with suggestions on a variety of growth strategies — potential acquisition candidates, new categories of consumer goods to be explored, ways to improve rural thrust and how to go about globalising their businesses. "We've found a wider variety of thought processes and ideas than ever in the past," adds an enthusiastic Godrej.

Another fairly uncommon, and bold, initiative is the young executive's board (YEB), which was formed in October 2001. It has eleven 20-somethings on board (the oldest is 32). For all strategic purposes, they are supposed to behave like any senior board, and give their suggestions on strategy, human resource policies, corporate governance and ways and means to make the future brighter for the group. They have been provided access to all information, documented and otherwise, that the directors of the group's management committee have access to.

Again, the idea is to get strong young perspective on board issues. Also, the group wants to strengthen communications and transparency within. "The idea is to have a bottoms-up approach in strategic planning, as opposed to the traditional top-down one in which plans are formed by the senior management and left to the managers below to implement, who grumble about not having their say in planning. It also benefits the youngsters because it is a tremendous learning opportunity for them, and it is they who will rise to be the future managers," explains Godrej.

Meanwhile a team of five business heads has been instituted, which has to come up with a group-wide strategic plan this year. It is this team's recommendations on various business strategies — which businesses to exit, which new ones to enter, and deliberations on new growth horizons — that will decide what the Godrej group will be five years from now.

Why this sudden need for action on the HR front? Godrej learnt its lessons from the break-ups with its various joint ventures. Not only did a lot of managers walk out along with JV partners, the group did not attract as many talented people with the advent of MNCs in India.

Their internal surveys on HRD climate and employee satisfaction reflected that young people in the organization felt underutilised, and uninvolved in strategic decision-making.

A think-tank of eight people from different functions and group companies has been formed to evaluate trends in science, engineering, infotech, marketing and management developments, that are likely to affect them in future. In the last four months, 38 top managers, including Godrej himself, have had to undergo an assessment centre evaluation where they were tested for their ability to think, relate, learn and act.

Moreover, the company's existing 360-degree evaluation programme — that so far included only peers, subordinates and superiors — has been widened to include feedback from vendors and suppliers on employees who interact with them. To ensure that all these initiatives evolve into more than just colourful exercises, Godrej has rehauled compensation too. The group has linked its variable remuneration to economic value added (EVA).

Come April, Godrej's managers and officers, including the chairman, will receive a performance remuneration that's linked to their contribution to the business' EVA in the last year. What would make the employees even happier is that there's no limit to how much they can make as variable remuneration — their imagination will be limited only by their efforts, if at all.

Godrej credits the changed focus of the group for the turnaround of his Oleo chemical business, which has gone from making losses of more than Rs 75 crore and no exports four years ago, to making a profit of Rs 40 crore and exports worth Rs 120 crore this year. Another business to have benefited is the consumer products one, which went through very bad years after its fallout with P&G. According to Godrej, the changed fortune of GPCL has more to do with the initiatives than with any fundamental changes in the product portfolio. A framework that can assist companies in their quest for strategic competitiveness is the strategic management process, the full set of commitments, decisions and actions required for a company to systematically achieve strategic competitiveness and earn above-average returns. This process is illustrated in Figure.

FIGURE: Strategic Management Process

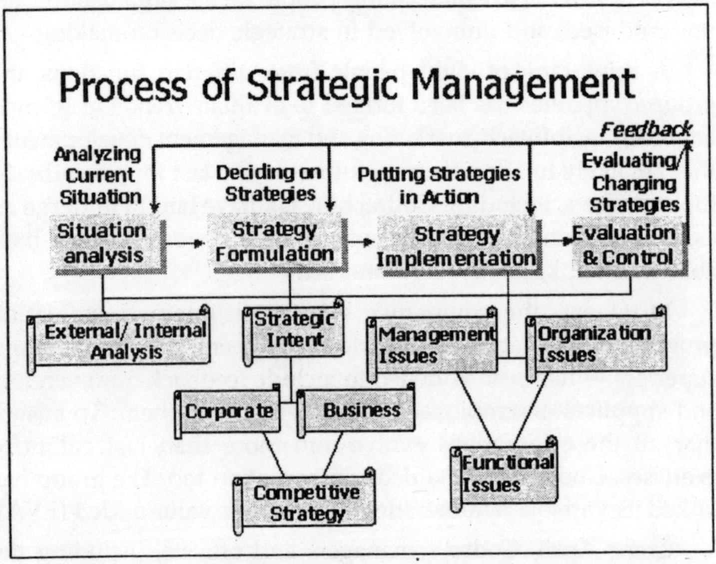

Figure above illustrates the dynamic, interrelated nature of the elements of the strategic management process and provides an outline of where the different elements of the process are covered in this text.

Feedback linkages among the three primary elements indicate the dynamic nature of the strategic management process: Situation Analysis, Strategy Formulation and Strategy Implementation.

Situation Analysis, in the form of information gained by scrutinising the internal environment and scanning the external environment, is used to develop the company's strategic intent and strategic mission.

Strategy Formulation is guided by the company's strategic intent and strategic mission, and is represented by strategies that are formulated or developed and subsequently implemented or put into action.

Strategy Implementation strategic competitiveness and above-average returns result when a company is able to successfully formulate and implement value-creating strategies that others are unable to duplicate.

Strategy Evaluation & Control links the elements of the strategic management process together and helps companies continuously adjust or revise strategic inputs and strategic actions in order to achieve desired strategic outcomes.

ESTABLISHING A MANAGEMENT INFORMATION SYSTEM

Information is a *critical resource* in the operation and management of organizations. Timely availability of relevant information is vital for effective performance of managerial functions such as planning, organizing, leading, and control. An information system in an organization is like the nervous system in the human body: it is the link that connects all the organization's components together and provides for better operation and survival in a competitive environment. Indeed, today's organizations run on information.

The term *information system* usually refers to a computer-based system, one that is designed to support the operations, management, and decision functions of an organization. Information systems in organizations thus provide information support for decision makers. Information systems encompass transaction processing systems, management information systems, decision support systems, and strategic information systems.

Information consists of data that have been processed and are meaningful to a user. A system is a set of components that operate together to achieve a common purpose.

Thus a management information system collects, transmits, processes, and stores data on an organization's resources, programmes, and accomplishments. The system makes possible the conversion of these data into management information for use by decision makers within the organization. A management information system, therefore, produces information that supports the management functions of an organization (Davis & Olson, 1985; Lucas, 1990; McLeod, 1995).

BASIC CONCEPTS

Data versus Information

Data refers to raw, unevaluated facts, figures, symbols, objects, events, etc. Data may be a collection of facts lying in storage, like a telephone directory or census records.

Information is data that have been put into a meaningful and useful context and communicated to a recipient who uses it to make decisions. Information involves the communication and reception of intelligence or knowledge. It appraises and notifies, surprises and stimulates, reduces uncertainty, reveals additional alternatives or helps eliminate irrelevant or poor ones, and influences individuals and stimulates them to action. An element of data may constitute information in a specific context; for example, when you want to contact your friend, his or her telephone number is a piece of information; otherwise, it is just one element of data in the telephone directory.

Computers have made the processing function much easier. Large quantities of data can be processed quickly through computers aiding in the conversion of data to information. Raw data enter the system and are transformed into the system's output, that is, information to support managers in their decision making.

Characteristics of Information

The characteristics of good information are relevance, timeliness, accuracy, cost-effectiveness, reliability, usability, exhaustiveness, and aggregation level. Information is relevant if it leads to improved decision making. It might also be relevant if it reaffirms a previous decision. If it does not have anything to do with your problem, it is irrelevant. For example, information about the weather conditions in Paris in January is relevant if you are considering a visit to Paris in January. Otherwise, the information is not relevant.

Timeliness refers to the currency of the information presented to the users. Currency of data or information is the time gap between the occurrence of an event in the field until its presentation to the user (decision maker). When this amount of time is very short, we describe the information system as a *real-time* system.

Accuracy is measured by comparing the data to *actual* events. The importance of accurate data varies with the type of decisions that need to be made. Payroll information must be exact. Approximations simply will not suffice. However, a general estimate of how much staff time was devoted to a particular activity may be all that is needed.

Value of Information

Information has a great impact on decision making, and hence its *value is* closely tied to the decisions that result from its use. Information does not have an absolute universal value. Its value is related to those who use it, when it is used, and in what situation it is used. In this sense, information is similar to other commodities. For example, the value of a glass of water is different for someone who has lost his way in Arctic glaciers than it is to a wanderer in the Sahara Desert.

Economists distinguish value from *cost* or *price* of a commodity incurred to produce or procure the commodity. Obviously, the value of a product must be higher than its cost or price for it to be *cost-effective.*

The concept of *normative value* of information has been developed by economists and statisticians and is derived from decision theory. The basic premise of the theory is that we always have some preliminary knowledge about the occurrence of events that are relevant to our decisions. Additional information might modify our view of the occurrence probabilities and consequently change our decision and the expected payoff from the decision. The value of additional information is, hence, the difference in expected payoff obtained by reduced uncertainty about the future event.

Information supports decisions, decisions trigger actions, and actions affect the achievements or performance of the organization. If we can measure the differences in performance, we can trace the impact of information, provided that the measurements are carefully performed, the relationships among variables are well defined, and possible effects of irrelevant factors are isolated. The measured difference in performance due to informational factors is called the *realistic value* or *revealed value* of information.

For most information systems, particularly those supporting middle and top management, the resulting decisions often relate to events that are not strictly defined and involve probabilities that cannot be quantified. The decision-making process often is obscure and the outcomes are scaled by multiple and incomparable dimensions. In such cases, we may either attempt to perform a multiattribute analysis or derive an overall *subjective value*. The *subjective value* reflects people's comprehensive impression of information and the amount they are willing to pay for specific information (Ahituv, Neumann, & Riley, 1994).

Information as an Aid to Decision Making

Simon (1977) describes the process of decision making as comprising four steps: intelligence, design, choice, and review. The *intelligence* stage encompasses collection, classification, processing, and presentation of data relating to the organization and its environment. This is necessary to identify situations calling for decision. During the *decision* stage, the decision maker outlines alternative solutions, each of which involves a set of actions to be taken. The data gathered during the intelligence stage are now used by statistical and other models to forecast possible outcomes for each alternative. Each alternative can also be examined for technological, behavioural, and economic feasibility. In the *choice* stage, the decision maker must select one of the alternatives that will best contribute to the goals of the organization. Past choices can be subjected to *review* during implementation and monitoring to enable the manager to learn from mistakes. Information plays an important role in all four stages of the decision process. Figure 1 indicates the information requirement at each stage, along with the functions performed at each stage and the feedback loops between stages.

Classification of Management Information Systems

There are various types of management information systems. Mason and Swanson (1981) describe four categories of management information systems: (1) databank information system, (2) predictive information system, (3) decision-making information system, and (4) decision-taking information system. The classification is based on the level of support that the information system provides in the process of decision making. Sachdeva (1990) comprehensively presents these four types of systems:

Databank Information System. The responsibility of this information system is to observe, classify, and store any item of data which might be potentially useful to the decision maker. Examples of the kind of data that might be recorded in such a database for a given village, region, or area are as follows:

- Number of farms
- Number of units of arable land (hectares, fedans, acres)
- Average farm size
- Amounts of selected farm inputs applied annually
- Production per year on a unit of land for selected crops

A second example of data that might be recorded in a database (this time involving data internal to the organization) is as follows:

- Number of extension staff by category and assigned to a particular village, region, or area
- Number of work hours devoted by staff to selected concerns for a particular village, region, or area
- Total extension salary costs and other expenses by village, region, or area

- Number of demonstrations conducted for selected farm technologies by village, region, or area
- Number of on-farm trials conducted for selected farm technologies by region or area
- Number of radio, TV, and print media releases regarding selected farm technologies by time period and region or area

Each of these databases can be summarized and converted to single tabular presentations of information of interest to management. When information from two or more time periods is compared, trends can be observed.

Predictive Information System. This system moves beyond pure data collection and the determination of trends over time. Predictive information systems provide for the drawing of inferences and predictions that are relevant to decision making. If data from the above examples were to be used in this way, it is possible to obtain information useful for making predictions or for drawing inferences. For example, tables containing the following information for a given village, region, or area might be produced:

- The ratio between the number of farms and the various categories of extension staff members
- The ratio between the amount of farmland and the various categories of extension staff members
- Amount of extension financial operating resources allocated per year to selected farmer problems or concerns
- Amount of extension financial resources, both salary and operating expenses, allocated per year to selected extension approaches to solving different farmer problems or concerns

Information obtained from these kinds of analyses is normally summarized in a two-way tabular format. And likewise, the information often is compared over time. Managers can then use such information to make predictions, for example to forecast costs of particular undertakings for budgeting purposes or as a basis for predicting results if a given change is made, such as change in the number of demonstrations with a given change in staffing.

Decision-Making Information System. This system goes one step further in the process of decision making and incorporates the value system of the organization or its criteria for choosing among alternatives. An extension organization's values are many and varied.

They include concerns for resolving farmer problems, increasing and providing for stability of farmer incomes, and improving the quality of farm life. But they also including and providing for stability of farmer incomes, and improving the quality of farm life. But they also include an intent to provide well for staff members (training, adequate salaries, etc.) and to aid in the process of bringing about rural economic development.

Table 1. Information Groups in India's Agricultural Extension System.

Levels	Groups	Types of Information Needed
Central	Extension commissioner, joint commissioners, directors, joint directors, etc. of the directorate of extension, ministry of agriculture	(1) Information on human resources, plans, and budgets for various extension services (2) Statewide monitoring and evaluation of activities completed
State	Director of agriculture, additional director, joint directors, etc. of the state department of agriculture	(1) Districtwide information on extension programmes, activities, expenditures, etc (2) Research-extension linkages and coordination with other allied departments such as animal husbandry and horticulture
District	District agricultural officers (DAOs)	(1) Information on extension resources and constraints at subdivision and block levels (2) Training requirements of staff at subdivision and block levels
Subdivision	Subdivisional agricultural officers	(1) Field demonstration programmes, activities planned and implemented by subject-matter specialists (SMSs) (zone) at the block level (2) Technical programme and constraints identified at the block level
Block (county)	Agricultural extension officers	(1) Performance of VEWs in terms of achievements in extension activities (2) Field-level problem of assessment of beneficiaries' response to various extension programmes

Information regarding these various attributes helps managers to make more enlightened decisions. Examples of ways that an extension organization uses information from a decision-making information system are as follows:

- Change in specific farm outputs (yields, practices) following selected extension activities
- Change in staff productivity following selected interventions (in-service training, better transport, etc)
- Comparison of relative costs and relative effectiveness of alternative extension delivery methods
- Analysis of economic returns to farmers who adopt recommended practices as compared to those who do not

Decision-Taking Information System. Examples of decision-taking information systems are not usually found in an extension organization.

This is a decision system in which the information system and the decision maker are one and the same. Management is so confident in the assumptions incorporated in the system that it basically relegates its power to initiate action to the system itself. Airplanes carry automatic pilot systems, which are an example of a decision-taking system.

Once activated, the system itself keeps the plane on course and at the proper speed and altitude (according to parameters determined by the pilot). Another example of decision-taking information systems is found in modem factory production. In automobile production, continuous inventories of parts are maintained by computer as cars move down an assembly line. Orders are placed automatically by the computer when additional parts are needed. This is done without the intervention of a manager.

The choice of an appropriate management information system (MIS) category primarily depends on the nature of the decisions it supports.

While unstructured decisions may use MIS-category (I), the highly structured ones, such as production schedules in an industry, may use MIS-category (iv). Further, Banerjee and Sachdeva (1995) observe that "as the deep structure of the decision problem becomes more and more understood, we may move to higher level of MIS i.e., from MIS-category (I) to MIS-category (ii); and MIS-category (ii) to MIS-category (iii); and so on."

ROLE OF MIS IN THE MANAGEMENT OF AGRICULTURAL EXTENSION PROGRAMMES

National agricultural extension systems, especially in developing countries, tend to be very large. For example, in India, the national agricultural extension system employs about 125,000 people. Extension managers at various levels need relevant information in order to make effective decisions. In the absence of such information, they act only on the basis of their intuition and past experience. Data that have been processed, stored, and presented properly will aid them in analysing situations and to make effective decisions.

As suggested above, at every phase of the management process, managers need information in order to make effective decisions. This we call *management information.* It does not include purely functional information or technical information, such as packages of practices for rice or wheat cultivation. Management information is the information required by managers as they make their decisions, such as the number of extension personnel employed by category, their training requirements, career development plans, job descriptions, budgets, forecasts, benchmark surveys, reports on socioeconomic conditions of people served, and existing facilities (Ramesh Babu & Singh, 1987).

The main purpose of management information systems is to provide management information to decision makers at various levels in the organization. Specifically, in an agricultural extension organization, MIS is needed:

1. To plan the most effective allocation of resources, for example, the allocation of extension personnel under a T & V extension system, the need for communications and training equipment and facilities, mobility, the amounts of required operational resources
2. To choose between alternative courses of action, whether to conduct a study on the impact of the T & V system with the resources on hand or hire an expert to investigate
3. To control day-to-day operations, for example, comparing the actual results achieved and those planned under the T & V system.

DESIGN OF A MIS IN AN AGRICULTURAL EXTENSION ORGANIZATION

The following are suggested steps to follow when designing a MIS for a national agricultural extension system.

Step One: Assessing Information Needs for Planning, Monitoring, and Evaluation

An investigation needs to be conducted into the types of decisions that extension managers have to make. For example, village extension workers (VEWs) seek solutions to their problems from their supervisors. In turn, supervisors need to be in a position to resolve these problems and to document how problems were solved for future reference.

State-level managers also need information to resolve problems. They are concerned with implementing extension programmes district by district. They need information on staffing, transport, research-extension linkages, staff training activities, and successes (or lack of them) in solving technical problems. Feedback is needed from field staff and farmers on farmer problems and on which recommended practices are helpful. State-level managers need to know something about the amounts, kinds, and combinations of media support (i.e., print, radio, television) that have been used for various efforts. They need to know if external factors have limited the success of particular efforts such as supply of credit or farm inputs and they need some assessment of farmers' responses to extension programmes (Raheja & Jai Krishna, 1991, p. 84).

Step Two: Deciding the Levels of Information Groups, Information Frequency, and Content

The number of information groups within an agricultural extension organization has to be decided because each group potentially will require a different type of information. As an example, in India, the reorganized national agricultural extension system can be grouped as shown in Table 1.

Data processing consists of identifying each item of data and systematically placing it within a scheme that categorizes data items on the basis of some common characteristic or feature. Data not organized into a meaningful pattern can serve almost no useful purpose to those who must use them to make decisions. A computer can help in processing the data effectively. Rao (1985) suggested the use of computers in agricultural extension in India. He proposed that computer programmes be focused on district and subdivisional levels. In that way, information collected can be viewed in terms of the crops that are likely to be grown, agroclimatic conditions, soil types, irrigation facilities, resources of the farmers, and availability of various farm inputs.

Documentation (storage and retrieval) involves storing items of information in an orderly manner. Storing information means recording it on storage media from which it can be made available when needed.

Storage media are materials such as ordinary office paper, magnetic tapes, magnetic disks, microfilms, film strips, and a few other devices. Once the information is recorded on these storage media, the system can generate, on demand, information required for making decisions, solving problems, or performing analyses and computations. Information retrieval refers to the ability to take different types of data in the storage media and to array information in some desired and meaningful format. A properly designed storage and retrieval system matches the related variables efficiently and accurately. In some cases, it even suggests alternative courses of action for management to take.

Presentation of information should be in a form and format suitable to the needs of extension managers. Generally, information is presented in reports, statistical summaries, analyses, and so forth in the form of text, figures, charts, tables, and graphs. The presentation of information should be precise, clear, and appealing.

Step Three: Ensuring System Flexibility and Adaptability

Flexibility means the ability to retrieve information from a system in whatever form it may be needed by decision makers. Therefore, data need to be collected in some detail so that they can be rearranged or summarized according to the needs of managers. But system design should not be too complex because it must first serve the needs of the lowest levels of management (i.e., subdistrict) that are likely to be instrumental in collecting important components of the original data. In addition, the system also must serve the needs of the district, regional, state or provincial, and national levels. Therefore, considerable care must be taken in assessing what types of information are required by management at the different levels. At the same time, effort must be made to ensure that the information collected meets acceptable standards of accuracy, timeliness, and coverage for each level.

Need for automation

An automated MIS system contains data just as a manual system does. It receives input, processes input, and delivers the processed input as output. Some input devices allow direct human-machine communication, while others require data to be recorded on an input medium such as a magnetizable material (specially coated plastic flexible or *floppy* disks and magnetic tapes). The keyboard of a workstation connected directly to a computer is an example of a direct input device. Use of automation makes it possible to store immense quantities of information, to avoid many of the errors that find their way into manual records, and to make calculations and comparisons that would be practically impossible in a manual system.

Organization of a database

Data are usually generated at the field level through transaction-processing systems, but once the data are captured, any echelon along the organizational hierarchy may use them, provided that information requirements have been well defined, appropriate programmes have been implemented, and a means has been arranged for the sharing of the data. This would imply that the same data can be used by different sets of programmes; hence we distinguish between the database (a set of data) and the applications (a set of programmes). In a decision support system (DSS), this set of programmes is the *model base* (Keen & Morton, 1978).

The term *database* may refer to any collection of data that might serve an organizational unit. A database on a given subject is a collection of data on that subject that observes three criteria: comprehensiveness (completeness), nonredundancy, and appropriate structure. Comprehensiveness means that all the data about the subject are actually present in the database. Nonredundancy means that each individual piece of data exists only once in the database. Appropriate structure means that the data are stored in such a way as to minimize the cost of expected processing and storage (Awad & Gotterer, 1992).

The idea of a large corporate database that can be flexibly shared by several applications or model bases has been realized by means of software packages specially devised to perform such tasks. These packages, called *database management systems* (DBMSs), are available in the market under different trade names such as ORACLE, SYBASE, INGRES, FOXBASE, and dBASE.

Networking and interactive processing

The two principal blocks that facilitate development and use of MIS are DBMS and *telecommunications.* The former makes data integration possible, while the latter brings information closer to the end users, who constitute nodes in a telecommunication network. The notion of telecommunications implies that some geographical distance exists between the computer site and the users' locations and that data are electronically transmitted between them. Remote applications may be executed between two floors in the same building, two offices in the same city, two offices on the same continent, or two places on opposite sides of the globe (Martin, 1990).

System alternatives and evaluation: Centralization versus decentralization

A completely centralized information system handles all processing at a single computer site, maintains a single central database, has centralized development of applications, provides central technical services, sets development priorities centrally, and allocates computer resources centrally. The system's remote users are served by transporting input and output data physically or electronically.

A completely decentralized system may have no central control of system development, no communication links among autonomous computing units, and stand-alone processors and databases at various sites. Each unit funds its own information-processing activities and is totally responsible for all development and operation.

An advantage of centralized information systems is that they provide for standardization in the collection of data and the release of information. There also are some *economies of scale. A* centralized system reduces the need for multiple hardware, software, space, personnel, and databases. It may be possible to recruit more qualified personnel in a central facility.

Observations indicate that user motivation and satisfaction are increased under a decentralized environment. This is attained because users feel more involved and more responsible, systems are better customized to their specific needs, and they usually get better response time in routine operations as well as in requests for changes.

It is likely that for national agricultural extension systems, neither a completely centralized nor a completely decentralized system is desirable. While it may be useful to decentralize hardware and software resources at different locations, the development of applications and provision of technical services may better be centralized.

End-user computing

The widespread use of personal computers and computer-based workstations has brought with it the age of end-user computing. End-user computing is a generic term for any information-processing activity performed by direct end users who actually use terminals or microcomputers to access data and programmes. The manager as end user may be provided with powerful software (like DBMS) for accessing data, developing models, and performing information processing directly. This has brought computing directly under the control of the end users and eliminates their dependence on the information systems specialist and the rigidities of predesigned procedures. They may now make ad hoc queries of information and analyse it in various ways. They may write programmes, or may often use ready-made programmes stored in the computer, using the computing power of a local PC or the mainframe to which it is connected.

Illustrative computer-based MIS

A national agricultural extension system is a nationwide system managed by the national government. In India, agriculture is a state subject under the division of powers between the national and the state levels. Nevertheless, the national government supplements the financial resources of the states and provides coordination at the national level. The state's administrative machinery is divided into districts, districts into subdivisions, subdivisions into blocks. A block is a group of villages and the basic unit for the administration of an agricultural extension programme. Data collected at the block level need to be integrated at higher administrative levels to provide an integrated view at the district and state levels to support planning, monitoring, and decision making.

However, the actual design may vary with the size of the state and other considerations. An integrated database for the entire state may be supported by a mainframe/minicomputer at the state headquarters. Suitable programmes for the analysis of data may be designed to provide an interactive decision support system at the state level. Each district and subdivision may be provided with a mini/micro computer, depending on the volume of data to be handled. The computers in the districts and subdivisions may be networked with the state computer. The local data may be stored and processed in the district/subdivision, and the shared data with appropriate level of aggregation may be transmitted to the state headquarters to update the integrated database. The districts and subdivisions would have direct access to the integrated database with proper authorizations assigned to them through their passwords. The blocks may have only the input-output terminals connected to the subdivision computer to feed data to the subdivision and make on-line inquiries as and when necessary.

SUMMARY

In this chapter, we have defined and described the basic concepts of a management information system. The characteristics of good information, namely, relevance, timeliness, accuracy, cost-effectiveness, reliability, usability, exhaustiveness, and aggregation level, have been described. The role of information systems in the process of decision making and the value of information have been explained. Four types of MIS, namely, databank information system, predictive information system, decision-making information system, and decisiontaking information system, have been presented. The role of MIS in management of agricultural extension programmes and the conceptual design of a MIS in an agricultural extension organization have been described.

Basic computer concepts have been explained. The advantages and disadvantages of centralized versus decentralized systems have been examined. The need for organizing databases and their integration and the need for programmes for decision analysis to evolve a decision support system have been explained. An assessment of hardware, software, and networking requirements for a typical computer-based MIS for a national agricultural extension system have been illustrated.

BIBLIOGRAPHY

Awad, E. M., & Gotterer, M. H. (1992). *Database management.* Danvers, MA: Boyd & Fraser.

Banerjee, U. K., & Sachdeva, R. K. (1995). *Management information system: A new frame work.* New Delhi: Vikas Publishing House.

Imboden, N. (1980). *Managing information for rural development projects.* Paris: Organization for Economic Co-operation and Development.

Keen, P. G. W., & Morton, M. S. S. (1978). *Decision support systems.* Reading, MA: Addison-Wesley.

Lucas, H. C., Jr. (1990). *Information systems concepts for management.* New York: McGraw-Hill.

Martin, J. (1990). *Telecommunications and the computer.* Englewood Cliffs, NJ: Prentice-Hall.

Mason, R. D., & Swanson, B. E. (1981). *Measurements for management decision.* Reading, MA: Addison-Wesley.

McLeod, R., Jr. (1995). *Management information systems: A study of computer-based information systems.* New Delhi: Prentice Hall of India.

Rao, C. S. S. (1985). Agricultural extension management system in India: Past, present and modalities in future. *Indian Journal of Extension Education.*

Sachdeva, R. K. (1990). *Management handbook of computer usage.* Oxford: NCC Blackwell.

Simon, H. A. (1977). The new science of management decision. New Jersey: Prentice-Hall.

Singh, Y. P., & Ramesh Babu, A. (1985). Basic management issues in extension. *Indian Journal of Extension Education.*

Wentling, T. L., & Wentling, R. M. (1993). *Introduction to microcomputer technologies. Rome: FAO.*

INDEX

C

Corporate Responsibility, 48, 52, 53, 54, 55, 59, 60, 61, 62, 67, 71, 72, 74, 75.

D

Distribution, 43, 193, 198, 251.

F

Financial Management, 66, 103, 104, 107, 113, 117, 129, 142.

G

Governance Reforms, 162, 165.

H

Historical Development, 7.

I

Information System, 263, 264, 265, 267, 270, 275, 278.
Institutionalism, 226, 227, 229, 231, 232, 233, 248, 249, 250.

L

Legal Risks, 145, 146, 178.

M

Marketing Revolution, 11.
Military Theorists, 20.

N

Non-profit Paradox, 108.
Nonprofit Organization, 37, 38, 39, 41, 42, 43, 115, 121, 122, 123, 127, 129, 130, 135, 147.
Nonprofit Strategic Management, 209.

O

Operations, 16, 53, 59, 60, 81, 93, 103, 164, 165, 188, 211, 228, 263, 272, 276.
Organisational Performance, 179, 188.

P

Performance, 1, 4, 13, 17, 19, 47, 48, 93, 96, 100, 104, 154, 177, 179, 189, 193, 202, 205, 209, 226, 258, 262, 263, 266.
Portfolio Theory, 9, 10.
Protections, 145, 146, 148, 171, 178.

S

Strategic Management, 7, 186, 192, 217, 219, 222, 223, 224, 225, 232, 256, 267, 278.
Strategic Planning, 2, 5, 24, 25, 33, 58, 86, 184, 185, 188, 210, 222, 261.
Strategy Hierarchy, 5, 212.

T

Technology Driven Strategy, 26.

♦♦♦

Ruffin Viclère MABIALA

La résurrection d'une nation brisée par les conflits

TOME I

Le guide des Affaires civiles de l'ONU

L'Harmattan

5-7, rue de l'École-Polytechnique ; 75005 Paris

http://www.librairieharmattan.com
diffusion.harmattan@wanadoo.fr
harmattan1@wanadoo.fr

ISBN : 978-2-336-29391-2

EAN : 9782336293912

DU MÊME AUTEUR

« LA JUSTICE DANS LES PAYS EN SITUATION DE POST-CONFLIT ; La Justice Transitionnelle », Editions l'Harmattan, Paris, France, novembre 2009, 351 pages

(En 2010, ce livre a été choisi par l'Institut Belge de Droit Comparé, en Belgique comme l'une des huit meilleures publications soumises en recension, pour les pays francophones. Il a fait l'objet d'un article publié dans la revue dudit institut Belge)

« LE DROIT D'INGERENCE », Tome-I (340 pages) & Tome-II (331 pages), Presses Universitaires de France, Thèse à la carte, Editions du Septentrion, Villeneuve d'Ascq Cedex France, 1999

(Ce livre a été publié parce qu'il a été choisi parmi les dix meilleures thèses de doctorat de l'année 1997, en France)

« Le conflit est une situation de crise politique, socioéconomique et/ou militaire, qui met en péril ou entraîne le dysfonctionnement des institutions de l'Etat et/ou, engendre des violations massives des droits de l'homme ou encore, produit des conséquences humanitaires d'une exceptionnelle gravité. »

Dr. Ruffin Viclère MABIALA, Ph.D.

REMERCIEMENTS

Mes remerciements les plus honnêtes s'adressent à ma partenaire et complice dans le mariage, en affaires et dans la vie. Il s'agit bien évidemment de celle qui me comble si bien en amour et en bienveillance : mon épouse, Sophie MABIALA, sans laquelle je serais comme une âme en peine. Elle a toujours collaboré très étroitement avec moi dans la réalisation de mes ouvrages. J'en profite de l'occasion pour remercier ses parents, Amane et Paul Niamazok pour avoir élevé la merveilleuse Sophie qui, depuis 24 ans, représente pour moi un modèle d'amour, de sagesse et d'inspiration.

Lorsque j'évoque la problématique des remerciements, je pense profondément à ma fille Tracy Amane Ratiba MABIALA et à mon fils Moth-Viclère Goumakana MABIALA pour la joie et le sens qu'ils donnent à ma vie.

C'est avec le plus grand plaisir et je dirai l'intérêt que je tiens aussi à remercier vivement pour leur soutien et/ou leur contribution : Pembé Pauline (ma mère), Gérald Jean-Baptiste, Kossi Tiassou, J Carter, Jean Berckman Kabirigi, Luc Duschene, Ludovic Koutinhoun Zanou, Maikabi Arzika Moussa et Walters Tohnji Tikum Samah.

Enfin, mes remerciements s'adressent à tous ceux et toutes celles dont je n'ai pas fait mention ici, afin de ne pas me perdre dans les méandres de leurs noms. Tous mes hommages aux parents qui ont transités vers l'orient éternel : Amane Jacquette, Bernard Mabiala (mon père), Gouma-Kana Lembé, Niama-Imono, Angélique et Marie Tsiahou, Nzem-Nzeu Laurent, Alain et Yvette Mabiala…

Dr. Ruffin Viclère MABIALA, Ph.D.
New York City, 2013

AVANT-PROPOS

La section des Affaires civiles, dans les missions de maintien de la paix de l'ONU, est peu connue du grand public, de l'homme de la rue et même de certains universitaires. Lorsqu'on évoque cette notion, les gens ont tendance à faire allusion au droit civil que l'on apprend dans les écoles spécialisées ou dans les universités, alors que ce sont les Affaires civiles sur fond de politique, économie, droit et administration publique. Ce livre vient combler ce vide. Il constitue une réponse à tous ceux qui, lorsqu'ils entendent le concept « Affaires civiles » de l'ONU se demandent souvent : « Affaires civiles ! De quoi parle-t-on ? »

Cette analyse est révélatrice de la lourde tâche qui pèse sur l'officier des Affaires civiles dans une mission de stabilisation ou de consolidation de la paix. Elle énumère les responsabilités des collectivités territoriales qui sont appelées à satisfaire les besoins des populations locales, sans-cesse croissants.

Les élus et tous les lecteurs de ce livre vont acquérir les connaissances essentielles pour mieux satisfaire les besoins des populations locales, pour les uns et acquérir une meilleure maîtrise du rôle d'un officier des Affaires civiles appelé à travailler avec les autorités territoriales, pour les autres.

Cette théorie de clarification sur les activités des officiers des Affaires civiles dans les missions de maintien de la paix de l'ONU est basée sur mon expérience personnelle, en tant qu'Officier des Affaires civiles, au Burundi et en Haïti.

Au Burundi, j'ai aussi eu l'occasion de travailler à la Commission d'Enquêtes des Nations unies, très connue sous l'appellation « Board of Inquiry (BOI). » J'ai, en outre, animé un forum sur la problématique des droits de l'homme à l'université de Bujumbura.

En Haïti, j'ai eu, à plusieurs reprises, la possibilité d'assurer temporairement la fonction de Chef de Bureau Régional, connu sous le sigle : CRO qui signifie, en Anglais, « Chief of Regional Office » du bureau intégré de Léogane, par intérim. Il m'a aussi été donné l'occasion de gérer temporairement les sections des Affaires civiles et Humanitaires du Bureau Régional de Jérémie, en absence de mon superviseur, aux moments forts de la crise humanitaire, en collaborant étroitement avec les autres sections substantielles de la mission. A l'époque, il nous a fallu gérer cent vingt mille (120.000) rescapés du séisme du 12 janvier 2010 sur le plan humanitaire. J'ai aussi été le point focal des projets à effets rapides (QIP), à Jacmel, dans le département du Sud-est, en Haïti.

J'ai présenté une conférence à l'Ecole de Droit de Jérémie sur le thème « la justice transitionnelle », le sous-titre de mon dernier ouvrage intitulé « la justice dans les pays en situation de post-conflit », publié en novembre 2009, aux Editions l'Harmattan[1]. Ce livre fait partie des huit ouvrages choisis en recensions en 2010, par l'Institut Belge de Droit Comparé ASBL. Un article sur l'analyse de mes recherches, a été publié dans la revue de Droit International et de Droit Comparé, dans cette même année par cet institut de renom. Il m'a été donné l'occasion de gérer l'« intake[2] », pendant les périodes électorales. Je venais en support à l'officier des Affaires électorales, submergé par le travail. Par contre, à Léogane, j'ai été, purement et simplement, le « point focal » des élections dans la région des Palmes, pour le Bureau Intégré des Nations unies.

A ce titre, j'ai participé à l'élaboration du plan de sécurisation des centres de votes de la juridiction sous notre tutelle, avec le bataillon Sri-lankais, dirigé par un Général des armées, mais aussi avec les UNPOL (la police des Nations unies) et les PNH (la Police Nationale d'Haïti). Ce poste m'a permis d'organiser, avec les autres composantes de la mission des Nations unies en Haïti, le D-JESC/JESC (Department Joint Electoral Support Center) qui n'est

---

[1] « En un mot, la justice transitionnelle est un processus politique, extrajudiciaire caractérisé par des rencontres entre les bourreaux et leurs victimes, hors des tribunaux traditionnels, mais devant une commission de vérité et réconciliation, dans le but de les réconcilier pour repartir sur de nouvelles bases, tout en consolidant la paix et le développement. » Dr Ruffin V. Mabiala « La Justice dans les Pays en Situation de Post-Conflit. La Justice Transitionnelle. » Edition l'Harmattan Paris, France, 2009.
Voir aussi article d'ONDO, Revue de Droit International et de Droit Comparé (RDIC), pp.410-416, Bruxelles, Belgique, 2010

[2] L'intake est le centre de traitement des résultats, ou plutôt, des bulletins de vote d'une collectivité territoriale donnée.

autre que le centre de traitement des informations et des problèmes qui surviennent dans le processus électoral.

Nous avons aussi organisé la distribution du matériel électoral : sensible et non sensible. Bien entendu, il nous appartenait aussi de collecter les bulletins de vote, sans oublier de faire le suivi de l'ensemble du processus électoral.

Dans « la résurrection d'une nation brisée par les conflits », je tente de dévoiler comment les officiers des Affaires civiles collaborent avec le gouvernement Central et les collectivités territoriales pour réformer une administration publique en situation de post-conflit. L'enjeu est de promouvoir la gestion efficiente des collectivités territoriales et par là, booster le développement durable local pour le bien-être de la population dont les besoins et les services attendus de leurs élus ne cessent d'augmenter.

Ce livre est par conséquent, un guide de gestion municipale au service d'un officier des Affaires civiles. C'est un conseiller pilote pour un maire qui veut avoir un agenda efficace de travail pour réussir son mandat. Il constitue aussi le cicérone du directeur général, secrétaires archivistes ou dactylo, caissiers payeurs, comptables, chefs de service internes des mairies des pays post-conflit.

Les mots : « préfet », « gouverneur » ou « délégué départemental » signifient la même fonction, celle de gestion d'une région, d'une province ou d'un département. C'est aussi le cas lorsque j'utilise les termes « maire » et « administrateur. » De même pour les mots « section communale » et « colline » qui désignent le même palier de décentralisation, celui qui succède à la commune. En fait, ce sont des appellations qui varient selon les pays.

Il est impératif que les Nations unies évitent de gérer et/ ou de s'ingérer dans les affaires intérieures des Etats souverains, tel que prévu par la charte de l'ONU dans le Chapitre I, article 2, paragraphe 7[3]. Dans le même ordre d'idées, l'ONU doit, en toutes circonstances, garder son impartialité et sa neutralité dans les règlements pacifiques des crises. La règle de non-ingérence est aussi valable pour tous les fonctionnaires des Nations unies, à commencer par le Secrétaire Général de l'ONU. Evidemment, l'article 100 de la charte de l'ONU sur les prorogatifs du Secrétaire Général précise clairement que le « primus inter partes/first among equals » des fonctionnaires mondiaux n'a ni l'autorité, ni le droit, ni la légitimité de se substituer ou de s'immiscer dans les affaires qui relèvent de la compétence exclusive des autorités et/ou institutions d'un pays indépendant et souverain. Dès lors, le monde verra naître ou apparaître une nouvelle religion que l'on baptisera du nom de « l'onusisme. »

Dans un conflit où deux points de vue s'affrontent dans l'expression violente du multi-ethnisme et des rivalités tribales ou religieuses, il n'y a pas

---

[3] Dr Ruffin V. Mabiala, Ph.D. "Le droit d'Ingérence", Presse Universitaire de France, Editions Septentrion, Villeneuve d'ASCQ, France, 1999.

de lutte entre les bons et les méchants. Mais, on a des communautés qui s'opposent et s'affrontent, en raison des fractures souvent inscrites dans leur histoire, la neutralité est la seule solution qui s'impose. Au cas contraire, la crédibilité et l'autorité des hautes instances internationales sont ternies.

En clair, à partir du moment où l'ONU intervient systématiquement contre une partie au conflit ; soutient une rébellion armée contre un gouvernement du moins, établi constitutionnellement ; cautionne une ingérence, immixtion ou interférence de quelque nature que ce soit dans un pays indépendant, elle sort de ces prérogatives de protection des populations civiles pour s'engager dans une guerre sans fondement contre un Etat souverain. Ce type d'interventions politiques canonnières est illégal et illégitime, puisqu'il n'est pas humanitaire.

Effectivement, il est difficile de transformer une intrusion meurtrière en victoire démocratique ou en succès humanitaire, car tout changement de pouvoir par la force ne peut guère entraîner l'avènement d'une ère de démocratie, de paix et de stabilité, sans faire couler inutilement le sang des humains innocents.

Je pense fermement que l'ONU est une lumière puissante et purificatrice même si l'ombre est là, terrible et terrifiante et c'est pour faire voir cette lumière, que j'ai entrepris de publier mon ouvrage sur : la réforme d'une administration publique et les enjeux du développement local en situation de post-conflit.

J'estime que l'ONU sera un jour la force civilisatrice qui bouleversera les données, les principes et les croyances de toutes les religions du monde pour devenir la Mecque de la justice, de la paix et de la vérité. Mais, il va falloir qu'elle arrête la désertification des terres du monde et transforme les chars de guerre et les fusils en instruments aratoires et en charrues pour les semailles, pour faire ce que Constantin avait fait au 4e siècle pour le christianisme.

Il faut « per fas et nefas[4] » que l'organisation mondiale emploi sa bombe atomique et sa bombe thermonucléaire pour transformer le désert du Gobi et le désert du Sahara en éden ou en terre fertiles pour que les peuples de l'univers tournent le dos aux religions fossiles et anhistoriques qui les ont trompées et qui les ont toujours conduites à la honte et dans l'abîme. Le monde attend que ce moment propice se matérialise dans la glaise de la réalité.

Toutefois, sans la présence de l'ONU sur la terre, peut-être que la vie aurait perdu de son lustre et toutes les régions du globe seraient des places infernales comme à l'époque du Carbonifère. Je n'entends point faire les panégyriques de l'ONU, mais je dis ce que j'estime être vrai et foncièrement vrai. J'aurais contre moi toute la meute infernale des Cerbère et des Hécate qui se sont toujours ligués contre le bien et le beau.

---

[4] « Qu'on le veuille ou non »

« La résurrection d'une nation brisée par les conflits », dessillera les yeux de plus d'un et les aidera à comprendre le travail colossal que réalise les Affaires civiles au sein des missions de maintien de la paix de l'ONU de par le monde au regard des activités qu'elles exécutent.

Dr. Ruffin Viclère MABIALA, Ph.D.
New York City, 2013

INTRODUCTION

Des écrivains à plume de Bersa se sont penchés sur les contours de l'ONU et les ont scrutés superficiellement, ce qui ne leur a jamais permis de dire la vérité et toute la vérité sur le colosse d'airain qui garde jalousement ses mystères comme un sphinx. Je viens aujourd'hui après avoir découvert la pierre de Rosette des affaires internationales pour parler, de long en large et avec le sérieux et la force scientifique qui m'ont toujours caractérisé, des Affaires civiles de l'ONU.

Ce coup de pioche à la base de l'armature de l'ONU en surprendra plus d'un, mais les esprits éclairés exalteront mon courage en disant : « MABIALA a entrepris une œuvre qui est une sorte de « prolem sine matre creatam[5]. » Ceux qui ne comprennent pas et qui sont toujours portés par le daltonisme intellectuel à voir le mal là où il y a le bien, gloseront pour me décourager, mais je veux bien leur dire comme les anciens : « Felix qui potuit cognoscere rerum causas[6]. »

Mais, pour mieux vous faire comprendre ce que représente l'ONU pour les hommes, je vais m'appliquer non seulement à retracer pour vous le schéma ou l'organigramme de cette organisation, mais encore à rechercher dans son sous-sol, certaines parties ou comités de celle-ci que vous ne connaissez pas ou dont on ne parle que très rarement. Il y a en effet des entités de l'ONU que vous ignorez. Elles font partie des Casques bleus. Ce sont les Affaires civiles.

Ensemble, nous allons faire une robinsonnade à travers les frondaisons de l'ONU pour palper les Affaires civiles et en donner une démonstration ad oculos.

Certains intellectuels à la petite semaine pensent que les Affaires civiles sont le PNUD sous un autre masque ou sous une autre dénomination. Ils se trompent parce que le PNUD est un programme de Nations unies pour le développement sur une échelle macro-économique tandis que les Affaires civiles constituent, entre autres, un programme de développement à caractère micro-économique. On pourrait, dans une certaine mesure, appeler les Affaires

---

[5] Ce concept Latin veut dire : œuvre jamais vue

[6] Ce concept Latin veut dire : Heureux celui qui veut connaître la cause des choses

civiles, microprojets, c'est-à-dire de petits projets pour apaiser la grogne des populations frustrées par l'occupation de leur pays. Les Affaires civiles sont là pour satisfaire les besoins de Maslow des peuples victimes des conflits et des cataclysmes naturels, par le biais des élus territoriaux.

On a remarqué qu'après une crise il y a de lourdes contraintes socio-économiques qui pèsent sur le dos des hommes. Les gens n'arrivent pas à se nourrir ni à nourrir avec satisfaction leur famille. Le chômage conjecturel sévit dans les pays après la guerre civile. Il faut aider les populations et c'est à cause de ce goût pour l'humanitarisme que l'ONU a mis sur pied la section des Affaires civiles. Quel amour pour le genre humain !

L'ONU a compris ces mots d'Albert Camus dans la Peste : « dans l'immense grange de l'univers le fléau battra le blé humains, il y aura plus de paille que de grains, plus d'appelés que d'élus. » Est-ce que les intellectuels de haut vol et dignes de ce nom peuvent voir sans douleur la misère humaine ?

Les penseurs de l'ONU sont des philosophes de la lignée de Victor Hugo dans les Misérables et de Fénelon dans les Aventures de Télémaque, encore faut-il que la souffrance des uns soit la souffrance des autres, la déchéance des uns soit la déchéance des autres et que tout soit centré sur l'homme, au point de parler d'anthropocentrisme existentiel au sein des Nations unies.

Le devoir de solidarité internationale naît de la mondialisation et la globalisation, mais fondé sur le principe de la fraternité universelle et de l'éthique de conviction et de la responsabilité veut que les sottises de l'homme, les défaillances des collectivités et même la volonté de Dieu incombent au monde. Ce même devoir engendre l'obligation pratique de cogestion dans la mise en œuvre d'une politique nationale de développement durable dans les pays en situation d'urgence politique complexe. C'est la conséquence de la responsabilité conjointe assumée à la fois par les autorités nationales et la communauté internationale, pour le bien-être de l'humanité. Evidemment, pour relever le défi de la refondation territoriale, économique, sociale et institutionnelle d'une nation post-crise ou post-catastrophe, il convient de construire une large concertation, qui va au-delà des frontières de la nation sélectionnée. Et si les Affaires civiles de l'ONU s'appelaient service d'aide aux victimes de guerres, de crises et des cataclysmes ! Ce vocable n'est-il pas plus classique et plus significatif? Faut-il suggérer à l'ONU de substituer les Affaires civiles par les services d'aide humanitaire rapide après les conflits et les cataclysmes ou les services de redressement des administrations défaillantes en vue de satisfaire les besoins du peuple. Les mots n'ont-ils pas une plus belle résonnance acoustique à l'oreille des gens ?

Il n'est pas donné à tout le monde de comprendre le sens intrinsèque de l'expression « Affaires civiles. » C'est pour faire comprendre aux lecteurs le travail sérieux que fait la section des Affaires civiles de par le monde et c'est pour avoir compris la somme des travaux qu'elle exécute à travers les missions qui lui sont confiées par le colosse onusien que j'ai entrepris de lever le voile épais qui la masque à la vue des profanes.

Quel est le bien fondé des Affaires civiles ? Pourquoi les Affaires civiles ?

L'origine étymologique du mot « civil » en dit long. Le terme civil dérive du mot parisyllabique latin « cives civis » qui signifie citoyen. En un mot on peut dire que les Affaires civiles ce sont les Affaires ou les choses qui concernent les citoyens. L'ONU a mis sur pied les Affaires civiles juste pour intervenir rapidement et sans failles dans la vie des citoyens d'un pays en transition politique, ravagé par la guerre civile ou par des cataclysmes naturels comme l'éruption d'un volcan, le séisme, le cyclone, l'inondation ou le tsunami.

Les Affaires civiles entretiennent ainsi des rapports ou des relations avec la société civile, les ONG et les gouvernements locaux via les Ministères. Avec le programme des QIP, elles entreprennent des travaux à haute ou faible intensité de main d'œuvre qui permettent d'embaucher les citoyens du pays d'accueil dans plusieurs domaines.

Les Affaires civiles interviennent surtout dans les secteurs de :

- la gouvernance efficace ;
- l'Etat de droit, la démocratie, la « sécurité démocratique » et la décentralisation ;
- la réforme de l'administration publique et le renforcement des capacités ;
- le Développement humain et durable ;
- la reconstruction des routes, le captage des sources d'eau potable et le drainage des marais ou des marécages ;
- la distribution des produits alimentaires et sanitaires à la population démunie.

Dans certaines missions, elles participent aussi dans le contrôle des frontières du pays concerné.

La présence des Affaires civiles aide à chasser les sorcières et les vieux crabes de l'ancien gouvernement qui sont corrompus jusqu'à la moelle, mais qu'on ne doit point tuer, au risque de retomber dans le même cycle de la violence. Toutefois, il est apodictique de demander aux envoyés de l'ONU d'encourager au besoin, l'arrestation de ces anciens fonctionnaires et de les punir par devant la justice transitionnelle. A travers le renforcement des capacités d'un Etat, les Affaires civiles accompagnent la recherche et la formation des gens compétents, honnêtes, sérieux et capables de travailler pour le développement durable de leur pays. Les Affaires civiles aident aussi les citoyens du pays dévasté par la guerre civile et par un cataclysme naturel à reconstruire ou à réhabiliter les routes détruites parce que sans désenclavement, l'économie va stagner et la misère va s'installer parmi les victimes de la guerre ou du cataclysme.

Elles interviennent aussi dans le captage des sources d'eau potable parce que si la population boit de l'eau insalubre elle va contracter des infections amibiennes et les enfants mourront de diarrhée et de typhoïde ce qui est contraire aux objectifs du millénium.

Les Affaires civiles interviennent parfois dans la distribution des produits alimentaires et sanitaires à la population. Tout cela est bien.

Après la rupture des stocks de marchandises dans les villes, le pillage des silos des commerçants, l'incendie allumé dans les champs par les seigneurs ou les caïds de la guerre, il faut aider la population locale à se sustenter ou à trouver quelque chose de comestible pour se nourrir et pour ne pas crever de faim ou de « starvation. » Après la guerre civile ou après un grand cataclysme presque tous les hommes forment un ensemble de ventres mous, ce pour employer ce terme cher au Président américain Richard Nixon. Il faut donner à manger aux gens, ce pour éviter le cannibalisme et l'anéantissement de la population. On sait très bien que « ventre affamé n'a point d'oreilles. » Cet adage populaire est vrai pour tous les pays du monde. On se rappelle ce qui s'est passé aux États-Unis après la dépression économique de 1929. Des foules affamées incendièrent et pillèrent les magasins, les banques et les granges aux USA.

Qui n'a pas lu les raisons de la colère de Steinberk ? Pour remédier à cette situation, le gouvernement américain fut obligé de distribuer de la nourriture dans les grandes villes. Qui peut oublier ce qui s'est passé en Haïti après le départ d'Aristide en 2004 ? On a vu des bandes d'individus brandissant des armes hétéroclites au nombre desquelles se trouvaient des piques, des machettes, des fusils, des coups de poing espagnols envahirent les rues de la capitale. Ces gens faméliques saccagèrent les magasins et les boutiques pour pouvoir trouver du riz et des produits alimentaires. La faim est mauvaise conseillère, dit-on.

Faut-il rappeler que le renforcement de l'Etat passe par des réformes structurelles obligeant à répondre aux besoins immédiats de la population par des paquets minimum de services accompagnés des mesures d'apaisement social, qui elles-mêmes sont fondées sur des actions structurantes qui visent en particulier :

- l'élimination des obstacles à l'inclusion sociale, suivie d'une réponse immédiate aux besoins des personnes les plus vulnérables, marginalisées et fragilisées par la sous-alimentation ;
- la relance de la production nationale dans le but d'augmenter les ressources de la nation et des ménages ;
- l'amélioration de l'accès aux services de base, à savoir, l'eau et l'assainissement, les infrastructures visant à réduire les risques ou conséquences des aléas naturels et les conflits, l'éducation avec comme priorité la gratuité et la réhabilitation des écoles détruites par la guerre,

ainsi que la distribution de manuels, etc. la santé avec pour priorité l'accès à l'eau potable et l'établissement de centres de santé dans les communes privées de telles services de base, etc. ;

- la création d'emplois, en particulier pour les ouvriers non qualifiés, comme résultat et conséquence des autres activités destinées à produire, avant toute chose, des biens et des services bénéficiant à la population.

La section des Affaires civiles constitue, pour ainsi dire, un instrument au service des missions de maintien de la paix, pour le renforcement des institutions, le développement de l'Etat de droit, la consolidation de l'autorité de l'Etat et la bonne gouvernance. Elle se focalise principalement sur le renforcement des capacités des autorités de base, notamment des élus communaux, des autorités déconcentrées et de la société civile organisée. Son domaine exclusif est l'appui institutionnel.

Cet appui comprend deux volets différents, mais qui se complètent : le fonctionnement des collectivités territoriales et la formation des cadres. Le volet fonctionnement concerne l'accompagnement, l'assistance et les conseils techniques en faveur des autorités locales et des institutions. Il permet d'observer les dysfonctionnements et les faiblesses des collectivités territoriales, base sur laquelle on élabore des modules de formation à adresser aux ayants droit.

Toutefois, cet aspect exclusif des Affaires civiles n'est pas sans dérogation. Certains secteurs relèvent du domaine partagé conjointement avec d'autres sections de la mission. Il s'agit du développement de l'Etat de droit qui est partagé avec les sections Droit de l'homme et Justice, ainsi que les UNPOL et les militaires, en s'appuyant sur la communication et les échanges entre les gouvernements locaux et la société civile, afin de promouvoir la démocratie participative, la transparence et la bonne gouvernance. Le développement de l'Etat de droit permet aussi d'impliquer la population dans la gestion de la chose publique, surtout lorsque ces réunions sont organisées de façon thématique. Les thèmes fréquemment soulevés sont : la sécurité ; la fiscalité ; le paiement des taxes ; la lutte contre la corruption ; la production, la commercialisation et la consommation de la drogue...

Les Affaires civiles participent aussi à la réalisation des Tables de Concertation[7] Départementales (TCD) ou Communales (TCC) et des Tables Sectorielles (TS) qui font intervenir d'autres composantes des Nations unies, y compris les Agences de l'ONU et les ONG internationales. Ces tables constituent un espace de réflexion sur les questions humanitaires, de protection et de sécurité civile, de l'environnement et du tourisme, de l'agriculture, de l'éducation, de la santé, des travaux publics… Elles regroupent, les directeurs

[7] L'idée de table de concertation Départementale ou communale et de table sectorielle, est née en Haïti avec un ancien ministre de l'Agriculture d'un des gouvernements du Président René Préval, en la personne du Ministre Gerald Maturin, en 1997

départementaux de chaque secteur d'activités, autour du préfet pour ce qui concerne les tables de concertation départementales, tandis que les sous-préfets et les maires cogèrent les tables de concertation communales. Dans tous les cas, les Affaires civiles ont besoin de l'expertise de la section humanitaires et des autres acteurs humanitaires pour faire fonctionner les tables de concertation et les tables sectorielles ou pour l'élaboration des plans de contingence.

Dans le cadre du renforcement du parlement, la section des Affaires civiles peut aussi bénéficier indirectement du soutien d'autres sections telles que la section justice qui appuie le gouvernement dans le cadre de la réforme de la justice. Une intervention stratégique et politique considérable est nécessaire de la part des Affaires civiles au niveau du parlement qui vote les lois, pour que celles-ci passent et soient applicables. Le rôle des Affaires politiques dans ce secteur n'est pas, non plus négligeable, car le parlement est une institution qui assume des fonctions éminemment politiques. Le staff national joue un rôle très important dans la phase qui consiste à faciliter les relations entre les Affaires civiles et les autorités locales, en dehors de l'assistance technique qu'il offre, en tant qu'officier des Affaires civiles, au même titre que les internationaux.

La Section des Affaires civiles a pour rôle d'assister le gouvernement à étendre et consolider l'autorité de l'Etat à travers le pays, y compris dans les zones autrefois contrôlées par des groupes armés. Cela inclut la bonne gouvernance et la mise sur pied d'une administration civile fonctionnelle, étape essentielle pour la stabilisation et la réconciliation ainsi que le retour des personnes déplacées et des réfugiés. Elle doit fortement s'impliquer auprès des communautés locales pour l'identification de projets prioritaires de développement.

Les Affaires civiles plaident aussi auprès des bailleurs de fonds pour assurer les financements de certains projets communautaires.

Au cœur du dispositif du renforcement de l'autorité de l'Etat, dans son aspect économique, avec la gestion des projets QIP « Quick Impact Projects », en français, les Projets à Effets Rapides, les Affaires civiles s'occupent de ce qui suit :

- l'identification des projets, sur proposition/de connivence avec les autorités locales ;
- l'élaboration et l'étude de faisabilité ;
- la recherche des financements ;
- le suivi de l'exécution ;
- la présentation, tout au moins l'obtention d'un rapport final pour chaque projet.

Il n'est pas vain de préciser que les Affaires civiles doivent se concentrer sur les interventions prioritaires destinées à satisfaire les besoins de la société, afin d'éviter de créer une nouvelle crise ou la reprise du conflit. Elles œuvrent aussi, pour renforcer la stabilité et la sécurité à court et moyen terme. A cette fin, il convient d'élaborer une stratégie spécifique de sécurisation et de stabilisation des collectivités territoriales pour consolider les acquis de la paix et des libertés retrouvées et créer les conditions favorables au développement intégral et durable.

En ce sens, les Affaires civiles interviennent dans la résolution et la prévention des conflits par :

- le renforcement du dialogue et la communication entre les communautés ;
- la résolution pacifique des crises ;
- la prévention des conflits en établissant un système d'alerte rapide « early warning System » ;
- la réconciliation des populations qui se sont entredéchirées...

Les Affaires civiles encouragent la réconciliation effective dans les régions et les communes, parfois à travers les réunions de l'Etat de droit qui servent d'outil pour renforcer la démocratie participative, sans laquelle les élus locaux et le gouvernement ne peuvent bénéficier de la confiance du peuple. L'officier des Affaires civiles soutient l'Etat dans son rôle de coordination et dans le cadre des relations institutionnelles. Cela signifie encourager les relations entre les personnalités locales, les autres acteurs institutionnels et la société civile. Dans ce pilier d'activités, les objectifs principaux de l'officier des Affaires civiles consiste à :

- contribuer à l'établissement d'institutions étatiques fonctionnelles et dynamiques ;
- augmenter les capacités de ces institutions étatiques dans la délivrance de services sociaux de base ;
- sensibiliser les acteurs provinciaux étatiques et municipaux sur la bonne gouvernance, la transparence et la responsabilité politique, sociale et économique.

Au plan purement politique, elles mettent en œuvre des tâches spécifiques caractérisées aux trois rôles centraux qui leur sont essentiellement dévolus :

- la représentation, supervision et facilitation transversales au niveau local ;
- la consolidation de la confiance, liée à la gestion de conflits et à l'appui à la réconciliation ;
- le soutien à la restauration et extension de l'autorité de l'état.

Cette responsabilité des Affaires civiles dans la réforme d'une administration publique et les enjeux du développement local en situation de post-conflit n'est plus un rêve ni une fiction, mais une réalité reconnue par la communauté internationale. Le rapport de la Banque Mondiale intitulé

« World Development Report 2011 : conflict, security and Development », publié le 26 mai 2011, souligne clairement que : « les institutions légitimes qui assurent la sécurité des citoyens, la justice et l'emploi » sont cruciaux pour mettre un terme au cycle de la violence dans un pays post-conflit. Mieux, ce rapport reconnaît l'importance de la communication stratégique et de la confiance dans le contexte de la consolidation de la paix. Ce qui signifie que la sécurité, la justice et l'économie sont liées. Et, ce sont les Affaires civiles, en charge des réformes sur la décentralisation politique, la privatisation et le changement des attitudes envers les groupes marginalisés et les minorités qui sont au centre du processus de consolidation de la paix, via la satisfaction des besoins primaires de la population.

L'Assemblée générale de l'ONU n'est pas en reste. Elle a légitimé l'action de la section des Affaires civiles en ces termes : « le Comité spécial est conscient du rôle important que remplissent les spécialistes des Affaires civiles dans les opérations de maintien de la paix, notamment par des activités de représentation à tous les niveaux de la mission, de suivi et de facilitation au niveau local, de renforcement de la confiance, de gestion des conflits, de réconciliation, [mais aussi] d'appui à la restauration et à l'extension de l'autorité étatique. Il relève que, bien souvent, pour parvenir à remplir correctement leur mission, les [Officiers des Affaires civiles] doivent entretenir un dialogue constant avec le gouvernement local et les populations. [Le comité] souligne que l'intégration de personnel local [dans la composante Affaires civiles d'une mission] joue un rôle déterminant. Il encourage le Secrétariat à continuer d'appuyer le travail des spécialistes des Affaires civiles, et lui demande de le tenir informé des progrès accomplis en la matière[8]. »

Bref, les profanes ne savent pas que les Affaires civiles ont un staff constitué de cadres bien préparés dans plusieurs domaines. Ce secteur d'activités comprend, entre autre, des juristes, des avocats, des administrateurs publics, des économistes, des comptables, des gestionnaires et des politistes.

« Le Guide des Affaires civiles de l'ONU », (Tome-1) est une monographie qui relate l'ensemble des activités des officiers des Affaires civiles dans une mission de maintien de la paix. Il met en évidence la nécessité du renforcement des capacités des autorités de base. C'est une approche qui consiste à montrer comment réformer une administration publique dans un pays en situation de post-crise.

La vocation du « Guide de Formation à l'intention des autorités locales » (Tome-2) est de renforcer les capacités des agents municipaux, à travers une série de formations choisies sur plusieurs thèmes. Toutefois, ce livre n'est pas une panacée encore moins une formation académique destinée à donner aux

---

[8] Voir « Rapport du Comité spécial des opérations de maintien de la paix », Assemblée générale de l'ONU, Session de fond de 2011 (New York, 22 février-18 mars et 9 mai 2011), A/65/19, Chapitre 96, page 26

élus de base ou aux lecteurs, le droit de revendiquer un niveau universitaire quelconque.

Aussi, c'est sans forfanterie que j'incite les intellectuels à lire mon ouvrage « la Résurrection d'une Nation Brisée par les Conflits » qui est une lampe d'Aladin qui permettra à tout un chacun de voir clair même à travers les ténèbres les plus épaisses. Que ceux qui n'ont aucune conscience comprennent enfin que sans l'ONU et les Affaires civiles, le monde marcherait à pas redoublés ou à grandes enjambés vers l'abîme et vers le néant.

Le guide des Affaires civiles de l'ONU

L'Organisation des Nations unies a été fondée dans l'esprit de préserver les générations futures du fléau de la guerre. C'est à ce titre qu'elle a toujours été appelée pour rétablir la paix lorsque les conflits éclatent, afin de créer un environnement propice dans lequel le processus de paix peut être consolidé et fournir une réponse adéquate aux situations post-conflit.

Les résolutions du Conseil de sécurité sur la création d'une mission sont inspirées des rapports fournis par le Secrétaire général sur la situation politico-militaire et humanitaire du pays en question. Le Comité spécial des opérations de maintien de la paix, composé de 144 Etats membres, connu sous le nom de « C34 » puisqu'il avait été crée, à l'origine, par 34 pays, se réunit annuellement, à New York, dans le cadre de la quatrième Commission. Cette Commission s'occupe des questions politiques spéciales et de la décolonisation à l'Assemblée générale. Elle prépare le contexte, les règles et les paramètres de la politique d'intervention de l'ONU.

En 2011, dans son rapport A/65/19, ce Comité spécial avait pour la première fois reconnu « le rôle important joué par les officiers des Affaires civiles dans les opérations de maintien de la paix des Nations unies, notamment dans la facilitation [du processus de paix] au niveau local, le soutien à la reprise de confiance envers l'Etat ; dans la gestion des conflits et la réconciliation et dans le soutien à la restauration et l'extension de l'autorité de l'Etat. » Il soulignait aussi l'importance du personnel local dans les rangs des Affaires civiles dans l'exécution du mandat et pour décrocher l'engagement du gouvernement et de la population locale.

Pour sa part, l'Assemblée générale approuve annuellement le budget de la mission, lors de la cinquième Commission, chargée des questions administratives et budgétaires.

Le Sous-secrétaire général (USG) pour les opérations de maintien de la paix (DPKO) est celui qui oriente la mission et conseille le Secrétaire général sur les questions qui y sont liées. Au sein du Secrétariat, il joue le rôle de point focal auprès des Etats membres.

Au fond, la responsabilité de l'ONU consiste à maintenir la paix et la sécurité internationales. Cela signifie préserver et renforcer les conditions nécessaires à une paix durable, d'où les accords de cessez-le-feu. Une mission peut être créée lorsque les parties au conflit s'entendent sur le déploiement d'une force de maintien de paix, qui doit surveiller le processus de paix qui émerge. La mission aide les signataires à mettre en œuvre des accords qu'ils ont forgés. Cela implique des efforts pour instaurer la confiance et réaffirmer les engagements en faveur du processus de paix dont les difficultés sont toujours présentes.

Par définition, une mission de maintien de la paix est un instrument de paix et de sécurité basée sur trois principes fondamentaux qui se renforcent mutuellement et qui fournissent une boussole aux Casques bleus : le consentement, l'impartialité et le non-usage de la force, auxquels il faut ajouter la crédibilité, la légitimité et l'appropriation nationale et locale. Le consentement des parties au conflit ou celui du gouvernement légitime apporte la liberté politique et la protection nécessaires pour réaliser efficacement le mandat. Son absence constitue une cause d'insécurité qui sape la légitimité de la mission et peut entraîner son retrait précipité. Le premier rôle des Affaires civiles est souvent de rechercher ou renforcer l'acceptation de la mission et expliquer le mandat, notamment, au niveau local où les gens ne sont pas toujours associés à la décision de faire intervenir les Nations unies. Ceci est possible grâce à la liaison et la coordination avec les autorités locales, les leaders communautaires et les acteurs de la société civile, mais aussi par le suivi et les rapports sur les attitudes et les perceptions de la communauté d'accueil ainsi que l'observation des conséquences prévues et imprévues de la mission. Les Affaires civiles s'appuient aussi sur les autres composantes, telles que : la section de l'information publique, pour informer la hiérarchie de tout changement ou des problèmes qui peuvent influencer l'acceptation de la mission et le consentement, pour ne citer qu'une section.

Quant à l'impartialité, il est important de préciser que les Affaires civiles n'ont pas le droit de mettre en œuvre leur mandat en faveur d'une partie au conflit ni de causer préjudice à l'une ou l'autre. Pour répondre aux exigences des différents conflits et à l'évolution du paysage politique du pays hôte, la neutralité est de mise. Elles doivent traiter équitablement tous leurs partenaires et les tenir aux mêmes normes, dans le but de maintenir leur crédibilité aux yeux de la communauté d'accueil, ainsi que le consentement des parties.

Apolitiques, les Affaires civiles n'ont pas le droit de faire l'apologie de la violence ou des violations de l'accord de paix et des normes internationales. C'est la condition première pour qu'elles soient perçues comme des acteurs justes et transparents. Elles sont tenues de s'abstenir de faire usage de la force, sauf en cas de légitime défense et pour la défense du mandat. Là encore, ce sont les hommes et femmes en uniforme, qui peuvent utiliser la violence comme mesure tactique de dernier recours en cas de légitime défense ou pour la protection du personnel et des biens des Nations unies, ou encore pour défendre le mandat.

Pour être crédible, une mission doit avoir un mandat réalisable avec les ressources suffisantes pour aider à gérer les attentes du pays. L'échec des Affaires civiles peut endommager irrémédiablement la réputation de toute la mission qui, par ailleurs, se déploie avec un niveau sans précédent de légitimité internationale. La légitimité est fonction de l'impartialité avec laquelle les Affaires civiles exercent leur mandat, notamment : l'usage de la force, la conduite du personnel des Nations unies et le respect qu'ils démontrent pour la culture, les coutumes et les gens de leur pays d'accueil, sans oublier la visibilité comme dividende de la paix réelle. Cette visibilité est souvent le résultat des projets QIP. Ceux-ci sont critiques pour le succès d'une mission. Les Affaires civiles, dans l'exécution de leur mandat, doivent toujours promouvoir l'appropriation nationale et locale, qui constitue un préalable à la consolidation de la paix durable, à la préservation du consentement et pour le renforcement de la légitimité de la mission. Leur mandat s'étend sur la gestion des conflits, le renforcement de la confiance et de l'espace politique.

Le Conseil de sécurité de l'ONU attend donc des Affaires civiles, qu'elles renforcent les capacités institutionnelles de l'Etat, y compris en fournissant des services spécialisés aux principaux ministères et institutions décentralisées et déconcentrées. Dans la pratique, cela se traduit non seulement par le renforcement des institutions nationales démocratiques, mais aussi, par le rétablissement de l'autorité de l'Etat sur l'ensemble du territoire concerné.

Le conseil exige souvent que les Affaires civiles mettent toutes leurs compétences techniques à la disposition de l'Etat et des gouvernements régionaux ou communaux pour les aider à suivre une approche intégrée de la gestion des affaires publiques. Les Affaires civiles doivent mettre l'accent sur le renforcement des capacités de l'Etat, y compris dans le domaine des frontières pour lequel le Conseil souligne la nécessité d'offrir au gouvernement d'accueil, un appui international coordonné. Sur le plan stratégique, le but fondamental poursuivi par la Section des Affaires civiles dans une mission de maintien de la paix est d'implanter une administration publique réformée, à travers les bases d'une politique efficace et responsable de l'autorité étatique. Cette autorité doit être établie au niveau central, provincial et municipal dans un environnement sécuritaire renforcé par l'Etat de droit, pour offrir de meilleurs services publics de base aux citoyens, notamment dans le cadre de : l'éducation, la santé, le logement, l'emploi, la sécurité alimentaire, l'eau et l'assainissement, et cetera. Cependant, sans une stratégie nationale sur la démocratie et la décentralisation, les progrès accomplis par les Affaires civiles et leurs partenaires risquent d'être peu visibles et marginalisés. Or, l'adoption de cette stratégie nationale accompagnée d'une législation pertinente y afférente est hautement politique. Mais, elle permet de garder le caractère unitaire de l'Etat et maintenir la cohésion entre les priorités nationales et internationales.

Les Affaires civiles sont donc censées se concentrer sur l'extension de l'autorité de l'Etat, pour contribuer à la promotion de la bonne gouvernance en tant que fondements de la stabilité à long terme. Elles ont pour vocation d'appuyer les efforts déployés pour améliorer la présentation des comptes, la stabilité politique et lutter contre la corruption, pour ne citer que ceux-là. L'enjeu est de fortifier les liens entre les autorités locales et nationales, en soutenant simultanément les niveaux centraux — gouvernement et Parlement — et les niveaux locaux, notamment : les régions, les communes et les sections communales ou les collines. En ce sens, la signature d'accords de coopération avec les principaux ministères partenaires, notamment celui qui gère les collectivités territoriales donnerait plus de marge de manœuvre aux Affaires civiles.

C'est à la lumière des priorités de l'Etat et conjointement avec le ministère de tutelle et selon des critères convenus, que les Affaires civiles doivent soutenir et fournir des formations aux élus Municipaux en vue d'améliorer le leadership, la planification et les capacités de gestion. Le but clairement défini est d'avoir des institutions fonctionnelles et efficaces, notamment grâce à la « crédibilisation » accrue et plus d'autorité et d'efficacité dans la fourniture des services à la population.

Les spécialistes des Affaires civiles ont pour ainsi dire, la mission de mettre à exécution les directives du Conseil de Sécurité de l'ONU, à travers leurs activités qui vont être tour à tour explicitées dans les prochaines pages de cet ouvrage. Cependant, il ne saurait être judicieux de parler de la section des Affaires civiles de l'ONU sans connaître la maison mère : sa structure et ses organes principaux. Donc, une présentation sommaire de l'Organisation des Nations unies (I) s'impose. Ensuite, il sera question de définir les concepts (II) d'usage dans le jargon « civiliste », de l'ONU.

Mais, afin de faciliter la compréhension des enjeux de la résurrection d'une nation brisée par les conflits, il semble inévitable d'examiner la structure organisationnelle de la section des Affaires civiles (III) avant de passer à l'élaboration des compétences requises pour assumer la fonction d'officier des Affaires civiles (IV).

Bien que n'étant pas une mission du développement, les Affaires civiles jouent souvent dans la cour des institutions traditionnelles du développement (V) avec le programme des projets QIP.

Une analyse spécifique et approfondie de la notion de renforcement des capacités en situation d'urgence ou de risque de catastrophe naturelle (VI), va boucler l'appétit et le bonheur du lecteur en quête de connaissance.

I. Présentation sommaire de l'Organisation des Nations unies

L'Organisation des Nations unies a été créée le 24 octobre 1945 à la Conférence de San Francisco par les représentants de 50 pays. L'acte fondateur de l'ONU est la Charte. C'est elle qui fixe les droits et les obligations des Etats membres. C'est aussi dans la Charte qu'il y a la création des organes et des procédures de l'organisation mondiale. En tant que convention internationale, la Charte des Nations unies codifie les grands principes des relations internationales, qu'il s'agisse de l'égalité souveraine des Etats ou de l'interdiction d'employer la force dans les rapports avec et entre les Etats qui, de toute manière, est incompatible avec les buts des Nations unies, sans oublier la gestion des catastrophes humanitaires et celles des problèmes d'urgence du même ordre.

Aussi prévoit-elle dans son préambule, les objectifs que l'Organisation des Nations unies doit atteindre, à savoir :

- « préserver les générations futures du fléau de la guerre qui, deux fois en l'espace d'une vie humaine a infligé à l'humanité d'indicibles souffrances ;
- « proclamer à nouveau notre foi dans les droits fondamentaux de l'homme ;
- « favoriser le progrès social et instaurer de meilleures conditions de vie dans une liberté plus grande. »

Dans le chapitre qui traite des buts des Nations unies, la Charte précise que l'ONU doit :

- Entretenir la paix et la sécurité internationale ;
- Réaliser la coopération internationale à travers la résolution des problèmes internationaux d'ordre économique, social, culturel, intellectuel et humanitaire, d'une part et par le développement du respect des droits de l'homme et des libertés fondamentales, d'autre part ;

- Encourager et faciliter les relations amicales entre les nations, sur la base du principe de l'égalité de droits des peuples et de leur droit de disposer d'eux-mêmes ;
- Constituer le centre qui abriterait l'harmonisation des efforts des six (6) organes de l'ONU pour atteindre des fins communes.

A. ORGANES DE L'ONU

De cinquante (50) pays signataires de la Charte à l'origine, l'Organisation des Nations unies compte de nos jours cent quatre-vingt-quatorze (194) Etats membres, y compris le Kosovo et le Sud Soudan, ainsi que six organes principaux qui sont :

- le Conseil de Tutelle ;
- la Cour Internationale de Justice ;
- l'Assemblée Générale ;
- le Conseil Economique et Social (ECOSOC) ;
- le Conseil de Sécurité ;
- le Secrétariat Général.

a. Conseil de tutelle

Le rôle fondamental du conseil de tutelle est d'administrer les territoires sous tutelle. Cependant, depuis l'indépendance de Palaos qui constitue le dernier territoire sous tutelle des Nations unies, ce conseil a officiellement suspendu ses activités en date du 1er novembre 1994.

Désormais, le conseil de tutelle ne se réunit plus qu'une fois par an, mais uniquement, lorsque les circonstances l'imposent. Il peut toujours se réunir à la demande expresse de son Président ou à la majorité des membres du conseil, de l'Assemblée générale ou du Conseil de Sécurité.

b. Cour Internationale de Justice (CIJ)

La Cour Internationale de Justice a été créée par la Charte des Nations unies en 1945, mais elle avait commencé ses activités un an plus tard.

Son siège se trouve au Palais de la Paix, à La Haye, au Pays-Bas, alors que tous les cinq autres organes principaux des Nations unies ont leur siège à New York, aux Etat Unis d'Amérique.

Les fonctions principales de la cour internationale de justice peuvent s'articuler en deux points :

- régler, conformément au droit international, les différends d'ordre juridique entre Etats ou qui lui sont soumis par les Etats membres ;
- donner des avis consultatifs sur les questions juridiques, à la demande des autres organes et institutions spécialisées de l'ONU qui sont habilitées à le faire.

Assistée du Greffe, son organe administratif, la Cour Internationale de Justice est composée de 15 juges indépendants, élus pour un mandat de neuf ans.

c. L'Assemblée générale

L'Assemblée générale de l'Organisation des Nations unies est, jusqu'à preuve du contraire, le principal organe de délibération, direction et représentation de l'ONU. A ce titre, elle occupe une place centrale et constitue un forum multilatéral de discussion unique sur tout l'éventail des questions internationales retenues par la Charte de San Francisco.

Composée des représentants des cent quatre-vingt-quatorze (194) Etats Membres, qui disposent chacun d'une seule et unique voix, elle joue un rôle important dans l'établissement des règles du droit international et dans sa codification. Chaque année, il se tient une session ordinaire intensive de l'Assemblée générale de l'ONU. Elle commence en septembre pour finir en décembre, avec possibilité de prolongement au-delà de cette période, si nécessaire.

En ce qui concerne ses fonctions et pouvoirs, il y a lieu de préciser qu'elle a été créée pour :

- « étudier les principes généraux de coopération pour le maintien de la paix et de la sécurité internationale, y compris les principes régissant le désarmement et faire des recommandations sur ces principes ;
- « discuter de toutes questions se rattachant au maintien de la paix et de la sécurité internationale et faire des recommandations sur ces questions, sauf lorsqu'un différend ou une situation est en cours d'examen au Conseil de sécurité ;
- « discuter de toutes questions rentrant dans le cadre de la Charte ou se rapportant aux pouvoirs et fonctions de l'un quelconque des organes de l'Organisation et, avec la même exception, faire des recommandations sur ces questions ;
- « demander l'établissement d'études et faire des recommandations en vue de développer la coopération internationale dans le domaine politique, d'encourager le développement progressif du droit international et sa codification, de faciliter pour tous la jouissance des droits de l'homme et des libertés fondamentales et de favoriser la coopération internationale dans les domaines économique, social,

humanitaire, de la culture intellectuelle et de l'éducation, et de la santé publique ;

- recommander des mesures propres à assurer l'ajustement pacifique de toute situation de nature à compromettre les relations amicales entre nations ;
- « recevoir et étudier les rapports du Conseil de sécurité et des autres organes de l'Organisation ;
- « examiner et approuver le budget de l'Organisation et déterminer la répartition des contributions entre les États Membres ;
- « élire les membres non permanents du Conseil de sécurité et les membres d'autres conseils et organes de l'Organisation et, sur recommandation du Conseil de sécurité, nommer le Secrétaire général. »

L'Assemblée s'adresse aux États à travers des recommandations sur les questions internationales relevant de sa compétence. Celles-ci n'ont malheureusement pas force exécutoire. Cependant, les initiatives de l'Assemblée générale dans les domaines : politique, économique, humanitaire, social et juridique ont toujours touché directement des millions de personnes dans le monde entier.

d. Conseil Economique et Social (ECOSOC)

Selon les termes de la Charte de 1945, le Conseil économique et social est d'abord et avant tout l'organe principal de la coordination des activités économiques, sociales et apparentées des 14 institutions spécialisées de l'ONU, des commissions techniques et des cinq commissions régionales. Il reçoit par ailleurs les rapports de 11 fonds et programmes des Nations unies. C'est l'instance principale d'analyse des questions économiques et sociales internationales qui élabore des recommandations pratiques pour mettre à la disposition des Etats Membres et à l'ensemble du système des Nations unies. Il est habilité à réaliser ou à faire des études et des rapports permettant de :

- promouvoir une élévation du niveau de vie, le plein-emploi et le progrès économique et social ;
- trouver des solutions aux problèmes économiques, sociaux et sanitaires internationaux ;
- faciliter la coopération internationale dans les domaines de la culture et de l'éducation ;
- favoriser le respect universel des droits de l'homme et des libertés fondamentales.

Le Conseil Economique et social contribue aussi à la préparation et à l'organisation de grandes conférences internationales dans le domaine économique et social et dans d'autres domaines apparentés. Il facilite le suivi de ces conférences, ce qui lui donne « la haute main sur plus de 70 % des ressources humaines et financières de l'ensemble du système des Nations unies. »

Chaque année, le conseil tient une session comprenant cinq débats :

- un débat de haut niveau. Celui-ci constitue l'instance où les ministres, les chefs du secrétariat des organisations internationales, les hauts fonctionnaires et les représentants de la société civile et du secteur privé examinent les questions épineuses qui préoccupent la communauté internationale dans le domaine du développement économique, social et environnemental. Depuis 2005, ce débat permet désormais de faire l'Examen ministériel annuel et celui du Forum pour la coopération en matière de développement. La déclaration ministérielle qui en découle porte les orientations sur la politique à mener et les recommandations concernant les mesures à prendre dans le secteur ;
- un débat consacré aux questions de coordination qui joue depuis quelques années un rôle de direction dans certains grands domaines d'action ;
- un débat au sujet des activités opérationnelles ;
- un débat concernant les Affaires humanitaires ;
- un débat sur les questions diverses.

Ce conseil réalise plusieurs activités importantes parmi lesquelles :

- observer le plein-emploi productif et le travail décent, ainsi que leurs incidences sur le développement durable ;
- encourager les Etats membres à faire du plein-emploi productif et du travail décent l'un des principaux objectifs des politiques nationales et internationales ;
- analyser les progrès réalisés dans la mise en œuvre de la Déclaration du Millénaire, y compris dans la réalisation des objectifs de développement convenus au niveau international et la concrétisation du partenariat mondial pour le développement auxquelles dépend la réalisation de ces objectifs du Millénaire ;
- mobiliser les ressources pour la création d'un environnement propice à l'élimination de la pauvreté ;
- promouvoir l'approche intégrée du développement rural dans les pays en développement dans le but d'éliminer la pauvreté et encourager le développement durable ;
- faciliter la contribution des ressources humaines dans les domaines de la santé, l'éducation et le développement ;
- Examiner le développement africain, ce qui a d'ailleurs débouché sur la création du Nouveau Partenariat pour le développement de l'Afrique (NEPAD) ;

- remédier à la fracture numérique entre les pays ;
- exécuter les consultations sur la coopération inter institutions financières, à travers le contrôle et l'évaluation de la mise en œuvre du Consensus de Monterrey, l'approfondissement du dialogue entre l'Organisation des Nations unies et les institutions financières et commerciales internationales, sans oublier le renforcement de leur collaboration en vue de la réalisation des objectifs de développement convenus au niveau international.

La participation aux réunions de ce conseil s'est élargie depuis la réunion de 1998, quand elle fut ouverte au Conseil général de l'Organisation mondiale du commerce, à la Conférence des Nations Unies sur le Commerce et le développement (CNUCED), au président du Comité du développement de la Banque mondiale et au président du Comité monétaire et financier international du Fonds monétaire international.

Depuis quelques années, malgré les progrès accomplis dans l'amélioration de son efficacité et les efforts mis en œuvre pour consolider son rôle parmi les organes responsables de la coordination du système des Nations unies, il y a de plus en plus de voix qui s'élèvent au sein de la communauté internationale pour demander fermement le renforcement de son rôle. Le souhait est de lui donner plus de pouvoirs au sein du système de la gouvernance des Nations unies et en ce qui concerne la gestion de l'économie mondiale. C'est ainsi qu'il s'est vu confier le rôle d'effectuer le suivi intégré et la coordination de l'application des textes issus des grandes conférences et réunions, organisées par les Nations unies. Par conséquent, depuis 2005, les pouvoirs du Conseil Economique et Social ne cessent de s'accroître. C'est à lui qu'incombe la charge :

- d'organiser les examens ministériels annuels sur les questions de fond, dans le but d'évaluer les progrès accomplis dans l'application des textes issus de grandes conférences et réunion organisées par les Nations unies, y compris celle des objectifs de développement convenus au plan international. Autrement dit, il appartient au Conseil d'établir le bilan des progrès accomplis dans la mise en œuvre du programme de développement des Nations unies, notamment dans la réalisation des objectifs du Millénaire pour le développement :
- d'offrir un cadre approprié permettant d'engager un débat sur les politiques et tendances mondiales dans les domaines économique, social, environnemental et humanitaire ;
- de tenir tous les deux ans, à New York, un forum sur la coopération en matière de développement afin d'examiner les tendances de la coopération internationale pour le développement. Cela signifie qu'il doit analyser les questions relatives à la qualité et la quantité d'aide, en vue de formuler des recommandations concernant les politiques et les

pratiques susceptibles d'améliorer la cohérence et l'efficacité dans le domaine du développement ;
- d'organiser des réunions ad hoc sur des crises humanitaires spécifiques qui sont sollicitées par les autorités internationales compétentes ;
- de continuer à expérimenter des interventions dans le domaine de la consolidation de la paix après les conflits.

e. Conseil de Sécurité

Le Conseil de Sécurité est l'organe exécutif de l'Organisation des Nations unies. Il est composé de quinze (15) membres dont dix (10) membres non-permanents, élus pour un mandat de deux ans, par l'Assemblée générale et cinq membres permanents qui sont : les Etats-Unis, la Fédération de Russie, la France, la Chine et le Royaume-Uni.

Dans le jargon onusien on utilise l'acronyme « P5 » pour désigner ces cinq membres permanents qui sont détenteurs du droit de veto. Ils disposent de la responsabilité principale dans les opérations du maintien de la paix et de la sécurité internationale.

La Charte de l'ONU donne au Conseil de Sécurité des pouvoirs spécifiques, tels que :

- le maintien de la paix et la sécurité internationale qui se justifie pour les raisons de rapidité et d'efficacité des actions de l'ONU ;
- l'établissement de sanctions internationales ;
- les interventions militaires ;
- l'initiative d'entreprendre des actions en cas de menace contre la paix, de rupture de la paix et d'acte d'agression.

Ce Conseil rend des décisions appelées résolutions. Ces dernières ont force exécutoire et les Etats Membres sont priés de les accepter et les appliquer. En revanche, les membres du Conseil de Sécurité doivent toujours être présents en permanence au siège, car ils peuvent être appelés à se réunir à tout moment, notamment en cas de crise exceptionnelle, ce qui n'était pas autorisé par la Charte de la Société des Nations (SDN), organe qui a précédé l'ONU.

Il fonctionne de la manière suivante :

- une « présidence tournante », selon l'ordre alphabétique anglais du nom des pays, pour assurer la Présidence pendant une période d'un mois chacun et ceux, à tour de rôle entre ses quinze (15) membres ;
- la possibilité pour les Etats non-membres du Conseil de Sécurité d'assister aux séances dudit Conseil lorsqu'ils sont mis en cause dans une affaire en cours de discussion, avec droit de réponse, mais sans droit de vote ;

- l'obligation de s'abstenir lors des votes du Conseil de Sécurité, pour les Etats Membres qui sont mis en cause dans l'affaire en discussion ;
- la participation du Secrétariat Général de l'ONU à toutes les séances du Conseil de Sécurité avec possibilité d'intervention, mais sans droit de vote.

Le Conseil de Sécurité est composé de plusieurs organes subsidiaires parmi lesquels :

- la commission de consolidation de la paix des Nations unies. Elle appuie les efforts de maintien de la paix dans les pays sortant d'un conflit, par la mobilisation des acteurs institutionnels comme, les gouvernements ou les ONG, mais aussi celle des ressources. Cette commission fait des recommandations stratégiques quant au développement ;
- le comité de sanctions qui est habilité à prendre des « mesures coercitives pour maintenir ou rétablir la paix et la sécurité internationales. » Ces sanctions peuvent être économiques ou caractérisées par une intervention militaire ;
- le comité contre le terrorisme. Il a la lourde tâche de tout mettre en « œuvre pour renforcer la capacité des Etats Membres à empêcher les actes de terrorisme sur leur sol, ainsi qu'au-delà » ;
- le comité 1540, du nom de la Résolution 1540, relative à la non-prolifération des armes de destruction massive. Il est chargé d'examiner la mise en œuvre par les pays membres ladite résolution. A cet effet, il doit périodiquement soumettre des rapports et, si nécessaire, faire des recommandations au Conseil de Sécurité à ce sujet ;
- le Conseil des droits de l'homme de l'ONU. C'est lui qui examine la question des droits de l'homme de tous les pays membres sur la base des documents que lesdits pays et les organisations indépendantes fournissent, en vue d'en améliorer le respect ;
- la force de maintien de la paix des Nations unies, communément connu sous le nom de Casques bleus, armée temporaire composée des militaires issus de différents pays membres, ayant pour rôle « le maintien ou le rétablissement de la paix et de la sécurité internationale » ;
- le fonds d'indemnisation des Nations unies, chargé d'étudier les demandes d'indemnisation et de verser des indemnités aux victimes koweïtiennes de l'invasion et occupation irakienne durant la première guerre du Golfe ;
- le Tribunal Pénal International pour l'ex-Yougoslavie qui siège à La Haye et qui est en charge de poursuivre et juger les présumés

responsables des violations graves des droits de l'homme durant les guerres en Croatie, en Bosnie-Herzégovine et au Kosovo ;

- Tribunal pénal international pour le Rwanda situé à Arusha. Il est conçu pour poursuivre et juger les présumés coupables des violations du droit international commis au Rwanda au cours du génocide de 1994 ;
- la commission de contrôle, de vérification et d'inspection des Nations unies qui s'occupe du dossier du désarmement de l'Irak et de ses armes de destruction massive. Il contrôle ce pays, au sens de l'empêcher de se procurer à nouveau ces mêmes armes ;
- le comité 1267, en charge des sanctions contre les talibans et Al-Qaïda, etc.

f. Secrétariat Général de L'ONU

Le Secrétariat Général est une institution au service des autres organes principaux de l'ONU. Il est composé d'environ 7 500 fonctionnaires recrutés sur le plan international et en poste dans divers lieux d'affectation à travers le monde. Le Secrétaire Général (SG) est le plus haut fonctionnaire de l'Organisation des Nations unies dont il est le chef par excellence. Il est nommé par le Conseil de Sécurité et ratifié par l'Assemblée générale pour un mandat de cinq ans renouvelable.

Le Secrétaire Général est chargé de remplir toutes les fonctions confiées par le Conseil de Sécurité, l'Assemblée générale, le Conseil économique et Social ou tous les autres organes de l'ONU. Sa fonction consiste aussi à attirer l'attention du Conseil de Sécurité sur toutes les affaires qu'il juge importantes.

Le Secrétariat Général est composé de plusieurs Départements dont celui des Opérations du Maintien de la Paix qui gère actuellement seize (16) opérations de maintien de la Paix et trois Missions Politiques à travers le monde, sans compter la Lybie et la Syrie :

- Organisme des Nations unies chargé de la surveillance de la Trêve (ONUST), c'est la première mission de maintien de la paix créée en 1948 au Moyen-Orient ;
- United Nations Military Observer Group in India and Pakistan (UNMOGIP), en français c'est le Groupe des Observateurs Militaires des Nations unies pour l'Inde et le Pakistan, 1949 ;
- United Nations Peacekeeping Force in Cyprus (UNFICYP) créée par la Résolution 186 du Conseil de Sécurité, en 1964 ;
- Force des Nations unies chargée d'observer le dégagement (FNUOD), établie en 1974 dans le conflit israélo-syrien sur le Golan ;
- Force intérimaire des Nations unies au Liban (FINUL), mise en place en 1978 par les résolutions 425 et 426 du Conseil de Sécurité ;

- Mission des Nations unies pour l'organisation d'un Referendum au Sahara Occidental (MINURSO), en septembre 1991. Il a été mis en place à la suite d'un accord entre le gouvernement du Maroc et le front POLISARIO ;
- Mission d'observation des Nations unies en Géorgie (MONUG), autorisée par la Résolution 858 du Conseil de Sécurité, en1993 ;
- Mission de l'Organisation des Nations unies au Congo-RDC (MONUC), créée par la Résolution 1279 le 30 novembre 1999, par le Conseil de Sécurité ;
- Mission des Nations unies en Angola (MINUA), créée en 2002, pour consolider la paix entre le gouvernement Angolais et l'UNITA de Jonas Savimbi ;
- Mission des Nations unies au Liberia (MINUL), établie le 19 septembre 2003, par la Résolution 1509 du Conseil de Sécurité ;
- Mission des Nations unies pour la Stabilisation en Haïti (MINUSTAH), créée en 2004, par la Résolution 1540 du Conseil de Sécurité ;
- Opération des Nations unies en Côte d'Ivoire (ONUCI), mise en place par la Résolution 1528 du Conseil de Sécurité, en 2004 ;
- Mission préparatoire des Nations unies au Soudan (MINUS), établie par la Résolution 1590 du Conseil de Sécurité du 24 mars 2005, pour appuyer l'accord de paix global signé le 09 janvier de la même année ;
- Mission Intégrée des Nations unies au Timor-Leste (MINUT), établie en 2006 par la Résolution 1704, dans le but de consolider la paix, promouvoir la gouvernance démocratique, faciliter le dialogue politique, lancer le processus de réconciliation et favoriser la cohésion sociale ;
- Bureau Intégré des Nations unies en Sierra Leone (BINUSIL), mise en place à travers la résolution 1734 du Conseil de Sécurité en 2006, Mission des Nations unies et de l'Union Africaine au Darfour (MINUAD), établie par le Conseil de Sécurité, à travers la Résolution 1769 du 31 juillet 2007 ;
- Bureau Intégré des Nations unies au Burundi (BINUB), crée en 2007, pour mettre en application la résolution 1719 du Conseil de Sécurité de 2006 ;
- Mission des Nations unies en République Centrafricaine et au Tchad (MINURCAT), mise en œuvre par la Résolution 1778 du 25 septembre 2007 du Conseil de Sécurité.

.Chacune de ces missions est soutenue par un mandat bien spécifique dans lequel les Affaires civiles de l'ONU puisent leur légitimité.

B. MANDAT DES AFFAIRES CIVILES

Le contexte politico-administratif des pays en situation de post-conflit est souvent, essentiellement caractérisé par un affaiblissement de l'Etat et par une instabilité politique et sécuritaire rendant le fonctionnement des collectivités territoriales très précaire. Aux carences d'une administration locale faible, vient se greffer un manque de moyens matériels auquel s'ajoute une rareté de ressources humaines qualifiées.

Entre autres, les élus locaux ont rarement une claire conscience de leurs prérogatives et des moyens d'intervention à leur portée. Pire encore, les assemblées municipales et les conseils/assemblées des collines ou sections communales sont totalement dépourvues ou n'ont pas assez de moyens, en termes de bureaux et matériels de base, pour travailler correctement. De plus, l'instabilité politique empêche de faire aboutir tout processus de décentralisation et de déconcentration et de faire réellement fonctionner certains prescrits de la Constitution de ces pays. On ne saurait quoi dire du manque accru de références légales qui retarde considérablement la bonne mise en place des institutions et le développement durable tendant vers une autonomie progressive des communautés locales.

A cet effet, les gouvernements de ces pays post-crise, plus particulièrement leurs Ministères des collectivités territoriales, doivent renforcer leurs structures et développer leurs capacités tant au niveau central qu'au niveau local, à travers les programmes d'appui institutionnel local, réalisés par la section des Affaires civiles. Ces programmes des Affaires civiles s'adressent non seulement aux collectivités territoriales, mais aussi aux institutions centrales.

Du coup, les gouvernements avertis font immédiatement appel aux compétences techniques des officiers des Affaires civiles qui répondent toujours favorablement dans le cadre d'un projet de renforcement institutionnel des structures centrales et des collectivités locales. Ce qui se fait dans le domaine législatif, le statut et les compétences pour concourir, essentiellement, au renforcement de la Direction des Collectivités Territoriales (DCT) du pays concerné, afin qu'elle puisse mieux exercer son mandat de tutelle. Globalement, cela se traduit par :

- l'inventaire des textes existants et du droit applicable régissant l'administration locale qui n'exclut pas les propositions de révision de certains textes ;
- l'élaboration ou la simplification d'un manuel sur l'organisation municipale ;
- la création d'une brochure informative/guide à l'intention des maires ;
- l'élaboration ou la mise à jour des modules de formation sur le cadre légale, la gestion municipale, les finances locales… ;

- l'appui aux structures de la direction des collectivités territoriales et aux services d'encadrement technique, par la rédaction des termes de référence et du cadre de travail, sans oublier une analyse institutionnelle de cette structure interne présente.

L'objectif est d'aboutir à des propositions de restructuration :

- l'encouragement à l'institutionnalisation des structures déconcentrées de l'Etat, par la formation des préfets, l'évaluation et la restructuration dans le cadre de l'administration, la comptabilité publique et le pouvoir de tutelle administrative ;
- la promotion de la coopération décentralisée, en favorisant et facilitant la coopération entre les mairies dudit pays et les collectivités territoriales étrangères.

L'assistance des Affaires civiles se prolonge aussi sur la rationalisation des finances publiques locales, en matière de recettes et dépenses, pour garantir l'équité sociale au sein de l'administration municipale et surtout pour assurer un contrôle des fonds propres de chaque commune. En ce sens, les Affaires civiles doivent fournir un appui substantiel à la modernisation des services financiers des communes, en vue de garantir la maîtrise des dépenses et recettes locales. Cela est possible grâce au développement d'outils financiers, de contrôle, de vulgarisation et de formation.

Concomitamment, les Affaires civiles doivent assister le gouvernement à établir un fonds de développement crédible des communes, élaborer les conditions d'accès à ce fonds et prévoir un mode de gestion et d'allocation de ses ressources. Il appartient aux Affaires civiles de mettre l'accent sur la bonne gestion des services de base, notamment, en ce qui concerne les différents modes de gestion des infrastructures de base. Le but est d'étudier, d'adapter et de mettre en œuvre ces infrastructures pour améliorer la desserte de services publics à la population et favoriser un meilleur développement économique local. C'est le cas, par exemple, des marchés communaux, des abattoirs, des gares routières…

Bref, les Affaires civiles jouent le rôle d'assistant technique et de facilitateur auprès du gouvernement central et des collectivités territoriales. Elles sont chargées de revoir, de mettre en forme, de planifier et de coordonner les différentes actions dans le cadre de la modernisation de l'Etat et de la réalisation de la décentralisation. Elles aident aussi à dispenser et assurer la coordination de tous les programmes de formation relative à la gestion et au fonctionnement des collectivités locales, des partis politiques et de la société civile.

Politiquement parlant, les activités menées par les officiers des Affaires civiles servent à rétablir la confiance, contrôler la gestion des conflits et soutenir le développement de l'espace politique et des institutions, notamment : les conditions sociales et civiques propices à la paix durable, l'engagement populaire et la confiance dans le processus de paix. Bien entendu, cela varie d'une mission à l'autre et selon le mandat puis le contexte.

Plus spécifiquement, les Affaires civiles concentrent leurs efforts à :

- assurer la liaison avec les collectivités locales et faciliter le développement de la compréhension culturelle ;
- faire l'analyse des conflits, donner l'alerte préventive, collecter les informations sur l'évaluation des besoins en matière de protection des civils et sur leur situation socio-économique ;
- identifier les partenariats potentiels et établir les possibilités de coopération et de coordination avec d'autres acteurs militaires et humanitaires ;
- organiser des activités de reprise de la confiance dans l'exécution des QIP, en s'appuyant autant que possible sur la participation, les priorités et les capacités des communautés et des autorités locales ;
- promouvoir les activités liées à l'amélioration de l'espace politique au niveau local, surtout en période de transition politique pré-électorale ;
- planifier des activités liées à la confiance et la gestion des conflits ;
- Soutenir les institutions publiques au niveau local, régional et central dans le cadre de la coordination avec les autres acteurs de tout bord, notamment dans un environnement politique mature ou en situation postélectorale.

Vers la fin de la mission, elles servent souvent à :

- évaluer les attitudes et préoccupations concernant les questions liées à la transmission du témoin aux autorités locales ;
- sensibiliser les communautés à gérer eux-mêmes, leurs attentes et les préoccupations de la population ;
- analyser continuellement le contexte local et prévenir les situations sécuritaires ;
- transférer les activités d'évaluation aux élus locaux et analyser les lacunes potentielles au niveau local.

Toutes ces activités des Affaires civiles puisent leurs sources dans les résolutions du Conseil de Sécurité portant création d'une mission de maintien de la paix. En réalité, c'est cette résolution qui définit le champ d'action de la mission, c'est-à-dire le mandat.

Par exemple, la résolution 1861 du Conseil de Sécurité du 14 janvier 2009, portant création de la mission de l'ONU pour le Tchad et la République centrafricaine (MINURCAT) demande aux Casques bleus de : « ...soutenir les initiatives des autorités nationales et locales au Tchad afin de résoudre les tensions locales et promouvoir les efforts de réconciliation au niveau local, afin d'améliorer l'environnement pour le retour des personnes déplacées à l'intérieur... »

La résolution 1856 du Conseil de sécurité du 22 décembre 2008 donne mandat à la mission de l'ONU en République démocratique du Congo (MONUC), dans les termes suivants : «... promouvoir la réconciliation nationale et le dialogue politique interne, notamment par la fourniture de bons offices et appuyer le renforcement de la société civile... » La mission des Nations unies en Afghanistan (MANUA) a reçu le mandat du Conseil de Sécurité à travers la résolution 1662 du 23 mars 2006, confirmée par la résolution 1746 du 23 mars de l'année suivante pour : « ...fournir un soutien politique de sensibilisation à travers une présence renforcée et élargie dans tout le pays ; offrir ses bons offices à l'appui de programmes de réconciliation menés par les Afghans… » S'agissant de la résolution 1769 du Conseil de sécurité du 31 juillet 2007, pour la MINUAD, au Darfour, elle demande à : « ...faciliter la préparation et la conduite du dialogue Darfour-Darfour et de la consultation, tel que stipulé dans l'accord de paix sur le Darfour... » Enfin, le Conseil de sécurité, par la résolution 1870 du 30 avril 2009 invite les Casques bleus de la MINUS, au Soudan, à : « ...renforcer ses capacités de gestion des conflits en remplissant, dès que possible, sa stratégie intégrée de soutien des tribus locales des mécanismes de résolution des conflits... » Une fois ce mandat définit, l'Assemblée générale détermine et autorise le budget de l'opération de maintien de la paix. Tous les Pays Membres apportent ainsi, une certaine contribution au financement du coût des opérations. La répartition des charges est faite par l'Assemblée générale selon un barème de participations propres aux opérations de maintien de la paix. Ce barème tient compte de la situation économique de chaque Etat Membre pour la détermination de leur quote-part.

Généralement, le Conseil de Sécurité demande aux Casques bleus, dans les limites de leur mandat, d'assister le gouvernement dans le renforcement des institutions de l'Etat, y compris en fournissant des services spécialisés aux principaux ministères de la République concernée. Grosso modo, une mission de maintien de la paix est appelée à :

- aider le gouvernement à renforcer les institutions de l'Etat, en particulier dans le domaine de la décentralisation ;
- appuyer le processus constitutionnel et politique ;
- favoriser le dialogue et la réconciliation nationale ;
- participer à la résolution des conflits et à la médiation au niveau communautaire ;
- fournir un soutien sur le plan logistique et au niveau de la sécurité dans la perspective des élections démocratiques et transparentes ;
- aider au rétablissement et au maintien de l'état de droit ;
- assurer la sécurité et l'ordre publics ;
- instaurer une coordination optimale de façon à lutter contre la criminalité et la violence ;

- encourager la bonne gouvernance, essentiellement dans la restructuration de l'administration publique locale.

Il s'agit aussi :

- de promouvoir la sécurité et la stabilité ;
- d'appuyer les institutions du pays accrédité dans le rétablissement de l'Etat de droit, à travers une réforme et/ou une restructuration de la police et de la justice d'un pays ;
- d'appuyer l'Etat dans les processus électoraux ;
- de contribuer à la promotion et au respect des droits de l'homme et à la mise en œuvre des programmes de désarmement, de démobilisation, de réinsertion et de réinstallation (DDRR).

Ce dernier aspect est souvent lié à la lutte contre la violence communautaire, qui reste centrée sur :

- les efforts de réalisation des projets à haute intensité de main-d'œuvre comme solution alternative à la violence armée ;
- l'ouverture de registre des armes ;
- la révision des lois en vigueur en matière d'importation ;
- la détention d'armes et la réforme du régime des permis de port d'armes.

C'est donc à l'intérieur de ce mandat que les Affaires civiles discernent la légitimité de leurs interventions. En effet, les termes du mandat précisent toujours les objectifs de la mission. Dans ce vaste champ d'action, les Affaires civiles se focalisent surtout sur l'appui institutionnel et le renforcement de l'Etat à travers le pays. Elles agissent aussi dans le cadre de la réforme de l'Etat de droit ainsi qu'au soutien des efforts du gouvernement dans le processus du dialogue et dans les démarches de réconciliation nationale. Les Affaires civiles mettent à la disposition du gouvernement concerné leurs compétences techniques pour l'aider à réaliser une approche globale de la gestion des frontières. Mais, il faut reconnaître qu'il n'appartient pas toujours aux Affaires civiles de déployer des patrouilles le long des frontières maritimes et terrestres, en appui aux activités menées par la police national dudit pays ni d'assurer la sécurité des frontières.

L'appui Institutionnel et le renforcement des capacités de l'Etat se font à deux niveaux : au niveau central et au niveau local. Au niveau central, les Affaires civiles fournissent des conseils et une assistance technique au gouvernement, en vue de renforcer les capacités législatives du parlement et les capacités exécutives des ministères. Tandis qu'au niveau local, il s'agit d'apporter une assistance technique aux autorités départementales, municipales, collinaires et autres, à travers des formations, séminaires, réunions-débats… Dans le domaine particulier d'appui à la gestion intégrée des frontières, il s'agit d'appuyer techniquement les autorités centrales et locales dans l'élaboration du plan de gestion des frontières. En outre, il s'agit de faciliter la mise en place des patrouilles le long des frontières terrestres et maritimes. La contribution économique des Affaires civiles dans le développement locale est caractérisée par la réalisation des projets à effet rapide. Ces financements de projets d'organisations ou d'institutions locales sur tout le territoire national du pays en question sont destinés à aider le gouvernement à renforcer les institutions étatiques pour :

- répondre aux besoins immédiats de la population, notamment en eau potable, assainissement et pour réhabilitation d'infrastructure...
- appuyer les autorités locales dans la mise en place des structures d'État à travers la réhabilitation des mairies et des palais de justice, ainsi que la formation des contrôleurs financiers et autres agents techniques des collectivités territoriales, bref, à produire des trousses de démarrages pour les mairies…
- aider les populations dans les zones sensibles avec la construction des écoles, le nettoyage de canaux, l'aménagement de parcs...

En gros, voilà ce que font les Affaires civiles pendant plusieurs années jusqu'à la fin de la mission de maintien de la paix qui prend fin selon trois modalités :

- action du gouvernement d'accueil ;
- action du Secrétaire Général de l'Organisation des Nations unies ;
- usage du veto par l'un des cinq membres permanents du Conseil de Sécurité de l'ONU.

Dans la première hypothèse, le gouvernement d'accueil décide de mettre un terme à la mission lorsqu'il estime, soit que celle-ci n'est plus nécessaire, ou soit que les objectifs prévus par le Conseil de Sécurité dans la résolution portant création ou renouvèlement du mandat de la mission ont été atteints. Dans ce cas, la procédure est simple. Il avise le Secrétariat Général des Nations unies de cette décision. Ce dernier, à son tour, fait des recommandations au Conseil de Sécurité qui prendra une nouvelle résolution pour mettre un terme au mandat. Cette dernière résolution doit aussi être publiée en bonne et due forme, selon les règles procédurales des Nations unies.

Le deuxième cas de figure est celui d'une décision unilatérale du Secrétaire Général de l'organisation des Nations unies, eu égard aux différents points du mandat ayant été exécutés. Le cas échéant, si le chef par excellence du Secrétariat de l'ONU estime que les objectifs de la mission sont atteints, il fait des recommandations au Conseil de Sécurité. Ce dernier, comme dans le cas précédent, décide en prenant une résolution qui va mettre un terme au mandat de la mission. Comme toujours cette résolution doit aussi faire l'objet d'une publication.

La troisième et dernière hypothèse est celle du veto d'un des cinq membres permanents du Conseil de Sécurité des Nations unies contre le renouvellement du mandat de la mission. En effet, il suffit qu'un de ces cinq membres permanent du Conseil de Sécurité décide qu'il ne faut pas renouveler le mandat ; fort de son droit de veto, la mission doit prendre fin. Puisque le mandat n'est pas renouvelé, les Affaires civiles et les autres composantes de la mission sont remerciées. Il arrive aussi que les Affaires Civiles payent les frais avant les autres sections, lorsqu'on applique le non-renouvellement, surtout si la hiérarchie juge sa présence non indispensable. Cela a été le cas de l'ONUB (Mission de l'Organisation des Nations unies au Burundi). Lorsque le BINUB (Bureau Intégré des Nations unies au Burundi) a remplacé l'ONUB en 2006, les Affaires civiles avaient été l'une des premières sections à plier bagage.

Toutefois, pour les missions de maintien de la paix le Conseil de Sécurité de l'ONU prévoit deux types de mandat : le mandat exécutif qui est très rare, mais qui entraine la substitution des autorités du pays par le staff de la mission des Nations unies. Ce mandat donne pleins pouvoirs à la mission des Nations unies, au point d'effacer ou de faire main basse temporairement sur la souveraineté de l'Etat d'accueil d'une mission. Ainsi, il est possible, le cas échéant, de faire le travail à la place des autorités locales, en grappillant, à l'évidence, légèrement sur la souveraineté du pays concerné.

Le mandat d'appui reste le plus courant. Il permet aux Casques bleus civils d'appuyer, soutenir et conseiller les administrateurs de base du pays bénéficiaire. Ce mandat d'assistance oblige à ne faire que des propositions, en se limitant uniquement, à prodiguer des conseils sur le management et le fonctionnement. En aucun cas les autorités sont obligées de suivre les conseils des Affaires civiles.

Pour mieux comprendre ces conseils qui peuvent être apportés aux collectivités territoriales, il va falloir se lancer dans un débroussaillage sémantique qui suit une courbe suffisamment logique, basée sur la définition et l'analyse des concepts.

II. Esquisse de définition et analyse des concepts

La mise aux points sur les notions clés du mandat d'une mission des Nations unies, fondatrice de l'intervention des Affaires civiles dans les missions de maintien de la paix consiste à expliciter les termes qui justifient les actions et les relations avec les collectivités territoriales et l'Etat. Il s'agit d'apporter une clarification sur les concepts de :

- affaires civiles ;
- renforcement des Capacités ;
- société civile ;
- gouvernance et bonne gouvernance ;
- collectivités territoriales ;
- l'Etat de droit.

A. L'EXPRESSION AFFAIRES CIVILES

Qu'est-ce que les Affaires civiles (AC) ?

Le mot est américain. On le retrouve notamment au sein de l'armée américaine qui en consacre des bataillons spéciaux, constitués des réserves des soldats des Affaires civiles, à l'instar du 411ème bataillon des Affaires civiles qui avait conduit l'évaluation de la reconstruction des égouts sanitaires à Bagdad, le 11 juin 2003. C'est une section à part entière tenue par des officiers militaires qu'il convient d'analyser (a) avant de rechercher la signification du concept « Affaires civiles » dans le langage onusien (b).

a. Le Terme Affaires civiles au Sens de l'Armée Américaine

Né après la Seconde Guerre mondiale, les membres de ce corps spécial des Affaires civiles de l'armée américaine ont, depuis lors, été pratiquement engagés dans toutes les guerres, dans tous les conflits et/ou dans toutes les situations du même genre, impliquant les Etats-Unis. Aussi, depuis cinquante (50) ans, ces hommes et ces femmes des Affaires civiles de l'armée des Etats-

Unis ne cessent de s'adapter aux changements de la nature des guerres, pour rester relativement constant, sinon se perfectionner pour être en mesure d'aider le commandement militaire à améliorer leurs relations avec les communautés locales et internationales, en vue de légitimer leurs missions vis-à-vis de la population. Ces soldats des Affaires civiles de l'Armée américaine partent en formation, au commandement des opérations civilo-militaires et psychologiques à Fort Bragg, en Caroline du Nord. Ils sont sous le commandement d'un général de division du cadre de réserve, qui lui-même est subordonné au commandement des opérations spéciales également situé à Fort Bragg.

L'unité des Affaires civiles de l'armée américaine est essentiellement composée des soldats et des experts civils travaillant pour l'armée : médecins, ingénieurs, policiers, pompiers, banquiers, informaticiens, agronomes et autres, qui fournissent une expertise critique à l'Etat en question et permettent aux gouvernements d'évaluer les besoins des projets d'infrastructure cruciaux tels que les routes, dispensaires, écoles, centrales électriques, installations de traitement d'eau, et cetera. Dans une situation de guerre, les projets choisis sont traités dans des centres civils et militaires, avant d'être attribués aux entrepreneurs locaux et c'est l'équipe des Affaires civiles qui fait périodiquement le suivi des travaux, en vérifiant essentiellement, la bonne gestion de l'argent dépensé.

En réalité, historiquement parlant, le terme « Affaires civiles » a émergé dans le vocabulaire de l'armée américaine avec l'expression anglaise « *Military Operations Other Than War* (MOOTW) » qui signifie « opérations autres que la guerre », pour faire une distinction avec les opérations de combat à grande échelle. Ce vocable s'inscrit dans la continuité historique d'une philosophie doctrinal appelée « *limited war* (LW) », c'est-à-dire « guerres limitées », ce qui renforce la théorie de « Low Intensity Conflict (LIC) », qui se traduit par : les « conflits de basses intensités. »

Cette conception va gagner ses lettres de noblesse vers la fin des années 1970 et au cours des années 1980 qui avaient été caractérisées par les débats stratégiques destinés à tirer les leçons de l'expérience vietnamienne et à mener la guerre contre une variété de conflictualités concernant : la prise d'otages, les attentats terroristes, les guérillas, la lutte contre le trafic de drogue, les opérations de maintien de la paix... En 1992, les Affaires civiles vont se fondre dans la doctrine d'Anthony Lake, du nom du conseiller à la sécurité nationale de l'ancien Président américain, Bill Clinton, avec la théorie des « rogue states », autrement dit « les Etats-voyous. » Cette philosophie sera officialisée en 1993, par le biais de la publication du manuel des opérations de l'armée de terre, intitulé « Field Manual100-5. » Ce sera la première fois que ce concept « opérations autres que la guerre » fera l'objet d'un chapitre spécifique étalant au grand jour les principes et la conduite à tenir dans une certaine catégorie d'opérations.

De nos jours, l'impact des résultats des bombardements militaires sur la population civile n'est plus à démontrer. Les interventions des forces armées occidentales au Kosovo, en Bosnie, en Irak, en Afghanistan, en Haïti, en Somalie, puis ailleurs, témoignent du poids qui pèse sur la population civile dans de pareilles circonstances. Ce qui fait que, de plus en plus, les succès des engagements militaires ne sont plus garantis lorsque la population locale est hostile ou récalcitrante. Une telle situation affaiblit non seulement le moral des troupes, mais aussi relâche, diminue le soutien national et international, au point qu'elle exige davantage d'effectifs pour sécuriser les lignes de communication et assurer la sauvegarde des forces intervenantes.

Or, c'est justement ce soutien, notamment celui de la communauté internationale qui facilite les opérations des forces engagées et aide les troupes à atteindre les objectifs politiques, mais aussi économiques et sociales, puis contribue de surcroît, à créer un environnement plus sûr.

Aussi, pour pallier cette éventualité l'armée américaine a créé, en son sein, un corps spécial appartenant à l'unité des Affaires civiles, qui est organisé, équipé et entrainé pour des missions civilo-militaires, en vue d'aider le commandement militaire à établir des relations avec la population civile.

Selon la « *Joint Doctrine for Military Operations Other Than War* » publié le 16 juin 1995 dans Joint Publication 3-07, « les opérations militaires qui se distinguent des opérations de combat à grande échelle » constituent une option stratégique intermédiaire entre la guerre et la paix, puisqu'elles répondent à la nécessité de contrer les menaces non conventionnelles et asymétriques. Elles permettent de prendre en compte la situation des civils, au sens de ne pas ignorer leur souffrance, ainsi que les risques qu'ils encourent lors d'une opération militaire. Cette doctrine puise ses fondements dans :

- le Code Lieber[9] de 1863 ;
- les accords de La Haye de 1899 établissant que la distinction entre les forces armées et la population civile sont déterminants, car même si la population peut participer aux hostilités, il n'en demeure pas moins qu'elle doit être protégée et ce, sur la base de ce qui deviendra les accords de 1954 concernant la protection, non seulement des personnes, mais aussi des biens culturels, en cas de conflit armé ;
- les Conventions de Genève de 1949 et leurs protocoles additionnels.

---

[9] Du nom du juriste et philosophe politique germano-américain, Francis Lieber, le Code Lieber, aussi connu sous le nom de : « Instructions for the Government of Armies of the United States in the Field » ou « Instructions Lieber » est un acte signé par le président Lincoln le 24 avril 1863, codifiant l'attitude à adopter de la part des forces de l'Union pendant la guerre de Sécession. C'est un texte du droit international humanitaire qui codifie la loi martiale, la juridiction militaire, le traitement des espions, traîtres et prisonniers de guerre.

Au fond, lorsqu'on se soumet à l'examen de la pensée, cette philosophie de l'armée américaine ne fait aucune distinction entre les opérations de combat et les opérations de maintien de la paix. Le moins que l'on puisse dire est que, ce sont des interventions mixtes comportant les relations des forces militaires avec les autorités civiles, les organisations non gouvernementales (ONG), les organisations internationales (OI) et les populations dans les zones d'hostilité. Ces interventions sont donc éminemment politiques, au point qu'elles peuvent se définir comme une mise en œuvre des compétences spécialisées de l'armée dans des domaines qui sont normalement du ressort du gouvernement civil.

En réalité, les Affaires civiles de l'armée américaine appuient directement, d'abord et avant tout le commandement militaire même si la population civile et les organisations civiles peuvent également bénéficier de ce soutien. Elles soutiennent l'administration et les organisations civiles, sachant que le commandement militaire profitera de ces prérogatives. D'ailleurs, selon la doctrine militaire américaine, les généralistes et les spécialistes des actions civiles peuvent être requis pour appuyer les opérations civilo-militaires, en fonction des exigences de la mission et des intentions du commandement dans une zone d'opérations indiquée.

Ce personnel, techniquement qualifié et expérimenté, apporte donc une expertise dans plusieurs domaines variés de compétences fonctionnelles que nous pouvons regrouper sous les appellations génériques de service : gouvernementaux, économiques, publics, spéciaux. Principalement, il s'agit de :

- soutenir les relations du commandement militaire avec les autorités et la population civile ;
- valoriser ou encourager la légitimité de la mission ;
- renforcer l'efficacité militaire.

La rapidité d'intervention et les compétences spéciales de ces soldats civilo-militaires assurent au commandement de l'armée de terre des Etats-Unis, à tous les niveaux, la liberté d'action nécessaire dans l'accomplissement de sa tâche, tout en réduisant les interférences avec la population, comme quoi l'enjeu est bel et bien politique.

« *Train for War, Adapt for Peace*[10] » est l'ancien slogan du département de la défense américaine qui a pris une autre dimension avec les différents types d'expériences des opérations autres que la guerre. Ces dernières sont venues alimenter le débat sur la nécessité d'adapter l'armée américaine à de nouvelles tâches civiles. Il s'agit de faire en sorte que, lorsque les objectifs politiques de l'intervention sont modifiés, les soldats puissent toujours assumer des missions en dehors de leur sphère de compétences.

---

[10] Entraîné pour la guerre, adapté pour la paix

Le double syndrome du Vietnam et de la Somalie ayant donné naissance à la notion de « *mission creep* » qui traduit l'idée d'« enlisement » ou de « glissement de la mission » justifie, à lui seul, la nécessité de la transformation d'une mission d'engagement des troupes en mission d'assistance humanitaire. Bien entendu, historiquement et culturellement, certains militaires américains sont réticents à assumer de telles responsabilités.

Le journal des forces américaines, « *National Military Strategy* », révélait en 2004, le contenu de ces récentes missions mixtes qui consistent à transformer très rapidement une opération strictement militaire en mission post-conflictuelle que les Anglais appellent « multi-mission capable. » Ce journal souligne aussi la possibilité de synchroniser les opérations de combats majeurs et les opérations de stabilisation, où les troupes qui mènent la bataille, peuvent également être amenées à assurer le rôle de « gardiens de la paix. » Pourtant, elles ont été entraînées, dans le cadre spécifique de la « Révolution dans les Affaires Militaires » (RAM), pour les combats de haute intensité et non pour entreprendre des activités de police et/ou de maintien de la paix.

L'unité d'action civile de l'armée américaine est donc adaptée à des missions sur mesure. Elle répond aux besoins initiaux des forces armées au début d'une opération de circonstance ayant une vocation internationale, tout au moins, celles à qui il conviendrait manifestement de donner une crédibilité au niveau international. En effet, elle :

- peut-être mobilisée et déployée rapidement n'importe où dans le monde ;
- complète les équipes locales des ambassades américaines, d'autres organismes gouvernementaux, ainsi que des forces multinationales, mission qu'elle accomplit par le biais d'une assistance dans la planification, la coordination et le contrôle des activités des Affaires civiles, destinées à appuyer des opérations civilo-militaires ;
- renforce les états-majors des commandements géographiques, de la terre d'affrontements et opérationnels, jusqu'au niveau des bataillons.

Dans le même ordre d'idées, il n'est pas vain de préciser que le soutien à l'administration civile consiste à remplir les obligations découlant des traités, accords ou de la législation internationale. Dans ces zones de combat, l'impératif principal des Affaires civiles est d'appuyer les opérations spéciales et les forces conventionnelles au niveau tactique, opérationnel et stratégique.

Composées essentiellement de réserves, ces Affaires civiles sont réparties entre quatre commandements subordonnés aux commandements régionaux des Affaires civiles qui appuient respectivement les quatre commandements géographiques, à savoir : le commandement de la zone pacifique et Europe auquel fait partie le Moyen-Orient et, celui de la zone située au sud des Etats-Unis, comprenant l'Amérique centrale et l'Amérique du Sud.

En ce qui concerne le soutien à l'administration civile, il convient de souligner qu'il se présente sous trois formes différentes et générales :

- assistance civile ;
- administration civile en territoire ami ;
- administration civile en territoire occupé, faisant appel aux spécialistes de l'unité de réserve des Affaires civiles de l'armée des Etats unis, tandis que les autres fonctions peuvent être assurées par des généralistes.

De ce fait, l'unité d'action civile conseille et assiste le commandement des opérations. En ce sens, elle dirige l'équivalent civil du commandement. En pratique, l'autorité nationale de commandement fixe le type et l'importance du soutien que peuvent fournir les forces américaines.

Formés en permanence sur la base d'une étude par pays, ces hommes et ces femmes ayant reçu de nombreux entraînements et des déploiements opérationnels en tant qu'officiers des Affaires civiles, fond montre d'une capacité opérationnelle à mener des opérations dans les régions qui leur sont assignées.

Cette spécialisation régionale acquise au cours de ces expériences, une fois associée à la sensibilisation culturelle spécifique, donne à ces soldats des Affaires civiles une maîtrise adéquate aux plans du théâtre des opérations, aux plans des circonstances, aux plans fonctionnels et dans la prise des initiatives du commandant en chef. Du reste, cela constitue un ensemble d'outils nécessaires à l'établissement de liens avec les communautés locales et internationales.

A l'origine, les opérations autres que la guerre couvraient uniquement les « opérations en temps de paix », à l'instar de l'assistance aux autorités civiles américaines et étrangères, aux opérations de combat de courte durée, en passant par des opérations post-conflit, à savoir :

- contrôle d'armes ;
- lutte contre le terrorisme ;
- assistance au département de la défense pour les opérations de contre-insurrection ;
- assistance et opérations humanitaires ;
- assistance militaire aux autorités civiles ;
- opération non-combattante d'évacuation ;
- opérations de la paix.

Toutes ces opérations propres aux opérations autres que la guerre forment deux groupes d'opérations : opérations de stabilité et opérations d'assistance. Leurs points forts sont :

- la clarté de la définition des objectifs ;
- l'unité des efforts ;

- la sécurité des troupes et de la population locale.

Trois autres critères viennent se greffer à celui de la clarté de la définition des objectifs.

D'abord, il y a le critère de légitimité qui justifie l'opération menée à laquelle les Affaires civiles de l'armée des Etats Unis jouent le rôle primordial consistant à façonner les perceptions locales et internationales de la légitimité de l'opération.

Ensuite, il y a le critère de persévérance qui permet de penser et d'évaluer chaque action en fonction de son impact sur une stratégie sur le long terme.

Enfin, il y a le critère de modération dans l'usage des armes, des tactiques, de la proportionnalité de la réponse à une menace. Ce principe se situe à l'extrême opposé de la « guerre totale » où tout est permis, y compris le recours immodéré à la violence et aux armes les plus destructrices. Certes qu'il n'interdit pas le recours à une force écrasante en réponse à une menace qui le justifierait, mais il reconnaît que l'usage de la force doit se faire avec prudence et modération dans la mesure du possible. En outre, il convient d'en faire l'ultime recours dans la résolution des conflits.

On ne saurait ignorer le principe de la versatilité « versatility », qui sous-tend tous les autres principes, à savoir la nécessaire flexibilité et la modularité des forces militaires américaines opérant dans les opérations autres que la guerre. La particularité de ce critère est de requérir une armée capable de transformer rapidement les missions de combat en missions de contre-insurrection ou de reconstruction, d'assistance humanitaire et pourquoi pas mener les deux simultanément, en vue de construire et de consolider la paix, après l'intervention militaire.

A titre d'illustrations, on peut citer l'intervention des éléments du *96th Civil Affairs battalion* d'active, rejoints par des réservistes et les agents d'USAID, pour rétablir les « services publics essentiels » avant qu'une nouvelle infrastructure politique ne soit mise en place en Grenade, en 1983, lors de l'opération appelée « *urgent fury.* »

En 1989, ce fut le tour du Panama avec l'opération qualifiée « *Just Cause.* » Le cas échéant, trois cents (300) réservistes sont intervenus avec 120 militaires d'active du *96th Civil Affairs Batallion*, au sein de *Civil-Military Task Force* qui avait pour mission de contribuer à la « reconstruction politique » et à la mise en place d'un gouvernement favorable aux Etats-Unis.

Nul n'est censé ignorer l'opération « *Provide Comfort »* en Irak, en 1991, où le *353rd Civil Affairs Command* et les unités du *432nd Civil Affairs Battalion*, ainsi que le *431st Civil Affairs Battalion* apportaient une assistance humanitaire à la population civile. Que dirait-on de l'opération « *Restore Hope »* en Somalie en 1992 ? Cette fois encore, le *96th Civil Affairs Batallion* et des groupes d'opérations psychologiques (psyops) opéraient des tâches d'assistance humanitaire aux côtés des troupes de combats.

Le cas le plus récent est celui d'Haïti en 1994, dénommée « *Uphold Democracy* » où des équipes aux Affaires civiles mises en place par l'ambassade des Etats-Unis et USAID ont assisté le gouvernement d'Haïti à entreprendre les tâches de reconstruction et de développement[11]. Après le séisme du 12 janvier 2010 qui a ravagé la capitale de ce pays, les officiers des Affaires civiles de l'armée américaine ont été, une fois de plus, très actifs dans les actions humanitaires.

Bref, avec la multiplication de ce type d'interventions, le rôle des militaires américains n'a cessé de devenir de plus en plus complexe. Ces derniers vont petit à petit s'orienter vers des activités de maintien de la paix, des fonctions humanitaires, de reconstruction d'Etats effondrés et de lutte contre le terrorisme. C'est aussi dans cette optique que l'armée américaine des Etats-Unis décida de se doter d'un corps spécial des Affaires civiles délégué à la gestion des activités traditionnellement considérées comme civiles, aux hommes et femmes qui sont qualifiés de « spécialistes de cultures étrangères. » Ils sont sélectionnés en raison de leur formation, ce qui les amène à mieux connaître et comprendre l'environnement sur lequel ils opèrent. Par conséquent, cela place certaines unités de l'armée américaine dans un environnement politique qui contribue à « délégitimer » et marginaliser ce savoir-faire non spécifiquement militaire au sein des troupes.

Malheureusement, l'inconvénient majeur du travail de ces officiers des Affaires civiles est d'être toujours, jusqu'à preuve du contraire, relayé au second plan au profit du personnel plus militarisé qui assume théoriquement ces besognes, malgré le fait que ces missions incluent la fonction de soutien à l'administration civile. Cette volonté d'isolation des devoirs civils, empêche de faire une véritable réflexion en termes d'avantage comparatif des unités spécialisées dans la gestion des questions relatives aux Affaires civiles et les actions purement militaires.

Selon la stratégie de l'armée américaine, l'unité des Affaires civiles a pour mission d'aider les commandants militaires, en travaillant avec les autorités civiles et les sociétés civiles dans la zone de commandement des opérations militaires. Elle a la responsabilité de diminuer l'impact de ces opérations sur la population civile innocente au cours du rétablissement de la paix et des opérations d'urgence. C'est en principe, l'unité d'expertise en matière civile qui sert de pont entre un commandant et la société civile dans la conduite des opérations militaires.

---

[11] Voir Alexandra de Hoop Scheffer, Politologue, Institut d'Etudes Politiques de Paris, « L'Irak, cinq ans après : entre reconstruction et déconstruction », Questions Internationales n°31, La documentation française, Paris, 2009 ;
« Le rôle des militaires dans la reconstruction d'Etats après les conflits ». Etude commandée par le Ministère de la défense, Centre d'Etudes en Sciences Sociales de la Défense (C2SD), Paris, janvier 2008.

Cette unité assure aussi la liaison entre la présence militaire et les habitants civils d'une zone de guerre ou de catastrophe. Son rôle est à la fois d'informer le commandant local de l'état de la population civile sur le moral et l'assistance à la population locale affectée par les opérations militaires, puis assurer la coordination avec les organisations non gouvernementales (ONG) et organisations intergouvernementales. Elle est aussi en droit de distribuer directement l'aide humanitaire.

De tout ce qui précède, les opérations civilo-militaires sont des fonctions de commandement et des fonctions opérationnelles. Bien entendu, l'aspect commandement constitue l'instrument d'aide au commandement. C'est l'outil par excellence qui permet de faciliter l'accomplissement de la mission civilo-militaire qui s'inscrit dans la catégorie des activités suivantes :

- contrôle de la population et des ressources ;
- aide humanitaire ;
- action militaire civique ;
- services d'urgence ;
- soutien aux nations étrangères ;
- appui à l'administration civile.

Nous sommes donc en droit de conclure que les Affaires civiles militaire produisent au commandant une expertise culturelle et évaluent les besoins de la population civile sur-le-champ de bataille. Elles gèrent aussi les questions relatives aux réfugiés et tiennent le commandant informé des cibles protégées telles que les écoles, églises, hôpitaux et autres, sans oublier les interfaces avec les ONG locales et internationales, ainsi que les organisations bénévoles privées. Ces Affaires civiles offrent au commandant militaire une superposition du champ de bataille unique dans toutes les activités civiles, les projets d'infrastructure en cours, la présence et la mission des ONG dans la région.

Toutefois, depuis les attentats du 11 septembre 2001, le jargon militaire américain a définitivement changé. On est passé du concept d'opérations autres que la guerre aux expressions *« stability operations » à « stability and reconstruction »,* puis « post-conflict reconstruction. » Si cette terminologie ne change pas grand-chose, il n'en demeure pas moins qu'elle traduit la volonté de s'écarter d'une définition négative du terme « opérations autres que la guerre » pour favoriser une conception plus constructive qui a le mérite de mettre l'accent sur l'effort de reconstruction après toute intervention militaire, sans véritablement changer le contenu et la nature des missions militaires[12].

[12] Voir Alexandra de Hoop Scheffer, Politologue, Institut d'Etudes Politiques de Paris, « La Réforme de l'Administration Publique (RAP) en situation post-conflit », Best Practices Section, Paris, Automne 2006

Qu'en est-il de ce concept Affaires civiles dans les missions de maintien de la paix ?

b. Le Mot « Affaires civiles » au Sens Onusien

La complexité des opérations de maintien de la paix a donné naissance à la nécessité d'établir une connexion constante entre les Casques bleus et les populations locales. Ce qui a permis de renforcer la compréhension de l'engagement des différents acteurs qui opèrent dans les collectivités territoriales, pour donner toutes les chances de réponses appropriées, face aux défis que présentent les situations de post-conflit. Dès lors, la section des Affaires civiles s'impose peu à peu, comme étant la composante la plus importante de toutes les équipes civiles dans les missions de maintien de la paix. Elle constitue, pour ainsi dire, « les oreilles et les yeux[13] » de la mission de la paix, au sein des populations bénéficiaires des services de la communauté internationale. Historiquement parlant, le premier déploiement des Casques bleus a eu lieu en 1948, lorsque le Conseil de sécurité autorisa le déploiement des observateurs militaires de l'ONU au Moyen-Orient, en vue de surveiller l'accord d'armistice entre Israël et ses voisins arabes en Palestine (ONUST). A ce jour, les Nations unies comptent environ 63 missions de maintien de la paix déjà déployées dans le monde, en vertu du chapitre VI de la Charte de l'ONU, consacré au règlement pacifique des différends. Ce chapitre stipule le non-usage de la force, sauf en cas de légitime défense. Il exige le consentement du gouvernement hôte et le cessez-le-feu.

Depuis 1990, la donne a changé. Fini avec les missions traditionnelles d'observation non armées. Le chapitre VII de la Charte des Nations unies prévoyant l'action en cas de menace contre la paix, de rupture de la paix et d'agression gagnèrent leurs lettres de noblesse. Dès lors, les Casques bleus peuvent faire usage de la force pour se défendre et défendre le mandat et les civils en danger imminent. Plus tard, il sera conforté par « l'agenda pour la paix », présenté par Boutros Boutros-Ghali, alors secrétaire général de l'ONU, le 17 juin 1992. Dans ce contexte, le Rapport Brahimi en l'an 2000 représentait un tournant important pour la vision renouvelée des missions du XXIe siècle, pour avoir initié les réformes majeures ayant abouti à l'accroissement caractérisé de la taille des missions à cause de la complexité des crises.

Les Casques bleus peuvent maintenant intervenir pour répondre à la déstabilisation créée par la détérioration de la situation politique, sécuritaire et

[13] Gustavo De Carvalho in « *The Role of Civil Affairs in United Nations Peacekeeping* », article publié dans ACCORD (African Centre for the Constructive Disputes), Durban, février 2010

humanitaire. Ils peuvent même être engagés dans un contexte où aucun accord de paix n'existe.

La publication de la doctrine Capstone en 2008 va dans le même sens. Elle est destinée à asseoir une doctrine directrice des opérations de maintien de la paix et apporte aussi certaines innovations. Les missions cherchent maintenant à rationaliser les ressources pour mieux répondre aux besoins de restructuration et de consolidation de la paix, avec un volet d'appui administratif et logistique.

De plus en plus, on parle « d'intégration » dans le cadre de missions multidimensionnelles et politiques, afin de maximiser l'impact collectif et individuel des efforts de l'ONU, grâce à un partenariat stratégique entre les acteurs du système des Nations unies. Plus récemment, en 2008, la nouvelle doctrine du Département des Opérations de Maintien de la Paix, connu sous l'appellation : Department of Peacekeeping Operations (DPKO), tente de définir un agenda politique pour la paix, lequel redynamise et reflète les perspectives du partenariat pour la paix. Cette doctrine vise à faire la paix rapidement et efficacement, en répondant aux défis opérationnels et politiques qui émergent, tout en construisant un cadre commun pour le renforcement de la paix, afin de répondre aux exigences de l'avenir.

Dans le jargon onusien, le mot « Affaires civiles » est apparu pour la première fois dans une mission de maintien de la paix comme composante à part entière, en 1992, avec la Force de Protection des Nations unies (FORPRONU), en ex-Yougoslavie, plus précisément en Croatie et en Bosnie Herzégovine. Avant ça, il y avait déjà l'Autorité Provisoire des Nations unies au Cambodge et les autres missions de l'ONU en Amérique centrale, de 1990 à 1993. C'était déjà une structure administrative civile qui s'occupait de la sécurité et des finances publiques, ainsi que l'information.

En son temps, Mr. Cedric Thornberry, le premier directeur d'une section des Affaires civiles, avait négocié une entente, le 5 juin 1992, avec le gouvernement bosniaque et les représentants des Serbes de Bosnie pour ouvrir l'aéroport de Sarajevo à des fins humanitaires pendant le siège de la ville, sauvant ainsi de nombreuses vies. A sa suite, le second directeur d'une telle section, Mr. Sergio Vieira de Mello, a lui aussi négocié plusieurs trêves temporaires, ainsi que l'évacuation des blessés de la ville et la reconnexion du gaz dans les maisons de Sarajevo pendant l'hiver. Ceci donne déjà une connotation aux tâches des officiers des Affaires civiles. Après la guerre, les Affaires civiles ont poursuivi leur mission avec l'Administration Transitoire des Nations unies pour la Slovénie Orientale (ATNUSO[14]), en Croatie, pour faciliter les processus politiques et avec la Mission des Nations unies en

[14] L'ATNUSO a été, créée le 15 janvier 1996 par la résolution 1037

Bosnie-Herzégovine (MINUBH[15]), en Bosnie-Herzégovine. Elles ont réalisé des analyses stratégiques permettant de faire avancer efficacement l'exécution du mandat. Les Affaires civiles ont également fait leurs premiers pas au Tadjikistan entre 1994 et 2000 pour traiter des questions de coordination civile. Elles ont marqué la Mission d'Observation des Nations unies en Géorgie (MONUG), entre 1993 et 2009.

Les Affaires civiles se focalisaient sur l'amélioration des liens entre les personnes, organisations et autorités sur les lignes de cessez-le-feu, avec un regard professionnel dans la réalisation des projets à impact rapide. Elles sont aussi passées par Chypre où elles ont expérimenté le soutien aux activités intercommunautaires, axées sur l'interaction politique avec les civils. Nous sommes vers la fin des années 1990. Les Affaires civiles ont aussi été mises à rude épreuve en Somalie, entre 1992 et 1993, pour soutenir la création d'un gouvernement somalien, en plus des tâches habituelles liées au développement des relations avec la population locale et aux efforts de planification. Ayant reçu un mandat exécutif le 10 juin 1999, les Affaires civiles de la Mission des Nations unies au Kosovo (MINUK), devraient gérer la mise en place d'une administration civile, organiser et superviser le développement des institutions démocratiques provisoires et autonomes, devant « assurer les conditions d'une vie pacifique et normale pour tous les habitants du Kosovo. » Cette « administration transitoire » avait des lourdes responsabilités, allant de l'administration des municipalités à la mise en place des structures pour la protection des droits des minorités. Il s'agissait de renforcer les capacités des institutions provisoires du gouvernement autonome du Kosovo.

Ces mêmes responsabilités avaient été confiées en octobre 1999, à l'Administration transitoire des Nations unies au Timor oriental (ATNUTO), au Timor-Leste, alors Timor oriental. Elles bénéficiaient aussi d'un mandat exécutif lors de la transition du pays vers l'indépendance. A l'époque les Affaires civiles étaient chargées d'établir une administration efficace et développer les services civils et sociaux, à travers leur soutien au gouvernement.

Depuis l'an 2000, les Affaires civiles s'imposent, de plus en plus, de l'Afrique à l'Afghanistan, en passant par le Népal, le Liban et Haïti, comme composante incontournable des missions de maintien de la paix avec une forte augmentation de ses officiers. Cette section est destinée à soutenir le développement des conditions sociales favorables à la paix. Elle s'affirme localement comme facilitatrice globale pour passer les points de vue et les aspirations de la population locale vers les décideurs au niveau local, national et international.

[15] Début : 21 décembre 1995 et fin : 31 décembre 2002

Désormais, les Affaires civiles jouent un rôle prépondérant dans la prévention des conflits et la réconciliation. Ce sont elles aussi, qui prévoient des mécanismes d'alerte pour protéger les civils et soutenir la société civile et les institutions étatiques. Elles contribuent beaucoup à l'extension et la consolidation de l'autorité de l'Etat et à la création des structures permettant le fonctionnement administratif, l'administration des ressources naturelles, la participation de la société civile et le renforcement des capacités favorables à la réconciliation et la consolidation de la paix.

Les Affaires civiles s'investissent aussi dans l'analyse de l'atténuation des conflits au niveau local et dans la reprise de la confiance. Elles s'impliquent davantage dans la promotion de la bonne gouvernance et participent activement à la mise en œuvre réussie des programmes de gouvernance. C'est maintenant les Affaires civiles qui soutiennent la gouvernance locale, démocratique, représentative, participative et efficace au niveau infra national. Non seulement, elles fournissent un appui aux institutions étatiques, elles proposent aussi des réformes des services civils et renforcent les capacités et la coordination.

Jusqu'à preuve du contraire, ce sont les Affaires civiles qui ont été chargées d'aider l'Etat ivoirien à redéployer l'administration et à restaurer l'autorité de l'État, tout en promouvant la culture de la paix à travers le soutien à la cohésion sociale et la résolution pacifique des conflits locaux. Elles assurent aussi la gestion globale et le secrétariat pour les projets à impact rapide, permettant de concevoir et construire les bases socio-économiques, indispensables pour offrir des services communautaires, via les processus participatifs.

Les informations et les analyses des Affaires civiles dans le cas du Burundi ont donné naissance aux profils municipaux et à la cartographie des rivalités politiques et ethniques résultant du manque de gouvernance efficace. Elles ont permis d'élaborer une stratégie de soutien gouvernement post-transition et d'identifier les occasions de renforcement des capacités.

Depuis 2005, au Sud-Soudan, les Affaires civiles s'orientent, énormément, vers la résolution, la prévention des conflits et la réconciliation. Elles exercent aussi l'appui à la gouvernance locale et contribuent à l'entretien et à l'amélioration de l'espace politique, sans compter leur appui dans la collecte d'informations, la diffusion et la facilitation. Leur déploiement généralisé favorise une plus grande surveillance du système d'alerte rapide et précoce des éléments déclencheurs des conflits. Cette cartographie des conflits permet de mieux les comprendre et de maîtriser les acteurs et les mécanismes en jeu, puis faire la planification d'urgence à des fins pacifiques en saison sèche, pendant les migrations, mais aussi de soutenir la paix et les comités locaux de réconciliation.

La gestion de l'information, des ressources naturelles et de l'environnement, ainsi que l'analyse, la formation et le renforcement des capacités constituent le lot des tâches des Affaires civiles au Darfour, depuis 2007.

Exceptionnellement, elles s'impliquent dans la promotion de la paix au niveau local dans une crise permanente.

C'est parfois les Affaires civiles qui s'occupent de la création des conditions de sécurité propices au retour volontaire et à la réintégration sociale des personnes déplacées. Elles soutiennent en outre, les initiatives des autorités locales pour résoudre les tensions locales et promouvoir les efforts de réconciliation au niveau local, sans oublier le renforcement de l'autorité de l'Etat. Le cas échéant, le rôle des Affaires civiles au Tchad et au Centrafrique avec la MINURCAT, entre 2007 et 2010, en dit long.

Quant au Népal, les Affaires civiles ont travaillé sur la surveillance des aspects non militaires du cessez-le feu et favoriser une atmosphère propice à une assemblée constituante libre et équitable pouvant organiser les élections, en particulier dans les zones rurales du Népal, où l'absence prolongée de l'Etat a laissé des séquelles durables et fortes.

En Somalie, les Affaires civiles travaillent en étroite collaboration avec les Affaires politiques et les autres acteurs de mission pour appuyer certains objectifs stratégiques, tels que : le renforcement du soutien populaire pour le processus de paix, l'amélioration de la sécurité humaine et la gouvernance, par la mise en place d'institutions civiles efficaces et responsables. Dans le plateau du Golan syrien, les Affaires civiles assurent la liaison et analysent les informations en provenance du terrain. Elles facilitent la coordination et la coopération civilo-militaire et participe à la sensibilisation culturelle des Casques bleus, pour atteindre efficacement les objectifs du mandat. En janvier 2012, les statistiques indiquent que près de 1009 officiers des Affaires civiles ont été déployés dans 17 pays accueillant actuellement une mission de maintien de la paix dans le monde, à savoir :

- Afghanistan, UNAMA créé par la résolution 1401 du 28 mars 2002 (148 officiers des Affaires civiles) ;
- Côte d'Ivoire, ONUCI créée par la résolution 1528 du 27 février 2004 (34 officiers des Affaires civiles) ;
- Chypre, UNFICYP créé par la résolution 186 du 04 mars 1964 (neuf officiers des Affaires civiles) ;
- Darfour, UNAMID créé par la résolution 1769 du 31 juillet 2007 (90 officiers des Affaires civiles) ;
- Haïti, MINUSTAH créée par la résolution 1529 du 29 février 2004 (105 officiers des Affaires civiles) ;
- Kosovo, UNMIK créé par la résolution 1244 du 10 janvier 1999 (53 officiers des Affaires civiles) ;

- Liban, FINUL/UNIFIL créé par les résolutions 425 et 426 de mars 1978 (18 officiers des Affaires civiles) ;
- Libéria, UNMIL créé par la résolution 1509 du 19 septembre 2003 (75 officiers des Affaires civiles) ;
- République Démocratique du Congo (RDC), MONUC créée par la résolution 1279 du 30 novembre 1999 (133 officiers des Affaires civiles) ;
- Sierra Leone, UNAMSIL créé par la résolution 1270 du 22 novembre 1999, est devenue UNIPSIL avec la résolution 1829 du 04 août 2008 (Neuf officiers des Affaires civiles) ;
- Somalie, ONUSOM/UNPOS créée par la résolution 733 du 23 janvier 1992 et AMISOM du 1er janvier 2007 (quatre officiers des Affaires civiles) ;
- Soudan, UNMIS créé par la résolution 1590 du 24 mars 2005 (140 officiers des Affaires civiles). Cette mission a changé de nom pour devenir UNMISS le 09 juillet 2011, le jour de l'indépendance du Sud-Soudan ;
- Syrie, UNDOF créé par la résolution 350 du 31 mai 1974 (un officier des Affaires civiles) ;
- Timor Leste, MINUT/UNMIT créée par la résolution 1704 du 25 août 2006 (179 officiers des Affaires civiles) ;
- Burundi, BINUB créé par la résolution 1719 du 25 octobre 2006 (deux officiers des Affaires civiles) ;
- République centrafricaine, BINUCA créé par la déclaration du président du Conseil de sécurité (S/ PRST/2009/5) du 7 avril 2009, en réponse à la recommandation du Secrétaire général de l'ONU, Ban Ki-Moon, formulée le 5 mars 2009. Le BINUCA, qui a remplacé le BONUCA le 1er janvier 2010, a pour objectif de coordonner les efforts de l'ONU dans le cadre de l'appui au processus de réconciliation nationale et au désarmement, démobilisation et réintégration (DDR), dont les paramètres avaient été établis par le dialogue politique inclusif de Bangui en 2008 et par les résolutions 1539 du 22 avril 2004 et 1612 du 26 juillet 2005 du Conseil de sécurité. Cette mission compte quatre officiers des Affaires civiles ;
- Libye, UNSMIL créé le 16 septembre 2011 pour trois mois renouvelables (trois officiers des Affaires civiles).

Le terme « Affaires civiles » utilisé dans le lexique de l'Organisation des Nations unies a une signification différente de celle des autres institutions, principalement, du vocable qui émerge du langage de l'armée américaine. En effet, à l'ONU, les spécialistes des Affaires civiles dans les opérations du maintien de la paix ne sont pas des officiers militaires détachés ou chargés des

Affaires civiles. Ce sont plutôt les membres du personnel civil de l'ONU qui sont à la pointe de l'interaction entre la mission et les responsables gouvernementaux centraux et locaux, la société civile et d'autres partenaires civils pour le compte de la communauté internationale.

Ces officiers civils des Affaires civiles des Nations unies travaillent sur les plans : politique et administratif, économique et social, pour faciliter l'exécution du mandat du Conseil de Sécurité de l'ONU sur tout le territoire couvert par la mission. Leur fonction est de soutenir la population et le gouvernement dans le renforcement des capacités et des structures de référence propice à la paix durable, prélude au développement économique.

La grande particularité des Affaires civiles de l'ONU est, non seulement le fait que l'équipe des Affaires civiles est composée de civils et non de militaires, mais surtout parce que cette équipe fait partie d'une section substantielle, à part entière. Cette section ne travaille pas pour les Casques bleus, mais les appuie, en travaillant en symbiose avec ces hommes et femmes en uniforme au sein des Nations unies.

Les officiers des Affaires civiles constituent souvent le premier contingent des civils à être déployé sur le terrain dans le but d'apporter un appui substantiel permettant d'éclairer et de faire le suivi de la démarche des Casques bleus en uniforme. A travers eux, il est possible de comprendre le climat qui règne au sein de la société civile et de la population. Ces experts aident à faciliter la mise en place d'une atmosphère de dialogue dans les relations entre les autorités locales et la population, à travers les réunions de l'Etat de droit dans les collectivités territoriales.

Par leur présence massive et remarquable sur le terrain, les officiers des Affaires civiles sont aussi responsables de l'exécution des évaluations rapides des besoins réels et immédiats de la population de chaque entité territoriale, notamment, en cas d'urgence politique ou de catastrophe naturelle. Ce qui leur permet de proposer des solutions adéquates utilisées pour résoudre les défis auxquels doit faire face une mission de maintien ou de stabilisation de la paix. En effet, il est de leur ressort de prélever la température politique au niveau local puis informer et conseiller la mission sur les meilleures interventions envisageables.

Les Affaires civiles collectent et rassemblent les informations. Elles assurent la liaison avec les partenaires locaux et les autorités de base, puis procèdent à l'expertise des préoccupations et revendications administratives, politiques et économiques issues des différentes régions du pays. Elles se hissent au centre de la résolution et la gestion des crises et agissent en vue de renforcer l'Etat central et les collectivités territoriales. Les Affaires civiles travaillent pour le rétablissement de la confiance vis-à-vis des institutions de la République. Elles constituent aussi une chaîne de communication servant à faciliter les échanges d'informations destinées à favoriser la bonne perception de la mission auprès des différentes couches de la population, ce qui est indispensable non seulement pour la mission de maintien de la paix en tant que tel, mais aussi pour le processus de paix et de réconciliation. En effet, ce sont les Affaires civiles qui véhiculent, au premier chef, l'image de la mission de maintien de la paix. Aussi, servent-elles d'avant-garde pour la protection de cette image à travers leurs interventions directes auprès des autorités à la base et en fonction de leur rôle de coordination.

Dans ce contexte d'utilisation plus cohérente des civils spécialisés dans certaines fonctions au sein d'une mission de maintien de la paix, les Affaires civiles se focalisent sur le renforcement des structures locales et le rétablissement de la confiance envers l'Etat. Elles apportent aussi un support constructif dans les processus de réconciliation et dans la restauration et l'amplification de l'autorité de l'Etat. Evidemment, elles interviennent non seulement dans l'analyse des conflits, mais aussi dans leur transformation. Ce rôle qui lui est dévolu se développe tellement qu'il crée parfois l'amalgame avec les attributions de la section des Affaires politiques.

Bref, la section des Affaires civiles devient de plus en plus une composante indispensable et indépendante plus ou moins autonome dans une mission de maintien de la paix. Elle travaille dans le domaine social, administratif, économique, et politique, pour faciliter l'exécution des opérations de maintien de la paix sur l'ensemble du territoire, comme il a été prévu par la résolution du conseil de sécurité portant création de ladite mission. Son rôle principal est de renforcer les capacités de la population et du gouvernement tant au niveau local qu'au niveau central. Sa fonction est aussi de consolider les structures conduisant à la stabilité et à la paix durable.

Ce sont les Affaires civiles qui organisent les réunions de sécurité regroupant les autorités locales, la police nationale et internationale, les autorités judiciaires et les militaires nationaux et internationaux. Le cas échéant, le rôle des Affaires civiles se limite à mettre ces partenaires ensemble pour analyser la situation sécuritaire dans une commune, mais la réunion est dirigée par le maire. C'est dans ce type de réunions que peuvent être décidées des opérations « coup de poing » dans certaines localités de la commune en question.

Dans le cadre de l'intégration de la mission de la paix de l'ONU, les Affaires civiles travaillent aussi avec les autres sections d'une mission, y compris les hommes et femme de la police et l'armée onusienne, notamment, lorsqu'il s'agit de faire une campagne de sensibilisation sur l'image de la mission pour laquelle ils/elles travaillent. Là encore, les Affaires civiles regroupent autour d'elles les officiers des droits de l'homme, de la Justice, des Affaires humanitaires, des UNPOL (United Nations Police) et parfois des Affaires électorales, pour répondre aux interrogations que se pose la population, notamment dans les écoles et universités.

Avec les UNPOL, il y a un échange constant d'information sur les questions de sécurité. Lorsque ces policiers des Nations unies sont en conflit avec les autorités locales ou la population, les Affaires civiles interviennent pour assurer la médiation et aussi, sensibiliser les uns et les autres sur le bien-fondé de la coopération entre eux.

De plus, puisqu'il s'agit d'une mission intégrée, les Affaires civiles s'entourent des autres sections ci-dessus citées pour rencontrer les autres partenaires locaux : préfets, maires, chefs des collines et des sections communales, autorités de police nationale et responsables de la justice locale pour travailler ensemble dans le cadre des réunions sur l'Etat de droit qui puis est, peut se faire de façon thématique.

Le travail des officiers des Affaires civiles est souvent recoupé, soutenu et appuyé par les travaux de divers autres acteurs de la mission. Il peut s'articuler sur les huit principaux rôles suivants :

- représentation de la mission, suivi et facilitation de l'exécution du mandat au niveau local ;
- réforme de l'administration publique d'un pays en situation de post-crise ;
- rétablissement de la confiance, gestion des conflits et soutien aux processus de réconciliation ;
- soutien à la restauration et l'extension de l'autorité de l'Etat et l'Etat de droit ;
- renforcement des capacités de l'Etat et des collectivités territoriales, à travers l'appui institutionnel ;
- assistance au parlement de la République concernée ;
- renforcement de la démocratie et la décentralisation ;
- appui dans la gestion des frontières.

Et, la liste n'est pas exhaustive. Par conséquent, les Affaires civiles constituent un ensemble de moyens d'appui à la gouvernance publique au niveau : central et local, assortie d'un lien ou d'une collaboration étroite avec la société civile, les ONG et la population, ainsi que les autorités centrales et locales, comme partenaires privilégiés. Elles sont concernées par la gestion de la cité ou la gouvernance civile en tant que répondants du corps administratif civil de l'Etat. Les Affaires civiles décrivent une sorte de coopération internationale entre la mission des Nations unies et les élus à la base, dans le cadre d'un appui institutionnel, incluant l'appui au parlement et la gestion des frontières, fondé sur la bonne gouvernance et le renforcement des capacités de l'Etat et des collectivités territoriales, notamment, en matière de :

- développement communautaire local, sur le plan économique et social ;
- démocratie participative ;
- fiscalité et des finances locales ;

- fonctionnement des municipalités ;
- formation continu des autorités territoriales à deux niveaux, celui du training et du monitoring.

De tout ce qui précède, il devient logique d'affirmer que la mission de la section des Affaires civiles se résume à susciter l'espoir d'une population dans le renouveau des institutions démocratiques post-conflituelles, pour redonner une nouvelle chance à un dialogue national, en mettant l'accent sur la gouvernance politique et la reconstitution de l'Etat, sans oublier la relance économique et les services de base. Dans cette optique, la section des Affaires civiles qu'on pourrait vraisemblablement appeler section des « Affaires publiques », vise naturellement la modernisation de l'Etat à travers le renforcement des capacités du gouvernement sur des problématiques spécifiques liées à l'humanitaire, la paix et le développement, en vue d'aboutir essentiellement à :

- des institutions démocratiques renforcées, permettant de restaurer l'Etat de droit et de garantir la justice pour tous, ainsi que la sécurité de tous les citoyens, sans oublier le respect des droits humains ;
- un Etat renforcé et modernisé dans une perspective de service public, favorisant ainsi la réduction des inégalités et la vulnérabilité de la population, le dialogue et la réconciliation ;
- une production des richesses nationales accrue et harmonisée malgré la croissance démographique, pour permettre de créer un cadre de vie acceptable pour tous, avec en prime, la stabilisation institutionnelle et sociale ;
- la disponibilité des services de base, augmentée sur la totalité du territoire national du pays concerné, avec une dimension géographique et humaine contribuant à l'inclusion et l'apaisement sociale ;
- une augmentation des revenus de l'Etat et des ménages permettant à la fois d'assurer une meilleure couverture des besoins humanitaires, économiques et sociaux et de créer un environnement favorable au relèvement du pays tout entier.

La section des Affaires civiles peut aussi se définir comme étant une section du « *outreach* », destinée à faire la liaison entre la mission, d'une part et les élus de base, les agences des Nations unies, les ONG internationales et nationales, la société civile, la population et les tous les autres acteurs humanitaires ou du développement, d'autre part.

L'officier des Affaires civiles est donc un spécialiste humanitaire auquel on peut faire appel en temps de crise, pour œuvrer dans d'autres domaines, tels que : la politique, les droits de l'homme, la justice, l'humanitaire, le genre, la conduite et discipline, le correctionnel, l'électoral, la démobilisation, le désarmement, la réinsertion et réinstallation (DDRR)..., surtout en cas d'absence ou de défaillance de la section concernée.

Tous ces paramètres laissent à croire qu'un officier des Affaires civiles est un agent de coordination, communication, facilitation et négociation. Son travail consiste à collecter les informations sur le terrain, à partir des entretiens avec les autorités de base et les acteurs clés de la collectivité territoriale. Ensuite, il les analyse pour élaborer une stratégie de réponse à un réseau de problèmes destinée à satisfaire les besoins fondamentaux d'une population.

Dans une mission de maintien de la paix, l'officier des Affaires civiles joue le rôle de réformateur, plutôt de « modernisateur » d'une administration publique, à travers le soutien qu'il apporte non seulement aux élus locaux, mais aussi à la société civile, dans le but d'améliorer les services publics et consolider la paix et la stabilité.

Sa fonction est, pour ainsi dire, d'aider les dirigeants locaux à mieux saisir les aspirations des différentes couches de la population qu'ils sont censés diriger. Aussi, il lui appartient de mobiliser divers secteurs de la population pour recevoir leurs inputs venant d'un processus participatif, pour les mettre au profit des élus locaux et permettre à ces derniers de développer de meilleures relations avec leurs mandants, puis être en meilleure position pour réaliser leur travail de représentation.

Par définition, la section des Affaires civiles est une équipe d'experts polyvalents dévouée à l'urgence politico-humanitaire, dans le domaine du renforcement de l'autorité de l'Etat, l'Etat de Droit et l'appui institutionnel, spécialement, dans un contexte de maintien ou de consolidation de la paix, incluant la résolution et la prévention des conflits, sans oublier la réconciliation des communautés déchirées par la crise.

Dans le même ordre d'idées, le concept « Affaires civiles » constitue l'ensemble des mécanismes permettant de réformer une administration publique post-conflictuelle, au niveau central, intermédiaire/régional et local/communal, en vue du développement politique et socio-économique, à travers l'appui institutionnel et la gestion des fonds. Les Affaires civiles se servent des projets à effets rapides, pour mieux satisfaire les besoins de la population et par la même occasion, renforcer l'autorité de l'Etat et l'Etat de Droit, avec anguille sous roche, l'amplification de la visibilité de la mission et la promotion de son acceptation par les bénéficiaires des services de l'ONU.

Donc, les officiers des Affaires civiles ont la lourde tâche de participer activement, ou plutôt, de contribuer techniquement au relèvement d'un pays dans la situation d'après-crise. Cela engage en général, plusieurs acteurs, tant au niveau interne qu'externe et les poussant à exercer une certaine influence dans l'arène politique et sur le système socio-économique, conformément à leurs propres intérêts et perceptions. Les choses se compliquent souvent lorsqu'il s'agit de faire le renforcement des capacités dans un pays en situation d'urgence politique complexe et/ou dans un contexte d'urgence due aux catastrophes naturelles.

B. THEORIE DU RENFORCEMENT DES CAPACITES

Si la paix et le développement durable constituent l'objet du mandat d'une mission de l'ONU, les moyens employés pour exécuter ce mandat restent, jusqu'à preuve du contraire, le renforcement des capacités, mis en œuvre par les officiers des Affaires civiles et les autres composantes d'une mission. Né dans les laboratoires des chercheurs et praticiens du développement, le concept « renforcement des capacités » n'a pas la même signification dans la langue de Molière que dans celle de Shakespeare. Les anglophones parlent de « *Capacity Building* » qui désigne une approche d'édification, de construction ou d'acquisition de nouvelles capacités.

Ce principe a été largement influencé par les théories organisationnelles, les sciences politiques, la gestion du développement et de l'économie, avant d'atterrir dans le lexique diplomatique, des bailleurs de fonds, des ONG et des institutions internationales, qui en donnent chacun sa propre définition.

Il fait sa première apparition dans le jargon diplomatique entre 1950 et 1960 avec la notion de développement communautaire. Il s'agissait, précisément, du renforcement des capacités sous forme d'auto-assistance au sein des collectivités rurales. A l'époque, le renforcement des capacités était caractérisé par la mise en valeur du potentiel des individus et par l'appui de leurs aptitudes grâce à la formation, la recherche et aux relations entre homologues dans le cadre d'aide ou de coopération technique. Cette nouvelle démarche visait surtout le renforcement des capacités humaines en vue de susciter en eux, un auto-perfectionnement. Les écoles, les centres de formation professionnelle et les universités constituaient les outils indispensables pour la transmission du savoir.

En 1969, intervient l'élaboration du premier rapport sur le développement international connu sous le nom de rapport de la Commission Pearson[16]. Cette commission avait fait une étude sur la création des capacités administratives dans les pays en voie de développement. Elle mettait fondamentalement l'accent sur la capacité de soutenir les changements politiques et économiques.

Cinq ans plus tard, en 1974, la notion de « responsabilisation » voyait le jour dans les locaux de l'Institut de recherche des Nations unies pour le développement social. Cette expression véhiculait l'idée d'établir des conditions ou des capacités permettant à une société donnée d'être dorénavant à la hauteur de ses propres problèmes. Ainsi, la rupture avec la pratique de

[16] La Commission Pearson est la première commission de la banque mondiale sur le développement international. Elle a été constituée en août 1968 par Robert S. Mc. Namara, alors président de ladite banque, pour examiner l'efficacité de l'aide au développement et formuler des recommandations concernant le fonctionnement futur de l'organisation. Cette commission avait été dirigée par l'ancien Premier ministre canadien et lauréat du prix Nobel de la paix Lester Bowles Pearson. Elle avait rendu son rapport le 15 septembre 1969

l'établissement d'objectifs appropriés pour l'avenir était consommée. Il était plutôt question de s'appuyer sur le diagnostic des points faibles et des possibilités du moment, ce qui laisse entendre le principe d'adoption de politiques appropriées et la surveillance constante au cours d'un processus de développement.

Le concept va évoluer encore plus en 1980, avec l'entrée en jeu du terme développement institutionnel qui caractérise l'intention d'enrichir non seulement le gouvernement et le secteur public, mais aussi le secteur privé et les ONG, dans le processus de restructuration et de changement institutionnel vu sous l'angle d'un processus à long terme. Dès lors, les balises installées par les théoriciens et praticiens de développement s'orientaient vers les formules d'adaptabilité et de réceptivité des établissements de développement, une stratégie qui dépasse le cadre d'organisations, pour se lancer dans l'analyse des perspectives sectorielles et des groupes d'établissements. Les notions de résultats et de durabilité emboîtent le pas pour se hisser au sommet du développement, d'où le slogan : agir avec efficacité et de façon durable pour aboutir au développement humain tant attendu.

En 1990, le bilan de toutes ces années de tergiversations entre création de capacités et développement institutionnel et organisationnel, fait état d'un constat d'échec, puisqu'il n'a pas donné le résultat escompté, celui du développement durable. Il est maintenant certain que le renforcement des capacités ne fait pas bon ménage avec les inégalités et la corruption qui atteignent des proportions endémiques dans certains pays, ou lorsqu'il n'y a aucune volonté politique, aucun espoir dans l'avenir, ou encore lorsque la violence, la haine et les abus de tous genres concernant les droits de la personne humaine sont érigés en politique de gouvernement.

Habituellement intitulé « aide technique » ou « coopération technique » le renforcement des capacités se limitait à fournir des services spécialisés sur ce que les personnes ne savaient pas faire et sur ce dont ils avaient besoin, autrement dit le savoir-faire notamment professionnel qui manquait et qu'il fallait transmettre aux destinataires. Or, cette politique ne n'était mise en œuvre que par des intervenants externes au pays bénéficiaire, entrainant ainsi une « infantilisation » de la population qui se voyait soumis à des privations.

Au bout du compte, les experts dressèrent un constat d'échec par rapport au contexte, au rendement et à la situation réelle qui se présente réellement sur le terrain. Il n'est plus à démontrer que le renforcement des capacités avait plutôt amélioré les capacités de certains gouvernements abusifs, les habilitant de surcroît à taire leur propre peuple. Et en prime, cette aide qu'ils recevaient de leurs protecteurs étrangers, les rendait encore plus riches, contrairement à l'objectif prévu d'améliorer les conditions favorables au développement, au changement social et/ou à la réduction de la pauvreté.

A présent, il est aisé de constater à travers le bilan des précédentes stratégies dans le cadre du renforcement des capacités que les théories et solutions intellectuelles, économique et techniques ne peuvent pas, à elles seules, apporter une réponse adéquate aux enjeux de lutte contre la pauvreté et la fracture sociale, la faim, la vie chère... Elles ne peuvent pas, non plus, solutionner l'ensemble des problèmes de développement humain dans une société.

Cependant, c'est en cette même année 1990 qu'apparaîtront les innovations ayant produit les termes, tels que : développement participatif et renforcement de l'autonomie de la population locale. L'émergence de ces concepts dans le jargon international a fait en sorte que le renforcement cible dorénavant, non seulement les individus, mais aussi les collectivités territoriales, les organisations, les secteurs spécifiques comme l'agriculture, la santé, l'éducation, l'environnement et parfois les sous-ensembles sociétaux. Ainsi, la création, le maintien ou la consolidation de capacités incarnées par le modèle de développement organisationnel ont cédé la place au système du développement sectoriel, puis à celui du développement institutionnel qui représente un vaste échantillon d'organismes et institution incluant les entrepreneurs du secteur non structuré et/ou la société civile. Désormais, l'objectif est d'enrichir les collectivités territoriales et les ONG locales, afin de les doter des moyens qui leur permettront de mettre en œuvre et de gérer leurs propres programmes, indépendamment des intervenants de l'extérieur. Cette démarche ne pourra se faire sans miser sur la stimulation, en vue d'une cohérence accrue à propos d'une ou plusieurs questions au sein de ladite collectivité. En un mot, il faut adapter la cible au but et tenir compte du processus d'exécution.

Le renforcement des capacités devient littéralement appuyé, soutenir les capacités existantes ; faire acquérir et maintenir les aptitudes aux gens, pour leur permettre de réaliser leurs propres objectifs de développement. Ce sont les anglophones qui lui apportent un vrai sens, celui qui touche à la notion de développement, notamment dans une situation post-conflit où le nouveau ne remplace pas forcément l'ancien et où le principe selon lequel : « hôte-toi de là que je m'y mets » n'est pas à l'ordre du jour.

Il est préférable d'avoir une formule permettant de faire cohabiter les notions d'adaptation, de lien, de relation et de cohésion entre les nouvelles et les anciennes connaissances de gestion de l'Etat, pourvu que cela tienne compte de l'auto-organisation de la société, son évolution, sa vision et ses valeurs, pour aboutir au développement durable. Bien entendu le développement dont il s'agit inclut plusieurs aspects, à savoir le développement : organisationnel, communautaire, rurale intégré, environnemental et durable, auxquels il faut ajouter le volet des capacités intangibles de transformation ou de résolution des conflits, ainsi que la mise en place des réseaux de communication.

Ce développement est à la fois systémique et structurel. Il s'adapte mieux à la notion anglophone de « Capacity Development. » Cela signifie qu'il s'agit d'un processus constant d'intégration et d'adaptation, de construction et de renforcement des capacités nouvelles à construire et de consolidation et/ou de maintien des capacités existantes, liées à d'autres valeurs de la société. Reste à savoir la signification du mot capacité.

Dans le contexte sociétal, le mot capacité désigne les aptitudes des autorités locales à exercer leurs fonctions, à résoudre les problèmes, à satisfaire les besoins de la population, à fixer et atteindre les objectifs du développement qui se présentent à divers niveaux de la société, à des entités de taille et de portée différentes, aux différents stades du processus dudit développement. Par conséquent, « le renforcement des capacités se définit [de façon générale] comme un processus endogène au travers duquel une société modifie ses règles, ses institutions et son mode de vie, accroît son capital social et améliore ses facultés de réaction, d'adaptation et d'autodiscipline[17]. »

En matière de développement, le renforcement des capacités se réfère souvent à l'assistance qui est fournie à des pays du Tiers-monde appelés à développer certaines compétences ou à améliorer leurs performances. La plupart des capacités sont construites par les sociétés elles-mêmes, parfois par le secteur public, parfois par le secteur non gouvernemental et souvent, par le secteur privé. Lorsque qu'il va au-delà de la formation, il peut comprendre le :

- développement des ressources humaines, au sens de la valorisation des connaissances et l'accès à l'information ;
- développement organisationnel, c'est-à-dire l'élaboration des structures de gestion, des processus et procédures, non seulement au sein des organisations, mais aussi dans le cadre de la gestion des relations entre les différentes organisations et les secteurs : public, privé et communautaire ;
- cadre institutionnel et juridique du développement, de l'évolution juridique et réglementaire pour permettre aux institutions à tous les niveaux et dans tous les secteurs, de renforcer leurs capacités.

Dans le contexte des affaires, notamment celui du commerce international, le renforcement des capacités est défini comme étant les activités soutenues par les bailleurs de fonds en vue d'améliorer l'aptitude des parties prenantes dans les pays en développement. Il s'agit d'élaborer des politiques

[17] « Gouvernance locale et renforcement des capacités. Quelques pistes de réflexion pour un développement territorial durable des collectivités rurales », par Tchabagnan AYEVA, doctorant en développement régional, Université du Québec à Rimouski, Centre de recherche sur le développement territorial (CRDT) Rimouski, septembre 2003, sous la direction de Bruno JEAN

commerciales ou de procéder à des analyses et identifier leurs intérêts dans les négociations commerciales internationales.

Au sens du volontariat, le renforcement des capacités est le processus qui permet de développer les potentialités des organisations bénévoles à répondre aux besoins de la communauté qu'ils desservent.

Selon le Programme des Nations unies pour le Développement (PNUD), le renforcement des capacités est un « processus par lequel les particuliers, les groupes, les organisations, les institutions et les sociétés accroissent leurs aptitudes à exercer des fonctions essentielles, résoudre des problèmes, définir et remplir des objectifs ; [...] à comprendre et à gérer leurs besoins en développement dans un contexte global et de manière durable[18]. »

En revanche, pour la Banque Mondiale[19], il s'agit d'investir dans l'ensemble du système et des institutions, notamment : les gens, les institutions et les pratiques censées agir ensemble pour qu'un pays ou une région puisse atteindre ses objectifs de développement.

C'est aussi la manière dont les acteurs nationaux et internationaux intègrent plusieurs facteurs qui ne sont pas toujours économiques tels que l'apprentissage, l'imagination, l'environnement... pour répondre à une demande de développement. Le but est de satisfaire les besoins d'une société, puis leur aptitude à s'adapter aux conditions locales, liées aux différentes capacités requises, à savoir intellectuelles, organisationnelles, sociales, politiques, culturelles, matérielles, pratiques et/ou financières.

Finalement, le renforcement des capacités est une réponse aux processus multidimensionnels du changement. Il ne se limite plus à faire des interventions techniques discrètes ou préétablies, destinées à apporter un résultat défini par avance. Mais, son objectif est d'accroître les compétences techniques, les connaissances, le développement des ressources humaines et autres moyens, permettant aux individus (sous-entendus les autorités à la base) et aux institutions (les collectivités territoriales), dans la perspective de durabilité et d'amélioration des aptitudes à résoudre les problèmes de la communauté. Il existe plusieurs approches de renforcement des capacités parmi lesquels :

- l'approche organisationnelle qui considère que le renforcement passe par une entité, une organisation ou un groupe de plusieurs organisations d'une communauté donnée. Elle s'appuie sur la théorie des organisations et du changement organisationnel pour laquelle le renforcement des capacités consiste à repérer et développer les composantes ou les éléments de capacité d'une organisation, c'est-à-dire, les compétences, les systèmes, le leadership, etc. ;

---

[18] PNUD, 1997 ; Taschereau, 1997, cité par Tchabagnan AYEVA, ibidem

[19] Voir Banque Mondiale (1997), cité par Tchabagnan AYEVA, ibidem

- l'approche institutionnelle ou approche stimulatrice de la création de connaissances et d'accès aux « règles formelles et informelles du jeu. » Elle met l'accent sur des composants, tels que : les lois, les règlements, les mentalités, etc., et vise à développer les facultés créatives, de changement et de mise en œuvre et d'apprentissage. Cette démarche se fonde sur les procédures et les règles qui régissent la société ;
- l'approche systémique, elle offre une vision pluridimensionnelle du renforcement des capacités. Ici, la société est considérée comme un ensemble de systèmes à plusieurs niveaux : individuel, organisationnel, sectoriel, de réseau et de l'environnement. Ces systèmes sont reliés à tel point que chacun se conjugue et se rattache à l'autre, les oblige à avoir connaissance et à pouvoir travailler sur la base des relations avec les autres. Ainsi, toute intervention dans le cadre du renforcement des capacités ne peut se faire qu'en tenant compte de toutes ces dimensions et auprès de ces divers acteurs, dans des processus, des liens et des relations de pouvoir ;
- l'approche participative est celle qui insiste sur les moyens utilisés pour atteindre les objectifs de développement. Le cas échéant, la procédure consiste à repérer et utiliser les compétences locales, en travaillant avec ces gens pour élaborer des modèles appropriés et qui sont adaptés aux besoins locaux. Cette approche est « autonomisante. » Elle est fondée sur un développement non hiérarchique, mais centré sur l'individu, contrairement à l'approche d'assistance étatique paternaliste ayant entretenu des décennies de défaitisme, de fatalisme et d'incapacité chronique des leaders de la communauté à exercer leurs responsabilités[20].

La question est maintenant de savoir comment mettre en application, comment faire fonctionner le principe de renforcement des capacités, quel que soit le type d'approche, ce qui pousse à présenter quelques exemples de techniques à mettre en œuvre :

- pour renforcer les capacités d'un organisme, c'est-à-dire, faire le développement organisationnel, la technique est de renforcer l'aptitude de cet organisme à remplir ses fonctions de gestion. Cela signifie promouvoir sa cohérence interne en favorisant les possibilités d'apprentissage et d'adaptation continus, afin de rendre l'organisme plus viable et plus durable, tout en ayant une incidence sur sa mission ;
- pour renforcer les capacités de la société civile, en tant qu'enjeu du développement institutionnel, le meilleur moyen est d'améliorer l'aptitude des parties intéressées pour qu'elle détermine et mène à bien des activités d'identification et de résolution des problèmes de la

[20] Consulter : www.capacity.org/definit_fr.html et www.gtz.de

communauté. La procédure consiste à rendre possible et stimuler l'amélioration de : l'interaction, la communication, les infrastructures et la résolution des crises. Sa finalité est d'accroître les aptitudes des parties intéressées à entrer dans l'arène politique et dans le système socio-économique, conformément à leurs intérêts, pour y laisser leurs marques ;

- pour renforcer les capacités d'un secteur ou d'un sous-secteur d'établissements autrement dit, faire le développement sectoriel, il est louable de renforcer l'aptitude du secteur ou du sous-secteur à améliorer son incidence en général. La méthode consiste à établir des relations de soutien et de compréhension mutuelle au sein du secteur ou des sous-secteurs. Dans ce cas, le résultat attendu est de réaliser une interaction confiante et significatrice avec les autres secteurs et acteurs sociaux, compte tenu des stratégies et des connaissances communes.

Finalement, tout projet visant à déterminer les priorités d'un programme d'élaboration des politiques de reconstruction de sociétés déchirées par la guerre ou par une crise d'extrême gravité doit tenir compte des paramètres suivants :

- « les conflits de pouvoirs peuvent n'avoir rien résolu et des élections ne règlent pas nécessairement les problèmes sous-jacents peuvent ne pas résulter sur des ententes durables de partage du pouvoir ;
- « la guerre peut avoir détruit ou discrédité les structures sociales traditionnelles et ce qui a succédé à ces dernières qui peuvent être faible et manquer de légitimité ;
- « les gouvernements d'après-guerre conscients des priorités et des défis qu'ils doivent affronter, peuvent être tentés par des solutions autoritaires qui vont à l'encontre de l'inclusion, du dialogue et de la crédibilité ;
- « les grandes espérances des gens peuvent contraster avec les faibles capacités de prestation du gouvernement ;
- « la marge permettant un dialogue neutre ou impartial peut être étroite ;
- « les acteurs du dehors peuvent continuer de viser à la désunion. »

D'emblée, l'objet du renforcement des capacités d'un Etat est de combler les déficiences auxquelles font face les services publics du pays en question. Il sert aussi à rendre l'Etat plus proche des citoyens, plus efficace et plus accessible à travers :

- l'adéquation des services aux besoins des populations ;
- l'utilisation efficace des ressources ;
- une gestion décentralisée de certains services publics, en faisant appel à une déconcentration des systèmes des services publics, notamment l'éducation, la santé, les infrastructures ;

- un rapprochement de la décision politique du territoire où elle s'inscrit et de la population à laquelle elle s'adresse ;
- la participation populaire.

Le renforcement des capacités nécessite donc un ensemble d'efforts normalisés en matière de développement des ressources humaines, additionnés à l'art d'apprendre aux Hommes ou aux groupes d'Hommes, aux organismes et/ ou aux institutions, aux collectivités territoriales, et cetera. Comment se suffire, sans réserver une place de choix à la société civile ?

C. LE TERME DE « SOCIETE CIVILE »

Compte tenu des potentialités locales et des défis auxquels il doit faire face, l'officier des Affaires civiles est appelé à s'assigner des objectifs à atteindre, afin de définir une projection future proche et/ou lointain. Et ceci, en fonction de la vision définie en synergie avec les gouvernants locaux et les acteurs de la société civile. Il est prié d'identifier les actions à entreprendre en vue de créer la route qui lui permettra de combler le fossé entre la situation qu'il trouve sur le terrain et la situation à laquelle la mission veut aboutir : le développement local.

Qu'est-ce que cette société civile indispensable et incontournable, mais qui malgré tout, n'est pas indépendante de l'État et vice versa ?

Avant de répondre à cette interrogation, il convient de préciser que dans toute nation il y a des institutions composées de l'ensemble des structures étatiques c'est-à-dire : les ministères, les collectivités territoriales (régions, communes, collines, sections communales…), les organes électifs, notamment le parlement (sénat et chambre de députés), l'appareil judiciaire, l'armée et les organisations en charge de la sécurité. Les fonctions attachées à ces structures donnent naissance aux fonctionnaires de l'Etat qui sont liés par la raison d'Etat même si l'Etat est le premier protecteur de l'intérêt général.

A côté de tout cela, il y a une institution spéciale qui n'est ni publique ni privée : les partis politiques qui sont des institutions dotées d'une force politique sociale organisée dont la mission fondamentale est d'aller à la conquête du pouvoir de gestion des institutions publiques. L'objectif d'un parti politique est de diriger l'appareil de l'Etat. Du coup, tous ceux qui font partie de ces deux groupes d'institutions ne sont pas inclus dans la société civile.

Par conséquent, comme nos prédécesseurs qui se sont alignés et inspirés des philosophies d'Hegel, de Tocqueville, de Gramsci et plus récemment de l'étude de Robert Putnam, publiée en 1993[21], nous estimons que la société civile est susceptible de comprendre les :

- individus ;
- ménages ;
- voisinages ;
- organisations locales ou communautaires ;
- cercles de réflexion ;
- groupes de bienfaisance et d'entraide ;
- organisations patronales ;
- coalitions et groupes de plaidoyer ;
- syndicats ;
- sociétés de services sociaux et groupes d'entraide ;
- confessions religieuses ;
- établissements de formation ;
- organismes de recherche ;
- secteurs privés ;
- medias ;
- associations et ONG nationales et internationales opérant sur le territoire concerné ;
- organismes donateurs d'organisations officielles ou non gouvernementales des pays riches et pauvres, qui sont impliqués dans un ensemble de réseaux et des relations mutuelles et de réciprocité au sein d'une société.

En revanche, lorsqu'on parle de la société civile organisée on voit surtout les :

- mouvements sociaux pour la défense de la démocratie, la résistance non-violente, la promotion des droits des minorités ou d'autres thématiques ;
- grandes organisations sectorielles telles que les syndicats, les organisations patronales, les organisations de femmes, les organisations paysannes, etc. ;
- organisations communautaires ;
- structures religieuses ;
- chefs coutumiers, les anciens et les notables ;
- partis politiques ;

[21] Robert D. Putnam, « *Making Democracy Work: Civic Traditions in Modern Italy* » Princeton: Princeton University Press, 1993, cité par Mick Moore, « Qu'est-ce que le renforcement des capacités ? C'est là tout le problème », article publié dans « Chapitre 1. Le renforcement des capacités et l'œuvre humanitaire », Centre de recherches pour le développement international, www.idrc.ca

- organisations professionnelles ;
- organisations des droits de l'homme ;
- ONG.

Donc, la société civile constitue l'ensemble des citoyens organisés ou non organisés, ayant la capacité d'influencer les pouvoirs publics. Malheureusement, cette définition est trop vaste. Elle risque de banaliser le concept. Pour cela, l'approche des droits de l'homme qui représente la société civile par l'ensemble des groupes apolitiques organisés semble plus appropriée.

En ce sens, la société civile est une force sociale non manipulable et non maniable, à l'intérieur de la population, mais qui est capable de constituer « la voix des sans voix », sur la base d'un engagement militant pour une cause donnée. Elle a pour mission de rappeler ce qu'on veut écarter, oublier ou détourner volontairement ou involontairement.

Pour être plus explicite, la société civile est un espace de réflexion qui s'auto-organise dans la société, en dehors du cadre de la famille, l'Etat et les marchés économiques, et dans lequel les gens n'agissent pas individuellement, mais dans le cadre associatif. Son objectif est de faire progresser les intérêts communs des citoyens se déclarant formellement et juridiquement membres de ladite association.

Elle représente un véritable corps social organisé sur une base volontaire, par opposition à la classe politique qui est largement auto-suffisante et autonome de l'Etat. La classe politique composée d'un ensemble d'organisations ou de groupes constitués de façon plus ou moins formelle, mais qui n'appartient ni à la sphère gouvernementale ni à la sphère commerciale.

La société civile est souvent composée des leaders d'opinion, interlocuteurs locaux constituant une source d'information importante sur les préoccupations, besoins et priorités et pour agir comme des puissants catalyseurs, en faveur de la consolidation de la paix. Cet aspect devrait intéresser, au premier chef, les officiers des Affaires civiles appelés à travailler avec la société civile et les institutions civiles comme les universités, dans un cadre plus large d'efforts de gestion des conflits, caractérisé par le renforcement des capacités. Les Affaires civiles ont deux raisons principales de s'intéresser à la société civile. La première est que : les acteurs de la société civile sont des composants à part entiers du tissu politique, économique et social du pays hôte. Ils constituent, de surcroît, le pilier vital de tout Etat démocratique.

La seconde raison est que les leaders de la société civile sont souvent des grands, sinon les plus importants défenseurs de la gouvernance démocratique. Ils prêchent généralement la paix et contribuent énormément dans les processus de transformation et de prévention des conflits. En outre, ils jouent ordinairement le rôle de canalisation et d'organisation des intérêts et des opinions publiques.

A ce titre, le soutien de la section des Affaires civiles à la société civile peut donc aider à communiquer avec la population et à surmonter les inhibitions liées au conflit et/ou la répression gouvernementale. Cet appui peut faciliter le renforcement de la participation de la société civile au processus de transition politique et démocratique, ainsi qu'à la consolidation de la Paix. Il est donc impératif et vital que les officiers des Affaires civiles développent des relations étroites avec la société civile. Ils ont besoin d'élaborer une cartographie des acteurs de la société civile afin d'identifier leurs forces, leurs faiblesses, leurs opinions et leurs motivations. Ainsi sont-ils priés d'établir la confiance avec la société civile et inventer des stratégies pour consolider ses liens.

Bien entendu, l'officier des Affaires civiles doit écouter la société civile avec beaucoup d'attention. Il doit respecter son expertise et les stratégies locales qu'elle présente, car selon nous, une société civile n'est jamais « faible » ni « non existante. »

Cependant, dans sa coopération avec la société civile, l'officier des Affaires civiles doit éviter de créer des attentes irréalistes ni de développer une politique de parti pris et/ou de favoritisme, y compris à travers les tendances politiques de ses interlocuteurs. Il ne faut surtout pas qu'il se substitue à leurs capacités, au risque de l'affaiblir. Il est d'ailleurs déconseillé d'éviter au maximum de recruter le personnel de la société civile sauf à ne pas violer le principe de la liberté de choisir son emploi.

Dans le même ordre d'idées, il serait contre-productif d'ignorer la perception par la société civile de l'ONU et particulièrement, de la section des Affaires civiles. Dans l'autre sens, les Affaires civiles ne peuvent ignorer leurs propres préjugés vis-à-vis de la société civile.

Cependant, dans le cadre du renforcement des capacités de la société civile, les Affaires civiles doivent soutenir les promoteurs de la société civile, notamment, ceux qui ont la :

- force et le potentiel d'influencer les résultats de la mission ;
- sagesse de proposer des solutions pertinentes pour la recherche de la paix, mais aussi, pour la résolution et la prévention des crises ;
- volonté de promouvoir le respect des droits fondamentaux ;
- capacité ou les moyens de contribuer à la réduction des conflits.

Cela se fait essentiellement par l'organisation des activités conjointes et en offrant un appui stratégique, ainsi que de bons offices, des formations et le soutien logistique et financier aux leaders politiques, économiques et sociaux.

Toutefois, il ne faut jamais oublier que la faiblesse de la société civile provient principalement de sa vulnérabilité de ces membres. D'où le devoir de protéger certains de ces membres qui n'ont pas les moyens d'assurer leur propre protection. Pour cela, il est nécessaire de marquer la présence des Affaires civiles à leurs côtés et de faire des plaidoyers en sa faveur. On peut aussi adopter la stratégie de la création de liens, la mise en réseau, l'appui à d'autres acteurs, et cetera. En un mot, l'engagement et le soutien de la société civile ne sont pas inclusivement une affaire des Affaires civiles, mais aussi des droits de l'homme et de la justice. Dans ce cas, le renforcement de la société civile passe par l'amélioration des connaissances sur les textes en vigueur et les techniques modernes de monitoring et des plaidoyers en faveur de la communauté, ainsi que sur la gestion du temps et les moyens d'assumer sa neutralité, son autonomie et son indépendance vis-à-vis des pouvoirs publics. De nos jours, la faiblesse ou l'absence de la société civile est synonyme ou tout au moins, créée les conditions propices aux abus en matière de droits de la personne et à : une mauvaise gestion des affaires publiques, la faiblesse de la démocratie et l'Etat de droit, l'effondrement de l'Etat, l'aggravation des conflits, la réduction de la stabilité, l'existence d'un régime totalitaire, les problèmes d'environnement et la guerre. Cela peut aussi entrainer une cooptation gouvernementale et ethnique, ainsi qu'un climat politique dangereux pour les dissidents et les organismes donateurs dont les programmes sont explicitement apolitiques.

Ceci n'est possible que si la société civile est :

- neutre ;
- apolitique ;
- indépendante ;
- autonome.

En revanche, une société civile forte est d'une importance cruciale pour le développement, notamment en situation d'urgence politique complexe pour marginaliser les autorités abusives existantes. Elle constitue la pierre angulaire de la démocratie, des droits de l'homme, des principes de pluralisme et de la culture d'intégration.

Son renforcement permettra d'aider à surmonter les défis énumérés ci-après par Paul Harvey[22] :

- « un processus très rigoureux par lequel la société civile se dégage de l'État ;
- « un recours aux groupements primaires au sein de la société civile. Les structures familiales, tribales et religieuses, de même que les structures politiques traditionnelles servent de stratégies de prise en charge pour réagir à l'effondrement de l'État ;

---

[22] Paul Harvey « Rehabilitation in Complex Political Emergencies: Is Rebuilding Civil Society the Answer ? » Disasters 22, no. 3 (1998), cité par Mick Moore, « Qu'est-ce que le renforcement des capacités ? C'est là tout le problème », article publié dans « Chapitre 1. Le renforcement des capacités et l'œuvre humanitaire », Centre de recherches pour le développement international, www.idrc.ca

- « des stratégies militaires, une grande pénurie et des déplacements qui sapent la société civile ;
- « des autorités locales abusives contestant la place de la société civile, pénétrant dans l'économie parallèle et tentant de gagner des appuis en recourant à des liens néo-patrimoniaux sur la base de l'ethnie ;
- « la force continue de la société civile au niveau local dans l'économie parallèle et au sein des établissements traditionnels. »

Il se dégage de ce commentaire, une société civile qui ne peut être ni étatique, ni militaire, ni politique et ni financier afin de conserver sa neutralité, son autonomie et son indépendance. Ce sont les critères permettant d'être l'instrument privilégié de la protection non pas de la population, mais plutôt le garant des intérêts de la population.

Il convient ainsi de :

- comprendre et s'engager avec la représentation locale de la société civile pour promouvoir la stabilité, les conditions de vie socio-économiques et la paix ;
- être conscient du fait que les organisations de la société civile ne sont pas à l'abri de tensions politiques et sociales et peuvent elles-mêmes, perpétuer des disparités qui reflètent le genre, les inégalités ethniques ou raciales des communautés … ;
- éviter de légitimer les groupes d'intérêts spécifiques ;
- étudier et comprendre la dynamique dans laquelle opère la société civile dans l'intérêt de la gestion de ses relations avec elle, de manière la plus significative possible ;
- agir en facilitateur pour faire émerger la société civile, pour qu'elle existe et s'engage, sans s'impliquer dans la direction ni soutenir la substance de leur travail, notamment, faire sa promotion ou assurer la censure de leurs messages ou leurs initiatives spécifiques.

Le renforcement de la société civile se fait dans le cadre de l'élaboration de mécanismes de « responsabilisation » et de transparence. Il sert à faire de la société civile un interlocuteur crédible et légitime de l'Etat. Ceci peut se faire par l'élaboration d'une cartographie des organisations de la société civile conduisant à la création d'une plate-forme nationale de la société civile qui aura une influence sur le gouvernement.

Evidemment, le rôle des Affaires civiles n'est pas de s'immiscer dans la politique intérieure d'un Etat souverain, mais de faire en sorte que les différentes expressions de la société civile devienne de plus en plus autonome. Par rapport à leurs objectifs et leurs stratégies, il est important qu'elle se constitue en acteur efficace dans le dialogue avec les institutions, par le canal de l'approche participative dans l'identification des besoins prioritaires de leur circonscription.

La société civile a aussi besoin des conseils sur les mécanismes d'évaluation des performances des institutions participatives. Par conséquent, il est important de faire le suivi des politiques publiques en encourageant et en facilitant le dialogue entre les autorités locales responsables de l'élaboration et l'exécution des budgets locaux et leurs mandants. Politique publique ! Ce nouveau concept du lexique onusien oblige les Affaires civiles, les droits de l'homme et leurs partenaires locaux à élaborer des politiques de participation non exclusives / sans discrimination, qui seront mises en œuvre avec efficacité, en visant le résultat.

La politique publique constitue, pour ainsi dire un dénominateur commun permettant à la section des Affaires civiles de mieux assurer son rôle de colonne vertébrale de la mission de maintien de la paix. Elle favorise l'esprit de responsabilisation, la sécurité et le maintien de l'état de droit, en impliquant directement les bénéficiaires dans le processus de conception et de réalisation des projets de développement de leur collectivité. C'est le nouvel outil, par excellence, au service des Affaires civiles et des droits de l'homme pour civiliser la population, à travers l'éducation des citoyens. Il permet d'humaniser l'Etat, via la décentralisation, tout en rendant les membres de la communauté plus citoyenne et responsable.

Il s'agit de mettre les bénéficiaires au centre du développement communal, sous un arbre à palabres, en traitant le problème à la racine, avec comme but de maximiser le bien-être d'un peuple, accroître le revenu par habitant puis, favoriser le plein-emploi et éviter la pauvreté subie.

La politique publique est, jusqu'à preuve du contraire, la méthode idéale ou plutôt, la plus efficace pour mettre en œuvre les droits économiques et socioculturels, tels que : assurer le droit au logement pour tous, permettre la circulation des personnes et des biens. Elle encourage la mise en place de réseaux de transport et garantit la situation sanitaire d'une population, par les campagnes de : prévention, soins et vaccinations.

Tout compte fait, sans rentrer dans les détails, la politique publique peut se définir comme une stratégie publique caractérisée par la composition d'actions coordonnées, conduites par les institutions et administrations publiques, avec un ensemble de moyens humains, financiers et matériels ; pour agir sur une situation structurelle ou conjoncturelle déterminée, telles que : infrastructure, santé, famille, logement, emploi, formation professionnelle, recherche, fonction publique, crise, déficit. Il permet d'atteindre un ensemble d'objectifs préalablement fixés, à savoir : l'égalité, la justice socioéconomique, la santé publique, le bien-être social, la résorption de la crise, le déficit budgétaire et autres.

De plus en plus, cette approche de politique publique est en train de devenir incontournable lorsqu'il s'agit d'obtenir une modification ou l'évolution d'une situation précise, puisque son évaluation est faite sur la base de la qualité et l'opportunité de l'intervention publique. Contrairement à la notion de service public, la politique publique oblige une évaluation après chaque intervention publique. Cette évaluation consiste à : analyser les résultats, c'est-à-dire déterminer si les objectifs assignés ont été atteints ; se fonder un jugement sur la valeur et les impacts de l'intervention et vérifier si les besoins que l'on cherche à satisfaire sont bien identifiés, en s'appuyant sur les données empiriques collectées.

Toutefois, la politique publique peut entrainer la création ou l'augmentation de certains impôts et taxes ou imposer des dotations budgétaires au profit des organismes, agences ou services, afin de leur permettre de réaliser les objectifs qui leur sont assignés. Bien entendu, la politique publique ne saurait être mise en œuvre sans une publicité adéquate, à travers les ondes officielles, afin d'inciter les citoyens à y participer massivement, surtout dans le cadre de la redistribution des richesses, notamment lorsque l'égalité des chances n'est pas assurée initialement.

Du point de vue stratégique, à travers le soutien de la société civile, il est possible de contourner le Ministère des collectivités territoriales pour résoudre les problèmes dont il est dans l'incapacité de trouver des solutions, sans pour autant violer le contenu du mandat de la mission.

Raison de plus, pour développer les compétences des citoyens et les capacités des organisations de la société civile à mieux comprendre et participer effectivement au processus de formulation et de suivi des politiques publiques constituées, notamment par l'ensemble de décisions prises et exécutées par l'Etat, les collectivités territoriales, les agences ou les tiers affiliés. C'est le meilleur moyen d'atteindre les objectifs publics avec une influence sur la vie des citoyens. Le but est de promouvoir la transparence, l'inclusion, le respect et la protection des droits des personnes dans le cadre des politiques gouvernementales.

Généralement, dans les Etats fragiles, la société civile souffre souvent d'un mutisme permanent. Même la diaspora s'implique peu dans sa reconstitution, sauf pour faire des plaidoyers en sa faveur, auprès des instances institutionnelles des pays où elle s'est installée et/ou par de petites contributions financières. Malheureusement, cela permet seulement à certaines associations à se fédérer politiquement autour de la contestation du pouvoir et de son exercice de façon autocratique. En conséquence, ces associations se limitent à demander un changement et/ou une alternance politique, ce qui ne dégage pas, pour autant, un projet sociétal.

Or, le ressort et le rôle de la société civile dans ses composantes multiples ne peuvent être réduits à une simple contestation du pouvoir, qui plus est : plus riche, plus divers et plus complexe. C'est en ces termes qu'il est important de renforcer les capacités de la société civile, en lui parlant de sa participation effective à la vie publique, comme constituant un grand et vrai enjeu national, pour que ladite nation reste démocratique, active et inclusive. Il s'agit d'aborder avec la société civile, une question importante, celle d'un autre rôle, d'une autre fonction, non seulement plus inclusive et plus participative, mais aussi dans un dialogue avec les pouvoirs publics, sur les problèmes liés aux politiques publiques, à leur définition et leur mise en œuvre. La société civile mérite d'être incitée à prendre conscience de son rôle, pour qu'elle se forge une idée de sa capacité institutionnelle et qu'elle connaisse les paramètres d'un plan d'action pour le développement.

Dans le même temps, il semble impératif d'encourager les autorités publiques à faciliter les processus participatifs, en leur expliquant les transformations consultatives visant à dégager des priorités d'action par la société civile, lesquelles seront avalisées par les autorités locales. Donc, il n'est pas vain que la société civile toute entière comprenne les exigences d'un processus participatif et ce qu'elle doit en attendre, en matière de bénéfices dans le cadre du développement et de la reconstruction d'une nation brisée par les conflits. Les thèmes pouvant être abordés dans cette optique de formation de la société civile sont, entre autres :

- les dispositions légales des structures de participation des collectivités territoriales ;
- le rôle de la société civile dans une société démocratique ;
- les actions prioritaires cernées et définies par les organisations de la société civile ;
- le dialogue national ;
- le renforcement d'un partenariat de confiance entre la société civile et les autorités politico-administratives, au niveau : central et régional ;
- les processus consultatifs départementaux ou communaux ;
- les enjeux de la participation des femmes dans le processus de développement ;
- la structuration d'une société civile dans une démarche participative ;
- l'élaboration d'un plan d'action pour le développement, à travers les outils tels que, l'analyse causale et budgétaire et les fiches d'évaluation des communautés des services de base.

Le but de ce renforcement de la société civile est aussi de montrer comment l'argent public est dépensé. Il faut donc encourager les conseils municipaux à tenir des assemblées municipales publiques pour présenter au public leur budget municipal et le solde de clôture de l'exercice financier précédent, dans le cadre des activités de sensibilisation des citoyens sur les systèmes de fiscalité locale. De même, l'appui aux initiatives anticorruptions en coordination avec les organismes locales doit être créé en partenariat avec la société civile. Dans tous les cas, il est essentiel que les acteurs nationaux prennent les devants dans la réalisation des évaluations, dans l'optique d'assurer la cohérence entre les besoins, les ressources et les priorités. Les

Affaires civiles n'interviennent qu'en cas de défaillance des partenaires locaux, sur demande des autorités nationales qui définissent la portée et l'objet de l'évaluation, et établissent le rôle et les responsabilités de chaque partenaire, ainsi que les résultats attendus.

Ainsi, un renforcement des capacités dignes de ce nom doit viser la reconstruction totale, avec l'implication de la société civile au vue de l'infrastructure post-conflictuelle. Il s'agit de renforcer les intérêts d'ordre non militaire pour créer une plate-forme pour la paix, en donnant à la société civile une marge et une voix pour exprimer son désir de paix et proposer sa stratégie de développement.

La société civile a toujours joué un rôle historique en matière d'aide sociale, mais elle est parfois cooptée et mal préparée à faire face à l'autoritarisme rampant d'un gouvernement, surtout lorsqu'elle est affaiblie et politiquement impotente.

Il est contre-productif d'ignorer ou négliger le rôle de la société civile aux côtés de l'Etat, notamment dans la prestation des services. Il y a là, de bonnes raisons de promouvoir des mécanismes non gouvernementaux de prestation d'aide en cas d'urgence, dans le but de rendre l'aide plus efficace et d'apporter de meilleurs rendements à court terme, de même qu'à plus long terme, en ce qui concerne la consolidation de la paix et la reconstruction après le conflit ou la catastrophe naturelle. En tant que cliente essentielle des ONG, elle est censée combler les écarts les plus importants creusés par l'Etat, en matière de services sociaux, notamment là où le gouvernement s'est écroulé ou quand il est l'une des forces en présence dans un conflit.

La société civile organisée peut même suppléer aux défaillances de l'Etat jusqu'à devenir le principal fournisseur de services sociaux publics, quitte à être la plus importante source d'emplois, particulièrement lorsqu'elle se joint aux organismes de secours et aux ONG, pour exécuter les programmes de plus grandes tailles prévus par les donateurs bilatéraux. En tant que telles, Les Affaires civils disposent des capacités d'affaiblir encore davantage les structures gouvernementales, en drainant ce qui reste des compétences professionnelles locales formées et qualifiées, qui sont attirées par les salaires faramineux et réguliers versés par les intervenants externes.

De nos jours, le renforcement des capacités ne se contente plus que d'exécuter des opérations caractérisant le raffinement conceptuel des faiblesses qui avaient été marquées par la pratique de renforcement d'organismes et de développement des ressources humaines. Il se transforme en un concept plus normatif, moins orienté vers la technique de renforcement des établissements ou du développement institutionnel, tout en encourageant l'aptitude des gens, des groupes, des institutions, des organismes et de la société civile à déterminer et affronter les défis au fil du temps. Cette donne indique qu'il y a refonte de la relation entre les donateurs et les pays en développement. L'objectif est de faire des capacités locales l'enjeu majeur sur lequel il faut concentrer tous les efforts. Il va falloir faciliter le développement d'organisations dans le cadre bien plus large que les efforts sectoriels ou nationaux, en vue d'améliorer les capacités de développement.

A vrai dire, les interventions s'inscrivent dans des contextes qui sont tellement différents qu'elles nécessitent des efforts de réaction qui varient en fonction d'un organisme ou d'une situation à l'autre. Cependant, il serait ahurissant de soutenir le renforcement des capacités qui ne prévoit pas de donner un espace de formation ou de consolidation de la société civile. Il est surtout déconseillé de ne pas faire fi de longues années d'expérience qu'elle a pu accumuler pour trouver le prétexte fallacieux qui donnera la possibilité d'agir sans elle.

Naturellement, le renforcement des capacités, signifie toute intervention visant à renforcer ou à créer des points forts dans une société. Il ressort de cet effort une société civile sur laquelle pourraient compter les collectivités territoriales et leur population pour compenser la vulnérabilité résultant d'un désastre survenu. Savoir quoi faire et quoi ne pas faire, puis lier l'intention à la réalité sont les préoccupations du renforcement des capacités.

Brièvement, le rôle fondamental de la société civile Organisée (SCO) au niveau étatique, régional et rural consiste à exercer un contrôle systématique sur leur représentant au parlement et dans les communes, en vue d'influencer les décisions et pour une application des prescrits de la décentralisation. C'est par là que passe la réussite d'un processus de développement local qui ne peut s'amorcer que par la base. Il n'est pas certain que les esprits les plus avisés de la société civile au niveau : étatique, provincial et rural soient tous sensibilisés sur cet enjeu capital. Parfois ces gens sont hésitants lorsqu'il faut s'engager dans la bataille pour apporter leur propre contribution et faire pression sur les pouvoirs : exécutif, parlementaire et judiciaire. Pourtant, il faut sortir l'Etat de sa lenteur symptomatique de sa situation sociopolitique de l'après-crise et de sa léthargie dans la consolidation de la démocratie et dans la lutte contre les inégalités et la fracture sociale qui en découle. D'où le renforcement de leurs capacités.

Sur le plan purement politique, force est de constater qu'il est fructueux de mobiliser les organisations de la société civile autour de leurs droits. Il s'agit de sensibiliser les groupements communautaires proche de la population, c'est-à-dire ceux qui attendent et demandent des services, en quelque sorte les vrais bénéficiaires. Le but est de faire participer la population qui est en droit de réclamer, dénoncer l'absentéisme des maires, par exemple, car le peuple souverain détient le pouvoir de destitution que personne ne peut contrer.

L'implication de la société civile suppose que des séances de formation soient données dans des domaines pertinents comme celui de la communication, pour apprendre aux participants comment revendiquer leurs droits, de façon pacifique et démocratique.

Cette implication dans le processus démocratique est indispensable à cause du rôle qu'elle joue, à savoir l'interface et l'agent d'information, de formation et d'éducation des populations à la base. Mais, pour qu'elle assume pleinement et efficacement cette fonction, elle a besoin de l'aide des Affaires civiles pour se structurer et former leurs acteurs. Ce travail de la section des Affaires civiles consiste à conseiller ces organisations à :

- développer des réseaux d'intégrité qui implique les personnes s'investissant comme catalyseur pour encourager les ONG et associations nationales existantes, à former des coalitions ;
- défendre la liberté d'expression et de réunion, ainsi que la liberté de manifester ;
- éduquer, sensibiliser et former les populations ;
- anticiper les problèmes socio-économiques et humanitaires, en attirant l'attention des gouvernants pour qu'ils élaborent des textes légaux encourageant les démarches participatives ;
- prévenir les conflits ;
- jouer le rôle d'arbitre entre l'Etat, les collectivités territoriales et les associations de défense des droits de l'homme ;
- rester en éveil sur les questions du genre ;
- veiller au respect scrupuleux des droits de la personne.

Autrement dit, le renforcement des capacités de la société civile signifie, entre autres :

- entretenir les partenariats avec elle, par composante sectorielle ;
- favoriser de manière substantielle les orientations et les mécanismes des projets de subvention de ladite société civile ;
- faire en sorte qu'elle soit bien conçue pour répondre aux besoins de la population ;
- encourager les activités et les projets mis en œuvre par des organisations de la société civile ;
- renforcer les sources d'informations relatives à la société civile et la démocratisation ;
- favoriser les meilleures pratiques et les enseignements tirés des programmes et des objectifs de politique nationale en faveur de la société civile ;
- soutenir le développement des politiques et des institutions qui se penchent sur les problèmes et les besoins des populations, en collaboration avec le gouvernement et d'autres partenaires stratégiques, y compris la société civile ;

- construire une synergie entre les organisations de la société civile œuvrant dans le domaine de la gouvernance démocratique et la décentralisation ;
- entretenir des partenariats plus larges dans les domaines de la gouvernance démocratique et des élections, communiquer et défendre les positions des partenaires internationaux et s'engager avec les partenaires du pays d'accueil de manière efficace ;
- assurer une gestion efficace de la composante société civile dans les programmes de la gouvernance Démocratique pour le Développement (GDD/DGD) ;
- promouvoir les relations contractuelles entre autorités de l'Etat et les organisations de la société civile et leur rôle pour assurer la pérennité de la société civile dans les pays sélectionnés ;
- faciliter le financement des organisations de la société civile en matière de financement par l'Etat et les autorités locales et en ce qui concerne les dons des particuliers et le secteur privé.

Qu'on le veuille ou non, la réforme de l'Etat est une entreprise trop importante pour la cantonner uniquement au niveau de la sphère de l'administration publique, du gouvernement et de la classe politique. C'est plutôt une affaire de tous les citoyens. Donc, il appartient à ces derniers de porter ce projet d'avenir qui intéresse, au premier chef, l'ensemble de la société civile. Mais, le devenir d'une nation dépend, en grande partie, du niveau d'appropriation de ses enjeux par les groupes organisés de la société civile.

Bref, pour capitaliser sur l'importance et l'influence de la société civile dans la réflexion globale sur les questions du développement et la protection de l'environnement et des droits humains en général, il est judicieux de centrer les préoccupations sur les politiques publiques dans les domaines ci-après :

- défendre l'organisation interne et l'obtention de la reconnaissance légale vis-à-vis des pouvoirs publics ;
- identifier les organisations crédibles et représentatives localement ; celles qui ont des activités de production, les réseaux d'associations de femmes et de paysans en particulier, pour faire face à la diversité et la multiplicité et s'appuyer sur ces connaissances locales ;
- soutenir la restructuration des Organisations de la Société Civile (OSC) dans le cadre d'une stratégie visant à favoriser la mise en commun des ressources et le renforcement des capacités, sur la base des idéologies communes, par exemple ;
- promouvoir les organisations qui visent l'autonomie communautaire et la résilience en termes de démarcation d'avec les partis politiques. Ce besoin fondamental d'indépendance devrait leur permettre de mieux

réclamer la transparence et la reddition des comptes, pour ainsi lutter efficacement contre la corruption ;

- multiplier les rencontres de discussion et d'échange sur le rôle de la société civile, en la spécialisant selon les domaines précis ;
- favoriser les partenariats entre divers acteurs et minimiser les écarts d'organisation et d'information entre les différents réseaux de la société civile ;
- renforcer les capacités institutionnelles de la société ci vile, tout en évitant de créer des attentes non comblées ;
- appuyer les organisations qui centrent l'action sur la formation, leréseautage,le partage d'expérience et de compétence ;
- encourager les bailleurs de fonds à ne pas se retirer rapidement, surtout lorsqu'ils ont commencé l'appui a un projet, au risque de mettre l'organisation bénéficiaire dans une situation encore plus délicate ;
- élaborer des critères permettant d'éviter de travailler avec les associations opportunistes qui se comptent par milliers et mettre en commun toutes les connaissances et l'expertise des différentes institutions au sein de la grande famille des Nations Unies, sans oublier de renforcer la concertation entre les membres de cette famille lors de la planification d'activités. Dans ce contexte de partenariat, il est important de s'assurer que la compréhension est la même entre partenaires, c'est-à-dire l'égalité entre partenaires et le partage des capacités ;
- éviter des engagements trop basés sur les individus plutôt que sur les organisations ;
- dans le cadre d'appui aux organisations des femmes, il convient de se concentrer surtout sur celles qui font la production agricole, la protection des enfants, la prévention des violences faites aux femmes, enfants et filles, sans oublier la participation politique des femmes dans la vie publique.

Toute société civile organisée replace les détenteurs des droits au centre des préoccupations dans l'élaboration, la définition et l'exécution des politiques publiques. Et, le renforcement des capacités fait appel à une synergie et une coordination entre les Affaires civiles d'une part, les partis et les leaders politiques, les autorités gouvernementales et locales, ainsi que la société civile d'autre part, ce qui implique une autre notion : la gouvernance.

D. LE CONCEPT DE « GOUVERNANCE »

Gouvernance ! Le mot est grec. Il dérive de « kyberman » qui signifie « naviguer » et « kybernetes » c'est-à-dire « piloter ». En un mot, la gouvernance traduit l'idée de conduire ou d'utiliser différents mécanismes permettant d'assurer la direction cohérente de la cité.

En réalité, c'est au XIIIème siècle que ce concept atteindra le sommet de sa popularité et prendra véritablement la connotation de gouvernance, au sens du « gouvernement », indiquant ainsi qu'il s'agit de la coordination des acteurs d'une entité et des dynamiques qui les animent.

Il ressort de cette étymologie, l'action de piloter un système ou de coordonner une démarche collective sur fond d'ordre organisationnel. La gouvernance fait davantage appel à la négociation entre les acteurs du système, qui ne sont pas toujours sur la même longueur d'onde. Elle décrit une régulation qui, désormais, ne repose pas exclusivement sur les mécanismes du marché et des interventions de l'Etat, mais de plus en plus sur une société civile organisée en tant que pièce maitresse du système. Faut-il rappeler que c'est, entre autres, la perte de confiance des citoyens envers leur gouvernement couplée de l'émergence d'une approche territoriale du développement, ayant entrainé la multiplicité des acteurs et des centres des décisions qui sont réellement à l'origine de l'apparition de la notion de gouvernance ?

La gouvernance vient du principe de « gouvernabilité. » C'est une politique qui place le « droit » et « l'ordre » au centre du développement, en englobant une série de mécanismes et de processus susceptibles de maintenir le système. Elle consiste à responsabiliser la population et à faire en sorte que la société et ses composantes s'approprient le processus.

La gouvernance est pour ainsi dire, la réponse adéquate aux nouvelles préoccupations des populations contemporaines qui militent en faveur du développement humain. Les gouvernements démocratiques n'ont désormais plus d'autres alternatives que de tisser des liens de partenariat avec la société civile et le secteur privé, multiplicité des acteurs oblige. De surcroît, la tendance actuelle est de se rapprocher le plus possible des besoins des individus, c'est-à-dire au niveau : local et régional. Il faut se placer au plus près des problèmes et des individus pour toute concertation sur l'environnement social, économique et politique, en vue d'un développement durable : le principe de la subsidiarité[23] gagne ainsi ses lettres de noblesse.

---

[23] D'origine latine, le mot subsidiarité est un principe politique et social qui vient de « subsidiarii » qui veut dire troupe de réserve, ou « subsidium » qui signifie réserve, recours ou appuis. Par rapport à cette étymologie, il reflète un double mouvement, à la fois de non-intervention relative à la subsidiarité qui veut que la responsabilité d'une action publique soit allouée à la plus petite entité capable de résoudre le problème d'elle-même, puis de la capacité d'intervention indiquant la suppléance qui veut que, quand les problèmes excèdent les capacités d'une petite entité, l'échelon supérieur ait, alors, le devoir de la soutenir, dans les limites du

La subsidiarité ou le primat du principe de proximité est caractérisé par la montée en puissance des approches territoriales en économie du développement. Elle implique la diminution progressive du développement de l'Etat providence qui met en cause le rôle traditionnel de l'Etat, et impose la nécessité d'une nouvelle approche du développement local durable. On parle d'ailleurs de la gouvernance locale pour désigner la place des collectivités territoriales, éléments-clés de ce processus de développement.

Il est actuellement possible d'apprécier une diversité des caractéristiques de la gouvernance, à savoir :

- démarche qui consiste à mettre l'accent sur les « réseaux » qui se tissent ou se consolident sur le plan territorial et sur les manifestations de « solidarité » observées çà et là et aussi sur les « décisions consensuelles » qui se prennent sans ingérence extérieure ;
- processus de diffusion de la politique caractérisé par un élargissement de l'exercice de la citoyenneté vers les acteurs sociaux qui soutiennent les modes décisionnels décentralisés accompagnés du respect de leur qualité de vie ;
- gestion des affaires publiques fondée sur le partage des pouvoirs entre acteurs territoriaux ayant pour conséquence la diminution de la centralité de l'État au profit d'une approche moins institutionnelle, mais plus collective soutenue par les populations locales ;
- mécanisme de coordination focalisée sur la coopération, les réseaux, les conventions, les alliances, le partenariat, destiné à gérer une pluralité d'acteurs plus ou moins autonomes, mais interdépendants. Du reste, ce mécanisme se distingue du marché, c'est-à-dire la régulation par les prix et par le gouvernement, à savoir la régulation par la hiérarchie ;
- forme de gestion des affaires sociales, attachée à la volonté de tenir compte de la nouvelle donne de pluralité au détriment de la bureaucratie publique ;
- capacité de gouverner des réseaux inter-organisationnels autonomes, en réduisant le rôle du gouvernement à celui d'un acteur parmi tant d'autres, sans pour autant le faire disparaître totalement. En fait, il ne faut surtout pas laisser les citoyens et la communauté suivre leur propre voie. Le risque est qu'ils ne tiennent pas compte de leurs multiples partenaires, y compris leurs partenaires institutionnels ;

---

principe de subsidiarité. Ces deux principes fonctionnent ensemble dans la relation entre l'Etat et les collectivités territoriales dans le cadre de la décentralisation. Ils permettent de veiller à ne pas faire à un niveau plus élevé ce qui peut l'être avec plus d'efficacité à une échelle plus faible, c'est-à-dire la recherche du niveau pertinent d'action publique. Cette théorie bien définie dans le lexique politique et sur le site Wikipédia, est une formule très utilisée dans le domaine du développement durable.

- processus de dialogue continu entre les acteurs d'un système institutionnel, sur la négociation simultanée et continue à propos des objectifs poursuivis et des moyens d'action retenus. Ceci établit inévitablement une relation d'interdépendance entre les acteurs impliqués qui de surcroît, se regroupent autour des fins partagées ;
- mode de pilotage politique capable de s'adapter à des environnements économiques en mutation et qui se construit à partir d'une trame complexe d'interactions entre acteurs. En ce sens, elle est différente système organisé entièrement autour d'un gouvernement mono centré qui rappelle les régimes totalitaires ou monarchiques ;
- modèle de gouvernance politique fondée sur une régulation spécifique du pouvoir et de la prise de décision qui émerge dans un système sociopolitique en tant que résultat « commun » de l'interaction de tous les acteurs en présence, dans une communauté donnée ;
- structure de gouvernance qui s'appuie sur un processus de coordination d'acteurs, de groupes sociaux, d'institutions pour atteindre des buts propres discutés et définis collectivement, dans des environnements fragmentés et incertains ;
- technique de coordination d'une pluralité d'acteurs et d'institutions différentes, organisée selon une structure intermédiaire d'apprentissage collectif, génératrice d'une dynamique collective spécifique. Elle permet d'apprécier les règles et routines qui créaient la spécificité d'un lieu vis-à-vis d'autres lieux et vis-à-vis du système productif qui l'englobe ;
- brassage d'acteurs, les uns amarrés dans la société civile, tandis que d'autres sont attachés aux appareils de gestion publique. Cela suppose que des interactions synergiques entre les acteurs publics, privés, communautaires et les citoyens, pour favoriser un véritable développement durable approprié à une société donnée.

Loin d'être une sorte d'abdication de l'État face à l'idéologie libérale, pour donner carte blanche aux privatisations, la gouvernance est plutôt une « réappropriation » par les acteurs sociaux, via l'activation des réseaux, des interactions et des alliances, liés par différentes instances de médiation et de coordination. Elle permet à l'Etat de s'adapter à la conduite d'analyses à l'échelle locale et au développement local durable à partir des collectivités territoriales. La gouvernance implique donc les facteurs suivants :

- démocratie élective caractérisée par des élections libres et transparentes ;
- démocratie participative évoquant la participation de la population et la société civile dans le processus de prise de décision ;
- administration intègre et efficace ;

- transparence dans la gestion de la chose publique.

L'objectif principal de la gouvernance est d'aboutir à la cohésion sociale pour atteindre le développement. Elle nécessite de grands efforts de négociation, de concertation, de mise en réseaux à l'échelle des collectivités territoriales : régions, microrégions, communes, collines, sections communales, zones, quartiers, localités…

La gouvernance regroupe trois notions essentielles :

- multi-acteurs, ce qui impose le système de partenariats ;
- multi-territoires, ce qui évoque le fait que ce soit du local au global ;
- multi-secteurs, ce qui englobe les paramètres concernant le social à l'économique.

C'est à travers ces dimensions qu'il est possible d'apprécier la gouvernance. Cela tient compte de la capacité d'innovation, de création et de développement permettant à un gouvernement de faire converger tous ces niveaux d'intervention socio-économique et politique. La gouvernance se fait en fonction des objectifs sociaux définis localement, mais aussi par rapport à l'aptitude d'instaurer des contrats sociaux, des réseaux, la confiance inter-individus et intergroupes qui incarnent ensemble la force d'agir d'un gouvernement.

Elle présume l'existence préalable d'une vraie décentralisation du pouvoir de l'État vers les collectivités locales et une déconcentration administrative et celle des services publics qui conditionnent les dimensions fondamentales suivantes :

- la capacité d'appréhender les problématiques socioéconomiques et environnementales du milieu, de façon hostile et transversale ;
- la participation active des citoyens aux processus décisionnels et à l'administration de la vie du milieu, incluant les populations traditionnellement marginalisées ;
- le développement de partenariats entre l'administration municipale et les acteurs des secteurs communautaires et privés, et cetera.

La gouvernance doit inclure et répondre à la problématique des pays en transition et en développement puisqu'elle est étroitement liée à plusieurs activités de développement concernant :

- l'élimination de la pauvreté ;
- la création d'emplois ;
- la protection de l'environnement ;
- l'intégration sociale ;
- la gestion économique ;
- les réformes de l'agriculture et la justice pour ne citer que ceux-là ;
- le contrôle des populations ;

- la question des femmes et des filles qui sont toutes dépendantes d'une gouvernance efficace.

Elle tient compte de l'influence des besoins, des contributions et de la responsabilité du secteur privé et/ou de la société civile qui joue le rôle de catalyseur. La gouvernance va au-delà de la gestion du secteur public qui ne vise qu'une seule perspective celle de l'Etat, pour s'étendre sur celle du peuple. Il ne s'agit nullement, de réinventer la roue en générant un nouvel ensemble d'activités de coopération, mais d'élargir le concept de gouvernance pour permettre de tenir compte de l'ensemble des interactions entre tous ceux qui participent à la prise de décision :

- entre l'Etat et la société civile ;
- à l'intérieur de la société civile ;
- à l'intérieur de l'appareil étatique ;
- entre l'État et le secteur privé et entre le gouvernement central et les collectivités territoriales.

Cela se traduit par la coordination de l'ensemble des établissements, des procédés et des traditions qui dictent l'exercice du pouvoir, la prise de décision et la façon dont les citoyens font entendre leur voix.

La gouvernance s'intéresse donc à :

- l'engagement des citoyens et la « responsabilisation » des gouvernements envers ceux-ci ;
- le développement des capacités aux fins de bonne gouvernance ;
- la réforme de la fonction publique ;
- l'implication du secteur bénévole.

Tout ceci nous conduit vers le développement participatif et la bonne gestion des affaires publiques au sens des principes et stratégies à appliquer et des actions à mener en reliant la gestion du secteur public à la gouvernance et au développement humain.

De nos jours, le temps où les populations se contentaient de la gestion au jour le jour de leurs problèmes de vie quotidienne n'est plus à l'ordre du jour. Elles revendiquent vivement, haut et fort, la gouvernance efficace des affaires publiques, qui passe par la gouvernance locale et qui s'applique à travers la décentralisation, avec l'espoir de disposer des espaces de liberté, de dialogue et de concertation. Toute nation a besoin de la libre expression de toutes les composantes de la population qui demeure, jusqu'à preuve du contraire, un signe d'appropriation de la démarche de développement local durable et de la bonne gouvernance.

La décentralisation se situe à la croisée de chemins entre les stratégies et politiques nationales de lutte contre la pauvreté et la promotion d'un développement humain en milieu urbain et rural.

Elle devrait s'accompagner ou, tout au moins, être porteuse d'un développement économique local durable dont le but est d'améliorer les conditions de vie des populations locales, ce qui, bien entendu, constitue une attente légitime surtout dans le cas de situation post-crise.

Par conséquent, les pouvoirs publics locaux doivent être d'abord des organisateurs et des promoteurs du développement durable qui implique l'idée d'un partenariat avec la communauté de base et la société civile, car c'est dans ce sens qu'il convient de comprendre le concept d'obligation de résultat et de la transparence dans la gestion des affaires publiques.

Toute politique de développement local durable basée sur la décentralisation doit avoir pour objectif de :

- présenter les orientations nationales en matière de développement rural et les stratégies qui en découlent ;
- servir de cadre de référence pour la conception, la mise en œuvre, la coordination et le suivi ainsi que l'évaluation des projets et programmes de développement rural que le gouvernement et ses partenaires envisagent d'entreprendre ;
- promouvoir l'harmonisation des démarches de ces différents programmes et projets ;
- décrire les mécanismes que le gouvernement entend mettre en place avec ses partenaires pour assurer la coordination et le suivi et l'évaluation des actions en matière de développement rural décentralisé.

Cela explique une vision prospective du développement communautaire où les populations sont appelées à jouer le rôle de premier plan, sur toutes les décisions relatives aux investissements, notamment dans les collectivités territoriales, tout en plaçant la gestion des ressources naturelles à la base des activités productives.

La gouvernance caractérise l'exercice du pouvoir politique et le contrôle dans le cadre de l'administration des ressources de la société aux fins du développement économique et social. Elle précise à la fois le rôle que jouent les pouvoirs publics dans la création du cadre des activités des agents économiques et dans la décision en matière de redistribution des avantages et de la nature des rapports entre gouvernants et gouvernés. Cette technique est principalement axée sur les aspects économiques et sociaux.

Il n'est pas gratuit ou fortuit d'affirmer que la gouvernance est avant tout la façon dont une unité sociale, de la société entière à la plus petite association bénévole s'organise politiquement pour formuler et exécuter les politiques publiques, identifier les priorités et résoudre les problèmes publics, allouer et gérer les ressources publiques. Elle est reconnue comme la méthode de gestion du pouvoir et des ressources publiques, dans un espace public. Cette technique s'apprécie : bonne ou mauvaise en fonction de la participation et la transparence, du devoir sinon de l'obligation de rendre compte de l'efficacité et l'équité, selon une approche normative.

C'est la manière de gérer un espace public, c'est-à-dire l'endroit où les acteurs de la société : société civile, associations et ONG, entrepreneurs public et privé, institutions et organisations formelles ou informelles entreprennent, en interaction, des actes qui ont des impacts sur les unités sociales. Dans ces unités, on trouve les familles, les communautés et la nation entière, ce qui nécessite un mode de gestion adapté, pour mieux répondre aux préoccupations de la population.

Théoriquement la gouvernance est le résultat des processus sociaux politiques internes à une société. C'est aussi le résultat des processus exogènes dont l'origine n'est pas clairement étudiée.

Elle n'est appréciable que lorsque la gouvernance est efficace. Par conséquent, si l'enjeu de la gouvernance est d'apporter un changement social, alors, ce changement qui se définit comme un « ensemble observable des mutations affectant tout ou partie de l'organisation sociale pendant une période donnée[24] », ne peut se réaliser, que dans le cadre d'une bonne gouvernance.

E. L'IDEE DE BONNE GOUVERNANCE

La gouvernance démocratique est un concept qui a émergé à partir des principes basés sur la compréhension d'un système efficace de gouvernabilité. Ce système est lui-même fondé sur : la représentativité, l'égalité des genres, les institutions transparentes, responsables et inclusives ; accompagné d'une dynamique des médias, responsables et capables avec une société civile organisée et engagée dans le processus politique. L'objectif global de cette gouvernance démocratique pour le développement (DGD) est de contribuer au renforcement des capacités des institutions nationales et sous national, des réseaux et des processus, qu'elles soient gouvernementales ou non gouvernementales, en tant que facteur essentiel de la perpétuation de la gouvernance démocratique.

La bonne gouvernance que d'aucuns appellent gouvernance ou gestion efficace du développement, traduit l'aptitude des pouvoirs publics à définir et mettre en œuvre des politiques cohérentes et à s'acquitter des fonctions qui leur incombent avec dignité, efficacité et responsabilité. Elle s'attache à la primauté du droit, aux valeurs efficientes de la gestion du secteur public, au rendement et à la productivité dans la lutte contre la corruption et la réduction de la pauvreté, ainsi que les dépenses militaires.

[24] Présentation de Djoumé Sylla Chargé de programme FENU, « La décentralisation entre deux courants de pensée : ses avantages et ses inconvénients », United Nations Development Programme PNUD), Bulletin d'information du PNUD au Mali, juillet 2004

Elle doit respecter et s'adapter aux paramètres du développement durable, afin de devenir le cadre de gestion des affaires publiques fondée sur la primauté du droit ou de l'Etat de droit, sur un système de justice équitable et efficace, puis sur la participation active et massive de la population dans la relation entre gouvernants et gouvernés. Cela nécessite la mise en place des mécanismes permettant de soutenir le système, en « autonomisant » les individus et en leur donnant une véritable appropriation du processus.

C'est donc une façon d'exercer l'autorité politique, économique et administrative dans la gestion des affaires de la cité. Elle englobe les structures organisationnelles et les activités de l'Etat, des collectivités territoriales, du parlement, du pouvoir judiciaire, des Organisations Non Gouvernementales et association, sans oublier les individus qui composent la société civile et le secteur privé. Cela se fait dans la mesure où ces derniers participent activement et influencent la formation des politiques publiques qui touchent à la vie de toute la communauté.

L'Etat est « une communauté politique organisée sous un gouvernement », et la gouvernance est « le processus par lequel les décisions sont prises et mises en œuvre » tandis que la bonne gouvernance est fondée sur les principes de participation, de consensus, de responsabilité de transparence, de réactivité, d'efficacité et d'efficience. En d'autres termes, il s'agit de bonnes pratiques dans le processus de prise de décision et de sa bonne exécution.

L'autorité de l'État dépend beaucoup de la confiance que les citoyens placent dans ses mécanismes de prise de décision sur la base du respect que l'Etat accorde à leurs intérêts individuels, sans être au-dessus de l'intérêt collectif. Ce « contrat social », pour reprendre les termes de Jean-Jacques Rousseau, caractérisé par la relation entre ceux qui gouvernent et ceux qui sont gouvernés, permet de définir la « bonne gouvernance. »

Par ailleurs, la déclaration du G8 (les Huit Pays le Plus Industrialisés au Monde) d'avril 2010 à Dili, au Timor Leste apporte de l'eau dans notre moulin. Il reconnait implicitement la nécessité de renforcer la bonne gouvernance dans les nations fragiles pour garantir une administration publique et la gestion financière ouverte et transparente. Selon ce G8, ce sont les principes de bonne gouvernance qui caractérisent l'efficacité et l'efficience de l'administration publique dans un Etat post-conflit et cette bonne gouvernance constitue une condition évidente de la stabilité et la paix.

La gouvernance efficace est liée à l'environnement institutionnel dans lequel les citoyens interagissent entre eux et avec les agences gouvernementales. Elle traduit la façon dont un gouvernement gère les ressources sociales et économiques d'un pays. C'est une saine gestion des affaires publiques, qui désigne un exercice du pouvoir, à divers échelons du gouvernement, de façon efficace, intègre, équitable, transparent et comptable.

La tâche qui incombe à la section des Affaires civiles est d'aider les gouvernants à articuler ces pratiques de gouvernance, à travers le renforcement des capacités, qui encourage le développement durable. Cette section contribue à promouvoir l'Etat de droit sans lequel le développement local durable est un leurre.

Le monde est arrivé à une époque où il faut absolument redéfinir la notion de leadership national et local, qui elle-même exige une nouvelle coopération au niveau : national et local, entre l'Etat, la société civile et le secteur privé, travaillant ensemble pour le bien collectif de toute une nation. De nos jours, la bonne gouvernance inclut aussi la notion de gouvernance locale qui traduit l'autorité exercée par les collectivités territoriales dans la gestion des affaires publiques locales dans un domaine préalablement défini par la loi.

Les particularités de cette gouvernance locale sont :

- processus par lequel les autorités locales sont choisies, contrôlées et remplacées, transition oblige ;
- caractéristiques de la capacité de l'Etat à élaborer et appliquer efficacement des politiques saines au niveau des collectivités territoriales ;
- respect par les citoyens et l'Etat, des institutions locales qui régissent les interactions économiques et sociales entre collectivités.

Les facteurs économiques, politiques et sociaux qui ont une influence sur la bonne gouvernance sont :

- les organisations et agences de l'ONU ;
- les régimes politiques ;
- le parlement ;
- les pouvoirs judiciaires ;
- les ONG et associations nationales et internationales ;
- la société civile ;
- les institutions publiques et privées ;
- le système formel et/ou informel de valeurs ;
- les normes et les règles de procédure utilisées pour gérer les ressources humaines, naturelles et économiques ;
- l'aptitude du gouvernement à formuler et mettre en œuvre des politiques, y compris changer les organisations, influencer les institutions et modifier la nature des interactions entre les organisations et les institutions, sans oublier la nature des interactions entre l'autorité politique et la société civile, incluant la liberté d'expression et le rôle des médias ;
- la modernisation du gouvernement et le renforcement de la société civile ;
- la démocratie multipartite ;

- le pluralisme et les questions reliées aux droits humains et aux libertés fondamentales ;
- la reconnaissance et l'application des principes démocratiques,
- la consolidation de la primauté du droit et du bon gouvernement.

Les critères d'évaluation de la bonne gouvernance se réduisent à :

- intégrité ;
- mise en œuvre des politiques économiques et sociales ;
- gestion du secteur public ;
- existence d'un cadre juridique et légale ;
- lutte contre la corruption ;
- réduction des dépenses militaires dans les cas d'urgence politique complexe ;
- engagement des citoyens et « responsabilisation » des gouvernements envers ceux-ci ;
- développement des capacités aux fins d'avoir un bon gouvernement ;
- réforme du secteur public ;
- transition du secteur bénévole ;
- cadre légal et juridique ;
- coopération avec les organisations de la société civile ;
- décentralisation ;
- rôle des médias et liberté d'expression ;
- interfaces entre secteurs public et privé ;
- sécurité, paix, résolution de conflits ;
- allocation des ressources ;
- égalité des genres.

Ceci explique l'aptitude d'un gouvernement à formuler et mettre en œuvre des politiques, y compris changer les organisations, influencer les institutions, corriger la nature des interactions entre organisations-institutions, selon les règles suivantes :

- participation. Elle se définit comme un processus participatif direct ou indirect, par l'intermédiaire des institutions légitimes ou de leurs représentants. La participation encourage la liberté d'association et d'expression. Elle est organisée, pour faciliter la participation de la société civile organisée ;
- primauté du droit. La bonne gouvernance exige un cadre juridique qui soit applicable de manière impartiale et des lois équitables, prévoyant la protection intégrale des droits de l'homme, en particulier ceux des minorités. Dans un Etat post-conflituel, l'impartialité requiert non seulement, un pouvoir judiciaire indépendant, mais aussi une force de police impartiale et incorruptible ;

- transparence, ce qui signifie que les décisions sont prises et appliquées dans le respect des règles et règlements. Donc l'information est disponible gratuitement et directement accessible à ceux qui seront touchés par ces décisions, qui elles-mêmes sont applicables. De son côté, la presse exerce son rôle d'informer dans les formes compréhensibles et accessibles à tous ;
- imputabilité. Cela requiert que l'Etat assume sa responsabilité envers toutes les parties prenantes dans un délai raisonnable qui satisfasse les besoins de la population ;
- consensus. Il oblige la médiation entre les différents intérêts dans la société pour privilégier l'intérêt collectif. Le consensus les perspectives du développement durable, mais la manière d'atteindre ces objectifs doit résulter de la compréhension du contexte historique, culturel et social d'une société ou d'une collectivité ;
- équité sociale et non-exclusion. Cette règle veut qu'aucun membre ou groupe de la société ne soit pas exclu de l'ensemble de la communauté à laquelle il appartient, y compris les plus vulnérables à qui il est accordé la possibilité de s'améliorer ou maintenir leur bien-être ;
- efficacité et efficience, ce qui soulignent la production des résultats en matière de processus et des institutions, pour répondre aux besoins de la société tout en faisant le meilleur usage des ressources disponibles. La notion d'efficience évoque l'utilisation des ressources naturelles dans le cadre du développement durable, ce qui inclut la protection de l'environnement ;
- responsabilisation. En tant qu'exigence clé de la bonne gouvernance, elle souligne l'obligation gouvernementale, du secteur privé et de la société civile à être responsables devant le peuple et l'Etat. A la question de savoir qui est responsable envers qui, la réponse varie selon que les décisions sont prises par une organisation ou une institution. En général, une organisation ou une institution est responsable devant ceux qui seront touchés par ses mesures selon qu'elles soient internes ou externes. Dans tous les cas, la responsabilité ne peut s'appliquer sans transparence ni Etat de droit.

En un mot, la promotion de la bonne gouvernance apporte aux citoyens ordinaires un accès plus direct aux institutions de la gouvernance. Elle facilite le flux de communication nécessaire entre les autorités locales et des citoyens pour encourager la « responsabilisation » et la transparence, ainsi que leur corolaire, l'approche participative dans la prise de décision. Par conséquent, les Affaires civiles doivent mener les actions servant à :

- évaluer les capacités et lacunes des communautés locales existantes, en faisant des recommandations aux bailleurs de fonds, au gouvernement central et aux partenaires de l'ONU, pour renforcer les zones prioritaires ;

- aider les autorités locales à accroître la « responsabilisation » des administrations locales par la promotion de la politique fiscale, les bases de revenus et les zones de prestation de services ;
- divulguer les canaux et les mécanismes existants de règlement des différends ;
- soutenir les relations entre le gouvernement central et les collectivités territoriales.

Cet appui à la gouvernance locale passe par :

- une collaboration tacite et effective entre les Affaires civiles et le Ministère des collectivités territoriales ;
- la mise en place d'un système de gestion financière et administrative de base ;
- l'élaboration des budgets communaux et présentation des rapports financiers mensuels ;
- le renforcement de connaissance en gestion administrative et financière, puis en comptabilité communale ;
- la formation et le déploiement des cadres municipaux dans divers domaines et dans l'utilisation des nouvelles technologies ;
- la revalorisation des potentialités fiscales municipales par le renforcement des capacités des collectivités locales à recouvrer les créances publiques locales des communes ;
- l'amélioration de la collaboration entre la Mairie, la Direction Générale des Impôts, la Cour des Comptes en matière des finances publiques locales ;
- le renforcement des capacités des institutions déconcentrées afin qu'elles puissent remplir efficacement leur rôle de coordination et d'assumer pleinement la tutelle sur les collectivités locales ;
- un appui de proximité, marqué par les formations de manière systématique et l'encadrement permanents des collectivités ;
- les visites de travail conjointes et régulières entre les Affaires civiles et le Ministère des collectivités territoriales dans les communes.

Les éléments-clés d'un système de gouvernance locale efficace et effectif, sur lesquels il convient de mettre l'accent sont :

- la procédure bien formalisée, c'est-à-dire un cadre légal ou Institutionnel ;
- la promotion du développement socio-économique de base, par l'approche participative ;
- la gestion transparente des affaires publiques locales par le biais d'une structure administrative politiquement neutre ;

- l'amélioration dans la satisfaction des besoins immédiats de la population ;
- la consistance, l'endurance et la continuité, même pendant des périodes d'instabilité ou de transition politique ;
- la collaboration avec d'autres secteurs, tels que : le secteur public, parapublic et privé, les ONG et la société civile, pour fournir de meilleurs services de base à la population.

Cette bonne gouvernance ne peut pas se réaliser sans l'existence d'un Etat légitime, responsable et engagé dans le combat pour l'implantation de la démocratie et l'impulsion du développement économique et social, puis le respect des droits de l'homme. Dans le même ordre d'idées, elle ne peut se faire sans l'apport de la société civile structurée, organisée et dynamique pouvant soutenir les collectivités territoriales.

F. LA NOTION DE « COLLECTIVITE TERRITORIALE »

Une collectivité territoriale peut se définir comme une institution politico-administrative territoriale décentralisée dans un Etat unitaire, lui-même décentralisé. C'est donc une division territoriale autonome, d'essence participative, concourant à l'exécution des politiques d'aménagement du territoire et à la gestion des affaires publiques. Elle constitue un excellent cadre de mobilisation et de participation de la population à laquelle elle doit fournir des services publics, en vue de promouvoir le progrès social, économique et culturel. La collectivité territoriale est aussi une zone de libre administration ayant des compétences qui lui sont attribuées par la Constitution et/ou par la loi.

Les collectivités territoriales sont caractérisées par :

- une dénomination, une population et une superficie bien délimitée du territoire national. Cela signifie qu'une collectivité territoriale est dotée d'une portion bien définie de la population. Et, cette population est établie sur une partie bien délimitée du territoire national et qui possède un nom propre ;
- un conseil exécutif qui s'occupe des problèmes locaux spécifiques distincts des problèmes nationaux et assure sa libre administration ;
- une Assemblée délibérante dont le rôle est de définir et orienter la politique de développement de la collectivité. Elle délibère sur toutes les questions nationales ayant des conséquences sur le territoire de la collectivité, puis statue sur toutes les propositions du conseil exécutif, prend toutes les dispositions nécessaires et contrôle tous les actes du conseil ;

- des ressources propres à leur disposition, octroyées par le pouvoir central sous diverses formes, notamment, les subventions, dotations, emprunts consolidés…, et/ou générés par une fiscalité appropriée, lui permettant de réaliser les compétences qui lui sont dévolues ;
- l'obtention des vocations et des compétences spécifiques définies par les textes légaux ;
- une autonomie administrative et financière qui responsabilise les autorités locales ;
- une personnalité morale ou juridique, en relation avec la notion d'affaires locales et qui lui donne le droit d'ester en justice, c'est-à-dire la capacité d'exercer des recours par-devant les tribunaux compétents, contre les interventions jugées arbitraires des autorités de l'administration centrale ou déconcentrée et contre d'autres collectivités ou contre des tierces. Certes qu'elle a des droits, mais elle a aussi des devoirs.

Le statut de personne morale des collectivités territoriales détermine leur niveau d'autonomie par rapport aux autres institutions publiques. Il balise et influence la nature des rapports politico-administratifs entre l'Etat et elles, puis entre différentes collectivités. Il lui octroie aussi certaines compétences administratives propres, ainsi que des compétences techniques, incluant les modalités d'exercice de ces compétences qui leur permet de disposer des attributions, telles que :

- l'autonomie administrative et financière dans les conditions définies par la loi, incluant les exigences de conformité de leurs actes ;
- les compétences attribuées par la Constitution et celles qui doivent être définies par la loi sans oublier celles dont l'exercice peut être contesté en justice, notamment en matière de responsabilité civile et pénale ;
- un patrimoine faisant partie de leur domaine privé ;
- des ressources financières comme les emprunts et le pouvoir fiscal ;
- le droit d'association qui sous-entend la coopération décentralisée.

Généralement, c'est la Constitution qui attribue explicitement ou implicitement la personnalité morale aux départements et communes, en conférant aux communes une autonomie administrative et financière, faisant partie des attributs de la personnalité morale, tout comme elle prévoit l'existence éventuelle de litiges entre l'Etat et les collectivités territoriales. La Constitution accorde souvent à ces dernières le droit de disposer du monopole d'intérêt public.

Les modalités d'exercice de ces compétences décrivent leur niveau d'autonomie par rapport à l'Etat, la gestion des rapports avec ces derniers et l'administration des rapports des collectivités territoriales entre elles.

Cependant, ce statut n'est pas non plus indépendant de leurs vocations et de la nature des compétences techniques à attribuer à chacune des collectivités territoriales. De même, la présence d'élus au suffrage universel direct, donnant ou non aux collectivités territoriales la légitimité pour intervenir directement sur le territoire, engendre de mini-Etats.

Leurs vocations et compétences sont donc constituées par les prérogatives Constitutionnelles. Elles découlent des nominations et de la composition des organes qui les constituent. Ces prérogatives sont de droit lorsqu'elles sont relatives à leur statut. Elles sont politiques lorsqu'il s'agit des compétences d'ordre stratégique, concernant les prises de décisions qui traduisent l'articulation des interventions de l'Etat sur le territoire. Mais, des prérogatives doivent être partagées avec d'autres institutions publiques dans le cadre de l'Etat unitaire décentralisé. Elles peuvent aussi être d'ordre technique puisqu'elles sont parfois spécifiques à l'une ou l'autre des collectivités territoriales et elles sont partagées avec l'administration centrale à des fins de fonctionnalité.

Pour déterminer les compétences des collectivités territoriales on utilise les paramètres énumérés ci-dessous :

- les provisions constitutionnelles et les tendances qui s'en dégagent ;
- la présence ou non d'élus directs, de préférence issus du suffrage universel, pour garantir la légitimité de leurs interventions ;
- l'emboîtement des divisions territoriales administratives et des collectivités territoriales ;
- la question de subsidiarité posée par la superficie du territoire ;
- un continuum à assurer entre les fonctions de l'administration centrale et les activités des collectivités territoriales, notamment dans les secteurs de la santé, de l'éducation… ;
- la qualité ou la quantité de services à assurer pouvant parfois requérir une présence forte de l'administration publique ;
- l'incapacité ou les défaillances structurelles de l'administration publique à fournir convenablement certains services collectifs à toute la population, le cas de curage, drainage, ramassage d'ordures, distribution de l'eau potable et bien d'autres ;
- l'importance de doter les collectivités territoriales de certaines fonctions pour garantir l'impact total souhaité dans leur mise en place ;
- la détermination précise des compétences, à chaque niveau de collectivités territoriales, surtout techniques.

Quant aux vocations générales des collectivités territoriales telles qu'envisagées dans les lois fondamentales des pays post-totalitaires. Elles peuvent se résumer par les indications suivantes :

- concourir à la mise en place des projets de société formulés par la Constitution ;

- participer à l'institutionnalisation du régime politique pour renforcer la souveraineté populaire ;
- contribuer à la cohésion socioculturelle et l'équité économique ;
- garantir la représentation politique territoriale de l'ensemble de la population dans les décisions locales et nationales ;
- défendre la concertation et la participation de toute la population aux grandes décisions locales et nationales ;
- stimuler les initiatives locales et l'approbation du développement économique, social et culturel ;
- assurer partiellement ou complètement la desserte de certains services publics ou collectifs.

Finalement, une collectivité territoriale est une structure administrative de l'Etat, chargée de protéger les intérêts, satisfaire les besoins fondamentaux et rendre des services publics à la population vivant sur un territoire précis. La collectivité territoriale bénéficie d'une autonomie administrative et financière qui lui permet de disposer de son propre personnel et budget, ainsi que des ressources propres, contrairement, aux ministères et autres services de l'État au niveau local, qui ne sont pas des personnes morales, mais qui constituent de simples administrations émanant de l'État.

Bien qu'elle détienne des compétences propres, qui lui sont confiées par le pouvoir législatif, cela ne veut pas dire pour autant, qu'elle peut constituer un Etat dans l'Etat, car elle ne possède pas de souveraineté et ne peut pas se doter de sa seule initiative, le statut d'organe nouveau. Etant entendu, qu'un organe est une structure chargée de faire fonctionner un ensemble de services, ou qui est destinée à remplir une fonction spécifique. C'est un instrument par lequel on accomplit une tâche bien déterminée.

Le pouvoir décisionnel d'une collectivité territoriale s'exerce par délibération au sein d'un conseil constitué de représentants élus et ses décisions sont ensuite appliquées par les pouvoirs exécutifs locaux. Elle exerce aussi un pouvoir réglementaire dans l'exercice de ses compétences, mais elle peut être soumise à un contrôle de tutelle.

Sa compétence est caractérisée par son aptitude à procéder, en tant qu'autorité administrative ou judiciaire, à certains actes dans des conditions déterminées par les lois et les règlements.

Le transfert des compétences dont elle bénéficie est défini par la transmission, cession ou dévolution du pouvoir d'agir ou de poser des actes à caractère administratif, qui pour l'essentiel, vise à développer la bonne gouvernance et à promouvoir les compétences locales dans le cadre de la mise en œuvre de la politique de la décentralisation. L'Etat Central confie aux collectivités territoriales, le soin de détenir et de gérer en ses lieux et places, des compétences initialement détenues et gérées par lui. Ce qui fait qu'en vertu du principe de subsidiarité, les services de proximité tombent sous le coup de la gestion de la collectivité territoriale la plus proche de la population, dans les limites fixées par la loi.

Généralement, ce transfert de compétences est toujours accompagné de transfert des ressources adéquates, pour permettre aux collectivités locales d'assumer leurs responsabilités. Cependant, ce ne sont pas toutes compétences qui sont décentralisées. Il y en a qui ne peuvent pas l'être. C'est la loi qui établit les critères pour déterminer les compétences susceptibles d'être décentralisées, pour lesquels nous retenons les trois principaux :

- externalité, elle renvoie aux effets d'un service en dehors du territoire où il est issu. En d'autres termes, c'est l'incidence causée par la production d'un service donné sur des agents externes, qui ne sont pas concernés. Une remarque tout aussi importante, nous fait dire que, plus ce critère d'externalité d'un service est petit, plus il est facile à décentraliser ;
- « tarificabilité », ce qui se rapporte à l'aisance avec laquelle un service peut être financé aux frais des usagers, en lieu et place de l'imposition des taxes. Commentaire, il est plus facile de décentraliser un service lorsque la « tarificabilité » est grande que lorsqu'elle est petite ;
- Technicité, elle se réfère au niveau d'expertise technique, requis pour fournir un service. Elle doit être faible pour faciliter la décentralisation.

Dans le cadre de la décentralisation, l'Etat Central détient le monopole de transférer certaines compétences aux collectivités territoriales en tout ou partie. Si une compétence n'est pas transférable, il peut arriver que ses fonctions le soient. C'est un partage de compétence entre l'Etat central et la collectivité territoriale qui en assure la fonction.

Les institutions de l'Etat, qu'elles soient déconcentrées ou décentralisées, ont pour vocation de contribuer à fortifier l'unité nationale. Elles éliminent toutes discriminations entre les populations des villes et des campagnes par : le droit au progrès, à l'information, à l'éducation, au travail et au loisir, pour tous les citoyens. Ces institutions doivent s'assurer de la distribution équitable de la richesse nationale, ce qui intègre et représente les intérêts des collectivités territoriales. Ces dernières participent à l'élaboration et au suivi de la mise en œuvre des politiques, des programmes et des projets publics d'aménagement du territoire, de la décentralisation et du développement économique, social et culturel.

Ainsi, elles doivent contribuer à la production de la richesse nationale, en mettant en place et en développant les structures garantissant l'équité économique, la paix sociale, les libertés fondamentales et le respect des droits humains. En ce sens, elles promeuvent et encouragent les initiatives économiques locales, départementales et communales, puis assurent la disponibilité et l'accessibilité des Services Sociaux de Base (SSB) aux citoyens, y compris pour les secteurs les plus vulnérables.

Ce sont les collectivités territoriales qui coordonnent et évaluent la prestation de services collectifs. Elles participent à l'organisation et l'amélioration du cadre et des conditions de vie de la population. Ceci inclue, fondamentalement, la desserte de services collectifs de proximité.

Selon le principe de subsidiarité, elles constituent les premières étapes du développement local et national, en mobilisant et canalisant la participation de la communauté, mais aussi en veillant à la protection et la défense des intérêts des habitants de leurs collectivités respectives. Après tout, n'est-ce pas les régions, les communes et, dans une certaine mesure, les sections communales ou collines, qui constituent le premier niveau de l'exercice de la démocratie locale et même nationale ?

Le développement durable est une forme de gestion des ressources planétaires, nationales ou locales, dont le but est de répondre aux besoins immédiats de la génération actuelle tout en sauvegardant les intérêts des générations futures. Par contre, le développement local est une stratégie d'intervention globale intersectorielle, participative et endogène d'accroissement durable pour le bien-être d'une communauté. Il est caractérisé par une succession des événements liés entre eux. Ces événements sont basés sur le leadership et les initiatives locales, dans le but de créer des richesses, tout en respectant l'environnement et procurant une meilleure qualité de vie aux populations locales. Cette approche veut :

- favoriser la résolution des problèmes sociaux par un auto-développement économique et social des communautés locales ;
- faire porter l'attention des autorités locales, régionales et nationales sur les problèmes les plus criards, liés à l'emploi, au manque d'infrastructures économiques et des services de base ;
- soutenir la mise sur pied, sur le plan organisationnel, d'entreprises communautaires de service ou de production de biens, de coopératives et de groupes d'entraide dans les principaux secteurs de la vie des communautés concernées, notamment, le logement, l'emploi, les services sociaux, l'environnement, etc. ;
- travailler en partenariat avec les principaux acteurs de la communauté locale, c'est-à-dire les organisations populaires et communautaires, la société civile et les syndicats, mais aussi les paroisses et l'élite locale, à l'instar des petits hommes d'affaires, les professionnels, etc. ;
- construire les structures autonomes à partir d'un effort local soutenu financièrement, au moins, en partie par l'Etat. Il s'agit des ressources étatiques fédérales, provinciales et municipales, ainsi que les fonds privés ou volontaires des communautés religieuses, par exemple, sur la base d'une corporation de développement communautaire.

L'affaiblissement de l'appareil étatique, causé par les crises justifie, à elle seule, la nécessité de renforcer les capacités de gestion des collectivités territoriales, notamment les communes. En outre, la gestion démocratique post-totalitaire, surtout après les premières élections libres et transparentes qui implantent les bases de la paix définitive et le manque de leadership, remet à l'ordre du jour le défi majeur de la satisfaction des besoins d'intérêt général de la population. De surcroît, les coups d'Etat électoraux ne font pas bon ménage avec la bonne gouvernance qui, disant-le, traduit la normalité, la responsabilité et l'Ethnique et/ou la morale.

Le renforcement des capacités des collectivités territoriales consiste à créer les conditions cadre pour :

- l'élaboration et l'adoption des textes réglementaires organisant la mise en œuvre des dispositions Constitutionnelles relatives aux collectivités territoriales et aux relations de celles-ci avec le pouvoir central. L'objectif est de disposer d'un cadre légal d'intervention cohérent favorisant le développement des entités territoriales décentralisées ;
- l'amélioration de l'environnement institutionnel des collectivités territoriales qui passent par le respect strict et l'exercice des rôles et des responsabilités de chacun des acteurs de la décentralisation ;
- le déploiement d'efforts afin de développer durablement les capacités du personnel de chacun des niveaux de l'administration locale par ledit renforcement des capacités et par la formation continue ;
- la formation et la sensibilisation des opinions publiques à l'échelle nationale et locale dans l'exercice de la citoyenneté active et à travers la promotion de l'action collective autour des enjeux de la décentralisation.

Les dispositions à intégrer dans le domaine du renforcement des collectivités territoriales sont caractérisées comme suite :

- préparer, planifier et coordonner les plans de développement et le budget y afférent ;
- élaborer les projets d'aménagement du territoire départemental et communal ;
- préparer et défendre le budget de la collectivité territoriale ;
- contribuer à l'élaboration des lois sur la fiscalité, selon ce que dit la Constitution ;
- faire le rapport sur les dépenses effectuées au cours de l'année fiscale ;
- participer à l'élaboration des politiques éducatives nationales ;
- promouvoir et faire respecter les droits humains ;
- supporter les différents acteurs locaux dans la recherche des voies pour la consolidation de la paix et la résolution des conflits dans les zones sensibles ;

- promouvoir les négociations dans le règlement pacifique des conflits sous la coordination conjointe des Affaires civiles et des autorités déconcentrées de l'Etat.

On sait pertinemment que dans les pays post-conflictuels, la disponibilité des ressources humaines pour les collectivités territoriales, notamment l'insuffisance tant qualitativement que quantitativement — les communes disposent d'un personnel qui souvent, manque de qualifications et de compétences — constitue un handicap au développement. A cela s'ajoute la faiblesse institutionnelle caractérisée par ce même déficit en ressources humaines. Toutes ces limitations structurelles importantes rendent indispensables le renforcement des capacités dans le but de mettre en place une administration territoriale moderne ayant les capacités d'assurer la coordination des services publics locaux et donner un appui substantiel aux structures locales.

A côté des autorités élues des collectivités territoriales, il y a aussi des autorités déconcentrées, notamment, les gouverneurs de province auxquels s'ajoutent les directeurs régionaux des ministères, sont ceux avec lesquels les Affaires civiles doivent travailler conjointement pour appliquer les politiques de réformes et de modernisation des services déconcentrés d'un pays brisé par les conflits. Ceci englobe :

- l'encouragement à l'élaboration d'un cadre juridique en faveur de ces autorités locales ;
- la formation du personnel de ces collectivités territoriales ;
- la coordination des activités avec les officiers des Affaires civiles sur le terrain ;
- l'appui aux autorités déconcentrées dans leur rôle de coordination et contrôle des activités des services déconcentrés ;
- la fourniture d'une assistance technique pour faire face aux doléances des collectivités territoriales ;
- la promotion de l'application des lois par les collectivités territoriales, pour le bon fonctionnement de leurs institutions ;
- la facilitation du contrôle de légalité des actes et mesures des collectivités territoriales transmises aux gouverneurs.

Pour cela, il convient de travailler en étroite collaboration avec ces responsables, pour assurer la bonne gestion financière des collectivités territoriales et la coordination des activités et des services déconcentrés. Dans le cadre du contrôle des finances locales il faut aider ces derniers dans la transmission des différents rapports financiers au Ministère de l'Intérieur et des collectivités territoriales pour les suites nécessaires.

En ce qui concerne le contrôle de la légalité, il est important pour un officier des Affaires civiles d'établir de bons rapports avec les chefs régionaux déconcentrés, afin d'encourager le bon fonctionnement des services administratifs et les techniques de leur circonscription. Il s'agit de les aider à rédiger des rapports mensuels concernant le fonctionnement des institutions et services territoriaux déconcentrés à mettre à la disposition du gouverneur, mais aussi assister celui-ci à assurer une liaison effective entre les différents ministères et les collectivités territoriales.

Il appartient aux Affaires civiles d'aider à diagnostiquer les problèmes éventuels, et donner des avis et des conseils, y compris sur les activités liées à la sécurité des personnes et des biens. Ce qui se traduit par une assistance dans la coordination des structures relevant de la compétence des autorités nommées par le gouvernement central, telles que : le Comité Départemental de Gestion de Risques et Désastres, la Table de Concertation Départemental, le Conseil Technique Départemental, Groupe de travail sur l'Etat de droit, Comité départemental sur la gestion des frontières, dans le cas d'Haïti.

La tutelle des autorités déconcentrées n'est pas civiliste, c'est-à-dire qu'elle ne s'exprime pas par la prise en main d'une tierce personne, des décisions notamment juridiques et patrimoniales qu'un homme ou une femme ne peut pas prendre en raison de son état physique ou mental, ou de sa condition de minorité légale, où la personne placée sous tutelle perd ses capacités à agir en adulte majeur.

Il s'agit d'une tutelle du point de vue administratif, qui s'entend d'un régime d'autorisation à obtenir par une personne morale de droit public, pour permettre à une autre institution de décider de son administration. C'est aussi une tutelle qui est exercée par une autorité hiérarchique d'une collectivité territoriale impliquant le contrôle de légalité des actes de la collectivité sous tutelle. Ce contrôle s'exerce dans le respect de la Constitution et de la législation sur les collectivités territoriales et organismes autonomes. Cette tutelle est caractérisée par :

- le pouvoir d'information de l'autorité de tutelle sur les délibérations, arrêtés, plans, budgets… des collectivités sous sa juridiction ;
- l'approbation d'un acte a priori, avant d'entrer en vigueur, notamment en ce qui concerne les décisions budgétaires, l'urbanisation, le patrimoine, la police municipale… ;
- les décisions entrées en vigueur automatiquement, à la signature du conseil et à la publication dudit acte, sauf opposition de l'autorité de tutelle. C'est le contrôle a posteriori ;
- la demande à un conseil d'une collectivité, d'un rapport sur sa gestion sans jamais s'immiscer dans la comptabilité de l'administration de la collectivité ;
- la compétence de réunir, à tout moment, les autorités civiles et armées pour des conférences d'orientation, d'information et de coordination ;
- l'obligation de veiller à l'égal accès des administrés aux services collectifs de l'Etat ou de la collectivité Territoriale.

Il va sans dire que le contrôle des actes des collectivités demeure une nécessité pour la sauvegarde des droits et libertés du citoyen, pourvu que cette tutelle ne soit pas trop présente et pesante, sur les collectivités territoriales. Contrairement aux partisans d'une décentralisation effective et totale, il est souhaitable de ne pas supprimer le contrôle administratif sur les collectivités, dans les pays en situation d'urgence politique.

Comme il sera aisé de le constater dans le schéma présenté à la fin du chapitre, le gouvernement doit garder à son actif les rôles politiques les plus éminents et les fonctions de supervision et de coordination qu'il exerce dans un esprit de concertation avec les partenaires sociopolitique. Cela permet au final, de créer ou maintenir les conditions qui rendent capables les unités locales d'administration ou les organisations non gouvernementales de prendre plus de responsabilités selon les principes de l'Etat de droit.

G. PRINCIPE DE « L'ETAT DE DROIT »

Les officiers des Affaires civiles sont censés organiser des rencontres sur l'Etat de droit, puisque cela fait partie du mandat qui leur a été assigné. La question est de savoir, de quoi parle-t-on, en fait ? Pour répondre à cette interrogation et aider le lecteur à comprendre cet aspect de la plupart des missions de l'ONU, il convient de commencer par définir le concept Etat de droit dans un pays en situation d'urgence politique complexe.

Historiquement parlant, la notion « Etat de droit » a fait son apparition progressivement vers la fin du Moyen-âge, sur fond de lutte politique, en suivant les étapes ci-après :

- en 1215, la Grande-Bretagne promulgue la Grande Charte qui fixe un certain nombre de règles et de droits, notamment la liberté d'entrée et de sortie du royaume, en vue de protéger les individus contre l'arbitraire ;
- en 1679 est apparu le texte institué habeas corpus sur les libertés fondamentales ;
- en 1689, la « Glorieuse Révolution » fait proclamer le fameux « Bill of Rights » qui pourvoit dans son article 1 : « Que le prétendu pouvoir de suspendre les lois ou l'exécution des lois par l'autorité royale, sans le consentement du Parlement, est illégal » ;
- en 1776, la déclaration d'Indépendance américaine affirme que le gouvernement repose sur le consentement du peuple et que les Hommes ont le droit de changer de gouvernement lorsqu'ils sont victimes d'abus et d'usurpations tendant au « despotisme absolu » ;
- en 1791, la Révolution française fait prolonger la tradition selon laquelle, la loi protège l'individu contre l'arbitraire, en affirmant qu' « Il n'y a pas en France d'autorité supérieure à la loi » ;

- au XIXe siècle, l'un des grands juristes allemands, Rechtsstaat traite la question de l'Etat de droit qui aboutira en 1871, à un système d'encadrement de la toute-puissance Etat par le droit, pendant que l'Empire se met en place ;
- entre 1920 et 1922 le juriste français R. Carré de Malberg, à travers la « Contribution à la théorie générale de l'Etat (1920-1922,) » introduit le concept Etat de droit dans le vocabulaire technique des juristes et des spécialistes de la philosophie du droit ;
- dans la période de 1970 à1980, le débat public s'empare du thème de l'Etat de droit pour affirmer le primat de la démocratie et des libertés individuelles. C'est l'époque où le système soviétique est en crise et M. Gorbatchev veut créer un « Etat socialiste de droit. » Les théories de la philosophie politique relancent le débat sur la tradition libérale qui intensifie, en même temps l'importance de la problématique des droits de l'homme au plan international. Les critiques contre le totalitarisme se multiplient au profit de la réhabilitation du principe de l'Etat démocratique dont la légitimité avait été mise en cause par la critique marxiste.

Dès lors, les penseurs se sont emparés du terme Etat de droit pour le moderniser. Et le débat s'installa. Certes qu'ils affirment unanimement que le concept Etat de droit est lié à la notion de souveraineté, mais ils se divisent profondément sur le titulaire de cette fameuse souveraineté.

Les deux tendances qui se démarquent sont celles de J. Bodin qui soutient la théorie selon laquelle la souveraineté est une puissance absolue qui s'exerce sur un territoire et sur une population, par le monarque et celle de J. J. Rousseau qui estime que la souveraineté appartient au peuple qui peut l'exercer à travers ses représentants : les parlements. Comme bémol, dans les deux hypothèses, le détenteur de la souveraineté se situe au sommet de la hiérarchie et c'est lui qui fixe les règles qui sont applicables par tous.

Cette idée d'un pouvoir auquel ne s'impose aucune règle sera progressivement contestée par la pensée contre-révolutionnaire qui en appelle aux traditions, pour limiter la puissance de l'Etat central et du monarque. Elle est tirée à hue et à dia par les théoriciens du droit naturel qui demandent que les lois soient conformes au droit naturel pour être légitimes. Selon eux, quelle que soit la souveraineté : nationale ou populaire, si elle est sans limite, elle aboutira inéluctablement à une absence de contrôle de constitutionnalité des lois. La France d'avant la Vème République en a fait le frais.

Très vite, la conception de l'Etat va évoluer au sens d'imposer aux institutions exerçant la souveraineté de prendre des décisions appropriées au droit et que, si le droit est modifié, que ce soit selon des procédures elles-mêmes légales.

Ainsi, l'Etat de droit deviendra un Etat où l'administration est soumise à des règles de droit dans ses rapports avec les citoyens. Ce qui donne au citoyen la possibilité de recours contre les décisions de l'administration. Du coup, apparaît la nécessité de créer des juridictions pour juger les différends entre les citoyens et l'Etat. Cela explique le droit d'affirmer que l'Etat de droit s'oppose à l'Etat de police que définit pour nous par R. Carré de Malberg[25] en ces termes : « l'Etat de police est celui dans lequel l'autorité administrative peut, d'une façon discrétionnaire et avec une liberté de décision plus ou moins complète, appliquer aux citoyens toutes les mesures dont elle juge utile de prendre par elle-même l'initiative, en vue de faire face aux circonstances et d'atteindre à chaque moment les fins qu'elle se propose. »

A l'inverse, l'Etat de droit selon lui, est « un Etat qui, dans ses rapports avec ses sujets et pour la garantie de leur statut individuel, se soumet lui-même à un régime de droit et cela, en tant qu'il enchaîne son action sur eux par des règles, dont les unes déterminent les droits réservés aux citoyens, dont les autres fixent par avance les voies et moyens qui pourront être employés en vue de réaliser les buts étatiques. »

De façon générale, l'état de droit est une situation juridique ou un système institutionnel dans lequel chacun est soumis au respect du droit, notamment :

- la hiérarchie des normes ;
- la séparation des pouvoirs ;
- les droits fondamentaux de tous, du simple citoyen à la puissance publique.

La théorie de la séparation des pouvoirs, chère à Montesquieu, met en lumière la distinction des pouvoirs entre exécutif, législatif et judiciaire, puis édicte la limitation mutuelle entre ces institutions. Ainsi, le pouvoir législatif incarné par le Parlement, limite le pouvoir de l'exécutif. Ce dernier n'est donc pas libre d'agir à sa guise. Il doit constamment s'assurer de l'appui des Parlementaires, qui eux, constituent l'expression de la volonté du peuple. Entre-temps, le pouvoir judiciaire permet de faire le contrepoids institutionnel à certaines décisions gouvernementales. Encore faudrait que l'indépendance de la justice soit effective.

---

[25] Raymond Carré de Malberg (1861-1935) est un juriste positiviste étatique, Français. Professeur agrégé en droit, R. Carré de Malberg prône la séparation entre le droit d'une part et la morale, le droit naturel et la politique d'autre part. Sous la IIIe République, il s'oppose au parlementarisme absolu et propose un exécutif fort et un législatif soumis au gouvernement. Cette thèse se justifie par le fait que l'Etat est une émanation des gens dans le besoin de mettre en commun leurs biens afin qu'ils soient gérés de façon commune. Selon lui, ce sont ces individus qui pour solutionner cette préoccupation ont pu trouver un consensus qui se caractérise par la création de l'Etat. Par conséquent, bien que n'étant pas supérieur au droit, l'Etat incarne tant bien que mal, la puissance absolue et constitue la personne juridique suprême. L'une de ses plus grandes réflexions concerne une étude sur la distinction entre la souveraineté populaire et la souveraineté nationale.

Aussi, pour mieux jouer le jeu de la démocratie, les acteurs de la décentralisation doivent impérativement appliquer les principes et les règles essentielles de la séparation des pouvoirs.

En guise d'illustration, les élus à la base doivent :

- être capables de distinguer clairement le domaine public du domaine privé, assurer les cessions et les concessions des terres domaniales dans le strict respect de la loi ;
- accorder des indemnisations justes et équitables en cas d'expropriation ;
- mobiliser la population à l'enregistrement des terres pour une diminution des litiges fonciers ;
- partager équitablement les richesses publiques ;
- lutter contre la corruption ;
- gérer correctement la question des terres des rapatriés et des déplacés.

Qui plus est, les autorités territoriales, notamment les maires qui sont les premiers officiers de police judiciaire, doivent être capables de faire la distinction entre les matières civiles et pénales. Elles sont censées identifier les compétences civiles et répressives des juridictions nationales et différencier les divers échelons de la hiérarchie judiciaire et leurs pouvoirs respectifs. Toutes les juridictions ne sont pas compétentes pour connaître des affaires civiles. De même, elles ne sont pas toutes habilitées à connaître des affaires pénales, étant donné que les délais et les voies de recours sont différents d'une matière à l'autre.

C'est en maîtrisant ces paramètres de base du droit que les élus locaux pourront être en mesure d'exécuter leur mandat dans les limites de leur compétence, tout en respectant les droits de leurs collaborateurs.

L'Etat de droit est aussi un Etat caractérisé par une hiérarchie des normes, ce qui veut dire que les circulaires, les décrets et les arrêtés doivent être conformes aux lois, lesquelles doivent être conformes à la Constitution. Cela sup pose un contrôle de la « constitutionalité » des lois qui limite le pouvoir des législateurs eux-mêmes. En ce sens, l'Etat produit le droit certes, mais il est lui-même soumis à ce droit qu'il a produit. Autrement dit, bien qu'il soit souverain, son action demeure limitée. Il y a là, le principe de « l'autolimitation » qui oblige l'Etat à accepter de lui-même de se soumettre à un ordre juridique qu'il ne peut décider de remettre en cause sans saper les bases de son action.

L'état de droit prescrit deux types de contrôle :

- le contrôle de constitutionnalité permettant au Conseil Constitutionnel (en France) ou à la Cour Suprême (aux Etats-Unis) de vérifier la validité de la loi par rapport à la Constitution ;
- le contrôle de « conventionalité » qui donne le droit au juge de contrôler la validité d'une norme interne au regard d'une convention

internationale et lui attribue le pouvoir d'écarter ladite norme en cas d'incompatibilité.

L'existence de la hiérarchie des normes constitue l'une des plus importantes garanties de l'état de droit. C'est le cadre dans lequel l'Etat définit les normes dont la validité est conditionnée par le respect de l'ensemble des principes du droit supérieur. C'est une sorte de pyramide au sommet de laquelle, figure la Constitution, suivie des engagements internationaux, de la loi, puis des règlements et dont la base est composée des décisions administratives ou des conventions entre les personnes du droit privé.

A l'évidence, cet ordonnancement juridique caractéristique de l'état de droit s'impose à l'ensemble des personnes juridiques, physiques ou morales qui encourent des sanctions juridiques en cas de violation ou de méconnaissance. Les principes de légalité et de l'égalité des différents sujets de droit soumis aux normes en vigueur et aux règles juridiqucs, assure la fonction de régulation qui est affirmée et légitimée dans les pays dits civilisés.

Au regard de la tradition française, héritée de la Révolution française, ce principe repose sur une approche déductive fondée sur une espèce de hiérarchie qui place la déclaration des droits de l'homme au sommet de cette pyramidale juridictionnelle. Elle reconnaît et soutient l'existence des droits naturels, inaliénables et sacrés, au côté de la Constitution, des lois et des textes réglementaires. Dans cette perspective, l'Etat de droit est caractérisé par la conformité du contenu des lois aux principes fondateurs des droits de l'homme. L'option d'absence de contrôle de « Constitutionalité » est synonyme d'inachèvement de l'Etat de droit, puisque la puissance parlementaire n'est pas soumise à l'examen de la conformité aux lois et à la Constitution.

Le juriste autrichien H. Kelsen, figure de proue du positivisme juridique, viendra conjuguer ces deux formules de l'Etat de droit. Il affirme la nécessité des normes juridiques qui doivent être produites par l'Etat, tout en distinguant l'Etat et le droit. Selon lui, la production des règles de droit n'est pas soumise qu'à des contraintes de forme, c'est-à-dire une hiérarchie des normes sans considération de leur contenu, mais les gouvernants sont toutefois responsables de leurs actes devant des tribunaux indépendants et les citoyens ont le droit d'ester en justice l'Etat.

L'égalité de droit permet à ce que tout individu, toute organisation ou toute institution, y compris l'Etat et les collectivités territoriales, puissent contester contre l'application d'une norme juridique, dès lors que celle-ci n'est pas conforme à une norme supérieure. Tous reçoivent en conséquence la qualité de personne juridique : on parle de personne physique, pour les citoyens et de personne morale, pour les autres. De ce fait, que ce soit l'Etat ou les collectivités territoriales, leurs décisions sont soumises au respect du principe de légalité, à l'instar des autres personnes juridiques. Dans ce contexte, tous les règlements et toutes les décisions prises par les pouvoirs publics doivent s'aligner sur le respect de l'ensemble des normes juridiques supérieures en vigueur : lois, conventions internationales et règles Constitutionnelles. Ils ne doivent pas non plus bénéficier d'un quelconque privilège de juridiction, ni d'un régime dérogatoire au droit commun.

Par conséquent, le principe de la hiérarchie des normes facilite l'encadrement de l'action de la puissance publique, en la soumettant au principe de légalité. Il donne aux personnes physiques et morales de droit privé, le pouvoir de s'opposer contre les décisions de l'Etat en s'appuyant sur les règles qu'il a lui-même décrétées. Ceci met en exergue le rôle primordial des juridictions dont l'indépendance devient une nécessité indéniable.

En effet, il n'y a pas d'état de droit sans l'existence des juridictions indépendantes et compétentes dont la fonction principale est de régler les conflits entre les différentes personnes juridiques. Cela est possible en appliquant à la fois le principe de légalité, qui découle de l'existence de la hiérarchie des normes et le principe d'égalité, qui s'oppose à tout traitement différencié des personnes juridiques.

Si l'action de l'Etat doit se soumettre à des règles juridiques qui garantissent les libertés des citoyens, alors il y a un lien étroit entre l'Etat de droit et la démocratie même s'il convient de reconnaître que tout Etat de droit n'est pas nécessairement un Etat démocratique. Le contraire semble plus plausible, car il n'y a pas de démocratie sans Etat de droit. Tout ceci exige une réflexion sur la nature du droit et sur la distinction entre la légalité et la légitimité des normes juridiques.

Au XVIIIème siècle le concept Etat de droit était fortement lié au libéralisme politique. C'était le meilleur moyen de faire face à l'arbitraire du pouvoir royal et aux contraintes qui pesaient sur l'activité économique de l'époque. L'objectif visé était de garantir les droits des individus et assurer le libre exercice de l'initiative individuelle, en se basant sur l'idée que ce libre exercice était le même pour tous. La lutte contre les inégalités sociales qui remettaient en cause l'exercice de la citoyenneté du fait, que les individus dont les droits économiques et sociaux ne sont pas respectés ne peuvent guère exercer la plénitude de leurs droits politiques, est venu renforcer la notion de l'Etat-providence. Cet Etat providence devient le prolongement de l'Etat-protecteur des droits économiques et sociaux qu'on appelle aussi les droits-créances. Ces derniers constituent le prolongement des droits civils et politiques ou les droits-libertés.

Cette nouvelle dimension de l'Etat de droit donne au gouvernement le droit d'intervenir dans les domaines économique et social qui pourrait constituer une menace pour les libertés civiles et politiques, selon certains penseurs libéraux.

L'idée de justice sociale a fait son apparition avec l'interventionnisme croissant de l'Etat dans la vie économique et sociale, ce qui fait disparaître des pans entiers des activités des gouvernements, au profit du marché. Désormais, le pouvoir discrétionnaire se transforme en pouvoir régulateur et le monopole administré bascule vers le marché régulé. Bref, l'identification entre « économie de marché libre » et Etat de droit est là et cela est en rapport avec la problématique du développement humain. Ce développement est caractérisé par la dynamique de l'Etat de droit, le primat du politique et de la démocratie participative et aussi, par la satisfaction des besoins de l'être humain, détaillés par la communauté internationale dans les objectifs du millénium.

Or, un tel modèle de développement ne peut fonctionner efficacement que s'il existe une séparation des pouvoirs et une justice indépendante. La Justice fait partie de l'Etat et, bien entendu, seule son indépendance à l'égard du pouvoir législatif et exécutif peut garantir son impartialité dans l'application des normes de droit.

L'Etat de droit est une réalité qui n'est ni statique ni immuable, mais une dynamique liée à l'activité politique. L'évolution des idées relatives à l'intervention de l'Etat dans l'économie oblige à ne plus être insensibles aux rapports de forces politiques et à l'état de l'opinion publique et la société civile. Par conséquent, le droit se trouve relié à la démocratie. L'ordre juridique perd sa légitimité lorsque les citoyens ne sont pas des acteurs du processus d'élaboration des lois non seulement sous la forme de l'élection des parlementaires, mais aussi dans la mesure où les pratiques et les règles délibératives permettent l'existence d'une véritable « démocratie juridique » et participative.

Cette dernière peut se traduire par l'organisation des débats dans les différentes régions, communes, collines ou sections communales, avec la participation des principales organisations et institutions sectorielles, ainsi que les citoyens et la société civile. Cela illustre parfaitement le fait qu'il soit possible d'exercer une citoyenneté éclairée et vigilante dans la production des règles de droit. Cette pratique consiste à élargir au niveau du citoyen ordinaire la procédure acquise de réflexion publique sur les grands sujets de société, tels que : les projets d'infrastructure, la politique de la santé, l'éducation, le logement, la vie chère… C'est le sens donné à la notion de participation de tous à la vie locale : les assemblées municipales, les référendums locaux, les comités de quartiers et autres, pour faire entendre « la voix des sans voix. » Cela évoque l'idée de gouvernance participative qui, elle-même, implique le principe de renforcement des capacités en vue du développement durable.

Si à l'origine, l'état de droit était un modèle purement théorique, à présent, il est devenu le thème politique considéré comme principale caractéristique des régimes démocratiques. De surcroît, il fait du droit un instrument privilégié de régulation de l'organisation politique et sociale. De ce fait, il subordonne le principe de légitimité au respect de la légalité, puis justifie ainsi, le rôle croissant des juridictions dans les pays qui se réclament de ce modèle, en imposant une certaine forme de relation entre les acteurs publics et privés. Il devient évident que l'Etat de droit interpelle la notion de gouvernance.

C'est dans cette optique qu'il est intéressant de réfléchir sur la théorie de B. Oppetit[26] selon laquelle « le concept Etat de droit » repose sur deux piliers.

Le premier est « le droit au droit : du point de vue formel, l'Etat de droit suppose l'existence d'un ordre juridique et d'une hiérarchie des normes bien établies ; mais il est également lié à l'adhésion du corps social à une exigence démocratique. A priori le constitutionnalisme [découlant de la philosophie libérale souligne que les revendications des droits économiques et sociaux relèvent davantage de la logique de l'Etat-providence. Ces revendications conduisent au renforcement de l'Etat,] alors que l'Etat de droit constitue par définition un instrument de limitation de l'Etat. »

Le second est « le droit au juge : la diversité et la hiérarchie des normes impliquent, pour leur respect, la mise en place des contrôles juridictionnels. Le contrôle de la constitutionnalité des lois assure l'intégrité de la pyramide des normes. Le recours pour excès de pouvoir, reconnu comme principe général du droit applicable même sans texte, sanctionne la légalité des actes administratifs. »

L'Etat de droit ne peut qu'être compris comme un Etat dans lequel tout le monde est soumis à la loi. En d'autres termes un espace territorial où le peuple et ses dirigeants sont censés respecter les normes de la République, où personne n'est au-dessus de la loi. Cette définition est valable dans le contexte d'un pays qui fonctionne normalement.

En revanche, dans le cas de situation post-conflit, les rencontres de l'Etat de droit peuvent se définir comme un espace d'échange permettant à une population de demander des comptes aux autorités locales. Dans ces conditions, l'Etat de droit se caractérise par le devoir d'information pour les dirigeants et le droit de savoir pour les bénéficiaires des services publics. C'est dans le cadre de l'Etat de droit qu'une population peut aussi faire des propositions aux gouvernants sur la manière dont ils doivent gérer les affaires de la société. L'Etat de droit permet alors à la population de pointer du doigt les erreurs de gestion et les manquements du pouvoir local obligé à rendre des comptes. C'est donc le moyen idéal de renforcer la démocratie participative.

Ainsi, les réunions de l'Etat de droit constituent une grande occasion pour les dirigeants de mobiliser la population sur les orientations qu'ils donnent à la cité, afin de lutter contre un certain nombre de maux qui freinent le développement local. Lors des rencontres sur l'Etat de droit, certaines autorités locales ont pu lutter contre la mauvaise culture de non-paiement des taxes en

---

[26] B. Oppetit : Philosophie du droit, Dalloz, Coll. Précis, 1999 (p. 96)

abordant les questions de fiscalité. Les Affaires civiles sont arrivées à créer des rencontres thématiques de l'Etat de droit sur des sujets sensibles comme l'environnement, la drogue à l'école…

Effectivement, la lutte contre la déforestation et le reboisement pour la protection de l'environnement passe mieux par la sensibilisation de la population, y compris, lors des rencontres de l'Etat de droit.

L'Etat de droit peut aussi devenir un espace de dialogue pour la prévention, la transformation et la résolution pacifique des conflits. Dans certaines communes, il a été possible de mettre ensemble les partisans du maire et ceux du député qui s'opposaient violemment, à travers leurs supporteurs respectifs. Au cours d'une réunion de l'Etat de droit, il a été démontré aux participants la nécessité de faire la paix, car l'absence de sécurité est une cause de non-investissement. Les relations entre la paix et le développement sont régis par la sécurité et l'investissement. Ce que les Nations unies ont bien compris.

En ce sens, elles développent souvent des projets appelés QIP (Quick Impact Projects), en français Projets à Effets Rapides. Dans une Commune plutôt chaude du Département de la Grand-Anse, en Haïti, il a fallu démontrer à la population que leur commune ne pouvait pas bénéficier de ces projets QIP parce qu'il était impossible de faire le monitoring en cas d'investissement, à cause des affrontements qui engendrent l'insécurité. Les Nations unies n'envoient pas son personnel civil à l'abattoir. Et, il est difficile et très couteux de mobiliser les forces militaires chaque fois que les Affaires civiles veulent faire le suivi des actions sur le terrain. Un comité de dialogue et de réconciliation avait été créé pour rapprocher les deux parties au cours d'une réunion de l'Etat de droit.

La population ayant vite compris la nécessité de faire la paix, les deux parties avaient donc fini par amorcer un dialogue et la commune a pu recevoir des financements pour des projets QIP, au cours de cette même année. Lorsque la violence avait repris le droit de cité dans cette même commune, la population elle-même, avait fini par solliciter une rencontre de l'Etat de droit dans le but de renforcer ce comité de dialogue et de réconciliation, afin de prévenir la recrudescence des affrontements.

C'est aussi dans le cadre des réunions de l'Etat de droit qu'avait été résolue la crise entre le cartel des maires d'une commune et les autorités de la police de ladite localité. En l'occurrence, dans cette autre commune de la Grand-Anse, les maires n'avaient jamais reçu l'appui de la police lorsqu'ils procédaient au prélèvement des taxes sur le charbon. La police locale demandait sa part du gâteau avant d'apporter son assistance à la Mairie. La tension persistante avait été évoquée lors d'une réunion de l'Etat de droit, en présence d'un haut responsable de la police qui va rappeler les policiers à l'ordre. Ces derniers sont payés pour servir, non pas pour se servir.

Du coup, un autre participant va soulever la question de la légalité et la légitimité de cette taxe sur le charbon de bois qu'il faut d'ailleurs bannir pour décourager les braconniers. Tout le monde s'est rendu compte que la taxe était illégale à la base parce qu'elle avait été créée par un arrêté municipal qui n'avait pas respecté la procédure d'approbation de l'autorité hiérarchique. Pire encore, la Constitution haïtienne dans ses articles 217 et 218, affirme que seul l'exécutif est compétent pour prendre des initiatives en matière de fiscalité et c'est la loi qui détermine les différents types d'impôts. Ce qui revient à dire que les arrêtés municipaux pris à ce sujet sont nuls et non avenus.

Si les rencontres sur l'Etat de droit dans les communes constituent un face-à-face entre les autorités locales et la population, les réunions sur le développement et la gouvernance locale qui ont été expérimentés dans le Département de la Grand-Anse, en Haïti[27] ont aussi constitué des espaces de réflexion regroupant les élus de base et les experts ainsi que les acteurs du développement, y compris la société civile et les notables de la commune. Elles ont ainsi permis d'explorer les voies et moyens de la création des richesses et les meilleures techniques du partage de ces richesses. Leur point commun est de placer les intérêts, ou plutôt l'amélioration des services à rendre à la population au centre des débats. Tout cela concourt au renforcement des capacités d'un Etat.

H. LA PRATIQUE DU RENFORCEMENT DES CAPACITES DE L'ETAT

Si la gouvernance politique implique le renforcement ou l'installation des institutions démocratiques pour contribuer à restaurer l'Etat de droit et de mieux garantir la sécurité de tous les citoyens, ainsi que le respect des droits de l'homme, le renforcement de l'Etat vise à moderniser une administration dans la perspective de service public, dans le but de favoriser la réduction des inégalités, le dialogue et la réconciliation.

Dans la pratique, le renforcement des capacités se focalise sur les interventions qui touchent essentiellement :

- les réformes du secteur public et la gestion économique et financière ;
- la gouvernance participative orientée vers l'appui au parlement, au pouvoir judiciaire et aux médias ;
- la gestion de l'aide et de « l'imputabilité » ;
- la décentralisation et l'appui au gouvernement local ;
- les interventions et le rôle de la société civile ;
- la planification et l'appui à la formulation de politiques.

[27] Voir chapitre sur « La Planification du Développement Local », dans la seconde partie de cet ouvrage.

Il donne à l'Etat l'aptitude d'assurer à tous les citoyens : la sécurité, la justice, les conditions favorables à l'exercice d'une activité économique, ainsi que les services publics comme l'éducation et les soins de santé, tout en respectant le libre exercice des droits sociaux, politiques et économiques. En fait, les structures de la gouvernance reposent sur la reddition de comptes. En contrepartie, les citoyens ont des obligations envers l'Etat, telles que : celle de payer les impôts, d'accepter le monopole de l'Etat sur les forces de maintien de l'ordre et d'accepter d'autres limitations de leur liberté prévues par la loi. Les Affaires civiles sont là pour faciliter cette transition socio-politico-économique d'un Etat post-conflictuel qui a perdu les réflexes de la démocratie et la décentralisation.

Cela se traduit par un soutien à la gouvernance locale et à la décentralisation pour favoriser l'accès aux services de base. Bien entendu, l'apaisement social est la conséquence de la disponibilité des services de base, augmenté sur l'ensemble du territoire d'intervention, avec une dimension géographique et humaine contribuant à l'inclusion sociale. C'est aussi le soutien à la scolarisation et à l'éducation, à la santé avec pour objectif la priorité aux soins de base et à l'immunisation. Il facilite l'accès à l'eau et l'assainissement, sans oublier la protection et la prévention dans les domaines, tels que : la violence basée sur le genre, les droits humains, les enfants et les filles…

Le renforcement d'un Etat fragile en tant que tel, est un processus endogène qui prend naissance à l'intérieur d'un système et dans la prise de décisions politiques et microéconomiques. Il inclut la volonté de la base et le respect de la proximité dans le processus d'identification, pour la satisfaction des besoins de la population. Il est destiné à renforcer les capacités des institutions et la légitimité de l'État. Toutefois, il est nourri par les relations qu'entretiennent l'Etat, la société civile, le secteur privé et les autres acteurs locaux, pourvoyeurs de services à la population.

Il s'avère donc impératif d'instaurer des relations de réciprocité entre un Etat et les groupes sociopolitiques qui participent de façon constructive à la vie de la société. Pour y arriver, il est nécessaire de construire des mécanismes politiques ouverts qui facilitent la négociation, la collaboration et la coopération entre les détenteurs du pouvoir étatique et les groupes organisés.

Ainsi, le renforcement de l'Etat consiste à promouvoir les processus politiques permettant l'instauration des relations négociées entre l'Etat et la société, puis des rapports de force entre les élites et les groupes sociaux. Il s'agit de donner à un Etat, les moyens de négocier et d'administrer les intérêts communs entre ses différents partenaires condamnés à poursuivre le même but dans une société, pour qu'il assaille sa légitimité. En effet, l'Etat doit contrôler les transformations de la société et satisfaire les attentes qui lui incombent. Il doit résister aux chocs internes ou externes associés à ces changements, sans faire recours à la violence.

L'Etat ne doit pas être résilient. Il ne peut pas, non plus, se disculper de sa responsabilité de gérer les tensions politiques qui sont de nature à imposer une renégociation des règles du jeu, par les mécontents. De même, il ne doit pas exclure les principales institutions et les groupes sociaux sous prétexte qu'ils peuvent chercher à remettre en cause son autorité, y compris par la violence. Le renforcement de l'Etat est un véritable jeu de rapports de force qu'il faut établir entre les élites et les groupes organisés au sein de la société.

La légitimité est à la fois un moyen et une fin pour le renforcement de l'Etat. Ce dernier s'affermit au fur et à mesure que les citoyens en perçoivent les avantages, à travers la capacité de l'Etat à gérer la relation entre lui et le citoyen, d'une part et les attentes qui en résultent, d'autre part. Ces processus sont souvent influencés par le niveau de légitimité que l'Etat détient aux yeux de la population.

Brièvement, le processus de renforcement d'un Etat s'appuie sur trois sources de légitimité :

- la légitimité induite par la performance, pouvant susciter la fourniture de services efficaces et équitables ;
- la légitimité dérivée de la conviction partagée au sein de la société du bien-fondé de la source de l'autorité. Ce sentiment est la conséquence du principe de la souveraineté populaire qui découle à son tour de l'autorité morale ou de la formation antérieure de l'Etat. Elle peut aussi provenir de la dynamique historique de l'Etat ;
- la légitimité résultant du processus selon lequel l'Etat de droit est prévu par la Constitution et/ou des mécanismes de reddition de comptes appropriés. Cette légitimité résulte de la reconnaissance ou du soutien de la communauté internationale.

Dans ces conditions, il est évident de conclure sur le fait que si la légitimité de l'Etat permet l'acceptation d'une autorité politique par la population, il n'en demeure pas moins qu'elle est elle-même, influencée par l'intégrité et l'efficacité de la fonction publique.

Il est envisageable de renforcer un Etat, en lui donnant un appui au niveau de ses propres structures administratives centrales et locales. Il s'agit de lui fournir le minimum de capacités, qui lui permettra d'établir sa présence. Le but est de faire en sorte que ces structures administratives composées de la fonction publique et du système de gestion des finances publiques fonctionnent raisonnablement bien, notamment au niveau de sa capacité de mobiliser des ressources. Cela se fait, en particulier, par le biais de la fiscalité. Cette dernière constitue le levier des négociations entre les citoyens et les responsables politiques quant à leurs droits et obligations mutuels. Lorsqu'un Etat dépend de la fiscalité pour ses recettes, il sera partie prenante à la prospérité de ses citoyens. En revanche, les citoyens qui entretiennent des relations avec l'Etat par le biais de la fiscalité sont généralement parties prenantes à la performance et à la capacité de rendre des comptes aux institutions de l'Etat. Ces citoyens sont même disposés à céder une partie de leur pouvoir à l'administration à qui elle exige des comptes. Faut-il rappeler que le budget de l'Etat ou de la collectivité Territoriale, ainsi que sa préparation sont au cœur du processus politique central qui consiste à allouer des ressources, souvent rares, à la population. L'Etat de droit est un excellent espace pour ces échanges.

La formation d'un Etat et son approche de renforcement des capacités ne sont pas des expressions descriptives ou des concepts normatifs servant à renforcer les capacités institutionnelles aux seules fins d'une exclusion politique, économique ou sociale de certaines communautés.

Le renforcement de l'Etat n'est ni un programme, ni un projet, ni mêmc un simple élément d'une phase après-conflit. Il se limite à un effort de construction de la paix et sous forme d'un processus non linéaire, c'est-à-dire jalonné d'avancées et de retours en arrière. Il est également asymétrique parce qu'il ne peut y avoir de symétrie ni entre les attentes sociales d'un peuple et la capacité ou la volonté de l'Etat à répondre ni même dans les relations entre l'Etat et la société.

Il s'agit plutôt d'un processus continu d'évolution et d'institutionnalisation d'une nation dont les racines remontent à son histoire. C'est une politique de négociations et parfois, de contestations ou de luttes qui s'opèrent sur le long terme, même si à vue d'œil, l'attention se focalise généralement sur des caractéristiques immédiates.

L'objectif du renforcement de l'Etat est donc de faire passer un pays d'une situation de fragilité à une situation de résilience où l'Etat est rompu à répondre aux besoins et aux attentes de sa population pour bâtir sa légitimité. Pour y parvenir, il convient de consolider, d'une part, les capacités organisationnelles et institutionnelles, d'autre part, la légitimité et les mécanismes politiques à mettre en œuvre pour gérer les attentes sociales et les ressources dont dispose l'Etat. C'est ce qu'il convient d'appeler le « développement de la résilience de l'Etat » qui n'est autre qu'une alternative au « renforcement de l'Etat. »

Cependant, sans la décentralisation, il est difficile, sinon impossible, de renforcer les capacités d'un Etat, car les fonctions assumées par l'Etat sont organisées et financées à différents niveaux administratifs et politiques. Par conséquent, développer la résilience suppose donc une intégration administrative territoriale et l'existence de mécanismes politiques efficaces, propres à gérer les attentes de l'Etat et de la société, à tous les niveaux de l'administration ; de l'échelon local à l'échelon national. Il faut donc définir un cadre favorable aux relations entre le centre et la périphérie, c'est-à-dire les relations entre l'Etat et les collectivités Territoriales. Ce cadre doit influencer les relations entre l'Etat et la société pour permettre de gérer, de façon constructive, les expressions de l'unité et de la diversité au sein de l'Etat et de la société.

Au sens du renforcement de l'Etat, la notion de construction de la nation renvoie à un sentiment commun d'identité nationale sur le plan ethnique, culturel ou politique dont l'Etat n'a pas le monopole. En effet, même les groupes rebelles peuvent « instrumentaliser » et revendiquer le principe d'identité nationale pour renforcer leur opposition contre l'Etat. A bien voir, le renforcement de l'Etat et l'identité nationale se renforcent mutuellement.

Il convient de noter que le renforcement de l'Etat ne crée pas pour autant de nouvelles institutions publiques. Il ne sert pas à renforcer les institutions existantes qui traduisent précisément les tâches du principe de « renforcement institutionnel », mais il se focalise sur le bon fonctionnement des institutions. Et, ce bon fonctionnement dépend non seulement de la nature formelle de ces institutions, mais aussi du contexte social dans lequel elles opèrent. En effet, ces institutions doivent être solidement ancrées dans la société, faute de quoi, elles serviraient de relais à des intérêts privés ou patrimoniaux.

Il est aussi lié à la notion de construction de la paix dont les activités recouvrent l'ensemble des actions menées par des acteurs nationaux et/ou internationaux en vue de prévenir des conflits violents et d'institutionnaliser la paix sur un territoire. Cette liaison vient du fait que la dynamique de renforcement de l'Etat, concoure souvent à la consolidation de la sécurité et la stabilité politique, et à l'établissement des fondements de la confiance ainsi que la réconciliation entre les différents groupes sociaux.

Cependant, il convient de préciser que la construction de la paix est d'abord et avant tout un processus de gestion des défis immédiats. Elle pourrait apporter au renforcement de l'Etat les moyens de surmonter les plus graves difficultés qui s'y présentent. Le renforcement de l'Etat par contre doit s'étaler sur le long terme, puisque la nécessité d'établir des relations toujours plus étroites entre l'Etat et la société, avec ses corollaires, les groupes sociaux qui sont appelés à perdurer. A cet effet, le rôle des acteurs extérieurs est de soutenir les acteurs internes qui favorisent une dynamique positive et sans exclusive de renforcement de l'Etat. Ils doivent ainsi aligner leur action sur la leur, tout en évitant que ces démarches externes ne deviennent des interventions qui portent atteinte aux processus endogènes positifs dudit renforcement. En résumé, le renforcement de l'Etat comprend essentiellement :

- le développement des capacités ;
- l'appui institutionnel ;
- la consolidation de la gouvernance efficace ;
- l'Etat de droit ;

- la démocratie participative y compris la concertation et la coordination ;
- la décentralisation ainsi que la sensibilisation et la mobilisation qui peuvent se faire à travers les discussions sur l'Etat de droit.

Mais, la « refondation contemporaine » d'un pays post-conflit doit tenir compte des aspects :

- d'urgence ;
- du relèvement immédiat ;
- de la reconstruction ;
- du développement.

Tous ces aspects sont parfaitement entremêlés les uns aux autres jusqu'à leur finalité qui n'est autre que le développement durable et harmonieux.

III. Structure organisationelle d'une section des Affaires civiles

Si le mandat d'une mission des Nations unies appellee toujours à « renforcer l'autonomie des institutions de l'État, en particulier en dehors de la capitale » du pays sélectionné, il appartient aux Affaires civiles d'exécuter cet appel au niveau central à travers son unité d'appui institutionnel, son bureau de soutien au Parlement et au niveau local, avec l'ensemble de ses bureaux régionaux. Ces bureau marquent de facto une présence permanente sur le terrain à partir d'un accord préalable avec les autorités établies et qui au demeurant, donne aux Affaires civiles une position unique, leur permettant de maintenir un dialogue mutuel, dynamique et productif, continu et confiant avec les autorités locales.

En principe, le plan de travail d'une section des Affaires civiles doit suivre les thématiques du plan d'action de la direction des collectivités territoriales pour répondre aux besoins du Ministère des collectivités territoriales. C'est un programme prévisionnel qui doit être mis en oeuvre, grace à des relations de proximité dans le respect des priorités du gouvernement. Ce programme doit être en conformité avec le mandat qui lui est conféré par le Conseil de Sécurité de l'ONU.

Il revient à la direction des Affaires civiles, la lourde tâche d'interpréter le texte prévoyant le mandat de la mission pour :

- clarifier les objectifs stratégiques de la section des Affaires civiles ;
- définir le contexte opérationnel des officiers des Affaires civiles, autrement dit, préciser le rôle des officiers des Affaires civiles dans les relations entre les autorités locales et le pouvoir central ;
- mesurer l'impact de l'exécution du projet de renforcement des capacités, harmoniser l'approche en matière d'appui institutionnel des officiers des Affaires civiles sur le terrain et ceux du bureau central de la mission ;
- appréhender les questions à aborder avec les autorités des collectivités territoriales de façon subtile et constructive ;
- harmoniser et maîtriser l'essence des rapports d'évaluation ;

- créer un mécanisme de partage d'informations entre les bureaux régionaux et leurs unités pour fonctionner comme un réseau d'échange ;
- définir le cadre de l'interaction entre les acteurs de la section des Affaires civiles en vue d'une grande efficacité des actions à entreprendre tant au niveau central que local ;
- déterminer les partenaires clés avec lesquels les officiers des Affaires civiles doivent fondamentalement travailler ;
- définir l'interaction entre le travail des Affaires civiles et la politique du gouvernement impliqué en matière de gouvernance et du développement ;
- clarifier le rôle/la fonction des officiers des Affaires civiles en matière d'appui institutionnel, d'appui au parlement et dans la gestion des frontières.

Les contacts réguliers que les Affaires civiles entretiennent avec les gouverneurs et administrateurs territoriaux, directeurs départementaux, élus de base, personnel municipal et fonctionnaires locaux, ainsi que la société civile et la population, entre autres, leur permettent d'identifier les questions émergentes. De là, elles explorent et soutiennent leurs homologues nationaux par des mesures appropriées, sous forme de propositions de solutions adéquates à ces nouveaux défis. Les Affaires civiles doivent ainsi, quotidiennement, faire des consultations auprès de leurs partenaires au sein de l'administration territoriale afin de renforcer les liens avec les institutions au niveau étatique, départemental et communal.

La présence permanente sur le terrain de ces officiers et les relations directes qu'ils entretiennent avec les autorités locales constituent un atout qui les positionne en interlocuteur privilégié chargé de maintenir un dialogue productif constant et, dans une certaine mesure, d'établir un niveau de confiance avec les autorités locales.

Ces interactions régulières, significatives et substantielles avec les instances locales et les autorités nationales constituent un moyen encore plus crucial pour établir le bon fonctionnement des différents paliers de l'administration publique d'un pays en reconstruction. Les Affaires civiles doivent exploiter ces interactions, eu égard aux maigres ressources dont elles disposent et nonobstant les capacités très limitées des collectivités territoriales.

Les Affaires civiles sont censées jouer le rôle de premier plan dans la coordination des efforts de toutes les sections pour faire en sorte que toutes les composantes de la mission travaillent de manière efficace avec les autorités régionales et municipales dans le traitement des questions prioritaires. Elles s'efforcent de dégager une synergie en faveur du dialogue politique, nécessaire à la construction d'un climat de confiance.

L'organigramme de la section des Affaires civiles prévoit au sommet de la section un bureau central dirigé par le directeur de la section des Affaires civiles et son adjoint. Ce bureau se trouve généralement dans la capitale du pays d'accueil. Il est en charge de :

- la gestion générale ;
- support institutionnel et de la gouvernance ;
- la liaison et l'assistance aux autorités locales via les bureaux régionaux et les unités centrales ;
- l'élaboration du rapport hebdomadaire intégré à transmettre aux hauts responsables de la mission ;
- la coordination avec les autres composantes de la mission et les bureaux régionaux ;
- la liaison avec le Parlement via son unité au parlement national.

Dans le contexte actuel, où la nécessité de générer des améliorations socio-économiques devient de plus en plus tangible compte tenu des phénomènes, tels que : la vie chère et la fracture sociale qui occasionnent encore plus de troubles sociaux dans les pays post-crise, les Affaires civiles sont invitées à travailler très étroitement avec les autres sections substantielles. Ceci pour que les activités de la mission respectent les principes humanitaires et les droits de l'homme, principalement ceux qui sont axés sur les droits socio-économiques, et se fassent sur la base d'une vision du développement durable.

Tout ce déballage introductif montre bien qu'une section des Affaires civiles peut-être composée de façon suivante :

- une Unité de Coordination et Rapports ;
- une Unité d'Appui Institutionnel ;
- un Bureau d'Appui au Parlement ;
- une Unité de Gestion des Frontières ;
- des bureaux régionaux dans chaque région.

A. UNITE COORDINATION ET RAPPORTS (UCR)

La création d'une section des Affaires civiles est non seulement fonction de sa taille, mais aussi des ressources, à la fois financières et humaines. Néanmoins, il existe quelques caractéristiques principales communes à toutes les sections des Affaires civiles des différentes missions de maintien de la paix, à travers le monde.

Dans toutes les sections des Affaires civiles, il y a toujours ou presque, une unité qui s'occupe de la coordination et des rapports des bureaux régionaux. Dans chaque region du pays d'accueil, les missions des Nations unies installment un bureau régional (BR) qui constitue le relais de la mission sur le territoire. En principe chaque section substantielle de la mission est représentée dans ce bureau régional qui assure la coordination de toutes ces sections. Le rôle de l'Unité Coordination et rapport est de faire la liaison entre les bureau régionaux et la hiérarchie de la mission.

Cette unité est placée sous la supervision de la direction de la section des Affaires civiles. C'est elle qui reçoit les rapports hebdomadaires intégrés de chaque bureau régional et ceux des autres unités des Affaires civiles, telles que : l'unité de la gestion des frontières (UGF), l'unité d'appui au parlement (UDP) et l'unité d'appui institutionnel (UAI).

L'Unité Coordination et Rapports est une sorte de caisse de résonnance qui récupère les informations du terrain via les bureaux régionaux pour les transmettre à la direction de la section des Affaires civiles. Une fois obtenue la clearance de la direction des Affaires civiles, cette synthèse est acheminée au bureau du Représentant Spécial du Secrétaire Général (SRSG) de l'ONU, sous forme de résumé intitulé « faits saillants » de la semaine. Ce résumé qui porte aussi le nom anglais de « highlight », est un document présenté sur une page afin de faciliter la lecture des autorités d'une mission. Il permet de connaître les grandes lignes d'actualité de la semaine. Ce document est suivi d'un rapport hebdomadaire intégré plus détaillé, qui fait une synthèse de quatre pages sur la mise en perspective des activités et des événements de la mission ainsi que les propositions d'actions.

Le rapport de l'UCR est aussi envoyé :

- aux chefs de sections substantives ;
- au chef d'appui à la mission ;
- au « force commander » (le grand chef des militaires
- de toute la mission) ;
- au « police commissionner » (le grand chef des policier
- onusien de toute la mission) ;
- au « desk office » de la mission à New York ;
- aux bureaux régionaux.

Le rapport constitue une partie essentielle de l'alerte rapide et précoce, utile pour identifier les interventions et résoudre les problèmes au stade préventif. Il contribue à l'efficacité du partage de l'information et l'archivage, mais aussi à la compréhension commune de la situation. Ce rapport facilite la cohérence des efforts, la connaissance de l'histoire de la situation locale qui cause des conflits, ainsi que les relations avec les interlocuteurs, les initiatives, puis permet de faire le suivi.

Les Affaires civiles produisent une série de rapports d'information de qualité et d'analyse, parmi lesquels les rapports : quotidiens, hebdomadaires, mensuels et trimestriels. Dans certaines circonstances, les rapports thématiques et occasionnels, les comptes rendus de réunions, des événements ou des incidents sont souvent nécessaires pour prendre les décisions opérationnelles, élaborer la stratégie et la politique urgentes, guidées par les réalités du terrain.

En revanche, la structure et la fréquence de ces rapports internes varient souvent selon les missions.

Fondamentalement, le rapport sert à :

- informer, expliquer, convaincre, instruire et obtenir des informations ;
- partager une analyse et souligner, ne serait-ce que brièvement, l'importance des facteurs ou des dynamiques en cours de discussion ;
- présenter une analyse sur les activités à entreprendre et sur ce qui se passe sur le terrain ;
- intégrer les questions du genre ;
- clarifier les sources et la fiabilité des données, c'est-à-dire indiquer les sources d'informations et les opinions qui ont été vérifiées ou non ;
- gérer les documents confidentiels et sensibles, ainsi que les risques auxquels sont exposés les informateurs ;
- faire des recommandations assez précises dans la conclusion afin de favoriser l'action et expliquer le bien fondé de ces recommandations qui sont souvent liées à l'impact attendu, sur la base de l'analyse.

L'officier des Affaires civiles doit régulièrement identifier et commenter de façon concise, les événements du terrain, les conditions et la dynamique, par une mise à jour de la situation communale, régionale ou nationale, y compris l'analyse de la dynamique entre le niveau national et local et les changements de l'environnement politique interne ou externe, qui influencent la crise. Lorsque l'environnement est relativement stable, il doit fournir des rapports thématiques, en regardant plus en profondeur les dynamiques spécifiques ou les acteurs.

Il doit aussi fournir en permanence une analyse locale du conflit par rapport à la présence de la mission, en expliquant l'impact des dynamiques locales, des événements et des acteurs de la mission. Son rôle est aussi d'apporter un éclairage confirmant ou infirmant l'efficacité des relations entre les facteurs principaux et la dynamique de réponse identifiée dans l'analyse existante. L'autre fonction de l'Unité coordination et rapport est de faire le suivi des activités de l'ensemble de la section des Affaires civiles afin d'alimenter deux bases de données : celle de la section des Affaires civiles, qui se fait de façon hebdomadaire et celle de la mission qui est établie mensuellement.

Toutefois, la base de données des Affaires civiles est inspire du programme d'exécution de la mission qui est couramment qualifié de MIP, abrégé du concept anglais « *Mission Implementation Programm.* » Le MIP est lui-même fondé sur un autre outil de suivi et de management de la mission, connu sous l'appellation de RBB qui traduit les termes anglais « Results Base Budget. » Cela signifie faire l'évaluation des résultats des activités accomplies pendant une période donnée, en vue de justifier l'utilisation du budget qui a été alloué à la mission. Ce RBB existe dans toutes les missions puisqu'il demeure, jusqu'à preuve du contraire, l'unique et commun instrument permettant de faire le monitoring des activités budgétisées de chacune des missions de maintien de la paix.

Dans sa fonction de coordination, l'Unité Coordination et Rapports se comporte en courroie de transmission pour gérer les relations entre le centre et la périphérie, à travers :

- l'organisation des réunions de coordination des Chefs de Bureaux Régionaux dans un intervalle de temps, qui varie selon les missions et les circonstances (en général entre les deux et six mois);
- l'organisation des forums avec les bureaux régionaux et l'Unité Appui au Parlement, afin de renforcer les relations entre les parlementaires et les autres responsables des collectivités territoriales ;
- les collectes d'information sur des sujets spécifiques comme par exemple, les polices municipales, militaires démobilisés ;
- l'organisation d'opérations spéciales qui ne relevant pas toujours de la compétence de la section des Affaires civiles, telle que : campagne de vaccination dans certains pays ayant accueilli une mission ;
- l'organisation de visites sur le terrain, à la fois des VIP (*Very Importante Personnalities)* de la mission et des invités extérieurs.

C'est aussi l'Unité Coordination et Rapports, qui présente les activités de la section des Affaires civiles aux sessions *« d'induction »* qui veut dire en français « introduction », aux Casques bleus nouvellement arrivés, ainsi que le personnel civil arrivant dans la mission. Elle participe, sur une base régulière, aux réunions et travaux du *« Joint Mission Analysis Center »* (JMAC) qui est une sorte d'intelligentsia pour ne pas dire service de renseignements de la mission de maintien de la paix des Nations unies.

Dans certaines missions, elle assume les fonctions de l'unité d'appui institutionnel et vice-versa, selon que l'une ou l'autre n'est pas établie.

B. UNITE APPUI INSTITUTIONEL (UAI)

L'UAI est composée d'une équipe formée de spécialistes motivés au siège de la mission. Elle dispose d'un réseau relais de ressources humaines multidisciplinaires sur le terrain. Ces hommes et ces femmes des Affaires civiles sont censés établir et entretenir des relations constantes avec les instances locales.

Qu'est ce que l'appui institutionnel ?

Dans ce binôme « appui institutionnel », le mot « appui » veut dire renforcement, développement, assistance, réconfort, secours, soutien, support moral ou technique, aide matérielle et logistique,... Bien entendu, l'appui matériel ou logistique se fait surtout à travers les programmes QIP.

Quant au concept « institutionnel », il dérive du mot « institution. » Et, institution peut être interprétée comme relatif à Etat, aux collectivités territoriales et aux services publics. Au sens plus large, il s'agit de tout organisme ou structure dont les membres partagent les mêmes objectifs et se dotent de règles et de moyens pour les atteindre. Il y a par exemple :

- le gouvernement central ou l'Etat, notamment le Ministère de l'intérieur ou le Ministère en charge des collectivités territoriales, ainsi que le Ministère du plan et de la planification, plus précisément, la Direction des Collectivités Territoriales (DCT) et à la Direction des Etudes de la Planification et du Suivi (DEPS) ;
- les collectivités territoriales, notamment les institutions décentralisées telles que la région, la commune, la section communale dont les autorités sont élues ;
- les Directions départementales, qui sont des institutions déconcentrées de l'Etat, dont les responsables sont nommées par le gouvernement ;
- la société civile.

Dans le cadre des institutions publiques, l'appui institutionnel peut se définir comme :

- le moyen permettant à l'Etat de se recentrer sur ses missions d'orientation, de programmation, de suiviévaluation et promotion des partenariats ;
- un accompagnement des Affaires civiles dans la définition, la mise en oeuvre et le suivi-évaluation des politiques sectorielles et sous-sectorielles des collectivités territoriales ;
- un ensemble des pratiques, outils et méthodes qui visent à impliquer des fonctionnaires dans la réflexion et le suivi-évaluation des actions ;
- un appui aux hommes et femmes qui travaillent dans une institution, dans le but de repérer et comprendre les enjeux et les individus qui vont permettre d'améliorer les méthodes de travail, pour créer des dynamiques d'évolution sur le plan politique, économique et social ;
- la capacité à faire travailler ensemble, de façon à faire évoluer les comportements et les capacités ;
- la cohérence d'outils et des pratiques pour mettre en adéquation les objectifs, l'organisation et les moyens d'une structure donnée ;
- une stratégie qui consiste à adapter les structures et les institutions à l'évolution des sociétés et de la situation d'un pays post-crise, pour une meilleure efficience et le renforcement des processus démocratiques ;
- la technique pour faire reconnaître par l'Etat les évolutions de la société civile afin qu'elle les intègre dans sa stratégie de développement.

Evidemment, l'appui institutionnel doit prendre en compte différents niveaux d'intervention : du local à l'international, en passant par l'Etat central.

Il va de soi que l'Etat ne saurait assurer ses fonctions que si l'appui institutionnel est également orienté vers le renforcement des capacités de la société civile et de ses représentants à être des interlocuteurs qualifiés. Donc, ce n'est pas sans fondement que certains experts disent que : l'appui institutionnel est une technique de renforcement des capacités des collectivités territoriales dont l'objectif est d'améliorer les performances des autorités décentralisées et déconcentrées, ainsi que la société civile et l'Etat, pour rendre plus accessibles les services rendus à la population, dans un Etat unitaire décentralisé, déconcentré et démocratique.

Au sens large, on dirait qu'il s'agit :

- de l'appui aux politiques de décentralisation et développement institutionnel qui passe par un appui aux stratégies nationales de décentralisation, à la réforme institutionnelle au niveau macroéconomique et au renforcement des capacités des collectivités locales ;
- du soutien à la bonne gouvernance et la gouvernance locale qui se traduit par un appui à la démocratie locale et aux processus électoraux, la promotion de la participation des acteurs locaux dans les processus politiques, le renforcement de la société civile ;
- du renforcement de la décentralisation des services, caractérisé par l'appui à la décentralisation des services proprement dite, le renforcement des capacités des collectivités locales à fournir, gérer et maintenir les services, l'appui budgétaire ou les facilités d'investissement octroyés aux communes ;
- d'élaboration des budgets communaux et programmes thématiques d'acteurs non étatiques et autorités locales dans le développement ;
- du développement local, ce qui signifie renforcer les capacités des structures des gouvernements locaux à promouvoir la planification participative et le développement économique et social ;
- du renforcement du développement participatif et des capacités par la sensibilisation et l'éducation au développement, la mise en réseau et l'échange de bonnes pratiques ainsi que le dialogue et l'échange d'informations, sans oublier la coopération… ;
- de la coopération décentralisée, basée sur les microprojets, à travers le développement économique local, le développement urbain, l'appui aux acteurs décentralisés, c'est-à-dire les collectivités territoriales ;
- de la promotion de la participation des collectivités locales dans le dialogue et les stratégies de coopération, à travers la programmation, la formulation, la mise en oeuvre et l'évaluation des programmes de coopération ;
- de la réhabilitation post-conflit et réconciliation ;

- de l'organisation et la gestion des services du Ministère de l'Intérieur, chargé des collectivités territoriales ;
- de la formation et le renforcement des capacités des services centraux et des collectivités territoriales ;
- de la gestion et la capitalisation de l'information dans le cadre d'activités événementielles ;
- de l'appui matériel et logistique dans les déplacements et la transmission des courriers et directives ministériels ;
- de l'harmonisation, la conception et le cofinancement, avec les fonds de QIP, des formations dispensées à l'intention des comptables communaux et des maires, dans les domaines pointus, tels que : le protocole, l'éthique et la gestion administrative et financière ;
- de l'organisation d'ateliers pour la préparation des budgets communaux ;
- de la contribution dans la réalisation des forums départementaux dans le cadre des campagnes nationales sur la transparence de l'administration locale et pour l'implantation des panneaux d'affichage public dans les départements, arrondissements, communes et sections communales ;
- de l'organisation de colloques internationaux sur le statut et la formation du personnel territorial, ainsi que les assises sur la coopération décentralisée ;
- du renforcement de l'appui du Ministère de tutelle aux communes dans le cadre des informations émanant des bureaux régionaux.

De tout ce qui précède, l'appui institutionnel peut se définir comme une forme d'assistance technique et logistique, caractérisée par la composition des outils, méthodes et pratiques, qui concourent à rendre plus efficace une institution ou une structure donnée dans l'atteinte de ses objectifs et pour la permettre d'améliorer la qualité des services rendus à la population.

De ce fait, l'assistance technique apportée par les officiers des Affaires civiles en appui institutionnel se positionne en interface ou encore en médiation entre les services de l'Etat et ses partenaires, y compris la population et la société civile. D'où, l'importance de faire circuler l'information en temps utile, de contribuer à ouvrir les discussions et d'aider aux synthèses et à la formulation d'alternatives — avantages/inconvénients — pour faciliter la prise de décision des autorités locales. En ce sens, l'officier des Affaires civiles a pour tâche essentielle de contribuer à la définition ou clarification, non seulement du mandat de la mission et ses objectifs, mais aussi de la stratégie, l'organisation et les moyens, nécessaires pour atteindre les buts de la collectivité concernée. Malgré cela, il doit trouver la bonne distance entre une forte implication pouvant basculer dans la substitution ou l'ingérence que certains observateurs peuvent d'ailleurs juger indispensable, d'une part et le recul nécessaire pour se limiter aux conseils, d'autre part. C'est pour cette raison qu'il est d'abord décrit comme un conseiller, qui ne doit pas imposer ses idées, mais qui doit savoir relativiser et composer dans le court, moyen et long terme, ce qui exige un « savoir-être indispensable, mais pas incontournable. »

Du coup, l'Unité Appui Institutionnel désigne, pour ainsi dire, l'assistance technique des officiers des Affaires civiles dans :

- la coordination et la planification des activités ;
- la mise en oeuvre des règles ou des lois régissant le fonctionnement des entités respectives de l'Etat hôte ;
- le rapprochement des collectivités et la société civile, afin de faciliter la cohésion entre ces diverses entités de l'Etat, notamment, mairie-justice-police sur la sécurité et l'Etat de droit, mairie-DGI sur la fiscalité et les finances locales, mairie-travaux publics sur l'urbanisme... le renforcement du processus de déconcentration et de décentralisation ;
- l'accompagnement des autorités élues dans l'exécution de leurs responsabilités ;
- la consolidation des mécanismes de coordination et les capacités de suivi et de contrôle des collectivités territoriales ;
- l'élaboration des budgets et des plans de développement communal ;
- la résolution et la prévention des conflits ;
- la promotion du dialogue communautaire ;
- l'amélioration de la gestion des finances publiques par les autorités locales ;
- l'établissement d'une fonction publique territoriale moderne ;
- l'affermissement de la capacité de planification du gouvernement central et des collectivités territoriales, afin de promouvoir le développement local ;
- l'amélioration des infrastructures, pour le bon fonctionnement des collectivités territoriales.

En d'autres termes, l'appui institutionnel veut dire : le renforcement des capacités administratives et financières pour la gestion des affaires publiques dans le cadre de la bonne gouvernance. Il est caractérisé par un mécanisme d'accompagnement des autorités locales, notamment les collectivités territoriales et les Directions régionales déconcentrées, pour leur permettre de s'approprier toutes les responsabilités qui sont les leurs, en vue de la satisfaction des besoins immédiats de la population locale.

Concrètement, l'officier des Affaires civiles :

- contribue à la rédaction des documents de politiques générales et des cadres stratégiques de lutte contre la pauvreté ;
- participe aux diagnostics communaux, à l'identification des besoins et à la réorganisation administrative ;

- s'investi dans la définition des politiques de gestion des ressources humaines ;
- participe aux tables de concertation et à la cohérence d'ensemble des documents produits par les collectivités territoriales en lien avec les orientations nationales et internationales ;
- intervient dans l'instruction et le suivi des projets visant à satisfaire les besoins de la communauté.

Ceci revient à dire qu'il travaille prioritairement dans les secteurs suivants :

- l'organisation institutionnelle ;
- les politiques sectorielles et communales ;
- la gouvernance ;
- l'appui organisationnel ;
- la concertation ;
- l'identification et la « priorisation » des besoins avec les autorités locales ;
- la recherche des causes de dysfonctionnement des administrations locales ;
- l'organisation ou facilitation de formations sur les différents thèmes détaillés dans le tome II de ce livre ;
- le « monitoring » ;
- le « coaching » ;
- le « reporting » ;
- la collecte et l'analyse des données spécifiques à l'appui institutionnel ;
- la résolution de conflits locaux ;
- l'amélioration des relations interinstitutionnelles ;
- l'appui logistique ;
- le renforcement de structures de coordination, telles que les délégations, les assemblées départementales les conseils municipaux, à travers les tables de concertation départementales et communales, les rencontres de l'Etat de droit…

Ses outils sont essentiellement :

- le diagnostic ;
- l'évaluation des besoins en formation ;
- les échanges d'expériences ;
- les ateliers et séminaires ;
- les notes de synthèse ;
- les études de faisabilité ;
- les évaluations de performance ;

- le suivi sur le terrain[28].

Dans le cas spécifique des Affaires civiles de l'ONU, les outils de travail les plus courants, pour les actions concrètes sont : les projets à impact rapide (QIP) et les analyses qui découlent des inputs venus des régions, ainsi que le suivi de terrain. Ils permettent d'élaborer la synthèse de l'Unité Appui Institutionnel et préparer le rapport de performance des municipalités.

En principe, l'UAI doit constituer la mémoire institutionnelle d'une section des Affaires civiles, pour éviter la dispersion des ressources. Son rôle entre autres, est de pousser les régions à consacrer suffisamment de temps à l'appui institutionnel, pour plus d'efficacité.

Dans l'autre sens cette unité doit faire en sorte que le gouvernement, notamment le ministère des collectivités territoriales avec lequel elle doit entretenir des réunions régulières, soit « demandeur » de ses services, pour faciliter son accès et tirer tous les bénéfices de l'expertise issue de ses ressources.

Toutefois, elle doit aussi établir des relations de partenariat avec les autres ministères, essentiellement celui des finances et du plan. L'UAI doit évidemment faire un travail de proximité pouvant se traduire par l'installation de certains experts de son équipe dans les ministères clés, principalement celui de l'intérieur avec lequel elle est amenée à agencer un cadre de coopération mission-ministère.

Ce cadre de coopération est un laissez-passer qui permet à l'Unité Appui Institutionnel de connaître la stratégie du gouvernement aux fins de mieux appuyer le renforcement des institutions nationales et être plus efficace. Cette implication de proximité est le meilleur moyen de conseiller le gouvernement et porter à sa connaissance les besoins, toutes les difficultés et les suggestions soulevées par les éléments des Affaires civiles de toutes les régions.

Au sens large du terme, cet accord de coopération légitime la présence permanente sur le terrain, des officiers des Affaires civiles qui sont appelés à tisser des relations continues, productives et ouvertes avec l'ensemble des autorités publiques.

Par rapport à son positionnement, l'Unité Appui Institutionnel est aussi bien placée pour assister le ministère des collectivités territoriales dans la prise en compte des réformes de l'Etat, par exemple pour élaborer une stratégie nationale sur la décentralisation, ce qui exige un cadre légal reconnu et validé pour que cela soit applicable.

L'UAI constitue aussi le pont entre la section des Affaires civiles et la communauté internationale : PNUD, Bailleurs de fonds… A ce titre, il lui

---

[28] 23e session de la conférence ministérielle de la francophonie, Vientiane-Laos, 20-21 Novembre 2007
Voir aussi site de la Mission des Nations unies pour la Stabilisation en Haïti, www.minustah.org et http://institutionnel.redev.info/

appartient de définir et redéfinir la valeur ajoutée de la mission, via celle des Affaires civiles : ses ressources humaines, sa logistique et la présence sur le terrain des hommes et des femmes qui parcourent toutes les routes et pistes du pays, pour observer et prendre note des vrais problèmes à remonter à la surface, au niveau central. Elle est censée assister le gouvernement dans la mise en place des mécanismes de coordination, à l'instar des tables sectorielles au niveau de l'Etat et stimuler l'organisation des réunions des bailleurs de fonds et des opérateurs, à travers des relations formelles.

Pour ce faire, elle doit prendre en compte les stratégies du Programme des Nations unies pour le Développement (PNUD), de l'UNDAF (« United Nations Devolopment Assistance Framework ») et des autres institutions internationales, puis utiliser les ressources et bases de données d'OCHA, mais aussi développer un partenariat avec les ONG et associations nationales et internationales. Il serait aussi très avantageux pour l'UAI d'exploiter les clauses des « Tables de Concertations » au niveau départemental et tisser des liens et des réseaux avec les acteurs locaux via les Bureau Régionaux.

En un mot, l'action des Affaires civiles se conjugue avec les termes comme « promotion », « soutien », « facilitation », « encouragement », etc. La « promotion » donne aux Affaires civiles un rôle basé sur le plaidoyer et la capacité à fournir une philosophie constructive, rétroaction et pertinente ou à conseiller les institutions locales afin d'encourager les réformes urgentes. La référence au concept « soutenir » évoque par contre, un rôle plus proactif qui peut se traduire en appui technique et logistique direct. Il intègre aussi le personnel des institutions clés du gouvernement au niveau central ou local.

Tandis que la « facilitation » suppose que les institutions étatiques ont un niveau faible des capacités qu'il va falloir renforcer, par le biais : des conseils techniques et l'élaboration des stratégies, dans un esprit de coopération pour atteindre les objectifs fixés. Pour terminer, le vocable « encouragement » rappelle la possibilité offerte aux institutions de l'Etat d'augmenter leurs responsabilités afin qu'elles acquièrent les aptitudes à rendre les services qu'elles sont censées fournir à la population.

Cependant, il est clair que les Affaires civiles ne doivent jouer aucun rôle majeur dans le processus global de résolution de conflit, ce qui relève principalement, de la compétence de la section des Affaires politiques, même si elles sont souvent les premiers acteurs internationaux sur le terrain post-conflit et qu'elles constituent le principal interlocuteur pour les autorités locales. Certes, dans cet environnement post-conflictuel, elles sont souvent sollicitées pour aider et soutenir le gouvernement central et les collectivités territoriales, ainsi que la société civile, mais elles doivent se limiter à prendre des initiatives dans le cadre du renforcement des capacités, c'est-à-dire des formations ciblées.

Ainsi, il est préférable de réduire les interventions directes et s'impliquer plutôt dans la facilitation des processus de développement des capacités, tout en offrant des outils d'orientation, matrice d'évaluation, fiches d'information ou notes de synthèses, etc., permettant de définir les politiques et planifier les activités au fil du temps, au lieu de simplement faire face aux urgences. Lorsque les gouvernements locaux et régionaux ont acquis un certain niveau de capacité de fonctionnement autonome, ils ont donc besoin d'assistance d'une nature plus discrète et subtile qui se focalise sur la mobilisation des ressources. Ces distinctions sont théoriques et conceptuelles plutôt que pratiques. Les différentes actions qui y sont liées tendent à se chevaucher, mais elles se complètent mutuellement pour apporter une certaine valeur ajoutée, telle que :

- offrir une perspective fraîche et novatrice sur les dynamiques enfermées dans des cercles vicieux classiques du fonctionnement des collectivités territoriales ;
- fournir des conseils à tous les acteurs en tant qu'observateur impartial du processus formé par une équipe combinée des nationaux et internationaux les plus efficaces, pouvant renforcer la confiance dans la proximité culturelle ;
- faire usage des connaissances techniques des officiers des Affaires civiles pour effectuer le transfert des meilleures pratiques dans les domaines spécifiques d'appui institutionnel ;
- recevoir, transporter et livrer les messages, à travers les barrières géographiques, institutionnelles et hiérarchiques, pour faciliter les échanges entre les acteurs locaux et centraux ;
- utiliser les moyens logistiques qui ne sont pas disponibles pour d'autres acteurs locaux afin de faciliter l'élaboration de la cartographie des besoins et des capacités, au niveau institutionnel ;
- promouvoir les synergies avec d'autres acteurs et les donateurs présents au niveau local.

En situation de post-conflit, les besoins des institutions étatiques sont généralement immenses et les attentes tout aussi énormes, au point que toute évaluation aboutie à une liste irréaliste et ingérable de priorités. Dans ce cas, pour mesurer les besoins et définir les priorités, il faut se donner des critères de base d'évaluer, tels que : les besoins sans lien avec les circonstances spécifiques de la situation préconflit, ainsi que la nature et le niveau des services qui ont été livrés à l'époque. Ce qui permet de façonner certains programmes critiques de formation que les Affaires civiles se doivent de mettre à exécution pour renforcer la confiance dans le système de gouvernement local.

La démarche d'évaluation des besoins institutionnels oblige à :

- émettre des hypothèses solides, mais qui facilitent une compréhension claire de l'architecture institutionnelle, des fonctions et des résultats attendus. Il convient de se débarrasser de toutes les hypothèses pré-fondées, même si elles sont plus familières ;
- faire une bonne planification pour identifier les acteurs concernés afin de les engager dès le départ, pour établir conjointement les termes de référence, les objectifs clairs et la division du travail entre ceux qui vont effectuer l'évaluation ;
- former des équipes d'évaluations qualifiées en recherchant les compétences techniques locales nécessaires à l'évaluation. En cas d'indisponibilité, il convient explorer la possibilité d'utiliser les ressources de la mission ;
- élaborer une méthodologie solide basée sur des objectifs clairs et définis, puis en fonction des critères objectifs et comparables comme le statut juridique de la propriété, la surface globale, le nombre de chambres, l'accès à l'alimentation et l'eau, l'existence de toilettes, la proximité du centre-ville, etc. ;
- avoir une cohérence dans le suivi, c'est-a-dire ne pas jeter le rapport d'évaluation dans les oubliettes, mais capitaliser sur les résultats. Il faut également engager ceux qui ont participé à la définition de la stratégie de suivi, à la determination des points d'action et à des acteurs responsables dans l'exécution. Il est important d'archiver correctement les conclusions et le rapport, pour en faire un document pour la mémoire institutionnelle des Affaires civiles et des autorités locales concernées.

Reste à savoir comment apprécier la bonne performance d'une section des Affaires civiles en matière d'appui institutionnel.

D'emblée, cela dépend largement de sa compréhension de l'ensemble des éléments qui entourent les officiers des Affaires civiles et qui, de surcroit, sont susceptibles d'interagir avec eux directement ou indirectement, mais aussi de leur capacité à s'adapter, au sens de rassembler tous les acteurs et toutes les forces internes et externes capables d'influencer la façon dont ils développent leurs activités, ainsi que les échanges avec les autres partenaires étatiques ou non étatiques.

Cependant, si les Affaires civiles ont peu de pouvoir sur cet environnement, notamment, sur ces forces externes, il n'en demeure pas moins qu'elles doivent, à tout moment, s'accommoder à leurs actions pour contribuer à l'amélioration de la bonne gouvernance. L'environnement dont il s'agit inclut :

- la situation politique difficile ;
- l'absence d'un gouvernement fort et crédible ;

- le mandat des élus locaux lorsqu'il arrive à terme, autrement dit l'alternance politique qui ouvre des perspectives d'organisation de nouvelles élections municipales et locales ;
- les risques de catastrophes naturelles ;
- la précarité de la situation économique.

Les Affaires civiles, en coopération avec les autorités nationales, sont aussi appelées à surveiller le rendement de certaines institutions locales. Ce travail permet d'évaluer la pertinence du traitement accordé aux besoins identifiés initialement. Il renvoie à apprécier l'efficacité globale de l'appui fourni au renforcement des institutions locales. Aussi convient-il de trouver des repères réalistes permettant d'orienter les activités et aligner leurs priorités. Par exemple, la matrice d'évaluation pour les administrations municipales basées sur la mesure des indicateurs standards, en Haïti.

Les Affaires civiles sont en droit de fournir un soutien logistique et administratif aux représentants des gouvernements locaux pour maintenir une présence dans leurs communes, afin d'accompagner le rétablissement des structures de la gouvernance locale, ainsi que la prestation de services de base à travers le transport des fonctionnaires et des matériaux locaux. Même la simple capacité de transférer des messages auprès des autorités locales au niveau central et vice-versa permet de combler une lacune majeure dans la communication institutionnelle. Dans ce processus, il faut éviter de se substituer et/ou réduire les possibilités de formater un mécanisme plus durable lorsque les institutions d'Etat auront développé une certaine capacité de fonctionnement de base.

Cela aide le gouvernement local à interpréter et appliquer les directives et initiatives du gouvernement central. Il faut aussi éviter une dépendance logistique et administrative entrainant l'échec du renforcement des capacités. Les responsables locaux ont souvent besoin d'avoir une présence physique dans les zones souvent abandonnées ou détruites pendant le conflit pour renouer avec leurs électeurs, en faisant attention aux perceptions négatives des gens qui pourraient penser que la Mission veut imposer à la population, un représentant quelconque. Pour cela, il faut simplement que les représentants des gouvernements locaux soient perçus comme agissant dans leur pleine autorité et sur la base d'une légitimité propre.

Les fonds des QIP peuvent servir à reconstruire les bureaux des gouvernements locaux, les postes de police ou les tribunaux… mais, étant donné que la demande dépasse presque toujours les ressources et les capacités disponibles, les Affaires civiles doivent avoir une politique claire sur les circonstances dans lesquelles il convient de fournir leur appui logistique et la manière de répartir leurs actifs.

Tout au long de la mission, les officiers des Affaires civiles continueront à expérimenter les activités de renforcement des capacités à petite échelle avec les interlocuteurs locaux, pour combler le vide laissé par la baisse progressive des acteurs du développement au niveau local, à travers :

- le suivi sur la capacité initiale d'évaluation des besoins, ce qui peut être réalisé par une combinaison de soutien direct, à savoir le transfert des compétences et des connaissances disponibles au sein des Affaires civiles ;
- la mobilisation des ressources financières et des compétences nationales ou extérieures et aussi, le soutien au niveau local dans la mise en oeuvre et la surveillance ;
- la formation des nouveaux élus sur des sujets comme la finance, l'administration locale, la budgétisation ou la gestion des structures étatiques, mais aussi dans le cadre des profils professionnels spécifiques des agents municipaux.

Toutefois, ces programmes doivent être conçus conjointement avec les autorités nationales. Dans la mesure du possible, c'cst l'expertise nationale qui en prendrait la paternité, mais les Affaires civiles se contenteraient de soutenir et/ou faciliter ce genre de projets exécutés seulement lorsqu'aucune autre solution alternative viable n'est possible.

Dans ses rapports avec les bureaux régionaux l'Unité Appui Institutionnel doit :

- formuler des directives claires à l'attention des bureaux régionaux pour impulser une véritable dynamique et une interaction entre la direction des Affaires civiles, la mission et les régions, en vue de définir ensemble les priorités et les axes de travail ;
- répondre aux préoccupations quotidiennes des bureaux régionaux, notammement celles qui nécessitent l'intervention du gouvernement ;
- suivre, évaluer et synthétiser les informations reçues via les rapports hebdomadaires et les rapports spécifiques, dans un souci de cohérence et de visibilité des activités de la Section des Affaires civiles ;
- transmettre aux régions les orientations de manière ponctuelle et sur la base de l'urgence, dans le but d'empêcher la dispersion dans les activités menées ;
- consolider le travail fourni par les régions afin de valoriser l'exploitation des données venant du terrain ;
- réunir les chefs de bureaux de façon régulière, pour discuter des orientations, décider des priorités et établir ou réaménager le calendrier de travail qui sera exécuté par la section, en fonction de l'évolution de la situation qui prévaut sur le terrain ;
- inviter les bureaux régionaux à des réunions thématiques pour mieux prendre à corps les besoins

- à satisfaire ; analyser les rapports des BR, notamment les rapports hebdomadaires et ceux des activités spécifiques, car ils constituent des vrais outils de consolidation et de planification ;
- transmettre les conclusions et les recommandations issues des réunions avec les bureaux, au sommet de la mission et aux ministères concernés ;
- rédiger les synthèses qui refléteront les actions des régions sur la base des rapports hebdomadaires et des rapports spéciaux qui conviendraient d'être partagées avec les Bureaux ;
- organiser des rencontres avec les autorités locales basées sur une démarche constructive et cohérente ;
- supputer les formations périodiques des collectivités territoriales et de leurs associations, puis définir les besoins en formations et en infrastructures publiques, pour l'avenir ;
- poursuivre dans une certaine mesure les activités de médiation et de gestion de conflits ;
- travailler avec la société civile comme acteur de la décentralisation ;
- évaluer les besoins des préfectures et des autres collectivités territoriales, allant au-delà d'un simple soutien logistique ;
- faire des propositions dans le projet de réforme de la fiscalité ;
- aider les collectivités territoriales à définir leurs investissements.

Ceci nous amène à conclure que le Renforcement de l'autorité de l'Etat et la Promotion de la bonne gouvernance dans le jargon onusien touche directement, au niveau central, les principales activités de l'Unité Appui Institutionnel, tandis qu'au niveau local, la responsabilité incombe aux Bureaux Régionaux des Affaires civiles.

Dans chaque cas, le renforcement des capacités de l'autorité de l'Etat et la promotion de la bonne gouvernance se comprennent de façon thématique.

En ce qui concerne le statut du travail public territorial au niveau central, l'UAI doit accompagner le Ministère des collectivités territoriales et ses partenaires dans la formation du personnel territorial. Cela inclut l'accès, les profils de poste, le déroulement de carrière, la formation initiale et continue, les barèmes de rémunérations, les différentes positions, et cetera. Ce travail vise concrètement le maintien d'un système d'échange d'informations à travers des réunions régulières et constructives avec les partenaires ministériels pour l'élaboration des propositions de projet de loi sur le statut de la fonction publique territoriale, par exemple.

L'UAI est appelée à faire régulièrement des recommandations pertinentes et précises dans des rapports thématiques permettant d'identifier les domaines où le Ministère doit renforcer son appui auprès de la préfecture ou à toute autre autorité locale.

En guise d'illustration, l'UAI peut :

- conseiller les autorités dans le domaine de formation sur le tas au niveau : national et local ;
- proposer les mesures en vue de renforcer l'autorité de l'Etat, en mettant un accent particulier sur la réforme de l'administration publique, la décentralisation, finance publique et impôts, ainsi que le service public ;
- fournir une assistance technique permettant d'améliorer la capacité des délégations départementales dans le contrôle administratif et financier des entités décentralisées, en offrant des services et en rédigeant des lois sur le gouvernement local ;
- organiser des séances de formation dans les régions sur l'administration publique, pour renforcer la capacité des gouverneurs et des maires ;
- organiser des réunions mensuelles avec le bureau du Ministère de l'Intérieur sur les stratégies de planification et de gestion.

En ce qui concerne le budget et les finances publiques, l'UAI pourrait :

- aider le Ministère des collectivités territoriales dans la réalisation d'un guide des procédures visant à l'amélioration de la préparation budgétaire, étant donné qu'il s'agit d'une administration naissante où tout est à refaire ;
- coordonner avec l'Unité d'Appui au Parlement pour la transmission des propositions de loi en lien avec les budgets et les finances locales, spécifiquement un projet de loi concernant l'amélioration de la fiscalité locale qui devrait passer par une commission intérieure et les collectivités territoriales (exception faite des pays comme Haïti où le parlement n'est pas compétent dans le domaine de fiscalité et dont l'initiative doit venir du gouvernement) ;
- appuyer le Ministère des collectivités territoriales dans la rédaction du protocole pour la mise en œuvre des programmes d'inventaire communaux, destinés à recueillir les informations nécessaires aux ratios pour le calcul des allocations versées aux budgets communaux ;
- aider à augmenter les recettes fiscales ;
- encourager les autorités à réaliser des états des lieux physiques et financiers des mairies ;
- contribuer à la réalisation d'une base de données pour l'enregistrement et le traitement des informations liées à des inventaires communaux ;
- Concourir à la mise en oeuvre d'un accord entre le Ministère de l'intérieur et la Commission Nationale des Marchés Publics (CNMP) pour déconcentrer les compétences de la CNMP, en appui et au profit des communes.

Sur le terrain, ce travail peut se concrétiser en apportant une assistance technique dans le secteur de la comptabilité municipale en :

- assistant les caissiers payeurs en matière de comptabilité ;
- s'assurant de la tenue quotidienne des livres comptables de la mairie ;
- contrôlant l'enregistrement des revenus et des dépenses municipales.

Ce travail qui se fait en partenariat avec les cadres du Ministère des collectivités territoriales consiste, entre autres à :

- assister le Conseil municipal, le secrétaire général, le caissier payeur en matière d'élaboration budgétaire ;
- contrôler le respect des principes et l'exécution des dépenses, en conformité avec les prévisions budgétaires, ainsi que l'exécution mensuelle du « payroll » de la mairie, à partir des rapports d'exécution présenter par la municipalité ;
- vérifier l'exécution des dépenses en conformité avec les règles de passation des marchés publics ;
- aider les mairies en matière d'élaboration de gestion de projets et dans le cadre de la mobilisation des ressources et de planification locale ;
- encourager la coopération entre les institutions de contrôle dans la réalisation conjointe des missions d'audit financier dans les mairies et la signalisation des irrégularités constatées à la cour pour les poursuites nécessaires.

Dans le domaine de la formation, les tâches de l'UAI consistent à :

- appuyer le Ministère de l'intérieur dans l'élaboration et la mise en oeuvre de nouveaux programmes de formation pour les cadres du ministère et pour ceux des collectivités territoriales (secrétaires et directeurs généraux, agents fiscaux, comptables payeurs, ingénieurs…) ;
- soutenir le Ministère dans la création des fiches de demandes individuelles et collectives de formation ;
- contribuer à la réalisation des carnets de formation et des fiches de bilan de stage du personnel du Ministère de l'Intérieur et des collectivités territoriales ;
- tester les procédures déjà élaborées dans un certain nombre de municipalités pilotes ;
- coopérer dans l'organisation des séminaires à l'intention des autorités locales et les membres de la société civile sur la décentralisation, les taxes et les frais locaux, ainsi que sur les responsabilités dont elles sont appelés à rendre des comptes ;
- aider à faire la collecte de ces fiches de demandes de formation qui sont élaborées, afin de les traiter ;
- contribuer à l'élaboration des fiches techniques dans la collecte des informations nécessaires à l'inventaire communal pour lister les

infrastructures communales indispensables aux calculs des ratios pour le versement des allocations destinées aux communes ;

- soutenir le ministère de l'intérieur pour qu'il soit en mesure de diffuser aux élus et aux agents communaux, les notions de base des marchés publics ;
- inciter à la préparation et utilisation des carnets de formation et des fiches de bilan de stage ;
- encourager la création d'une base de données pour le partage d'information entre les ministères et les communes.

Ce partage d'informations doit aussi se faire entre les ministères et l'Unité Appui Institutionnel. Cette denière doit :

- utiliser les synthèses hebdomadaires accompagnées des fiches de signalement contenant des recommandations pertinentes et précises pour aider le Ministère de l'Intérieur à mettre en oeuvre les moyens d'améliorer la gestion des collectivités territoriales ;
- adapter les rapports trimestriels des bureaux régionaux aux attentes et priorités du Ministère des collectivités territoriales, en matière d'évaluation de la gestion communale ;
- contribuer à l'identification des acteurs impliqués dans l'appui institutionnel, afin d'aider le Ministère de l'Intérieur à promouvoir la coordination et aider à la programmation ;
- faire de l'échange d'informations un outil pour faciliter des réunions régulières et constructives avec les partenaires ministériels et créer une synergie qu'il faut continuer à développer en faveur de l'appui aux communes ;
- élaborer des rapports thématiques pour permettre aux Ministères d'identifier les domaines où ils doivent renforcer leur appui à la Délégation et/ou à toute autre autorité locale.

La communication n'est pas en reste. Dans ce domaine, l'Unité Appui Institutionnel doit notamment :

- promouvoir la transparence de l'administration locale en aidant à médiatiser l'installation des panneaux d'affichage et/ou par les spots radiotélévisés ;
- valoriser et médiatiser régulièrement les activités réalisées au profit de l'amélioration de la gouvernance ;
- contribuer à l'élaboration d'un plan de communication du Ministère de l'Intérieur, mettant en valeur les projets et les activités, tout en ciblant les canaux de communication les plus appropriés ;
- participer à la réalisation des carnets de formation et des fiches de bilan de stage du personnel dudit Ministère et des collectivités territoriales ;

- conseiller le Ministère de l'Intérieur dans l'élaboration des procédures de délivrance et de renouvellement d'agrément des organismes de formation du personnel des collectivités territoriales ;
- aider les partenaires nationaux et internationaux à partager les informations et harmoniser les programmes de formation, pour une plus grande cohérence dans la programmation et pour éviter les duplications.

L'UAI assume aussi la fonction de support et d'encadrement de l'Etat et des collectivités territoriales. En ce sens, elle :

- accompagne le Ministère de l'Intérieur et les bureaux régionaux dans les visites auprès des communes en difficultés ;
- facilite l'assimilation par les élus locaux, des connaissances acquises dans les formations ;
- sollicite la mise en place de directives et d'outils pour une meilleure pratique des connaissances acquises et le respect des règles ;
- encourage le renforcement du rôle de contrôle et d'appui du Ministère de l'Intérieur ;
- adapte les fonctions des experts nationaux et internationaux de l'UAI détachés au Ministère de l'Intérieur et/ou aux autres ministères concernés, conformément aux attentes du gouvernement ;
- pousse le Ministère de l'Intérieur à être très réactif quant aux problèmes posés par les collectivités territoriales ;
- soutient la soumission pour agrément au Ministère de l'Intérieur, des projets, des directives et des outils à l'attention de l'administration locale, avant leur réalisation.

En matière d'appui institutionnel, l'élaboration des monographies que d'aucuns appelleraient livres blancs, semble être le passage obligé. Toute politique de développement devrait en faire appel et en tirer profit. Faut-il rappeler qu'une monographie est un état des lieux de la situation politique, économique et social d'un pays, département, commune ou section communale. Le livre blanc montre les points faibles et les points forts de la collectivité territoriale concernée. Il s'élabore en partenariat avec les autorités locales, dans le but de faciliter, sinon attirer les investisseurs qui ont vraiment besoin de ces informations précises et précieuses.

Dans son rôle de pont entre la mission et la communauté internationale, l'Unité Appui Institutionnel doit prévoir une stratégie de support du PNUD. Celle-ci consiste à développer avec le PNUD un dialogue continu sur toutes les questions relatives à la gouvernance, déconcentration et décentralisation, puis à la compréhension commune des rôles et responsabilités de la mission et du PNUD dans ces domaines, pour que les contreparties nationales bénéficient d'un appui coordonné. C'est aussi à l'Unité Appui Institutionnel d'établir la feuille de route pour un support continu dans les domaines susmentionnés après une éventuelle réduction des effectifs du staff de la mission de maintien de la paix. Tout comme l'Unité Coordination et Rapport, l'Unité Appui Institutionnel a comme instrument de travail privilégié la synthèse des rapports des bureaux régionaux auquel il convient d'ajouter le rapport de performance des municipalités.

La synthèse hebdomadaire de l'Unité Appui Institutionnel et le rapport de performance des municipalités sont des outils de pilotages pratiques et simplifiés pour la communication entre la direction des Affaires civiles et les bureaux régionaux, d'une part et entre les régions et le siège de la mission d'autre part. Contrairement à la synthèse de l'Unité Coordination et Rapport qui traite tous les aspects des rapports intégrés des bureaux régionaux, la synthèse de l'Unité Appui Institutionnel se focalise uniquement sur les enjeux qui concernent l'appui institutionnel.

Cette synthèse constitue aussi un outil de communication entre les bureaux régionaux et le gouvernement central d'un côté et de l'autre, avec les partenaires sur le terrain. En outre, elle favorise les échanges entre les bureaux régionaux et facilite le partage d'informations écrites en vue de :

- avoir une vision d'ensemble des résultats sur le court, moyen et long terme, puis conserver les preuves d'échanges entre partenaires ;
- traiter l'ensemble des informations venues des bureaux régionaux ;
- faciliter la prise des décisions qui s'imposent tant au niveau gouvernemental qu'au niveau de la hiérarchie de la mission et faire le suivi des démarches engagées.

Ainsi, les rapports hebdomadaires des bureaux régionaux permettent à l'Unité Appui Institutionnel de dresser des « Notes de Synthèses » sur les différents thèmes en rapport avec les fonctions des autorités de base et des Affaires civiles telles que la fiscalité, les évaluations quantitatives des communes, l'absentéisme…

Cependant, l'Unité Appui Institutionnel n'a aucune compétence d'évaluer ou de juger leurs collègues Officiers des Affaires civiles sur le terrain. Son rôle est de faire ressortir les interactions et les questions/remarques qui restent sans réponse auprès des décideurs gouvernementaux, à travers les « notes de synthèses » et tous ceux de la mission qui reçoivent la synthèse hebdomadaire de ladite unité. Comment traite-t-on les informations au niveau de cette unité ?

Le traitement des informations venant des BR ne sont pas stockées dans une sorte de banque de données quelconque, pour ressortir seulement en cas de besoin. En fait, l'unité traite les rapports des bureaux régionaux et fait le suivi des informations qu'elle reçoit par le truchement de ces derniers. Elle assure la transmission d'informations aux ministères concernés, au premier rang desquels se trouve le Ministère des collectivités territoriales. Elle prodigue des conseils techniques aux partenaires sur le terrain. C'est aussi sur cette base que sont diligentées les propositions de projets de formation ou d'assistance multiple.

L'Unité Appui Institutionnel donne la preuve que le travail des bureaux régionaux est pris en considération et très au sérieux, en même temps, stimule la recherche de la substance dans les contributions hebdomadaires afin de les rendre plus simples et plus faciles à exploiter. La synthèse de l'UAI permet, à coup sûr, de déterminer les priorités des interventions pour l'organisation des visites sur le terrain, visites destinées à aider les bureaux régionaux à solutionner certains problèmes d'efficacité et de performance de la section des Affaires civiles.

A travers cette synthèse, l'UAI interpelle le Ministère des collectivités territoriales tout autant que la direction des Affaires civiles, mais aussi les bureaux régionaux. Elle peut faire des recommandations de duplications à l'attention de ces derniers. Cette synthèse sert aussi à faciliter l'élaboration d'un tableau statistique sur les liens avec les partenaires locaux, sans pour autant porter un jugement de valeurs ou une évaluation du travail des autres officiers de la section.

Il va de soi qu'il est plus facile de faire le suivi lorsque le mandat de la mission est exécutif (mandat de substitution de la mission au Kossovo), que lorsqu'il s'agit d'un mandat d'appui, d'assistance ou de soutien qui dépend du bon vouloir ou de la volonté politique du gouvernement en place et des collectivités territoriales. Avec le Ministère des collectivités territoriales, la synthèse, via les « notes de synthèses » permet la transmission d'informations et de prodiguer des conseils ou de faire des propositions de projets de formation ou d'assistance multiple, dont les bureaux régionaux constituent la principale source d'informations. Bien entendu, le ministre en charge des collectivités territoriales ne lit pas les rapports des bureaux régionaux qui sont des documents internes à la mission, mais il reçoit un extrait de la synthèse de l'Unité Appui Institutionnel sous forme de fiches de signalement dont le contenu est le suivant :

- la date ;
- le service concerné ;
- le nom de la commune ;
- l'objet du signalement ;
- le contenu ;
- les observations/recommandations.

Les synthèses de l'UAI ont permis de pointer du doigt les grands problèmes qui gênent le bon fonctionnement des mairies dans certains pays :

- Absentéisme ;
- dysfonctionnement ;
- ingérence des députés et sénateurs ;
- interférence des élus des sections communales,
- l'équivalent des collines ;

- conflits entre les autorités locales.

Et la liste n'est pas exhaustive.

Les Affaires civiles sont censées soutenir les projets de municipalisation et départementalisation dans les régions, ce qui constitue l'application d'un programme national au niveau des communes ou des provinces, sur l'aspect éducationnel économique, politique et social. Ces projets ne devraient pas se contenter seulement de la construction de grands ensembles administratifs dans le domaine infrastructurel, mais plutôt encourager le redressement et les réparations spéciales des régions détruites par la guerre, ainsi que les torts spécifiquement faits à certaines populations, dans le but de rétablir l'âme d'une nation. La municipalisation ou la départementalisation qui se fait toujours en liaison avec toutes les collectivités d'un pays est aussi le moyen de faire la promotion des valeurs et des idées destinées à faire avancer l'Etat de droit.

L'Unité Appui Institutionnel doit surtout renforcer sa présence auprès du Ministère des collectivités territoriales, plus particulièrement en appui à la Direction des Collectivités Territoriales (DCT) et à la Direction des Etudes de la Planification et du Suivi (DEPS), mais aussi auprès du Ministère de la Planification. Elle est donc conviée à entretenir une étroite coopération s'il le faut, en maintenant son personnel intégré au sein de ces instances du Ministère et en capitalisant sur l'appui apporté par les bureaux régionaux des Affaires civiles. Reste à savoir comment évaluer les résultats de ce renforcement des capacités ou de l'appui institutionnel ?

Le meilleur système d'évaluation est celui qui permet de mesurer la gouvernance locale, à travers le rôle joué par la société civile dans le cadre de la démocratie participative et de la décentralisation. Elle peut se faire aussi sur la base des performances des administrations communales. En ce sens, les composantes principales qui sont généralement utilisées par la majorité des pays sont :

- la gestion financière ;
- l'administration interne ;
- la fourniture de services ;
- la démocratie et la participation ;
- les activités législatives, essentiellement ceux des assemblées parlementaires.

Chaque composante contient un certain nombre d'indicateurs, chacun étant pondéré d'un coefficient représentant son importance. Dans la pratique, il s'agit d'organiser des entretiens avec les responsables municipaux ou ceux des collectivités territoriales pour la collecte de données administratives.

Pour garantir un niveau égal de capacité et de qualité de gouvernance parmi toutes les municipalités du pays, le gouvernement mexicain, par exemple, utilisa le principe d'autoévaluation par les équipes municipales elles-mêmes.

L'Etat considère 39 indicateurs répartis en quatre grandes catégories :

- la capacité institutionnelle dans le cadre de la bonne gouvernance ;
- le développement économique durable ;
- les services publics pour tous ;
- la gestion de l'environnement.

Le cas échéant, pour chaque catégorie, l'évaluation porte sur les actions entreprises par la municipalité et les ressources dont elle dispose pour améliorer la situation de la communauté.

Les résultats sont ensuite présentés sous la forme de tableau de bord avec trois couleurs :

- rouge pour les indicateurs sur lesquels la municipalité étudiée a de mauvais résultats ;
- jaune lorsque les résultats sont moyens ;
- vert pour indiquer que les résultats sont bons.

Ces résultats sont affichés dans un jargon simpliste, pour faciliter la compréhension des populations locales concernées. Cette méthode encourage les municipalités à plus de « redevabilité » envers leurs citoyens qui, en retour, sont d'une manière ou d'une autre, impliqués activement dans la gestion des affaires publiques.

Un système identique d'auto-évaluation couplé au renforcement des capacités a été appliqué aux Philippines. Il permet aux collectivités territoriales — communes et départements — de mieux comprendre leurs capacités et leurs contraintes dans la fourniture de services au profit de leur population. Contrairement à la technique du gouvernement Mexicain, cette méthode utilise 111 indicateurs répartis en cinq grandes catégories :

- la gouvernance ;
- l'administration ;
- les services sociaux ;
- le développement économique ;
- la gestion de l'environnement.

Ici, les données sont collectées une fois par an par des équipes d'experts départementaux qui bénéficient de la participation et du soutien total des maires et de leurs équipes municipales. Ensuite, ces informations sont enregistrées et stockées dans une base de données en ligne. Elles génèrent des rapports annuels pour chaque commune ou département.

Au final, ce rapport est disponible à la consultation par n'importe quel citoyen, transparence du système oblige. En revanche, en Afrique de l'Ouest, la méthode d'évaluation consiste à faire un diagnostic concernant le fonctionnement de la collectivité territoriale en question, tant au plan organisationnel et institutionnel qu'au plan financier et économique. Il procure ainsi aux décideurs et aux populations les informations dont ils ont besoin pour prendre les décisions qui les concernent en toute connaissance de cause.

Il s'agit donc d'une contribution à la décision très précieuse, notamment dans le cadre de la planification du développement de la collectivité, dans le contexte de la décentralisation et de la démocratie participative[29].

Par contre, en Haïti, les Affaires civiles utilisent une matrice d'évaluation semestrielle pour élaborer le rapport de performance des administrations municipales. Ce rapport paramétré et analytique est une relation raisonnée dans laquelle l'officier des Affaires civiles fait le point sur les activités, les réalisations et la situation, puis apporte des éléments en vue d'une décision à prendre.

Il ne s'agit nullement, d'un questionnaire à remettre aux administrations municipales pour qu'ils le remplissent, mais d'un document permettant à l'officier des Affaires civiles de structurer son dialogue avec les autorités municipales de façon constructive et orientée vers le renforcement de leurs capacités, à travers un appui pratique et technique dans les domaines suivants :

- la gestion administrative et financière ;
- la fourniture de services à la communauté ;
- les relations institutionnelles ;
- le rôle de la mairie dans la planification et le développement de son territoire.

L'idée de fond est non seulement de mesurer la performance des administrations municipales du pays hôte, en visualisant l'impact des interventions menées en faveur de la gouvernance locale, mais aussi de fournir aux Affaires civiles elles-mêmes une « boussole » qui leur permet de mieux orienter leurs actions et de fixer les priorités, dans le but de développer des stratégies de mise en oeuvre du mandat de la Mission avec des objectifs clairs à court et moyen terme.

Il s'agit de compiler, autant que possible, de façon cumulative les remarques et les recommandations faisant référence aux valeurs quantifiées et qualifiées de la performance des administrations municipales. Ces valeurs doivent correspondre à des critères aussi rigoureux et non susceptibles d'interprétation arbitraires. Ce qui permet aussi à l'officier des Affaires civiles de se familiarisent avec les indicateurs de la matrice et encore plus avec les paramètres qui permettront d'orienter l'échange sur des questions très spécifiques avec les autres partenaires du développement.

Dans un rapport, les recommandations ne sont jamais accessoires, mais plutôt fondamentales afin d'aller au-delà des constats et de contribuer aux

---

[29] Alexandra Wilde, Shiprah Narang, Marie Laberge, Luisa Moretto, « Guide de l'Utilisateur pour Mesurer la gouvernance », édité par Joachim Nahem, Centre pour la gouvernance d'Oslo, PNUD http://www.undp.org/oslocentre/flagship/democratic_governance_assessments.html

solutions pouvant, effectivement, renforcer les administrations municipales et améliorer leurs performances. Il est clair qu'il ne sera pas toujours possible de proposer des solutions, mais l'appréciation professionnelle des officiers des Affaires civiles constitue souvent une partie intégrante du travail de la mission.

Par contre, il est important pour un officier des Affaires civiles d'éviter de formuler des recommandations vagues sans cibler précisément un interlocuteur ou un fait donné, au risque de « déresponsabiliser » les Affaires civiles. Au contraire, ces recommandations doivent être réalistes et pragmatiques, identifiant ainsi qui doit faire quoi et quel rôle les Affaires civiles devront jouer pour faciliter la solution.

Tout compte fait, avec l'Unité Coordination et Rapport, ainsi que leurs sources d'informations, à savoir les bureaux régionaux, l'Unité Appui Institutionnel fait de la section des Affaires civiles une section multidisciplinaire de coordination des activités d'une mission de maintien de la paix. Leur travail est aussi soutenu et complété au niveau législatif par une autre unité spécialement conçue pour travailler avec les parlementaires : l'Unité Appui au Parlement.

ORGANIGRAMME DU TRAVAIL DE L'UNITE COORDINATION ET RAPPORTS

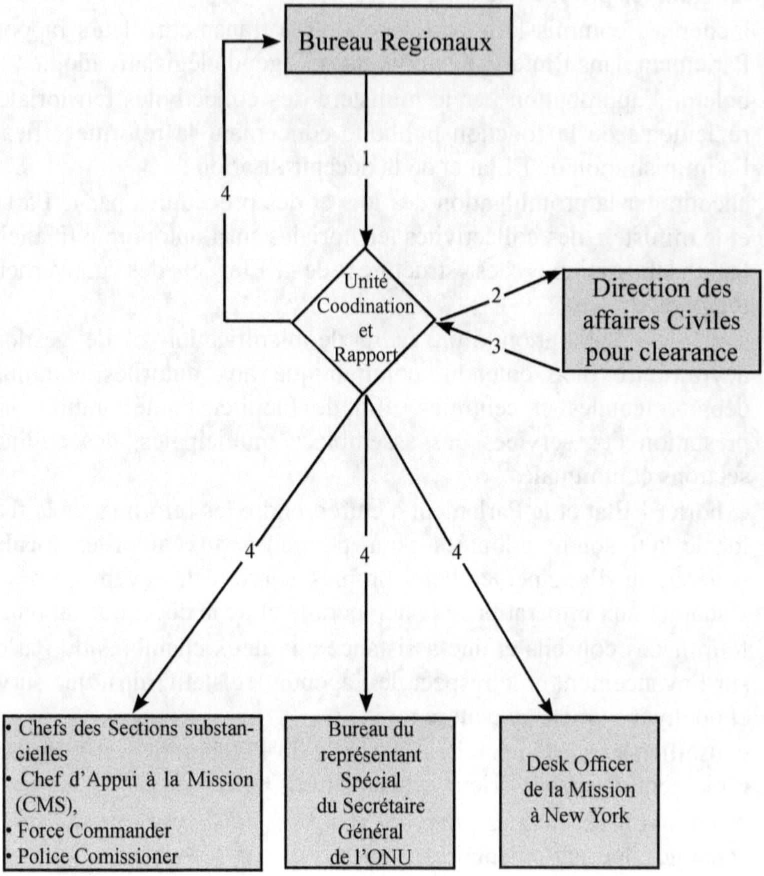

Elaboré par: Dr Ruffin Viclère Mabiala, Ph.D.

C. BUREAU D'APPUI AU PARLEMENT (BAP)

De plus en plus, les missions de maintient de la paix s'organisent pour faire en sorte qu'il y ait un bureau dans chaque institution politique afin de faciliter la coopération entre le siège de la mission et le gouvernement Central. Il n'est pas surprennant de trouver un bureau des Affaires civiles dans l'enceinte du parlement. Cette unité spécialisée que l'on peut appeler unité d'appui au parlement, s'occupe notamment de :

- suivre les développements des activités du parlement ;
- pousser le parlement à adopter chaque année, un agenda législatif reflétant les priorités de cette année ;
- inciter les commissions parlementaires à transmettre leurs rapports au Parlement dans l'intervalle prévu dans l'agenda législatif adopté ;
- obtenir l'approbation par le ministère des collectivités territoriales des règlements de la fonction publique concernant la réforme efficace de l'administration de l'État et de la décentralisation ;
- encourager la promulgation des lois et des procédures par le Parlement et le ministère des collectivités territoriales sur l'autonomie financière et la « viabilisation » des structures de l'Etat et des gouvernements régionaux ;
- soutenir l'élaboration d'un cadre de planification et de gestion qui devrait être bien entendu, communiqué aux autorités communales, départementales et centrales, afin de faciliter l'amélioration dans la prestation des services des assemblées municipales, des collines ou sections communales ;
- exhorter l'Etat et le Parlement à entreprendre les réformes de la fiscalité locale qui soient adoptées pour permettre aux autorités locales de générer ou d'augmenter leurs propres sources de revenus, en vue de s'adapter aux impératifs de la démocratie et de la décentralisation ;
- fournir des conseils et une assistance aux deux chambres du Parlement sur l'avancement et le respect de l'agenda législatif, ainsi que surveiller et appuyer sa mise en oeuvre rapide ;
- conseiller les parlementaires à propos de l'élaboration et le respect du règlement d'ordre intérieur et les relations publiques ;
- promouvoir les bonnes pratiques d'autres législatures, ce qui inclut les échanges interparlementaires, caractérisés par des visites à l'étranger ;
- offrir une assistance technique et logistique en matière d'organisation des conférences, des forums sur des questions pertinentes et/ou des formations si nécessaire.

C'est, par exemple, le cas pour la fourniture des moyens de transport de l'ONU (hélicoptères et véhicules) qui sont mis à la disposition des parlementaires pour faciliter la communication avec leurs circonscriptions respectives, ou encore l'apport d'un appui administratif, notammement :

- l'approvisionnement en ordinateurs, imprimantes, photocopieuses, internet, etc. ;
- servir de liaison entre parlementaires et organisations internationales partenaires du pays d'accueil, essentiellement dans le cadre de la recherche du financement des projets ;
- procurer une assistance technique dans les domaines de la formulation et la rédaction de projets d'intérêt national, par exemple, fournir des fonds pour l'embauche de consultants qui vont apporter leur expertise dans l'élaboration des propositions de loi venant du parlement lui-même d'une part, l'analyse et la préparation des projets de loi venant de l'exécutif, d'autre part ;
- apporter un appui technique aux parlementaires et aux commissions parlementaires en travaillant en étroite collaboration avec les législateurs pour identifier les besoins de la population et essayer d'y répondre graduellement ;
- aider à accélérer le processus d'adoption des principales lois de réforme dans des domaines clés, tels que : la réforme de la justice, la gouvernance locale, la décentralisation qui constitue une condition préalable aux élections indirectes, les élections en général, la lutte contre la corruption, le salaire minimum, les questions du genre et des droits de l'enfant, la loi sur les partis politiques et « la fonction publique parlementaire » qui ouvre la voie vers la reconnaissance des fonctionnaires parlementaires de carrière, et cetera. Cela veut dire conforter les capacités législatives du Parlement, en facilitant le processus d'adoption des projets de loi de réforme, qui sont essentiels tant pour le gouvernement que pour la mission de stabilisation et de maintien de la paix ;
- apporter une assistance ponctuelle dans le cadre des projets de loi et la mobilisation de fonds ;
- appuyer le processus de ratification des traités internationaux.

Le mandat de ce Bureau d'Appui au Parlement (BAP) a toujours été de renforcer les institutions démocratiques nationales, par un appui technique, politique et logistique.

Ce bureau s'emploie à consolider la capacité législative par une assistance directe, en servant de liaison entre les unités spécialisées de la mission et le parlement ou/et entre les parlementaires. C'est également ce bureau qui assure la liaison entre les parlementaires et les partenaires des Affaires civiles. Il mobilise les parlementaires sur le travail de la mission à travers les campagnes de sensibilisation, caractérisées par des rencontres entre la communauté internationale et les parlementaires.

Le Bureau Appui au Parlement partage de façon systématique les développements législatifs avec l'ensemble des partenaires internationaux. Il effectue principalement le monitoring parlementaire, c'est-à-dire le suivi des développements politiques et législatifs des activités et des événements qui dominent la vie politique parlementaire pendant les sessions ordinaires ou extraordinaires. Ce bureau se charge de faire la rédaction des analyses et des recommandations.

Le bureau d'appui au parlement gère l'évolution des programmes d'appui institutionnel destinés à renforcer non seulement les relations entre l'exécutif et le législatif, mais aussi à renforcer les capacités législatives du Parlement luimême.

Son rôle est d'accroître la transparence dans le travail parlementaire, à travers les forums, l'assistance aux commissions, puis favoriser la mise à disposition des élus et des bibliothèques législatives. Il appartient à ce bureau de suivre les développements politiques au sein des deux chambres afin de leur fournir une assistance ponctuelle en cas de besoin. Le BAP travaille de concert avec une autre équipe de la mission de maintien de la paix, en l'occurrence la division des Affaires politiques et de la planification.

Concrètement, le Bureau d'Appui au Parlement intervient dans les actions suivantes :

- organiser des rencontres régulières avec les députés et les sénateurs pour échanger sur les lois à adopter et la ratification des nominations des hautes autorités de l'Etat, à l'instar des premiers ministres ;
- faciliter les rencontres entre les commissions des chambres et les unités spécialisées pour discuter du processus de ratification de divers traités et conventions ;
- appuyer la réalisation des activités législatives du Parlement ;
- mettre à la disposition des membres du comité d'organisation des ordinateurs et autres matériels de bureaux, afin de faciliter l'avancement des travaux ;
- plaider auprès des organisations internationales, bailleurs de fonds, pour aider les Commissions de l'Intérieur et les collectivités territoriales des chambres du Parlement à réaliser des forums de consultation autour de la proposition de loi sur le fonctionnement et l'organisation des collectivités territoriales ;
- faire régulièrement des suggestions et conseils aux Commissions de l'Intérieur des chambres parlementaires.

Dans le cas d'Haïti dévasté par le séisme du 10 janvier 2010, le rôle du Bureau d'Appui au Parlement peut s'étendre à contribuer aux efforts pour rétablir immédiatement le fonctionnement minimal du Parlement. Cela consiste, par exemple, à fournir de tentes, des kits d'hygiène, la papeterie, ou les moyens de transport. Ce support consiste aussi à soutenir les secrétariats généraux des deux Chambres.

De tout ce qui précède, le renforcement des systèmes nationaux des institutions démocratiques au niveau Parlementaire permet précisément de :

- stimuler la confiance et la compréhension entre le parlement et la mission, en faisant la promotion du rôle et du mandat de la mission au niveau parlementaire, à travers, notamment l'organisation des réunions avec les Présidents des deux chambres et avec les parlementaires eux-mêmes ;
- promouvoir, grâce à la participation des parlementaires, le processus de renforcement des institutions démocratiques, y compris dans le cadre des élections, de la décentralisation, des réformes économiques et constitutionnelles au sein de la population ;
- établir et maintenir un dialogue constructif et ouvert avec les députés ;
- rendre compréhensif le rôle de la mission de l'ONU et ses activités dans le milieu parlementaire ;
- renforcer les capacités institutionnelles la durabilité du Parlement en assurant l'adoption par les deux chambres d'un règlement administratif et financier, mais aussi d'un statut du personnel parlementaire ;
- consolider la relation exécutif-législatif par la définition d'un programme législatif concerté et qui doit être pleinement respecté, en renforçant un contrôle constructif des activités du gouvernement par les législateurs.

Les rencontres publiques avec les parlementaires et les autorités locales sur le processus de renforcement des institutions démocratiques, par exemple, les lois sur le fonctionnement et l'organisation des collectivités locales ; ainsi que les ateliers de travail en faveur des parlementaires, des partis politiques et des représentants de la société civile.

Tout ceci peut avoir des retombées positives sur le processus de réformes Constitutionnelles. De ce fait, les pouvoirs exécutifs et législatifs doivent s'engager à collaborer de façon constructive sur les réformes institutionnelles clés sans aucune confrontation. Le contraire pourrait conduire à de longs blocages législatifs inutiles et sans fondement.

Les ateliers entre les organes exécutifs et législatifs sur l'évaluation à mi-parcours de chaque agenda législatif sont pour le moins essentiels. A cet effet, l'agenda législatif et le calendrier peuvent être proposés par l'exécutif, en consultation avec les deux chambres parlementaires.

Ainsi, il sera possible, tout au moins plus facile de prévoir la mise sur pied des projets de loi préparés par l'exécutif, en conformité avec le calendrier législatif. De même, il semble nécessaire d'organiser des réunions constructives régulières et des audiences avec les représentants des gouvernements et autres acteurs intéressés, ainsi que des séances de formation dirigées vers les hauts gradés et autres personnels parlementaires sur des sujets visant à renforcer les capacités. L'essentiel est de permettre le soutien efficace aux travaux législatifs quotidiens.

L'Unité Appui au Parlement doit pour ainsi dire :

- offrir de bons offices aux Présidents des deux chambres du Parlement pour non seulement stimuler la confiance et la compréhension, mais aussi, pour renforcer le principe du consensus ;
- guider le Parlement sur la mise en oeuvre du règlement intérieur et une meilleure utilisation, en adoptant particulièrement les meilleures pratiques des autres administrations nationales ;
- conseiller et appuyer le Parlement en matière d'organisation des réunions thématiques entre les parlementaires et les donateurs, les agences des Nations unies et les Organisations Non-Gouvernementales nationales et internationales afin de promouvoir le dialogue sur les questions relatives au processus de réformes et des questions politiques controversées ;
- organiser des rencontres régionales dans les départements, avec les parlementaires sur le renforcement des institutions démocratiques et les procédures ;
- encourager le dialogue sur des thèmes spécifiques pour faciliter la constitution du consensus sur les questions politiques litigieuses, en organisant des réunions avec les députés, conjointement avec la section des Affaires politiques ;
- fournir un soutien de coordination aux partenaires internationaux engagés dans le soutien du Parlement concerné et assurer une liaison avec l'équipe de pays
- Membres de l'Organisation des Nations unies sur le suivi d'activités spécifiques ;
- tenir au courant la haute hiérarchie sur des questions de fond qui nécessitent une attention urgente et une intervention de haut niveau.

Une fois la mission terminée, les observateurs nationaux et internationaux devraient être en mesure de constater les résultats suivants :

- organisation des réunions régulières ordinaires des commissions parlementaires avec une forte participation de la primature se tiennent ;
- adoption par le Parlement des projets de loi sur les réformes fondamentales de l'Etat est acquise ;
- les travaux législatifs au cours des séances plénières sont menés de manière plus cohérente et plus orientée vers les résultats ;
- la professionnalisation de l'administration des deux chambres apparaît visiblement ;
- la gestion du budget du Parlement sera efficace et transparente ;

- la primature aura pu acquérir une meilleure connaissance des thèmes abordés. Les thèmes vont être choisis et débattus au Parlement ;
- le consensus sera atteint sur les questions litigieuses ;
- la bonne entente et le dialogue seront maintenus entre les parties, y compris au sein des commissions du Parlement ;
- les rapports du Parlement sont ponctuels et efficaces ;
- les actions visant à soutenir le Parlement seront cohérentes les unes avec les autres, tout comme avec le programme de développement stratégique élaboré par le gouvernement, sous les auspices de la communauté internationale ;
- le programme de développement stratégique et les mécanismes de mise en oeuvre sont définis et compris par toutes les parties, le Parlement et les partenaires ;
- les pays Membres de l'organisation des Nations unies sont dorénavant informés sur les débats ;
- les initiatives au sein du Parlement en question sont en relation avec les activités des agences sur le terrain ;
- les parlementaires ont désormais une plus grande connaissance des activités des agences des Nations unies.

Il n'est pas innocent de reconnaitre, dans la pratique, le bureau d'appui au Parlement est généralement confronté à des défis qui sont directement liés aux crises politiques qui animent le Parlement — blocage et éclatement —, notamment :

- les arrêts du travail et les apathies chroniques des commissions parlementaires sur le plan Législatif ;
- la faillite de l'administration, le discrédit des parlementaires dans l'opinion publique et parfois, l'existence d'un Parlement fort et indépendant de l'exécutif au plan institutionnel ;
- la création de majorité entrainant la rupture avec le leadership des partis politiques en ce qui concerne la politique dans les chambres des députés ;
- les situations de quorum obligatoire et insatisfaisant et les difficultés d'adoption de la politique générale des nouveaux gouvernements ;
- le manque de moyens des législateurs pour s'acquitter de leurs responsabilités législatives ;
- la faiblesse du débat et l'absence du processus de consultation entre les parlementaires et les groupes d'intérêt ou l'électorat ;
- le manque d'intérêt de certains parlementaires pour le travail législatif ;
- le retard dans la mise en oeuvre des programmes législatifs convenus entre le gouvernement et le Parlement ;

- la politisation prolongée de l'échiquier politique provoquant une impasse législative et le dysfonctionnement du parlement.

Ce sont tous ces maux que l'on retrouve dans la plupart des parlements des pays post-conflictuels. Pour y faire face, il faut mettre en place une véritable stratégie institutionnelle qui prend en compte l'aspect réforme parlementaire. Il s'agit par exemple de la création par la mission via les Affaires civiles, d'une table de coordination des bailleurs de fonds et des programmes d'appui au Parlement afin de :

- parler d'une seule voix lors des négociations avec les deux chambres ;
- centraliser les demandes d'assistance émises par les deux chambres ;
- établir une division du travail entre partenaires internationaux ;
- assurer la cohérence de l'assistance au Parlement.

Cette optique se justifie par le fait d'encourager l'adoption de lois.

Bien qu'il faille reconnaître que les objectifs du Bureau d'Appui au Parlement sont louables, il reste encore beaucoup d'obstacles à franchir. Elle travaille aussi étroitement avec l'Unité Gestion des Frontières (UGF) qui n'est pas commune à toutes les missions de maintien de la paix des Nations unies, car certain de ces pays ont de sérieux problèmes de frontières avec leurs voisins. Il peut même arriver que l'unité UGF soit mise sous la tutelle d'une section autre que celle des Affaires civiles.

D. UNITE DE GESTION INTEGREE DES FRONTIERES (UGF)

Dans certains cas, la mission des Nations unies, spécialement la section des Affaires civiles a aussi la lourde tâche d'assister le gouvernement dans la gestion des frontières, comme c'est le cas de la Mission des Nations unies pour la Stabilisation en Haïti (MINUSTAH).

Cet aspect est une innovation du Conseil de Sécurité des Nations unies qui peut toujours faire l'objet d'une polémique. D'aucuns diront que la gestion des frontières relève du domaine militaire ou policier, mais lorsqu'on se soumet à l'examen de la pensée, on se rend à l'évidence que le domaine des frontières concerne principalement, les taxes, l'immigration, la douane et la sécurité du territoire. Donc, il y a réellement un aspect administratif, politique, sécuritaire et stratégique, très important. D'ailleurs, la mise en oeuvre des piliers du mandat des Affaires civiles en matière de gestion des frontières constitue un volet essentiellement stratégique dans certains pays post-conflits. C'est avec l'Etat de droit, deux (2) secteurs d'activités obligeant que l'on y consacre beaucoup de temps et d'efforts, en s'appuyant et en appuyant les autorités de base pour un meilleur contrôle des airs et des frontières terrestres et maritimes. En retour, il faudrait s'attendre à des retombées telles que :

- amélioration de la sécurité ;

- diminution des activités et trafics illicites ;
- augmentation probable des recettes fiscales.

L'Unité de Gestion Intégrée des Frontières travaille avec les institutions nationales et internationales impliquées dans le domaine de la douane (lutte contre la contrebande), de l'immigration (lutte contre les trafics de personnes) et de la sécurité (lutte contre les trafics de drogue et d'armes) dans le but de renforcer les capacités de l'Etat aux points de passage terrestres, maritimes et aériens.

La création d'une telle unité au sein d'une mission a pour base légale les résolutions du Conseil de sécurité des Nations unies qui demande à la mission de fournir une expertise technique au gouvernement dans la mise en place d'une stratégie intégrée de la gestion des frontières.

En Haïti, par exemple, c'est la résolution 1780 qui donne aux Affaires civiles le droit de l'impliquer dans le secteur des frontières dont les points frontaliers se matérialisent officiellement par dix ports maritimes, quatre frontières terrestrès et deux aéroports internationaux.

Il va sans dire que cette pléiade des passages constitue une menace constante pour la stabilité de ce pays ainsi que des états environnants dans une zone où le trafic de stupéfiants constitue la clé de voûte du commerce illicite avec son corollaire d'insécurité et de corruption.

Comme tous les pays sous-développés, Haïti dispose de peu de moyens aussi bien sur le plan des infrastructures que dans le cadre du personnel qualifié pour engager une lutte efficace contre les menaces de toute sorte. C'est pourquoi le but de cette unité est d'aider les autorités locales à atteindre les objectifs suivants :

- étendre l'autorité de l'Etat sur l'ensemble du territoire ;
- faciliter en appui à la police nationale, la mise en place de patrouilles le long des frontières maritimes et terrestres ;
- encourager la concertation entre le pays sélectionné et ses voisins dans le cadre d'un partage d'informations ;
- inciter l'Etat à lutter contre les trafics de drogue, d'armes et autres activités illicites, en sécurisant les frontières dans le but de réduire sinon éradiquer ces trafics illicites en collaboration avec les pays voisins ;
- contribuer à renforcer les contrôles frontaliers ;
- soutenir le gouvernement à travers la mise en place de mécanismes de coordination visant à assurer ou renforcer le développement socio-économique durable des zones frontalières ;
- augmenter les recettes fiscales de l'Etat.

La réalisation de ces objectifs passe vraisemblablement par :

- l'établissement des relations de travail avec les institutions principales concernées par la gestion des frontières, c'est-à-dire : le ministère des finances, l'administration générale des douanes, la direction générale des Impôts, les autorités portuaires, la police nationale, la direction de l'immigration et de l'emigration, le service maritime et de navigation du pays concerné ;

- la participation active aux réunions de la table ronde des donateurs sur la gestion des frontières ;
- l'élaboration des documents de stratégies internes ;
- l'identification des experts nationaux et internationaux en gestion des frontières ;
- la coordination du groupe de travail de la mission de l'ONU sur la gestion des frontières ;
- le maintien d'une liaison constante avec les bureaux régionaux des Affaires civiles et les autres composantes de la mission, concernées par la gestion des frontières, à l'instar des policiers des Nations unies (UNPOL) ;
- la réalisation de l'inventaire des projets de réhabilitation des infrastructures frontalières ;
- l'exécution de l'inventaire des initiatives de renforcement des capacités sur le territoire concerné ;
- la rédaction des rapports d'activités.

Pour cela, il va falloir :

- aider le gouvernement à mettre en place sa stratégie de gestion intégrée des frontières ;
- Établir des groupes de travail mixtes entre le gouvernement et la mission pour plancher sur les différentes parties du document ;
- obtenir l'accord du gouvernement sur l'élaboration d'un document de stratégie intégrée de gestion des frontières ;
- assister le gouvernement à publier de manière officielle ce document de stratégie intégrée de gestion des frontières ;
- créer ou consolider les acquis des groupes de travail sur la gestion des frontières ;
- soumettre les documents de ce groupe de travail à l'approbation du gouvernement ;
- faire le monitoring des préparatifs pour le déploiement des équipements sur les frontières maritimes, terrestres ;
- organiser des travaux relatifs à la colocation, au déploiement des bateaux de patrouille et la mise en place des comités régionaux de gestion de frontières ;
- engager le suivi et la formation des institutions gouvernementales en charge de ce secteur ;
- maintenir des contacts réguliers avec les autorités gouvernementales et les bailleurs de fonds au sein de la table de concertation sur la gestion frontalière ;
- renforcer la législation en la matière pour se mettre en adéquation avec les conventions internationales.

Ce laborieux travail au niveau central ne peut véritablement prendre corps et montrer son efficacité en apportant les fruits escomptés que s'il est complété au niveau régional, par d'autres activités, telles que :

- l'établissement des relations de travail avec les directions départementales des institutions étatiques comme la police, la douane, les impôts, les autorités portuaires et aéroportuaires, le service de l'immigration ;
- l'installation des mécanismes ad hoc de coordination avec les autorités gouvernementales à travers des réunions régulières ;
- la coordination des réunions de travail sur la gestion des frontières au niveau des bureaux régionaux de la mission ;
- l'identification, la réalisation et le suivi des projets de réhabilitation ou de construction des infrastructures frontalières régionales ;
- la rédaction des rapports des activités régionales sur la gestion des frontières devant parvenir au sommet de l'Unité de Gestion des Frontières ;

- la rédaction et la mise à jour d'une matrice des frontières et des projets des bailleurs de fonds.

Finalement, le renforcement de la gestion des frontières par l'Unité de gestion des frontières est caractérisé par une mise en oeuvre progressive de la gestion révisée de la mission aux frontières étatiques. Le résultat attendu n'est ni plus ni moins d'améliorer les rôles, les responsabilités et la structure de gestion des frontières dont les principales mesures consistent à :

- recommander des changements qui visent à mieux soutenir les efforts du gouvernement à adopter et mettre en oeuvre une stratégie intégrée de gestion des frontières ;
- apporter les modifications nécessaires pour améliorer et intégrer le support au gouvernement dans sa stratégie de gestion des frontières ;
- réorganiser le système afin d'inclure les personnels de toutes les composantes ;
- utiliser plus efficacement les ressources de la gestion des frontières ainsi que les informations dans le processus de décision ;
- recruter des spécialistes supplémentaires dans le domaine douanier, de l'immigration et de la sécurité frontalière pour soutenir les efforts du gouvernement ;
- fournir plus d'expertise et d'assistance technique ;
- encourager et faciliter les efforts du gouvernement à établir un mécanisme officiel chargé d'élaborer et de mettre en oeuvre une stratégie de gestion intégrée des frontières, puis faire appliquer ce mécanisme lors de sa constitution ;
- soutenir les initiatives du gouvernement par l'intégration des activités de la mission avec les réformes dans la gestion intégrée des frontières ;
- faciliter la mobilisation des ressources pour contribuer au développement du gouvernement dans sa capacité de gestion des frontières ;
- établir un mécanisme officiel habilité à formuler et mettre en oeuvre un plan intégré de gestion des frontières ;
- mettre en place un dispositif de support financier pour les réformes ;
- entreprendre les travaux conduisant à un programme intégré et efficace de gestion des frontières, basé sur les meilleures pratiques internationales ;
- identifier et hiérarchiser les lacunes de la législation pour les adresser au Parlement ;
- déterminer les réformes nécessaires par priorité et fournir les moyens de les accomplir ;
- élaborer et faire approuver le projet de code douanier et le code maritime, pour les mettre en oeuvre immédiatement ;

- établir et fournir une orientation générale sur les questions frontalières aux autorités régionales ;
- induire des formations pour mettre à la disposition de gestionnaires des frontières des points focaux de la mission ;
- pousser les donateurs à former et équiper les personnels du gouvernement de la douane et de l'immigration, ainsi que fournir de l'assistance et de la formation à la police des douanes ;
- aider les institutions frontalières à mieux se faire connaitre de ses usagers dans le cadre des campagnes de sensibilisation.

Il n'est pas surprenant de constater que cette unité rencontre généralement de sérieuses difficultés pour faire avancer le travail dans ce domaine, à commencer par les impasses politiques qui freinent souvent les engagements à long terme. Cela est suivi par le manque de volonté politique permettant de lancer les réformes nécessaires dans un pays où il faut pratiquement tout refaire.

Dans certaines missions on note parfois une absence de législation adéquate pour faciliter la coordination effective entre les différents ministères et les institutions impliquées dans la gestion des frontières. A cela s'ajoute l'insuffisance des ressources financières utiles au renforcement des capacités, pour sortir le secteur de la dépendance accrue de l'aide extérieure, pouvant retarder l'exécution de certains projets.

Il y a aussi une carence considérable des ressources humaines qualifiées. Et que dire du système de gestion de l'information sécuritaire qui se trouve dans un état désuet, inadapté et d'ailleurs inadéquat ?

En ce sens, il est toujours recommandé d'encourager les autorités nationales à trouver des issues rapides aux crises politiques généralement liées à l'exercice ou l'apprentissage de la démocratie et à l'usage abusif des libertés fondamentales que l'on transforme, assez souvent, en libertinage et qui, du reste, empêchent le pays à aller de l'avant.

Il va de soi que l'unité de Gestion des Frontières maintient des contacts permanents au sommet de l'état et de la mission, avec les bailleurs de fonds, en vue de renforcer l'appui à la gestion des frontières, ce qui peut se faire avec l'aide des experts nationaux et internationaux déployés sur le terrain, bien entendu, dans un souci du renforcement des capacités.

E. LES BUREAUX REGIONAUX

Au niveau local le travail des Affaires civiles se résume au rôle que jouent les bureaux régionaux. Pour mieux comprendre ces fonctions, il convient de procéder par une analyse thématique. Evidemment, en ce qui concerne le renforcement des capacités matérielles, il faut reconnaître qu'au vu des priorités du Ministère des collectivités territoriales et compte tenu de la répartition géographique des différents partenaires opérant dans le pays touché, mais aussi pour répondre aux attentes des maires et satisfaire les besoins locaux, il est nécessaire d'orienter l'appui de manière durable. Cela se fait, en conseillant et en faisant le suivi des formations dans les communes et/ou les provinces.

L'enjeu est de renforcer le leadership, la planification et la gestion, à travers des formations allant dans le sens de :

- faciliter l'assimilation, par les élus locaux, des connaissances acquises au cours des formations ;
- évaluer la compréhension et l'application des législations et des directives émanant du gouvernement, via le ministère des collectivités territoriales au niveau : municipal et provincial ;
- prendre attache avec le ministère de tutelle, afin que les législations, les directives de la hiérarchie, les règles, procédures et pratiques administratives soient mieux comprises et appliquées ;
- encourager l'approche participative et l'équilibre des genres au niveau des collectivités territoriales en vue d'une meilleure planification et prise de décision, y compris à travers les groupes de travail et les réunions communales ;
- soutenir la méthode démocratique participative dans la planification et la prise de décision, y compris avec la société civile pour qu'elle participe activement aux débats ayant trait aux affaires locales ;
- initier la tenue des réunions du conseil technique qui regroupent les chefs de service et les directeurs régionaux des différents ministères pour discuter sur la coordination et le fonctionnement des institutions étatiques de la région ;
- renforcer la réalisation des tables de concertation qui ressemble à des réunions du conseil technique élargies aux ONG et associations nationales et internationales, ainsi que la société civile. Ce sont les institutions publiques et privées qui y participent avec les acteurs du développement pour discuter des questions qui touchent le développement du local ;
- appuyer la mise en place des tables de concertations communales qui regroupent les autorités communales, c'est-à-dire les membres du conseil municipal, les juges, le chef de la police, les directeurs d'école, les chefs des centres hospitaliers, les ingénieurs agronomes, les ONG et la société civile. Il ressemble à un mini-sommet de la table de concertation départementale ;
- assister les collectivités locales dans l'élaboration de leurs plans de développement et, si possible, les aider à trouver des financements, y

compris les Projets à Effet Rapide (QIP), qui sont justement acceptés et mis en oeuvre pour aider les municipalités ;

- appuyer les communes dans la rédaction et la soumission des différents rapports financiers et administratifs ;
- travailler avec les maires pour mettre en place un système de gestion administrative et financière moderne et durable ;
- promouvoir une compréhension commune et partagée des règles et des procédures entre les conseils et les assemblées ;
- inciter la coopération entre les conseils municipaux et les responsables des autres paliers de la décentralisation, tels que les collines ou les sections communales ;
- encourager les conseils municipaux à gérer un plan de travail concernant l'appui aux communes ;
- organiser régulièrement des réunions constructives pour discuter des affaires sociales ;
- établir et maintenir un dialogue constructif et ouvert avec les autorités concernées.

En matière de Budget et Finance, les bureaux régionaux sont appelé à :

- appuyer les communes dans la mise en oeuvre et le respect du guide des procédures budgétaires validées par le gouvernement et pour que les budgets municipaux soient approuvés et rendus publics ;
- inciter les communes et l'administration fiscale locale à développer des relations basées sur l'échange d'informations régulier et sur les priorités communales ;
- contribuer à l'amélioration des services de la Direction Générale des Impôts (DGI), en présentant aux décideurs les difficultés et les dysfonctionnements, ce qui sert à faciliter l'augmentation des recettes ;
- encourager les élus locaux à prendre toutes les mesures nécessaires pour que la fiscalité locale soit en conformité avec la législation et les procédures en vigueur ;
- promouvoir le leadership communal par la sensibilisation de la population sur la fiscalité locale et la transparence dans l'utilisation des ressources locales. Il est important de montrer que les ressources publiques sont gérées de façon transparente ;
- faire respecter le calendrier des opérations de recensement mis en oeuvre par le ministère de tutelle, en partageant avec lui les données sur les propriétés taxables qui sont collectées, organisées et mises à jour ;
- faire en sorte que les ressources permettant de faire face aux salaires et à la fourniture des services publics de base proviennent des ressources propres de l'institution ;

- encourager la rédaction et la soumission à temps des rapports financiers mensuels, ainsi que d'autres rapports circonstanciels ;
- fixer un cadre réglementaire pour une harmonisation et une standardisation des budgets municipaux ;
- offrir des précieuses informations en termes d'orientations et de perspectives budgétaires permettre aux acteurs d'élaborer et exécuter leur budget municipal sans difficultés ;
- faciliter le travail de toutes les structures municipales impliquées dans le processus d'élaboration de budget ;
- assurer la bonne tenue de la comptabilité des engagements et des ordonnancements et celle de la comptabilité générale.

Que dire de la tâche des Affaires civiles dans le domaine des infrastructures ?

Les bureaux régionaux sont en droit de faire une mise à jour de l'évaluation des besoins avant de donner un appui à la remise en état et à l'équipement des bâtiments publics. Les partenaires doivent donc être informés et mobilisés sur les besoins de réhabilitation et d'équipements et que les infrastructures ciblées soient fonctionnelles pour que les QIP soient exécutés pour répondre aux besoins prioritaires non couverts par d'autres partenaires.

Le plus gros défi qui se présente aux Affaires civiles dans les bureaux régionaux est celui de transparence et de la lutte contre la corruption. Les Affaires civiles doivent collaborer avec les instances concernées telles que : la cour des comptes, la direction générale des impôts, la société civile et les autorités locales afin de mobiliser et informer toutes les énergies dans la lutte anticorruption. A cet effet, il paraît fondamental que les groupes de la société civile, les leaders d'opinions et les médias, exercent un contrôle pour une meilleure transparence des élus locaux et que les autorités locales perçoivent la portée de la corruption, les sanctions qui lui sont associées et comment les institutions nationales la gèrent.

Les Affaires civiles sont tenues de prendre en compte le principe d'intercommunalité, du « codéveloppement » et de la coopération décentralisée, ce qui les oblige à aider les municipalités à prospecter pour des partenariats avec d'autres communes du pays, avec la diaspora et avec d'autres collectivités publiques étrangères, y compris dans la fourniture de services de base. Ainsi, convient-il d'encourager les rencontres régulières entre les maires pour discuter des questions d'intérêt commun entre les partenaires. C'est dans cette optique qu'il faut soutenir les projets sur l'intercommunalité, le « codéveloppement », la coopération intercommunale et la coopération décentralisée qui sont pour certains préparés pour être examinées et discutées avec le ministère de tutelle ou d'autres ministères intéressés.

Il appartient aussi aux Affaires civiles d'apporter un support particulier aux autorités déconcentrées de l'Etat, à travert le maintien d'un dialogue efficace avec les gouverneurs et les vice-gouverneurs sur les affaires courantes, ainsi que sur les nouveaux sujets de préoccupation. En ce sens, les Affaires civiles sont invitées à leur fournir des conseils sur les moyens d'affirmer leur rôle de contrôle et de coordination, y compris au niveau des conseils techniques départementaux, ainsi que dans les relations avec les autorités locales. Cela peut se traduire par l'organisation des réunions aussi souvent que nécessaires, pour examiner de façon régulière et approfondie les préoccupations quotidiennes. Il s'agit de pousser les préfets à exercer un leadership efficace au Conseil Technique Départemental (CTD) de leur région, puis maintenir des relations régulières et constructives avec les autorités locales.

La politique de tables de concertation devrait être prise au sérieux par les officiers des Affaires civiles, en encourageant les pouvoirs publics à élaborer un cadre juridique pouvant les rendre permanentes pour des raisons stratégiques qui vont être détaillées ci-après. Au risque de se répéter, la table de concertation est une structure participative ou un espace de rencontre des multiples acteurs travaillant dans le domaine du développement au niveau du département ou de la commune, dans le but de faciliter l'échange d'informations entre ces acteurs. C'est aussi pour une meilleure prise de décisions et d'articulation des différentes interventions. Elle est chargée de planifier, promouvoir, orienter et se concerter dans la recherche d'une certaine cohérence des activités de développement au niveau des collectivités territoriales, en tenant compte des spécificités et priorités locales.

Ces tables peuvent permettre de rentabiliser la décentralisation, par l'implication et la contribution des représentants de tous les secteurs dans le processus de développement local, qui du reste, participent à la prise de décision, la planification, l'exécution, le suivi et l'évaluation des actions de développement de la collectivité. Encore faut-il que les contraintes d'ordre politique ne freinent pas l'établissement et le fonctionnement de ces structures de façon permanente.

L'objectif d'une table de concertation, notamment communale est de :

- garantir la concertation communale en matière de développement, d'aménagement du territoire et d'urbanisme ;
- présenter des propositions relatives à l'élaboration des plans aux mesures propres à assurer le développement durable de la commune ;
- servir de plate-forme communale dans l'établissement du diagnostic communal et régional et pour l'identification des orientations d'aménagement et des projets de développement sectoriels et/ou globaux à retenir ;
- travailler, en collaboration avec les organisations de base de la société civile, à l'identification des problèmes et besoins intéressant la commune ou le département ;

- recueillir et compiler les problèmes vécus et les besoins exprimés par la population des habitations, bourgs, quartiers et sections communales ;
- assurer le suivi des activités relevant de leur compétence et leur mission, ainsi que la mise en oeuvre des orientations de la politique nationale au niveau de la commune ;
- nommer des représentants pour participer à d'autres structures de concertation au niveau supérieur ;
- appuyer la mairie et les instances compétentes dans l'élaboration et la mise en oeuvre du plan d'action communal, appelé à se transformer en plan stratégique de développement communal, tout en constituant une base d'informations pour l'élaboration d'un schéma communal d'aménagement et l'élaboration du programme annuel d'investissements publics.

Composée des entités étatiques de la planification, l'éducation, la justice, la santé, l'agriculture, l'environnement, les travaux publics et responsables des projets… ; auxquelles il convient d'adjoindre les institutions non étatiques telles que : les ONG nationales et étrangères, les institutions de coopération internationale, les associations et membres de la société civile ; sans oublier les élus locaux. La table de concertation communale a pour mission de :

- se servir du conseil consultatif pour le département ou la commune ;
- être un forum principal notamment dans la coordination stratégique, l'orientation de la direction stratégique et l'identification des secteurs prioritaires de la collectivité ;
- dénombrer tous les acteurs de développement, concernant les personnes et institutions publiques ou privées oeuvrant dans le département et/ou la commune, en vue de constituer une base de données ;
- sensibiliser les intervenants à se concerter en vue d'arriver à un développement participatif et durable ;
- cataloguer les potentialités départementales et/ou communales en matière de ressources naturelles, d'infrastructures et des activités économiques ;
- inventorier et encadrer les services sociaux de base, présents dans la collectivité afin d'améliorer leur fonctionnement et leur rendement ;
- diagnostiquer les problèmes et besoins de la collectivité en vue de proposer des solutions adéquates ;
- identifier les axes prioritaires sur lesquelles il va falloir bâtir une stratégie de recouvrement en vue de proposer un plan communal de développement conséquent ;
- assurer la cohérence permanente des actions de tous les intervenants avec le schéma de développement communal ;

- faciliter les échanges et la circulation des informations entre les prestataires de services et les bénéficiaires.

En ce qui concerne la structure d'une table de concertation, la simplicité et la flexibilité, doivent être les maîtres mots dans l'élaboration de son organigramme, pour lui permettre de mieux accomplir sa mission. Pour son fonctionnement, une table de concertation a besoin d'un appui technique venant du Ministère de la planification. Il ne doit pas se réunir plus d'une fois par mois, sauf en cas de rencontre extraordinaire, sur convocation de son président et/ou du secrétaire. Cependant, il doit tenir compte des conclusions des tables sectorielles.

La table de concertation doit être financée par la mairie pour la commune et par le préfet pour le département. Cependant, au cas où ces derniers ne seraient pas en mesure de supporter l'intégralité des coûts relatifs à la logistique d'une rencontre, concernant notamment le secrétariat, la collation, l'impression de documents, etc., les Affaires civiles devraient en faire les frais. Au cas contraire l'appui financier de l'un des partenaires présents dans la commune, étatiques ou non étatiques, serait sollicité. Ce financement peut se faire sur une base de roulement, entre le secteur privé et public.

En matère de support et tables de concertation, il est à noter que les Affaires civiles apportent un appui à la section humanitaire, pour le renforcement des tables de concertation, par exemple, faire en sorte qu'elles se déroulent sur une base régulière, en présence de tous les secteurs intéressés aux discussions sur les priorités du développement régional et tenir compte des besoins locaux exprimés par les municipalités, notamment :

- le gouverneur exerce un rôle d'appui effectif ;
- les réunions aient lieu sur une base mensuelle au moins ;
- tous les secteurs soient effectivement représentés ;
- les actions de suivi soient identifiées et acceptées par tous les participants.

Dans ce domaine le Chef du Bureau Régional joue un rôle spécial qui mérite d'être élucidé.

F. ROLE PARTICULIER DES CHEFS DE BUREAUX REGIONAUX (CBR/CRO)

Les bureaux régionaux travaillent avec les autorités locales, en assurant le suivi du développement des Affaires politiques et sécuritaires, du fonctionnement de la société civile et des institutions, ainsi que l'évolution du développement économique et social. Ils constituent des piliers indispensables à la coordination des activités de l'ensemble du bureau régional et assurent les fonctions de points focaux pour les autres unités substantives non représentées dans la région.

A cet effet, le responsable régional de la section des Affaires civiles est le Chef du Bureau Régional (CBR), en anglais CRO, dans la plupart des missions de maintien de la paix. Il/elle devient, par ricochet, le porte-parole de la mission dans sa région. C'est lui qui coordonne la mise en œuvre du mandat de la mission dans la région et dirige les réunions hebdomadaires avec toutes les composantes de la mission. Il gère le remplacement ou la substitution des sections substantives non représentées dans son bureau régional. Le CRO doit s'assurer, par exemple, que les UNPOL (Police des Nations unies) reçoivent l'appui des autres composantes de la mission dans leur travail d'assistance à la police nationale et locale du pays d'accueil.

La fonction du CRO est aussi de s'assurer que toutes les unités travaillent de manière coordonnée, particulièrement en ce qui concerne les échanges des informations. Il/elle coordonne les réunions sur la sécurité, notamment pendant les élections, avec les autorités locales et les sections de la mission. Il anime les groupes de travail sur l'état de droit et la protection civile. Il/elle organise des rencontres pour traiter, entre autres, des questions concernant les actions des gangs, des trafiquants de tous genres, la formation de polices municipales et de polices de substitution dans certaines entités territoriales.

Le/la CRO participe à la mise en place des opérations conjointes : police nationale, Casques bleus (la police onusienne et les militaires). Leurs interlocuteurs privilégiés au niveau des collectivités territoriales sont :

- les maires et les agents municipaux ;
- les représentants des sections communales ou des collines ;
- les gouverneurs et les vice-gouverneurs, avec leurs équipes ;
- les représentants de la société civile et les ONG, ainsi que les associations nationales ou internationales ;
- les représentants des ministères présents dans la région, notamment les directions régionales.

Le chef du bureau a une fonction particulière, celle de promouvoir l'établissement de l'Etat de droit dans les régions. Théoriquement, le CRO :

- co-préside avec le gouverneur de province, le groupe de travail régional sur l'Etat de droit et la sécurité ;
- crée de nouveaux jalons sur l'Etat de droit ; renforce l'autorité de l'Etat de droit au niveau des municipalités ;
- identifie les problèmes et fournit des recommandations au groupe de la mission.

Sous l'impulsion du coordonnateur de l'Etat de droit de la mission et du Chef des Affaires civiles, il effectue la promotion du travail des sections intéressées par des questions d'intérêt commun, par exemple, les visites des centres de détention, les informations et les bases de données sur les crimes et les criminels, le développement local, la situation humanitaire surtout en cas de catastrophe humanitaire, et cetera.

Les réunions régulières sur l'Etat de droit doivent être organisées avec les sections concernées et les composantes, notamment les UNPOL, les droits de l'homme, la justice et les militaires, en partenariat avec les acteurs locaux, à savoir : la délégation, la police et le bureau du procureur au niveau de chaque juridiction. Généralement, ces réunions au niveau régional se tiennent trimestriellement.

Par la suite les sections concernées de la mission et les autorités locales sont censées faire le suivi des questions évoquées et des progrès tangibles accomplis dans l'application des recommandations adoptées et dans le fonctionnement de la chaine pénale. Entre-temps, les interlocuteurs locaux s'engagent dans des efforts communs et prennent les commandes pour l'observation de l'état de droit. Dès lors, il suffit d'utiliser la même recette pour que « les mêmes causes produisent les mêmes effets », c'est-à-dire que les problèmes similaires soulevés soient résolus par le même procédé dans d'autres départements du pays.

Cela permet de faire des recommandations réalistes, sur la base d'un référentiel. On tire alors les leçons pour que les « bonnes pratiques » soient regroupées et diffusées, afin de souscrire à leurs réplications ou duplications.

Sous un autre registre, il convient de donner un appui efficace aux équipes de « vetting », principalement les UNPOL, les officiers des droits de l'homme et la justice, grâce à une action de sensibilisation. Le CRO doit coordonner efficacement leurs activités pour faire en sorte que tous poursuivent les mêmes objectifs et que, cela soit fondé sur une stratégie cohérente convenue. Les activités bien coordonnées permettent d'éviter les duplications insensées, car les informations, dans de pareilles circonstances, sont recueillies, harmonisées et accessibles à tous pour la bonne marche de la mission et pour l'exécution du mandat.

Les Affaires civiles sont tenues de faire la promotion de chaque processus inclusif électoral. Ainsi, dans les régions, le CRO mobilise toute son équipe d'officiers des Affaires civiles pour :

- surveiller et faire des rapports sur l'évolution politique et sécuritaire dans le contexte des élections ;
- coordonner le support de la mission sur le plan de la sécurité et la logistique au comité national électoral qui émane du gouvernement et de ses organes décentralisés, dans l'organisation des élections ;
- coordonner l'appui de la mission pour l'organisation des élections au niveau régional ;
- promouvoir la sensibilisation des membres des assemblées parlementaires, des partis politiques et la population, sur les règles et les procédures électorales en vigueur ;

- soutenir le processus électoral et les besoins qui y sont attachés.

Sous l'impulsion du CRO, les Affaires civiles sont condamnées à entreprendre les activités suivantes :

- rédiger des rapports ponctuels et précis permettant de comprendre la situation et agir en temps
- réel, afin de réduire les risques politiques et sécuritaires ;
- organiser de manière efficace et pacifique le déroulement des élections municipales locales, parlementaires et présidentielles ;
- tenir les élections directes et indirectes de manière organisée, efficace et pacifique afin que les municipalités et les autres collectivités territoriales aient leurs assemblées constituées ;
- mettre en accord les politiciens locaux sur la tenue d'élections libres, équitables et transparentes et avoir une bonne compréhension du processus électoral ;
- fournir un support logistique adéquat aux instances nationales sur l'organisation des élections.

Le CRO et son équipe doivent contribuer à la construction d'un climat de confiance et faire la promotion du dialogue politique au niveau régional. Autrement dit, ils doivent s'investir dans la prévention et la résolution des conflits, ainsi que dans le processus de réconciliation nationale, ce qui se traduit de façon suivante :

- établir le dialogue et renforcer la confiance avec les responsables locaux, partis politiques, représentants de la société civile et les autres décideurs locaux ;
- rencontrer les responsables locaux et les partis politiques afin d'établir des rapports sur les développements politiques cohérents, au profit de la hiérarchie de la mission ;
- analyser et maintenir un aperçu des facteurs politiques qui pourraient avoir un impact sur la stabilité ou l'exécution du mandat et faire la prévention des crises ;
- favoriser la construction du dialogue et de la confiance dans les zones à risques ou enclins à des tensions, en particulier à travers des réunions régulières avec des représentants communautaires, les dirigeants de la société civile et les responsables locaux ;
- mener les activités de règlement pacifique ou de transformation des conflits pour désamorcer les tensions politiques.

En ce sens, il convient de se donner les moyens de présenter des rapports ponctuels et précis sur l'évolution des événements politiques, puis les mettre à jour à partir des analyses détaillées des facteurs politiques concernés. Le cas échéant, le CRO et ses collègues des Affaires civiles sont invités à contribuer activement à :

- établir des relations constructives, efficaces basées sur la confiance avec les acteurs clés ;
- permettre une meilleure compréhension par les interlocuteurs locaux, du mandat de la mission et la possibilité d'acquérir une plus grande prise de conscience de ses activités ;
- réduire les tensions et identifier les solutions locales, pour aider à maintenir le dialogue et la confiance ;
- engager directement les autorités locales dans les initiatives de constructions ou de consolidation de la confiance et du dialogue ;
- trouver un terrain d'entente et une adhésion des acteurs politiques à des normes de bonne conduite.

Il est du devoir du chef de bureau régional de renforcer la coordination et l'intégration régionales, ce qui fait de la section des Affaires civiles une unité de coordination des régions, pour le compte de la mission. Dans la pratique, ils exécutent les tâches ci-après :

- fournir des rapports hebdomadaires régionaux intégrés et consolidés sur les développements régionaux ;
- produire des rapports analytiques sur des questions spécifiques d'intérêt national ou local ;
- collaborer avec la section des Affaires politiques et l'intelligentsia (JMAC) de la mission pour que les exigences prioritaires de la Mission d'information soient respectées, avec un accent sur les développements politiques et la sécurité dans les régions ;
- tenir le Représentant Spécial du Secrétaire Générale de l'Organisation des Nations Unies et la haute administration au courant des questions de fond qui nécessitent une attention urgente et des interventions de haut niveau ;
- surveiller la mise en oeuvre des Projets à Impacts Rapides (QIP) ;
- présider le comité de révision ou d'attribution des QIP ;
- assurer la coordination de toutes les sections de la mission et des composants au niveau régional ;
- soutenir la liaison avec la section information du public pour accroître la visibilité de la mission et la conduite des activités de sensibilisation ;
- agir en qualité de représentant des sections qui ne sont pas représentées au niveau régional ;
- exécuter les tâches de coordination du domaine de la sécurité régionale ;
- servir d'évaluateur supplémentaire de l'ensemble du personnel substantif des autres composantes civiles ;
- travailler en étroite collaboration avec la section des Affaires humanitaires, les agences onusiennes et les ONG, pour veiller à ce que les activités de la mission respectent les principes humanitaires et de

développement, puis fournir un appui aux activités humanitaires et de développement ;

- renforcer la coordination au sein de « *United Nations Country Team* » (UNCT) qui regroupe les chefs de la mission et ceux des agences onusiennes, au niveau régional ;
- encourager la participation des agences de l'ONU à des réunions régionales de coordination ;
- assurer la coordination des services opérationnels et de logistiques (JOC) de la région, afin de répondre adéquatement aux risques majeurs, notamment les catastrophes naturelles dans la région ;
- veiller à ce qu'un plan régional de réponse aux risques et désastres naturels ou autres soit adapté et intégré au plan officiel départemental.

Le chef de bureau régional veillera à ce que la mission donne un appui adéquat aux autorités départementales, pour une réponse intégrée efficace, en cas de catastrophe. Et ce travail ne peut s'accomplir que si et seulement si les critères suivants sont réunis :

- l'existence des rapports hebdomadaires ponctuels et précis ;
- l'identification des questions d'actualités ;
- l'analyse des implications possibles ;
- l'élaboration des recommandations sur les questions d'intérêt ;
- la mise en oeuvre des analyses approfondies sur les principales tendances et les facteurs ;
- l'obtention par les bureaux régionaux des comptes rendus de la mission du HQ sur les questions pertinentes de développement national ;
- la signalisation au moment opportun, des questions clés, accompagnée des recommandations pertinentes sur les mesures à prendre ;
- la diffusion régulière des rapports sur l'exercice des projets QIP, le suivi de ces projets et les quelques leçons à retenir, pour contribuer à l'amélioration du programme ;
- l'utilisation responsable des fonds disponibles engagés et l'exécution des projets de manière opportune et efficace ;
- la sélection des projets QIP dans le but de poursuivre les objectifs stratégiques de la mission au niveau régional ;
- la coordination soutenue et le partage d'informations se font entre les composantes des sections régionales pour le maintien de l'unité de message et de l'objet par lesdites composantes ;
- la visibilité des activités des Affaires civiles dans la région ;
- la meilleure compréhension par les interlocuteurs locaux du mandat de la mission ;
- la mise en oeuvre des programmes de sensibilisation dans les écoles et les universités de la province ;

- la garantie de support adéquat aux sections substantives respectives dans la région ;
- la vulgarisation au sein du staff, du plan régional adopté pour les réponses aux désastres naturels ;
- l'adaptation du plan de la mission au plan départemental et national permettant de répondre adéquatement aux situations de désastres naturels et autres risques majeurs.

Les équipes des Affaires civiles sont mixtes, composées des internationaux et nationaux très mobiles et dotées d'expertises diverses, essentiellement dans le domaine de l'économie, le droit et la politique, mais aussi d'une connaissance approfondie du terrain. Les Affaires civiles s'appuient ainsi sur ces solides ressources humaines et logistiques qui représentent une force à la disposition des gouvernements d'accueil pour les accompagner dans la mise en oeuvre de la bonne gouvernance, l'Etat de droit et du renforcement institutionnel, ce qui nécessitent des compétences spécifiques.

L'une des plus grandes responsabilités d'un chef de bureau régional ou de la section des Affaires civiles est : la création et l'activation du comité de gestion d'une crise que l'on appelle en langage onusien, le RJOC (*Regional Joint Operation Center).* C'est une cellule de crise destinée à gérer la crise ou tous autres risques de désastre et de catastrophe naturelle. Il est composé des autorités locales, de tous les chefs de section d'un bureau régional, des casques bleus en uniforme (militaire et UNPOL), de la police du pays d'accueil, des agences de l'ONU oeuvrant dans le domaine humanitaire, des ONG nationales et internationales, ainsi que du service de protection civile national, lorsqu'il en existe un. Un devoir d'explication de texte au sujet du RJOC s'impose à nous.

En effet, force est de constater que le CRO joue un rôle fondamental dans le cadre du fonctionnement du JOTC. Le JOTC[30] est un centre commun et intégré de l'information qui a pour but d'aider à la prise de décisions sur la base de rapports ayant trait à des évènements récents ou en cours, dans le but de coordonner le soutien des militaires et policiers de l'ONU, mais aussi dans le cadre les activités humanitaires ou liées à la sécurité. En tant que principal point focal pour toutes les demandes des organisations humanitaires à des fins militaires et policières et le soutien de la logistique de la mission de l'ONU, ainsi que pour l'assistance technique aux activités de secours humanitaire, le JOTC constitue le mécanisme qui permet de :

- donner une réponse intégrée à toutes les crises humanitaires ;

[30] Le JOTC (*Joint Operations & Tasking Centre*, en français, le centre des opérations et des tâches Conjointes) a été créé en Haïti, pour la première fois en partenariat avec OCHA, après le tremblement de terre de janvier 2010.

- garantir une utilisation plus efficace de l'aide humanitaire et coordonner les actifs militaires, policiers et logistiques de la mission ;
- agir dans la transparence, en donnant un aperçu global pour les participants partenaires au premier rang desquels se trouve OCHA, en tant que co-fondateur ;
- appuyer les organisations humanitaires dans des processus simples d'accès à l'assistance militaire, policières et logistique de la mission.

Il agit non seulement comme une entité centrale de gestion et de réaction aux urgences humanitaires, mais aussi comme un support aux activités d'aide humanitaire par la mission, mais aussi coordonne l'assistance logistique, sécuritaire et l'ingénierie, du fait qu'il assigne, contrôle et évalue les opérations sur le terrain et transmet les feedbacks aux partenaires. JOTC est le principal support du EJOC[31] qui se définit comme étant le centre de gestion de crise d'urgence à long terme au niveau national, activé uniquement en cas de survenance des crises majeures, telles que :

- les catastrophes naturelles comme les tempêtes, ouragans, séismes, inondations ;
- les incidents de sécurité, du genre kidnapping ou prise d'otage ou encore les événements de masse soutenue et de désordre public, etc. ;
- les élections.

Dans le cas particulier des élections, il prend le nom de JESC (*Joint Elections Support Committee*/Comité Conjoint de Support Electoral) dont les mécanismes de fonctionnement sont identiques à ceux du EJOC.

Quelle que soit la nature de la crise, le EJOC est dirigé et soutenu par les entités concernées parmi lesquelles le gouvernement du pays hôte, à travers son Centre d'Opérations d'Urgence National ; les agences de l'ONU et les partenaires internationaux, notamment EJOINT (*Emergency Joint Operations Centre*) et, bien entendu, les Affaires civiles représentées par leur chef de section. L'EJOC est activé à l'avance ou pendant une crise pour assister les départements à travers des multiples interventions et en fournissant des informations à la haute direction de la mission et à la communauté internationale dans son ensemble.

Au niveau régional, l'équivalent de l'EJOC est le RJOC (Centre d'Opération Régional/*Regional Joint Operations Centers*), principalement dirigé par le CRO et le bureau régional des Affaires civiles, en collaboration avec les partenaires humanitaires, notamment OCHA. Le CRO est soutenu par toutes les entités de la mission dans la province : militaires, police, sécurité, logistique, humanitaire, etc.

---

[31] EJOC : *Expanded Joint Operations Center* ou centre élargi des opérations conjointes de gestion des crises

Ses fonctions dans ce cas particulier de crise consistent à :

- recueillir les informations sur la crise et élaborer des rapports régulièrement pour les transmettre à qui de droit ;
- recevoir les requêtes d'assistance et aider avec l'exécution ;
- solliciter l'intervention des forces militaires et la police de la mission ;
- concevoir les plans d'intervention en temps réel avec l'appui technique de JOTC et EJOC ;
- diffuser l'état de la situation sécuritaire dans la région ;
- renforcer la coordination entre les différentes composantes de la mission et les autorités locales du gouvernement, ainsi que les ONG ;
- assurer le support de la mission aux comités départementaux de gestion des risques et des désastres, notamment la DPC, en Haïti ;
- centraliser les informations et établir un réseau de communications claires entre les acteurs concernés.

Le succès du RJOC dépend de plusieurs facteurs, parmi lesquels :

- l'identification des points focaux et des protocoles d'interaction entre les structures concernées ;
- la création des procédures pour le suivi des informations provenant du terrain au niveau des communes et des collines ;
- la mise à jour régulière et partagée des listes de contacts ;
- la détermination et le renforcement des capacités logistiques des intervenants ;
- l'information et la formation sur les techniques d'évacuation en faveur des membres des équipes d'évaluation rapide, ainsi que la planification et la mise à jour des « *rosters* » de ces équipes pendant la phase d'alerte et en général ;
- le soutien des structures locales dans la mise en place et la diffusion des procédures standards pour ouverture et fermeture des abris temporaires ;
- la meilleure notification des points et conférences de presse, par le biais d'un interlocuteur unique ;
- l'obtention d'un représentant de l'unité d'ingénierie de la mission dans le RJOC afin de faciliter l'évaluation rapide des demandes, des équipements nécessaires et des capacités disponibles ;
- la garantie d'une communication plus directe entre EJOC et RJOC, ce qui fait du CRO, le principal point de contact pour obtenir et valider les informations relatives aux demandes d'aide de la mission au niveau local.

Toutefois, les informations relatives aux activités menées au cours d'une urgence par la communauté humanitaire ont besoin d'être vérifiées par OCHA, avant de les inclure dans le rapport du RJOC.

Ce comité siège en permanence pendant toute la durée de la crise, dans les locaux de la mission des Nations-unies. Il doit : analyser la situation en temps réel, faire des évaluations rapides des besoins des sinistrés ou des victimes, décider de l'opportunité des interventions appropriées qu'il faut engager, faire le suivi des interventions sur le terrain, recevoir les instructions de la hiérarchie et se charger de leur mise en oeuvre, c'est-à-dire informer la population et la hiérarchie de l'évolution de la situation et des dispositions prises. C'est lui qui décide en dernier ressort, de la stratégie d'assistance convenable, en tenant compte des propositions venues d'en haut. Il est fermé à la fin de l'urgence. Tout ceci nous oblige à jeter un regard expérimental sur les compétences requises et les fonctions d'un officier des Affaires civiles.

IV. Compétences requises et fonctions générales des officiers des Affaires civiles

Les crises sont des facteurs d'affaiblissement des capacities de n'importe quel gouvernement central ou régional à élaborer et appliquer des politiques pouvant être bénéfiques à la population. La relation entre les Affaires civiles d'une mission des Nations unies et les collectivités territoriales dans les pays d'intervention est à rechercher dans le cadre de la compréhension des vocations et des competences politiques des Départements et communes essentiellement, mais aussi des sections communales ou des collines. Cette relation étroite tire sa légitimité dans les différents mandats du Conseil de Sécurité de l'ONU qui s'expriment souvent dans les termes identiques à ceux-ci :

- « Aider le gouvernement […] à rétablir l'autorité de l'Etat et favoriser la bonne gouvernance au niveau local et promouvoir le développement institutionnel[32] »
- « Élargir son assistance, dans les limites de son mandat, pour renforcer les institutions de l'État, en particulier à l'extérieur de [la capitale], y compris en fournissant des services spécialisés aux principaux ministères[33] ».

A. LES FONCTIONS GENERALES DES OFFICIERS DES AFFAIRES CIVILES

Il y a des caractéristiques principales qu'il faut prendre en compte pour renforcer les capacités de gestion administrative des collectivités territoriales si l'on veut obtenir des résultats satisfaisants : « payroll », feuille de présence,

[32] Résolution 1542 du Conseil de Sécurité de l'ONU du 30 avril 2004 sur la Mission des Nations unies pour la Stabilisation en Haïti.

[33] Voir les résolutions successives qui reconduisent le mandat de la mission de l'ONU en Haïti, notamment la Résolution 1780 du Conseil de Sécurité adoptée le 15 octobre 2007

présence des maires dans la commune, arrêtés municipaux publiés par la mairie, tenue des documents et des archives…

Concrètement, les Affaires civiles ont pour mission d'assister les gouvernements locaux à faire la promotion du développement socio-économique à la base et de faciliter l'élaboration d'un plan de développement communal qui prévoit et classifie les priorités de la commune. Dans le même temps, elles encouragent la réalisation des tables de concertation départementales ou communales, à travers une approche participative.

Les mairies qui n'intègrent pas cette approche participative dans les questions qui concernent le développement local passent souvent à côté de l'opportunité d'ouvrir un véritable dialogue ouvert avec les forces vives de la commune. Pour être effectivement fonctionnelles et opérationnelles, les mairies doivent travailler avec la société civile et les autres acteurs locaux, afin de développer une stratégie de développement local répondant aux aspirations de la population. Les statistiques indiquent que les mairies qui adoptent un Plan de Développement Communal (PDC) sans aucune consultation des acteurs sociaux sont moins performantes que celles qui entretiennent un dialogue avec leurs communautés. L'approche participative est à ce titre, un indicateur de performance et un instrument de dialogue et de réconciliation. Cependant, une mairie opérationnelle n'est pas forcément celle qui fait toujours de bonnes performances.

Les mairies non opérationnelles et dysfonctionnelles se caractérisent au niveau du développement local, par l'absence de plan de développement communal (PDC) et de Table de Concertation Communal (TCC) opérationnelles. Elles se distinguent par le manque de ponctualité dans la soumission des rapports financiers (toujours en retard) et le non-respect de l'équilibre des opérations budgétaires. Au niveau des finances locales elles enregistrent souvent des bas taux de recensement des propriétés bâties ou non bâties, entrainant ainsi un taux de recouvrement des recettes locales négligeable. Le Plan de Développement Communal (PDC), est un instrument de planification qui définit les priorités d'une commune à travers une approche participative. Tout comme les tables de concertation (TCC) et les tables sectorielles (TS), le Plan de Développement Communal (PDC) peut être adopté sous l'impulsion de la section des Affaires civiles.

Dans le domaine de la gestion des finances locales, le renforcement des capacités passe inévitablement par le soutien des comptables payeurs, des agents fiscaux et par l'appui des conseillers ou Contrôleurs Financiers Territoriaux (CFT), comme on les appelle en Haïti. Dans ce contexte, l'appui aux mairies doit inclure une stratégie permettant l'augmentation des recettes fiscales, afin de leur consentir plus d'autonomie et de leur donner la possibilité d'investir encore plus dans les services à rendre à leurs populations. Sans ces prouesses, la décentralisation prônée par toutes les institutions internationales sera un leurre.

La formation des comptables payeurs et le soutien apporté aux Contrôleurs Financiers Territoriaux (CFT) permettent de faire des progrès importants en matière de tenue des livres et des documents comptables ainsi que dans la présentation des rapports financiers. La corrélation entre ces deux (2) indicateurs est positive pour deux (2) raisons. D'une part, cela donne l'opportunité aux mairies d'entretenir une documentation comptable en ordre et d'autre part, elle souscrit à la présentation des rapports financiers à temps sinon avec un retard raisonnable, c'est-à-dire ne dépassant pas un mois.

Néanmoins, cette corrélation n'est pas systématique, car la bonne tenue des livres comptables ne se traduit pas forcément par la soumission ponctuelle des rapports financiers.

Au sens inverse, il peut arriver qu'une mairie qui ne tient pas des documents comptables en ordre, puisse soumettre ses rapports financiers à temps. Les Conseillers financiers jouent un rôle prédominant dans la formulation et la soumission de ces rapports financiers. D'où le besoin d'un accompagnement rapproché des comptables payeurs par les contrôleurs financiers, en collaboration avec les Affaires civiles dans le domaine ci-après :

- l'élaboration et l'exécution des opérations budgétaires ;
- l'exécution du budget en matière des revenus locaux ;
- la tenue des livres et des documents comptables ;
- le recouvrement et recensement des taxes foncières et des taxes sur l'habitation ;
- la tenue des livres et des documents comptables ;
- la rédaction et la soumission des rapports financiers.

Le manque de dynamisme dans ces secteurs ci-dessus cités, entraine des conséquences évidentes d'affaiblissement des recettes locales, ce qui affecte la capacité des mairies à gérer un budget au-delà des simples allocations du Ministère des collectivités territoriales.

Il est impératif et important d'encourager les mairies à procéder au recensement et à la réévaluation des propriétés foncières de leur commune, afin que cela se traduise en effort d'amélioration et de recouvrement des taxes foncières. Le but est de réaliser une augmentation des recettes locales. Ce travail devrait se faire en coordination avec la direction générale des impôts.

Force est de constater que les faiblesses dans la collecte des impôts viennent parfois du fait qu'il existe fréquemment des conflits entre ces mairies et la Direction Générale des Impôts (DGI). Cet élément affecte négativement les finances locales d'une municipalité. Il engendre des conséquences visibles qui reflètent le niveau très bas des services en matière d'entretien des routes et d'assainissement. Le cas échéant, les Affaires civiles sont appelées à jouer le rôle de médiateur de la République, pour inciter à la collaboration entre les différentes institutions. Elles doivent aussi assister les autorités de base dans leur rôle de coordination et dans le cadre des relations institutionnelles. Il s'agit principalement de faciliter les relations des autorités municipales avec les autres acteurs institutionnels de la commune.

En outre, il convient d'appuyer la création ou de faire la promotion de l'unité de protection ou de sécurité civile. En réalité, les relations interinstitutionnelles et la protection civile revêtent d'une importance capitale dans le cadre du fonctionnement d'une collectivité territoriale. La mairie est une institution centrale dans la gouvernance locale et dans la coordination des activités de sécurité civile. A ce titre, elle est appelée à jouer un rôle de médiation et de coordination pour lequel elle n'est pas toujours préparée et équipée. Pour ce faire, il convient d'organiser des réunions avec ses partenaires institutionnels afin de renforcer la coordination et de traiter des sujets d'intérêt commun.

Cette faiblesse cache mal le problème de conflictualité dans les communes. Ces dernières connaissent des conflits interinstitutionnels, souvent d'origine politique, liés aux difficiles relations avec la Direction Générale des Impôts (DGI). C'est aussi le manque d'engagement qui empêche certaines mairies d'entretenir des relations formelles avec les autres institutions présentes dans la commune. A ce sujet, la promotion des réunions de sécurité et de l'Etat de droit organisée par les Affaires civiles dans les communes, devrait donner suite à des initiatives locales porteuses.

La difficulté systématique de la majorité des mairies de fournir des services de base à la population est souvent clairement établie. Le manque de moyens matériels et financiers en est la cause principale. Cependant, il nous appartient de reconnaître que les mairies ne prennent pas souvent les dispositions pouvant leur permettre de collecter certaines redevances. C'est le cas pour le ramassage des ordures. Cela montre la passivité qui semble caractérisée beaucoup d'administrations municipales qui pourraient être bien plus efficaces si et seulement si, elles osaient utiliser les pouvoirs que la loi met à leur disposition. En ce sens, il revient aux Affaires civiles de jouer le rôle de catalyseur en matière de vulgarisation des droits et des responsabilités des administrations municipales.

Il est du ressort des Affaires civiles d'analyser le fonctionnement des services liés à l'urbanisme, tels que :

- la gestion des marchés qui est une très importante source de revenus pour certaines communes ;
- le fonctionnement des services d'urbanisation, c'est-à-dire le service de génie municipal ;
- le domaine des transports et de communication, notamment la réhabilitation ou le pesage des routes communales, la signalisation et autres ;

- l'assainissement qui inclut le ramassage et le traitement des ordures, le curage des caniveaux, le traitement des rivières et des bassins versant pour le cas particulier d'Haïti…

Par expérience, le secteur dans lequel les mairies s'impliquent tant soit peu c'est la gestion des marchés. Le plus souvent, elles contrôlent entièrement les recettes des marchés. C'est avec ces revenus qu'elles fournissent des services d'assainissement, tels que : le ramassage et le traitement des ordures, ainsi que le curage des caniveaux, et cetera. Pratiquement, toutes les maires essaient de rendre des services en matière de transport et de communication, notamment dans le cadre de la réhabilitation, l'entretien et le pesage des routes communales, ainsi que la signalisation.

Les maires ont tendance à prendre au sérieux le domaine du génie municipal et de l'urbanisme. Malheureusement, une analyse des services fournis par les mairies dans les pays post-conflit montre que ces services municipaux de génie ou d'urbanisme présentent des indices généralement négatifs. D'ailleurs, certaines de ces mairies ne disposent même pas d'un service de génie municipal ou de voirie qui soit opérationnel et actif dans la gestion des cimetières et des terrains communaux, ainsi que dans la livraison des permis de construire, selon les règles établies par la loi. Ce niveau de dysfonctionnement est assez uniforme dans plusieurs pays sortis de crise.

Nombreuses sont les municipalités qui accusent, assez souvent, des difficultés dans la gestion administrative ainsi que dans la tenue des documents et archives ou des livres comptables. Elles ne tiennent pas leurs documentations selon les principes administratifs de la bonne gouvernance, ce qui a un impact négatif lors des passations de pouvoirs.

En situation de post-conflit, l'absentéisme est sans doute un des problèmes les plus saillants. Les mairies en reconstruction fonctionnent généralement, sans aucun système d'enregistrements des présences. Quand bien même celui-ci existerait, il n'est pas du tout appliqué. Du coup, ces mairies évoluent parfois avec la moitié de leur potentiel en ressources humaines. Or, la performance des administrations municipales est aussi fonction de la présence assidue des employés municipaux.

L'absence chronique des maires est pour ainsi dire une circonstance aggravante. En guise de stratégie de moindre mal, certaines mairies s'arrangent pour qu'au moins, un maire soit présent dans la commune.

Selon toutes hypothèses, la présence des maires et le fonctionnement des conseils municipaux restent problématiques. Ils doivent être pris à bras le corps. Quand bien même ces conseils municipaux fonctionneraient, ces rencontres ne semblent pas toujours aboutir à des décisions qui se traduisent en arrêtés municipaux.

Très souvent, l'un des indicateurs qui révèlent le dysfonctionnement d'une administration municipale est le faible taux des réunions du conseil municipal.

Très peu de conseils municipaux se réunissent au moins une fois par mois et produisent un procès-verbal. Cela traduit souvent un dysfonctionnement interne entre les membres du conseil. Il arrive aussi que les administrateurs ou maires titulaires ne se sentent pas toujours tenus à agir de façon collégiale et donc prennent des décisions de façon informelle et non dûment enregistrées. Cette tendance à gérer la chose publique dans l'informel se remarque par le nombre ou le pourcentage excessivement faible des mairies qui adoptent des arrêtés selon les normes prévues par la loi.

En effet, peu ou très peu de conseils municipaux se réunissent de façon régulière et dans le respect des règles constitutionnelles. Cela s'explique parfois par la complexité de la procédure. Cette dernière est souvent mentionnée comme étant la principale responsable du manque d'encadrement juridique des décisions prises par le conseil municipal. Cependant, l'absence de connaissances des différentes opportunités données aux mairies dans ce domaine est aussi responsable. Or, il existe une corrélation directe entre le bon fonctionnement des conseils municipaux et leur performance. Aussi serait-il avantageux pour les Affaires civiles d'assister les ministères en charge des collectivités territoriales dans l'élaboration d'un guide pratique pour les maires, essentiellement sur les questions des arrêtés municipaux.

De ce fait, l'accompagnement des mairies dans l'adoption et la publication des arrêtés devient l'une des meilleures approches du renforcement de la bonne gouvernance et de la transparence. Il ouvre la voie à une bonne compréhension des responsabilités qui incombent aux maires. En un mot, le renforcement des conseils municipaux comme organe de prise de décision et la formalisation de certaines de leurs décisions par des arrêtés, est une priorité qui rendrait les mairies réellement opérationnelles et performantes. Ainsi, les Affaires civiles ont fort à faire pour capitaliser sur la bonne performance des conseils municipaux et pour encourager ceux-ci à exercer leur pouvoir et leur autorité, à travers la publication des arrêtés. L'objectif principal est de faire l'accompagnement des mairies afin d'orienter leur potentiel administratif vers le renforcement de leur autonomie financière, en se focalisant sur l'augmentation des revenues locaux.

Techniquement, en matière d'opérationnalité et de fonctionnement d'une collectivité territoriale, il semble important pour les officiers des Affaires civiles d'observer, de vérifier :

- l'existence d'un organigramme dont l'absence a pour conséquence, le manque de répartition claire des tâches, ce qui accentue le taux d'absentéisme des employés et demeure l'une des causes du dysfonctionnement d'une mairie ;
- le système de gestion administrative surtout au niveau du Payroll ;

- le fonctionnement du conseil municipal auquel il faut inclure la présence des maires à la mairie, ainsi que la rédaction et la publication des arrêtés municipaux ;
- la tenue des documents et archives ;
- la fréquence de la présentation des rapports financiers ;
- la capacité de recensement et de recouvrement des recettes locales, pour connaître le talon d'Achille de la gestion financière et comptable de la municipalité en question. Cela permet de mesurer le manque d'implication des autorités locales dans le processus d'augmentation des recettes locales qui passe forcément par un recensement et une réévaluation annuelle des propriétés foncières, en vue accroître la performance des administrations municipales ;
- les résultats au niveau de la gestion financière et comptable, en matière d'exécution des opérations budgétaires, notamment en ce qui concerne l'exécution des dépenses, l'entretien des livres comptables et la gestion des revenus locaux ;
- la capacité des comptables payeurs d'être en possession et de maîtriser les chiffres relatifs à la gestion financière et comptable, ce qui constitue un indicateur important de performance. Toutefois, pour les Affaires civiles, il ne s'agit pas de contrôler la gestion financière des communes, mais plutôt de se familiariser et sensibiliser les maires et les services de finances, avec l'importance que ces indicateurs ont pour leur propre travail. Cela passe par l'organisation des séances de travail conjointes avec les comptables payeurs, les contrôleurs financiers et si possible, les maires. La coopération avec les Affaires civiles, comme partenaire et non pas comme évaluateur est très attendue ;
- le rôle des agents fiscaux appelés à travailler avec la Direction Générale des Impôts (DGI) pour faire le suivi sur le paiement des taxes foncières et sur les contribuables récalcitrants, en faisant une mise à jour régulière des données. Il est dommage de constater qu'il existe toujours des mairies qui ne disposent pas d'agents fiscaux. Leur opérationnalité est donc compromise. Il appartient aussi aux mairies de faire le suivi sur les listes des contribuables et les redevances attendues ;
- la gestion des marchés, car le manque de contrôle dans ce secteur peut justifier le manque d'efficacité dans la provision des services d'assainissement. Nombreuses sont ces mairies en difficulté qui ne disposent généralement pas de service pour le ramassage des ordures, tandis que d'autres l'ont pour la bonne forme seulement ;
- le niveau des services fournis par le génie municipal et l'urbanisme, notamment les défaillances en ce qui concerne l'opérationnalité des services d'assainissement et les performances dans le secteur de construction et de réhabilitation des routes. Evidemment, l'analyse des

différents pays post-crise montre très souvent, une faiblesse généralisée des services municipaux du génie civil et d'urbanisme. Le renforcement de ce secteur s'avère indispensable, car il permet aux mairies de rendre effectivement des services tangibles à la population. Dans cette optique, le travail des Affaires civiles consiste à envisager des stratégies visant à capitaliser le recrutement et le déploiement des ingénieurs municipaux dans les collectivités territoriales afin de faciliter la mise en oeuvre de ces services ;

- la performance des services de sécurité civile, en charge de la prévention et la gestion des risques et des catastrophes naturelles. Le manque d'un comité de protection civile qui soit véritablement fonctionnel est un handicap pour la commune, surtout dans les pays exposés aux risques de catastrophes. Il s'agit de connaître la capacité communale de réaction à travers une estimation des besoins probables, en cas de désastre. En clair, il faut élaborer un plan de contingence qu'on peut aussi appeler plan d'urgence ;
- la formalisation d'un plan de développement communal et la création des mécanismes de coordination effective à travers les tables de concertation départementales ou communales et les tables sectorielles, sont d'une nécessité indéniable ; l'élaboration et l'exécution des projets de développement dans la commune ;
- les relations interinstitutionnelles dont les faiblesses, surtout de nature politique, reflètent une faible approche participative aux questions du développement local. C'est cette approche participative dans la gestion des affaires publiques, qui montre que la mairie reste ouverte au dialogue avec ses communautés.

Malgré cela, la prudence reste de mise, car le fait qu'une mairie présente des valeurs faibles sur l'absentéisme des employés ne reflète pas nécessairement la bonne tenue de ses documents et archives. Dans le même ordre d'idées, le bon niveau des indicateurs en ce qui concerne le fonctionnement des conseils municipaux et la publication des arrêtés ou la présence régulière des maires dans la mairie n'est pas paradoxalement, relatif à l'apport des bénéfices tangibles à une administration.

De même, au niveau de la gestion financière et comptable les contradictions, telles que : les indicateurs négatifs dans le domaine du recensement et du recouvrement des taxes foncières n'affectent pas mécaniquement et négativement le taux de recouvrement des revenus locaux. Aussi, l'indicateur relatif à la soumission des rapports financiers peut paraitre positif, alors que celui relatif à la tenue des livres et documents comptables est négatif. Il appartient à l'officier des Affaires civiles d'examiner profondément ces faiblesses et ces points forts, au cas par cas, pour mieux comprendre comment aider les maires à renforcer leur administration.

B. FONCTIONS SPECIALES DE L'OFFICIER DES AFFAIRES CIVILES : ASPECT POLITIQUE DE SA MISSION

Les officiers des Affaires civiles sont des Casques bleus civils déployés au niveau national, régional et local, où ils servent de lien entre les autorités locales, la mission de l'ONU et les communautés. Ils ont pour mission de renforcer les conditions sociales et civiques nécessaires pour consolider les processus de paix dans un pays. Leur rôle de « facilitateurs », animateurs et « résolveurs » de problèmes se traduit principalement par :

- une mission de liaison, surveillance et facilitation au niveau local, ce qui les obligent à soutenir et exploiter le travail des acteurs locaux dans la construction de la dynamique de paix et du développement. Cette mission consiste à observer les préoccupations et les priorités des citoyens ordinaires, afin de s'engager avec eux et avec les structures gouvernementales dans le processus de consolidation de la paix post-conflit ;
- le renforcement de la confiance, la gestion des conflits et la réconciliation, ce qui les place à la pointe du travail d'une mission de surveillance, permettant de comprendre et soutenir le processus de consolidation de la paix. A ce titre, les officiers des Affaires civiles développent et innovent en matière de nouvelles méthodes et des approches pour faciliter la mise en oeuvre du mandat et ses orientations politiques ;
- le soutien à la restauration et l'extension de l'autorité de l'Etat par leur flexibilité et leur capacité à s'adapter à des facteurs, besoins, moments et endroits distincts ; dans des contextes et des phases différentes de l'exécution du mandat. En effet, le travail des Affaires civiles se résume à créer et entretenir des réseaux sociaux locaux qu'elles utilisent pour recueillir des informations qui vont générer des évaluations, des analyses et des rapports pour le reste de la mission.

Les Affaires civiles interviennent dans le processus national de reconstruction et de réconciliation nationale, pour harmoniser ou unifier les sociétés profondément divisées et meurtries par les guerres. Elles contribuent à l'instauration de la démocratie là où auparavant, il n'y avait que tyrannie, guerre, violations excessives des droits de l'homme... leur mission est d'aider l'Etat à exercer une autorité légitime[34].

L'indéniable succès de l'ONU peut être constaté au Salvador, Cambodge, Mozambique, en Slavonie orientale (la Croatie), Namibie, Sierra Leone et au

---

[34] Voir Cedric Thornberry, universitaire, juriste, journaliste et fonctionnaire international, qui avait été le premier directeur d'une section des Affaires civiles pour la mission UNPROFOR (« United Nations Protection Force » en Ex-Yougoslavie) en Févier 1992, dans « Civil Affairs in the development of UN peacekeeping », International Peacekeeping, vol1, no. 4, 1994

Burundi où aucune recrudescence de violences n'est intervenue. Même après le départ de la mission, on constate plutôt plusieurs réussites des processus électoraux et des transitions politiques avec succès.

Les Affaires civiles exécutent des tâches souvent transversales, telles que la protection des civiles et autres tâches spécifiques touchant les relations entre citoyens ou entre les citoyens et l'État. Elles constituent un canal de communication des priorités et perceptions aux différents secteurs de la population et à la mission. Elles contrôlent aussi les conditions et les évolutions au niveau local en faveur du travail politique et opérationnel réalisé par la mission à l'échelon national. Le rôle des Affaires civiles est aussi d'analyser les conflits et donner l'alerte à travers leurs rapports hebdomadaires.

Elles assurent le suivi des progrès accomplis pendant la mise en oeuvre du mandat, ainsi que les éventuelles conséquences involontaires qui surgissent. Leur travail est aussi de faciliter celui des autres composantes de la mission, à travers leur rôle de coordination, de cohésion et de cohérence entre les partenaires internationaux et locaux.

L'appui à la gestion des conflits, la réconciliation et de confiance les poussent à soutenir le développement des conditions sociales propices à une paix durable, en appuyant la réconciliation et la résolution des conflits. C'est ce qui favorise également l'engagement populaire et la confiance dans le processus de paix. Ces efforts sont entrepris dans le cadre de la facilitation au dialogue entre les groupes d'intérêt et pour la sensibilisation directe auprès des communautés. Ils se concrétisent en travaillant avec la société civile et les autorités de base sur l'identification et le suivi des projets à impact rapide (QIP), ainsi que pour la promotion et la protection des intérêts des groupes marginalisés ou minoritaires.

En outre, il appartient aux Affaires civiles de soutenir le développement de l'espace politique au niveau local, ce qui contribue à la gouvernance légitime, représentative et participative. Ceci se traduit par des campagnes d'éducation civique, l'organisation des forums politiques et l'installation du dialogue entre d'un côté, les différentes couches de la population et de l'autre, le gouvernement.

Le soutien à la restauration et l'extension de l'autorité étatique consistent à renforcer la présence de l'Etat et ses fonctions administratives, à travers la création et le développement des systèmes et processus permettant de renforcer les liens entre les collectivités territoriales, mais aussi entre les autorités locales et leurs communautés. Et la gestion des ressources disponibles entre les partenaires nationaux et internationaux, pour répondre aux besoins des communautés locales entre aussi dans ce cadre.

a. Les officiers des Affaires civiles Dans la Fonction d'Ambassadeur

Un ambassadeur dans le contexte des opérations de maintien de la paix est une personne mandatée par un organisme international pour apporter un message de paix et de réconciliation ou réaliser une mission humanitaire et/ou de développement. Son rôle est de négocier avec le gouvernement central ou les collectivités territoriales et défendre les intérêts de son mandat. Il est en droit de se tenir au courant de l'évolution de la situation politique, socio-économique et humanitaire du territoire qu'il couvre, pour en informer les décideurs de la mission de l'ONU.

Ici, l'ambassadeur est aussi responsable de l'unité et la cohérence du bureau régional qu'il gère. Il est chargé de faire fonctionner l'administration du système onusien, à savoir coordonner et animer l'action des services civils et militaires qui composent le bureau régional — rôle spécialement révolu au chef de bureau, mais qui peut être accompli par n'importe quel officier des Affaires civiles. — Il assure aussi le rôle de représentant de toute la communauté internationale, à travers sa fonction d'intermédiaire entre les services de la mission de maintien de la paix et les populations des communes qui relèvent de sa compétence. L'ambassadeur est aussi chargé de promouvoir des relations amicales et développer les relations économiques, culturelles, scientifiques, militaires et sécuritaires avec les autorités à la base et la société civile, pour une meilleure exécution de son mandat.

L'administration civile de la majorité des pays en urgence politique grave, est divisée en quatre niveaux : central ou ministériel, régional, municipal et sous communale. Mais, le renforcement des capacités et le transfert des responsabilités se font essentiellement avec les trois premiers, pour atteindre les objectifs suivants :

- la stabilité durable qui consiste à renforcer les structures administratives locales ;
- la réinsertion sociale et le rétablissement des institutions qui fonctionnent, ainsi que les infrastructures politiques, controversées et sensibles à la manipulation ;
- la reconstruction par la promotion de la participation significative du public de toutes les communautés, dans le cas particulier de conflit ethnique ;
- la compréhension profonde de la complexité locale et des sensibilités politiques tout en conservant leur objectivité et leur engagement à atteindre les résultats ;
- l'identification non seulement des homologues locaux, mais aussi des partenaires internationaux notamment, les institutions spécialisées et les organisations régionales qui sont prêtes à assumer des tâches de développement.

Il apparaît clairement que les officiers Affaires civiles opèrent au niveau : politique, social, administratif et sous national pour faciliter la mise en oeuvre, dans l'ensemble du pays, du mandat de maintien de la paix et, par la même occasion, appuyer les populations et le gouvernement dans le renforcement des conditions et des structures propices à une paix durable.

Dans ce sens, le travail des Affaires civiles croise, soutient et s'alimente des activités d'une variété d'autres composantes de la mission et d'acteurs internationaux basés sur des rapports de travail clairement définis et bien coordonnés, y compris un soutien mutuel pour servir de socle à des actions efficaces de toute la mission. Le personnel de cette section dirige souvent les bureaux régionaux ou locaux de la mission et sert de coordinateurs régionaux, lorsque les responsables de la mission leur attribuent cette responsabilité.

La division du travail entre les Affaires civiles et les autres acteurs est adaptée aux besoins et aux ressources disponibles dans chaque contexte. Elle est déterminée par les processus de planification continus qui aboutissent à des approches efficaces et des principes généraux issus de ce partenariat avec les Affaires civiles.

Dans le domaine de la représentation, supervision et facilitation transversales au niveau local, les Affaires civiles agissent en qualité de représentant de la mission et travaillent en liaison avec les acteurs locaux dans les opérations globales, mais aussi sur une gamme d'activités parmi lesquelles l'identification des priorités et des perceptions de différents secteurs de la population concernant la mission elle-même, mais aussi à propos du processus de paix. Elles surveillent les conditions de développement au niveau local, afin d'appuyer le travail politique et opérationnel, par l'analyse des conflits et le déclenchement du système d'alarme au niveau de la communauté, sans oublier qu'elles fournissent des repères ou indices établis, permettant de contrôler les possibles conséquences imprévues des activités de la mission.

Une collecte des données a lieu pour soutenir les stratégies et la planification des activités de la mission, par les Affaires civiles, dans le but de faciliter le travail des partenaires des Nations unies qui ne sont pas représentées au niveau local. Dans un contexte politique plus mûr, l'appui dans la restauration de l'autorité de l'état est si pertinent qu'il est important d'établir des partenariats et une planification rapprochée avec les acteurs sur le long terme.

A ce titre, les Affaires civiles planifient les mécanismes d'évaluation des besoins post-conflictuels employés par le groupe de développement de l'Organisation des Nations unies et la Banque mondiale et en faveur du processus d'appel consolidé, composé par le Bureau de la Coordination des Affaires humanitaires des Nations unies (OCHA) ; du Bilan Commun de Pays (BCP) menés par le groupe de développement des Nations unies, ainsi que les mécanismes participatifs de planification et de choix de priorités à plus long terme, à l'instar du « Document Stratégique de Réduction de la Pauvreté (DSRP). »

Ce plan stratégique dénommé DRSP évalue la pauvreté et décrit les politiques macroéconomiques, structurelles et sociales, ainsi que les programmes qu'un pays peut mettre en oeuvre pendant plusieurs années, pour promouvoir la croissance et réduire la pauvreté. Dans cette optique, il est souvent judicieux de combiner les financements extérieurs et les sources de financement connexes. Ce plan préparé par le gouvernement d'accueil, dans les pays à faibles revenus, grâce à un processus participatif impliquant les acteurs nationaux et les partenaires extérieurs du développement, notamment le Fonds Monétaire International (FMI) et la Banque mondiale.

Dans le contexte politique en transition, les Affaires civiles se concentrent sur l'appui au développement de l'espace politique au niveau local, ainsi que les activités relatives à la consolidation de la confiance et la gestion des conflits. Tandis que, lors du processus de retrait des effectifs onusiens, les Affaires civiles reviennent à une fonction de liaison et de supervision transversale plus large.

En clair, le travail de représentation et de liaison des Affaires civiles au niveau local signifie essentiellement s'assurer que l'ensemble des acteurs gouvernementaux et non gouvernementaux disposent des informations précises concernant le mandat et les opérations de la mission qui, elle-même, dispose d'informations précises concernant les rôles, revendications et perspectives des diverses structures et groupes qui opèrent au niveau local, y compris leurs attitudes à l'égard de la mission ou leurs demandes à propos de la conduite des soldats de la paix. Cette pertinence engendre : la collecte de données et la supervision, ce qui concernent le rassemblement des informations utiles à l'appui d'autres acteurs civils et militaires de la mission, mais aussi aux agences des Nations unies ou aux institutions de l'Etat. Ceci, avant de donner des orientations claires concernant :

- le processus formel d'évaluation d'enjeux spécifiques à l'égard des repères établis et de proposer des suggestions quant à la formulation de ces repères ;
- le système d'alerte rapprochée permettant de fournir des renseignements efficaces et disponibles au moment utile et en temps réel, au sujet des conflits potentiels et imminents au niveau local. Cela peut mener à une action pour prévenir le conflit ou diminuer les risques d'escalades qui exigent la consolidation de confiance dans un rôle de résolution de conflit ;
- l'appui à la coordination, cohésion et cohérence politique parmi les acteurs de la mission au niveau : local et régional ;
- l'appui à la coordination avec/entre les partenaires externes au niveau : local et régional ;

- la facilitation du travail des autres acteurs externes ;
- l'analyse de l'impact global de la mission et celle des conflits concernant une variété de sujets politiques, sociaux et économiques au niveau local qui, par ailleurs, risquent d'avoir un effet rapide ou durable sur la stabilité, en particulier quand leurs enjeux touchent la dynamique au niveau national.

Cette analyse peut inclure l'identification de moteurs du conflit et une analyse de leur nature, puis une évaluation des obstacles à la paix, ainsi que des recommandations à propos des réponses au niveau : local et national.

Faire face aux moteurs précis d'un conflit veut dire s'engager sur des questions, telles que : l'accès à emplois, la résolution de conflits concernant des biens immobiliers, les conflits fonciers...

Il s'avère que les Affaires civiles sont souvent les seuls interlocuteurs qui représentent et assurent la liaison entre la mission et les communautés locales. Le cas échéant, leur rôle consiste à :

- s'assurer que les autorités locales et la population sont informées de l'importance et des objectifs de la mission, concernant le processus politique, le contenu des accords de paix et les résolutions du Conseil de Sécurité ;
- développer et favoriser les bonnes relations entre la mission et la population locale ;
- répondre à toutes les perceptions erronées et gérer les ambitions parfois démesurées de certains élus de base ;
- réunir les informations sur les priorités, les perceptions et les préoccupations des différents groupes à l'égard de la mission, du mandat et du processus en cours ;
- promouvoir la compréhension des objectifs de la mission et faire l'analyse du conflit et de la consolidation de la paix dans le contexte du pays ;
- établir des relations avec les acteurs clés pouvant influencer le processus de paix ;
- planifier les activités conjointes, ou solliciter des commentaires sur les activités prévues par la mission.

Les interlocuteurs locaux des Affaires civiles sont les :

- administrateurs de communes ;
- sages et les chefs traditionnels ;
- élus et les autorités déconcentrées des collectivités territoriales ;
- organisations de la société civile ;
- chefs religieux ;
- journalistes ;
- hommes d'affaires ;

- associations des femmes ;
- groupes des jeunes ;
- organismes communautaires ;
- réfugiés et/ou personnes déplacées (IDP) ;
- ONG nationales ;
- citoyens ordinaires.

La liaison avec ces autorités se concrétise par :

- des réunions planifiées ;
- la participation aux réunions tenues par les groupes locaux eux-mêmes, ainsi qu'aux conférences ou tables rondes organisées par des tiers ;
- les rencontres informelles ;
- l'organisation des conférences de presse avec les médias et les appels radio avec la contribution de la section information publique de la mission ;
- les campagnes de sensibilisation en faveur du grand public ;
- les réunions publiques organisées par les Affaires civiles, mais dirigées par les autorités locales.

Les réunions publiques nécessitent une bonne préparation. Elles incluent la consultation des intervenants clés, censés prendre conscience de l'objectif visé et leur rôle. C'est ce moment qui convient non seulement d'établir l'ordre du jour, mais aussi de prévoir les questions qui pourront être soulevées lors de la rencontre, afin de ne surprendre personne, puisque les sujets sensibles ou litigieux auront été discutés à l'avance. Cette démarche contribue énormément à générer l'appropriation du processus et la légitimité à l'événement. De surcroît, elle symbolise l'ampleur du respect que les Affaires civiles portent vis-à-vis de la culture locale, des coutumes et personnalités.

En revanche, la gestion de ce type d'actions publiques varie d'un contexte à l'autre. La règle fondamentale est d'intégrer les attentes de la communauté locale. L'implication des principes coutumiers dans l'ordre de procédure, le rôle des dignitaires locaux et la manière dont la réunion est facilitée, peuvent engendrer la crédibilité de la réunion aux yeux des Autochtones. Dans ces conditions, le message à véhiculer ne peut pas être compromis par le cadre et les dispositions pratiques.

L'officier des Affaires civiles a besoin du temps pour construire son réseau d'interlocuteurs et comprendre leur rôle dans la société et dans le contexte sociétal dans lequel il évolue. Il doit s'entourer d'une équipe formée. Dans son rôle de d'officier de liaison et de coordination, il doit prendre en compte les faits suivants : ses interlocuteurs ont des attentes, parfois, irréalistes de ce qu'il peut leur apporter, ne serait-ce que, par défaut d'informations sur le rôle de la mission et ses financements QIP. Ils ne comprennent pas souvent la situation ou ne font pas confiance à la mission.

Aussi est-il important de divulguer l'information sur le mandat et discuter avec les homologues nationaux pour dissiper les fausses idées reçues et gérer les attentes plus ou moins démesurées ; les interlocuteurs ignorent aussi souvent la valeur de la mission des Affaires civiles et le profit qu'ils peuvent tirer de la coordination et la planification. Un travail d'explication s'impose, afin de montrer l'intérêt et la valeur ajoutée pour les collectivités locales.

Les circonstances qui sauvent l'officier des Affaires civiles sont souvent :

- l'amélioration de la sécurité ;
- le partager d'information ;
- l'assistance technique et les conseils, ainsi que le renforcement des capacités en matière de formation ;
- la facilitation des réunions impliquant différents acteurs nationaux et internationaux, permettant d'examiner entre autres, comment les objectifs des différents acteurs convergent et peuvent mieux se réaliser ;
- la connexion entre les besoins locaux et les programmes nationaux ;
- la mobilisation des acteurs et des ressources pour régler les problèmes locaux ;
- l'encouragement des partenaires locaux à participer au processus politique ;
- l'identification et l'exécution des projets QIP dans un esprit de collaboration et de coopération avec des partenaires nationaux ;
- le fait de diversifier les interlocuteurs et les interrogatoires constitue un atout important.

Ces fonctions de liaison et représentation de la mission obligent les Affaires civiles à s'organiser pour la facilitation et mobilisation des partenaires. En effet, les officiers des Affaires civiles sont appelés à faciliter le travail des autres partenaires des Nations unies, surtout ceux qui ne sont pas représentés sur le terrain. Le but est d'assurer la coordination et garder la cohésion et la cohérence entre les acteurs de la mission, notamment avec les casques bleus en uniforme, ainsi que les partenaires internationaux et locaux. Cela facilite : la collecte d'informations, les analyses et les évaluations des besoins, les processus de consultation ou la livraison des messages aux interlocuteurs locaux.

Les Affaires civiles conservent souvent le contrôle de la gestion des réunions de coordination et incitent leurs partenaires à contribuer activement. La mission de surveillance des Affaires civiles est axée sur la mise en oeuvre du mandat et dans la collecte d'informations, selon une méthode appréciée par les autorités locales. Ce qui semble possible dans le cadre de la formation des élus de base qui devrait bénéficier de la participation des responsables nationaux dans la conception et la réalisation des interventions. La condition et que cela se fasse dans la logique du développement des capacités, afin de permettre aux bénéficiaires de s'acquitter efficacement de leurs tâches.

Les facteurs sur lesquels les officiers des Affaires civiles devraient s'appuyer sont :

- le leadership et l'engagement de leur hiérarchie ;
- le dévouement des partenaires à collaborer dans l'élaboration des stratégies ;
- la réflexion et la planification des compétences de chacun des membres ;
- la flexibilité et la capacité de s'adapter aux changements de penser et d'expérience, mais aussi dans l'application des initiatives ;
- une parfaite complémentarité au sein de l'équipe ;
- la promotion de l'appropriation nationale.

La facilitation implique aussi un soutien logistique des acteurs qui sont présents au niveau local, notamment en l'aidant à accéder à certaines ressources dans les zones éloignées. La grande difficulté se situe au niveau de la demande qui dépasse très souvent les capacités des spécialistes des Affaires civiles à répondre aux appels de secours. Cette difficulté de trouver un équilibre entre les besoins quotidiens et l'offre oblige parfois les officiers des Affaires civiles à se donner des objectifs réalistes sur une liste de priorités, dans le but d'encourager la restauration et l'extension de l'autorité de l'Etat hôte.

b. Les Diplomates de la Restauration et l'Extension de l'Autorité de l'Etat

Si la diplomatie est l'art de conduire des négociations en situation post-conflictuelle sans faire recours à la violence, il n'en demeure pas moins qu'elle se rapporte habituellement à la diplomatie internationale qui, dans le cas des missions de maintien de la paix, est conduite par les officiers des Affaires civiles, dans le cadre des relations entre les collectivités territoriales et les hauts dignitaires de la mission, en suivant la feuille de route arrêtée par le Conseil de Sécurité de l'ONU : le mandat.

Doué d'un sens de la conciliation, des connaissances politiques, juridiques, historiques et économiques étendues, avec une certaine ouverture d'esprit et de bonnes capacités d'adaptation accompagnées d'une grande mobilité, l'officier des Affaires civiles organise ses activités sur la base des missions bien définies par le Conseil de Sécurité. C'est son rôle d'assurer l'analyse et l'interprétation politique, économique et culturelle de sa juridiction de travail, car, en tant que diplomate, il doit avoir un bon esprit d'analyse et de synthèse, faire montre d'une excellente capacité de communication, être réaliste et pouvoir travailler en équipe. Il rassemble ainsi l'ensemble des éléments dont il dispose sur place, au contact des autorités locales et en fait une synthèse qu'il soumet à l'appréciation de son supérieur hiérarchique.

En matière de soutien à la restauration et l'extension de l'autorité de l'état, on peut brièvement dire que les Affaires civiles appuient le développement d'un espace politique au niveau local, ce qui contribue à une gouvernance légitime et représentative. Elles proposent un soutien opérationnel aux activités des institutions de l'Etat, selon les besoins. Bien entendu, ce soutien au développement implique plusieurs activités, telles que : l'éducation civique, l'organisation des forums politiques avant un scrutin électoral et l'aide à la création ou à l'encouragement du dialogue entre les différents secteurs de la population, la société civile et le gouvernement.

Ce soutien implique le développement d'espace politique au niveau local, à travers les activités suivantes :

- organisation destiné à encourager les rencontres avec les hommes et femmes politiques, les officiers locaux, les candidats aux élections et/ou les autres acteurs pertinents, pour que ceux-ci présentent leurs programmes ou à la population locale et aux groupes d'intérêt ;
- appui au dialogue et à la coopération entre les autorités et les groupes d'intérêt pertinents qui symbolisent un dialogue visant à créer un espace politique transparent, où les interêts divers intéressés ont une tribune à partir de laquelle ils peuvent commenter ou suggérer des activités au gouvernement. Cela comprend aussi l'appui au gouvernement central dans le cadre du développement des stratégies ou structures de dialogue, mais aussi la société civile organisée qui représente souvent un pilier important pour faciliter la consolidation des institutions démocratiques. Cela permet aussi de promouvoir une « responsabilisation » accrue, en encourageant la participation civique, la démocratie participative, le soutien des capacités et l'assistance dans les liaisons avec les donateurs ;
- soutien au développement de structures de responsabilité et de transparence, ce qui implique le partage de méthodologies appropriées aux processus participatifs de planification avec les autorités locales. Cela concerne aussi le recrutement d'un personnel ayant des connaissances spécialisées dans les domaines pertinents d'appui à l'administration publique couplée d'une expérience avec les programmes du PNUD. Il y a aussi les institutions financières internationales, les donateurs bilatéraux et multilatéraux qui sont souvent coordonnés par l'intermédiaire d'une convention de gouvernance conclue avec les autorités nationales. Cela demande une mobilisation et un soutien de ces acteurs, en coordination et en tenant compte de la dimension politique des efforts de renforcer les institutions d'Etat ;

- évaluation préliminaire des besoins de consolidation des capacités et d'appui. Cette aspect qui comporte une appréciation de l'envergure du soutien externe dans le cadre : des conseils politiques spécialisés, de la consolidation des capacités dont la formation du renforcement des institutions et du soutien à la réforme et aux infrastructures, ainsi que la réforme législative et Constitutionnelle ;
- appui aux processus de décision, de planification et de politique dans le but d'appuyer les processus de décision et la politique par la collecte ciblée de renseignements et de données au bénéfice des autorités. Cette pratique touche les conseils concernant les méthodologies à employer dans le choix de priorités, la planification et les processus budgétaires. Il s'agit aussi d'identifier les tendances dans l'ensemble du pays en matière de besoin de soutien de la politique ou des conseils à la restructuration ;
- assistance logistique et administratif qui signifie faciliter le retour des représentants du gouvernement local à leur circonscription, en cautionnant la provision d'une assistance administrative fondamentale dans la création de calendriers, la préparation de minutes des réunions, le développement de systèmes d'archivage, l'appui à l'initiation de mécanismes de gestion d'information ou de coordination de base. Cela inclut le partage de leurs ordinateurs et autres équipements de communication, pendant la restauration ou la création des capacités organisationnelles ;
- renforcement des capacités à petite échelle, caractérisé par la mise en oeuvre au niveau local, des programmes de consolidation des aptitudes conjointement avec les autres acteurs du développement. Cela veut dire entreprendre des activités de supervision ou de facilitation dans la planification ou encore appliquer ces projets avec les autres acteurs au niveau local sur des sujets comme les finances locales, l'administration municipale, les budgets, la gestion des structures d'Etat et autres. Bien entendu, ces programmes sont conçus en collaboration avec les autorités nationales, dans la mesure du possible, ils sont émis par une autre institution d'Etat, telle que : la commission des services civils ou une institution semblable ;
- aide aux efforts de mobilisation des ressources.

Cela signifie appuyer au niveau local, les efforts entrepris par les autorités du gouvernement central et les membres de la mission à mobiliser l'intérêt des donateurs, de telle sorte que ces intérêts des agences de donation soient en harmonie avec la stratégie centrale et les priorités, notamment les plans de pays, conclus avec les autorités nationales.

A travers la Résolution 1542 du 30 avril 2004, le Conseil de sécurité demande à la Mission des Nations unies en Haïti (MINUSTAH) d'« appuyer le processus constitutionnel et politique en cours en Haïti [...] et de promouvoir les principes de la gouvernance démocratique et du développement des institutions », ainsi que d'« aider le gouvernement de transition à rétablir l'autorité de l'État sur toute l'étendue du territoire haïtien et à favoriser la bonne gouvernance au niveau local. »

Dans ce domaine de la restauration de l'autorité de l'Etat, le rôle des Affaires civiles se résume à restaurer la confiance entre les citoyens et le gouvernement. Cette relation créée la force légitime de l'autorité de l'Etat. Il ne s'agit plus simplement, de renforcer les capacités institutionnelles, mais aussi de l'interaction entre les institutions de l'Etat et la société civile. C'est ce qui fait que les principes de la bonne gouvernance deviennent effectifs. Le manque d'engagement simultané de la société civile et des institutions gouvernementales engendre le risque d'échec de l'appropriation locale. D'où l'émergence de l'imposition d'une solution externe, car l'efficacité dans le processus de consolidation de la paix reste précaire.

Les circonstances dans lesquelles opèrent les Affaires civiles, plus précisément la nature exacte du mandat de la mission, tel que traduit dans leur plan de travail. La disponibilité des ressources humaines, logistiques et financières jouent un rôle déterminant dans leur démarche pour soutenir l'extension de l'autorité de l'État.

Les Affaires civiles fonctionnent aux côtés des autres acteurs impliqués dans l'appui institutionnel et la bonne gouvernance.

Il s'agit de la police, des militaires et des partenaires extérieurs comme : le PNUD, la Banque mondiale, les donateurs bilatéraux, les ONG internationales et d'autres. Cette prolifération d'acteurs rend parfois difficile la restauration et l'extension de l'autorité étatique en matière d'établissements des processus efficaces de planification et des arrangements de partenariat avec une multitude de différents acteurs externes. Sur le terrain, chacun a sa propre démarche, son calendrier, ses financements des mécanismes et son mandat. Il faut simplement jouer sur la valeur ajoutée qu'ils apportent et le rôle qu'ils peuvent jouer en réalité.

Les Affaires civiles déploient aussi leurs compétences techniques spécialisées dans l'administration publique ou la gouvernance démocratique, en travaillant avec les institutions locales et les autres acteurs, pour comprendre et identifier leurs besoins. Elles utilisent leur présence à l'échelon central pour mobiliser les partenaires de la gouvernance à élaborer une stratégie ou un partenariat et faire en sorte que les priorités et les besoins soient en rapport avec le cadre national global déjà en place. Les Affaires civiles deviennent une partie intégrante de la réponse, grâce à un partenariat formalisé avec les partenaires qui fournissent l'expertise technique dans les domaines de la prévention des conflits, la consolidation de la paix et la gouvernance décentralisée.

Il est important de comprendre comment les partenaires fonctionnent pour être en mesure d'apprécier correctement ce qu'ils peuvent apporter et dans quelles circonstances et conditions, la disponibilité des ressources et les contraintes vécues, dans le but de gérer les attentes. Il s'agit de bâtir une relation avec d'autres partenaires du développement, basée sur la confiance mutuelle et la compréhension des potentialités et limites respectives. La confiance des acteurs locaux permet de poursuivre des objectifs clairs et réalisables, en matière d'appui institutionnel et de restauration de l'autorité étatique. C'est de cette façon que les Affaires civiles seront en mesure de s'engager de manière productive avec les acteurs internationaux.

Du coup, l'officier des Affaires civiles est le chef de file dans le domaine de la gouvernance démocratique locale puisqu'il contrôle la politique de la gouvernance et contribue à façonner le dialogue national à ce sujet. Il appuie les efforts déployés pour améliorer les capacités locales à offrir les services de base, surtout pour les femmes et les pauvres et pour s'assurer que leurs voix sont incluses dans les décisions politiques. En particulier, l'officier des Affaires civiles intervient à travers les plaidoyers, le développement des capacités, les conseils politiques et le soutien technique, le partenariat et le partage d'expériences et les bonnes pratiques. Il est censé promouvoir la gouvernance démocratique dans quatre domaines principaux :

- accroître les possibilités de gens à participer à la décision
- politique, en particulier ceux des femmes, des pauvres et des réfugiés ;
- rendre les institutions étatiques plus démocratiques, responsables, en répondant aux besoins des citoyens et en soutenant le parlement national et les conseils municipaux, les administrations publiques et l'Etat de droit ;
- promouvoir les principes de la gouvernance démocratique, en particulier la lutte contre la corruption, les droits de l'homme, la possibilité « d'autonomisation » des femmes et l'égalité de chances et devant la justice ;
- réaliser des évaluations de la gouvernance démocratique sur l'ensemble du territoire, pour identifier les besoins et évaluer les progrès dans l'atteinte des objectifs.

Pour certaines institutions internationales comme la Banque mondiale, les Affaires civiles peuvent coopérer pour :

- la promotion de la bonne gouvernance et la consolidation de la paix ;
- la consolidation de la stabilité macro-économique et la croissance économique ;
- l'amélioration de l'accès aux services sociaux et la réduction de la vulnérabilité ;
- la promotion de la réconciliation ;

- l'encouragement de la gouvernance économique et la lutte contre la corruption ;
- la gestion financière et « l'imputabilité » ;
- l'amélioration de la budgétisation et des dépenses ;
- le soutien aux institutions clés pour établir des processus efficaces ;
- le renforcement des capacités institutionnelles.

Tous ces détails ne sauraient exclure les demandes d'explications de la part des profanes, sur la nécessité de la réhabilitation et l'extension de l'autorité de l'État. En fait, la restauration de l'autorité étatique et le lien entre le maintien de la paix et la nécessité de stabiliser les Etats fragiles constituent, de plus en plus, une exigence essentielle pour maintenir la paix. Ils ont été reconnus par le Conseil de Sécurité de l'ONU qui demande, par exemple, au gouvernement afghan, via la résolution 1974 du 22 mars 2011 « d'améliorer la gouvernance » et « poursuivre la réforme de l'administration publique et les législatives en vue d'assurer la bonne gouvernance. » Idem pour la résolution 1892 du Conseil de Sécurité, du 13 octobre 2009 qui veut que la mission en Haïti renforce « les institutions étatiques, en particulier en dehors de Port-au-Prince [la capitale], y compris par la fourniture d'une expertise spécialisée aux principaux ministères et institutions. »

Dans les circonstances exceptionnelles qui prévalaient au Kosovo et au Timor-Leste, Le Conseil de Sécurité n'avait pas hésité d'autoriser les missions de maintien de la paix, à assumer provisoirement les fonctions administratives et législatives de l'Etat, à travers la création d'une administration transitoire, sur la base d'un mandat exécutif qui génère une dynamique extrêmement complexe. La question de l'appropriation nationale et locale est mise à rude épreuve. Soulignons, au passage que cette option de dernier recours est uniquement applicable sur les territoires pratiquement dépourvus de toute institution de l'Etat.

Pour comprendre l'intérêt que les Affaires civiles attachent à la restauration et l'extension de l'autorité étatique dans un pays faible il faut consulter les archives du DPKO (Department of Peacekipping Operations) consacrant la doctrine Capstone du 18 janvier 2008, sur « l'intégration des civiles et militaires dans les missions de maintien de la paix de l'ONU. » Cette théorie dit ceci : « dans le but de générer des revenus et de fournir des services de base à la population, l'Etat doit être capable d'exercer un contrôle sur son territoire national. Multidimensionnelle, une opération de maintien de la paix des Nations unies peut soutenir la restauration et l'extension de l'autorité de l'Etat [ce qui inclut le renforcement de] la politique participative, ainsi que le soutien opérationnel aux activités immédiates des institutions étatiques. Le cas échéant, il peut également inclure le renforcement des capacités à petite échelle ou le soutien [le plus large possible du processus constitutionnel ou institutionnel de restructuration.] »

En d'autres termes, le succès de la consolidation de la paix est lié à la capacité de l'Etat d'exercer un contrôle sur ses institutions ou à fournir des services de base à la population. Mais, en échange de cette autorité légitime, l'Etat doit assurer la stabilité et minimiser le risque de rechute dans le conflit. En clair, ce raisonnement sous-entend l'existence d'une fonction civile qui se trouve au coeur des activités de la section des Affaires civiles, appelée à poursuivre une approche cohérente de soutien des institutions de l'État.

La nature des opérations de maintien de la paix a ces dernières années, radicalement changé avec la prédominance des conflits intra-étatiques et non étatiques. Au lieu de maintenir la paix entre les Etats ou l'Etat et la rébellion, l'ONU est appelée à intervenir pour des situations qui caractérisent l'échec ou l'absence de l'Etat sur la politique, l'économie et le social, à l'instar des émeutes de la fin en Haïti, en 2008, marquées par l'incapacité de l'Etat à gouverner le pays.

Dans ces circonstances, pour le citoyen ordinaire, l'Etat perd effectivement la légitimité suffisante pour les gouverner. Ainsi, celui-ci représente désormais une partie à la crise au lieu d'en être le régulateur. Pour ces raisons, les Affaires civiles sont obligées de renforcer la restauration de l'autorité de l'Etat, afin de redonner confiance et reconstruire la légitimité, ce qui les amène souvent à s'immiscer dans le processus de consolidation de la paix.

c. La Politique de la Consolidation de la Paix conduite par les officiers des Affaires civiles

« La politique, au sens de « Politeia », renvoie à la Constitution et concerne donc la structure et le fonctionnement (méthodique, théorique et pratique) d'une communauté, d'une société, d'un groupe social. La politique porte sur les actions, l'équilibre, le développement interne ou externe de la société, ses relations internes et ses rapports avac d'autres ensembles. Elle est donc principalement ce qui a trait au collectif, à une somme d'individualités et/ou de multiplicités. C'est dans cette optique que les études politiques ou les sciences politiques s'élargissent à tous les domaines d'une société (économie, droit, sociologie, ainsi de suite). » Or, la consolidation de la paix est un processus profondément politique. Elle implique une gamme d'activités visant à identifier et résoudre les causes primaires des conflits, puis fournir les outils pour reconstruire sur de nouvelles bases solides, afin d'éviter une récidive. La consolidation de la paix renvoie ainsi à des techniques permettant de rendre la paix permanente, à travers la réduction des risques de rechute. Son but ultime est la réconciliation des parties belligérantes en vue de l'installation d'une paix durable. Cela suppose qu'il faut faire un travail de fond qui implique la satisfaction des besoins des populations locales sur la base des priorités figurant dans le plan du gouvernement légitime. Mais, il faut l'exécuter en partenariat avec tous les autres organes de l'Etat.

En revanche, le maintien de la paix s'impose et impose des sanctions internationales en cas de non-respect des résolutions du Conseil de Sécurité ou des accords de paix signés par les parties, dans le but d'aider les pays déchirés par des conflits à créer les conditions d'une paix durable. Le cas échéant, le personnel des Nations unies : soldats et officiers militaires, policiers et personnel civil, au premier rang desquelles se trouvent les Affaires civiles, surveille et observe les processus de paix. Il aide les parties au conflit à mettre en oeuvre les accords de paix qu'elles ont signés.

Cependant, ces deux concepts différents de la diplomatie préventive qui vise à empêcher que les différents conflits localisés, inhérents à toute société, ne prennent pas de proportions graves. Elle cherche à atténuer, sinon étouffer tous les facteurs susceptibles d'aggraver la crise. Toutefois, certains de ces facteurs, d'ordres forts divers, sont : la pauvreté, la corruption, les violations des droits de l'homme, l'absence d'autorité de l'Etat, l'irresponsabilité des gouvernements et des forces armées, ainsi que les inégalités socio-économiques adressées par les Affaires civiles de l'ONU, à l'exception des violations des droits humains.

Pour ce qui est de la consolidation de la confiance, la gestion de conflits et le soutien à la réconciliation, les Affaires civiles soutiennent activement le développement des conditions sociales propices à une paix durable, en appuyant les activités de réconciliation et de résolution de conflits aux niveaux : national et local, tout en incitant l'engagement et la confiance populaires dans le processus de paix. Ces efforts se caractérisent par :

- la réunion ou la facilitation du dialogue entre les groupes d'intérêts ;
- la sensibilisation directe de la population, en collaboration avec les autres acteurs de la mission, dans la conception et l'émission des messages pertinents et cohérents ;
- l'appui aux efforts de groupes de la société civile à la recherche de la paix et à la réconciliation ;
- l'identification et la mise en oeuvre et contrôle des projets à effet rapide ;
- la promotion ou protection des intérêts des exclus, menacés, marginalisés et autres ;
- les groupes minoritaires.

C'est un travail de mobilisation qui regarde la participation au processus de mise en place d'une démocratie représentative, caractérisé par un soutien opérationnel aux activités des institutions étatiques. Cette approche peut revêtir une variété de formes selon les exigences de mise en œuvre du mandat et compte tenu des capacités continues de l'ensemble du système des Nations unies, à répondre à la consolidation d'institutions et aux besoins d'appui à la gouvernance, dans le contexte post-conflictuel.

En outre, cette consolidation de la confiance est très liée à la sensibilisation de la communauté. Ce qui implique un contact direct entre la population et les Affaires civiles, ainsi que d'autres acteurs, tels que : la société civile. Certes qu'elle est souvent faite sous forme de réunions publiques, mais elle offre une occasion de proposer des renseignements formels permettant de promouvoir les discussions sur les questions politiques centrales ou les textes sur les accords de paix ou encore les résolutions du Conseil de sécurité. Cette sensibilisation offre aussi l'occasion de transmettre des messages ciblés à des groupes spécifiques, conçus en collaboration avec la section d'information du public connue sous le nom PIO.

L'entretien de bons rapports entre la mission et la population fait aussi partie du rôle de la sensibilisation de la communauté. Il est associé au rôle de soutien à la cohésion et cohérence entre les acteurs de niveau local et régional. Cette activité peut incorporer le briefing des acteurs de la mission, en particulier les casques bleus formant le corps habillé, sur les enjeux culturels et le contexte civil de la mise en œuvre du mandat. C'est dans cette lancée que les Affaires civiles ont héritée de la gestion des projets à effet rapide (QIP) leur permettant ainsi d'identifier, de façon efficace, les projets potentiels grâce à leur présence extensive au niveau local. En fait, ces projets sont conçus pour consolider la confiance dans la mission, le mandat ou le processus de paix.

La consolidation de la confiance inclut aussi l'appui aux efforts de la société civile de promouvoir la culture de la paix. Le cas échéant, les Affaires civiles encouragent la création d'une culture de paix et de réconciliation, par l'organisation des initiatives des communes, fondées sur le dialogue, la résolution de conflits, les événements sportifs, et cetera. Cela se traduit aussi par l'assistance dans l'identification des donateurs ou le soutien technique, ou encore en proposant un appui opérationnel et l'amélioration des capacités restreintes aux organismes de la société civile, notamment dans les situations où ces organisations servent de partenaires à la mise en œuvre de Projets à effet rapide. Les Affaires civiles contribuent ainsi à la facilitation des rapports entre les groupes de la société civile et les donateurs internationaux.

Dans le même ordre d'idées, le soutien au dialogue entre les parties en conflit fait partie des responsabilités des Affaires civiles qu'elles concrétisent par une assistance à l'initiation, la facilitation ou la structuration du dialogues entre les différents groupes d'intérêts, afin de consolider la confiance, résoudre ou prévenir les crises. Ce dialogue, au niveau local, alimente souvent le processus national et est parfois lié aux efforts qui encouragent le développement d'un espace politique. Pour terminer, la protection des intérêts des membres de groupes exclus ou menacés, en facilitant l'accès équitable aux droits aux ressources ou à la participation de certains groupes, tels que : les personnes déplacées à l'intérieur du pays ou les groupes ethniques minoritaires. Le risque est de miner la mise en place d'une paix durable qui constitue un enjeu crucial. Les Affaires civiles assurent aussi l'interface entre ces acteurs et le corps habillé des Nations unies par l'appui et les conseils dans la planification de leur travail. En d'autres termes, ce sont les Affaires civiles qui évaluent les besoins et les priorités de la population locale, dans le but de lier les processus de développement avec les sensibilités et les réalités locales. Elles suscitent la prise de conscience de la population par rapport à leurs propres et multiples réalités régionales, en fournissant une plateforme permettant d'entendre divers intervenants dans les négociations. Le tout sert à la reconstruction de la nation et l'identification des besoins, sans oublier l'élaboration des priorités.

Les Affaires civiles soutiennent les gouvernements locaux à articuler les plans des priorités et les programmes en rapport avec les processus nationaux. Elles facilitent le contrôle des progrès accomplis par rapport aux repères de base.

Les Affaires civiles aident ainsi les Casques bleus en uniforme à créer un environnement propice à la consolidation de la paix, en réglant les conflits au niveau : local et intercommunautaire. Cela souscrit à : renforcer la confiance dans le processus de paix, faciliter les processus de réconciliation et favoriser l'amélioration de l'espace politique du pays. Elles contribuent à créer et maintenir un environnement politique favorable à la paix, notamment par le biais du dialogue politique ou la résolution pacifique des conflits, mais aussi en encourageant les relations entre l'Etat et la société sur tout le territoire.

Les Affaires civiles coordonnent les efforts de la communauté internationale, en général et renforcent les mécanismes nationaux de coordination, en particulier. Elles s'assurent que tous leurs partenaires civiles et militaires : nationaux et internationaux, sont bien imbus du contexte culturel et communautaire au sein duquel ils travaillent. Elles mobilisent les acteurs humanitaires et ceux du développement, en leur offrant une interface pouvant faciliter leurs opérations sur le terrain, notamment dans les endroits où ils ne sont pas représentés. Ce sont aussi les Affaires civiles qui règlent les lacunes du processus de paix, à travers la réhabilitation des infrastructures publiques et la fourniture d'un soutien logistique, principalement dans le domaine des transports et de la communication avec les partenaires impliqués dans le processus de paix.

Le rôle des Affaires civiles est celui d'une catalytique destinée à jeter les bases du développement communautaire durable, par le renforcement des capacités des autorités de l'Etat, ce qui inclut : l'évaluation des capacités, l'appui à la planification, la formation et la participation effective entre les autorités locales et centrales, d'une part et entre les autorités locales et la population locale, d'autre part.

Le rapport du Secrétaire général sur la « consolidation de la paix au lendemain immédiat d'un conflit », publié le 11 juin 2009, nous amène à placer les Affaires civiles au premier rang des leaders de la consolidation de la paix et de la réforme d'une administration en situation de post-conflit. Il prévoit, notamment :

- le renforcement de la sécurité de base, c'est-à-dire la protection des civiles, le désarmement, la démobilisation et la réinsertion, couplés de la promotion de l'Etat de droit et l'engagement des réformes dans le domaine sécuritaire ;
- l'appui aux processus politiques, particulièrement les processus électoraux, la promotion du dialogue inclusif et la réconciliation, ainsi que le développement de la gestion pacifique des conflits au niveau : national et sous-régional ;
- le soutien à la bonne gouvernance, pour favoriser la bonne prestation de services de base comme l'eau et l'assainissement, la santé et l'éducation primaire, sans oublier la facilitation au retour sûr et durable des personnes déplacées et des réfugiés, ainsi que leur réintégration et leur réinsertion ;
- l'appui à la restauration des fonctions essentielles de l'État, en particulier l'administration publique de base et les finances publiques au niveau : local et national ;
- la promotion de la relance économique, ayant comme corollaire, la création d'emplois en faveur des jeunes et des anciens combattants démobilisés, ainsi que l'augmentation des moyens de subsistance, essentiellement dans le secteur agricole, les travaux publics et la réhabilitation des infrastructures communautaires de base.

Généralement, la consolidation de la paix passe inévitablement par le renforcement du dialogue entre les parties en conflit. Raison pour laquelle les Affaires civiles initient souvent la facilitation et/ou la structuration du dialogue entre les différents groupes en conflit. Elles apportent un soutien logistique et accueillent les rencontres, en offrant ces espaces aux débats, puis elles élaborent l'ordre du jour du dialogue au niveau local. Ce dialogue peut s'alimenter et/ou devenir le précurseur d'un processus de paix au niveau national. Il est de leur devoir d'encourager et responsabiliser les acteurs locaux à prendre les devants de la scène dans ce processus, afin de faciliter et/ou soutenir les mécanismes de surveillance conjointe des progrès accomplis par rapport aux accords conclus précédemment. Cela permet non seulement d'assurer l'engagement continu des parties dans la mise en œuvre parfaite des accords, mais aussi d'alerter les intervenants sur de nouvelles tensions ou une rupture dans l'exécution desdits accords.

Toutefois, pour soutenir ce dialogue, il faut d'abord et avant tout :

- comprendre le contexte et évaluer la profondeur des divisions entre les parties, à travers l'analyse des conflits. Cela évoque des consultations approfondies avec les participants ;
- identifier les défis potentiels et prévoir une stratégie de réponse aux difficultés pouvant survenir dans le processus ;
- choisir les animateurs crédibles dotés de la connaissance du contexte de conflit sur le plan culturel et linguistique, mais aussi ceux qui ont une certaine compétence à faire face aux crises. Ces animateurs devraient être soucieux de la transparence, la discrétion, la cohérence et la fiabilité. Ils sont censés intervenir de façon limitée et offrir assez d'espace de parole aux acteurs. Leur mission est de structurer les interventions en cas d'hostilité de haut niveau entre les participants ;
- laisser les participants diriger le processus, c'est-à-dire établir le programme, le rythme et le style de celui-ci. Il appartiendra aux participants d'en assurer, probablement, le suivi et d'en faire leur propriété ;
- faire des suggestions permettant d'inclure les participants sur la base d'un large éventail de points de vue et des perspectives pour garantir l'équilibre entre les modérés et les extrémistes ;
- prévoir la sécurité et l'accessibilité des participants dans l'espace de discussions, qui du reste, a un impact sur la dynamique du pouvoir entre les participants, ce qui peut influencer le processus de dialogue ;
- réaliser des sondages auprès des participants pour obtenir leurs opinions sur la procédure.

La mission des Affaires civiles consiste à s'attaquer aux causes structurelles des conflits en travaillant avec des partenaires qui disposent des ressources, d'une expertise et des suggestions de sortie de crise dans le domaine spécifique de la transformation des conflits. Ces partenaires interviennent aussi dans la sélection des interventions ayant le caractère de réducteur de tension et de déclencheurs de la confiance dans un processus de paix. La faisabilité est conditionnée par les éléments ci-après : le contexte, l'accès à l'emploi ou à la terre, les litiges de propriété, la dégradation environnementale, la concurrence sur les ressources naturelles… Tout ceci ne peut avoir du succès que si la stratégie de réponse prévoit un paramètre de protection et d'éducation civique des populations civiles.

d. Protection et Education Civique des Populations Civiles

Bien que l'Etat hôte soit responsable de la protection des populations civiles vivant sous une menace imminente de violences physiques au sein de ses frontières nationales, il n'en demeure pas moins que le rôle des Affaires civiles reste une contribution précieuse.

Les campagnes d'éducation civique servent à initier ou appuyer les programmes d'éducation civique au niveau local à propos d'une variété des sujets pertinents associés à la mise en oeuvre du mandat, tels que : les élections, les questions politiques, la structure du gouvernement, les principes de bonne gouvernance, etc. dans le cadre de la coordination avec les autorités locales et/ou les acteurs de la société civile.

Les Affaires civiles effectuent des analyses détaillées sur les risques de menaces qui pèsent sur les populations civiles à l'intérieur du pays. Elles élaborent des stratégies civiles permettant de répondre globalement et de façon coordonnée à la vulnérabilité de la population ciblée. Ce sont aussi les Affaires civiles qui transmettent les informations venant de la communauté de base. En gérant le processus de coordination globale, elles constituent un lien externe à la mission entre les communautés locales et les acteurs de la société civile, ainsi que les ONG et les agences.

L'interprétation du mandat indique que les Affaires civiles assurent la protection dans le cadre du soutien au processus politique, en encourageant la lutte contre la violence physique. Ce sont des efforts destinés à établir un environnement protecteur.

Les dirigeants politiques locaux, les élus de base et les communautés sont assistés par les Affaires civiles lorsqu'il s'agit d'identifier, de planifier et prendre des mesures concrètes pour protéger les populations locales des risques de conflit. Les Affaires civiles encouragent ainsi la réconciliation et la gestion des conflits au niveau local, en assurant la promotion du dialogue et en apportant d'éventuelles réponses aux déclencheurs potentiels de la violence contre les populations civiles. Elles plaident pour la résolution pacifique des conflits. C'est aussi les Affaires civiles qui facilitent la prévention des crises en faisant l'interface entre les populations civiles menacées, les Casques bleus en uniforme et d'autres partenaires de la mission. Dans leur rôle de coordination, elles conseillent leurs partenaires au niveau : local et régional, sur la conduite à suivre lors de leurs interventions. Elles contribuent, sans aucun doute, à renforcer leurs capacités dans le domaine de la paix, pour mieux répondre aux besoins de protection et de prévention, puis atténuer les conséquences involontaires des opérations militaires. C'est pour ces raisons que les Affaires civiles soutiennent les autorités, les communautés et la société civile dans l'amélioration des conditions de vie sociale et civile au profit de la paix et, en s'attaquant aux causes profondes des risques de rechute. D'ailleurs, le rôle des Affaires civiles dans ce domaine est reconnu par l'Assemblée générale qui souligne, à juste titre, « qu'il est important que les missions coopèrent étroitement avec les pouvoirs publics du pays hôte, les autorités locales et la population pour faire en sorte que leur mandat et leurs activités de protection des civils soient bien connus et compris.

À cette fin, il invite les [acteurs] de maintien de la paix dont le mandat comprend cette protection à continuer de mettre en oeuvre, par l'intermédiaire de leurs [spécialistes] et en étroite coordination avec les autorités du pays, par des stratégies d'information et la sensibilisation, conformément à la résolution 1894 du 11 novembre 2009 du Conseil de sécurité. Le Comité spécial salue certaines pratiques, telles que : le détachement dans les missions d'équipes mixtes de protection, d'interprètes de proximité et de spécialistes des Affaires civiles, ce qui permet d'améliorer l'analyse au plan local et aide à gérer les attentes des populations quant au rôle et aux limites de la mission[35]. »

En dehors de la protection des civiles contre la menace imminente de violences physiques, il y a la protection assurée par les acteurs humanitaires qui vise à garantir le respect des droits de la personne, conformément au droit international humanitaire et au droit international des droits de l'homme incluant le droit des réfugiés. Le cas échéant, les types de problèmes identifiés comme risques d'exposition des populations civiles, ainsi que les réponses à apporter, qui diffèrent souvent considérablement et constituent des sources essentielles d'interface avec les acteurs humanitaires sur le terrain. D'où la nécessité d'une éducation civique de la population.

Comprendre et analyser de façon critique le cadre institutionnel et la dynamique politique qui sous-entend la dynamique institutionnelle, ainsi que les programmes individuels des principaux intervenants, permet de mieux cibler les interventions des officiers des Affaires civiles dans le cadre du soutien aux autorités de l'Etat. Il s'agit de :

- aider les autorités locales et nationales dans le cadre de la politique et des processus décisionnels ;
- analyser les besoins institutionnels et évaluer les capacités menées avec les partenaires locaux, afin d'être en mesure de fournir des conseils judicieux sur les méthodes de détermination des priorités, la planification et la budgétisation, favorisant les processus de planification inclusives. Cela et renforce la confiance des institutions de l'Etat ;
- identifier les besoins qui existent au niveau local, puis mobiliser le soutien des acteurs ayant une expertise technique ;
- travailler en coordination avec les acteurs du développement possédant les connaissances techniques spécialisées dans l'administration publique, pour répondre aux besoins spécialisés à plus long terme.

---

[35] Voir « Rapport du Comité spécial des opérations de maintien de la paix », Assemblée générale de l'ONU, Session de fond de 2011 (New York, 22 février-18 mars et 9 mai 2011), A/65/19, Chapitre 182, page 44

Le soutien à la mobilisation des ressources et l'intérêt des donateurs à soutenir les besoins identifiés au niveau local pourraient être négligés au plan : national et international, alors que cela fait partie des prérogatives des officiers des Affaires civiles. Ces dernières s'appuient sur leur présence à la fois sur le terrain et au siège de la mission et en facilitant la circulation des informations dans le cadre des efforts de coordination globale, sans toutefois se positionner en intermédiaire, mais plutôt en partenaire ou en facilitateur dans le processus.

Les Affaires civiles peuvent développer des programmes d'éducation civique pour sensibiliser et cultiver la compréhension de la population locale sur les processus politiques et leur rôle en tant que constituants dans ces processus. La réussite de ces campagnes de sensibilisation dépend de la crédibilité et la légitimité de la mission. La réalité veut qu'il faille :

- associer tous les éléments pertinents de la mission et avoir l'autorisation formelle des élus de base avant son lancement ;
- impliquer les acteurs locaux dès la phase initiale de planification et s'assurer de la pertinence du résultat souhaité ;
- définir les objectifs clairs et simples de la campagne et identifier les indicateurs pour mesurer son impact ;
- cibler un public spécifique et l'aspect linguistique doit être choisi sur mesure et en fonction du message ;
- faire passer le message, à travers les personnes respectées par le public ou au moins les associer ;
- tester le message et réaliser des événements pilotes pour affiner l'approche avant de lancer une campagne à grande échelle ;
- encourager l'approche participative et engager le public dans un dialogue ouvert ;
- s'abstenir de réagir aux provocations et rester centré sur le message à livrer ;
- utilisez la campagne pour établir les contacts et maintenir un réseau actif d'interlocuteurs.

Au sein de la mission, les Affaires civiles ont foncièrement pour mission de canaliser les renseignements et les analyses rassemblées par les différents partenaires, ce qui implique une communication de développements et une dynamique au niveau local, pour transmettre les messages aux acteurs politiques concernant les processus engagés au niveau national. Il faut une approche stratégique coordonnée et un dispositif efficace de partage des renseignements et d'analyses dans les deux sens : centre-périphérie.

Le travail des Affaires civiles, notamment au niveau administratif et social, se rapproche de celui des droits de l'homme. D'où la nécessité de partager les données et les analyses pertinents, compte tenu des soucis de confidentialité des informations. Cela exige qu'un suivi technique doit être transmis aux officiers des droits de l'homme, mieux placés pour suggérer le meilleur plan d'action, y compris dans le transfert de certains cas sur les mécanismes des droits de l'homme des Nations unies.

Les officiers des Affaires civiles fournissent des renseignements concernant les attitudes et perceptions de différents groupes au niveau local à la section Information du Publique. Ils participent à la conception des messages à communiquer à la population dans les médias, dans le but d'assurer la cohérence des messages transmis directement au public et à travers les médias.

Le travail accompli par les Affaires civiles au niveau : social et administratif dans l'ensemble du pays permet de démilitariser au fur et à mesure les problèmes auxquels les militaires font face. C'est le cas du dialogue ou l'interaction des militaires et civiles dans les zones tampons. La coordination civilo-militaire contribue au développement de planification conjointe civile-militaire, y compris par rapport à la protection des civils et l'harmonisation des plans d'urgence humanitaires.

Les Affaires civiles proposent des conseils concernant le cadre stratégique et politique des opérations et la liaison des UNPOL avec la communauté. Elles gardent l'oeil sur les processus d'initiation et sur le développement des projets de police, selon les besoins. Cela permet de faciliter la cohérence et la continuité de l'ensemble des acteurs de la mission au niveau local.

Ce rôle est important pour la fonction de planification des missions à toutes les phases du déploiement de la mission, ainsi que pour l'équipe de planification d'une mission intégrée. Les Affaires civiles fournissent, pour ainsi dire, des renseignements pertinents aux planificateurs concernant les conditions sur le terrain, afin de vérifier ou modifier les hypothèses d'intervention. Elles servent aussi le développement des repères, pour contrôler le progrès de la mission et pour surveiller cette progression par rapport aux balises, tout au long de la mission, y compris dans la phase du retrait des effectifs.

L'assistance apportée par les Affaires civiles à la section électorale sur des questions pertinentes, telles que la restauration de l'autorité de l'État, par des initiatives visant le développement d'un espace politique au niveau local en dit long. Dans ce domaine on parle aussi du partenariat avec les membres de l'équipe de pays des Nations unies, ce qui inclut la planification stratégique avec les agences, afin de maximiser les ressources déployées par les Nations unies, en matière de personnel, d'expertise et de fonds aux programmes. C'est aussi utile dans le cadre de l'identification des besoins et le contrôle de la mise en oeuvre de programmes au niveau local, ce qui s'avère indispensable, en particulier pour assurer la durabilité des activités une fois que l'opération de maintien de la paix commence à se retirer. Une telle problématique mérite d'être analysée en profondeur.

C. PROBLEMATIQUE

Dans la plupart des pays post-conflit, la situation politicoadministrative présente souvent un climat de désolation tant au niveau central qu'au niveau local. Effectivement :

- habituellement l'administration est complètement désorganisée ;
- les ministres se substituent continuellement aux directeurs généraux ;
- les orientations politiques sont peu ou mal définies ;
- les directions n'ont pas toujours la capacité d'agir, beaucoup des membres du personnel qui sont sousemployés et ayant besoin de formations ;
- les infrastructures sont vétustes, de même pour les équipements qui d'ailleurs sont très insuffisants ;
- le chaos s'installe partout dans le pays…

Que dire des services déconcentrés, tels que : les délégations et les vice-délégations ? Au bas mot, ils ne sont jamais à la hauteur des défis à relever ; non seulement, ils n'assument pas leurs fonctions de représentation du gouvernement, mais aussi ils n'exercent aucun contrôle de légalité des collectivités territoriales sous leur tutelle. A l'évidence, la situation au niveau local n'a jamais été meilleure. Les collectivités territoriales présentent une image hétérogène dont les communes caractérisent :

- un exécutif physiquement placé, sans aucune assemblée délibérante ;
- des modes de fonctionnement différents d'une commune à l'autre ;
- peu ou pas du tout de dynamisme et de « performance » ;
- abondant total ou partiel de leur ministère de tutelle ;
- un personnel contractuel, de surcroît peu qualifié.

Quant aux autres paliers de la décentralisation qui viennent après les communes, notamment les collines ou les sections communales. Leurs prérogatives ne sont mêmes pas définies dans certains pays. Mieux, ils sont dépourvus de services publics.

Les Affaires civiles ont souvent d'énormes défis à relever dans ces pays post-crise, parmi lesquels :

- réformer une administration publique post-conflictuelle ;
- aider le pays à passer d'une situation de faibles intensités de guerre civile à la réconciliation et à la paix durable ou d'une situation d'instabilité politique totale à une situation pacifique ;
- assurer la transition entre la culture non démocratique héritée de l'avant-crise et/ou l'avant-guerre à une société démocratique participative respectueuse des règles d'alternance et de transparence dans la gestion de la chose publique ;

- transformer l'Etat de non-droit en Etat de droit, fondé sur le respect de la hiérarchie des normes, la séparation de pouvoir et les droits de l'homme ;
- lutter contre la corruption et la vie chère pour supprimer la fracture sociale, ce qui entraînent l'instabilité et l'insécurité et engendre des « laissés-pour-compte » ;
- établir ou renforcer la décentralisation et la déconcentration administrative, politique et financière ;
- transformer la faiblesse d'un régime en politique nationale pouvant rendre l'Etat plus fort.

Il s'agit de construire ou réhabiliter les infrastructures politiques et matérielles d'un pays caractérisé par :

- l'absence de cadre légal et institutionnel ;
- le manque ou l'insuffisance de ressources humaines qualifiées, compétentes et motivées ;
- le contexte sociopolitique souvent dépourvu de tout consensus et de toute volonté politique, pas très visible en matière de démocratie et du développement ;
- le système de gouvernance locale plutôt lourd ;
- la faible capacité des gouvernants à assumer pleinement leurs missions de coordination et de tutelle ;
- la maigre mobilisation des ressources locales ;
- les conflits entre autorités locales sur la gestion des fonds de développement local ;
- la mauvaise gestion administrative et financière ;
- le manque de volonté politique de certains leaders élus à opter pour le changement social profond.

De nos jours, la première préoccupation d'un gouvernement en situation de post-conflit est d'établir les bases d'une nouvelle société, en dotant le pays de moyens structurels capables de lui permettre de prendre en charge son propre destin.

Cette construction d'un nouvel Etat post-conflictuel est pour ainsi dire, une exigence de premier ordre, une exigence constitutionnelle qui doit répondre à la lutte historique de tout peuple contre le totalitarisme, l'injustice, la misère, la famine, les maladies, l'analphabétisme, la dégradation de l'environnement, les violations des droits de l'homme et les discriminations de toutes sortes. C'est une transition politique qui doit se caractériser par la mise en place de nouveaux piliers institutionnels, cadrant et structurant l'établissement d'une démocratie participative pouvant canaliser les énergies disponibles vers la transformation permanente de l'environnement physique, politique, économique et social.

A cet effet, la réforme institutionnelle qui se veut objective et réaliste devrait permettre de définir un cadre de gestion de la transition politique, en se présentant comme outil principal pour changer la nature de l'ancien Etat traditionnel connu pour ses caractéristiques fondamentales : conflictuel, oligarchique, dépendant, centralisateur, tyrannique, excluant, corrompu et surtout distant des besoins de la population. Il faut renforcer les prescriptions portant sur la démocratisation, la décentralisation et la modernisation des trois (3) pouvoirs traditionnels, à savoir l'exécutif, le législatif et le judiciaire, en vue du développement humain.

Une réforme approfondie de l'administration publique constituera le fondement essentiel de l'organisation de l'Etat post-totalitaire. La mise en place d'institutions indépendantes et des collectivités territoriales décentralisées, qui seront toutes imbriquées dans des mécanismes décisionnels et participants selon leurs compétences spécifiques à cette démocratisation, de la société s'impose comme une nécessité indéniable.

Or, si après la guerre, la réconciliation est un des éléments moteurs de la mobilisation nécessaire à la reconstruction nationale, il n'en demeure pas moins vrai que, l'instauration d'un régime basé sur : les libertés fondamentales et le respect des droits humains, la paix sociale, l'équité économique, la concertation et la participation de toute la population aux grandes décisions engageant la vie nationale favorisent le développement économique durable.

Dans le binôme développement durable, le mot « développement » indique la modernisation structurelle tandis que celui de « durable » indique la continuité dans l'utilisation des ressources. Ce qui revient à dire que le développement durable est pour l'humanité, un défi qui se partage entre trois dimensions complexes : celle de la protection des intérêts des générations actuelles et futures qu'il faut agencer, celle des intérêts des pays industrialisés et ceux en voie de développement, auxquels il convient d'inclure les pays émergents et enfin ; celle de l'amélioration de la qualité de vie des gens tout en préservant les écosystèmes.

Il y a un lien très étroit entre le développement et la démocratie. C'est de cette corrélation qu'il faut puiser l'argumentation qui permettra au processus de modernisation de l'Etat de décoller. Si la croissance économique précède la politique démocratique, cette dernière doit à son tour être précédée de la formation de l'Etat au sens du renforcement des capacités.

Les compétences des acteurs de la décentralisation : Préfets, maires, y compris les maires adjoints, secrétaires ou directeurs généraux, caissiers payeurs, comptables, planificateurs, secrétaires dactylos, leaders et cadres de mouvements associatifs... sont au coeur de cette problématique de mise en oeuvre et d'approfondissement de la démocratie et du renforcement de l'Etat dans ces pays en transition politique. Dans cette perspective d'opérationnalisation du développement humain, il est important de rendre ces acteurs territoriaux capables d'assumer leurs responsabilités et d'exercer leurs fonctions dans le cadre d'une gouvernance démocratique décentralisée.

Dans ces conditions, la nécessité d'adopter une démarche inclusive, capable de réunir et de mobiliser toutes les catégories sociales, tous les groupes sociaux, tous les groupes d'intérêts sur la base du principe selon lequel « l'union fait la force » s'impose fermement.

La reconstruction ou la « refondation » d'un Etat post-guerre ou post-crise ne peut se faire que par la gouvernabilité et par la réussite dans le processus du renforcement de l'Etat.

Le soutien du secteur privé est indispensable pour enrayer la fragilité de l'équilibre politique qui prévaut dans des situations de ce genre. En effet, dans une société non institutionnelle, le secteur privé est parfois la seule institution relativement organisée pour encourager l'institutionnalisation de l'Etat.

Malheureusement, même ce secteur sur lequel il faut compter est souvent divisé. Il est souvent composé des hommes et des femmes d'affaires pragmatiques qui n'hésitent pas à financer les processus électoraux pour ensuite recevoir les dividendes de leurs investissements. Dans ce secteur, on dénombre aussi les indécis composés des libéraux et les conservateurs qui sont prêts à envisager de participer à une version modernisée de la gestion de la chose publique, mais ils ne font pas toujours confiance en l'Etat. Enfin, il y a le clan de ceux qui bénéficient de l'impunité, qui n'ont aucun intérêt à ce que la règle de droit s'applique. Ils s'opposent systématiquement et ne veulent ou ne peuvent pas donner une chance de réussite au processus de reconstruction ou de consolidation de la paix et de la stabilité. En coopération avec les autorités centrales et locales, la société pourrait constituer une force sur laquelle il faudrait s'appuyer. Cette problématique fait appel à une méthodologie adaptée à des situations post-conflictuelles.

D. METHODOLOGIE DE L'OFFICIER DES AFFAIRES CIVILES

Tout édifice du développement durable se construit de bas en haut, c'est-à-dire à partir de la base. Pour que les résultats dégagés bénéficient d'une réelle légitimité, il faut que la collaboration de tous les secteurs de la population soit privilégiée. La méthodologie des officiers des Affaires civiles est une démarche organisée rationnellement pour constituer l'ensemble des techniques qu'ils utilisent pour atteindre les objectifs de la mission. Si le mandat de la mission de maintien de la paix prévoit des objectifs, il reste, en revanche, silencieux sur la démarche qui permettra d'aboutir au résultat. De ce fait, il appartient à l'officier des Affaires civiles d'élaborer une stratégie qui le conduira vers la réalisation des attentes du Conseil de Sécurité de l'ONU.

L'officier des Affaires civiles est prié d'identifier les problèmes et de repérer ses acteurs potentiels de travail. C'est son rôle d'organiser des rencontres et des entretiens dont le but ultime est de recueillir les informations qui vont alimenter ses rapports hebdomadaires. Les informations reçues sont analysées pour donner naissance à des stratégies de réponses aux problèmes qui agacent les populations, via les autorités locales et la société civile. Reste à savoir quelles sont ses sources d'informations et comment obtenir une base de données fiable, surtout si la question d'identification des partenaires et des interlocuteurs locaux n'est pas réglée.

a. Identification des Acteurs du Terrain

L'une des phases essentielles de la méthode de l'officier des Affaires civiles consiste à cataloguer ses partenaires sur une cartographie. Cet outil indispensable constitue le meilleur instrument d'analyse de la situation. Il permet non seulement de comprendre la diversité et la complexité de ses interlocuteurs, ainsi que les liens qui les gouvernent ; mais aussi ouvre la porte à la découverte des stratégies d'interaction les plus efficaces et appropriés pour la résolution des problèmes.

Lorsqu'il arrive sur le terrain, l'officier des Affaires civiles doit chercher à comprendre le contexte de la situation qui prévaut dans la collectivité. Il a besoin de déchiffrer le fonctionnement de la population locale, notamment comment elle est structurée, la place la culture dans l'organisation de la société… Dans le cas de conflit, par exemple, il doit connaitre les facteurs qui divisent les populations ou les individus afin d'imaginer les facteurs de conciliation ou de réconciliation.

Avant toute chose, l'officier des Affaires civiles doit pointer du doigt, puis clarifier la problématique à laquelle il doit faire face. Ensuite, il doit reconnaître les acteurs clés de la commune ou du département. Dans une situation de crise, il s'agit de déterminer les parties prenantes et les notables qui peuvent influencer le processus de résolution du problème. Cela veut dire, chercher à savoir : quel acteur est directement affecté, bien entendu, positivement ou négativement par la situation ; lequel possède des intérêts personnels liés au problème ; qui peut appuyer ou empêcher le travail de l'officier des Affaires civiles et quel sont les pouvoirs des uns sur les autres et vice-versa.

En d'autres termes, la compréhension des acteurs veut dire indiquer le rôle de chaque interlocuteur, son positionnement, ses intérêts, ses motivations et ses capacités. Il s'agit ni plus ni moins, de mesurer leur utilité, notamment en ce qui concerne leur pouvoir de décision, d'accès à l'information, ainsi que l'influence et les informations qu'il détient.

L'officier des Affaires civiles doit aussi se pencher sur l'analyse des relations et les liens entre les différents acteurs du terrain. Ainsi, il lui appartient d'apprécier les capacités d'influence des uns et des autres, c'est-à-dire savoir qui a besoin de qui ou qui soutient qui ?

Naturellement, il doit aussi connaitre ce sur quoi repose cette influence et quelles sont les sources de tension et les facteurs de pérennité de la situation, pour faciliter la recherche de solutions. C'est après tout cela qu'il peut définir des stratégies d'engagement qui consistent à rencontrer les acteurs avec lesquels il pourra s'appuyer pour mettre à exécution son plan de travail.

b. Collecte d'Informations et Préparation à l'Interview

Sans information, l'officier des Affaires civiles est paralysé. De ce point de vue, les rencontres avec les interlocuteurs pour les interviewers relèvent d'une importance capitale. Jusqu'à preuve du contraire, l'interview demeure l'un des moyens réguliers le plus efficace pour la collecte d'informations. C'est un processus qui permet aux partenaires de faire part aux Affaires civiles, les événements ou les problèmes dont elles doivent ou veulent être au courant. Elle demeure une méthode d'analyse ou d'évaluation des informations ou encore une prise de contact pour vérifier les informations ou pour valider les analyses précédentes.

C'est pour comprendre et gérer les dynamiques sociétales que l'on détermine si un processus de paix est finalement tenable ou le contraire. Les Affaires civiles collectent les informations, surveillent les progrès accomplis par rapport aux repères de progrès d'un processus de paix, entreprennent des évaluations dans différents secteurs, analysent les faits et élaborent des rapports sur une gamme de questions, telles que : les seigneurs de la guerre, les perceptions de la mission, le mandat et le processus de paix, les capacités et les faiblesses institutionnelles, ainsi que les relations politiques entre le centre et la périphérie.

Il existe plusieurs types d'informations, de données et d'analyse qui alimentent les mécanismes de partage d'information en faveur du travail politique et opérationnel des officiers des Affaires civiles. Tout processus de collecte d'informations devrait permettre d'éviter le gaspillage d'efforts, d'énergie et de ressources, dès lors qu'il se soumet aux étapes suivantes :

- identifier le type d'informations nécessaires pour atteindre l'objectif ;
- compiler les informations déjà disponibles venant de différents partenaires ;
- évaluer la qualité ou l'exactitude des informations existantes ;
- souligner systématiquement, les erreurs ou les lacunes des archives d'information, ainsi que le manque de faits, les perspectives et les opinions pertinents ;

- rechercher les opinions différentes ou supplémentaires, notamment celles des femmes ou des minorités exclues ;
- entrevoir une technique pour combler les lacunes dans les informations reçues, puis déterminer les meilleures sources et techniques pour solutionner les crises ;
- envisager, si nécessaire, la possibilité d'établir de nouveaux contacts, en utilisant de nouveaux instruments d'analyse et techniques inédites ;
- protéger les informateurs et ceux qui partagent l'information, ainsi que ceux qui les collectent ;
- éviter les sensibilités sociopolitiques, à l'instar de la collecte de renseignements sur la religion ou l'origine ethnique, qui sont souvent considérés avec suspicion dans les pays où l'identité fait partie des causes du conflit ;
- adopter un système adéquat pour organiser, gérer et analyser les informations recueillies avant de les partager avec les personnes concernées ;
- diversifier les sources et les techniques de collecte d'informations et prévenir les préjugés par des techniques de combinaisons, du reste, soutenues par des approches qualitatives et quantitatives destinées à améliorer la qualité et la viabilité des informations.

La collecte d'informations peut se faire aussi par le biais des rencontres individuelles ou des entrevues dont la procédure nécessite de :

- avoir toutes les informations sur les gens connectés à la situation, surtout lorsque l'officier rend visite à des communautés vulnérables ou des témoins. C'est le premier pas à franchir ;
- choisir son approche en déterminant l'objectif, les questions appropriées et les probables réponses sur les sujets délicats ;
- tenir compte du contexte et des différences culturelles locales, ainsi que les tabous ou les sensibilités ;
- vérifier le jugement personnel sur le contenu, puis considérer la composition de son équipe en matière d'âge, sexe, ancienneté, et cetera ;
- choisir les lieux de rencontres respectant la vie privée des interlocuteurs et garantissant leur sécurité ;
- prendre des notes plutôt que faire des enregistrements audio des entretiens et dans la mesure du possible, se faire accompagner, afin de discuter ensemble immédiatement après l'entrevue, pour faire le point de ce que les deux interviewers ont entendu et noté comme idées principales ;

- établir une zone de confort au début de l'entrevue, en se présentant et en expliquant le mandat et le but de la visite, au cas où cela n'a pas été dit à l'avance ;
- préserver le principe du consentement éclairé, c'est-à-dire informer son interlocuteur de l'usage qui sera fait de ses informations, puis respecter le droit de l'interlocuteur de partager ou retenir ses informations à propos du sujet discuté. Evidemment, il appartient à l'interlocuteur d'apprécier le moment propice de prendre le risque d'échanger ses informations avec l'officier des Affaires civiles ;
- prévenir les attentes au sujet des résultats, sauf à ne pas susciter des espoirs irréalistes, afin d'obtenir le consentement éclairé. De toute évidence, il est extrêmement important d'être cohérent, de ne pas faire des promesses irréalisables aux partenaires, mais de faire le suivi des actions et des dispositions entreprises ou discutées ensemble, sans oublier de traiter et partager les informations avec une sensibilité remarquable ;
- terminer la rencontre en rappelant comment ces informations vont être utilisées pour que l'interlocuteur soit conscient de ce qui adviendra de l'entretien, en matière de références, commentaires, suivi... pour l'officier des Affaires civiles. Bien entendu, il faut s'assurer que le contact sera gardé.

Il existe une panoplie d'informations susceptibles d'être recherchées par l'officier des Affaires civiles, parmi lesquelles :

- les cartes ;
- la topographie et la démographie, essentiellement la zone géographique, population, capitale régionale, les grandes villes, groupes ethniques ;
- l'histoire et les événements majeurs ayant marqué la crise ;
- la structure économique, c'est-à-dire : la production, les services, l'agriculture, l'évolution des prix alimentaires, l'emploi, l'état des infrastructures, des ressources humaines et l'éducation, la santé, et cetera ;
- l'Etat central, les collectivités territoriales et leurs maîtres, les ministères et leurs locataires, les tribunaux et les titulaires des postes avec les coordonnées, la direction et les membres de l'assemblée, y compris l'affiliation des contacts du parti, les lois votées et celles qui sont en attente ;
- les représentations locales dans les assemblées régionales et nationales ;
- les informations sur les notables, les chefs traditionnels, les organisations religieuses, ONG et autres groupes de la société civile ;
- les partis politiques et leurs leaders, ainsi qu'un aperçu sur le degré d'influence des détails d'informations thématiques spécifiques.

Un conseil : l'officier des Affaires civiles ne doit jamais personnaliser les événements, même lorsque les perceptions sont négatives à son sujet. Il ne doit en aucun cas répondre avec patient, émotion ou colère ni même essayer de corriger ce qu'il qualifie d'injuste ou d'inapproprié. La meilleure approche est de se concentrer sur la façon dont les objectifs ultimes de la coordination peuvent être mieux réalisés.

Cette attitude devrait être la même lorsque certains interlocuteurs sont traumatisés par le conflit et/ou d'autres ressentent une anxiété sur l'avenir ou la lenteur des progrès ou encore lorsqu'ils cherchent à profiter politiquement d'une prise de position oppositionnelle en public. Il convient de toujours garder la tête sur les épaules, en restant calme et cohérent dans ses messages, pour montrer le respect à l'égard de la personne avec laquelle on communique. Il faut surtout garder à l'esprit que l'officier des Affaires civiles représente l'Organisation des Nations unies. De ce fait, sa responsabilité est de s'assurer qu'il comprend les préoccupations de ses interlocuteurs. S'il le faut, il doit même noter les doléances et les perspectives qui lui sont présentées, pour donner le sentiment à l'interviewé qu'il a été entendu.

Il est possible que les interlocuteurs prétendent à tort qu'ils représentent les opinions de toute la communauté ou se présentent faussement comme les représentants d'une collectivité territoriale spécifique, dans le but d'accéder à des ressources, des privilèges ou des prestiges ou encore pour bien d'autres raisons. Voilà pourquoi il est toujours conseillé d'avoir un interlocuteur dans chaque communauté ou groupe ethnique. En outre, il convient d'observer la façon dont ces différentes entités se constituent : officiellement, officieusement ou occasionnellement ou encore lorsqu'elles sont préexistantes.

Dans certaines circonstances, l'impartialité des Affaires civiles peut-être mise en cause. Dans ce cas, la solution idéale consiste à envisager de planifier soigneusement ses réunions, en amenant les acteurs locaux à prendre conscience qu'ils sont écoutés et que les Affaires civiles travaillent avec eux tous, sans exception. L'usage des services d'un interprète indispensable. Celui-ci doit :

- être généralement mieux informés que l'officier, sur les habitudes et coutumes culturelles locales. En plus, il peut l'avertir des problèmes potentiels de communication et proposer des formulations d'apaisement, efficacité et accessibilité dans la transmission du message ;
- servir d'instrument pour instaurer la confiance avec les interlocuteurs locaux, notamment lorsqu'il est accepté par eux ;
- adapter le langage des Affaires civiles à la sensibilité et à la culture locale, pour éviter de créer des malaises chez les interlocuteurs qui seraient très attachés à la traduction littérale des propos tenus.

Comme, là où les avantages existent, les inconvénients ne manquent pas, alors les risques encourus, en utilisant les services d'un interprète sont aussi présents :

- la traduction peut être non professionnelle ou erronée, au point de défigurer le message et mettre l'huile sur le feu ;
- la possibilité de recourir à un interprète supplémentaire improvisé, lorsque le premier est compétent uniquement, dans la langue nationale ou le dialecte local parlé par les interlocuteurs ;
- l'interprète peut parfois se tromper dans l'adaptation du message, notamment lorsqu'il se sent à l'aise avec sa manière, le choix des mots ou le message qu'il souhaite transmettre ;
- la traduction littérale n'est pas toujours appropriée à une adaptation culturelle ;
- un interprète originaire de la région de travail ou issu de l'ethnie locale, la culture ou le parti politique peut entraîner des soupçons et peut éveiller des hostilités parmi les interlocuteurs, au point de compromettre le dialogue ou de réconciliation.

Face à ces risques, les officiers des Affaires civiles sont tenus de :

- connaître leurs interprètes du point de vue des faiblesses et des forces qui les caractérisent, mais aussi leur profil académique. Cela signifie évaluer leurs compétences professionnelles, tout particulièrement leurs réactions dans une situation différente et particulière, en ce qui concerne principalement l'élaboration d'une stratégie de communication ;
- son affection à la langue locale, en apprenant quelques mots, ne serait-ce que pour saluer les interlocuteurs au début et à la fin de la réunion ;
- apprendre à reconnaître les formalités de la communication locale, les styles et les normes ;
- utiliser un vocabulaire simple couplé d'une rupture des messages dans un intervalle de temps raisonnable et qui soit facile à comprendre ;
- laisser l'interprète finir de traduire avant de reprendre la parole ;
- éviter l'argot et les expressions idiomatiques, mais faire usage des mots utilisés dans le langage courant ou même terre à terre. Le but étant de se comprendre ;
- choisir les résumés, la longueur du message ou les courtes phrases, ainsi que la traduction au mot-à-mot, selon le niveau de confiance vis-à-vis de l'interprète, ainsi qu'à la sensibilité par sa façon de communiquer ;
- adapter les intonations et le langage corporel puisqu'ils font également partie du message diffusé par l'interprète ;
- écoutez attentivement les interlocuteurs et ne pas hésiter à solliciter des explications, car demander la confirmation ou l'infirmation de la

compréhension, ainsi que poser des questions, font partie des règles du jeu dans la communication ;

- éviter les sujets qui fâchent, surtout lorsque l'interprète n'est pas vraiment accepté par les interlocuteurs. Il faut plutôt adapter le message de façon appropriée.

L'interview se prépare en amont et fait appel à une discipline et une sensibilité exemplaire, si l'on veut aboutir à une analyse rigoureuse qui doit figurer dans le contenu du rapport ou dans la stratégie. Le suivi fait aussi partie des phases essentielles d'une interview.

La préparation en amont est une étape décisive de la recherche de l'information. Elle permet de recueillir l'essentiel des informations sur un sujet, une situation, une personne, des faits, un contexte... Elle est caractérisée par la planification de l'approche de l'interviewer. C'est le moment où l'officier des Affaires civiles se pose des questions simples telles que : pourquoi faire une interview ? Quel est son objectif ? Quelles sont les questions qui méritent d'être posées ?

Le plus grand avantage de l'interview est d'offrir aux interlocuteurs la possibilité de se préparer à l'avance, à toute réponse délicate, controversée ou tendue. Il est prudent de savoir qui doit faire l'interview, déterminer le nombre d'interviewers et interviewés, ainsi que leurs capacités linguistiques, puis tenir compte des différences culturelles, des questions du genre et de la personnalité des homologues. Parfois, il est nécessaire de faire recours aux interprètes qu'il faut sélectionner sur le volet et protéger. Pour toute interview, le lieu et le respect de la sphère privée sont à prendre en considération. Elle commence par la création d'une zone et une atmosphère de confort et de confiance pour son interlocuteur. Se présenter avant d'expliquer le mandat de la mission et le rôle spécifique des Affaires civiles, ainsi que les raisons et les objectifs de l'interview, font partie des formalités d'usage qu'il ne faut jamais négliger.

En outre, il convient de définir les paramètres et les limites de confidentialité, en indiquant comment l'information sera traitée par la suite. Il n'est jamais inutile d'informer l'interviewé au sujet de ce qu'adviendront les informations qu'il livrera. En ce sens, l'officier des Affaires civiles doit savoir gérer les attentes quant au suivi et à la suite à donner, tout en évitant de créer des espoirs démesurés.

Lors d'un entretien, il faut impérativement avoir le sens de l'écoute, ce qui suppose qu'il faut laisser l'interlocuteur parler, raconter son expérience ou sa version des faits. Le cas échéant, la patience et le calme sont de mise, car l'officier des Affaires civiles est censé avoir une conduite et une attitude rassurantes.

Il n'est pas de son intérêt de poser des questions dirigées. En revanche, il est en droit de demander des détails spécifiques dans le but de pouvoir restituer correctement tous les faits.

A la fin de l'interview, il est toujours intéressant de souligner à nouveau ce qui a été dit et convenu à propos de la confidentialité et l'accord informé de l'interlocuteur. Il convient aussi de s'assurer que les attentes quant à la suite à donner sont bien claires. Puis, il faut se mettre d'accord sur les modalités pour rester en contact.

Les mesures de confidentialité sont d'une grande importance pour la protection des interviewés principalement, pour les groupes présentant des vulnérabilités particulières, tels que : les femmes et les filles, les enfants, les victimes et autres. Une fois l'interview terminée, l'officier des Affaires civiles doit analyser les informations qu'il a reçues. En quoi faisant :

- la préparation à un compte rendu ;
- l'évaluation de la fiabilité de ces informations ;
- l'identification des contradictions ;
- la mise en contexte de ces informations par rapport à d'autres éléments ou informations concernant le sujet.

Il doit chercher à savoir si l'information retenue confirme ou infirme son analyse antérieure. Dans son compte rendu, l'officier des Affaires civiles doit expliquer l'utilité de sa rencontre et indiquer l'impact souhaité.

Le rapport doit être structuré en fonction de son objectif. Il doit inclure une analyse qui permet une « contextualisation » des faits et pourquoi ne pas indiquer les prochaines étapes du suivi. Bien entendu, il est important de le relire s'il le faut, le réécrire et le réduire au minimum. C'est à partir de ces rapports que des actions peuvent être entreprises par l'officier des Affaires civiles et sa hiérarchie, en faveur ou en défaveur de la population via les autorités locales et la société civile. Cela s'appelle la stratégie de l'officier des Affaires civiles.

c. Démarche Stratégie de l'officier des Affaires civiles

Définir une stratégie c'est non seulement élaborer la liste des objectifs en fonction des priorités, mais aussi établir un plan qui amène l'officier des Affaires civiles à creuser le fossé entre la situation qu'il trouve sur le terrain et celle qu'il laisse après lui. Cette différence caractérise la réalisation des objectifs de la mission. Elle est conditionnée par la prise en compte des ressources réelles disponibles et de toutes les contraintes contextuelles de la collectivité Territoriale.

L'avantage d'établir une stratégie claire est d'abord et avant toute la « priorisation » et la focalisation. Cela veut dire être rigoureux dans le processus de prise de décision, avoir une approche proactive, puis identifier et/ou faciliter la prise de décisions difficiles.

L'autre privilège est de servir la communication et la coordination dont les attributions entraînent l'amélioration et la cohésion interne ; consolident les prévisions et créent la confiance extérieure. Elles aident aussi à gérer les attentes, favoriser le suivi, l'évaluation et/ou la révision du plan. Cela présage de faire le monitoring et l'analyse des activités en cours, ainsi que leurs résultats. Il s'agit de favoriser l'adaptation au changement des circonstances pendant l'exécution des travaux.

Toute stratégie nécessite une planification efficace. Bien qu'il n'existe pas de modèle type de planification, il convient de reconnaître que tout processus de planification doit définir les objectifs à atteindre et énoncer les résultats stratégiques. Ce qui signifie générer des possibilités, c'est-à-dire les moyens d'atteindre les résultats. Cela inclut l'évaluation des possibilités, séparément par rapport au contexte, aux ressources, aux relations...

De même, il est important de mesurer l'impact du soutien des Affaires civiles par rapport aux réalités du terrain, afin de générer des options pour accroître positivement cet impact et réduire ses effets négatifs.

En outre, la planification permet de « prioriser » l'ensemble des possibilités d'actions qui vont être explorées sur la base de critères objectifs. Pour chaque situation, il peut exister différentes possibilités de l'aborder en particulier. Tout dépend de l'influence et du pouvoir des acteurs et aussi, selon l'approche qui a été retenue. Dans ce domaine, les plus pertinentes idées/actions ne sont pas toujours celles qui sont les plus employées. Seul le processus de planification permet d'identifier toute la gamme d'options possibles. Ce processus fait valoir la documentation et la communication.

La première hypothèse est nécessaire pour la communication stratégique, interne et externe. Elle sert aussi à réviser et ajuster le programme en fonction des changements dans le milieu dans lequel évolue l'officier des Affaires civiles. Le second postulat indique que quelle que soit la structure ou le format utilisé pour la communication formel ou informel, il est essentiel d'inclure le raisonnement et les facteurs contextuels qui justifient le choix effectué de l'officier des Affaires civiles. Quoi qu'il en soit, la révision et l'adaptation sont les maîtres mots de tout processus de planification, mais n'oublions jamais « qu'on ne change pas la carte qui gagne », tout en évitant la monotonie et le dogmatisme qui abrutissent l'homme.

La stratégie des Affaires civiles vise une meilleure préparation des pouvoirs publics, les obligeant à laisser un impact très visible sur les conditions de vie des populations, à travers la mise en oeuvre d'activités humanitaires d'accompagnement sélectionnées. Ceci permet de distribuer immédiatement et de façon concrète les dividendes de la démocratie et de la stabilité, notamment aux populations non violentes et pour la poursuite des objectifs de paix, de sécurité, de justice et d'équité sociale.

Au demeurant, les critères d'une stratégie tiennent aux résultats, aux moyens logistiques et financiers, au temps et au mandat de la mission. Cependant, pour élaborer une stratégie, il faut :

- connaitre la logique entre les activités et les objectifs ;
- identifier les hypothèses et les assomptions qui sont en dessus de la logique mise en place ;
- générer des actions à entreprendre ;
- prioriser les besoins ;
- identifier les objectifs de façon claire et précise, afin d'avoir une idée correcte de ce que l'officier des Affaires civiles veut atteindre.

Le succès d'une mission de maintien de la paix dépend en grande partie de l'approche stratégique commune, fondée sur des dispositions efficaces dont le but est de faciliter le partage bidirectionnel d'information et d'analyse entre les Affaires civiles et les Affaires politiques. Dans ce jeu diplomatique, les Affaires civiles constituent une source clé d'information au niveau local. Elles peuvent également aider à vérifier et affiner l'analyse menée au niveau central.

La relation entre les Affaires civiles et la section Information Publique est caractérisée par l'approvisionnement en informations sur les attitudes et les perceptions de différents groupes au niveau local, ce qui contribue à la conception de messages qui sont délivrés à la population par les médias.

Aussi, une bonne coordination avec la section Information Publique est essentielle pour assurer la cohérence des messages transmis de la mission. En tant qu'épine dorsale d'une opération de maintien de la paix le contingent militaire doit interagir avec les Affaires civiles et bâtir un partenariat efficace pour se familiariser avec le personnel civil. Les casques bleus civils participent ainsi aux mécanismes de coordination pour faciliter la circulation des informations et leur liaison avec les autorités locales.

Au niveau : local et régional, les Affaires civiles conseillent les forces armées sur les questions civiles, les normes culturelles et le contexte le plus large de l'exécution du mandat, permettant de comprendre quelles sont les interventions appropriées et/ou inappropriées. Elles s'impliquent dans la gestion des malentendus entre les communautés et les unités militaires.

Leurs performances au niveau : social et administratif dans le pays d'accueil peuvent également aider à démilitariser les problèmes rencontrés par l'armée sur le terrain, en encourageant le dialogue ou l'interaction civique dans les zones tampons, par exemple. Dans l'autre sens, les militaires peuvent être impliqués dans le processus de sélection et de gestion des QIP, surtout lorsque cela nécessite une expertise technique du génie civil. Bref, les Affaires civiles organisent et planifient des activités civilo-militaires conjointes destinées à renforcer la protection des populations civiles.

Quant aux UNPOL, elles ont pour mission d'assurer l'ordre et la sécurité publique, en renforçant les capacités de la police nationale à assurer la sécurité et faciliter l'accès à la justice, conformément aux normes internationales des droits de l'homme et aux règles de l'ONU. Ils s'occupent aussi de la protection du personnel, du matériel et des installations de l'ONU.

Dans le cadre de la coordination, les officiers des Affaires civiles soutiennent les UNPOL sur le plan stratégique et politique des opérations de police et assurent la liaison avec les communautés locales, en facilitant la cohésion et la cohérence entre les acteurs de la mission au niveau local. Elles favorisent la compréhension du contexte politique et socio-économique dans lequel les UNPOL opèrent. Ces derniers sont en droit de présenter des projets QIP en faveur de la police nationale. Ils escortent parfois les officiers des Affaires civiles dans les opérations d'aide humanitaire et de coordination de la sécurité des camps des déplacés, mais aussi interviennent dans les mécanismes d'alerte et de prévention des crises.

En matière des droits de l'homme, une coordination étroite avec les Affaires civiles est nécessaire auquel participe la section électorale. Il en est de même pour la section du genre. Quant aux officiers du désarmement, de la démobilisation et la réinsertion, ils sont parfois représentés au niveau local, aux côtés ou par les officiers des Affaires civiles qui peuvent jouer le rôle de facilitateur pour la mobilisation et la participation de la population locale. Le désarmement, la démobilisation et la réinsertion (DDR) font partie d'un processus complexe ayant des ramifications sur les aspects politiques, militaires, humanitaires et socio-économiques impliquant la section des Affaires civiles dans le renforcement de la confiance, afin de favoriser la stabilisation et le progrès du pays vers plus de sécurité et de développement[36].

L'intégration avec les agences de l'ONU offre des avantages notables permettant d'harmoniser les ressources dans le cadre d'une vision commune. C'est le meilleur moyen d'élaborer une stratégie pour la consolidation de la paix, même si ces agences partenaires sont souvent régies par des mandats, des calendriers, des structures de décision et des financements considérablement différents de celles de la mission.

En guise d'illustration, les horizons temporels des acteurs humanitaires sont plutôt orientés dans l'immédiat, vers le soulagement temporaire de besoin, alors que les Affaires civiles suivent un calendrier politique et encouragent les acteurs locaux à s'adapter à des perspectives à plus long terme dans leurs interventions. Raison de plus, pour harmoniser les activités autant que possible, compte tenu des intérêts et des objectifs différents qui y sont impliqués. La démarche stratégique des Affaires civiles consiste à :

- entreprendre des consultations séparées avec les jeunes, leurs aînés, les hommes et les femmes pour permettre à toutes les couches de la population, y compris les exclus, de se faire entendre ;
- ventiler les données selon l'âge, le sexe, l'ethnie, la religion, etc., dans leur analyse des informations et leurs rapports ;

[36] Consulter le site web suivant : www.unsystem.org

- examiner les questions de diversité, d'identité, du genre pour développer une compréhension des expériences, des priorités et des doléances des différents groupes ;
- tenir compte des attitudes et des pratiques culturelles liées au conflit et à la réconciliation tout en considérant la mitigation de la crise ainsi que les mécanismes traditionnels de gestion des différends ;
- développer un espace politique favorable à la paix et promouvoir la restauration et l'extension de l'autorité Etat, sans oublier de soutenir la participation des femmes et des minorités culturelles ou ethniques dans l'administration civile. Cela inclut leur nomination dans la sphère des dirigeants de la communauté ou du gouvernement ;
- s'appuyer, en matière de protection civile, sur les questions de genre et de diversité, pour comprendre les risques, la vulnérabilité et le rôle que les différents groupes jouent dans la transformation et la prévention des conflits ;
- garantir la représentation de toutes les couches de la société dans leurs réseaux d'information, y compris les minorités, les femmes et les groupes marginalisés, dans le but de mieux évaluer les principaux enjeux sur lesquels ils travaillent et le rôle que ces groupes jouent dans la prise de décision et leur influence ;
- prendre en compte les questions du genre et de la diversité ;
- élaborer les rapports et briefing servant d'instrument pour comprendre le contexte socioculturel dans le but de promouvoir une approche culturellement sensible ;
- soutenir les projets QIP présentés par les groupes marginalisés, ce qui entraine la confiance dans la mission, le mandat et le processus de paix ;
- examiner les structures sociales, les dynamiques et les pratiques culturelles, dans le but d'intégrer les questions de diversité et du genre, puis faire la promotion de la sensibilité culturelle. Cela signifie chercher à savoir quel est le processus et les circonstances de prise de décision et qui détient le pouvoir de prendre cette décision ? La réponse à cette interrogation permet de connaitre les autoritaires, s'il y a eu consensus, le type de démarche conjointe ou le contraire, la collaboration des parties, les participants, à savoir : les hommes, femmes, groupes, aînés, supérieurs, ainsi que leur classe sociale, c'est-à-dire les travailleurs formels et informels, chef de famille ou de clan, etc. ;
- identifier les inclus et les exclus de cette structure de la prise de décision au niveau local, régional ou national ;
- connaître les normes en vigueur sur le plan religieux et culturel, ainsi que les attitudes et les pratiques en matière de sexe, âge, handicap, religion, ethnie et autres orientation sexuelle ;

- faire des voeux au cours des réunions, négocier, conclure ou amender les accords en fonction des réalités du terrain, admettre ces erreurs et présenter des excuses tout en sauvant la face.

Il est difficile de résoudre un différend sans s'informer sur les mécanismes formels et informels ou les moyens traditionnels de réparation et de compensations matérielles punitives, sans comprendre les rôles traditionnels des femmes et des hommes dans le processus. De même, il faut saisir les mécanismes de discrimination dans le système juridique et les méthodes coutumières ; le manque d'accès aux services publics et les bases de l'exclusion : personnes déplacées, anciens combattants, l'ethnie, la religion, sexe, la tribu, clan.

L'écoute des homologues nationaux et locaux permet souvent d'identifier les partenaires appropriés et de s'assurer que leurs interventions sont sensibles à la diversité et au contexte culturel local.

Evidemment, la récupération d'un conflit est d'abord un défi national qui relève de la responsabilité et des facteurs internes. L'appropriation locale peut façonner le rythme, les progrès et les résultats. Elle se réfère au degré dans lequel les acteurs nationaux sont impliqués dans la prise de décision, la conception et la mise en oeuvre des activités et des processus clés.

L'appropriation locale ne doit pas être confondue à la position des élites gouvernementales et politiques ou celle des « initiés » ou encore des « étrangers. » C'est une volonté dérivant des autorités régionales et locales de la société civile et des citoyens ordinaires, se mesurant au niveau national, y compris le gouvernement central et l'Etat. Ici, il est question de durabilité. Celle-ci est issue du contexte et de la pertinence culturelle, mais aussi du développement des capacités locales à limiter ou empêcher la dépendance, la transition pacifique ou la sortie de crise. Elle conditionne l'amélioration des liens entre les efforts de paix locaux et nationaux.

Venant de la base, un processus initié sur fond des besoins locaux, mais contrôlé par la population locale a plus de chances d'aboutir, à condition que le processus soit démocratique et participatif. Le nombre des voix s'exprimant et la possibilité de contradictions sont des indicateurs de réussite.

Les circonstances d'aggravation des conflits qui sont sensibles à la prévention sont :

- la méfiance entre le gouvernement et ses citoyens ;
- les tensions entre les communautés ou les groupes ;
- la polarisation et/ou la politisation des acteurs de la société civile ;
- les contradictions entre les pratiques et/ou les priorités des principaux acteurs locaux et les normes du droit international accompagnés les principes des Nations unies et les intérêts des autres acteurs ;
- la méconnaissance de la profondeur des divisions ;

- la croyance à la théorie selon laquelle, le fait de rassembler les gens aura automatiquement un impact positif ;
- la ré-application des relations de pouvoir inégales, caractérisée par le choix des acteurs à inclure ou à exclure, ainsi que la nature de leur participation ;
- le soutien injuste, apporté à un statuquo ;
- les idées ou les modèles préconçus.

La mission des Affaires civiles peut se résumer à favoriser les discussions entre les différents acteurs ou protagonistes pour faciliter le processus de consultation et fournir une plateforme pour les populations locales en vue de les permettre d'entrer dans un processus national de discussions. Cette approche communautaire consiste à donner des informations et promouvoir des débats publics sur les questions clés, concernant les besoins et les priorités qui s'avèrent indispensables pour jeter les bases d'un engagement populaire, nécessaire au renforcement des institutions étatiques à long terme.

L'appropriation locale et le degré d'approche inclusive sont à la base de la construction de la confiance dans le soutien national pour le changement. Elle est orientée vers le rétablissement et le développement des capacités locales. Pour y arriver, il convient d'abord de faire une évaluation détaillée des systèmes locaux, des structures, des forces et des faiblesses de ceux-ci, afin de comprendre ce que ces acteurs considèrent comme manque de capacités ou barrières. Ensuite, il faudrait susciter une volonté politique de se réunir autour des objectifs communs. Cela signifie adopter une approche participative, impliquant les intervenants locaux dans le processus de planification, de liaison, de coordination et de consultation ; indispensables pour la collecte d'informations sur les besoins et les perceptions avenirs.

Il est important de connaître les circonscriptions et les populations locales marginalisées, leurs préoccupations, leurs besoins, leurs priorités et leurs intérêts ; pour faire une analyse du niveau sociopolitique, économique et culturel. L'objectif est de calibrer une approche conséquente, censée soutenir l'articulation des griefs, les racines des causes et les solutions locales aux conflits.

A l'évidence, il est déconseillé de saper les capacités locales ou de les remplacer, mais plutôt, les valoriser et faire usage de cette expertise locale. Pourquoi ne pas s'appuyer sur ces processus et structures existantes, formelles et informelles, pour atténuer les impacts négatifs imprévus ? En effet, vu la complexité de l'environnement de conflit, les actions ou la simple présence des Casques bleus civils ou militaires peuvent être nuisibles, au point d'exacerber la communauté locale et au sens large, le processus de paix ; ce qui engendre souvent des effets négatifs et des conséquences imprévues.

Le rôle des Affaires civiles n'est-il pas d'anticiper et d'atténuer ces méfaits par la compréhension du contexte dans lequel elles opèrent ? L'interaction entre leurs interventions et le contexte et/ou les effets de leurs agissements sur cette interaction ne servent-ils pas à minimiser les impacts négatifs et maximiser les impacts positifs ?

Il est prouvé que même l'aide humanitaire avec son corollaire, l'afflux des étrangers travaillant pour des organismes internationaux, son impact sur les prix, les salaires et les profits de l'économie locale, ainsi que sur l'inflation dans l'immobilier et les produits de première nécessité peuvent provoquer des conséquences positifs et/ou négatifs sur la dynamique d'un conflit.

La théorie de la « sensibilité au conflit[37] » oblige à comprendre comment travaillent et interagissent les Affaires civiles par rapport aux pouvoirs existants : coutumes, valeurs, systèmes et institutions, car les efforts pour la paix peuvent parfois involontairement alimenter les conflits. Si cette sensibilité aux conflits n'est pas fondée sur l'analyse régulière du contexte qui devrait être intégré dans la planificatio, à travers la mise en oeuvre et le suivi des activités des experts locaux et par l'analyse d'un certain nombre de facteurs, tels que : les tensions socio-économiques et politiques, la probabilité de reprendre la violence, etc., il est fort probable que la mission échoue lamentablement.

Même dans le domaine de formation, il faut absolument se concentrer sur une gamme de compétences clés, telles que : l'analyse des conflits, la planification stratégique, la négociation, la médiation et la facilitation ; la mobilisation et la coordination ; l'encouragement et le soutien des acteurs locaux, c'est-à-dire l'Etat, les collectivités territoriales et la société civile compris.

Politiquement parlant, voici quelques facteurs généraux de planification pouvant servir de fil conducteur à une équipe des Affaires civiles :

- analyser les tâches de la mission prévues dans le mandat, pour saisir le niveau de complexité et la dynamique politiques, le consentement du pays hôte et l'engagement des parties au processus de paix ;
- connaître la nature, la gravité et la portée du conflit, ainsi que la taille géographique du pays d'accueil et la taille de la population, sans oublier les infrastructures, les structures et leurs capacités administratives ;
- comprendre la politique sous-régionale lorsqu'elle se rapporte à la crise, tout au moins, ce qui peut empiéter sur le processus de paix. En clair, il convient de tenir compte de la présence d'autres acteurs internationaux ;
- mesurer le niveau de décentralisation politique ou de fragmentation de l'élite politique, ainsi que la masse de pluralité parmi les acteurs politiques et les tensions sous-jacentes entre eux, sans oublier le degré

[37] Voir Théorie du « Do No Harm », http://www.cdainc.com/dnh/docs/DoNoHarmHandbook.pdf et Le Consortium sensibilité aux conflits, http://conflictsensitivity.org/

de transparence du gouvernement et d'autres factions du processus de décision ;

- s'informer de l'existence de la Constitution et le volume de représentation politique autour de la formation de cette Constitution, ainsi que l'existence des sources des médias indépendants et multiples ;
- maîtriser les structures du système de gouvernance régionale et locale ;
- renforcer les activités encourageant la confiance et la réconciliation ;
- promouvoir le rôle, la force, la diversité et la capacité de la société civile ;
- étendre l'autorité de l'Etat et sa quantité de responsabilité, ainsi que les capacités des institutions de la gouvernance au niveau : local et régional ;
- développer des facteurs sociaux pouvant affecter le conflit au niveau local ou entre groupes sous nationaux.

Les Affaires civiles sont utiles pour mettre en place les différents mécanismes de planification de l'ONU et pour assurer le monitoring du développement ultérieur des plans opérationnels détaillés et les stratégies pour la réalisation des objectifs.

Fondamentalement, une stratégie comprend :

- une liste prioritaire des objectifs et des résultats souhaités ou les réalisations escomptées ;
- l'ensemble des activités et les résultats prévus par rapport aux ressources réelles disponibles, ainsi que les contraintes contextuelles ;
- une logique claire qui relie les deux.

L'analyse d'un conflit oblige à expérimenter les phases ci-après :

- avoir tous les détails possibles sur la dynamique au niveau : local et national ;
- alimenter et améliorer l'analyse des objectifs prévus à l'avance par le biais de la « priorisation » ;
- fournir un cadre de référence pour la présentation des rapports et des analyses ;
- prévoir un plan stratégique pouvant être actualisé en fonction des informations nouvelles ou par rapport à une compréhension évolutive de la situation ;
- identifier et exploiter les points d'intervention et d'impact des acteurs concernés, notamment les politiciens, la société civile et les autres acteurs nationaux et internationaux ;
- pour générer plusieurs options de la façon la plus créative possible, mais sans porter des jugements.

Le cas échéant, les officiers des Affaires civiles agissent comme mobilisateurs, « facilitateurs » ou catalyseurs, essentiellement pour les acteurs nationaux afin de :

- hiérarchiser les interventions par rapport au mandat et à l'échéancier de la mission, sur la base des ressources disponibles incluant ainsi les compétences et les capacités du personnel disponible, mais aussi les capacités des autres acteurs sur lesquelles reposent ou les interventions des intervenants nationaux ;
- clarifier noir sur blanc, les objectifs et les résultats escomptés, ainsi que les relations qui les gouvernent ;
- identifier et expliquer les possibilités de sortie de crise ;
- prévoir les activités, les échéanciers, les responsabilités et les ressources ;
- élaborer les indicateurs d'impact et si possible, le processus pour y arriver ;
- assurer le monitoring, afin de faire les mises à jour ou les révisions qui s'imposent.

Néanmoins, aucune stratégie, aucune planification ne peut être efficace sans avoir les informations viables que l'on pourrait acquérir à travers des interviews. Ce qui oblige l'officier des Affaires civiles à communiquer, négocier et assurer la coordination.

d. Méthode Communicationnelle de l'Officier des Affaires Civiles et Processus de Concertation entre Acteurs

La communication est un instrument important dans la recherche d'informations. L'officier des Affaires civiles doit la maîtriser pour améliorer ses performances. Il est d'ailleurs conseillé, mais ce n'est pas indispensable de parler la langue locale. C'est un des moyens les plus efficaces de la transmission des messages, du savoir et pour l'échange d'information. Quand elle est persuasive, elle vise à promouvoir le changement ou à influencer une opinion ou un comportement.

L'officier des Affaires civiles doit être conscient des messages qu'il communique. Dans ce domaine, tout mot, tout geste traduit un message : quelle que soit la forme d'expression qui lui est attribuée : silencieuse, implicite, confidentielle, directe ou publique.

Pour que la communication soit effective, l'officier des Affaires civiles doit, comme préconditions :

- connaître son institution, ses objectifs, ses partenaires et le terrain sur lequel il opère ;

- comprendre le cadre, le contexte politique et les sensibilités, ainsi que la culture du pays hôte ;
- tisser de bonnes relations avec les autorités locales et les leaders de la société civile.

La connaissance des partenaires se caractérise par la maîtrise de leur sensibilité, leur vulnérabilité et leur degré d'influence dans la collectivité Territoriale. La « real politics » oblige l'officier des Affaires civiles à faire une analyse politique permettant d'identifier leurs dimensions, étant donné que les effets de la communication peuvent être implicitement liés à ces sensibilités.

Dans le cadre de la sensibilité et la motivation à écouter, la réputation personnelle ou la politique de l'interlocuteur devrait être connue d'avance par l'officier des Affaires civiles, tout comme son accès aux bénéfices politiques et économiques, notamment à propos des biens, de l'argent, de l'appui politique qu'il peut apporter, sans oublier d'observer son image comparativement à ceux de ses adversaires.

La connaissance de l'institution doit amener l'officier des Affaires civiles à identifier ses capacités et à déterminer clairement ses objectifs. Dans ce domaine, il est toujours nécessaire de tenir compte des perceptions du passé et du présent, afin de mieux positionner son travail. En effet, les idées que les partenaires ont de la mission affectent les relations avec eux. Du coup, il convient de définir le type de relation à adopter et être cohérent avec l'approche choisie, tout en étant préparé à des changements inattendus. Le choix peut se faire parmi :

- l'échange d'informations ;
- la coopération et/ou la coordination ;
- l'interdépendance ;
- l'opposition, c'est-à-dire créer un espace dans lequel les désaccords pourront être communiqués et compris, mais dans un esprit de respect mutuel.

Dans tous les cas, il est important de toujours faire preuve de respect et établir la confiance avec son interlocuteur, tout en étant fidèle à son identité et à ses principes.

Le langage des Affaires civiles doit toujours être persuasif. Elles doivent prendre en considération différentes stratégies, entre autres, la :

- distinction entre les positions et les intérêts, les besoins et les souhaits… ;
- nécessité de mettre l'accent sur les bénéfices mutuels et les profits à tirer ;
- reconnaissance ou création des liens avec leurs projets, leurs besoins ou leurs inquiétudes.

Les officiers des Affaires civiles agissent sur des thèmes fédérateurs et transversaux, au coeur notamment de l'appui institutionnel : la concertation.

On comprend bien qu'avant d'être technique sur le fond, l'appui institutionnel semble d'abord être un enjeu de communication, quelle que soit la matière considérée :

- le rôle de l'Etat ;
- la décentralisation ou la déconcentration ;
- l'élaboration des politiques sectorielles et sous-sectorielles, puis les budgets communaux ;
- les cadres stratégiques de lutte contre la pauvreté ;
- les partenariats public et privé ;
- les restructurations de services publics ;
- les politiques de gestion des ressources humaines, etc.

Pour chacun de ces thèmes, l'assistant technique en appui institutionnel est confronté à un travail :

- de diagnostic des données existantes ;
- de mise en relation des différents acteurs concernés par le thème, à différents niveaux ;
- d'accompagnement, d'animation de la réflexion et de la définition d'alternatives ;
- de suivi et évaluation des dynamiques mises en oeuvre.

Pour progresser sur ces différents sujets, l'appui institutionnel doit reposer sur :

- l'instauration de relations de confiance sans lesquelles rien ne se fera ;
- la prise en compte d'intérêts divergents, ce qui entraine la gestion de compromis ;
- la volonté de construire dans la durée et de ne pas faire seul, ce qui oblige à générer des dynamiques ;
- l'expression du réalisme, afin que les travaux intellectuels et stratégiques trouvent leur place dans les réalités du terrain.

Ce processus de concertation entre acteurs permet à chacun de faire part de ses expériences quel que soit le thème. Et, c'est sur la base des expériences de chacun, qu'il est possible de confronter les points de vue, les outils et les pistes de travail qu'il faut alimenter avec les textes, les notes thématiques et les fiches pratiques. Du coup, l'appui institutionnel peut s'exercer à différents niveaux, ceux :

- des relations internationales, pour les négociations entre Etats ;
- au plan national, dans le cadre de la définition des politiques ;
- au plan local, en ce qui concerne les négociations avec les collectivités territoriales ;
- au plan interne, par rapport à l'institution d'accueil, le cas de la commune par exemple, dans la restructuration de services, l'élaboration d'un organigramme…

Selon les cas de figure, la concertation entre acteurs pourrait se faire « verticalement », entre Etat et bailleurs de fonds ou entre Etat et secteur privé. Lorsqu'elle se fait « horizontalement », il s'agit des bailleurs de fonds entre eux, pour traiter des questions de développement ou entre Etats et entre ministères. « Pour mettre en oeuvre un processus de concertation il faut au moins être à deux et il faut que chacun ait un intérêt à la concertation. Il n'est pas toujours facile, lorsque l'on est en situation de fournir des appuis institutionnels, de mettre en évidence l'ensemble des paramètres [constituant] la base de la concertation, soit parce que l'on prend un train en marche, soit parce que l'on ne dispose pas du tout des informations utiles. »

Mais, il faut veiller à ce que tous les acteurs qui détiennent le pouvoir de bloquer la mécanique soient pris en compte. Il s'agit de comprendre les avantages et inconvénients d'une réforme, en matière d'influence, de notoriété, de financements et d'accès à l'information. Cela permet d'apprécier les stratégies des différents acteurs et mesurer la faisabilité du processus de concertation, en particulier pour les moyens qui seront disponibles pour mettre en oeuvre les décisions ou les mesures qui seront prises.

La concertation doit se faire dans un souci d'efficacité et se mettre au service d'une véritable dynamique locale. Il n'est pas nécessaire d'inventer des simulacres de concertation sous forme de « vernis démocratique », servant à séduire, mais qui ne permettent pas l'avancement de la situation locale. L'initiative de concertation entre acteurs est trop souvent à l'actif des officiers des Affaires civiles. Certes, les partenaires sont convaincus de l'importance des processus de concertation entre acteurs, mais il n'est pas rare de voir ce type de procédé se heurter à des blocages en raison des résistances corporatistes de ceux qui craignent la remise en cause de leur pouvoir.

Si les concertations vont bon train, les réunions sont conduites à différents niveaux de la région et au niveau national, puis des documents de politique sont rédigés et des restitutions sont organisées à ces différents niveaux…

Malheureusement, l'étape qui consiste à transformer l'essai en intervention concrète dans lequel pourraient s'inscrire les financements externes n'aboutit que rarement. Mais, en appui institutionnel, les officiers des Affaires civiles sont comme « des travailleurs de l'ombre », obligés à naviguer entre plusieurs dossiers à la fois ; à gérer dans l'urgence, les notes de fonds, pour une autorité qui veut y voir plus clair sur les options qu'il a en matière de décentralisation ou de privatisation ; à participer à des réunions de travail parfois fastidieuses sur le système d'information du ministère, alors qu'il sait que les statistiques sont fausses et/ou non utilisées, tout en suivant le déroulement de missions d'appui à tel ou tel projet et en aidant la secrétaire à faire fonctionner son ordinateur…quand il y a du courant !

De tout se qui précède, il semble que les rôles joués par les officiers des Affaires civiles reposent sur des capacités à :

- accomplir les fonctions pédagogiques, en montrant aux différents acteurs, l'intérêt des démarches et outils mis en place, afin que les actions mises en oeuvre ne soient pas considérées comme extérieures et aient des chances de se poursuivre indépendamment de lui ;
- assurer une fonction de médiation par l'usage des compétences techniques d'abord, pour être pris
- au sérieux. La diplomatie étant l'art du compromis, elle sert à favoriser la création des dynamiques permettant de mettre en oeuvre la médiation, pour atteindre les résultats attendus ;
- jouer le rôle de gestionnaire des ressources humaines, c'est-à-dire savoir repérer et s'appuyer sur les compétences et les motivations existantes pour avancer ;
- gérer la concertation avec l'ensemble du personnel du système des Nations unies, pour la plus grande efficacité et pertinence des actions de coopération.

Le but est de générer un climat de confiance, qui rendrait tout le reste possible.

La concertation a pour objectif d'initier auprès des acteurs concernés, une capitalisation, des échanges et des débats sur les différentes approches, façons de faire et types d'appui à apporter face au changement institutionnel des pays en développement. Celui-ci doit être perçu comme un processus dynamique, qui suppose un accompagnement des évolutions en cours, principalement autour de la définition des règles du jeu, du partage des fonctions entre les acteurs et du renforcement des capacités de ces acteurs. Parmi les sujets abordés figurent, notamment le rôle de l'Etat, les relations publiques-privées et l'Etat-collectivités locales, puis leurs modalités : concertation, médiation, négociation …

Cette dernière est très utilisée par l'officier des Affaires civiles qui doit souvent ménager, à la fois coopération et concurrence pour atteindre les objectifs de la mission.

e. La « Négociation » dans le Jargon de l'officier des Affaires civiles

La négociation peut se définir comme étant une forme de communication qui permet à l'officier des Affaires civiles de parvenir à un accord, en se basant sur des bénéfices mutuels, à travers la discussion. Elle passe parfois par la médiation qui est caractérisée par l'intervention d'un tiers. Dans la négociation, l'officier des Affaires civiles dispose de deux alternatives : soit il recherche un accord créatif, en s'appuyant sur les positions et les intérêts communs ; soit il veut aboutir au meilleur accord possible, ce qui s'obtient par la coopération et les concessions. Sont considérées comme positions, les arguments évoqués pour convaincre l'autre, ou plutôt les déclarations explicites et précises de ce que chaque partie souhaite obtenir à l'issue de la négociation, sans oublier leur approche de la situation.

Les positions ont parfois l'avantage de représenter les prédispositions à satisfaire les intérêts et les besoins réels qu'elles sous-entendent. C'est par le dialogue que l'officier des Affaires civiles peut diagnostiquer ces préoccupations réelles, pour les contrebalancer avec la découverte des itinéraires alternatifs de sortie de crise et atteindre les résultats. Ainsi, le rôle de l'officier des Affaires civiles peut se résumer à la recherche d'une compréhension mutuelle entre les intérêts et les besoins les plus profonds que chacune des parties souhaite satisfaire. Evidemment, ces exigences reflètent souvent les envies, les inquiétudes ou les craintes qui justement, expliquent généralement les positions exprimées.

Dans une négociation, lorsqu'un camp campe sur ses positions, le chevauchement entre les enjeux et les intérêts n'apparaît pas clairement. Le cas échéant, la solution idéale serait d'élargir la discussion et examiner de plus près les faits, afin de mieux comprendre ce que les parties essayent de réaliser. C'est à partir de cela qu'il est possible de percevoir les intérêts communs qui du moins, ne sont pas en concurrence.

Normalement, les homologues des Affaires civiles sont plus explicites quant à leur situation que sur leurs intérêts. L'officier des Affaires civiles doit devoir lire entre les lignes et utiliser toutes les informations à sa connaissance pour tirer les marrons du feu.

L'un des facteurs décisifs à la négociation est l'ouverture aux questions de clarification permettant de faciliter la compréhension. Les acteurs de la négociation, établissent souvent des limites qu'ils décident de ne pas franchir. Cela représente environ le minimum d'intérêts qu'ils comptent protéger. Toutefois, la ligne de fond est soumise à un dilemme : lorsqu'elle est mise trop basse, l'on est susceptible d'accepter un accord que l'on ne souhaite pas réellement.

Dans ce cas, il est parfois préférable de ne pas s'engager dans un accord du tout. En revanche, lorsque la ligne de fond est trop élevée, il est fort probable que l'accord qui en découle soit effectivement bon. Il est cependant possible d'envisager une ligne de fond de façon naturelle, c'est-à-dire en pensant à ce qui serait un résultat positif par rapport à l'alternative de ne pas aboutir à un accord du tout. Dans le jargon de la négociation, on parle de « meilleure solution de rechange à un accord négocié. » Cela signifie que la viabilité de la solution peut avoir un impact important sur la force de l'officier des Affaires civiles dans une négociation.

Il est donc nécessaire de prévoir la position qui sera la sienne et celle de son homologue en cas de non-accord, afin de mieux connaître ses limites et celles de l'autre et par là, orienter le débat vers certaines contraintes de base de la négociation. La force de la position de chacune des parties dans la négociation est directement liée à l'attrait de la solution de rechange, même s'il y a beaucoup d'autres facteurs qui peuvent directement influencer les alternatives.

Visiblement, chaque partie négocie pour un résultat plus bénéfique que les limites à ne pas franchir qu'il s'était fixé. Alors, il est essentiel de prévoir ses bornes pour éviter d'aboutir à un « mauvais » accord. Mais le fait de prédire les limites ou la capacité de négociation de son homologue et qui consiste à générer des options conduit souvent à un « bon » accord.

Grosso modo, une négociation se complique quand :

- la hiérarchie et les relations de pouvoir sont inégales ;
- le favoritisme ou la partialité s'impose ;
- les conflits d'intérêts prennent le dessus ;
- la faible participation ou mauvaise représentation des parties ;
- les rivalités personnelles et les conflits institutionnels sont grands.

Ces paramètres limitatifs renforcent la capacité de négocier à tel point qu'envisager les façons d'améliorer la maîtrise de ses limites est un effort précieux permettant d'utiliser le moins possible d'alternatives. Par contre, exagérer sur la force ou la faiblesse de ses limites est une tactique contre-productive. Le négociateur averti va néanmoins essayer d'étudier les possibilités d'affaiblir son homologue, en jouant sur les barrières à ne pas dépasser et en prenant le soin de ne pas porter atteinte aux bonnes relations qui sont capitales dans la coordination.

f. Enjeux de la Coordination

Au regard des termes de référence de l'officier des Affaires civiles, la section des Affaires civiles est en définitive, une section de coordination. Cette tâche est certainement la plus lourde qui pèse sur le dos d'un officier des Affaires civiles en général et du chef de bureau, en particulier. Faisant partie de la tradition onusienne du « mythe de Sisyphe[38] », la coordination est l'outil de travail de l'officier des Affaires civiles qui lui permet de :

- rendre compatible les programmes spécifiques de chaque entité, dans le but d'harmoniser l'ensemble des activités de la mission, y compris les agences ;
- éviter la duplication ;
- organiser les activités des composantes de la mission, afin de maximiser le résultat ;
- économiser le temps et les ressources, tant sur le plan matériel que financier ;
- réduire la confusion, en uniformisant le message à la population hôte.

---

[38] Titre de l'essai rédigé par Albert Camus, publié en 1942

Elle peut se définir comme étant un processus collectif interdépendant, mais respectueux de l'autonomie et du plan de travail de chaque entité de la mission. La coordination sert à maximiser les résultats tout en minimisant le gaspillage des ressources.

Le concept coordination contient en soi une dimension de la négociation. En effet, toutes les entités d'une mission n'ont pas les mêmes objectifs, parfois elles ont plutôt des programmes spécifiques qui deviennent incompatibles. Puisque, « l'union fait la force » alors, il convient de reconnaitre que la coordination est plus efficace qu'une approche individuelle ou isolée. Elle repose sur un calcul souvent implicite des coûts et profits de chaque partenaire pouvant influencer les résultats.

De ce fait, le coordonateur en l'occurrence l'officier des Affaires civiles doit analyser les intérêts spécifiques de chaque groupe, leurs positions, les objectifs qu'ils visent, afin de faire valoir les intérêts communs. Il doit se fonder sur les bénéfices que chaque partie peut tirer du processus de coordination pour mieux rassembler et créer « l'engagement conjoint », résultat des croyances partagées permettant de faire face à un sujet pluriel issu des obligations et objectifs conjoints, ce qui nécessitent une action commune, liée, unifiée, conformément au principe de réaction commune. Cela l'oblige à mettre impérativement en avant, les avantages de la coordination, en montrant comment cette démarche peut aider l'ensemble des partenaires à atteindre leurs objectifs et profiter davantage de la relation de coordination.

La réussite d'une mission de maintien de la paix dépend de la coopération et l'intégration de l'ensemble des activités de tous les autres acteurs forts ou faibles, réunissant leurs efforts collectifs dans un contexte particulier. En raison de leur flexibilité et de leur portée, due à leur présence active et la motivation, les Affaires civiles prennent le « lead » de la force et la cohérence de l'ONU, pour faire l'interface entre les acteurs politiques et ceux de sécurité, d'une part et de l'autre, les acteurs humanitaires et ceux du développement, à travers la planification efficace et le partage d'informations. La coordination se fait d'abord avec les acteurs internes de la mission, c'est-à-dire : les militaires, les UNPOL et les autres composantes de la mission. Elle intègre aussi les agents de développement et les acteurs humanitaires, notamment les ONG. Une bonne coordination devrait aussi intégrer les acteurs nationaux qui travaillent pour les mêmes objectifs explicites, tels que les autorités locales ou nationales et les associations, ainsi que les organisations non gouvernementales du pays.

Elle est surtout caractérisée par un soutien mutuel destiné à éviter la duplication des interventions, à travers l'échange d'informations avec d'autres acteurs. Il faut savoir qui fait quoi et où. La coordination permet d'atteindre des objectifs communs, par la combinaison des efforts et des contributions de tous les partenaires.

Coordonner suppose planifier et la planification est un instrument efficace d'une part, pour entretenir un partenariat et d'autre part, pour faciliter l'identification des objectifs communs et prévoir la distribution des tâches. La coordination ne sera fonctionnelle que si et seulement si, les structures et procédures sont efficaces, mais aussi si des relations solides pouvant amener les membres à travailler en équipe sont réunies. Les structures et procédures de coordination peuvent être ad hoc ou formelles, selon les partenaires et selon qu'elles soient convenues de manière centralisée.

Quant aux mécanismes de coordination, ils varient d'un contexte à l'autre. Il est important d'identifier, et, si possible, de construire les structures de coordination sur les cendres de celles qui ont survécu à la crise, ou celles qui ont été établies par les partenaires locaux ou internationaux avant le déploiement de la mission. Ce que les Affaires civiles peuvent donc faire c'est de chercher à encourager et, si nécessaire, renforcer ces structures existantes, initiées par les locaux ou les prédécesseurs sur le dossier.

La coordination prend souvent la forme de rencontres d'informations sur les acteurs : ce qu'ils font, avec quel groupe ou sous-groupe, dans quels secteurs spécifiques… C'est une occasion pour les Affaires civiles de proposer une stratégie liée au contexte, aux acteurs et aux faits. Cela ressemble à une séance d'information et de débats, parfois tenues en présence des autorités locales et des organismes de la société civile sur les questions touchant : la sécurité, l'information du public, les droits de l'homme, les élections, et cetera. A travers la coordination les Affaires civiles soutiennent les autorités locales et la société civile, ce qui concourt à promouvoir la transparence dans l'unité pour les uns et pour les autres.

Cependant, la coordination a ses propres défis. Ceux-ci sont abordés selon le niveau de politisation de l'environnement socioétatique et par rapport au libre-échange des informations. La coordination peut aussi se faire à travers la circulation par courriel et des documents écrits, sur la base du travail que les différents acteurs mènent avec des membres inscrits dans une liste préétablie de distribution. C'est une démarche peu recommandable à l'officier des Affaires civiles tout comme celle qui consiste à travailler quotidiennement par le biais des contacts bilatéraux journaliers avec les partenaires.

Dans ce domaine, ce qui compte est d'instaurer des bonnes relations de travail avec toute l'équipe, mais aussi le respect des principes de coopération. C'est ce qui permet de travailler dans des endroits reculés, avec des collègues venant de différentes organisations et cultures. Il faut développer des relations personnelles fortes pour faciliter le travail d'équipe. Malgré tout, il faut aussi tenir compte du fait que les membres qui ne viennent pas toujours de la même organisation n'obéissent pas à des méthodes de travail identiques et parfois, ils sont très ou peu efficaces. De surcroît, ils apportent des expertises différentes.

Pour y remédier, une bonne équipe de coordination doit refléter les caractéristiques suivantes :

- donner la possibilité à chaque acteur d'apporter pleinement sa contribution et bien clarifier le rôle de chacun ;
- comprendre et respecter la motivation des autres, puis inclure la contribution de chaque acteur ;
- garder la même vision et poursuivre des objectifs communs ;
- échanger les informations par le biais d'une communication ouverte et informelle pour plus d'efficacité ;
- ne pas paniquer en cas de désaccord, mais les adresser sans mauvais sentiments, car ce sont des situations normales.

En effet, le manque de liberté d'expression dans le cadre du partage d'informations constitue souvent un facteur de complication pour la coordination. Les causes de l'échec de la coordination sont multiples : la bataille sur l'exclusivité du rapport sur un événement, les problèmes particuliers, la concurrence des acteurs constituant des sources des informations distinctes... Dans ce cas, il convient de :

- se focaliser sur la confiance et développer des relations personnelles ;
- toujours attribuer le crédit au méritant et de manière appropriée ;
- se rassembler autant que possible sur les grands objectifs acceptés par l'équipe et sur la vision commune ;
- analyser les facteurs incitatifs et dissuasifs régissant la coopération avec les différents acteurs et se concentrer sur les motivations ;
- établir un niveau minimum d'échange des informations et instituer des mécanismes formels permettant de les garantir ;
- se concentrer sur les idées constructives et les partenaires volontaristes.
- A bien voir, la coordination va de paire avec la planification.

Et l'exercice de planification consiste à identifier les points d'intervention. Dans ce domaine, il n'existe aucune formule simple et rapide pour trouver des points de levier qui, par ailleurs, ne sont pas souvent intuitifs à cause de la complexité des connexions.

Généralement, les interventions réussies impliquent les facteurs à l'origine de l'évolution de la crise, ceux dont la modification entraînerait un changement significatif dans le système. Mais, il faut avant tout identifier les liens et leurs faiblesses, afin d'imaginer les possibilités de briser ces liens entre les facteurs. Il faut aussi déterminer les dynamiques positives qui peuvent être renforcées, étant donné que le mandat, les ressources, les structures, l'accès à l'information… place l'officier des Affaires civiles en position d'influencer le conflit directement ou en mobilisant d'autres partenaires.

Les situations, telles que : les élections, le départ des vieux acteurs et l'arrivée des nouveaux, les changements dans la dynamique internationale ou régionale, l'accès à des nouvelles informations, peuvent également influer sur l'analyse du conflit. Cette analyse est appelée à être régulièrement mise à jour autant que la situation change. En ce sens, le partage de l'analyse s'impose avec les membres de l'équipe ayant participé aux discussions, car c'est avec eux que se feront les adaptations.

Toutefois, une analyse en forme narrative et concise est plus appropriée et facile à comprendre au lieu des représentations graphiques difficiles à partager avec les profanes au processus. Pour maximiser le potentiel de réussite d'une coordination ou d'une facilitation, l'officier des Affaires civiles doit utiliser des techniques qui lui donneront la possibilité :

- d'augmenter les avantages du consensus, afin de changer les modes de calcul et d'influence, fondés sur les coûts et profits ;
- de développer les procédés et les compétences de gestion des réunions de coordination ;
- de renforcer les compétences en leadership ;
- d'accroître les capacités d'écoute.

Aussi, la coordination est conditionnée par :

- le partage d'informations ;
- la priorisation des problèmes à prendre à coeur ;
- l'élaboration de propositions constructives et pertinentes ;
- la prise de décisions collectives, mais sur la base de critères communs ;
- le suivi et l'évaluation des réunions de coordination.

Il existe plusieurs méthodes de coordination, parmi lesquelles :

- la communication informelle ;
- la diplomatie bilatérale ;
- le cadre informel de discussion au sein du groupe ;
- les petits groupes de travail ;
- les réunions « intenses » ;
- les rencontres pour le partage des informations, en vue de faire l'analyse et le suivi communs des activités entreprises.

Les principaux critères de bonne gestion d'une réunion de coordination sont les suivants :

- préparer la rencontre ;
- imposer le timing pour la réunion et pour la prise de parole, gestion du temps oblige ;
- faire respecter les règles, tout en gérant les comportements difficiles ;
- identifier les points de divergence et les points de convergence, puis proposer des alternatives ;
- définir un processus de résolution des problèmes posés ;
- encourager la participation.
- La facilitation prend de mauvaises tournures lorsque :

- les objectifs sont mal définis ;
- la taille du groupe est trop importante ;
- l'ordre du jour est imprécis ;
- les participants adoptent des comportements perturbateurs ;
- la durée de la réunion est imprévisible[39].

Pour qu'une information soit utilisée efficacement, il faut des partenaires, auquel cas, elle sera sous-utilisée, faute d'ignorance sur son existence.

Les Affaires civiles sont bien placées pour obtenir les informations à travers les sondages d'opinion publique, les groupes de discussion et méthode publique de consultations.

La combinaison de ces méthodes dépend souvent du type d'informations requises, sans oublier les ressources, les capacités et les compétences disponibles.

Les Affaires civiles peuvent être appelées à recueillir des renseignements de base pour suivre les progrès par rapport aux repères.

L'analyse comparative est un type de processus de surveillance basée sur des points de référence par rapport auquel le changement et les progrès peuvent être mesurés. Il consiste à prédéfinir un objectif qui va ensuite être utilisé pour le monitoring ou l'évaluation des progrès accomplis dans le cadre de la consolidation de la paix. Il existe un ensemble de repères qu'il faut prendre en considération parmi lesquels :

- encourager le principe de contribution et d'attribution, en établissant des liens de causalité entre les entrées, sorties, les résultats et l'impact, ce qui se fait sur la base des contributions aux interventions particulières en rapport avec le résultat souhaité, en particulier dans l'environnement où une variété de facteurs constitue un enjeu. Le but est d'éviter d'isoler certaines activités à partir des facteurs pouvant conduire à des résultats inattendus ;
- privilégier les méthodes quantitatives et qualitatives utilisées de manière complémentaire pour maximiser les avantages comparatifs respectifs en relation avec le contexte particulier dans lequel ils sont appliqués. Les approches quantitatives facilitent le traitement des données linéaires, tandis que les techniques qualitatives aident à analyser les considérations d'ordre supérieur, telles que : l'évaluation des théories du changement et la pertinence d'une approche particulière de programmation ;
- l'utilisation des processus d'identification des repères et des indicateurs, notamment lorsqu'il y a de multiples acteurs impliqués à l'échelle du système d'évaluations.

---

[39] Voir Liam Mahomy, Trainer-Fieldview solutions, « Tailored in-mission skills training for Civil Affairs Officers », MINUSTAH, Haiti, du 6 au 9 juin 2011, Port-au-Prince

L'objectif est de forger une compréhension commune des résultats à atteindre, notamment dans la prise de décision stratégique des processus engagés. Certes, la conciliation des perspectives concurrentes est très difficile, mais ceux qui aident à formuler des points de repère devraient faciliter leurs applications, en contribuant à atténuer les éventuels malentendus méthodologiques et analytiques lors de la mise en oeuvre.

Toutefois, les interventions des Affaires civiles peuvent avoir des conséquences non intentionnelles, en matière d'impact social, économique et environnemental, ce qui peut marquer une population donnée. Il est donc nécessaire de surveiller les conséquences inattendues et imprévues se référant aux effets secondaires générés par les interventions des officiers des Affaires civiles dans ce type de système complexe. Ces conséquences involontaires peuvent être prévues ou intentionnelles ou encore surgir par surprise totale. C'est un phénomène naturel et prévisible dans toute intervention. Il doit être anticipé en consultation avec les homologues locaux et par rapport aux différentes façons dont la communauté locale pourrait réagir à l'intervention. Les Affaires civiles doivent également se préparer à réajuster leurs interventions éventuelles en fonction des possibles conséquences négatives qu'elles peuvent détecter.

g. Les Premiers « Pas » de l'officier des Affaires civiles

Lorsqu'un officier des Affaires civiles atterrit sur le terrain, les premières démarches à entreprendre sont : connaître et comprendre le cadre juridique global et l'architecture institutionnelle de l'Etat ou de la collectivité territoriale de son lieu d'affectation. Il doit faire sa propre évolution historique, en termes de dynamique du pouvoir, pour comprendre comment il lui sera possible de renforcer leur efficacité, tout en gagnant la confiance de la population locale. Pour cela, il a besoin des instruments/informations suivants :

- la Constitution/loi fondamentale de l'État. Ce document décrit l'architecture institutionnelle de l'Etat et permet d'apprécier le niveau de centralisation et/ou de décentralisation de l'Etat et pourquoi pas le niveau effectif de la mise en oeuvre des dispositions constitutionnelles ;
- le respect du cadre légal. Les lois en vigueur dans le pays d'accueil, la compilation des textes de loi sur les collectivités territoriales, le recueil de textes normatifs entourant l'action locale, ainsi que les notes circulaires, instructions administratives et autres principes de gestion dans le cadre de leur action de coaching et/ou de monitoring, notamment sur les collectivités territoriales ;
- la structure du gouvernement central. Elle sert à connaître les fondements de la division du travail et les responsabilités entre les principaux ministères impliqués dans le gouvernement local, afin

d'identifier les interlocuteurs appropriés. C'est ce qui facilite l'échange de communication et/ou l'identification de solutions viables pour un problème spécifique ;

- les autorités locales et leurs attributions légales. Ici, il est question de connaître l'origine du pouvoir des autorités décentralisées et déconcentrées ; s'elles sont élues ou nommés, si ces pouvoirs sont reconnus par la loi ou par des institutions gouvernementales locales... Ceci est nécessaire pour comprendre le rôle qu'ils joueront dans le domaine de la gouvernance locale, la place des autorités traditionnelles ayant une influence sur l'histoire et la morale, mais aussi la solidité de ces pouvoirs. Il s'agit aussi d'apprécier leur impact potentiel sur les activités des institutions d'appui de l'Etat ;
- la gestion locale des finances publiques. Il convient de prendre connaissance des grands principes de gestion communale, fondés sur respect de la loi fiscale et du budget de la commune avec lesquels il faut se familiariser. Il s'agit de savoir si les autorités locales perçoivent des impôts directement ou reçoivent seulement les allocations de l'Etat. Cela permettra de comprendre le niveau d'autonomie de ces collectivités territoriales, puis comment les mécanismes de transfert d'argent entre le niveau local et central vont être utiles dans la prévention des conflits institutionnels. C'est un élément qui permet aussi de saisir la structure budgétaire des communes et l'autonomie dont elles disposent dans la fixation des priorités, ainsi que les exigences du renforcement des capacités ;
- le statut de la fonction publique qui sous-entend celui des fonctionnaires territoriaux. Est-il réglementé par une loi spécifique ou associée à des fonctionnaires nationaux ? Y a-t-il des règles concernant le recrutement ou s'agit-il des arrangements contractuels ? Quelles sont les grilles de salaires, et cetera. Ces aspects constituent un ensemble des indicateurs qui ouvre la porte à l'appréciation de la motivation du personnel et son professionnalisme, étant donné que la gouvernance locale est plus prévisible et moins sujette à la corruption lorsqu'il existe des règles clairement établies ;
- le statut juridique des organisations de la société civile. Comment l'Etat traite et définit les organisations de la société civile, sous quels mécanismes ? Ces interrogations ouvrent la voie à la définition d'une approche et l'identification des interlocuteurs appropriés au niveau local.

Toutefois, dans certains cas de situation de post-conflit, le processus de prise de décision est limité dans la capitaleet dans les grands centres urbains, surtout si la structure théorique de l'Etat est centralisée. En pareilles circonstances, l'officier des Affaires civiles sera impliqué à la fois dans la restauration de l'autorité de l'Etat et dans son prolongement, en soutenant la présence étatique dans les zones où elle n'a jamais existé et lorsqu'elle a été absent pendant un temps plus ou moins prolongé. Il est clair qu'il est plus facile de promouvoir les principes de la bonne gouvernance dans le cas d'un Etat décentralisé puisque le niveau des responsabilités de l'autorité locale est beaucoup plus élevé en vertu du lien évident entre la bonne gouvernance locale et la décentralisation. En effet, sans aucune autonomie administrative ni financière, les systèmes de gouvernance locale ne seront pas en mesure de satisfaire les besoins des citoyens. Et, sans une bonne gouvernance locale, les subventions et les aides financières de l'Etat et de la communauté internationale, ainsi que le transfert des responsabilités aux différents paliers de la décentralisation, courent le risque de se dissiper.

Toutefois, il n'est pas question de faire la promotion d'un modèle d'Etat en particulier, prudence oblige. Les implications politiques sensibles au contexte propre peuvent parfois porter atteinte à la souveraineté nationale. Par exemple, le peut effectivement mettre un fardeau excessif et supplémentaire.

Sur les maigres ressources disponibles, tant humaines que financières. Adieu à la viabilité de l'Etat, ce qui entraine le risque de replonger la nation dans la controverse et peut occasionner l'émergence du conflit.

h. Défis et Stratégies de Réponses Possibles

Le travail des Affaires civiles ne peut être apprécié si la population locale ne reçoit pas les dividendes de paix qui ne sont autres que les bénéfices immédiats de la participation au dialogue, telles que : l'amélioration de la sécurité, la baisse de tension, la prévention des dommages à la propriété et la qualité de vie sociale, surtout lorsque les acteurs locaux méconnaissent la valeur de la participation aux efforts de gestion des conflits.

Si le dialogue initial peut se concentrer à bâtir ou rétablir le contact et les relations entre les parties, il n'en demeure pas moins qu'il faut qu'il soit lié à un processus plus vaste qui règle les questions concrètes, au cas contraire, l'intérêt des participants s'estompera et pourrait finir par déclencher de nouveaux conflits. Par conséquent, même si les Affaires civiles n'ont pas les ressources ni le mandat de traiter globalement les causes profondes des conflits, ils peuvent néanmoins, contribuer à mobiliser les ressources ou la volonté politique, pour traiter les questions spécifiques liées à la sécurité, la justice, la vie chère, la précarité, la fracture sociale, l'emploi, la gestion des ressources naturelles, etc. ; à travers des plaidoyers auprès des structures de la mission, du gouvernement, des donateurs, des partenaires et des agences internationales.

Le dialogue ou la réconciliation mal conçu ou géré peut creuser à nouveau, la division et approfondir les préjugés, surtout si les questions clés ou celles qui s'avèrent potentiellement difficiles pour faire avancer le dialogue ne sont pas identifiées. Cependant, il ne doit pas être trop ambitieux, mais réaliste sur les compétences et les capacités au sein de l'équipe, pour s'assurer de la compétence et l'expérience nécessaire à l'apaisement des tensions.

En réalité, la gestion des conflits demeure le terrain de prédilection des Affaires politiques. Les Affaires civiles interviennent dans ce secteur lorsqu'il n'y a pas d'autres ressources humaines ou institutions plus appropriées, au risque de désemparer les acteurs locaux. Ce rôle de premier plan est une option de dernier recours, qui doit être menée sans maladresse, notamment dans la présentation des modèles de gestion des conflits, en donnant aux participants l'espace d'examiner si et comment, ces approches répondent à la situation en cours d'analyse.

Il n'est pas vain de souligner que la stratégie de réponse aux défis rencontrés par les Affaires civiles se conjugue avec les éléments suivants :

- légitimité. Dans certains cas les Affaires civiles auront besoin de reconstruire une légitimité compromise et la confiance entre les institutions gouvernementales et les citoyens. Une nuance doit être faite entre la confiance dans les institutions en tant que telle et celle accordée à des personnes qui représentent ces institutions. La légitimité des Affaires civiles est issue de leur appartenance à l'ONU. Elle devrait être dépensée en faveur des institutions étatiques, pour aider les collectivités territoriales à acquérir la légitimité dans leurs circonscriptions locales sans compromettre la leur, par des liens trop étroits avec les représentants de ces institutions, surtout lorsqu'elles ont une réputation négative. La crédibilité d'un processus post-conflictuel dépend des capacités de l'officier des Affaires civiles à établir un équilibre entre faire une critique constructive et soutenir des personnes représentant les institutions, avec les efforts de transmettre quelques-unes des préoccupations majeures de la circonscription locale ;
- faible niveau d'engagement des autorités locales. Lorsque les autorités locales sont nommées par l'une des parties en conflit, sur la base de considérations politiques, il est possible que certains responsables locaux soient résistants aux changements et hostiles à la promotion des principes de la bonne gouvernance. Il ne serait pas surprenant qu'elles considèrent l'intervention extérieure comme une ingérence injustifiée. Dans ces circonstances, il convient d'adopter une approche efficace et réactive à l'administration publique. Malheureusement, ces attitudes sont susceptibles de persister même après des élections libres et transparentes, en particulier dans le contexte des démocraties immatures ;
- absence ou incohérence du cadre juridique. Ce sont des situations où la Constitution et/ou les autres lois organiques ne fournissent pas

suffisamment de clarté sur la mise en place des institutions. C'est aussi le cas des dispositions irréalistes par rapport au contexte de conjoncture de crise où il faut soutenir les réformes, leur nature et la procédure, quand bien même, les résultats ne seraient pas attendus dans le court ou moyen terme. En outre, dans cette incertitude juridique, il faut rester cohérent avec l'objectif ultime de promouvoir la bonne gouvernance au sein des institutions étatiques ;

- existence d'une crise institutionnelle. Dans ce cas, il faut faciliter le dialogue par des solutions négociées et s'engager dans la diffusion de ces tensions et conflits entre les institutions ayant des responsabilités et des mandats en compétition. C'est souvent le cas entre la DGI et la mairie ou lorsque les parlementaires se voient confier des sommes colossales d'argent pour faire le développement dans les communes, ou encore entre les élus locaux et le représentant du gouvernement central chargé de ce domaine ;
- défaut et/ou faiblesse des infrastructures. Les conflits entraînent souvent la destruction des installations et équipements, ainsi que la mémoire institutionnelle, sous la forme d'archives, des documents et dossiers perdus. Dans ces conditions, les projets à impacts rapides serviront à rétablir un certain niveau de base de l'espace de travail et des capacités auquel il faut ajouter la formation pour la restauration de la mémoire institutionnelle, notamment les dossiers administratifs internes : la masse salariale, les dossiers financiers, les stocks d'équipements et de propriétés. Lorsqu'ils sont définitivement perdus ou n'avaient jamais existé, il est impératif de les reconstituer en priorité. Il en est de même pour les documents d'état civil comme les actes de naissance, décès, état civil, etc. requis par les citoyens comme pièce d'identité, les titres fonciers et de propriété. Même s'il faut reconnaitre la complexité de ces questions controversées, qui de surcroît nécessitent à la fois l'expertise technique adéquate et la sensibilité politique pour être traitées, l'officier des Affaires civiles a tout à gagner en essayant de la faire ;
- incompétence professionnelle, sureffectif du personnel et bas salaires. Ces questions nécessitent une réforme radicale de la fonction publique entrainant, notamment : la rationalisation des effectifs, l'introduction d'un processus de recrutement public et transparent, création ou restauration des écoles publiques d'administrations, amélioration de la grille salariale... Toutefois, la résistance politique et le manque chronique de ressources obligent parfois les Affaires civiles à se contenter de ne faire que des évaluations des capacités, en vue de leur renforcement par la formation. Elles se contentent parfois de se limiter à développer des outils et mécanismes pour surveiller la performance des

administrations publiques. Le but est d'augmenter les capacités à répondre de façon ad hoc à des problèmes structurels ;

- faibles revenus. Si les recettes d'un pays brisé, ayant accumulé des années des échecs endémiques sont mal organisées, comment peut-on penser que la base de revenus ne puisse pas être pauvre. Bien entendu, les institutions responsables de la collecte des impôts, dans ces pays n'ont pas d'actif de taille économique, industriel ou commercial et battent les records en matière de corruption. C'est sans compter que la population est dépourvue de culture de payement des impôts et que ceux qui le peuvent, sont réticents à le faire, puisqu'ils ne reçoivent aucun service en retour. Or, sans ces revenus générés localement, les institutions d'Etat ne seront jamais en mesure de fournir les services de base à cette communauté dont la démographie est galopante. Cela traduit le manque de confiance que les citoyens ont en leurs dirigeants. Il appartient aux officiers des Affaires civiles d'effectuer des analyses précises de ces circonstances particulières, avant de se lancer dans la promotion ou la facilitation des initiatives qui peuvent restaurer à niveau la confiance nécessaire : la promotion de la transparence, les initiatives anticorruption, les approches participatives, dans la définition des besoins et des priorités locales, etc. ;
- incompréhension des responsabilités liées à la gouvernance. En situation de post-conflit, on trouve paradoxalement beaucoup plus de connaisseurs de la procédure d'accès au pouvoir qu'autres experts, puisqu'on regarde que le droit et ses avantages. Peu sont ceux qui comprennent la responsabilité envers leur circonscription. Malheureusement, ces statistiques se retrouvent également parmi les électeurs qui pensent seulement en termes d'avantages individuels, plutôt que des services collectifs. C'est la conséquence directe de l'absence de l'Etat, ou d'une présence qui se manifeste autrement que par les abus de pouvoir, l'incompétence et/ou la négligence. Pour venir à bout de ces attitudes profondément enracinés et intrinsèques à une conception traditionnelle de la dynamique du pouvoir, l'officier des Affaires civiles doit travailler à la fois sur un changement d'attitude et de perception, ainsi que sur l'adoption de meilleurs mécanismes de « responsabilisation », sans oublier de promouvoir le type de culture de service public prévoyant des droits et des devoirs entre les administrateurs et leurs administrés. Il s'agit d'établir fermement la différence entre payer une taxe légitime et donner un pot-de-vin. Le lien entre le pouvoir de l'autorité et le devoir de fournir un service au public, ainsi que l'amélioration de la sécurité et l'Etat de droit, facilitent la diffusion d'informations concernant les outils juridiques disponibles pour la lutte contre les abus de pouvoir ou l'obligation de fournir les

services non dus à la population. Les instruments de cette stratégie sont les campagnes de sensibilisation et d'éducation civique ;

- collaboration avec les autorités locales controversées. Il arrive souvent que la restauration de l'autorité étatique exige de travailler avec des représentants des administrations locales qui ne sont pas appréciés par la population et compromet l'impartialité de l'ONU. Dans ce cas, il faut rester sensible à ce contexte politique et affirmer son impartialité, tout en restant vigilants sur le respect des individus, de l'Etat de droit et des principes de la bonne gouvernance ;
- gestion des attentes. Les attentes suscitées par la présence d'une Mission de l'ONU dans le pays hôte, exigent souvent des solutions rapides dont la lenteur caractérise un manque de volonté politique, d'engagement, d'incompétence et se présente comme un signe marquant la poursuite des objectifs autres que ceux énoncés dans le mandat de l'ONU.

Il est donc important d'instaurer un dialogue honnête et ouvert qui expose clairement les limites du mandat, celles des opérations de maintien de la paix et en matière des ressources humaines et financières. L'objectif de la coordination est de prévoir un ensemble cohérent d'intervention, une méthodologie commune, ainsi que des instruments de coordination et de suivi pouvant être illustré par un exemple technique.

Dans les nations brisées par les conflits, on attend beaucoup d'un expert en appui institutionnel. Tout le monde s'accorde à dire que pour occuper ce type de fonctions, il faut avoir au préalable une expérience professionnelle de terrain. Par rapport à cela, il est possible de dégager le profil des compétences nécessaires à l'appui institutionnel, selon les tâches et fonctions à remplir, via celui de l'officier des Affaires civiles. D'ailleurs, toute cette rhétorique constituera un verbiage inutile si ce profil n'est pas établi.

E. PROFIL D'UN OFFICIER DES AFFAIRES CIVILES

Pour élaborer le profil de l'officier des Affaires civiles, il convient d'abord et avant tout de connaître ce qu'une section des Affaires civiles cherche à accomplir et comprendre comment ces objectifs peuvent influencer son comportement. Il faut ensuite rechercher les principes éthiques qui facilitent et/ou contraignent sa façon de travailler et/ou les stratégies qu'il doit mettre en oeuvre pour atteindre les objectifs prévus dans le mandat. Le tout pour aboutir à la détermination des qualités essentielles d'un officier des Affaires civiles.

Selon notre approche, le cadre normatif sur lequel se fondent la légitimité et la légalité d'une opération de maintien de la paix est :

- la Charte des Nations unies ;

- le droit international et le droit international des droits de l'homme ;
- le droit international humanitaire ;
- les mandats du Conseil de Sécurité.

Les autres facteurs additionnels de la légitimité sont le consentement des parties et/ou celui du gouvernement hôte, ainsi que la participation et le soutien des Etats Membres. Naturellement, ses facteurs peuvent être affectés par la conduite du personnel sur le terrain et par les résultats obtenus par les Affaires civiles. Sous un autre registre, ces facteurs peuvent constituer des causes d'illégitimité. Quant aux facteurs de crédibilité, il y a :

- la perception de la section des Affaires civiles par la population ;
- l'appropriation nationale pour la direction, la gestion et la coordination du processus de développement appelé à contribuer et à prévenir les risques de retour à une situation de crise ;
- le contenu ou le type/la force du mandat ;
- le gap entre la nécessité de changements et les résultats immédiats ;
- la force de la mission et ses capacités, dans le cadre des Affaires civiles. Le budget alloué pour les QIP sont essentiels ;
- la cohérence interne et externe des acteurs agissant dans le cadre du mandat, notamment les composantes de la mission ;
- les capacités de communication ;
- la pérennité du travail des Affaires civiles ;
- la prise en compte de la complexité de la diversité locale. Cette prise en charge est à encourager à tous les niveaux.

Il est important de noter qu'une fois que cette crédibilité est perdue, il est très difficile de la reconquérir, ce qui fait que les Affaires civiles marchent sur des oeufs. Elles doivent absolument éviter de faire des interventions qui vont :

- nuire directement à la population ;
- entretenir des relations exécrables avec les autorités locales et la société civile ;
- attiser ou créer des conflits au sein et entre les communautés ;
- intégrer les officiers des Affaires civiles dans les réseaux de la mafia du pays ;
- légitimer les conflits ;
- endommager ou remplacer les capacités locales.

Bien au contraire, un bon officier des Affaires civiles est celui qui est capable de créer une appropriation nationale et locale qui facilite :

- la mise en oeuvre du mandat et son acceptation ;
- la pérennité du travail fourni ;
- le renforcement des capacités des autorités locales et de la société civile.

Il doit tenir compte de la complexité et de la diversité locale, puis comprendre que son travail sur le terrain peut générer des effets négatifs ou influencer les résultats de ses propres efforts. D'où la nécessité de respecter certaines valeurs et principes d'éthique comme :

- l'intégrité ;
- l'indépendance ;
- l'impartialité ;
- le professionnalisme ;
- la compétence ;
- le respect des droits de l'homme ;
- la non-discrimination ;
- le respect de la diversité ;
- l'interdiction d'abus de pouvoir ;
- le non recours à la force sauf en cas de légitime défense ou la défense du mandat ;
- l'obtention du consentement des parties dans la résolution des conflits ;
- la sensibilité personnelle et culturelle ;
- l'efficacité ;
- la patience ;
- l'humilité ;
- la flexibilité ;
- la créativité ;
- l'appui à l'appropriation locale ;
- l'approche positive de la résolution des problèmes et des conflits ;
- la vision à long terme.

Pour nous résumer, la patience, l'humilité et la flexibilité devraient être axées sur des résultats positifs. Cela signifie s'engager à sa tâche et aux objectifs à long terme, mais aussi avoir une attitude positive, tout en mettant l'accent sur l'« autonomisation » des populations locales et leur appropriation du processus. Le respect de la diversité contribue à avoir un esprit d'équipe et de consensus ; une ouverture d'esprit, la créativité, la ténacité et l'attitude de travailler durement. En outre, la volonté est un comportement personnel et exemplaire avant, pendant et après les heures de travail, afin de projeter et de maintenir une image positive de la mission au sein des communautés locales et des intervenants extérieurs, prêts à renforcer les relations positives, le respect mutuel et la bonne compréhension de la mission par la population locale. Il convient d'être conscient de la différence du pouvoir économique des populations hôtes en tant que bénéficiaires.

Enfin, il faut agir avec intelligence, dans la tolérance et avec sensibilité.

Les valeurs ethniques, religieuses, politiques, tribales et du genre, constituent souvent des caractéristiques des conflits, car ceux-ci transforment les relations sociales et les schémas d'exclusion à la fois à travers la création de nouveaux groupes vulnérables comme : les personnes ayant un handicap physique, les femmes chefs du ménage, les personnes déplacées ou rapatriées, ainsi que les minorités, jouent un rôle plus important dans le domaine public au niveau, à la fois local et national. C'est pour cette raison que les Affaires civiles sont priées de soutenir la participation et l'inclusion des diverses circonscriptions, tout en appuyant les efforts formels et informels qui concourent à la paix afin de tirer parti de nouvelles modalités qui s'ouvrent en période d'urgence politique.

La sensibilité culturelle nécessite la compréhension et la considération des croyances en vigueur : les normes, traditions, attitudes et pratiques en matière de planification et d'exécution des activités et l'interaction avec les communautés. Le défaut de tenir compte du contexte culturel local peut aboutir à des interventions inefficaces ou inutiles. De plus, cela risque d'endommager les relations avec les autorités et les communautés locales.

Cependant, être sensibles à une culture ne signifie pas qu'il faille considérer que toutes les structures locales ou traditionnelles, les mécanismes ou les processus sont fondamentalement bons, car les coutumes ou les pratiques locales peuvent parfois constituer des sources d'inégalités, d'injustices, d'exclusion sociale ou humaine, ou encore de violation des droits fondamentaux. Les Affaires civiles devraient donc promouvoir l'harmonisation entre les lois statutaires et coutumières, en travaillant avec les autorités traditionnelles, afin de développer une approche culturellement sensible, tout en respectant les principes de l'ONU. L'aspect culturel d'un pays post-conflictuel relève d'une importance capitale dans la résolution des différentes problématiques qui émergent dans ces circonstances. Dans ce domaine, l'officier des Affaires civiles doit savoir prendre du recul sur sa propre identité culturelle afin de mieux percevoir ses valeurs et croyances et oeuvrer en vue d'apprécier et de respecter les cultures distinctes de la sienne.

Le but d'une telle sensibilisation culturelle est de promouvoir la communication interculturelle et d'avoir une meilleure compréhension de ses actions, de ses perceptions et de celles d'autres catégories de gens qu'il trouve sur place. C'est de cette façon qu'il peut mieux interagir avec des communautés ayant d'autres cultures, surtout lorsqu'il s'agit d'apporter un soutien à un peuple en quête de paix et du développement durable.

L'Homme est le produit de son héritage culturel, ce qui influence non seulement sa façon de concevoir le monde qui l'entoure, mais aussi de se comporter par rapport à l'autre. De ce fait, l'officier des Affaires civiles est prié de s'approprier la culture du pays hôte avec beaucoup d'humanité et de respect. Ses informations sur les pratiques culturelles spécifiques lui donneront un aperçu sur les caractéristiques et les enjeux de cette culture et lui permettront d'identifier les besoins et les préférences de ces communautés. En outre, il sera outillé pour éviter de réduire cette population à la simple expression d'une norme culturelle.

En réalité, les conflits engendrent des comportements potentiels, des facteurs de stress et parfois des difficultés d'adaptation à la nouvelle société en construction, ainsi que des attitudes de repli ou de rejet de la paix et la réconciliation causées par : les traumatismes de guerre, l'instabilité politique, les changements de statuts socio-économiques, les violences physiques et psychologiques, les déplacements des réfugiés, les séparations des familles, les injustices de tous genres, et cetera.

Dans ce contexte de gestion des différends, l'officier des Affaires civiles est censé connaître le cadre socio-économique du terrain, le niveau d'éducation, la résidence rurale ou urbaine de ses partenaires, l'identification de ses interlocuteurs avec le cadre religieux..., auxquels il convient d'ajouter des attitudes d'approches appropriées, telles que :

- être conscient de sa propre culture et de son influence potentielle ;
- éviter de juger le comportement des gens en référence à ses propres normes de culture ;
- prendre soin de ne pas opiner et/ou généraliser sur les influences culturelles civilisatrices ;
- admettre la relativité des comportements et des croyances des gens au sein de la même culture ;
- comprendre l'importance des croyances culturelles et religieuses ;
- accorder une importance spéciale à la communication verbale et gestuelle ;
- approfondir ses connaissances culturelles du terrain par des séances d'information et/ou formation.

De toute évidence, la diversité culturelle et le développement sont intimement liés. L'expérience a montré que les sociétés dans lesquelles la diversité est respectée et encouragée montrent des signes de développement économique et social. De surcroît, la diversité est une des compétences de l'ONU que tout personnel doit savoir développer, raison de plus pour en faire bon usage dans la recherche des solutions de sortie définitive de crise.

Les fonctions de la section des Affaires civiles dessinent un profil idéal permettant de sélectionner les officiers des Affaires civiles sur la base des « qualifications », des compétences et des expériences suivantes :

- être titulaire d'un diplôme universitaire, au moins une licence en administration publique, en sciences politiques, en droit, en relations internationales, en économie ou toutes autres disciplines similaires ou connexes, qui touchent aux enjeux de développement local et durable ;
- avoir une certaine expérience pratique en administration publique et gestion, essentiellement relative aux questions du renforcement organisationnel, aux réformes de l'Etat ou celles qui mettent l'accent sur le développement institutionnel ;

- posséder une excellente capacité à transférer, transmettre les connaissances, notamment en matière d'andragogie, ainsi que des compétences avérées et une certaine intégrité ;
- disposer d'excellentes compétences en communication interpersonnelle et maîtriser au moins une langue de travail des Nations unies, entre le français et l'anglais ;
- détenir une bonne connaissance de l'usage des nouvelles technologies de l'information, notamment les applications du Microsoft Office ;
- faire montre d'une affinité ou d'un intérêt dans l'aide humanitaire, les situations post-crise, le volontariat comme un mécanisme pour le développement durable, sans oublier le système des Nations unies lui-même.

Il ne faut pas oublier qu'il revient à la section des Affaires civiles d'apporter des conseils et une expertise dans la restructuration et la formation du personnel et dans l'amélioration de la gestion administrative et des conditions de travail des autorités de base. Avec les collectivités territoriales les Affaires civiles agissent particulièrement dans le renforcement des services publics en milieu rural. Quant aux institutions publiques centrales, leur travail contribue à la réorganisation des services existants, y compris les préfectures et sous-préfectures.

Dans une mission de maintien de la paix, le succès est conditionné par une meilleure interaction entre les différentes unités qui composent le bureau régional pour traiter directement les besoins et problèmes qui sont d'ordre juridique, politique, économique et social, sur fond de planification, conception et harmonisation des formations. Ces exigences sont par la suite soumises à l'attention du ministère de l'intérieur pour information et/ou pour actions. Ce dernier peut créer des commissions spéciales pour traiter ces dossiers.

Le fonctionnement de la section des Affaires civiles exige pour ainsi dire une interaction ou une connexion avec les autres composantes du Bureau Régional et un partenariat avec le ministère des collectivités territoriales, celui du plan, de l'économie et des finances, sans oublier les autres entités publiques, telles que : la cour des comptes et la direction générale des impôts, ainsi que les hauts fonctionnaires et par l'élaboration d'une analyse des ressources humaines et la direction des collectivités territoriales.

L'une des attributions stratégiques des Affaires civiles est le devoir de « redynamiser » le ministère et la direction des collectivités territoriales dans la création de commissions spéciales de règlement des conflits. Ainsi, les officiers des Affaires civiles travaillent essentiellement avec l'Etat et les gouvernements locaux. Ils sont polyvalents puisqu'ils coopèrent aussi avec les ONG et les autorités déconcentrées de l'Etat, ainsi que la société civile.

Entre officiers, il n'y a pas de distinction dans la section même si le chef de bureau dispose des tâches supplémentaires de coordination et d'intégration. Les professionnels, les volontaires et les NPO (National Program Officer) sont recrutés sur la base des mêmes critères et font le même travail en tant qu'Officier des Affaires civiles. Ils sont invités à combler le vide des autres sections non représentées dans les bureaux régionaux, notamment celui laissé par la section des Affaires politiques, qui n'a presque jamais eu de personnel sur le terrain et oblige ses dirigeants à toujours solliciter les services des Affaires civiles. La section des Affaires civiles une section fourre-tout, composée d'experts de tous genres et venant de tous horizons et de n'importe quels domaines de la vie professionnelle, alors qu'elle devrait engager fondamentalement les politistes, administrateurs publics, juristes et économistes. Ensuite, en cas de carence, faire recours à d'autres secteurs d'activité ayant atteint un certain niveau d'études et ayant une certaine expériencc ou expertise en matière de gestion administrative de la société.

Quatre domaines d'expertise sont essentiels pour être un bon officier des Affaires civiles :

- la résolution et la prévention des conflits ;
- l'administration publique ;
- l'appui institutionnel ;
- la gestion des projets de développement financés à travers les programmes QIP.

La diversité des Affaires civiles est l'une de ses forces intrinsèques. Le personnel national apporte les connaissances locales et facilite les relations avec les autochtones. Par conséquent, il appartient au personnel international de comprendre ces normes culturelles, pour bâtir rapidement la confiance avec leurs homologues locaux.

Le spécialiste des Affaires civiles doit comprendre la dynamique locale pour être capable de construire la crédibilité de la mission aux yeux de la communauté d'accueil. Il doit se préparer à vivre dans des zones isolées avec des conditions de vie de base : sans confort matériel ni capacités technologiques ou sociales — le choix alimentaire et autres fournitures limitées, puis peu d'options de loisirs, — occasionnant le stress et limitant ainsi son engagement professionnel. En tant qu'Homme de terrain, il doit agir en leadership et en décideur capable de gagner la reconnaissance et la confiance de ces interlocuteurs et de la communauté d'accueil, même lorsqu'il est dans le contexte d'instabilité permanente ou exposé à des situations traumatisantes ou émotionnelles.

Dans le domaine du renforcement des institutions de l'Etat et de la gouvernance, les progrès ne se mesurent pas sur des mois, mais plutôt sur des années, voir des décennies. Aussi, l'officier des Affaires civiles doit apprécier la portée de son travail et sa valeur ajoutée supplémentaire dans le temps et l'espace. Il doit être en mesure de travailler sous pression, dans un environnement très stressant, puis s'adapter à différents voisinages, pour accomplir ses tâches principales : la gestion des conflits, l'appui institutionnel et la gestion des projets/programmes.

De tout ce qui précède, il n'est pas exagéré de conclure en précisant que la section des Affaires civiles est un département substantiel d'une mission de maintien de la paix de l'ONU. Elle est chargée de la coordination, l'intégration et la consolidation des activités de l'ensemble de la mission pour lesquelles tout officier des Affaires civiles est pour ainsi dire formaté, préparé et habilité à assurer. A ce titre, son rôle est aussi d'appuyer les autres sections substantielles en travaillant avec elles, en leurs fournissant des points focaux ou en les remplaçant.

Du coup, la mission de la section des Affaires civiles est de moderniser une administration de crise en une administration démocratique et décentralisée, à travers l'appui institutionnel, tant au niveau central qu'au niveau local. Elle possède comme partenaires essentiels : le gouvernement central, les parlementaires, les collectivités territoriales et la société civile organisée. Les Affaires civiles se focalisent particulièrement sur les questions de gouvernance locale et nationale, sur le développement de l'Etat de droit et l'autorité de l'Etat, ainsi que sur la gestion et le fonctionnement des instances de l'Etat. Dans ces conditions, le renforcement des capacités locales et institutionnelles devient un paramètre indispensable et incontournable. Il se conduit par une série de formations à donner aux autorités locales pour améliorer leurs qualités opérationnelles.

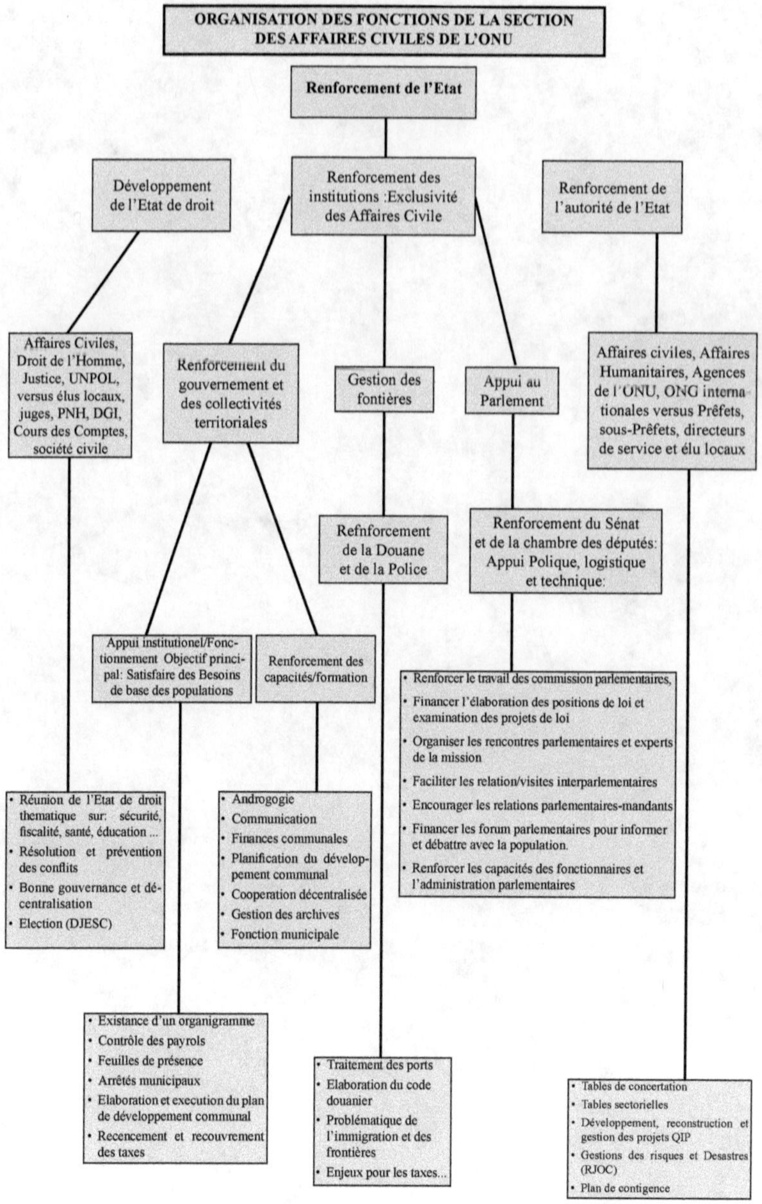

Elaboré par: Dr Ruffin Viclère Mabiala, Ph.D.

V. Les Affaires civiles dans l'axe du développement : gestion des QIP (Quick Impact Projects/projets à effets rapides)

Le mandat d'une Mission des Nations unies est donné par le Conseil de sécurité dans le but d'atteindre l'objectif global de restauration de la paix et la sécurité et poursuivre un processus constitutionnel et politique. Dans certains cas, cet objectif global consiste à préserver les acquis de la stabilisation et réconciliation, permettant la réalisation des activités humanitaires, de relèvement et de reconstruction.

Le Conseil de Sécurité demande souvent aux missions de faire le plein usage des moyens et des capacités existants pour soutenir les efforts humanitaires et de relèvement. C'est ainsi qu'il offre aux Affaires civiles des moyens supplémentaires pour mettre en oeuvre des projets à impact rapide dont le but est d'améliorer la confiance de la population locale envers la mission. Cela suppose l'exécution du travail très efficace et visible des projets à forte intensité de mains d'oeuvre qui aident à créer des emplois et offrir des services sociaux de base. Il encourage à fournir un soutien logistique et une expertise technique, selon les moyens disponibles, pour renforcer les capacités des institutions pour la primauté du droit au niveau : national et local. Il appartient aux Affaires civiles de mettre en place un plan d'action pour le relèvement et le développement national qui constituent des instruments pour assurer la coordination des efforts de reconstruction et de développement.

Cependant, les Affaires civiles jouent très souvent sur le terrain de prédilection du PNUD, celui du renforcement des capacités, de la gouvernance, de la démocratie, de la décentralisation et des institutions. La grande différence entre ces deux entités du système des Nations unies est que les Affaires civiles appartiennent au DPKO et interviennent dans le cadre précis des opérations du maintien de la paix ou de stabilité tandis que les Hommes du PNUD opèrent sur un terrain présumé stable.

L'autre distinction qui n'est pas le moindre est que les Affaires civiles disposent des Projets à effets Rapides dont le financement varie entre quinze miles (15.000) et cent miles (100.000) selon les missions, tandis que le PNUD exécute des projets dont les financements sont plus colossaux.

Il convient de reconnaitre en outre que les Affaires civiles sont dispersées sur l'ensemble du territoire sur lequel elles interviennent alors que le PNUD effectue des missions ponctuelles dans les coins et recoins du pays d'intervention. Il travaille beaucoup plus avec le gouvernement central, alors que les Affaires civiles font simultanément plusieurs tâches à la fois.

Le nombre des officiers des Affaires civiles aussi fait la différence et joue sur la proximité des besoins locaux, sans oublier la connaissance et les rapports étroits entre les Affaires civiles et les autorités à la base. Aussi, une mission d'intégration Affaires civiles-PNUD n'est qu'à l'avantage des uns et des autres. Cela éviterait la duplication et la confusion, car ces deux instances indépendantes et différentes l'une de l'autre, se complètent puisqu'elles sont toutes attachées au renforcement des capacités des Etats, notamment sur le volet formation qui n'existe pas dans le cadre des Affaires civiles militaires américains.

C'est une particularité des Affaires civiles de l'ONU. Il existe des secteurs pour lesquels la mission, par le canal de la section des Affaires civiles réalise des projets qui rentrent dans le cadre du développement. C'est de la microéconomie, fondée sur la gestion de petits Projets à Effets Rapides. Aussi, il serait intéressant de comprendre comment les Affaires civiles interviennent-elles concrètement, dans ce cadre du développement et de la reconstruction d'un pays post-conflit.

A. IMPACT DES PROJETS QIP

Les risques de détérioration de la confiance vis-à-vis du public dans la mission, le mandat ou le processus de paix en cours, sont des faits qui s'ajoutent souvent à la dégradation des conditions de vie déjà exacerbée par : la perte de maisons, écoles, bureaux gouvernementaux et d'autres infrastructures publiques, ainsi que les camps des réfugiés pendant le conflit ou les catastrophes naturelles. Cela constitue un environnement propice aux crises supplémentaires, les maladies, l'augmentation de la criminalité et de la violence politique.

Si les QIP sont limités et leurs financements ne suffisent pas à changer durablement la situation d'un pays sorti de crise, il n'en demeure pas moins qu'ils permettent d'améliorer considérablement l'environnement pour la mise en oeuvre efficace du mandat, puis aider à améliorer les conditions de sécurité. Grâce à leur popularité et leur grande visibilité, les QIP peuvent faire une différence dans la stimulation et dans le maintien de la confiance du public dans la Mission, dans la durabilité du processus de paix et en dépend et ce pour la reconstruction d'un avenir meilleur dans le pays hôte.

L'évolution constante de la portée et l'intensité des tâches confiées aux Affaires civiles font des QIP un instrument indispensable pour répondre à un certain nombre de besoins immédiats de la population et des institutions en augmentant ainsi la confiance de la population locale vis-à-vis de la mission et dans le processus de stabilisation et de la paix.

L'impact des projets à effets rapides est hautement rentable pour une Mission. Les QIP sont très utiles pour les activités de récupération et pour générer des opportunités économiques. Ils permettent également la mise en oeuvre des mesures rapides pour éviter la propagation des maladies épidémiques, pour répondre aux besoins fondamentaux de la population, surtout celles qui sont aussi touchées par les catastrophes naturelles. Une aide accrue du gouvernement pour répondre aux besoins les plus urgents de reconstruction grâce à des projets à impact rapide peut également être garantie, à travers les QIP qui restent aussi indispensables pour la reconstruction et contribuent du même coup, au développement local.

De ce fait, le budget alloué au programme de projets à impact rapide par l'Assemblée générale de l'ONU ne cesse d'augmenter d'année en année. Le plafond des dépenses par projet atteint dans certains pays, la somme de 100 000 dollars US. Cela permet de maximiser l'impact et l'efficacité de ces projets pour atteindre les objectifs prévus par le conseil de sécurité.

B. INTERETS DES PROJETS QIP

Les efforts d'aide à la reconstruction et au développement communautaire qui suivent le conflit augmentent souvent les besoins des interventions rapides pour réduire les risques de propagation des maladies, la recrudescence des combats ou de violences et rendent difficiles les réhabilitations les plus urgentes des infrastructures publiques, ainsi que la prestation des services publics. Dans le même ordre d'idées, la création d'activités génératrices de revenus et de moyens de subsistance pour la plupart des victimes d'une crise reste un facteur clé dans le processus de stabilisation, de paix et de reconstruction.

La force d'une administration publique dans le domaine de prestation efficace des services publics en matière de l'Etat de droit et de la bonne gouvernance fait partie des conditions préalables du développement durable d'un pays post-guerre. Cela oblige les Affaires civiles à identifier les infrastructures, les formations, la fourniture de services publics de base et la mobilisation sociale comme principaux domaines d'intervention pour les financements des projets QIP.

La nécessité d'aborder la faiblesse chronique des services publics de base et des infrastructures au niveau local se pose donc comme une urgence incontournable dans les pays post-crise. D'ailleurs, l'un des objectifs des QIP est de faciliter non seulement la livraison des services publics de base, mais aussi de permettre de renforcer les institutions locales possibilités d'emplois qui s'avèrent indirectement profitables à la population dans le moyen ou le long terme.

Les QIP constituent l'instrument politico-stratégique par excellence, destiné à accroître la visibilité et promouvoir l'acceptation d'une mission de maintien de la paix, tout en essayant de renforcer l'autorité de l'Etat et l'Etat de droit, à travers la satisfaction des besoins d'une population en situation d'urgence politique grave.

En ce qui concerne le domaine d'infrastructures, il est caractérisé par la gestion des fonds onusiens pour la réalisation des projets à effets rapides se focalisant sur :

- la réhabilitation ou la construction de bâtiments publics ;
- les projets de protection du rivage visant à protéger les sources d'eau dans le but de faire la prévention des inondations et des érosions des champs, ainsi que l'augmentation de la production agricole locale ;
- la réhabilitation de l'agriculture et des routes locales mineures, notamment celles qui donnent accès aux marchés dans les communes et les sections communales en tant que source de revenus pour les municipalités ;
- les projets de gestion de l'eau potable, utiles pour la santé publique ;
- l'électrification de base et l'éclairage solaire pour renforcer la sécurité et le bien-être des voisinages ;
- la réhabilitation dans les prisons, afin de renforcer la sécurité et améliorer les conditions de vie des prisonniers ;
- le creusage des puits d'eau et les pompes, la collecte des eaux de pluie, la canalisation, les fontaines de distribution d'eau, impliquant des partenaires d'exécution ayant une expertise dans le domaine de l'eau potable, pour la consommation d'une bonne qualité de l'eau dans le court, le moyen et/ou le long terme ;
- la réhabilitation ou de construction des mairies, des tribunaux, des écoles ou des salles de classe ;
- les autres infrastructures publiques, telles que : les équipements de base pour être fonctionnels dans la prestation des services.

Il faut noter que toute construction ou réhabilitation des bâtiments publics devrait être autorisée par l'institution publique compétente, afin de garantir les conditions minimales qualitatives. Et, il faut assurer la coordination avec d'autres donateurs potentiels pour éviter les duplications.

Cependant, pour maximiser l'influence positive des QIP sur la population, les officiers des Affaires civiles choisissent les projets à réaliser sur la base des programmes à forte intensité de main-d'oeuvre et s'efforcent de respecter les délais de faisabilité qui ne devraient pas excéder trois mois.

a. Enjeux des Projets Créateurs d'Emplois/Générateurs de Revenus

Bien qu'ayant une portée raisonnablement limitée, les QIP sont des projets communautaires dits « income-generating/ job-creating », c'est-à-dire générateurs de revenus. Ils sont destinés à répondre aux besoins les plus immédiats des populations et constituent un des moyens de subsistance des gens. A ce titre, ils peuvent créer des opportunités renouvelables et durables de revenus minimum pour les bénéficiaires directs, tout en bénéficiant globalement à l'ensemble de la communauté. Pour illustration, les projets à encourager sont les projets :

- agricoles de petite taille, à l'instar des plantations ou des magasins communautaires, des coopératives agricoles, des fabriques de transformation des fruits et légumes, des équipements agricoles, etc. ;
- de pisciculture, notamment les bassins de pisciculture, l'élevage ou l'aviculture ;
- de reboisement au niveau communal ;
- de formation professionnelle, car ces projets se traduisent par la création d'emplois comme la couture ;
- de recyclage des ordures faisant partie des efforts durables dans le cadre de la fertilisation organique, des briques pour la gravure et bien d'autres ;
- de fabriques des briques et des tuiles, et cetera.

Pour cette catégorie de projets, la durabilité est un facteur clé, ce qui devrait être dûment reflétée dans la proposition de projet. Si nécessaire, la consultation et l'autorisation des pouvoirs publics au niveau approprié devraient être recherchées pour ces projets générateurs de revenus.

b. QIP Pour la Formation et le Renforcement Des Capacités

Le renforcement des institutions clés du gouvernement au niveau : central, départemental, municipal et collinaires demeure crucial pour garantir la stabilité et la paix à long terme. C'est aussi une condition sine qua non du développement local. Il se traduit essentiellement par les formations, les forums ou les séminaires à l'attention des autorités locales, des fonctionnaires et agents municipaux ainsi que des représentants de la société civile. Les secteurs les plus sollicités par les bénéficiaires et reçoivent le financement QIP sont les suivants :

- la formation de l'administration locale de base, le budget et la décentralisation fiscale, la gestion des frontières, etc. ;
- la formation sur la gestion de bureau et de gestion de projet ;
- le renforcement des capacités visant à promouvoir la transparence et de la reddition des comptes, avec leurs mécanismes de suivi ;

- la formation destinée à renforcer la primauté du droit et soutenir le respect des droits humains.

Ces formations doivent être coordonnées avec les autorités gouvernementales au plus haut niveau pour assurer la normalisation et la maximisation de l'efficacité. Elles doivent être axées sur les résultats et accompagnées d'une évaluation complétée par la mise en oeuvre des mécanismes de suivi et de contrôle des actions permettant de créer des moyens d'évaluation de l'impact des projets. Ces projets doivent être adaptés aux groupes spécifiques ciblés, à la situation et aux nécessités des populations locales, car la sélection d'une proposition de projet est conditionnée par les avantages immédiats, mais aussi à moyen et à long terme de son impact.

Les Affaires civiles tiennent également compte du rapport coût-efficacité.

L'identification des besoins de formation doit être guidée par des évaluations adéquates. Les Affaires civiles doivent prendre en compte la réalité sur le terrain et être orientées vers les besoins des municipalités et de la société civile, tout en tenant compte du bénéfice que doit tirer la population. Ces projets peuvent aussi être choisis dans le cadre de la coordination entre le gouvernement central et les autorités de base, afin de renforcer le processus de décentralisation, mais aussi pour s'assurer que les normes minimales et la durabilité sont remplies. Aussi doivent-ils faire partie des activités prévues par le gouvernement et les autorités compétentes décentralisées ou déconcentrées, sous la rubrique du développement des capacités des bureaux et du personnel sous leur responsabilité directe ou indirecte.

Dans ce domaine, on considère aussi : l'impact à l'échelle du pays, la haute qualité de la formation, le matériel et les résultats. Ceci est documenté par des circonstances particulières, de haut niveau et par le nombre des participants, stagiaires et/ou formateurs, et cetera.

C. PROCESSUS DE MISE EN OEUVRE DES QIP

Le cycle d'un projet QIP commence par la phase d'évaluation. Cette phase permet à l'officier des Affaires civiles d'identifier les bénéficiaires, d'analyser leurs besoins et d'arpenter les défis potentiels pour la mise en oeuvre du projet. L'évaluation nécessite souvent des enquêtes de terrain et d'autres méthodes participatives de collecte de données. La consultation des bénéficiaires n'est pas à exclure. Elle s'avère d'ailleurs capitale. Par exemple, à Léogane, en Haïti, il a fallu que la section des Affaires civiles rencontre les jeunes de la commune, les associations locales, y compris les organisations des femmes ainsi que les autorités locales et les représentants du gouvernement dans la région des Palmes pour que la réhabilitation de l'auditorium, situé en plein centre-ville soit adoptée à l'unanimité. Evidemment, en matière de visibilité, ce projet ne peut que faire la promotion de la mission.

Une fois que les résultats d'évaluation sont disponibles, en tant que chef de projet, l'officier des Affaires civiles doit conceptualiser le projet. Généralement, il bénéficie de l'expertise de la firme d'exécution du projet QIP dans l'élaboration et la rédaction du budget. Cette phase consiste à non seulement rédiger le document et l'échéancier du projet, mais aussi à élaborer une stratégie et déterminer les indicateurs permettant de mesurer l'impact potentiel dudit projet.

Ensuite, il faut faire la recherche des financements. Cela signifie contacter les bailleurs de fonds pour faire le lobbying du projet. C'est le rôle particulier des Affaires civiles en tant que bailleur de fonds lui-même, pour ce type de projet. Le projet est soumis à une unité spéciale des Affaires civiles. Par la suite, il est crée un « Comité Régional de Revue des Projets » qui évalue la portée et la nécessité du projet, avant de donner son approbation. Après l'aval de ce comité connu sous le sigle « PRC », de l'anglais « Project Review Committee » l'officier des Affaires civiles transmet le dossier à l'Unité QIP pour l'obtention des « clearances » des chefs de la mission, ce qui précède la phase de décaissements.

Dès que les financements sont disponibles, on passe à la phase d'exécution du projet. L'officier des Affaires civiles et les ingénieurs de la firme d'exécution sont donc conviés à élaborer un plan d'exécution détaillé servant de tableau de bord pour toutes les activités, y compris la gestion du budget.

Ce plan est essentiellement contenu dans le formulaire de demande. Ils établissent aussi un lien avec le plan de suivi détaillé sur le rendement et l'évaluation. Ces deux outils permettront à l'officier des Affaires civiles de comprendre si les objectifs vont être atteints au moment opportun et si l'impact souhaité va se réaliser. Les écarts éventuels constituent des gaps à adresser au cours du suivi.

D. PRINCIPES D'EVALUATION ET DE SELECTION DES QIP

Dans l'exécution des QIP, les Affaires civiles favorisent souvent les partenaires qui ont déjà une expérience avec la gestion des projets, notamment avec la mission. C'est à eux que la priorité est accordée, pour exécuter d'autres projets similaires dans d'autres endroits. Cela permet de garantir une plus grande « responsabilisation » et facilite l'élaboration et l'obtention des rapports narratifs et financiers liés à l'exécution du QIP.

En règle générale, lorsque certains projets spécifiques nécessitent des fonds supplémentaires pour atteindre les objectifs initialement prévus, il appartient au partenaire d'exécution de trouver le cofinancement, à travers ses propres ressources ou par le canal d'autres donateurs. En effet, le partenaire doit avoir la capacité d'obtenir un cofinancement si nécessaire, puis assembler une pluralité de ressources financières, ce qui constitue la condition de base pour la durabilité du projet après sa mise en oeuvre.

L'identification et l'approbation des QIP sont basées sur des besoins bien spécifiques d'une communauté spécifique. Toutes les propositions sont d'abord examinées par le Chef de la Section des Affaires civiles ou son adjoint, pour les projets de faible montant. Dans certains cas, il faut que le projet soit examiné et approuvé par le Représentant Spécial Adjoint du Secrétaire Général de l'ONU, pour des sommes dépassant la limite habituelle.

Toutefois, toutes les composantes militaires, policières et civiles auront accès à ces fonds afin d'entreprendre des projets à impact rapide en faveur du mandat de la Mission, mais via la section des Affaires civiles.

Afin d'éviter tout chevauchement avec les projets financés par d'autres institutions de financement, au moins un représentant de la section humanitaire devrait participer à la Commission de Révision des Projets (PRC), dont la composition devrait intégrer au moins cinq autres sections différentes de la mission. Le mandat ou les responsabilités de ces sections doit être lié aux activités du projet. Il s'agit par exemple de :

- la Section justice en matière de réhabilitation ou construction des tribunaux ;
- les UNPOL concernant les commissariats de police ; genre dans les projets d'appui aux groupes des femmes vulnérables ;
- « child protection » pour la protection de l'enfance en ce qui concerne les projets ayant pour cible les enfants et les filles.

En cas d'absence du point focal de la section directement concernée, alors que son expertise est indispensable. Cela oblige les Affaires civiles à rechercher des informations supplémentaires pour donner plus de poids au PRC.

Néanmoins, tous les projets bénéficient souvent de la même considération dans les programmes QIP des Affaires civiles. Toutes les propositions de projet doivent indiquer clairement comment cette aide de la mission sera médiatisée. Cet aspect est toujours pris en considération dans le processus de sélection des projets.

Les bureaux régionaux doivent se prononcer pendant le PRC, sur la distribution des fonds entre les différentes catégories :

- infrastructures et prestation des services publics ;
- moyens de subsistance, de création d'emplois et de construction ;
- formation et de renforcement des capacités, en fonction des besoins spécifiques de chaque collectivité Territoriale.

Chaque bureau régional désigne un officier des Affaires civiles comme point focal pour les projets QIP. Le chef du Bureau Régional (CRO) est responsable de donner l'autorisation et coordonner l'identification et la gestion de ces projets. Il est aussi le secrétaire du PRC. C'est lui qui examine les propositions de projet pour la validité avant de les présenter au chef de section des Affaires civiles qui doit donner la clearance. Le PRC la pièce maîtresse de la procédure opérationnelle, standard, technique et financière.

E. COORDINATION DES ACTIVITES DE SUIVI ET D'EVALUATION

Le suivi et l'évaluation du QIP sont réalisés pendant la mise en oeuvre du projet. Le suivi permet de fournir les informations sur l'exécution du projet, tandis que l'évaluation se concentre sur l'impact du projet sur la population locale.

Il peut arriver que les bénéficiaires donnent leur avis au cours de l'exécution du projet, notamment pour savoir s'ils pourront réellement récolter les fruits de l'exécution de ce projet. Cela peut se faire à travers un sondage d'opinion et donne le droit aux Affaires civiles de suggérer des modifications à la conception initiale du programme, bien entendu, en accord avec le partenaire d'exécution.

Pour plus d'efficacité et de transparence dans la gestion des finances, il est souhaitable de scinder le budget par périodes d'activité avec les partenaires surtout, mais parfois avec les bénéficiaires. Ces initiatives vont contribuer à jeter un regard neuf sur le projet, afin d'identifier les défis et concevoir de nouvelles stratégies. Un projet correctement suivi et dont l'évaluation est également faite est une garantie des enseignements à tirer pour le bilan ou le rapport final qui servira de pièce maîtresse pour les projets antérieurs.

Après le séisme en Haïti, les besoins étant très énormes, les Affaires civiles ont désormais la possibilité de gérer des sommes exorbitantes atteignant la bagatelle de cent mille dollars pour la réhabilitation des rivières et les réparations des ponts et autres édifices publics. Ce qui est loin des quinze ou trente mille dollars américains ($15 à 30,000US) habituelles.

En un mot, il existe une panoplie des normes à respecter dans la gestion des QIP. Ces règles figurent dans un document appelé « Accord », dans le jargon des Affaires civiles.

a. Définition de l'Accord

L'accord est un contrat qui régit la mission des Nations unies, à travers la section des Affaires civiles, d'une part et le partenaire qui exécute le projet QIP, d'autre part. Ce dernier est aussi dénommé « Partenaire chargé du QIP » dans le protocole d'accord.

L'Accord établit les clauses et conditions selon lesquelles les Affaires civiles et le partenaire coopéreront aux fins de l'exécution du Projet à Effets Rapides qui devrait être décrite en annexe dudit accord.

b. Communication dans le cadre de la Gestion des QIP

Dans la gestion des QIP, toute correspondance entre les parties impliquées dans l'application ou l'interprétation de l'accord doit être envoyée par courrier postal avec un accusé de réception ou délivrée en mains propres contre un reçu.

L'accord est souvent accompagné d'un « formulaire de demande » figurant en annexe. Celui-ci contient la description et le budget détaillé du projet et le chronogramme des activités de réalisation du projet. En cas de différence ou de contradiction entre l'accord et le formulaire de demande, c'est l'accord qui prévaut, puisqu'il s'agit d'un contrat.

c. Durée de l'Accord

L'accord entre en vigueur à la date de sa signature par les parties, sauf en cas de résiliation conformément aux paragraphes prévus à cet effet, dans le même document. Il reste en vigueur jusqu'à l'achèvement du projet en question et à l'accomplissement par les parties de toutes leurs obligations prévues par ledit accord.

Le partenaire chargé du QIP s'engage à exécuter le projet conformément au chronogramme d'activités figurant à l'annexe de l'accord. Il lui appartient de prendre toutes les mesures possibles et faire tous les arrangements nécessaires pour la fourniture des biens, des services, de la main-d'oeuvre et de tous autres apports indispensables à l'exécution du projet.

d. Contribution de la Mission des Nations unies

Dans la pratique, la mission de l'ONU verse au partenaire chargé du QIP la somme équivalent au montant du budget, que le partenaire s'engage à utiliser conformément à l'accord. Cet argent sert exclusivement à couvrir les dépenses nécessaires à l'exécution du projet telles qu'elles sont détaillées au budget figurant à l'annexe de l'accord. Cette contribution est versée en deux ou trois échéanciers. Il y a la possibilité d'opter pour un paiement de 80% des frais totaux du projet et 20% additionnels pour terminer les travaux. La seconde hypothèse est de faire deux versements de 40% du montant global du budget chacun et un versement de 20% pour la finition des travaux. Les 80% sont versés directement par chèque ou par virement bancaire au partenaire, dans la quinzaine qui suit la signature de l'accord. Le dernier versement de 20% fait suite à la réception et l'acceptation des rapports des activités et financiers par la mission de l'ONU. Après quoi, la mission ne saurait être tenue de ne faire aucun autre versement en sus de ladite contribution conclue entre les parties.

Le partenaire chargé du QIP sera responsable de toutes autres dépenses ou tous autres coûts excédant la contribution prévue dans le budget initial. La mission est en droit de suspendre ou annuler les versements prévus dans l'accord, en cas de non-respect par le partenaire chargé de l'exécution de ses obligations.

e. Responsabilités du Partenaire d'Exécution du QIP

Le statut juridique du partenaire chargé du QIP est celui d'un entrepreneur indépendant vis-à-vis de la mission de l'ONU. Ses agents, employés, mandataires, contractants, y compris son personnel, ne sont aucunement considérés comme agents, employés, mandataires ou contractants de la mission de maintien de la paix. C'est donc au partenaire chargé du QIP de se conformer aux dispositions de l'accord et de prendre toutes les dispositions qui s'imposent pour s'assurer que son personnel s'y conforme.

Par conséquent, le partenaire chargé du QIP répond de la compétence professionnelle et technique de son personnel. Il relève de sa compétence et sa responsabilité de choisir aux fins de l'exécution du projet, des personnes qualifiées et efficaces, qui possèdent de surcroît, des hautes qualités morales et éthiques. L'exécutant s'abstiendra de toute action pouvant porter préjudice à la mission de maintien de la paix et doit exécuter ses obligations en vertu de l'accord, tout en ayant pleinement égard aux intérêts de celle-ci.

Au cas où le partenaire chargé du QIP aurait connaissance d'un événement ou d'une circonstance qui compromet ou risque de compromettre l'exécution du projet, il doit promptement informer les Affaires civiles. C'est à lui qu'incombe la responsabilité d'accomplir toutes formalités et pour obtenir tous les permis, licences et autres autorisations requises pour l'exécution du projet.

Il faut préciser que le partenaire chargé du QIP s'expose à des poursuites sur les actions, réclamations ou responsabilités de toute nature, y compris les frais et dépenses y ayant trait, pour des actes ou omissions de sa part ou de son personnel au cours de l'exécution de l'accord. Il se porte garant de la mission de l'ONU contre de telle poursuite, action, réclamation ou responsabilité.

Cette clause vise, entre autres, toute action, réclamation ou responsabilité ayant pour origine des accidents du travail.

Pendant la durée de l'accord, le partenaire chargé du QIP reste tenu de contracter et maintenir en vigueur ou de s'assurer que son personnel a contracté et maintient en vigueur, selon qu'il est requis par la législation locale, toutes assurances appropriées couvrant les accidents de travail subis par son personnel. Il prend sur sa charge toutes réclamations de son personnel résultant de décès, blessures, dommages des personnes ou des biens liés à l'exécution du projet.

En cas de dommage, vol ou perte d'équipement, matériels ou véhicules financés par la contribution, le partenaire chargé du QIP doit immédiatement informer les Affaires civiles. Dans le même temps, il doit fournir à celles-ci un rapport complet et précis sur les circonstances du dommage, vol ou perte. Ce rapport doit lui-même être accompagné de tout rapport de police y afférant et/ou le constat du juge.

f. Administration Financière et Audit

Il appartient au partenaire chargé du QIP de s'assurer que le public et les bénéficiaires du projet sont informés de l'impact du projet et de l'origine de la contribution, tant pendant l'exécution du projet, jusqu'à la remise de l'édifice aux autorités. S'il en faut, il bénéficie du soutien de la mission, pourvu que cela soit prévu dans le budget. La publicité peut se faire par les moyens ci-après :

- affiches ou panneaux sur le site du projet ;
- inscription sur façade nouvellement construite ou réhabilitée ;
- signes sur les équipements ou matériels utilisés pour le projet ;
- communiqués de presse.

L'exécutant du projet QIP est non seulement responsable, mais aussi comptable vis-à-vis de la section des Affaires civiles de la gestion de la contribution de manière efficace, efficiente et rentable. C'est à lui de mettre en place tous systèmes de contrôles et des méthodes appropriés pour la bonne exécution des travaux. Il tient les livres comptables et autres dossiers précis et à jour, concernant toutes les dépenses financées par la contribution. Pour chaque dépense, le partenaire chargé du QIP est tenu de conserver les pièces justificatives, y compris les originaux de toutes factures et tous reçus relatifs à la transaction concernée. Toute conversion de devises requises pour la mise en oeuvre de l'accord se fait au taux de change officiel en vigueur au moment de la transaction concernée. A moins qu'il n'en soit convenu autrement par écrit entre les contractants, le partenaire chargé du QIP est prié d'informer promptement la mission de tous intérêts accrus de la contribution.

Il est tenu de les refléter dans les livres comptables et dans un projet d'avenant au Budget du projet qu'il soumettra à l'accord de la section des Affaires civiles. Dans le même ordre d'idées, à moins qu'il n'en soit autrement convenu par écrit entre les parties, le partenaire chargé du QIP conservera les livres comptables et autres dossiers relatifs au projet pendant plusieurs années, au moins deux ans après l'achèvement du projet. Il pourra les mettre plus tard, sur demande écrite, à la disposition des auditeurs ou autres représentants désignés de la mission.

Les officiers des Affaires civiles ont le droit de visiter à tout moment le (s) site (s) d'exécution du projet, afin d'inspecter et/ou évaluer et/ou conduire un audit des activités du projet. Le partenaire chargé du QIP doit prendre toutes les mesures et effectuer tous les arrangements nécessaires, afin de faciliter ces visites.

g. Rapports d'activités

Dans le cadre du suivi de l'exécution des travaux, environ deux semaines après le lancement desdits travaux, l'officier des Affaires civiles doit exiger du partenaire chargé de la gestion du QIP un rapport d'activités de mi-parcours qui détaillera les informations suivantes :

- les activités réalisées et les résultats atteints conformément au descriptif du projet et au chronogramme d'activités ;
- tous les cas ou le descriptif du projet et/ou le chronogramme d'activités n'a pas été respecté, avec justifications à l'appui. Ce détail devrait être accompagné d'un exposé des mesures prises pour rattraper le retard et/ou atteindre les résultats prévus ;
- toutes circonstances qui, à la connaissance du partenaire chargé du QIP, seraient de nature à compromettre la bonne exécution du projet ou son achèvement et toutes propositions de l'exécutant pour faire face à ces circonstances.

L'officier des Affaires civiles doit aussi recevoir un rapport financier reflétant toutes les sommes reçues de la mission de l'ONU, bien entendu, à travers la section des Affaires civiles, au titre de la contribution ; toutes les dépenses financées par la contribution et tous soldes non utilisés. Ce rapport financier doit être certifié par le responsable du service financier du partenaire exécutant le QIP. Il doit aussi être accompagné de toutes pièces justificatives, y compris toutes factures et tous reçus. Ce rapport financier indiquera précisément et de manière détaillée le nombre, la description et le prix de tous matériels, équipements, fournitures et autres biens, ainsi que de tous services financés par la contribution. Il précisera tous intérêts accrus de la contribution et tous gains ou pertes réalisées lors de toutes opérations de change effectuées aux fins de l'exécution du projet.

Environ, deux semaines après la date d'achèvement du projet ou la date de résiliation de l'accord conclu entre l'exécutant et les Affaires civiles, le partenaire chargé du QIP doit soumettre à la mission de l'ONU deux rapports finaux. Le premier est un rapport d'activité décrivant :

- les activités réalisées et les résultats atteints conformément au descriptif du projet et au chronogramme d'activités ;
- tous les cas où le descriptif du projet et/ou le chronogramme d'activités n'ont pas été respectés, preuve à l'appui ;

- une évaluation documentée de l'impact du projet sur le (s) groupe (s) ou l'entité bénéficiaire ;
- un exposé des leçons à tirer de l'exécution du projet.

Le second est un rapport financier final portant sur le coût total du projet. Il est censé contenir les informations mentionnées dans le rapport de mi-parcours, cette fois pour toute la durée du Projet.

L'officier des Affaires civiles doit être très vigilant pour éviter les doubles emplois ou le gaspillage de ressources.

Mais, il appartient pour cela, au partenaire chargé du QIP d'assurer la pleine coordination des activités financées par la contribution et des autres programmes ou projets pertinents qu'il a sous sa responsabilité.

Lorsque le partenaire estime que des activités ou des dépenses non prévues par l'accord, mais dans les limites du budget original sont nécessaires pour la bonne exécution du projet, il est prié d'en informer immédiatement les Affaires civiles. Il devra ainsi obtenir l'approbation écrite de ceux-ci avant d'effectuer de telles activités ou d'engager de telles dépenses.

h. Règlement des différends

Les parties s'engagent à faire de leur mieux pour régler à l'amiable tout différend, litige ou réclamation découlant de l'accord, de sa nullité ou de sa violation ou ceux qui y sont relatif.

Tout différend, litige ou réclamation qui n'est pas réglé à l'amiable dans les soixante jours de la réception par l'une des parties de la demande de règlement à l'amiable faite par l'autre partie sera soumis par l'une ou l'autre partie à arbitrage conformément au règlement d'arbitrage de la Commission des Nations unies pour le Droit Commercial International (CNUDCI) alors en vigueur. Toutefois, le tribunal arbitral ne doit pas être habilité à accorder de dommages et intérêts à titre de sanction. Mais, les parties sont liées par la sentence arbitrale rendue au terme dudit arbitrage comme valant règlement final et définitif du différend, litige ou réclamation.

i. Privilèges et Immunités

Aucun des termes de l'accord ne saurait être considéré comme constituant une renonciation explicite ou implicite, à quelque privilège ou immunité que ce soit, dont peuvent jouir les Nations unies, y compris ses organes subsidiaires, tels que la mission de maintien de la paix.

j. Résiliation

La mission de l'ONU peut à sa discrétion, résilier l'accord à tout moment par préavis écrit d'au moins quinze (15) jours au partenaire chargé du QIP, au cas où les Affaires civiles estiment que le commencement, la continuation ou l'achèvement du projet, ou encore la réalisation des objectifs sont ou peuvent être compromis.

Elle est également en droit de résilier l'accord par préavis écrit, avec effet immédiat en cas de violation par le partenaire chargé du QIP d'une des conditions de l'accord, y compris au cas où le partenaire chargé du QIP manquerait de soumettre un des rapports prévus dans l'accord. Il est aussi possible que la mission résilie l'accord en cas de force majeure, par préavis écrit d'au moins sept jours au partenaire chargé du QIP. En outre, sans préjudice des dispositions contenues dans l'accord, la mission de l'ONU peut décider de consulter le partenaire chargé du QIP au cas où de son avis, des circonstances existent qui compromettent ou risquent de compromettre le commencement, la continuation ou l'achèvement du projet, ou encore, la réalisation de ses objectifs. Les parties se consulteront sur la possibilité d'éliminer de telles circonstances ou d'en minimiser les effets.

Dans les dix jours suivant l'expiration ou la résiliation de l'accord, le partenaire chargé de l'exécution est prié de retourner aux Affaires civiles tout solde non utilisé de la contribution, y compris de tous intérêts accrus de la contribution.

k. Cas de Force Majeure Dans l'Exécution des QIP

Lorsque survient un cas de force majeure empêchant le partenaire chargé du QIP à honorer tout ou partie ses obligations et responsabilités prévues par l'accord, il est tenu d'en aviser dès que possible les Affaires civiles, par écrit et en détail.

Une fois dûment, informée conformément aux clauses présentes dans l'accord, la mission a le droit, à sa seule discrétion, de prendre toute mesure qu'elle jugera appropriée ou nécessaire dans ces circonstances, notamment de consentir à une modification raisonnable du chronogramme d'activités, ou de résilier l'accord conformément au paragraphe de résiliation. L'expression « force majeure » utilisée dans un accord s'entend des catastrophes naturelles, guerres (déclarées ou non), invasions, révolutions, insurrections ou de tous autres actes de nature ou de portée similaires.

l. Cas Particuliers Pouvant Subvenir dans la Gestion de QIP

Il existe des cas particuliers dans la gestion des QIP. Il est possible que le partenaire chargé du QIP se rétracte et refuse de gérer les finances et les employés temporaires chargés de l'exécution du projet qu'il a lui-même élaboré et présenté un budget conséquent, comprenant toutes les lignes budgétaires d'exécution de QIP. Il est anormal qu'une mission soit confrontée à une situation où le contingent qui a préparé le projet se sent inconfortable de prendre la responsabilité de gérer les hommes et les dépenses. Les Affaires civiles ont été obligées de trouver un autre partenaire pour exécuter les dépenses et prendre en charge le personnel qui a travaillé sur l'ouvrage.

Dans ce cas, il est possible de suggérer ce qui suit : l'accord doit être modifié pour refléter le fait qu'il y ait un partenaire d'exécution et une agence d'exécution ; le partenaire d'exécution devrait avoir une personnalité juridique et un compte bancaire qui lui permettra de recevoir l'argent et répondre des dépenses qui seront faites.

L'acquisition des Projets à Impact Rapide n'est pas vraiment compliquée. Le cas échéant, il est nécessaire de présenter trois proformas pour la plupart des articles coûteux ou trois proformas pour tous les articles si l'officier des Affaires civiles choisit un seul fournisseur.

m. Processus d'Evaluation de l'Impact des QIP

Le Conseil de Sécurité créé les missions pour travailler à la restauration de l'ordre et la stabilité politique dans les pays en situation d'urgence politique. Etant donné que l'instabilité sape sérieusement l'autorité de l'Etat et sa capacité à fournir les services publics de base à ses citoyens, les Affaires civiles reçoivent une allocation budgétaire pour la mise en oeuvre des projets à impact rapide (QIP) en vue de combler ces déficits. Le but est d'exécuter les projets à petite échelle, rapidement réalisables, puis bénéficiant à un grand nombre de la population. Ces projets sont utiles pour établir et renforcer la confiance dans la mission, son mandat et le processus de paix. Ils servent fondamentalement à répondre aux besoins spécifiques de la majorité de la population plongée dans une pauvreté endémique et soumise au manque de services publics.

La Section des Affaires civiles utilise l'approche de QIP pour essayer de « gagner les coeurs et les esprits » lors de l'exécution du mandat de la mission. Malheureusement ces processus rencontrent souvent de nombreux défis, une résistance et l'opposition. D'où la nécessité de faire une évaluation annuelle, en vue de rechercher les objectifs suivants :

- évaluer l'impact des projets à effets rapides` ayant été mise en oeuvre dans le pays, notamment : l'adhésion/l'acceptation de la mise en oeuvre du mandat de la mission ;
- prouver que les mécanismes QIP sont appropriés pour le dialogue et la confiance vis-à-vis des populations locales ;
- évaluer la qualité et la durabilité des résultats des projets à moyen et à long terme, sans oublier l'appropriation par les bénéficiaires, les populations locales ou les institutions ;
- analyser la gestion du cycle de projet QIP pour identifier les forces et les faiblesses dans ladite gestion, à différentes étapes du cycle et au niveau régional, pour déboucher sur les recommandations basées sur des erreurs critiques.

La méthodologie peut être la suivante :

- faire l'analyse des données en termes quantitatifs et qualitatifs ;
- faire une évaluation, en utilisant les sources officielles et officieuses de la collecte de données. Toutefois, les informations officielles seront recueillies à partir de la base de données QIP, notamment les documents de projet et des périodiques ;
- organiser des visites de terrain sur les sites des projets pour recueillir de nouvelles informations ;
- s'entretenir avec des membres du personnel semistructurel et structurel impliqués dans QIP, les partenaires d'exécution, les communautés bénéficiaires, les autorités locales, et cetera.

Il s'agit notamment d'identifier les projets contribuant à :

- la promotion de l'acceptation de la mission par la population ;
- le renforcement de la confiance et/ou du processus de stabilisation ou de consolidation de la paix ;
- l'amélioration de l'environnement favorable à l'exécution du mandat de la mission.

Une telle étude vise aussi à examiner les questions liées à l'efficacité de gestion des QIP et l'impact sur les conditions de vie de la population et sur le fonctionnement des institutions publiques nationales.

Les projets à impact rapide sont susceptibles d'avoir une connotation politique introduisant ainsi une perspective différente en termes d'analyse, ce qui rend leur évaluation quasi distinctive des limitations pouvant affecter la profondeur et l'objectivité des résultats. Ceci pourrait aussi influencer l'analyse des données qualitatives dans la mesure où il peut y avoir une propension à se concentrer sur les résultats positifs et minimiser ceux qui sont négatifs, au lieu de présenter une image équilibrée des réussites et des échecs.

Pour réduire l'impact de cette limitation et minimiser ses effets perfides, la recherche se fait en utilisation le maximum de sources d'informations externes. Cela donne une image équilibrée des réussites et des échecs couplés avec la possibilité de gérer toutes les parties prenantes impliquées dans les succès et les échecs dans les collectivités territoriales. L'évaluation doit contenir :

- une synthèse historique, un contexte et l'ensemble des projets de QIP. Tout ceci dans l'introduction ;
- un aperçu statistique contenant le nombre de propositions de projets soumis aux Affaires civiles, ceux qui ont été transmis au comité d'analyse et ceux qui ont été approuvés et exécutés ;
- la quantité de projets actuellement en cours, ceux ayant dépassé trois mois de délai de mise en oeuvre et le nombre de projets achevés ;
- le pourcentage du total des fonds alloués dans une période d'un an ;
- le nombre et le montant des projets réalisés dans chaque catégorie, à savoir : les infrastructures des services publics, les moyens de subsistance et les emplois générés, la formation et le renforcement des capacités ;
- une explication du nombre exceptionnellement élevé ou faible des projets réalisés.

L'évaluation de la gestion du programme QIP se résume à :

- expliquer si l'identification du projet a eu effectivement lieu, mais aussi comment les différentes composantes de la mission et/ou agences d'exécution ont contribué à l'identification des divers projets ;
- étudier la gestion du processus d'examen des projets, y compris si les projets ont été traitées de façon opportune et transparente, avec instructions claires aux candidats de projet ;
- examiner le processus de sélection d'approbation des projets, notamment si les décisions prises ont été efficaces et avérées, pour éviter les duplications et les chevauchements en relation avec les interventions d'autres acteurs ;
- évaluer la mise en oeuvre et le suivi des fonds ayant été décaissés par le bureau des finances. Le suivi doit être entrepris par l'unité des Affaires civiles qui s'occupe des projets QIP et le comité d'évaluation prend des mesures pour atténuer les problèmes ou les retards ;
- vérifier la procédure de clôture des projets et l'évaluation de manière approfondie et en temps opportun.

Cette évaluation doit être accompagnée d'une médiatisation, pour expliquer comment l'exécution des QIP a apporté des réponses aux besoins spécifiques des femmes dans le cadre de l'égalité du genre, exemples à l'appui.

L'évaluation de l'impact des QIP se fait en utilisant les techniques suivantes :

- promouvoir l'acceptation de la mission par les populations et soutenir sa crédibilité en montrant les progrès dans la mise en oeuvre de ces tâches ou la confiance ;
- mesurer la confiance au processus de stabilisation et/ ou de consolidation de la paix, notamment en exhibant les dividendes en matière de sécurité, essentiellement ;
- améliorer l'environnement pour la mise en oeuvre du mandat, en générant un soutien à la mission, y compris, à travers la satisfaction des besoins immédiats de la population ;
- vérifier l'efficacité et l'efficience de la gestion du cycle de projet ;
- faire des analyses qualitatives et quantitatives de l'impact des projets QIP sur les conditions de vie de la population et sur le fonctionnement des institutions nationales ;
- fournir une analyse assez détaillée, incluant des exemples soutenus par des explications sur les projets particuliers qui ont eu un fort impact, ceux qui n'ont pas eu d'impact significatif ou même ceux qui ont eu un impact négatif.

Le système des QIP n'est pas exempt de reproches. En effet, imaginer qu'un officier des Affaires civiles s'accorde avec le partenaire d'exécution à qui il octroie des faveurs dans l'attribution des marchés et en retour, il reçoit des dividendes ! Que se passe-t-il si un partenaire gonfle les prix ou falsifie les factures en complicité avec l'officier des Affaires civiles ? Est-il possible qu'un point focal pactise avec la corruption qui se pratiquerait dans la gestion des QIP, sans avoir les coudées franches de ses supérieurs hiérarchiques ? Peut-il profiter de la naïveté ou l'incompétence de ceux-ci ? Ici, la moralité, l'intégrité et l'honnêteté des officiers des Affaires civiles sont souvent soumises à dure épreuve dans ce domaine.

Un bureau qui reçoit une somme colossale d'un million de dollars US, il va de soi que dans la région l'on trouve des monuments remarquables qui tapent à l'oeil, car la visibilité est la première préoccupation pour toute mission, en matière de QIP. Au cas contraire, il y a lieu de quoi s'interroger. Dans le même ordre d'idées, on est en droit de se poser des questions lorsque certaines autorités reçoivent de l'argent des fonds QIP et ne réalisent rien ou presque. L'absence du système de poursuites judiciaires, d'instruments juridiques et de coercitions est une porte ouverte à tous les abus. Très rares sont les cas qui prouvent le contraire. Comment se fait-il que des autorités détournent l'argent des QIP sans crainte d'être poursuivis ? Il faut qu'il y ait des mécanismes permettant à une mission non seulement de se faire rembourser, mais aussi d'ester en justice et se constituer partie civile, pour que justice soit rendue, au grand bonheur des bénéficiaires des services de la mission.

De même, il appartient à l'auteur de dénoncer le silence total des missions en cas de non respect du contrat ou de violation de l'accord. Ce vide juridique ne laisse aucune alternative au partenaire à l'acception de saisir les instances judiciaires nationales qui sont parfois corrompues. D'ailleurs, cela pose un sérieux problème de compétence juridictionnelle et c'est politiquement néfaste pour une mission concernant son image. Les officiers des Affaires civiles ne devraient pas être inamovibles, mais se soumettre aux rotations des membres de ladite équipe, pour ne pas être suspectés de bénéficiaire d'un favoritisme insensé. De même, lorsque le remplacement d'un officier suscite une polémique, il y a lieu à se poser des questions.

Bref, dans l'exécution des projets QIP, il est possible de rencontrer des obstacles administratifs et financiers. Pour contourner ces barrières et continuer à réaliser des projets financés par les fonds QIP et permettre d'assister certaines populations défavorisées, il est recommandé d'envisager des possibilités d'avoir un autre intermédiaire acceptable pouvant exécuter les projets dans le même endroit. En d'autres termes, au lieu de mettre en oeuvre le projet avec le partenaire défaillant directement, une autre organisation digne de confiance peut être chargée de la mise en oeuvre des projets avec l'approbation et en Coordination étroite avec l'institution compétente.

Il faut donc s'assurer que l'argent ne soit pas déboursé directement au partenaire irresponsable avec lequel on devrait toutefois discuter de l'approbation d'un exécutant indépendant.

Bien qu'il faille contourner ce partenaire, il n'en demeure pas moins qu'il soit non seulement impliqué dans le processus d'appel d'offre, mais aussi il conserve le droit de regard technique sur le suivi, ce qui lui donne la possibilité d'effectuer des visites de terrain.

Dans un souci de transparence, il serait souhaitable que les points focaux des QIP évitent des relations très étroites avec les caïds de leur région d'affectation. De même pour les politiciens trop puissants et les membres de la société civile les plus influents des alentours. En outre, les audits doivent être externes et indépendants de la mission concernée. Il devrait venir d'une agence des Nations unies ou secrétariat à New York.

Grosso modo, le but de l'auteur est d'expliquer dans quelle mesure les projets QIP peuvent permettre d'atteindre les priorités géographiques et thématiques fixées au départ. Ensuite comment cela s'inscrit dans le plan global de la mission et des stratégies plus larges, pour la sensibilisation de la communauté. Cela inclut l'analyse de la validité continue de ces priorités et de l'efficacité des stratégies plus larges de sensibilisation communautaire.

La mission des Affaires civiles s'inscrit dans un programme à court, moyen et long terme, axé sur la participation communautaire comme socle de la reconstruction et du développement fondamental permettant aux populations locales de devenir artisans et acteurs clés de leur propre développement. C'est donc, dans le souci de répondre aux impératifs non seulement post-urgence, mais aussi pour offrir à un peuple des services sociopolitiques et économiques améliorés, conformément aux valeurs et aux moeurs internationales qu'il faut renforcer les capacités et consolider les acquis de la paix. Cela ne peut se faire sans s'assurer de la proximité communautaire et offrir des programmes efficients dans un contexte culturel et linguistique approprié qui garantisse le renforcement des capacités, même en cas d'urgence de risque et de catastrophes naturelles.

VI. Interventions humanitaires des Affaires civiles : gestion des situations d'urgence, des risques et de catastrophes naturelles

Une catastrophe naturelle est un ensemble de dégâts causés par un phénomène naturel, affectant des populations, des infrastructures et/ou des secteurs productifs de l'activité économique avec une gravité dépassant les capacités locales de réponse. Son ampleur est telle qu'elle nécessite l'intervention de l'administration centrale et parfois de la communauté internationale, afin d'augmenter les efforts et les ressources disponibles, pour réduire ou limiter à la fois les pertes en vies humaines et en dégâts matériels En pareilles circonstances, les Affaires civiles sont conviées à poursuivre leur collaboration auprès de l'Etat et des collectivités territoriales, en apportant leur soutien aux communes et collines ou sections communales, pour la reconstruction des zones sinistrées et le renforcement des services publics. Il se pourrait que le gouvernement soit amené à prendre des mesures exceptionnelles d'intervention et/ou de réhabilitation de la situation après l'événement. Le cas échéant, la mesure phare qui s'impose inévitablement à la majorité des gouvernements est : l'Etat d'urgence. C'est une hypothèse qui décrit une situation dans laquelle l'Etat décrète et applique un régime restrictif de certaines libertés fondamentales, en utilisant les pouvoirs exceptionnels de l'exécutif. Ce dispositif se justifie par la situation de catastrophe naturelle avérée ou imminente et requiert l'adoption de mesures urgentes.

A. SITUATION GENERALE

Le rôle des Affaires civiles est de permettre aux élus de base et à leur personnel de mieux gérer l'urgence, mais aussi de mieux connaître leurs lacunes. Bien évidemment, seule une forte volonté politique ouvrirait la voie à la modernisation du pays et à une administration territoriale cohérente. Les Affaires civiles sont là pour aider à trouver des solutions pour offrir une vie décente aux populations qui sortent d'une crise ou d'un conflit. Que doivent-elles faire pour assurer cette responsabilité fortuite et inopportune de solidarité,

destiné, entre autres, à renforcer la section des Affaires humanitaires qui est souvent surchargée ou dépassée par l'évolution des événements ?

Les officiers des Affaires civiles doivent entre autres, avoir une certaine expertise en matière d'intervention rapide, puisqu'ils sont appelés à appuyer toutes les autres sections. Parfois, ils doivent combler l'absence des officiers des Affaires humanitaires ou remédier les défaillances et les faiblesses du secteur. Ainsi, il est important de mettre à la connaissance des officiers des Affaires civiles une approche leur permettant de prendre certaines initiatives en cas de désastre naturel.

Dans la pratique, il s'agit d'aider l'Etat, les autorités de base et les autres acteurs nationaux à mettre en place un plan national de gestion des risques et des désastres qui aura des représentations au niveau départemental, communal ou collinaire. Le plus souvent, dans les pays très exposés, il est de coutume d'agir en amont et en aval, en créant une structure étatique qui prendrait le nom selon les pays, de comité permanent de protection civile. Ce comité aura à gérer les risques et les catastrophes afin d'en atténuer les conséquences sur les personnes, les biens et l'environnement. Il devrait être composé des autorités dont les responsabilités sont légalement reconnues par la loi. Cette loi leur donnerait une compétence sur tout ou partie des zones affectées. Ce sont des ramifications du système national de gestion des risques et désastres dans les collectivités territoriales. En pareilles circonstances, c'est le développement économique local qui permet véritablement de stabiliser les populations sinistrées dans les provinces plutôt que dans les grandes agglomérations.

Ce comité doit faire partie des institutions publiques du pays. Cela doit être un organisme dont le personnel est composé essentiellement d'agents publics. Il s'agit des personnes physiques élues ou faisant l'objet d'un acte de nomination ou lié par un contrat de droit public, afin d'exercer un emploi pour le compte d'une institution ou d'une personne publique de l'administration publique nationale. Ce sont des fonctionnaires lorsqu'ils sont nommés à un emploi permanent à temps complet et titularisé dans un grade de la hiérarchie administrative. Ils peuvent parfois dépendre d'un organisme international ou d'une ONG. Dans ce domaine, il ne serait pas vain de miser sur le volontarisme.

Ce comité de la protection civile qu'on peut aussi appeler comité d'urgence est censé élaborer un plan national d'intervention dont la mise en oeuvre des mesures qui y sont contenues est ordonnée par l'Etat.

Dans les situations d'urgence, les individus et les groupes ont non seulement des vulnérabilités évidentes, mais ils ont aussi des capacités qu'il convient de prendre en compte. Il appartient donc aux intervenants de gérer cette vulnérabilité, les syndromes et les causes de la crise. Pour cela, il faut déterminer les capacités qu'il faut enrichir pour réduire ces vulnérabilités. L'objectif de l'appui des Affaires civiles est de fixer le cadre et les processus susceptibles de mettre les gens et les autorités locales sur la voie de leur propre perfectionnement.

Cette idée d'investir dans les capacités à long terme, a une incidence considérable sur l'aptitude des populations concernées à refaire leur vie après le départ des secouristes.

En réalité, la tâche semble être difficile pour un intervenant externe qui n'est pas toujours censé maîtriser comment perfectionner le bénéficiaire, qui lui est étranger.

En matière de prévention des risques et désastres, l'absence ou la faiblesse de la participation des destinataires à la planification et à la mise en oeuvre des projets entraine à coup sûr, un décalage entre les objectifs et les résultats. La meilleure approche est celle qui permet aux populations bénéficiaires de l'assistance, de partager, d'améliorer et d'analyser leurs connaissances de la vie et des conditions locales. Autrement dit, elles doivent être impliquées d'une manière ou d'une autre. Il appartient à ces populations d'évaluer leurs besoins de planifier, d'agir et de surveiller le processus de prévention et de résolution de la crise. Cela implique une méthodologie systématique visant à se renseigner sur les destinataires de l'assistance humanitaire et le contexte de la situation qui prévaut.

Ensuite, il convient de discerner puis de renforcer les capacités des gens et des collectivités territoriales dans le cadre d'une évaluation participative, notamment en milieu rural. L'accent doit porter tout autant sur le processus que sur les fins. C'est une forme particulière de la gouvernance locale effective fondée sur la démocratie participative et l'Etat de droit.

Au niveau national, cela oblige à définir un mode d'organisation générale de l'ensemble du système et des structures qui en font partie ; les rôles et les responsabilités de chacune de ces structures avant, pendant et après la situation d'urgence. Concrètement, il s'agit de préparer un plan d'intervention qui définira les grandes actions d'urgence, les rôles et les responsabilités de chaque institution, organisation et ONG, par rapport à ses fonctions.

Au niveau régional, le plan de contingence consiste à déterminer à la fois le mode d'organisation, les grandes fonctions et les procédures des interventions au moment des urgences. Ce qui fait appel à l'élaboration d'un plan de contingence au niveau départemental et au niveau communal, pour mieux gérer la crise. On parle même du plan de contingence au niveau collinaire. Ce plan de contingence est un outil de gestion utilisé par le comité de la gestion de crise dans les situations d'urgence. Il permet de garantir les dispositions adéquates devant être prises en anticipation d'une crise. Ce plan doit contenir l'ensemble des orientations nécessaires à prendre en prévision d'une urgence probable dans le but d'en atténuer les effets.

L'élaboration du plan de contingence contribuera sans aucun doute, à garantir la bonne préparation pour répondre de façon coordonnée et adéquate à une situation d'urgence. Son succès dépendra énormément à la clarification des buts des stratégies, des rôles et des responsabilités, ainsi que des moyens nécessaires qui vont être mis en oeuvre.

Pour plus d'efficacité, cette planification doit suivre un processus participatif impliquant idéalement tous les acteurs qui auront à travailler ensemble au moment de la crise. En un mot, le plan de contingence définit les mécanismes de gestion : rôles et responsabilités, dans le cadre d'une intervention humanitaire d'urgence, puis identifie les ressources nécessaires, à travers des hypothèses de planification qui tiennent compte du contexte du territoire en question. Son intérêt est de partager les informations sur :

- la planification d'urgence et les stratégies de réponse au niveau des collectivités territoriales et au niveau central ;
- les centres d'opération d'urgence d'une crise humanitaire ;
- les leçons apprises suite aux précédents désastres ;
- la connaissance des acteurs et ressources d'une collectivité ;
- la mise en place des stratégies de réponse et les différents centres d'opération d'urgence ;
- la manière de coordonner les opérations ;
- le plan de réponse militaire pour faire face aux catastrophes naturelles ;
- le rôle des clusters.

Le plan de contingence se situe entre la préparation et la réponse à une catastrophe. Il met en exergue les moyens de rétablir la situation : prévenir et atténuer la souffrance d'un peuple frappé par une crise. « Puisque la règle du jeu s'établit avant le match », alors il est important de prévoir la coordination et la préparation du processus d'élaboration du plan de contingence. Cela suppose la faisabilité d'une analyse de contexte à partir d'un montage des scénarios présentant les défis et les enjeux. Cela permettra de définir les hypothèses de planification afin d'élaborer des stratégies et des objectifs précis de gestion des catastrophe probables.

Ce processus de planification doit être consolidé, en activant et en faisant le monitoring du groupe de gestion qui doit prévoir entre autres, le déclenchement des opérations. Il faut donc définir un plan d'alerte, le cadre opérationnel, le cadre de coordination, de maintenance du plan et de suivi-évaluation, sans oublier le budget. Ce budget doit se faire sur la base d'une identification des besoins et en fonction du plan de réponse, de communication, d'évacuation et de diffusion d'alerte.

Il est important d'identifier les ressources et le savoir-faire à l'échelon local, pour ne pas passer à côté de véritables occasions d'intégrer :

- la société civile ;
- les ONG ;
- les organismes communautaires ;

- les syndicats ;
- les organismes religieux ;
- les corps professionnels ;
- les fondations ;
- les gouvernements locaux dans la gestion des secours liée à la consolidation de la paix et la sécurité.

L'objectif de ce renforcement des capacités locales lors des cas d'urgence est de mettre en valeur les capacités qui conviendraient et non celles des gens à l'égard de qui c'est contre-indiqué. Il faut éviter que les programmes d'aide en cas d'urgence ne soient pas en contradiction avec la politique déclarée à laquelle se sont engagés les donateurs et les bonnes intentions fréquemment exprimées.

Le premier réflexe dans ce cas est d'organiser une rencontre élargie qui réunira autour d'une seule table, tous les acteurs de la vie d'une commune ou d'un département, de préférence et en fonction de l'ampleur de la crise. Il ne faut pas se leurrer, la participation des journalistes, juristes et agents de l'ordre est extrêmement indispensable, contrairement à l'impression que cela peut avoir aux yeux du profane.

En tant que quatrième pouvoir après l'exécutif, le législatif et le judiciaire, la presse joue un rôle encore plus important pour la diffusion de bonnes informations et à temps réel, en vue de lutter contre la désintoxication, les rumeurs, les diffamations et les fausses nouvelles qui peuvent jeter l'huile sur le feu et ajouter l'incompréhension et la panique au sein d'une population en difficulté. Dans tous les cas, il vaut mieux les avoir avec soi que contre soi, dans des circonstances pareilles.

Quant aux juristes, ils sont les garants du respect des lois, des droits de l'homme et de la dignité humaine. Ils sont éventuelles poursuites pour violations de la loi. C'est une sorte de prévention juridique dans le feu de l'action. Il faut surtout éviter que la catastrophe engendre de nouveaux riches.

Le respect de la dignité est une préoccupation essentielle qu'il faut prendre en compte même en situation d'urgence et de détresse collective. C'est sur la base de cette dignité humaine que le largage des vivres et autres aides humanitaires à Port-au-Prince après le tremblement de terre du 12 janvier 2010 a été critiqué. Même si c'était le seul moyen de desservir les populations menacées par la famine dans certaines localités non accessibles, il n'en demeure pas moins que leur dignité reste à préserver. Ironie de l'histoire, les populations qui avaient reçu cette assistance qui tombait du ciel, à travers des hélicoptères américains ne s'étaient pas plaintes pour autant. En fait, l'urgence n'exclut pas la prudence et le respect des textes sur les droits fondamentaux.

Dans le même ordre d'idées, la police nationale et l'unité de police des Nations unies (UNPOL), y compris les militaires, devraient être les bienvenus à une rencontre de cette importance. Ils jouent un rôle principal dans une situation de crise. Ce sont les garants de la sécurité des collectivités territoriales. Ils doivent être informés et consultés sur les modalités d'appui sécuritaire, notamment sur la Sécurité des convois, les transferts et les distributions de l'aide humanitaire, ce qui n'exclut pas l'élaboration d'un plan stratégique d'urgence pour de développement.

Il est aujourd'hui prouvé que la fin de la guerre ne signifie pas toujours l'existence de la paix. La fin des hostilités est un pas vers la stabilité, car la vraie paix est d'abord et avant tout économique. Elle dépend de la capacité du gouvernement à satisfaire les besoins d'une population appauvrie par la crise.

B. PLAN STRATEGIQUE D'URGENCE SUR LE DEVELOPPEMENT

Dans les situations d'urgence, l'appui institutionnel aux collectivités territoriales doit se focaliser sur un accompagnement spécifique dans les domaines prioritaires de l'urbanisme et de la construction dans l'ensemble des communes. Les maires sont invités à prendre conscience de la responsabilité pénale des élus dans la délivrance d'actes relevant de leurs compétences. Les Affaires civiles doivent ainsi contribuer au montage d'un cahier des charges pour la reconstruction, dans le cadre d'une expérience de coopération intercommunale associée à une plateforme de coopération décentralisée avec certains partenaires étrangers.

Généralement, lorsqu'il y a une catastrophe, sur tout ou partie du territoire national, des dommages importants sont inévitablement subis. Les départements non touchés sont parfois forcés de recevoir beaucoup de réfugiés, solidarité oblige. Cette situation vient souvent aggraver les problèmes que confrontaient déjà certaines collectivités territoriales.

Le défi des régions est de trouver des moyens adéquats pour faire face à ce phénomène par la conception d'un plan départemental de développement durable.

Dans un premier temps, il serait judicieux de concevoir une stratégie permettant de faire face à cet afflux de victimes. Il s'agit essentiellement, de soutenir les familles d'accueil qui, en général, épuisent toutes leurs réserves dans un temps-record, au point de consommer même les semences agricoles des saisons prochaines. Pire encore, les rescapés rejettent ipso facto le logement dans des camps des déplacés, au profit des familles d'accueil et/ou des amis.

Dans un second temps, il est préférable d'accélérer la croissance économique de ces régions par le renforcement des activités de développement, tels que : l'appui en crédit agricole, le développement des financements solidaires et des projets de microcrédit. Il faut miser sur la consolidation de la décentralisation de toutes les institutions nationales pour en finir avec l'épiphénomène de « République capitale », sans oublier l'appui aux familles d'accueil en nourriture, vêtements, kits d'hygiène et de cuisine pendant plusieurs mois sinon plusieurs années. L'urgence est de déterminer les actions prioritaires du plan d'urgence. Celui-ci portera sur un véritable programme d'urgence concernant la réhabilitation et le développement. Il peut se concevoir en plusieurs sous-programmes. C'est le cas du secteur socio-économique dont les catastrophes engendrent des pressions sur les ressources alimentaires disponibles et qui, dans la plupart des cas sont déjà insuffisantes.

L'espace physique d'accueil est généralement défectueux et le ralentissement des activités économiques dans le secteur tertiaire pousse les familles à orienter leurs économies sur l'alimentation uniquement. Il y a aussi un arrêt des activités génératrices de revenus pour certains migrants, ce qui aggrave le chômage et augmente le phénomène de mendicité. Il n'est pas vain de noter le manque d'accès à des services de base par rapport au lieu de provenance et d'accueil des migrants. Tout cela s'ajoute à l'augmentation des prix des produits de première nécessité.

Les conditions socio-économiques difficiles d'une population en détresse peuvent être solutionnées par un investissement considérable dans les secteurs de la pêche et du tourisme, essentiellement dans les zones côtières. L'idée est d'encourager la création massive de nouveaux emplois dans les communes.

L'expérience en matière de gestion des situations d'urgence indique que, lorsque les conditions d'accès à l'emploi et l'établissement adéquat pour la poursuite de leurs études, ainsi que l'obtention des services sociaux de base, tels que : l'eau potable, l'électricité, routes… sont réunies les victimes admises dans un lieu donné pensent y rester définitivement.

Dans ces conjonctures, les résidants habituels ne manifestent aucune répulsion à leur égard, bien que cela aggrave davantage la misère dans leurs communautés. Il convient de comprendre que ni les Affaires civiles ni leurs partenaires locaux ne sont des professionnels, encore moins d'industriels de l'urgence. Par conséquent, il est préférable de se concentrer sur des actes qui s'inscrivent dans la logique de la durée et selon une certaine cohérence pour faire coïncider les bonnes intentions avec les actes, en vue d'atteindre les fameux objectifs du millénium.

Force est de reconnaître que les programmes de distribution massive d'aliments que l'on voit ici et là peuvent aboutir à tuer les économies agricoles des pays dévastés par les catastrophes naturelles ou d'autres situations d'urgence du même ordre. Voilà pourquoi, il faudrait absolument miser sur la distribution de semences et d'outils aratoires et sur l'encadrement technique des agriculteurs dans le cadre d'un programme d'augmentation de la production locale. Cette politique a l'avantage de garantir la sécurité et la souveraineté alimentaire qui permettront à terme, de ne plus dépendre de l'aide alimentaire internationale d'urgence. A cet effet, le développement des microcrédits : à l'agriculture, à l'agro-transformation et à la commercialisation de la production agricole, notamment à l'exportation sont des prototypes à encourager.

L'aide en cas d'urgence peut miner les capacités locales au lieu de la renforcer. Ce qui oblige à savoir avec qui travailler (par exemple, les femmes, les leaders traditionnels ou les ONG locales), mais aussi à comprendre comment œuvrer avec eux. En effet, la problématique homme-femme est un sujet de préoccupation particulièrement important qui contraint de mettre les femmes à l'abri de la violence lors de certains cas d'urgence. Il serait judicieux d'épargner ces groupes sociaux à être pris pour cible dans le but de ne pas accroître leur fardeau, notamment en ce qui a trait aux enfants, à l'entretien et à l'alimentation de leurs familles.

Pour couronner le tout, il est essentiel d'appuyer les activités socio-économiques et les programmes de crédit, notamment, en donnant des crédits aux groupements de femmes et associations mixtes pour améliorer leurs revenus. Pour illustration, on peut soutenir la création des mutuelles de solidarité et entretenir les initiatives entrepreneuriales dans les secteurs de transformation des produits agricoles et du développement de filières, d'implantation de moulins de canne, de maïs, manioc et autres produits de base de ces localités. Toutefois, dans l'optique d'une vision de développement à long terme, il est important de mettre en place les crédits pour les petits commerçants et appuyer la création d'investissements et d'emplois dans les collectivités territoriales, notamment dans le domaine de la sous-traitance. La mise en place des infrastructures de base : routes, électricité, ports, aéroports internationaux… font partie des priorités même en situation de crise.

C. ACTIONS PRIORITAIRES A ENTREPRENDRE APRES UNE CATASTROPHE

Le renforcement des capacités consiste à appuyer les victimes de la crise qui de surcroit, sont souvent dépourvues de matériels de résidence. Dans le secteur de la santé, par exemple, la distribution des Kits alimentaires, d'hygiènes et de cuisine, ainsi que la fourniture des matelas, vêtements, couvertures de laine, de drap, etc. sont indispensables pour soulager leur douleur.

Cependant, le mieux serait de renforcer les dispensaires et les centres de santé en matériels et équipements médicaux, mais aussi en personnel qualifié. Mieux encore, le renforcement des services de santé passe par la transformation de petits centres de santé en hôpitaux communaux pour accélérer sinon agrandir la proximité des services de santé.

A l'évidence, la catastrophe humanitaire apporte toujours son lot d'émotions : stress post-traumatique, pessimisme et anxiété dus à la perte d'un parent ou d'un proche, ainsi que l'augmentation de l'agressivité de la part des gens qui supportent mal les privations causées par la situation d'urgence.

Pour cela, une assistance psychosociale doit être prévue en faveur des rescapés. Elle inclut l'organisation des activités récréatives pour les victimes. On peut aussi compter sur l'éducation en faveur de toutes les couches de la société, ceux-là qui sont souvent touchées par la crise : écoliers, étudiants, cultivateurs, commerçants, chômeurs, artisans, enseignants, agents de santé, leaders religieux, enfants, femmes, hommes, jeunes, adultes et vieillards.

La situation d'urgence créée par les déplacés qui amplifient les effectifs scolaires dans les sales classes, elles-mêmes déjà surchargées, entraine parfois l'arrêt des études pour certains étudiants. L'urgence révèle souvent l'inadaptation des programmes scolaires et l'ensemble du système éducatif national qui, dans bien des cas, est inapproprié. Ce qui ressort généralement est un système d'écoles à deux vitesses avec des moyens et des programmes disproportionnés en fonction des régions.

Le besoin de plus d'écoles publiques et la formation des maîtres s'imposent. La lutte contre la centralisation excessive des pôles de décisions et des moyens de l'Etat concernent les grandes écoles, universités, industries. Il est souhaitable de soutenir l'ouverture de plus d'universités et d'écoles professionnelles, de sport et d'industries dans les départements, afin de désengorger la capitale et les autres « métropoles » très urbanisées. Le développement des programmes de parrainage et de subvention scolaire est aussi substantiel. Pour ce qui est du logement ou plutôt des abris provisoires, il s'agit d'effectuer la réhabilitation de résidences privées et étatiques, à savoir les bâtiments subissant des dommages au niveau de chaque département.

Ce programme d'appui en matériels pour abris provisoires et accessoires s'accomplit par un pré-positionnement des matériaux d'urgence dans tous les départements et communes. Il s'accompagne d'une campagne de sensibilisation communautaire sur les différentes menaces pour lesquelles la population est exposée. La réalisation des campagnes radiophoniques et autres moyens de communication aide énormément.

Dans certains cas spécifiques d'urgence, il est nécessaire de faire preuve de rigueur pour changer profondément le mode de gouvernance étatique irresponsable et inefficace, caractérisée par la corruption et le népotisme, en attribuant plus de pouvoir aux gouvernements locaux. Les décisions doivent émaner de la base. La gestion des catastrophes est aussi une opportunité de lutter contre la mauvaise gestion de l'espace physique et public, essentiellement de la manière de construire et de protéger les espaces publics et l'environnement.

Travailler sur l'urgence ne peut pas être une option planifiée, mais imprévue, car les désastres et leurs conséquences surprennent tout le monde. Cela n'empêche que dans la gestion de l'urgence, il faut toujours envisager de prévoir l'avenir, y compris dans le secteur de l'agriculture.

Le renforcement des capacités de ce secteur oblige à fortement encourager la politique qui consiste à subventionner l'agriculture des pays post-conflit. L'objectif est d'effacer une fois pour toute la théorie selon laquelle l'agriculture des pays industrialisés serait définie comme un instrument ou une arme de la politique étrangère et commerciale. Le monde n'est plus à l'époque de la guerre froide ou de l'émergence des pays arabes à la conquête de leurs ressources ou encore celle où l'or vert comme monnaie d'échange contre l'or noir servait d'outil de pression sur la Russie et la Chine engouffrée dans les crises cycliques de pénurie alimentaire.

La mondialisation et la globalisation exigent un certain pragmatisme qui sollicite un élan de la solidarité internationale. Un accent doit être mis sur la protection et la réhabilitation environnementale, car il convient de protéger les sources en eau, de réhabiliter les espaces dégradés et de gérer les déchets solides. Concrètement, il s'agit de réaliser des campagnes de reboisement à différentes échelles de provinces et de communes.

Dans le même ordre d'idées, l'appui en crédit agricole est un aspect non négligeable pour une politique visionnaire. Le but est d'améliorer le fonctionnement des exploitations agricoles par la libéralisation du crédit agricole. Cela signifie appuyer certains groupements d'agriculteurs en crédit, pour faciliter la production au niveau local.

L'urgence peut appeler l'urgence. Il faut donc éviter que la catastrophe naturelle n'engendre pas une autre catastrophe, celle qui provoquerait des émeutes de la faim. D'où la nécessité de redéfinir la stratégie de relance économique basée sur les performances de l'agriculture. Cette stratégie viserait à distribuer des engrais et des intrants agricoles aux cultivateurs pour les saisons futures. Des mesures d'accompagnement destinées à agir contre la cherté de la vie doivent être prises, notamment sur le prix des produits importés que pourrait occasionner la baisse du pouvoir d'achat et l'augmentation des prix des denrées de base.

Le gouvernement du pays en question doit se servir d'une base de données pour cibler les régions fertiles du territoire national et les cultivateurs qui contribuent au processus de la production locale en vue de renforcer l'efficacité de la politique de distribution des engrais et d'intrants agricoles. Le but est de protéger la production nationale, pour aller vers l'autosuffisance alimentaire. Puisqu'il s'agit de gérer l'urgence à très court terme, il est souhaitable d'appliquer la sélectivité de l'aide en fonction des réalités existantes dans chaque région afin d'apporter la bonne assistance au bon endroit et mieux soutenir la population.

Il n'est pas vain de prendre en compte le domaine d'implantation des magasins communautaires et de boutiques d'intrants agricoles. Cela sert à faciliter l'accès aux intrants agricoles dans plusieurs pôles au niveau des provinces, puis épauler l'approvisionnement des produits de première nécessité aux différentes communes provinciales. Cela peut se traduire par la construction de magasins communautaires et de boutiques d'intrants d'approvisionnement en produits de première nécessité et intrants agricoles.

Lorsqu'on parle d'autosuffisance alimentaire, il ne s'agit pas seulement de l'amélioration du secteur agricole, mais aussi celui de l'élevage. Le renforcement de la production agricole passe par l'accompagnement des paysans et des agriculteurs, en mettant à leur disposition des semences, de banques d'outils, de crédits en faveur de petits marchands par la modernisation des moyens de production. Il serait intéressant, par exemple, d'encourager l'extension des cultures vivrières et développer le domaine de l'agroforesterie dans le cadre de la production de bois de manière durable. Soulignons au passage qu'il convient aussi de prendre en compte la conservation de sols, à travers la réhabilitation de ceux-ci et les cultures fruitières de rente.

Dans le même temps, il convient de maintenir un regard sur l'agro-transformation qui consiste à former les travailleurs des ateliers locaux dans la fabrication des équipements utilisés pour la transformation des produits très consommés dans ces pays (exemple la fabrication des machines pour gratter le manioc ou l'arbre à pain), pour le cas d'Haïti.

Ensuite, il faut travailler avec les utilisateurs et les consommateurs de ces produits pour leur ouvrir des voies pour écouler cette production, notamment dans les pays développés.

En conséquence, dans le cadre de la préparation aux risques et désastres, un officier des Affaires civiles doit être aguerri à la méthode d'organisation et de gestion de l'information pour soutenir la préparation des plans de contingence locaux. A cette occasion, il doit mener des activités visant à réduire l'impact des désastres naturels. Par exemple, en collaboration avec les autorités locales, notamment ceux de la sécurité civile et les partenaires humanitaires, il peut réaliser une mission qui aurait pour objectifs :

- aider à la mise à jour des données sur les risques d'inondation dus à la saison cyclonique ;
- définir des produits informatifs sur le pré-positionnement des « clusters » et connaître les gaps/lacunes, pour la prise de décisions ;
- installer et présenter des formations sur les produits standards d'Information Management Unit (IMU), c'est-à-dire les 3W « who, what, where », « Contact Management System (CMS) », gestion des listes de contacts, planification des réunions, organisation de la réponse humanitaire, gestion du site web…

Pour les cas spécifiques de gestion des risques d'inondation, il s'agira de :

- aider à la mise en place ou faire la révision des formulaires existant sur la collecte des données des abris provisoires, collecter les données avec les partenaires sur le terrain ;
- mettre en place les outils de saisie des données ;
- assurer la formation GPS, outil de saisie de données… ;
- produire une cartographie actualisée des zones inondables et des abris provisoires d'évacuation ;
- identifier et préciser l'ordre de priorité des activités de mitigations qui sera soumis à l'approbation des autorités compétentes de la mission.

Ladite mission mènera donc des activités standards de gestion de l'information telles :

- formation et installation des formulaires et systèmes de collecte d'informations que l'on appelle dans le jargon humanitaire (« template » 3W) ;
- formation et installation du « Contact Management System (CMS) » ;
- formation sur le « template » pour la planification des réunions ;
- formation sur la gestion des listes de contacts ;
- formation sur l'utilisation du site et des pages Web, notamment l'édition, la visualisation des informations, la mise à jour des données...

Les Affaires civiles sont priées d'aider l'Etat et les collectivités territoriales à être plus opérationnelles non seulement pour l'accueil et le traitement des victimes, mais aussi pour l'obtention et la distribution efficace de l'aide humanitaire, dans le respect des droits de la personne humaine et de la dignité avec une prise en compte de la problématique de sécurité.

Cela n'est possible que si la section des Affaires civiles, elle-même est structurée et organisée.

De façon générale, les défis humanitaires dans les pays en situation d'urgence humanitaire et politico-économique peuvent se résumer, tels que présentés ci-après :

Dans le domaine agricole

- le manque d'infrastructures agricoles ;
- l'absence d'encadrement technique ;
- l'indisponibilité de l'eau pour l'irrigation des terres ;
- l'irresponsabilité de l'Etat sur toutes ses formes ;
- le défaut de conscience professionnelle des cadres formés ;
- la migration intérieure ou l'exode rural ;
- les problèmes climatiques.

Dans le domaine de l'Education

- le manque d'établissements scolaires de qualité ;
- l'absence de contrôle du système scolaire ;
- la non-informatisation du système scolaire et universitaire ;
- l'insuffisance de capacité de certaines responsables d'écoles privées.

Dans le domaine de la santé

- l'insuffisance du personnel de santé qualifié dans les hôpitaux et les centres de santé ;
- le défaut d'éducation sanitaire de la population ;
- l'insécurité alimentaire ;
- le manque de ressources matérielles ;
- l'incapacité de réagir rapidement et efficacement face aux situations épidémiques ;
- l'augmentation continue du taux de mortalité maternelle et infantile.

Dans le domaine du tourisme

- le manque d'infrastructures routières surtout interarrondissements et intercommunales ;
- l'absence de ports et autres sites touristiques d'accueil ;
- la défaillance des structures pour une plus grande commercialisation de l'artisanat, c'est-à-dire magasin pour artisans et galerie d'art ;
- l'insécurité globale ;
- la mendicité dans les rues et devant les hôtels ;
- les difficultés d'approvisionnement en matières premières (aliments de base).

Les propositions de solutions sont multiples. En matière d'agriculture, l'objectif des Affaires civiles est d'encourager les élus locaux à mettre en place une agriculture forte, rentable et compétitive. Cela passe par l'identification des terres propices à l'agriculture avec de bonnes conditions environnementales et un plaidoyer pour la « priorisation » de l'agriculture dans le budget national, couplé à l'enseignement des notions agricoles dans les différentes écoles et institutions du pays.

La solution aux problèmes de tourisme impose la planification des démarches suivantes :

- construction des axes routiers du pays hôte ;
- la restauration des sites touristiques et l'aménagement des plages ;
- l'encadrement des artisans et artistes ;
- l'établissement d'un système de sécurité du département ;

- l'augmentation des chambres d'hôtels qui doivent être plus agréable avec de meilleures conditions d'accueil et sanitaires (fatras dans l'environnement de ces hôtels).

Une telle stratégie devrait aller de pair avec la promotion des valeurs touristiques et la réorganisation de ce secteur, par la mobilisation des ressources humaines, matérielles et financières, ainsi que par le regroupement des acteurs dudit domaine en associations touristiques. L'Etat de son côté, doit diminuer les taxes et autres barrières administratives pour encourager les investissements dans ce secteur.

Quant au domaine d'infrastructures, il est essentiel pour les Affaires civiles de soutenir les autorités à :

- réaliser la construction de routes intercommunales en asphalte ou béton pour aboutir à une révolution routière où les communes sont liées par des autoroutes de la communication ;
- se lancer dans la production de courant électrique capable d'alimenter toutes les communes du pays ;
- élaborer un plan d'urbanisme pour toutes les mairies qui ont besoin ou la mise à jour des plans qui existent déjà et pourquoi pas, la construction d'un complexe administratif devant loger les bureaux publics de la commune, sans oublier la mise en place des infrastructures de base pour chaque mairie.

Dans le secteur de l'éducation, le soutien des Affaires civiles doit surtout s'orienter vers :

- l'éducation primaire et fondamentale obligatoire et gratuite ;
- l'informatisation du système éducatif ;
- la résolution du problème de fond de pension des ressources humaines, ainsi que celle des autres défis, notamment le manque de capacité des directeurs dans certaines écoles privées.

Pour terminer, le système de santé doit être caractérisé par la construction ou la réhabilitation des hôpitaux de référence, bien équipé dans chaque commune. Il est souhaitable que les Affaires civiles se mobilisent pour encourager les programmes qui prévoient au moins un centre de santé par commune et un dispensaire moderne dans chaque section communale. Il faut ajouter à cela :

- le renforcement du personnel qualifié à tous les niveaux ;
- plus de médicaments disponibles dans ces établissements ;
- la prise en charge des cas de malnutrition ;
- des meilleures conditions de travail pour le personnel médical de chaque structure, sans oublier d'appliquer le dispositif légal contre les usurpateurs de titres réservés aux professionnels de santé.

Toutefois, en absence du plan stratégique de distribution, il est difficile de cibler les vrais bénéficiaires de l'assistance.

D. ELABORATION D'UN PLAN STRATEGIQUE DE DISTRIBUTION

Le défi majeur de la distribution efficace de l'aide humanitaire est de pallier à l'accessibilité difficile que ce soit par voies aériennes, terrestre ou maritime. Ces difficultés liées, en particulier au mauvais état des routes reliant les différentes collectivités territoriales qui handicapent souvent la circulation des biens et des personnes. On ne saurait négliger la dispersion des habitations qui compliquent davantage la distribution des rations sèches et d'autres produits au niveau de chaque département, sans oublier le phénomène de détournement dans la chaine de distribution. Du coup, la définition d'un plan stratégique pour assurer une bonne prise en charge des rescapés devient alors une préoccupation majeure.

Elle permet non seulement de donner un accompagnement de proximité aux victimes d'une catastrophe naturelle dans les collectivités territoriales, mais aussi d'assurer un bon « ciblage » des victimes en vue d'éviter la confusion et les frustrations au sein des populations des différentes communes.

Enfin, c'est le meilleur moyen d'harmoniser et de concilier les actions des différents secteurs de la communauté. Ainsi, la distribution d'aide dépend des zones d'intervention. Lorsqu'il s'agit d'un milieu urbain, les habitations sont rapprochées et la population serait desservie sans trop de difficultés à cause de l'accessibilité. En revanche, dans le milieu rural les habitats sont généralement dispersés et les routes sont inaccessibles, ce qui entraine des difficultés d'approvisionnement.

Par conséquent, les stratégies seront différentes selon qu'on se trouve en milieu rural ou urbain. Sur l'aspect sécuritaire les catastrophes naturelles peuvent provoquer une augmentation de la délinquance, notamment : les viols, les vols de bétail, les dévastations de champ...

Il appartient aux autorités locales de :

- assurer le transport, le stockage et la sécurité des vivres ;
- coordonner la distribution ;
- organiser l'harmonisation des listes ;
- prévoir le terrain de stockage et de distribution ;
- identifier les bénéficiaires ;
- garantir la sécurisation de la distribution.

Les organisations de base et la société civile devraient être parties prenantes dans ce processus d'identification, de planification, de distribution, de sécurisation et de contrôle de l'aide humanitaire.

Le rôle des institutions d'appui est de faciliter la liaison entre le comité en charge de la gestion de l'urgence et leurs éléments sur le terrain, pour accompagner les autorités locales et les organisations de base dans la préparation des listes servant de base à la préparation et la distribution des cartes de bénéficiaires à chaque victime.

L'urgence humanitaire c'est l'acheminement des ressources tant bilatérales que multilatérales par l'entremise d'ONG internationales ne constituent pas une fin en soi. Au contraire, elle peut entraîner un changement de cap tendant à « déresponsabiliser » des leaders nationaux et locaux, à saper la capacité locale et à créer une dépendance plus poussée du pays en question.

Lors des cas d'urgence et des situations de relèvement après l'urgence, il est souhaitable que les programmes de secours ne restent pas caractérisés par leur externalité. Il faut davantage miser sur une approche adaptée de la « responsabilisation » du personnel expatrié pour ne pas susciter des tensions parmi les organisations locales ou entre les réfugiés, les déplacés et les autres victimes, ainsi que la population au sein de laquelle ils sont accueillis, concernant l'accès aux ressources extérieures.

CONCLUSION

La fonction des Affaires Civiles se ramène essentiellement, à aider le gouvernement du pays hôte à rétablir une administration post-crise et l'autorité de l'Etat sur l'ensemble du territoire national, en surveillant et en fournissant une assistance technique aux gouvernements régionaux et locaux sur une large gamme de programmes. C'est une lourde responsabilité qui se consiste à :

- A- appliquer leurs connaissances théoriques et pratiques, pour évaluer et formuler des recommandations pour la conception ou la révision des institutions régionales et locales, sans oublier la gestion des programmes de consolidation de paix ;
- A- aider au renforcement du pouvoir d'Etat et promouvoir la gouvernance efficace par le renforcement des capacités et la promotion des activités de bonne gouvernance ;
- A- assurer le monitoring, l'encadrement et l'assistance technique aux fonctionnaires du Gouvernement local nouvellement installé par des visites et de contacts réguliers ;
- A- assurer le suivi du processus de transfert de pouvoir ou de passation de service entre gouverneurs et entre cartels municipaux entrant et sortant ;
- C- coordonner les activités régionales des Affaires civiles de l'ensemble du bureau, notamment veiller à la cohérence et la synergie de tout le bureau et maintenir une interaction quotidienne avec d'autres éléments du bureau régional
- E- effectuer des recherches et formuler des recommandations dans le cadre du recrutement et de l'amélioration du personnel de la fonction publique à qui il faut garantir la formation ;
- E- encourager les initiatives de développement local, en donnant des conseils sur la modernisation des infrastructures et en facilitant les actions conjointes entre la direction générale des impôts, les contrôleurs des finances et les représentants du Gouvernement local pour l'établissement des rôles d'imposition municipale ;

- E- effectuer des visites régulières dans les communes pour évaluer les progrès accomplis dans la perception des impôts locaux et la budgétisation ;
- F- favoriser les liens entre les institutions locales ;
- F- fournir des conseils sur le renforcement de la sécurité des ports et des frontières maritimes ;
- F- fournir des informations précises, opportunes et factuelles, à travers des rapports périodiques sur l'évolution de la situation politique, les questions économiques, les changements institutionnels et/ou tous autres faits importants pouvant avoir un impact sur le relèvement du pouvoir étatique ;
- F- favoriser le renforcement de la confiance, le dialogue, la compréhension et la coopération entre toutes les parties concernées par la situation du pays, à savoir : les partis et acteurs politiques, la société civile, les associations et ONG nationales et internationales, la population, les confessions religieuses… ;
- F- former les préfets et sous-préfets sur les techniques de base dans l'exercice de fonctions de supervision et de coordination sur les institutions d'Etat locales ;
- F- faciliter la mise en place d'un cadre institutionnel au profit des dirigeants élus et nommés par le Gouvernement qui seront responsables de la performance ;
- G- gérer la section des Affaires Civiles du bureau régional ;
- I- identifier les besoins de formation et déterminer les programmes de formation à concevoir, tout en développant les outils de formation pouvant rendre plus efficace les services Gouvernementaux par leur impact sur le renforcement des institutions ;
- I- identifier les nouvelles menaces au processus politique et démocratique ;
- I- informer sur le mandat et les activités de la mission de maintien ou de consolidation de la paix et sur le rôle des autres agences de l'ONU, si nécessaire ;
- I- identifier et recommander, après consultation avec les autorités locales, la rénovation des infrastructures essentielles des collectivités territoriales, à travers les « Projets à Impact Rapide » ou toute autre source de financement disponibles ;
- M- maintenir le contact et assurer la liaison sur une base quotidienne avec des représentants des Gouvernements régionaux et locaux, les fonctionnaires, la société civile et les organisations d'aide internationale ;

- M- maintenir des contacts étroits et des relations de travail entre le délégué, vice-délégués et les directeurs régionaux des ministères de tutelle ;
- P- promouvoir le développement de la force de travail et les pratiques anti-discriminations et anticorruption, ainsi que les questions de décentralisation et d'autres domaines ayant un impact sur le renforcement des institutions de l'Etat ;
- P- participer à la coordination des activités du Groupe de travail sur l'état de droit et de la sécurité, ainsi que la promotion de la primauté du droit dans les communes ;
- P- promouvoir la politique et le dialogue intersectoriel et de la confiance à la mission d'assistance et aux autres composants de la politique régionale ;
- P- présider la réunion de coordination des affaires régionales et des questions de sécurité ;
- P- participer aux tables de concertation et fournir une assistance à l'accomplissement de la stratégie régionale de réduction de la pauvreté et l'augmentation des richesses ;
- S- surveiller et élaborer des rapports sur la conformité des actes des autorités de base avec les lois et autres règlements Gouvernementaux relatifs à la gouvernance locale et l'exécution de la politique de l'Etat au niveau régional, concernant les fonctionnaires du Gouvernement local, puis sur la collecte des impôts locaux et la budgétisation ;
- S- soutenir le dialogue des cultures et des ethnies ;
- S- suivre et rapporter les activités des partis politiques et d'éventuelles alliances électorales ou politiques.

Ce laborieux travail de débroussaillage préliminaire créait les conditions permettant d'envisager une réflexion sur les différents types de formations essentielles à porter à l'attention des partenaires des Affaires Civiles, au premier rang desquels se trouvent les autorités de base, en charge des Collectivités Territoriales. Toutefois, les thèmes qui seront développés dans cette partie, sont choisis en fonction des besoins et des faiblesses des Collectivités Territoriales, mais aussi sur la base de notre expérience de terrain. Il s'agit notamment de : la fonctionmunicipale (I), la gestion des affaires de la Mairie (II), la méthode de formation des adultes (III), la communication (IV), transformation des conflits (V), la gestion des ressources humaines (VI), les notions fondamentales des droits de l'homme (VII), la planification du développement communale (VIII), les finances communales (IX), la décentralisation (X), la coopération décentralisée (XI).

TABLE DES MATIÈRES

DU MÊME AUTEUR 7

REMERCIEMENTS 11

AVANT-PROPOS 13

INTRODUCTION 19

Le guide des Affaires civiles de l'ONU 29

I. Présentation sommaire de l'Organisation des Nations unies 33

A. ORGANES DE L'ONU 34
a. Conseil de tutelle 34
b. Cour Internationale de Justice (CIJ) 34
c. L'Assemblée générale 35
d. Conseil Economique et Social (ECOSOC) 36
e. Conseil de Sécurité 39
f. Secrétariat Général de L'ONU 41
B. MANDAT DES AFFAIRES CIVILES 43

II. Esquisse de définition et analyse des concepts 51

A. L'EXPRESSION AFFAIRES CIVILES 51
a. Le Terme Affaires civiles au Sens de l'Armée Américaine 51
b. Le Mot « Affaires civiles » au Sens Onusien 60
B. THEORIE DU RENFORCEMENT DES CAPACITES 71
C. LE TERME DE « SOCIETE CIVILE » 78
D. LE CONCEPT DE « GOUVERNANCE » 92
E. L'IDEE DE BONNE GOUVERNANCE 98
F. LA NOTION DE « COLLECTIVITE TERRITORIALE » 104
G. PRINCIPE DE « L'ETAT DE DROIT » 113
H. LA PRATIQUE DU RENFORCEMENT DES CAPACITES DE L'ETAT. 122

III. Structure organisationelle d'une section des Affaires civiles 129

A. UNITE COORDINATION ET RAPPORTS (UCR).. 131
B. UNITE APPUI INSTITUTIONEL (UAI) 134
C. BUREAU D'APPUI AU PARLEMENT (BAP) 158
D. UNITE DE GESTION INTEGREE DES FRONTIERES (UGF) 164
E. LES BUREAUX REGIONAUX 169
F. ROLE PARTICULIER DES CHEFS DE BUREAUX REGIONAUX (CBR/CRO)... 175

IV. Compétences requises et fonctions générales des officiers des Affaires civiles 185

A. LES FONCTIONS GENERALES DES OFFICIERS DES AFFAIRES CIVILES 185
B. FONCTIONS SPECIALES DE L'OFFICIER DES AFFAIRES CIVILES : ASPECT POLITIQUE DE SA MISSION 193
a. Les officiers des Affaires civiles Dans la Fonction d'Ambassadeur.......... 195
b. Les Diplomates de la Restauration et l'Extension de l'Autorité de l'Etat . 201
c. La Politique de la Consolidation de la Paix conduite par les officiers des Affaires civiles 207
d. Protection et Education Civique des Populations Civiles 212
C. PROBLEMATIQUE 217
D. METHODOLOGIE DE L'OFFICIER DES AFFAIRES CIVILES.............. 220
a. Identification des Acteurs du Terrain... 221
b. Collecte d'Informations et Préparation à l'Interview................................ 222
c. Démarche Stratégie de l'officier des Affaires civiles 228
d. Méthode Communicationnelle de l'Officier des Affaires Civiles et Processus de Concertation entre Acteurs 237
e. La « Négociation » dans le Jargon de l'officier des Affaires civiles.......... 241
f. Enjeux de la Coordination 243
g. Les Premiers « Pas » de l'officier des Affaires civiles 249
h. Défis et Stratégies de Réponses Possibles 251
E. PROFIL D'UN OFFICIER DES AFFAIRES CIVILES 255

V. Les Affaires civiles dans l'axe du développement : gestion des QIP (Quick Impact Projects/projets à effets rapides) 265

A. IMPACT DES PROJETS QIP 266
B. INTERETS DES PROJETS QIP... 267
a. Enjeux des Projets Créateurs d'Emplois/Générateurs de Revenus 269
b. QIP Pour la Formation et le Renforcement Des Capacités........................ 269
C. PROCESSUS DE MISE EN OEUVRE DES QIP... 270
D. PRINCIPES D'EVALUATION ET DE SELECTION DES QIP 271
E. COORDINATION DES ACTIVITES DE SUIVI ET D'EVALUATION 273
a. Définition de l'Accord 273

b. Communication dans le cadre de la Gestion des QIP 274
c. Durée de l'Accord 274
d. Contribution de la Mission des Nations unies 274
e. Responsabilités du Partenaire d'Exécution du QIP 275
f. Administration Financière et Audit 276
g. Rapports d'activités 277
h. Règlement des différends 278
i. Privilèges et Immunités 278
j. Résiliation 279
k. Cas de Force Majeure Dans l'Exécution des QIP 279
l. Cas Particuliers Pouvant Subvenir dans la Gestion de QIP 280
m. Processus d'Evaluation de l'Impact des QIP 280

VI. Interventions humanitaires des Affaires civiles : gestion des situations d'urgence, des risques et de catastrophes naturelles 287

A. SITUATION GENERALE 287
B. PLAN STRATEGIQUE D'URGENCE SUR LE DEVELOPPEMENT 292
C. ACTIONS PRIORITAIRES A ENTREPRENDRE APRES UNE CATASTROPHE 294
Dans le domaine agricole 298
Dans le domaine de l'Education 299
Dans le domaine de la santé 299
Dans le domaine du tourisme 299
D. ELABORATION D'UN PLAN STRATEGIQUE DE DISTRIBUTION 301

CONCLUSION 303

Politique
aux éditions L'Harmattan

Dernières parutions

GUERRE ET ÉCONOMIE : DE L'ÉCONOMIE DE GUERRE À LA GUERRE ÉCONOMIQUE
Kempf Olivier
Les relations entre l'économie et la guerre sont depuis l'origine structurelles, l'économie permettant la guerre et la guerre affectant l'économie. Comment considérer la guerre face à l'économie ? Que signifie vraiment cette guerre économique que les médias nous annoncent ? Ce livre permet de poser les analyses actuelles que suscite le rapport contemporain entre la guerre et l'économie.
(Coll. Défense, 27.00 euros, 276 p.)
ISBN : 978-2-343-00037-4, ISBN EBOOK : 978-2-296-53243-4

RÉGULER LES PRIX AGRICOLES
Berthelot Jacques - Préface de Mamadou Cissokho
Les vagues de flambée des prix agricoles mondiaux sont dues à l'effondrement des stocks céréaliers de l'UE et des États-Unis, suite à la folle promotion des agrocarburants et à la dérégulation de leurs politiques agricoles. Étant donné les hausses de revenus considérables en matière de céréales et oléagineux, l'engagement du G20 de lutter contre la volatilité des cours n'a aucune crédibilité. Concernant l'Afrique de l'Ouest, l'UE doit cesser d'imposer un accord de libre-échange et l'OMC ses contraintes, afin de stimuler une promotion sur la base de prix stables.
(17.00 euros, 170 p.)
ISBN : 978-2-343-00491-4, ISBN EBOOK : 978-2-296-53236-6

DE L'HÉGÉMONIE DU NORD AU TRIOMPHE DES SUDS
Vers l'inévitable catastrophe démographique et environnementale
Monnier Yves
Par la suite d'une uniformisation des comportements démographiques dans le Nord et dans les Suds, la population mondiale devrait se stabiliser autour de 10 milliards d'habitants vers 2100. L'auteur tente d'évaluer le coût environnemental de cette pression et définit les tendances des transformations socio-économiques et des bouleversements humains qui accompagneront cette ultime poussée. Aujourd'hui le Nord et les Suds sont coresponsables du destin du monde, aucun ne peut prétendre à l'innocence.
(Coll. Les Tropiques entre mythe et réalité, 17.50 euros, 174 p.)
ISBN : 978-2-336-29353-0, ISBN EBOOK : 978-2-296-53176-5

DE SMITH À MARX : DEUX APPROCHES DU CAPITALISME
Mesin André
Tout semble opposer ces deux auteurs majeurs : quoi de commun entre le champion de la gauche anticapitaliste et celui de la droite libérale, voire hyperlibérale ? Pourtant, une lecture attentive de leurs oeuvres majeures (*Le Capital* et *Richesses des Nations*) révèle quelques convergences au-delà de divergences réelles. Voici un ouvrage pour ceux qui souhaitent mieux connaître ces deux auteurs.
(Coll. Pour Comprendre, 14.50 euros, 142 p.)
ISBN : 978-2-296-99838-4, ISBN EBOOK : 978-2-296-53127-7

PASSAGE AU CRIBLE DE LA SCÈNE MONDIALE – L'actualité internationale 2012
Sous la direction de Josepha Laroche
Cet ouvrage réunit des textes portant sur l'actualité internationale de l'année 2012. Elle forme un ensemble homogène qui éclaire le lecteur sur les lignes de force parcourant la scène mondiale. Il

met l'accent sur la vulnérabilité de tous les États. En effet, qu'il s'agisse d'États faillis comme le Mali ou bien au contraire de l'hégémon américain, voire d'un simple État en formation comme la Palestine, le constat reste le même : tous participent aujourd'hui du chaos international.
(Coll. Chaos International, 17.00 euros, 170 p.)
ISBN : 978-2-343-00309-2, ISBN EBOOK : 978-2-296-53118-5

PUBLIC (LE), NOUVEL ACTEUR DES PROJETS D'AMÉNAGEMENT ?
Coullange Anaïs
L'expression de démocratie participative aura fait un temps florès dans le discours politique. Mais qu'en est-il de la réalité de la participation des citoyens lors de l'élaboration des projets d'aménagement ? Dépassant le simple aspect procédural, à travers l'exemple de l'urbanisme et des modalités permettant d'associer les habitants, ce sont le concept même de participation et la place que le politique entend donner (ou non) au citoyen qui sont ici questionnés.
(Coll. Master Collectivités territoriales et politiques publiques, 15.00 euros, 146 p.)
ISBN : 978-2-343-00131-9, ISBN EBOOK : 978-2-296-53070-6

VOUS N'EXISTEZ PAS – Négationnisme et mensonges d'État
Torossian Sévag
Le négationnisme est la dissimulation du crime de génocide. Cette infraction est concomitante au crime : en même temps que le criminel opère, il efface les preuves du génocide. Sous l'angle du mensonge d'Etat, ce concept couvre ainsi une définition plus large que celle retenue actuellement par le droit positif. Un an après l'invalidation de la loi Boyer par le Conseil constitutionnel, l'auteur revient sur la pénalisation du négationnisme du génocide arménien.
(14.00 euros, 134 p.)
ISBN : 978-2-343-00351-1, ISBN EBOOK : 978-2-296-53191-8

DEMAIN L'OCCIDENT !
Essai
Valdman Edouard
Si l'Occident veut poursuivre sa course, dans un monde à présent multipolaire, il lui faut trouver de nouvelles formes d'expression. Il doit unir le puritanisme américain, créateur du libre-échange et du marché, à une Europe fédérée qui a su préserver en son sein l'héritage de la création, de la beauté et de la gratuité. Il doit aussi accueillir la Loi juive, à même de regagner son rôle de tronc spirituel commun. Quelle forme originale prendra cette alliance si elle se réalise ?
(15.50 euros, 152 p.)
ISBN : 978-2-336-00919-3, ISBN EBOOK : 978-2-296-51557-4

CAMPAGNE (LA) PRÉSIDENTIELLE DE 2012 – Votez pour moi !
Sous la direction de Dominique Labbé et Denis Monière
2 241 messages, c'est le volume de la communication des cinq principaux candidats à la présidentielle de 2012. Ce livre en présente les caractéristiques grâce à l'analyse de contenu et à la lexicométrie : orientation de la communication, mise en valeur de soi et critiques des autres, thématiques et style des candidats. L'importance de la négativité dans les campagnes récentes est ainsi mise en valeur, confirmant la prédominance de la polémique et du dénigrement sur le contenu positif dans la communication politique.
(Coll. Logiques politiques, 19.00 euros, 182 p.)
ISBN : 978-2-336-00671-0, ISBN EBOOK : 978-2-296-53029-4

VILLE (LA) DURABLE APRÈS LE GRENELLE DE L'ENVIRONNEMENT
Sous la direction de Jean-Luc Pissaloux et Gérald Orange
Cet ouvrage traite explicitement de la ville durable : conséquences du Grenelle de l'environnement sur les administrations locales, nouvelles sources de financement, construction d'indicateurs, écoquartiers, biodiversité, risques environnementaux... sans oublier de nouveaux outils en gestation comme les quotas individuels de carbone.
(Coll. Grale, 27.00 euros, 262 p.)
ISBN : 978-2-336-29035-5, ISBN EBOOK : 978-2-296-51710-3

RÉVOLUTION (LA) IMPOSSIBLE – Mes années avec Socialisme ou Barbarie
De Diesbach Sébastien
Fin des années 40 : deux blocs se partagent le monde, mais une bande de jeunes refuse ce choix : être du bord des bureaucrates à l'Est ou des capitalistes à l'Ouest. L'ouvrage raconte l'histoire de ces iconoclastes et de leur organisation, dont l'auteur fit partie, *Socialisme ou Barbarie.* C'est aussi l'histoire de l'auteur, déchiré entre la fidélité à ses camarades et l'attraction des nouveaux courants culturels, comme le jazz, l'alpinisme, la littérature américaine, ou encore le nouveau cinéma.
(Coll. Questions contemporaines, 25.00 euros, 248 p.)
ISBN : 978-2-343-00071-8, ISBN EBOOK : 978-2-296-53013-3

TRIPLES A DE LA BIO-ÉCONOMIE
Efficacité, sobriété et diversité de la croissance verte
Le CLUB des Bio-économistes, ouvrage coordonné par Claude Roy
Dans cinquante ans tout au plus, ce qui fonde notre civilisation et notre confort sera menacé de rareté (eau, alimentation, énergie...) ou de dérèglement (climat). Or face à ces menaces, les ressources renouvelables de la terre, des forêts, et les hommes qui les cultivent et les valorisent, détiennent une part cruciale des réponses. Comment ? Ces réflexions nous livrent un exceptionnel concentré de développement durable, riche de données et de synthèses, pour voir loin et large, et pour assumer l'avenir avec cohérence.
(Coll. Développement durable, 30.50 euros, 294 p.)
ISBN : 978-2-296-99739-4, ISBN EBOOK : 978-2-296-51161-3

RENOUVEAU DU NUCLÉAIRE APRÈS FUKUSHIMA
Monfort Julie, Du Castel Viviane
L'énergie nucléaire, controversée suite à l'accident de la centrale nucléaire de Fukushima, revient sur le devant de la scène, tant ses avantages supplantent les risques potentiels. La raréfaction des hydrocarbures, les incertitudes géopolitiques, la volatilité des prix amènent une conjoncture qui favorise l'énergie nucléaire à usage civil.
(Coll. Géoéconomie et Géofinance, 22.00 euros, 224 p.)
ISBN : 978-2-296-99797-4, ISBN EBOOK : 978-2-296-51185-9

ÉTAT-PROVIDENCE ET LES JEUNES
Chevalier Tom - Préface de Bruno Palier
La jeunesse est de plus en plus présente au cœur des préoccupations publiques. En témoignent l'insistance du président François Hollande à se présenter comme le président de la jeunesse et sa proposition d'une allocation d'autonomie. Cet ouvrage compare les deux périodes où la question de la mise en place de cette allocation a été discutée, et explique comment la politique familiale a été privilégiée, aux dépens de ce type de prestation favorisant l'indépendance des jeunes.
(Coll. Inter-National, 19.00 euros, 194 p.)
ISBN : 978-2-296-99741-7, ISBN EBOOK : 978-2-296-51137-8

SAUVER LA SÉCURITÉ SOCIALE – Question de générations
Peraldi Olivier, Jeger François
Près de 70 ans après sa naissance, faut-il sauver la Sécu ? Retraites de plus en plus coûteuses, car de plus en plus longues, nouvelles pathologies, mais aussi nouveaux enjeux tels le renoncement aux soins et la pénurie des médecins... La Sécurité sociale concentre toutes les interrogations sur le modèle de société laissé aux générations suivantes, semant le doute chez les jeunes quant à la solidarité intergénérationnelle.
(15.50 euros, 148 p.)
ISBN : 978-2-336-00184-5, ISBN EBOOK : 978-2-296-51089-0

MONTÉE DE L'EXTRÊME DROITE EN FRANCE
Le cas du département de la Somme (CD inclus)
Nkunzumwami Emmanuel
Le présent ouvrage présente et analyse les évolutions de la sociologie électorale en France au cours du quinquennat de Nicolas Sarkozy. L'auteur apporte ici un éclairage sur les évolutions comparées

des formations politiques engagées sur le terrain des batailles électorales. Le lecteur pourra ainsi suivre les évolutions du paysage électoral dans les communes, les cantons et les circonscriptions, ainsi que l'implantation de plus en plus forte de l'extrême droite dans le département de la Somme.
(31.00 euros, 264 p.)
ISBN : 978-2-336-00576-8, ISBN EBOOK : 978-2-296-51106-4

BELLES-MÈRES (LES) ET LA POLITIQUE
Réguer-Petit Manon - Préface de Florence Haegel
Plus d'un million d'enfants mineurs vivent aujourd'hui dans une famille recomposée. Mêlant des approches quantitatives et qualitatives, ce livre explore pour la première fois l'impact de la beau-parentalité sur les systèmes de valeurs des femmes et le rôle des belles-mères dans la transmission de valeurs et de préférences politiques.
(Coll. Inter-National, 19.00 euros, 188 p.)
ISBN : 978-2-336-00330-6, ISBN EBOOK : 978-2-296-51096-8

CHUTE (LA) DE LA SARKOZYE – Chronique de la fin d'un quinquennat
Debbasch Charles
Avec ce livre, Charles Debbasch achève l'analyse de la société française et internationale durant le mandat de Nicolas Sarkozy. Il livre ses réflexions sur les mutations de la France dans la période charnière marquée par la campagne présidentielle et l'échec de Sarkozy : cette chronique aidera à mieux comprendre les lignes de force de la France contemporaine.
(33.00 euros, 328 p.)
ISBN : 978-2-296-99743-1, ISBN EBOOK : 978-2-296-51111-8

QUE RESTE-T-IL DU SOCIALISME ?
Tarondeau Jean-Claude
Cet ouvrage retrace l'histoire de l'utopie qui, au XIXe siècle, donne naissance au socialisme et décrit les principales expériences qui ont été menées en son nom. Les expériences socialistes limitées comme celle des Acadiens ont disparu rapidement, les plus grandes ont engendré des dictatures qui se sont effondrées comme en URSS ou qui ont renoncé au socialisme comme en Chine. Il montre enfin comment le socialisme d'aujourd'hui s'adapte aux réalités et rejette les utopies qui l'ont fait naître.
(Coll. Questions contemporaines, 18.50 euros, 190 p.)
ISBN : 978-2-336-00547-8, ISBN EBOOK : 978-2-296-50753-1

INTERNATIONALE (L') DE L'INTELLIGENCE – Pour une mondialisation éclairée !
Guyot Gilles - Préface de Francine Demichel
«Si l'on veut que la mondialisation ne soit pas pilotée selon les impératifs financiers, il est temps que se développe l'internationalisation des savoirs.» L'»internationale de l'intelligence» est la solution aux dérives actuelles de la mondialisation et l'enseignement supérieur français, très dynamique dans ce domaine, a une carte à jouer pour le plus grand bien de notre pays.
(22.00 euros, 232 p.)
ISBN : 978-2-336-00557-7, ISBN EBOOK : 978-2-296-50757-9

DOUZE (LES) TRAVAUX D'HERCULE DU NOUVEAU PRÉSIDENT
Sous la direction de Hubert Lévy-Lambert et Laurent Daniel
Ce livre explique les enjeux qui sous-tendent les décisions politiques attendues du nouveau Président. Il est orienté vers la recherche d'une réduction rapide du déficit public et du déficit extérieur. Les lecteurs y trouveront matière à réflexion sur certains choix stratégiques comme le recrutement de nouveaux fonctionnaires, le retour de la retraite à 60 ans, l'encadrement des loyers ou l'abandon de la TVA «sociale». La plupart des auteurs sont membres de «X Sursaut», regroupant plusieurs centaines de polytechniciens.
(Coll. Questions contemporaines, 24.00 euros, 234 p.)
ISBN : 978-2-296-99503-1, ISBN EBOOK : 978-2-296-50726-5

L'HARMATTAN ITALIA
Via Degli Artisti 15; 10124 Torino

L'HARMATTAN HONGRIE
Könyvesbolt ; Kossuth L. u. 14-16
1053 Budapest

L'HARMATTAN KINSHASA
185, avenue Nyangwe
Commune de Lingwala
Kinshasa, R.D. Congo
(00243) 998697603 ou (00243) 999229662

L'HARMATTAN CONGO
67, av. E. P. Lumumba
Bât. – Congo Pharmacie (Bib. Nat.)
BP2874 Brazzaville
harmattan.congo@yahoo.fr

L'HARMATTAN GUINÉE
Almamya Rue KA 028, en face du restaurant Le Cèdre
OKB agency BP 3470 Conakry
(00224) 60 20 85 08
harmattanguinee@yahoo.fr

L'HARMATTAN CAMEROUN
BP 11486
Face à la SNI, immeuble Don Bosco
Yaoundé
(00237) 99 76 61 66
harmattancam@yahoo.fr

L'HARMATTAN CÔTE D'IVOIRE
Résidence Karl / cité des arts
Abidjan-Cocody 03 BP 1588 Abidjan 03
(00225) 05 77 87 31
etien_nda@yahoo.fr

L'HARMATTAN MAURITANIE
Espace El Kettab du livre francophone
N° 472 avenue du Palais des Congrès
BP 316 Nouakchott
(00222) 63 25 980

L'HARMATTAN SÉNÉGAL
« Villa Rose », rue de Diourbel X G, Point E
BP 45034 Dakar FANN
(00221) 33 825 98 58 / 77 242 25 08
senharmattan@gmail.com

L'HARMATTAN TOGO
1771, Bd du 13 janvier
BP 414 Lomé
Tél : 00 228 2201792
gerry@taama.net

Achevé d'imprimer par Corlet Numérique - 14110 Condé-sur-Noireau
N° d'Imprimeur : 102564 - Dépôt légal : octobre 2013 - *Imprimé en France*

www.ingramcontent.com/pod-product-compliance
Lightning Source LLC
LaVergne TN
LVHW011448061026
849535LV00004BA/1009